www.brookscole.com

www.brookscole.com is the World Wide Web site for Brooks/Cole and is your direct source to dozens of online resources.

At *www.brookscole.com* you can find out about supplements, demonstration software, and student resources. You can also send email to many of our authors and preview new publications and exciting new technologies.

www.brookscole.com
Changing the way the world learns®

UNDERSTANDING DATA COMMUNICATIONS AND NETWORKS

THIRD EDITION

WILLIAM A. SHAY
University of Wisconsin–Green Bay

THOMSON

™

BROOKS/COLE

Australia • Canada • Mexico • Singapore • Spain
United Kingdom • United States

THOMSON

BROOKS/COLE

Publisher: *Bill Stenquist*
Editor: *Kallie Swanson*
Editorial Assistant: *Aarti Jayaraman*
Technology Project Manager: *Burke Taft*
Executive Marketing Manager: *Tom Ziolkowski*
Marketing Assistant: *Jennifer Gee*
Advertising Project Manager: *Vicky Wan*
Project Manager, Editorial Production: *Kelsey McGee*
Print/Media Buyer: *Doreen Suruki*

Permissions Editor: *Sommy Ko*
Production Service: *Penmarin Books*
Copy Editor: *Cynthia Kogut*
Illustration: *Accurate Art*
Cover Designer: *Denise Davidson/Simple Design*
Cover Image: *Guy Grenier/Masterfile*
Cover Printing: *Phoenix Color Corp.*
Printing and Binding: *RR Donnelley*
Compositor: *UG / GGS Information Services, Inc.*

Printed in the United States of America
2 3 4 5 6 7   07 06 05

For more information about our products, contact us at:
Thomson Learning Academic Resource Center
1-800-423-0563
For permission to use material from this text,
contact us by: **Phone:** 1-800-730-2214
Fax: 1-800-730-2215
Web: http://www.thomsonrights.com

Library of Congress Control Number: 2003109625

ISBN 0-534-38317-3

Brooks/Cole—Thomson Learning
10 Davis Drive
Belmont, CA 94002
USA

Asia
Thomson Learning
5 Shenton Way #01-01
UIC Building
Singapore 068808

Australia/New Zealand
Thomson Learning
102 Dodds Street
Southbank, Victoria 3006
Australia

Canada
Nelson
1120 Birchmount Road
Toronto, Ontario M1K 5G4
Canada

Europe/Middle East/Africa
Thomson Learning
High Holborn House
50/51 Bedford Row
London WC1R 4LR
United Kingdom

Latin America
Thomson Learning
Seneca, 53
Colonia Polanco
11560 Mexico D.F.
Mexico

Spain/Portugal
Paraninfo
Calle/Magallanes, 25
28015 Madrid
Spain

TO MY PARENTS, JACK AND MADELINE—THANKS FOR EVERYTHING

CONTENTS

PREFACE

PURPOSE

The second edition of this book appeared five years ago, and much in the fields of data communications and computer networks has changed since then.

- Web-based software has become commonplace.
- The need for secure connections to Web sites is widespread.
- Security concerns and tools for dealing with security threats have increased.
- New encryption standards have been created, and old ones have been compromised.
- Quality-of-service issues have spawned the need for new protocols to run alongside existing ones.
- New connection technologies such as DSL, USB, and FireWire have become common.
- Ethernet networks have evolved to gigabit rates.
- Audio compression schemes such as MP3 and gaming have changed forever how people use the Internet.
- Wireless technologies have become a viable alternative for many.
- Protocols that were once common or thought to have promise for the future are rarely used.

We don't live in the same world that existed when the previous edition was published, and this new edition reflects these changes.

Although much of this book's content has changed, its purpose is still fundamentally the same. It is designed for junior-level students in a computer science program who have a minimum of two semesters of software design and a knowledge of precalculus and discrete mathematics. It covers standard topics found in a typical introductory course in data communications and computer networks, such as transmission media, analog and digital signals, data transmissions, compression and encryption methods, network topologies, network security, LAN protocols,

Internet-based protocols and applications, circuit-switching technologies, and Web applications. The goals of this book are to help the reader understand the following:

- The differences, advantages, and disadvantages of various transmission media
- Analog and digital signals, modulation and demodulation techniques, and how modulation devices such as modems, cable modems, and DSL modems work
- The effect of noise on transmissions and how protocols detect when information has been damaged
- How protocols respond to cases where noise causes information to be damaged or even lost
- Standards such as AES, ATM, DES, EIA-232, HDLC, IEEE 802.3, IEEE 802.5, IEEE 802.11, IPv6, JPEG, MP3, MPEG, OSI, SONET, TCP/IP, X.25, standards organizations, and why standards are needed
- Data compression techniques, types of data that can be compressed, and a comparison of the different methods used
- Worms, viruses, and other threats to networked computers
- The need for security and the effectiveness of various encryption methods
- Differences between public and private key encryption systems
- How to establish secure connections to remote sites
- The need for flow control and various ways of implementing it
- Local area network protocols and contention strategies for shared transmission media
- Wireless standards
- Methods of connecting local area networks
- Routing strategies
- The need for protocols to support real-time video applications and respond to quality-of-service issues
- How to design and set up a variety of working client/server applications
- How increased Web use and the proliferation of multimedia applications have affected existing protocols and what is being done to deal with it

CONTENT AND ORGANIZATION

Major changes have been made to the third edition. Some were based on comments I received from readers, and the rest on the evolution of technology. Many involve clarification of figures or an improved description of protocols. The rest involve expansion of topics that have become commonplace, inclusion of new developments, and the removal of old topics that no longer play a significant role in this field.

Perhaps the most obvious change is the restructuring of the book into thirteen chapters as follows:

Chapter 1   Introduction to Communications Standards and Protocols

Chapter 2   Transmission Media and Codes

Chapter 3   Analog and Digital Signals
Chapter 4   Making Connections
Chapter 5   Data Compression
Chapter 6   Data Integrity
Chapter 7   Data Security
Chapter 8   Flow Control
Chapter 9   Local Area Networks
Chapter 10   Connecting Networks
Chapter 11   Internet Protocols and Applications
Chapter 12   Internet Programming
Chapter 13   Circuit Technologies

This restructuring should provide the instructor better guidance in focusing on specific topics necessary to meet the needs of his or her course. Some of these chapters correspond to chapter subsets from the previous edition; some were formed by combining sections of different chapters from the previous edition, and of course many chapters contain a lot of new material. The most significant changes include new or expanded coverage of the following:

- Media, including conductive metals, optics, wireless, and satellite communications
- DSL technologies
- Universal Serial Bus (USB) and FireWire (IEEE 1394 standard) Protocols
- Synchronous Optical Network (SONET)
- Arithmetic, facsimile, and MP3 compression techniques
- Advanced Encryption Standard (AES) and the Rijndael Algorithm
- Pretty Good Privacy security program
- Secure Sockets Layer, Transport Layer Security, and X.509 Certificates
- Firewalls
- Security threats
- Ethernet, Fast Ethernet, and Gigabit Ethernet standards, and an overview of the 10-gigabit Ethernet standard
- 802.11 Wireless LAN standard
- Switched Ethernet
- Virtual LANs
- Layer 3 and 4 protocols, including classless interdomain routing, routing and routers, multicasting, quality-of-service issues, Real-Time Transfer Protocol, and IPSec
- Internet applications
- Project-based CGI programming, including working examples of a Web-based ordering system using Linux and Perl Scripts
- Frame Relay Protocol

Although it would be difficult (almost impossible) to cover all these subjects in a one-semester course, the range of topics allows instructors flexibility in choosing the topics best suited for their students.

This text offers a mix of theory and application. The theory provides a solid foundation for further study, and the application brings students closer to the realities of communications systems and networks. It also gives them valuable experience. All students should benefit from the applications, while the more theoretical material will challenge the more ambitious students. In addition, Chapter 12 presents actual models of working client and server programs on which the student can build.

Each chapter serves as a base on which to build the next. For example, when studying multiplexing, contention, or compression, students should have an understanding of how signals propagate through different media. When studying local area networks, they should understand problems of contention on multiple-access lines, noisy channels, and flow control. When studying wide area network protocols, they should understand local area network protocols and why these are not suitable for larger networks. Chapters are summarized as follows.

Chapter 1 provides an introduction to the field, touching on current issues and applications in the field of communications and networks. It describes the need for standards, lists relevant standards organizations, and then summarizes a long-standing protocol model, the Open System Interconnect. It finishes with projections of what we might see in the future.

Chapter 2 presents different types of transmission media (cable, wired, wireless, satellite, optical fiber), their advantages and disadvantages, and various codes used to assign meaning to data. Chapter 3 develops analog and digital signal types, modulation techniques needed to convert between them, and the effect that noise has on bit rates. It also discusses modems, cable modems, and DSL technologies.

Chapter 4 focuses on making connections, namely transmission modes, communications carriers (telephone system, SONET, and T1), interface standards (EIA-232, USB, and FireWire), and how multiple devices access common media (multiplexing methods and various contention protocols).

Chapter 5 covers data compression techniques suited to compressing different types of data and how they exploit different types of redundancy in the data. Chapter 6 deals with the integrity of transmitted data and includes error detection and correction techniques such as parity, CRC, and Hamming codes.

Chapter 7 discusses data security, including encryption techniques (both public and private key), encryption standards, key-exchange algorithms, authentication methods, X.509 certificates and secure connections, firewalls, and various threats (viruses, worms, hackers, and denial of service attacks).

Chapter 8 introduces flow control algorithms that outline how devices handle an exchange of information and account for lost or damaged data. It also outlines some techniques used for the formal verification of protocol correctness. Chapter 9 then presents LAN protocols, including several flavors of Ethernet (original, Fast Ethernet, and Gigabit Ethernet), Token Ring, and the IEEE 802.11 Wireless LAN standard.

Chapter 10 is about the ways various networks can be connected. It covers layer 2 connections (bridges and switches), address learning, spanning tree algorithm, switched Ethernet, and VLANs. It also deals with layer 3 connections and discusses various routing algorithms (Dijkstra, Bellman-Ford, RIP, BGP, and more). It also describes problems caused by network congestion and deadlock.

Chapter 11 is the Internet chapter. Both versions 4 and 6 of the Internet Protocol are covered, as well as quality-of-service issues, multicasting, and other protocols designed to provide some real-time service requirements to the Internet. It also covers TCP (connection management, flow control, and congestion management) and concludes with an outline of several common Internet applications (Telnet, SSH, FTP, and SMTP).

Chapter 12 is for those who wish to build student projects into the course. It provides working examples of client/server applications. Examples include socket programming, CGI programming using C and Perl, and sample code that illustrates how file transfers, search engines, and online ordering systems work.

Chapter 13 deals with circuit-based technologies such as ISDN, X.25, Frame Relay, and ATM.

The questions at the end of each chapter are divided into two groups. The first group, Review Questions, contains questions for which answers can be obtained directly from the corresponding chapter. These questions encourage the reader to go back through the text and pick out what the author or instructor believes is important. I believe this method to be better pedagogically than only summarizing important topics at the end, which encourages students to read textbooks as they would a novel—linearly. Learning complex material, however, often requires reading, rereading, and going back through the text to sort out and understand different concepts. A colleague related a conversation she had with a student having some difficulty with course work. The student had a part-time job during which he had some free time. Rather than fight boredom, he decided to bring his textbook to work and read when he had the opportunity. Later in the semester his performance improved, and he related to the instructor that after reading the material four or five times, it actually began to make sense.

Review questions are not enough though. The second group, Exercises, contains questions that challenge readers to apply what they have learned and to compare, make logical deductions, and consider alternatives. The answers are not always simply stated and may be more elusive but that's typical of real problems.

INSTRUCTOR SUPPLEMENTS

- An *Instructor's Solutions Manual,* with answers to review questions and exercises, is available to qualified instructors from the publisher.

- Sample exams are available to qualified instructors upon request. (email: shayw@uwgb.edu).

- Instructional aids are available via the author's Web site, http://www.uwgb.edu/ shayw/udcn3. These include book figures in pdf format, corrections of any errors detected after printing, all copies of program code described in Chapter 12, and numerous Web links to other resources, organized by chapter.

ACKNOWLEDGMENTS

An undertaking such as writing a text is rarely, if ever, an individual effort. Many people have contributed and have given me valuable ideas, information, and support during this project. I especially would like to recognize the following people, who provided valuable advice during the writing of the first two editions.

Abdullah Abonamah
University of Akron

David Kieper
University of Wisconsin–Green Bay

George W. Ball
Alfred University

Lance Leventhal

Mehran Basiratmand
Florida International University

Judith Molka
University of Pittsburgh

Ron Bates
DeAnza College

Dan O'Connell
Fredonia College–SUNY

Bruce Derr

Jon L. Spear
Syracuse University

Mohammad El-Soussi
Santa Barbara City College

Janet M. Urlaub
Sinclair Community College

James E. Holden
Clarion University

David Whitney
San Francisco State University

Dr. Sub Ramakrishnan
Bowling Green State University

Dr. J. Archer Harris
James Madison University

Dr. Seyed H. Roosta
Mount Mercy College

Dr. Paul N. Higbee
University of North Florida

Dr. Brit Williams
Kennesaw State University

Dr. Gene Hill Price
Old Dominion University

Stan Wine
*Hunter College and
New Era of Networks, Inc.*

Dr. J. Mark Pullen
George Mason University

To those who took the time to review the manuscript for the third edition or provided me with useful suggestions on how to improve the second edition, many thanks. I took all of your comments and suggestions seriously and incorporated many into the final manuscript.

I am grateful to the reviewers of this edition:

Irvin Jay Levy
Gordon College

Mark Pullen
George Mason University

Aby Tehranipour
Eastern Michigan University

Camelia Zlatea
De Paul University

My thanks also to all the people at Brooks/Cole, including my editor, Kallie Swanson, and Aarti Jayaraman, her editorial assistant, as well as Penmarin Books for managing the production, Cindy Kogut for copy editing, and George Barile at Accurate Art for illustrating the new edition. Your contributions and efforts helped make a manuscript into a book. My family—Judy, Dan, and Tim—merit special thanks. You made sacrifices so that I could use my "free time" to prepare the manuscript. We will make up for it, I promise. Finally, to those who eventually read this text, I would very much appreciate your opinion. Please feel free to send any comments to Bill Shay, Department of Information and Computing Sciences, University of Wisconsin–Green Bay, Green Bay, WI 54311–7001, or via email at shayw@uwgb.edu.

BILL SHAY

CHAPTER 1

INTRODUCTION TO COMMUNICATIONS, STANDARDS, AND PROTOCOLS

The love of learning, the sequestered nooks, and all the sweet serenity of books.
—**Henry Wadsworth Longfellow** (1807–1882), U.S. poet

Knowledge is of two kinds. We know a subject ourselves, or we know where we can find information upon it.
—**Samuel Johnson** (1709–1784), British author

1.1 WHY STUDY COMMUNICATIONS?

Why should we study computer and data communications? The many reasons range from "It is an absolutely fascinating field" to "I have to know how to connect my computer to the company's network." But one of the most compelling reasons is that communication technology has invaded virtually every aspect of daily life, from professional and educational uses to purely recreational ones. It has become so pervasive that we either take it for granted or are simply not aware of its applications.

A BRIEF HISTORY

The field of communications is certainly not new: People have been communicating since early humans grunted and scratched pictures on cave walls. For thousands of years people communicated using little more than words, parchments, stone tablets, and smoke signals. The primary forms of sending information were based on the auditory and visual senses. You either heard someone speaking or saw the letters and symbols that defined a message.

Communications changed drastically in 1837, when Samuel Morse invented the telegraph. This invention made it possible to send information using electrical impulses over a copper wire. Messages were sent by translating each character into a sequence of long or short electrical impulses (or in less technical terms, dots and dashes) and transmitting them. This association of characters with electrical impulses was called **Morse code.** The capability to send information with no obvious verbal or visual medium began a sequence of events that forever changed the way people communicate.

In 1876 Alexander Graham Bell took the telegraph one step further. Rather than converting a message into a sequence of dots and dashes, he showed that a voice could be converted directly to electrical energy and transmitted over a wire using continuously varying voltages. At the wire's other end the electrical signals were converted back to sound. The result was that a person's voice could be transmitted electronically between two points as long as a physical connection existed between them. To most people whose lives were based on only what they could see and hear, this invention was absolutely incredible and seemed magical.

The earliest telephones required a different pair of wires for each phone to which you wished to connect. To place a call, a person had to first connect the telephone to the correct wires and then hope the person on the other end was there listening. There were no bells or signaling devices to interrupt dinner. That changed with the invention of the switchboard (Figure 1.1), a switching device that connected lines between two telephones. Callers simply picked up the phone and recited the number of the person they wished to call. Telephones had not yet evolved

Figure 1.1   Early Switchboards

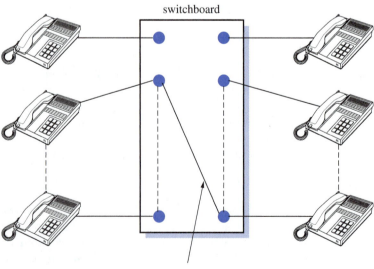

switchboard

connection was manually established by
a switchboard operator

to the point where people had to perform manual activities such as dialing numbers or pushing buttons. Establishing connections was voice activated. That is, an operator heard the number and then used a switchboard to connect one person's phone lines with another person's lines.

During the next 70 years the telephone system grew to the point where the telephone became a common device in a home. Most of us do not even think about how the telephone system works. We know we can dial a number and be connected to just about anywhere in the world.

Another event important to communications occurred in 1945 with the invention of the first electronic computer, ENIAC (Electronic Numerical Integrator and Calculator). Designed for computing ballistics tables for World War II, it was the first device that could actually process information electronically. Although ENIAC played no direct role in data or computer communications, it did show that calculations and decision making could be done electronically, an important capability in today's communications systems.

The relation between computers and communications began to emerge after the invention of the transistor in 1947 allowed smaller and cheaper computers to be built. The new generation of computers that emerged during the 1960s made new applications such as processing and routing telephone calls economically feasible. In addition, more businesses were buying computers and developing applications, and the need to transfer information between them began to grow.

The first communication system between computers was simple but reliable. Basically, it involved writing information from one computer onto a magnetic tape, throwing the tape into the back of the car, then transporting the tape to another computer. (People today still do the same thing, although disks, CD-ROMs, and DVDs have replaced the tape.) Once there, the other computer could read the information on the tape. This was a very reliable form of communication, assuming the person driving the car didn't get into an accident or leave the windows open while driving through a car wash.

Another milestone in electronic communications occurred with the development of the personal computer (PC). The capability to have computing power on a desk generated an entirely new way of storing and retrieving information. The 1980s saw the infusion of millions of PCs into virtually every business, company, school, and organization and into many homes as well. The fact that so many people now had computers generated the need to make information even more easily accessible.

The 1990s saw the emergence of the **World Wide Web,** an application that makes information from around the world easily accessible from one's desk. With the click of a mouse button, computer users can access files, programs, video clips, and sound bites. Online services such as America Online or Yahoo provide access to a wealth of services to their users, such as chat rooms, bulletin boards, airline reservation systems, and more.

As a side note, many mistakenly believe that the concept of a data network originated in the late 1900s with the creation of the Internet. It often surprises people to know that a data network was built in France in the late 1700s, about 200 years before the Internet! A series of towers was constructed, each having a pendulum clock and a panel that was black on one side and white on the other. A person at one tower would, in time with the clock, flip the panel exposing its black or white side. Another person at a remote tower watched through a telescope and could do the same with the local panel. Messages were coded according to the sequence of black and white images and could be transmitted from tower to tower. The first message that was transmitted spanned approximately 16 kilometers and took about four minutes. Reference [RHo94] provides a fascinating read regarding this network and some of the motivating forces behind its construction.

As we begin the 21st century, new technologies are still changing how we do things and how we see the world around us. The integration of media and communication services, along with the eventual conversion to digital broadcasts, promises to open up a whole new world of interactive entertainment and educational opportunities. The Internet access that cable companies are offering for home use increases the speed with which we can download information. In effect, this makes more information available to us. Palmtop computers and wireless technologies give us more flexibility to take our computing, learning, and entertainment activities to places previously not possible. The sheer numbers of people taking advantage of these technologies also increases the visibility of ethical and legal issues. Pornography and violent material long opposed by many becomes increasingly more difficult to control. Copyright infringement issues escalated in 2000 when the technology evolved to allow the sharing of popular music in digital, compressed formats. Issues are currently emerging that involve videos in addition to music.

Computers and communications have progressed to the point where businesses, schools, and many individuals can no longer function without them. Our almost total dependence on them demands that we understand them and their abilities and limitations.

APPLICATIONS

Transferring data between computers is just one area of communications. For example, most people are aware that a television uses an antenna or cable to bring signals into a home. But that is the last step in a worldwide communication system that began in 1962 with Telstar, a communications satellite designed to transfer telephone and television signals between the United States and Europe. Telstar showed that transmitting information between continents was both technologically and economically feasible.

Many communications satellites transmit television signals today. Figure 1.2 shows a common system. A transmitter in one part of the world sends a signal to an orbiting satellite, which relays the signal to receivers in other parts. Signals from the receiver are sent to broadcast towers and are transmitted locally using a frequency approved by the Federal Communications Commission (FCC). An antenna receives the signals and relays them to the television set in your home.

Television antennas are becoming a less common way to receive signals. Many homes subscribe to a cable television service that brings signals into the home using optical fibers and coaxial cable. In addition, many people purchase their own receiving dishes and receive satellite signals directly.

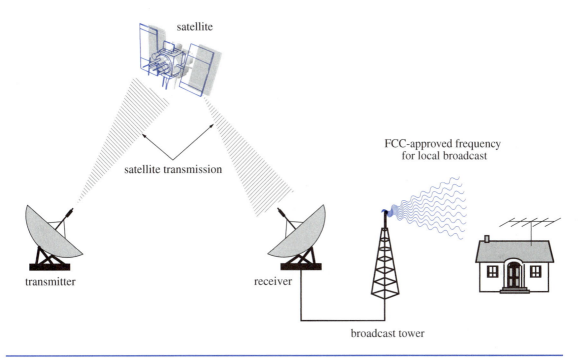

Figure 1.2   Broadcast Television Reception

Other communications applications use **local area networks (LANs)** and **wide area networks (WANs),** systems that allow multiple computers to communicate over short (LAN) or long (WAN) distances. Once connected, users can send or receive data files, log in to remote computers, send mail (**email,** or electronic mail), or connect to the World Wide Web. With email, a person can send personal or business messages, spreadsheets, databases, and even family photographs from one computer to another. The email system stores messages on a computer disk where someone else can read them.

The phenomenal growth of email, which sends and receives messages electronically, has caused some people to predict it will eventually replace the postal service. This is not likely to happen in the foreseeable future, but email is used extensively by many professionals and, with the widespread use of the Web, by individuals for personal reasons as well.

With email, it is possible to send a message to remote locations from the privacy of your own home; Figure 1.3 illustrates one possible arrangement. A person with a PC and modem at home can access his or her Internet service provider via a telephone line, cable service, or even satellite dish. This computer is connected to a wide area network that allows a message to be sent across the country or to other countries and eventually to a remote Internet service provider or perhaps a company computer through a company LAN. The result is an electronic transfer between two points across potentially very large distances.

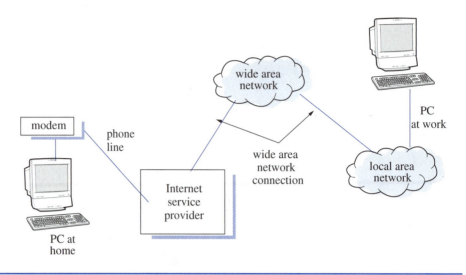

Figure 1.3 Electronic Mail Connections

The following additional applications are described only briefly here. We will discuss some of these topics more fully in later chapters.

- **Facsimile machines (fax).** A fax machine creates an electronic equivalent of an image on a sheet of paper and then sends the image over telephone lines. A fax machine at the other end recreates the original paper's image. The fax is widely used to send letters, charts, and diagrams in minutes or even seconds.

- **Voice and video communications.** LANs were originally used to connect PCs and various devices primarily to transfer data and software. Oftentimes, communications systems were developed to transmit voice and video images. Some companies even managed their own telephone systems or private branch exchanges (PBX) (discussed further in Chapter 4). Video communications can be used to play a tape or receive a video transmission from outside and relay the signals throughout a company or organization. Video communication has special needs because it typically requires the sending of 30 images per second, and each image requires a large amount of information to maintain crisp pictures with true color. However, emerging technologies have made gigabit (1 billion bits) per second transfer rates common in many LAN environments. As a result, the PC and LAN have evolved to open up a whole new set of activities. With a headset and microphone, a user can plug into a PC, dial a telephone number, and initiate a conversation with a person on a remote telephone. Mini cameras mounted on the PC's monitor can transmit images of the individual speaking. Digital imaging can also be used to transmit video images to PC users. This has many applications. For example, a company may sponsor a series of training programs. The department in charge can announce that it will be transmitting a "how to" video on the proper care and maintenance of chia pets at a specified time. Interested individuals need only use PC software to select a channel at that time and watch the broadcast as it is being transmitted.

- **Teleconferencing.** Many people are no doubt painfully aware of the number of business meetings or conferences that occur each day. One of the most difficult aspects of planning such meetings is making sure everyone who needs to be present can attend. When the necessary people are in different parts of the country, they must make arrangements to travel to the meeting site. Teleconferencing involves setting up video cameras and televisions at different locations so that people at each location can see and hear each other. In effect, they "attend" meetings or conferences without leaving their individual locations. Figures and charts needed for presentations also can be broadcast for all to see. Through teleconferencing, management can save travel costs and reduce lost employee time due to traveling.

- **Cellular telephones.** The telephone system is certainly the most extensive communications system. Until the 1960s, however, the two communicating sites had to be connected physically. At that time, the telephone system started to use satellite and microwave towers to send signals. Still, for a while those making and receiving the calls had to use a telephone that was connected physically to a local office. That changed with the invention of the cellular telephone, a device that connects to the telephone system using radio waves. It allows people to make telephone calls from their cars, the office picnic, the ballpark, or even from the remote areas of the country—any place that has sending and receiving towers nearby. Cell phones have also provided consumers an interface to the Web and the capability to send text messages. Section 4.2 discusses cellular telephones further.

- **Information services.** Those with a PC and modem can subscribe to many different information services. Bulletin boards (data banks) allow the free exchange of some software, files, or other information. Other services allow users to get stock quotations and make transactions electronically or to examine airline schedules and make reservations. Web search engines search databases for documents based on keywords or topics. They then return links to sites that the user can access with the click of a mouse button. Newsgroups allow individuals with a common interest to post questions and answer them. This has become an important resource for people looking for technical advice on a variety of software packages or, in fact, for advice on just about anything.

- **E-commerce.** The Internet, and the development of a variety of programming tools, has changed forever the way that many do business. Ordering from remote locations is not new, as people have used telephones to place catalog orders for decades. However, e-commerce applications have resulted in a proliferation of online sites competing for the consumers' dollar. Almost anything—from books, CDs, clothing, and the once-popular Beanie Babies to automobiles—can be purchased by connecting to a site, filling out a form (including your charge card number, of course), and submitting it. In fact, in December 2002 the Northern California town of Bridgeville, an old logging community, was up for bid on eBay, with the highest bid at approximately

$1.8 million. Although not quite the same as the Louisiana Purchase, this certainly changes the perception of what can be purchased via the Internet. In general, many find this approach the preferred way of doing business; of course, others are less enthusiastic. A recent survey in a technologies class polled the students and asked "What is the biggest advantage of purchasing online"? and "What is the biggest disadvantage of purchasing online"? The most common answer to both questions was "You don't talk to anyone."

- **Peer-to-peer networking.** Peer-to-peer networking is when a group of computers can all communicate without the use of a centralized server. This technology received national attention a few years ago when Napster raised awareness of copyright issues related to the exchange of music files. Many users rely on peer-to-peer networking to play Internet games interactively, and services such as Kazaa allow uses to share audio files, video clips, and even entire movies (often before they are released to the general public).

ISSUES

These new technological developments have created many issues of concern. For example, we have used the word *connect* and its various forms many times in the previous discussion. But how do we connect? What do we use to make a connection? Do we use wire, cable, or optical fiber? Can we connect without them? Chapter 2 discusses many options.

Communications technology is like traffic planning. Roads allow you to get where you want to go, but they must be able to handle large amounts of traffic, especially in a large city. Designers must strike a balance between flow and cost. A 10-lane highway circling the city will provide better traffic flow than a 6-lane highway, but are more lanes worth the extra cost? The answer probably is yes in the largest cities but no in the smaller ones. Communications systems are similar. They must allow a certain amount of information to be transmitted, but just how much depends on the applications. The amount of information we need to send will affect how devices are connected. Chapter 10 discusses different ways of connecting devices.

Once we decide how to connect, we must establish some rules for communication. City streets are of little use without traffic signals or laws to control traffic. The same is true for communications systems. Whether the primary medium is a cable or the air, we need to know that many sources will want to send information. We need some rules to prevent messages from colliding or to specify what to do when they do collide.

Ease of use is another concern. Most people will not use a technology if it is difficult to use. For example, many people who purchased VCRs never learned to program them, at least until "VCR plus" became available. Now some VCRs can be programmed by voice. For a communication system or network to be viable, the information must be readily accessible. But how accessible do we want it? Should anyone be able to look at it? If it's an online library catalog, yes. If it's financial information for your retirement or investment account, no.

Communications systems must be secure. We must realize that the easy exchange of information invites unauthorized and illegal use of it. How can we make information accessible to those who need it yet prevent anyone else from seeing it? This is especially tough when the unauthorized people have many resources and make concerted efforts to break security measures. As the sensitivity of the information increases, security measures become more sophisticated. No system, however, is perfectly safe. Consequently, laws that provide for severe penalties were passed to help deter such activities. Chapter 7 deals with security.

Even if we deal with all the issues and manage to connect computers to provide the most efficient, cost-effective, secure, and easy transfer of information, one problem remains: Not all computers are compatible. In some cases transferring information from one computer to another is like moving a transmission from one car to another. If both cars are Ford Escorts built in the same year you can do it, but if one is an Escort and the other is a Grand Prix you will have some problems.

One area of great interest is the open system. If fully implemented, an **open system** allows any two computers to exchange information provided they are connected. Given the diversity among computer systems, this is not trivial. Tremendous strides have been made toward reaching that goal in recent years. Section 1.4 describes open systems and a model called the **Open Systems Interconnect (OSI)** model. Although that particular model has proved to be a commercial failure, many still see it as an important model because it outlines a structure of communications systems and provides important insight into how various components of a communication system fit together.

Finally, we return to the opening question: Why study data communications and networking? Simply, it's a field that is experiencing and will experience tremendous growth. There is a desperate need for people who understand it and can help shape its future.

1.2 COMPUTER NETWORKS

During the 1950s, most computers were similar in one respect. They had a main memory, a central processing unit (CPU), and peripherals (Figure 1.4). The memory and CPU were central to the system and had connections to devices such as disk and tape drives and computer terminals. Since then, new generations of computing have emerged in which computation capability and data storage are distributed across many devices. A user may retrieve a program from one place, run it on any of a variety of processors, and send the result to a third location.

A system connecting different devices such as PCs, printers, and scanners is a **network.** Typically, each device in a network serves a specific purpose for one or more individuals. For example, a PC may sit on your desk providing access to information or software you need. A PC may also be devoted to managing a disk drive containing shared files. We call it a **file server.** Often a network covers a small geographic area and connects devices in a single building or group of buildings. Such a network is a *local area network* (LAN). A network that covers a larger area such as a state, country, or the world is called a *wide area network* (WAN).

Most networks involve many people using many PCs, each of which can access any of many printers or servers. With all these people accessing information, their

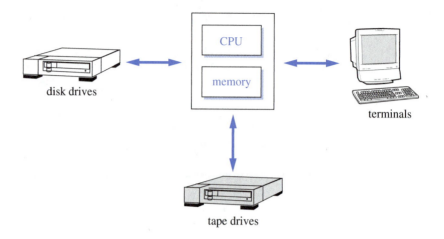

Figure 1.4   Communicating Devices in a Computer System

requests inevitably will conflict. Consequently, the devices must be connected in a way that permits an orderly transfer of information for all concerned. A good analogy is a street layout in a large city. With only one person driving, it matters little where the streets are, which ones are one-way, where the traffic signals are, or how they are synchronized. But with thousands of cars on the streets during the morning rush hour, a bad layout will create congestion that causes major delays. The same is true of computer networks. They must be connected in a way that allows data to travel among many users with little or no delay. We call the connection strategy the **network topology.** The best topology depends on the types of devices and user needs. What works well for one group may perform dismally for another.

COMMON BUS TOPOLOGY

Figure 1.5 shows the traditional **common bus topology** (or simply **bus topology**) connecting devices such as workstations, mainframes, and file servers.* They communicate through a single bus (for example, a coaxial cable). The traditional approach gave each device an interface that listened to the bus and examined its data traffic. If an interface determined that data were destined for the device it serves, it read the data from the bus and transferred it to the device. Similarly, if a device wanted to transmit data, the interface circuits sensed when the bus was clear and then transmitted data. This is not unlike waiting on a freeway entrance ramp during rush hour. You sense an opening and either quickly dart to it or muscle your way through, depending on whether you're driving a subcompact or a large truck.

Sometimes, two devices would try to transmit simultaneously. Each one detected an absence of traffic and began transmitting before becoming aware of the

---

* Chapter 10 shows that there are alternative ways to implement common bus topologies using devices called switches and hubs.

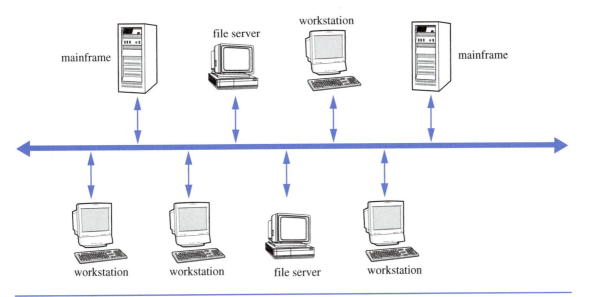

Figure 1.5   Common Bus Topology

other device's transmission. The result was a collision of signals. As the devices transmitted, they continued to listen to the bus and detect the noise resulting from the collision. When a device detected a collision, it stopped transmitting, waited a random period of time, and tried again. This process, called **Carrier Sense Multiple Access with Collision Detection (CSMA/CD)** is discussed along with other ways of accessing common media in Chapters 4 and 9.

One common bus network (and one of the original LAN standards) is the **Ethernet.** Its original configuration used a common bus such as we have described; however, recent changes in technology have provided numerous other ways in which to connect Ethernet devices while still preserving the bus logic. Chapter 9 discusses several versions of Ethernet in detail. Regardless of how it is implemented, a major advantage of an Ethernet is the capability to add new devices to the network easily.

STAR TOPOLOGY

Another common connecting arrangement is the **star topology** (Figure 1.6).* It uses a central component that allows other devices connected to it to communicate with each other. Such devices are commonly called hubs or switches; we'll distinguish between them in Chapter 10. Control is centralized: If a device wants to communicate, it does so only through the central switch. That switch, in turn, routes the

---

* The star topology can also be viewed as a hierarchical topology with the central node acting the role of the "root" in a tree. We will see in Chapter 10 that many devices are often connected to a single switch or hub, a device providing connectivity in hierarchical fashion.

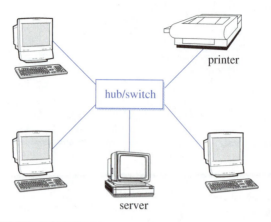

Figure 1.6   Star Topology

data to its destination. Centralization provides a focal point for responsibility, an advantage of the star topology. In early networks, the bus topology had advantages over a star topology. The lack of central control made adding new devices easy because no device needed to be aware of others. In addition, the failure or removal of a device in a bus network did not cause the network to fail. In a star topology, the failure of the central switch breaks the connection. However, changing technology and the development of reliable equipment has provided the technical and economical means to make multiple star topologies a common part of a larger topology.

RING TOPOLOGY

In a **ring topology** (Figure 1.7), devices are connected circularly. Each one can communicate directly with either or both of its neighbors but nobody else. If it wants to communicate with a device farther away, it sends a message that passes through each device in between.

A ring network may be either unidirectional or bidirectional. **Unidirectional** means that all transmissions travel in the same direction (for example, clockwise in Figure 1.7). Thus, each device can communicate directly with only one neighbor. **Bidirectional** means that data transmissions travel in either direction, and a device can communicate directly with both neighbors.

An early ring topology was IBM's Token Ring network, which connected PCs in a single office or department. In a **token ring network,** communications are coordinated by passing a **token** (a predefined sequence of bits) among all the devices in the ring. A device can send something only when it receives the token. Applications from one PC can therefore access data stored on others (file servers) without requiring a separate central device to coordinate communications. A disadvantage of the ring topology is that it requires more maintenance. For example, what happens if the token gets lost or damaged? Any device looking for the token will fail to

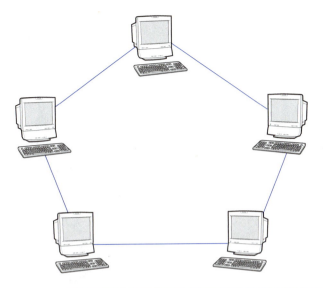

Figure 1.7   Ring Topology

see it and will not be able to send its data. There are ways of dealing with such problems, and we discuss them and other aspects of token rings further in Sections 4.7 and 9.6. The ring topology also has advantages. For example, requiring a device to wait for a token prevents two or more different devices from transmitting at the same time and causing a collision. This is a characteristic of the Ethernet protocol, which we also discuss in Section 4.7 and Chapter 9. As networks have evolved, the advantages of the Ethernet have outweighed any disadvantages; as a result, various versions of the Ethernet have dominated the LAN market.

FULLY CONNECTED TOPOLOGY

The **fully connected topology** (Figure 1.8) has a direct connection between every pair of devices in the network. This is an extreme design. Communication becomes very simple because there is no competition for common lines. If two devices want to communicate, they do so directly without involving other devices. The cost of direct connections between every pair of devices is high, however. Furthermore, many connections may be vastly underutilized. If two devices rarely communicate, the physical connection between them is seldom used. In such cases, a more economical approach is for the two to communicate indirectly, eliminating the underused line.

COMBINED TOPOLOGIES

Many computer networks use combinations of the various topologies. Figure 1.9 shows a possible combination. It has a common bus, which connects many devices directly. Groups of users such as research scientists, accountants, or sales personnel

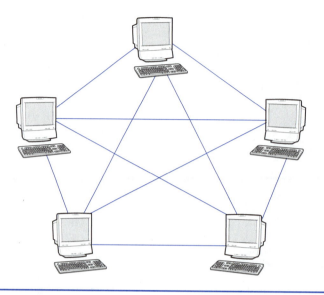

Figure 1.8 Fully Connected Topology

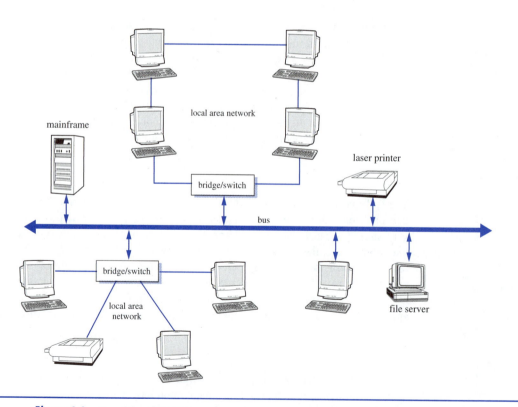

Figure 1.9 Combined Topology

may have specialized needs and want a separate LAN for much of their work. Periodically, however, they may want to access information from other LANs.

A possible design identifies several LANs connecting PCs and other devices in a ring, star, or bus topology. Devices within a LAN communicate according to the rules defined by its topology. If a PC must communicate with a device in another LAN, it can do so using a bridge or switch that connects the two LANs. Bridges and switches are devices that provide technologies to connect devices within and across LANs; we discuss them further in Chapter 10.

1.3 STANDARDS AND STANDARDS ORGANIZATIONS

THE NEED FOR STANDARDS

You might think that the primary problem in establishing communications between two computers is simply making sure that the data bits get from one computer to the other. However, because computers are often very different from one another, the transfer process is actually much more complex, like moving an automobile transmission from a Cadillac to a Toyota. All automobiles are based on the same principles, but different models have unique features appealing to a different style and market; the same is true of computers, except the user may be a little more fanatical (PC users hate Macs, and Mac users hate PCs). Companies design and manufacture computers in different styles and for different applications. Most follow the same general principles, but specifics reflect the thinking and philosophy of many people. Computers have different architectures, understand different languages, store data in different formats, and communicate at different rates. Consequently, there is much incompatibility, and communication is difficult.

This incompatibility raises a basic question: How can computers communicate at all? They communicate using a model similar to one used, for example, by trade representatives from different countries. Each person speaks a different language, so they need translators. Furthermore, they need to observe a **protocol** that defines the rules and the manner in which they begin and proceed with discussions. If all involved do not agree to a protocol, the discussions become chaotic. An orderly discussion occurs only if the participants follow the rules. Similarly, if computers are to communicate, they need protocols to determine which one "speaks" and translators to account for different languages. The next step is to define the protocols. Here lies another problem: Protocols are great, but if the principal parties involved follow different protocols, they might as well follow none. If the necessary people could agree on a common protocol, it would become a standard protocol and everyone could use it. Unfortunately, this is a lot like getting everyone to agree on a computer architecture, which we know didn't happen. Getting a diverse group of people to agree on anything is difficult. Different groups have different goals and ideas about which protocol best meets those goals. Consequently, many different standards have evolved and been used over the years.

There are two types of standards. **De facto standards** are those that exist by virtue of their widespread use. That is, they have become so common that vendors know that products consistent with them will have a large market. Many IBM products have become de facto standards. The second type of standard is one that is formally recognized and adopted by a standards organization that has achieved national or worldwide recognition. Those who wish to see their work become a standard write a proposal and submit it to a standards organization for consideration. Typically, if the proposal has merit and widespread acceptance, the standards organization will make suggestions and send it back to its originators for modifications. After several rounds of suggestions and modifications, the proposal will be adopted or refused. If approved, the standard gives vendors a model on which to design new products.

STANDARDS ORGANIZATIONS

The use of standards organizations certainly puts some order in the rapidly expanding field of communications. Hundreds of standards are approved for different aspects of communications, however, making incompatibility among different types of devices an ongoing problem. For example, many PC users purchase a modem (a device allowing a computer to send and receive signals over a telephone line) to connect to a company or university computer or to an Internet service provider. The problem is that more than a dozen standards describe different ways of sending and receiving signals over the telephone line, and if different modems use different standards, there will be no communication. Manufacturers, however, understand this and typically make sure the modems they produce implement certain standards to meet market demands. Chapter 3 discusses this problem fully.

The following organizations are important to the field of computer networks and data communications:

- **American National Standards Institute (ANSI).** ANSI (www.ansi.org/) is a private, nongovernmental agency whose members are manufacturers, users, and other interested companies. It has nearly 1000 members and is itself a member of the International Organization for Standardization, or ISO (described later in this list). ANSI standards are common in many fields. Examples include the Fiber Distributed Data Interface (FDDI) and the Synchronous Optical Network (SONET) standards for optical fiber. Another standard (discussed in Chapter 2) is the American Standard Code for Information Interchange (ASCII), used by many computers for storing information.

- **International Electrotechnical Commission (IEC).** The IEC (www.iec.ch/) is a nongovernmental agency devising standards for data processing and interconnections and safety in office equipment. It was involved in the development of the Joint Photographic Experts Group (JPEG), a group that devised a compression standard for images.

- **International Telecommunications Union (ITU),** formerly called **Comité Consultatif International de Télégraphique et Téléphonique (CCITT).** The English equivalent is the International Consultative Committee for Telephony and Telegraphy. ITU (www.itu.int/) is an agency of the United Nations and has three sectors. ITU-R deals with radio communications; ITU-D is a development sector; and the one relevant to this book, ITU-T, deals with telecommunications. ITU members include various scientific and industrial organizations, telecommunications agencies, telephone authorities, and the ISO. ITU has produced numerous standards dealing with network and telephone communications. Two well-known sets of standards are the V series and X series. The V series deals with telephone communications. Chapter 3 discusses some V standards that describe how a modem generates and interprets analog telephone signals. The X series deals with network interfaces and public networks. Examples include the X.25 standard for interfacing to a packet-switched network (discussed in Chapter 13), the X.400 standard for electronic mail systems, and the X.509 standard for digital certificates (discussed in Chapter 7). There are many other X and V standards.

- **Electronic Industries Association (EIA).** The members of EIA (www.eia.org) include electronics firms and manufacturers of telecommunications equipment. It is also a member of ANSI. The EIA's primary activities deal with electrical connections and the physical transfer of data between devices. Their most well-known standard is RS-232 (also called EIA-232), a long-time standard that PCs used for communicating with other devices such as modems or printers. The EIA-232 standard is discussed in Chapter 4.

- **Telecommunications Industry Association (TIA).** TIA (www.tiaonline.org) represents providers of communications and information technology products and services for the global marketplace. It is accredited by ANSI and develops standards for a wide range of communications products. Examples include optical cable, wires, and connectors used in local area networks.

- **Internet Engineering Task Force (IETF).** IETF (www.ietf.org) is an international community whose members include network designers, vendors, and researchers, all of whom have an interest in the stable operation of the Internet and in its evolution. It is divided into work groups that handle various technical aspects of the Internet, such as applications, operations and management, routing, security, and transport services. These working groups have been charged with the responsibility of developing and reviewing specifications intended as Internet standards. One important result of IETF's work is the next-generation Internet protocol that is presented in Chapter 11.

- **Institute of Electrical and Electronic Engineers (IEEE).** The IEEE (http://standards.ieee.org) is the largest professional organization in the world and consists of computing and engineering professionals. It publishes many different journals, runs conferences, and has a group that develops standards. Perhaps its best-known work in the communications field is its Project 802 LAN standards. Discussed in Chapter 9, the 802 standards define the communication protocols for bus, ring, and wireless networks.

- **International Organization for Standardization (ISO).** The ISO (www.iso.ch) is a worldwide organization consisting of standards bodies from many countries, such as ANSI from the United States. One of ISO's most significant activities is its work on open systems, which define the protocols that would allow any two computers to communicate independent of their architecture. One well-known model is the Open Systems Interconnect, a seven-layer organization of protocols. Some once believed OSI would be the model used for all future communications. With the explosion of the Internet and Web applications, that is unlikely. However, it is often studied as a model for layering protocols. We will discuss the OSI model in the next section.

- **National Institute of Standards and Technology (NIST).** Formerly the **National Bureau of Standards (NBS),** the NIST (www.nist.gov) is an agency of the U.S. Department of Commerce. It issues standards the federal government uses for equipment purchases. It also develops standards for many physical quantities, such as time, length, temperature, radioactivity, and radio frequencies. One important standard with security applications is the Data Encryption Standard (DES), a method of encrypting or changing information into a form that cannot be understood. The DES standard had been manufactured in chips used in communications devices. The standard is complex as well as controversial (some believe the National Security Agency purposely weakened it to prevent encryption techniques that it could not solve). It has also been broken and, by itself, is no longer a viable encryption method, but there are other techniques based on it. We discuss DES further in Chapter 7.

- **International Business Machines (IBM).** Although not a standards organization, we list it because so much of its work has become a de facto standard. Notable examples include its Systems Network Architecture (SNA) and the Extended Binary-Coded Decimal Interchange Code (EBCDIC). SNA is a protocol model designed to allow IBM computers and equipment to communicate. It predates OSI and is no longer common, but in many ways it is similar to the OSI model. The EBCDIC code (discussed in Chapter 2) is an alternative to ASCII for storing data and is commonly used on IBM mainframes (although IBM's PCs commonly use the ASCII code).

These organizations are by no means the only standards bodies, but they are the ones most pertinent to data communications and networks.

1.4 OPEN SYSTEMS AND THE OSI MODEL

We have stated that protocols allow otherwise incompatible systems to communicate. Given two specific systems, the definition of a protocol is fairly straightforward. The problem becomes bigger and more difficult as the number of different types of systems increases. A set of protocols that would allow any two different systems to communicate regardless of their underlying architecture is called an *open system*. The ISO has addressed the problem of allowing many devices to communicate and has developed its Open Systems Interconnect (OSI) model. If fully developed, it would allow any two computers to communicate provided they were connected.

The OSI model has not been a commercial success, having been overshadowed by the protocols on which the Internet runs. Consequently, some have argued that the OSI model is dead and is no longer of use. Others counter that even though it's not a commercial success, it does define a framework in which communication protocols can be studied and understood. Specifically, it allows individuals to study a wide variety of communication protocols and understand how they relate to one another. Like any complex program or system, there is a structure upon which the components are built. Furthermore, understanding each component is far different than understanding how they work together to produce an effective communication system. For this reason we provide an outline of the OSI model.

The OSI model is a seven-layer model (Figure 1.10). Each layer performs specific functions and communicates with the layers directly above and below it. Higher layers deal more with user services, applications, and activities, and the lower layers deal more with the actual transmission of information.

The purpose of layering the protocol is to separate specific functions and to make their implementation transparent to other components. This layering allows independent design and testing of each component. For example, the data link layer and physical layer perform separate functions. The physical layer performs a service to the data link layer. The data link layer does not care how the service is performed, just that it is done. Thus, if changes occur in how the physical layer is

Figure 1.10   ISO's OSI Layered Protocol

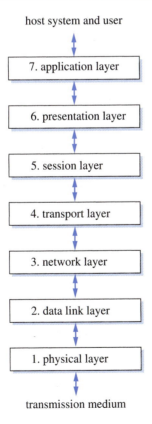

host system and user

7. application layer

6. presentation layer

5. session layer

4. transport layer

3. network layer

2. data link layer

1. physical layer

transmission medium

implemented, the data link layer (and all higher layers) is unaffected. This approach applies to any two consecutive layers and provides a level of abstraction analogous to that covered in many software design courses.

Compare the process to a meeting among several heads of state. Each leader needs to make his or her thoughts known, but the ideas often must be recast in appropriate diplomatic language to avoid offending someone. Furthermore, if they all speak a different language, one language must be chosen as the primary form of communication. Figure 1.11 illustrates a possible three-layer protocol involving a crisis that two of the leaders are trying to resolve. One leader adamantly states that he is not going to tolerate the situation. The diplomat recasts the message into a less-threatening tenor, and a translator translates the message to the chosen language. On the other side, another translator translates back to a specific language. The diplomat receives the message and tells the head of state what it really means.

In a sense, the two leaders are communicating directly, even though the message actually passes through other individuals. The OSI model works similarly. The lowest layer, the physical layer, deals with actual data transmission. The highest layer deals with the computer system connected to the network. Each layer in between

Figure 1.11   Communication Protocol between Two Heads of State

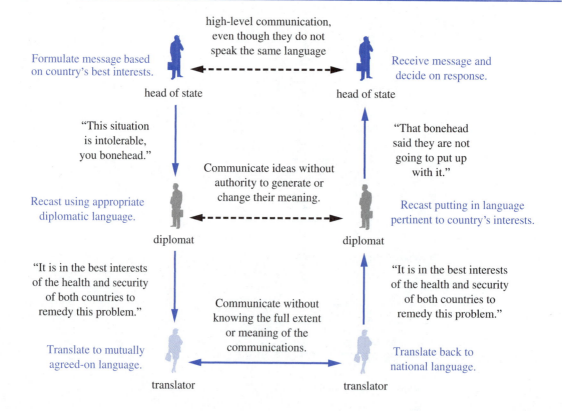

corresponds to a different level of abstraction in data communications and defines certain functions and protocols.

Two otherwise incompatible sites, each running the OSI model, can communicate with each other (Figure 1.12). Logically, each layer communicates directly with its counterpart at the other site. Physically, each layer communicates with the layers immediately above and below it. When a process wants to send information, it starts by handing it over to the application layer. That layer performs its functions and sends the data to the presentation layer. It, in turn, performs its functions and gives the data to the session layer. This process continues until the physical layer receives the data and actually transmits it.

On the receiving end, the process works in reverse. The physical layer receives the bit stream and gives it to the data link layer. The data link layer performs certain functions and sends the data to the network layer. This process continues until the

Figure 1.12   Communication Using the OSI Seven-Layer Protocol

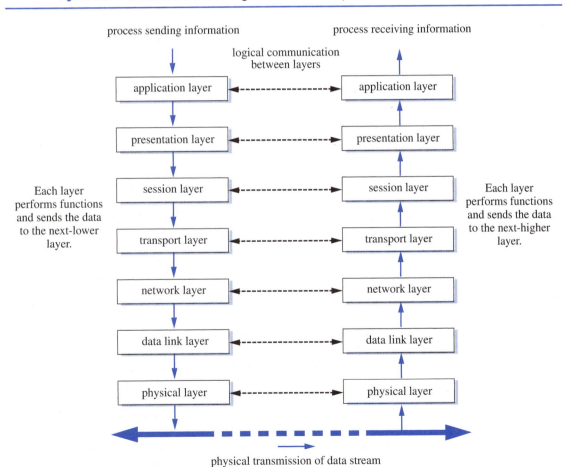

application eventually receives the information and gives it to the receiving process. The two processes appear to communicate directly, with each layer appearing to communicate directly with its counterpart at another network node. In reality, all data are broken into a bit stream and transmitted between physical layers.

This process is a bit like sending a letter, where you communicate with the letter's recipient by addressing the envelope and dropping it in a mailbox. As far as you are concerned, the activity is then complete: The communication is independent of how the letter is eventually routed or whether it goes by truck, plane, train, boat, or carrier pigeon. You know the letter will arrive and you can simply wait for a response.

OVERVIEW OF THE MODEL

The highest layer, the **application layer,** works directly with the user or application programs. Note that it is not the same as an application program. The application layer provides user services such as electronic mail and file transfers. For example, in a file transfer protocol the application layer on one end should appear to send a file directly to the application layer on the other end independent of the underlying network or computer architectures.

The application layer also defines the protocols that allow access to a full-screen text editor running on a remote server. The reason is that different types of editors use different control sequences for cursor control. For example, just moving the cursor may involve arrow keys or special key combinations. Ideally, we would like to make such differences transparent to the user.

The **presentation layer** is responsible for presenting data in a format its user can understand. For example, suppose two different computers use different numeric and character formats. The presentation layer translates data from one representation to another and insulates the user from such differences. In effect, the presentation layer determines the difference between data and information. After all, networks exist so users can exchange information, not raw bit streams. Users do not want to be concerned with different formats; they would prefer to concentrate on the informational content and what it means to them.

The presentation layer can also provide security measures. It may encrypt data before handing it to the lower layers for transfer. The presentation layer at the other end would decrypt the data after receiving it. The user need never know the data had been altered. This is especially important in wide area networks (ones that span large geographic distances), where unauthorized access is a serious problem.

The **session layer** allows applications on two different computers to establish a **session,** or logical connection. For example, a user may log on to a remote system and may communicate by alternately sending and receiving messages. The session layer helps coordinate the process by informing each end when it can send or must listen. This is a form of synchronization.

The session layer also handles error recovery. For example, suppose a user is sending the contents of a large file over a network that suddenly fails. When it is operational again, must the user start retransmitting from the beginning of the file? The answer is no, because the session layer lets the user insert checkpoints in a long stream. If a network crashes, only the data transmitted since the last check-point are lost.

The session layer also brackets operations that must appear to the user as a single transaction. A common example is the deletion of a record from a database. Although the user sees the deletion as a single operation, it actually may involve several. The record must be found and subsequently deleted by altering pointers and addresses and perhaps entries in an index or hash table. If a user is accessing a database through a network, the session layer makes sure that all low-level operations are received before the deletion actually begins. If the database operations were applied one at a time as they were received, a network failure could compromise the database's integrity by changing some pointers but not others (you may recall your introductory data structures class, where incorrect programs did not change all your pointers) or by deleting a record but not a reference to it.

The fourth layer is the **transport layer.** It is the lowest layer that deals primarily with end-to-end communications (the lower layers deal with the network itself). The transport layer may determine which network to use for communication. A computer may be connected to several networks that may differ in speed, cost, and type of communication, the choice often depending on many factors. For example, does the information consist of a long continuous stream of data? Or does it consist of many intermittent transfers? The telephone network is appropriate for long, continuous data transfers. Once a connection has been established, it is maintained until the transfer is complete.

Another approach divides the data into small **packets** (subsets of the data) and transfers them intermittently. In such cases, a constant connection between two points is unnecessary. Instead, each packet may be transmitted independently through the network. Consequently, when the packets arrive at the other end they must be reassembled before their contents are passed to the layer above. One problem is that if the packets follow different routes, there is no guarantee that they will arrive in the order in which they were sent (just as there is no guarantee that a letter mailed on Monday will arrive before one mailed on Tuesday) or that they will all arrive. Not only must the receiver determine the correct order of incoming packets, but also it must verify it got them all.

The **network layer** deals with routing strategies. For example, in a bidirectional ring network, there are two paths between any two points. A more complex topology may have many routes from which to choose. Which ones are fastest, cheapest, or safest? Which ones are open or uncongested? Should an entire message follow the same route, or should parts of it be transferred independently?

The network layer controls the **communications subnet,** the collection of transmission media and switching elements required for routing and data transmission. The network layer is the highest layer in the subnet. This layer may also contain accounting software for customer billing. Remember, networks exist to allow users to communicate. As with most services, someone must pay. The fee depends on the amount of data transmitted and possibly the time of day. The network layer can maintain such information and handle billing.

The **data link layer** supervises the flow of information between adjacent network nodes. It uses error detection or correction techniques to ensure that a transmission contains no errors. If the data link detects an error, it can either request a new transmission or, depending on the implementation, correct the error. It also controls how much information is sent at a time: too much and the network becomes congested; too little and the sending and receiving ends experience excessive waits.

The data link layer also recognizes a format. Data are often transmitted in **frames,** which consist of a group of bytes organized according to a specified format. The data link layer marks the beginning and end of each outgoing frame with unique bit patterns and recognizes these patterns to define an incoming frame. It then sends error-free frames to the previous layer, the network layer.

Finally, the **physical layer** transmits data bits over a network. It is concerned with the physical or electrical aspects of data communications. For example, is the medium copper cable, optical fiber, or satellite communications? How can data be transferred physically from point A to point B? The physical layer transmits data bits received from the data link layer in streams without regard to their meaning or format. Similarly, it receives bits without analyzing them and gives them to the data link layer.

In summary, the lowest three layers deal primarily with the details of network communications. Together, they provide a service to the upper layers. The upper layers deal with end-to-end communications. They define the communication protocols between two users but are not concerned with the low-level details of data transmission. Some network implementations may not use all seven layers or may combine some of the functions from different layers. Try to remember that OSI is just a model (albeit an important one), and many network protocols are not OSI compliant. However, it is an important place to begin because it helps us understand where many network functions belong within a protocol. Table 1.1 contains a summary of the functions we have discussed so far.

CONNECTION STRATEGIES

Before we expand on some of the layers, we provide an overview of network operations. We know that two computers must be connected (by wire, optical fiber, satellite, or other wireless technology) to communicate. How the information travels

Table 1.1 Summary of OSI Layers

LAYER	FUNCTIONS
7. Application	Provides electronic mail, file transfers, and other user services
6. Presentation	Translates data formats, encrypts and decrypts data
5. Session	Synchronizes communicating users, recovers from errors, and brackets operations
4. Transport	Determines network, may assemble and reassemble packets
3. Network	Determines routes, manages billing information
2. Data link	Detects or corrects errors, defines frames
1. Physical	Transmits physical data

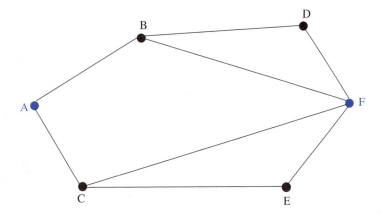

Figure 1.13   Sample Computer Network

through the network is a design issue. For example, consider the network in Figure 1.13. If node A wants to communicate with node F, how does the information travel from A to F? Take care to distinguish this problem from determining the route, or network path. If the lines represent physical connections, there are four routes along which data may travel from node A to node F. (Can you list them?) The network layer will determine which one is best, but the issue here is how the information travels via the chosen route. This is sometimes called the *connection strategy*.

There are three strategies: circuit switching, message switching, and packet switching. In **circuit switching,** once a connection is made between two nodes, it is maintained until one of them terminates it. In other words, the connection is dedicated to the communication between the two parties. Circuit switching is common in the telephone system (Figure 1.14) because the channel allocated to one telephone connection cannot be used by another.

How does it work? A person at node A wants to talk to someone at node F. The person at A requests a connection to F. In a telephone network, dialing a number makes the connection. In a computer network, the user enters appropriate commands to connect to a specified location. Either way, logic at node A must determine the next node in a route that leads to F. This process involves factors such as the cost of the connection and the availability of different paths. For example, a telephone call from San Francisco to Los Angeles is not normally routed through Miami. However, if the lines between the two cities are congested, the connection may be indirect—for example, through Sacramento.

In Figure 1.14, node A has determined that C is a better choice than B in the route from A to F. Thus, node A connects to node C. Node C, in turn, proceeds similarly. It might choose node F, or it might decide to go through node E. Again, cost and existing connections affect the choice. In this case, node C connects to node E. Finally, E connects to F. The connection is made, and node F may be willing to accept it. In the telephone system, you accept a connection by picking up the receiver

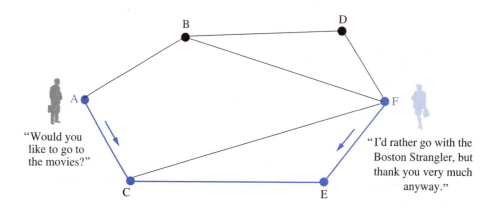

Figure 1.14   Dedicated Circuit Connecting A and F

and saying "Hello." In a computer network, appropriate commands are used to accept connections. If node F does not respond (e.g., busy signal or no answer), node A terminates the request.

If node F accepts the connection, information may be exchanged. The person at node A asks, "Do you want to go to the movies?" The person at node F responds by saying, "I'd really love to go with you, but my canary just died and I'm in mourning. Ask me some other time when I'm out of town."

Circuit switching requires that the route be determined and the connection made before any information is transmitted. Also, the network maintains the connection until a node terminates it. This type of connection is most useful when the communications between the two nodes are continuous, that is, when node A "says" something and node F "hears" almost immediately, with virtually no transmission delay. This approach is not always the best way to communicate, however. First, if node A calls node F, F must answer. Otherwise, A cannot send any information. Second, suppose nodes A and F exchange information infrequently. (Did you ever experience long periods of silence during a telephone conversation?) In that case, the connection is underused.

Message switching is an alternative to circuit switching. A network uses message switching to establish a route when a message (a unit of information) is sent. For example, suppose node A sends the message "Will you go to the movies with me?" to node F. Node A attaches the location or address of F to the message and looks for the first node in the route. As Figure 1.15, shows, node A chooses node C. As before, the choice depends on cost and the availability of connections. Node A sends the message (along with the address of F) to C. The message is stored there temporarily, while logic looks for another node. It sends the message to node E, where it is again stored temporarily. Finally, logic at E locates node F and sends the message to its final destination. Because the message is stored in its entirety at each node, networks that use this method are also called **store-and-forward networks.**

How are message switching and circuit switching different?

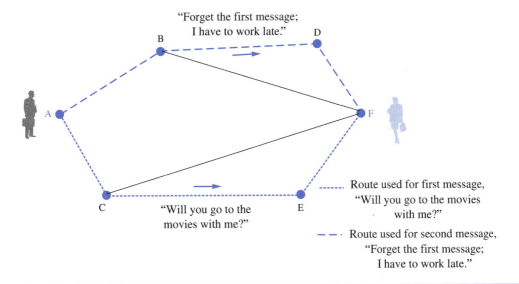

Figure 1.15 Message-Switched Network

- In message switching, the message is stored temporarily at each node. In circuit switching, the node simply acts as a switching device to route the data. For example, your telephone conversations are not stored at intermediate locations (unless someone is listening and recording your conversation!). The transmission delays resulting from message switching make this connection strategy unsuitable for telephone networks. Delays in voice transmission would make conversations very difficult.

- In circuit switching, a single route is dedicated to the exchange of all messages between two nodes. In message switching, different messages may travel over different routes. Suppose node A wanted to send a second message, "Forget the first message; I have to work late," to node F. Because routing is often time dependent, A might choose B for the first node in the route. The message then goes to nodes D and F. Different messages thus can share common connections over time, providing a higher utilization.

- Circuit switching requires that both parties be ready when data are sent. Message switching does not. The message may be sent and stored for later retrieval.

The third connection strategy, *packet switching,* minimizes the effects of problems caused by long messages. Long messages may exceed the buffering capacity at a node, or connections between adjacent nodes may be tied up for long periods. A failure in a connection may mean the loss of the entire message. Consequently, message-switched networks are no longer common and have given way to the more efficient packet-switched networks. Let's see how they work.

Suppose a user at node A wants to send a message to node F. If the message is long, it is divided into smaller units called **packets.** Their size is design dependent.

Each packet contains its destination address or some other designator indicating where it should go and is routed there by network protocols. When the packets all arrive, they are reassembled to form the original message. Like message switching, a physical connection between the two endpoints is not maintained. The smaller size of the packets facilitates the necessary buffering at intermediate network nodes.

The two common routing methods in packet-switched networks are the datagram and the virtual circuit. In the **datagram** approach, each packet is transmitted independently. That is, network protocols route each one as though it were a separate message. This allows routing strategies to consider the changing conditions within the network. Congestion on certain routes may cause rerouting. (Chapter 10 discusses routing strategies in more detail.)

In the **virtual circuit** approach, network protocols establish a route (virtual circuit) before sending any packets. The delivery of the packets using the same route ensures that the packets arrive in order and without error. The process is similar to circuit switching, with one important difference: The route is not dedicated. That is, different virtual circuits may share a common network connection. Logic at each node must store received packets and schedule them for transmission.

Datagrams have a disadvantage because independent routing requires more overhead. In such cases, a virtual circuit may be more efficient. Another disadvantage of datagrams is that packets may not arrive in the order in which they were sent. This is a disadvantage for applications such as real-time audio or video streaming where sound is heard or images are seen as they actually occur. Such applications typically require that the packets that contain the audio or video data arrive in the same order in which they were sent.

Figure 1.16 shows the problem. Suppose the user at node A wants to send a message consisting of three packets to node F. Logic at node A decides to route packets P_1 and P_2 to node C. However, as it examines possible routes for P_3, it determines that the route through C has become congested. Therefore, it sends P_3 to node B. Packets P_1 and P_2 then travel to nodes E and F, while packet P_3 goes

Figure 1.16   Packet-Switched Network

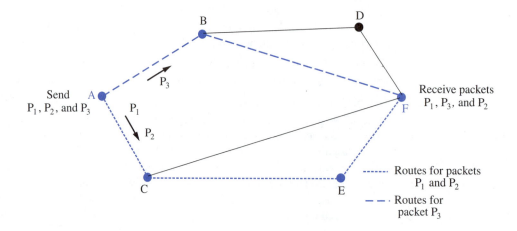

Send A $P_1, P_2,$ and P_3

P_3

P_1

P_2

B

D

F Receive packets $P_1, P_3,$ and P_2

C   E

------ Routes for packets P_1 and P_2

— — · Routes for packet P_3

Table 1.2   Comparison of Connection Strategies

STRATEGY	ADVANTAGES	DISADVANTAGES
Circuit switching	Speed. It is appropriate when transmission delays are unacceptable.	Because network connections are dedicated, all other routes must avoid them. Both users must be present during communications, such as during a telephone conversation.
Message switching	Routes are not dedicated and may be reused immediately after the transmission of a message. The recipient need not accept the message immediately.	Messages generally take longer to reach their destination. Problems also can occur with long messages, because they must be buffered at intermediate nodes. The end of a message travels a route chosen earlier based on conditions that may no longer be true.
Packet switching (datagrams)	If congestion develops, the datagram approach to packet switching may choose alternate routes for parts of the message. Thus, network routes are utilized better.	More overhead exists because each packet is routed separately. Routing decisions must be made for each packet. Packets may arrive out of order in the datagram approach.
Packet switching (virtual circuits)	All packets follow the same route and always arrive in order. This strategy is particularly useful for real-time streaming. Also, there is less overhead in routing packets.	Routes that packets follow may, after a time, no longer be optimal. New routes would have to be renegotiated.

directly from B to F. Depending on network traffic, F could receive the packets in the order P_1, P_3, P_2 and must reassemble them in the correct order.

On the other hand, the sensitivity to changing conditions may be an advantage. Routing P_3 differently made the packets arrive out of order, but P_3 may have arrived much sooner than it would have otherwise. In networks with a lot of traffic, a good route may turn bad quickly if every node begins to send over it—just as a major expressway from the suburbs to the center of a large city is a good route at 5:00 A.M. but very congested at 7:00 A.M.

We will discuss routing strategies and protocols for packet-switched networks more fully in later chapters. For now, Table 1.2 provides a comparison among the connection strategies we have presented.

PHYSICAL LAYER

The physical layer deals primarily with transmission media and how signals are transmitted. Typical media are twisted wire pair, coaxial cable, optical fiber, satellites, microwave towers, infrared, and radio waves. Each option has different electrical, electromagnetic, or optical properties that make it suitable for different situations. Those properties also put limitations on how much information can be transmitted per unit of time and determine the likelihood that they are subject to interference from external sources. Another issue is whether the signals are analog or digital. Most people are aware of the move toward digital transmissions, but what does that actually mean? A full description of transmission media and related topics in analog and digital transmissions, bandwidth, signal-to-noise ratios, broadband, baseband, voice grade transmissions, and even Fourier analysis can fill volumes. We discuss some of these topics further in Chapters 2 and 3.

DATA LINK LAYER

While the physical layer transmits and receives data, the data link layer sits above it and makes sure that it works correctly. For example, what happens if two nodes simultaneously try to transmit data along the same line (contention)? How does a node know the data it has received are correct (error detection and correction)? Could electrical interference such as that caused by an electrical storm or voltage fluctuations have changed some bits? If the interference changed a packet's destination, how does a node know it did not receive something it should have?

Contention occurs when two or more nodes want to transmit over the same medium at the same time. There are several ways of handling it. Some bus networks use a method called **collision detection.** Collision detection does not prevent multiple nodes from transmitting simultaneously over a common medium. Rather, it is a response to simultaneous transmissions, or collisions. Typically, if a device sends something that collides with another transmission, sensing circuits detect the collision, and the device tries to send again later.

Sometimes a device tries to avoid collisions by listening to the bus activity. If the bus is busy, the device does not transmit. If the circuits detect no activity on the bus, the device goes ahead and transmits. If two devices both sense no activity on the bus and transmit simultaneously, a collision occurs. We call this method of resolving contention *Carrier Sense Multiple Access with Collision Detection* (CSMA/CD). In effect, it reduces the number of collisions but does not eliminate them. Section 4.7 discusses this approach in more detail.

Token passing is another contention scheme that prevents collisions. Here, a unique bit stream, called a *token,* circulates among all network nodes. If a node wants to transmit, it must wait until it receives the token and must append the token to the end of the message. It also changes token control bits to indicate that the token is in use. The message is sent to its destination, and the receiving node now has the token. Depending on the protocol, that station may seize the token and send a message if it has one, or it may send the token to the next node.

Ring networks often use token passing, as shown in Figure 1.17. The token circulates clockwise around the ring. Node E currently has the token; therefore, only it can send a message. Because the token is unique, collisions cannot occur. Drawbacks do exist, however: A token may get lost or duplicated or may be hogged by a node. Chapter 9 discusses ways of dealing with such events.

Token passing is not limited to rings. It can be used with any network topology by numbering the nodes and circulating the token among them in numerical order. Device numbering is easiest to do in ring or linear networks, however. Section 4.7 discusses token passing and some of its variations, and Section 9.6 discusses it in the context of the token ring standard.

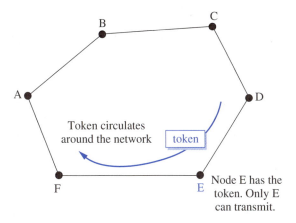

Figure 1.17   Token Ring Network

The physical layer transmits bit streams across the network. But how does the receiver know whether it has received the correct data? Bad connections, faulty lines, or electrical interference all can affect transmissions. The data link layer executes error detection and correction algorithms. With **error detection,** the receiving data link layer determines whether an error has occurred and, if so, typically requests that the information be retransmitted. With **error correction,** the data link layer has the capability to set the damaged bits to their correct value.

Perhaps the simplest detection method uses a **parity bit,** an extra bit attached to each sequence of data bits, or frame. For example, an **even parity** makes the total number of 1 bits (including itself) even. That is, if the frame has an odd number of 1 bits, the parity bit is 1. If it has an even number, the parity bit is 0. (There is an analogous definition for odd parity.) Consider the frames in Figure 1.18. The first frame has four 1 bits. Therefore, its even parity bit is 0. The second frame has five 1 bits, so its even parity bit is 1. The parity bit is transmitted with the frame and the receiver checks the parity. If it finds an odd number of 1 bits, an error has occurred.

The problem with parity bits is that errors can go undetected. For example, if two bits change during transmission, the number of 1 bits remains even. Thus, parity bits can detect single but not double errors. More sophisticated techniques exist that deal with multiple-bit errors. Chapter 6 discuss several of them in greater detail.

Figure 1.18   Parity Bits

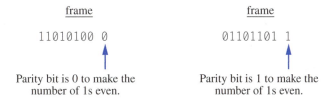

NETWORK LAYER

The network layer provides the transport layer with the capability to establish end-to-end communications. This capability allows the transport layer to do its tasks without worrying about the details of sending information back and forth between the two stations. It is a lot like making a telephone call without worrying about the details of telephone switching equipment. This process, which often requires communication across multiple intermediate nodes, can be quite difficult. There are several common protocols, but they are too complex to discuss here; we describe them in later chapters.

The network layer contains algorithms designed to find the best route between two points. We mentioned route determination when we described switching techniques. We indicated that route determination considers factors such as connection costs and availability of lines as it tries to find the quickest and cheapest route to a particular node. For example, Figure 1.19 shows a network containing several routes from A to F. Each line connecting two nodes represents the cost, indicated by the numbers on the lines. Going from A to F through B and D results in a total cost of 16. Going through B and E instead results in a cost of only 12. In general, the network layer determines which route is best. Perhaps more accurately, network-layer protocols running at network nodes collectively determine which route is best. There are many different ways to approach routing, which we explore in Chapter 10.

Successful routing is often more difficult than it seems at first. Courses in discrete mathematics and data structures typically cover algorithms designed to find the best or cheapest routes through a graph. They make assumptions that are often not true in real networks, however. They assume that a graph's nodes and the costs of edges connecting them do not change. In dynamic environments both assumptions are often false. New devices and nodes can enter the network regularly and

Figure 1.19   Route Costs

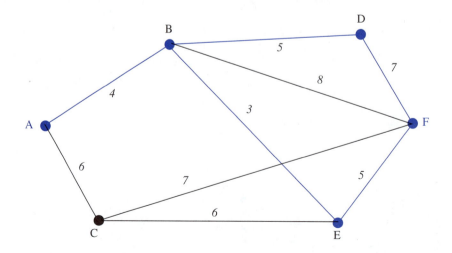

affect both existing routes and their costs. Algorithms must be robust enough to respond to changing conditions.

Even when algorithms do respond to changing conditions, other problems occur. A good route may attract a lot of traffic and overload the computers on it. The resulting congestion often results in some of the traffic being eliminated. This seems a severe solution, but when a network node has too much information to handle, it often has little choice. In this case, the network-layer protocol must be able to inform the sender when part of a message is lost.

Other problems can occur when information traveling one route is detoured because changing conditions generated a new best route. The information then may travel that route, only to be detoured again. In an extreme case, information can be detoured continually, causing an endless flow of information throughout the network to bounce from node to node. It is the electronic equivalent of a panhandler looking for a place to call home.

TRANSPORT LAYER

The transport layer represents a transitional layer. The three layers below transport deal primarily with network communications (Figure 1.20). Each node between a sending and a receiving node executes its protocols to ensure the information is being transmitted correctly and efficiently. The transport layer and the three layers

Figure 1.20   End-to-End Connection with Intermediate Nodes

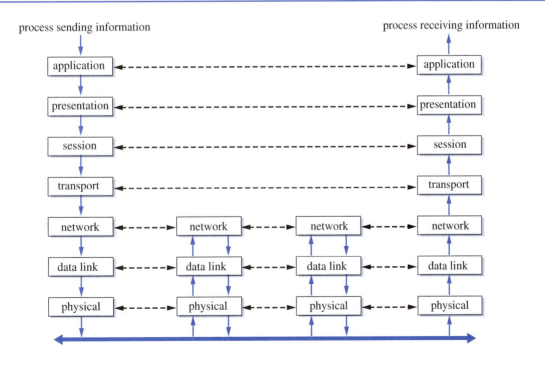

above it provide user services. They execute primarily at the sending and receiving nodes to ensure information arrives at the destination and to acknowledge its arrival to the sending node.

One of the transport layer's functions is to provide a reliable and efficient network connection. It allows the three layers above it to perform their tasks independent of a specific network architecture. At the same time, it relies on the lower three layers to control actual network operations. It makes sure information gets from the source to the eventual destination. The major responsibility of this layer is to provide the session layer with a network connection, or transport connection. Most important, the transport layer provides reliable and efficient communications. In practice, networks are sometimes unreliable; that is, there is no guarantee that the connections will not fail. What happens if a data packet is lost? What if a packet is significantly delayed? How do these problems affect users? The transport layer insulates the session layer from many details of the network. We discuss the specifics of a common transport protocol, TCP (Transmission Control Protocol), in Chapter 11.

Transport functions include multiplexing, buffering, and connection management. With *multiplexing* (Figure 1.21), several transport users share a single node. For example, a user might establish several connections to a network simultaneously through a single workstation. One connection is to log in to a remote machine, another to download a file, and a third to access a website. Each interacts with the transport layer to send and receive data, and the transport protocol makes sure that incoming data are routed to the appropriate user.

The transport layer also handles **buffering** at network nodes. An interesting aspect here is that buffering may occur at either the destination or the source node.

Figure 1.21   Multiplexing

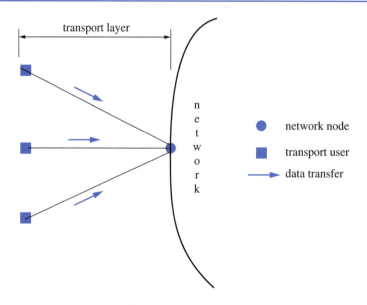

When a sending transport layer receives data from the session layer for transmission, it divides it into units called **transport protocol data units** (TPDUs). The transport protocol sends them to the receiving transport layer (via the lower layers), where they eventually are routed to the receiving session layer.

A transport protocol typically requires the acknowledgment of each received TPDU. This acknowledgment is especially useful in packet-switching networks, in which packets may be delayed or even lost because of a network failure. Suppose transport user A wants to send several TPDUs to user B. In some cases, the TPDUs are buffered at the source and queued for transmission by the lower layers. The transport layer waits for an acknowledgment for each TPDU but does not remove them from the buffer. If the protocol requires an acknowledgment for each TPDU, the sending transport layer waits for it. If it does not occur within a set period of time, the sender retransmits the TPDU, which is possible only if it is still in the buffer.

When a receiving transport layer receives a TPDU, it holds the TPDU until the session layer is ready for it. Keep in mind that there is no guarantee the session layer will accept it immediately. If the receiver knows the sender is buffering all TPDUs, it may elect to use a single buffer to save space. The disadvantage of this choice is that the receiver may have no room for subsequent TPDUs until the one being held is delivered to the session layer. In this case, the receiver ignores the TPDUs and refuses to acknowledge their reception. The sender receives no acknowledgment and eventually retransmits the TPDUs.

Connection management is the protocol by which the transport layer establishes and releases connections between two nodes. At first glance, making and releasing connections may seem easy, but it is deceptively tricky. For example, suppose the transport layer is trying to establish a connection between users A and B. You might think the connection is as simple as (1) user A requesting a connection to user B and (2) user B indicating readiness for a connection, after which (3) a connection occurs (Figure 1.22). This is a **two-way handshake protocol** for establishing a connection. The problem is that it does not always work because of potential delays in either A's request or B's response. However, these problems and their solutions are best described after we've had a chance to discuss some additional protocols. We therefore defer additional discussions of connection management until Section 11.4.

Figure 1.22   Two-Way Handshake

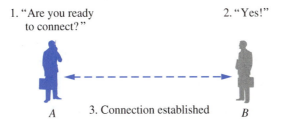

1. "Are you ready to connect?"

2. "Yes!"

3. Connection established

A   B

SESSION LAYER

The next three layers deal primarily with user services and functions. (The previous four layers focused on communications.) The session layer contains the protocols necessary for establishing and maintaining a connection, or session, between two end users. The difference between the transport and session layers is often unclear at first. The transport layer provides the session layer with a connection between two nodes, and we just stated that the session provides a connection between users. What is the difference? Figure 1.23 shows an analogy that should help clear up any confusion.

In the figure, an executive is asking a secretary to call a customer. The executive is analogous to the session layer, and the secretary to the transport layer. Thus, the request in (a) is similar to requesting a session. The executive requests the connection but does not get involved with technical details such as looking up the phone number or dialing it. In (b), the secretary makes the call and thus initiates procedures to establish the transport connection. The process of dialing and initiating

Figure 1.23   Requesting and Establishing a Session Connection

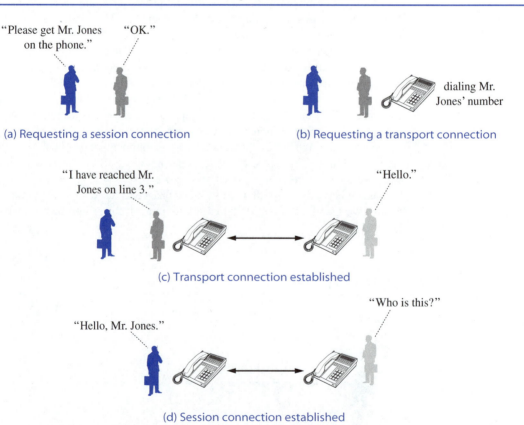

"Please get Mr. Jones on the phone."   "OK."

(a) Requesting a session connection

dialing Mr. Jones' number

(b) Requesting a transport connection

"I have reached Mr. Jones on line 3."

"Hello."

(c) Transport connection established

"Hello, Mr. Jones."

"Who is this?"

(d) Session connection established

the connection is independent of the way the telephone company's switching circuits actually route the call. But again, transport layers don't care about such details. When the call is completed in (c), the transport connection is made. However,
the session is not established until the executive finally gets on the phone in (d).

Figure 1.24 shows another example related to computer communications. A
large company with offices all over the world has all its essential information on a
database at a central location. Each office (airline reservation systems, major bro-
kerage companies, banks, and so on) has its own server that communicates with the
company's database over a network. Through the server, regional office employees
frequently access the database over short periods of time. These are the sessions that
the session layer provides. Because of the frequent access, the transport layer maintains a single transport connection between the server and database. Each session
uses the same transport connection, a system that is more efficient than negotiating
a new connection every time a user wants to access the database.

Don't interpret Figure 1.24 as a form of multiplexing. A transport connection
services only one session at a time. A second session can use the transport connection only when the first session is finished.

If the transport connection is disrupted because of a network failure, the session
layer can request another transport connection without disrupting the session. This
recovery is analogous to the executive in Figure 1.23 being disconnected from the
client and then waiting on the telephone while the secretary calls a second time.

Figure 1.24   Multiple Sessions Using One Transport Connection

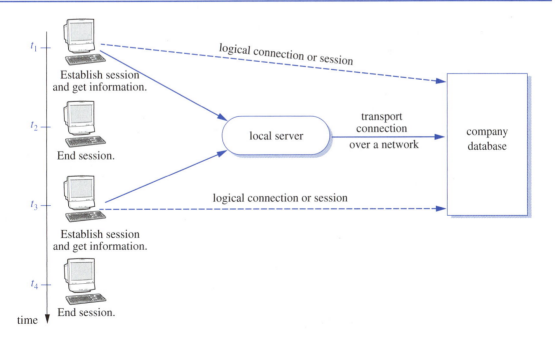

The session layer provides other abilities, but we will not describe details here. For example, the session layer can allow both sides to send information at the same time (**full duplex**) or can force them to take turns sending (**half duplex**). It can also organize information into units so that if a disruption in the connection occurs, the user does not have to restart from the beginning. This is useful if such a disruption occurs while downloading a large file. When the connection is reestablished, the transfer can resume at the point of interruption. The session layer can also define activities that must be done on an all-or-none basis. An example is a remote database update that involves changing several records. An ill-timed disruption in service could cause some records to be changed while leaving others intact, causing inconsistency. The session layer can ensure that all changes are made or, in the case of a problem, that none are.

PRESENTATION LAYER

Computer networking would be much simpler if all computers spoke the same language. We are not talking here about languages such as C, Ada, Java, C++, or COBOL. We are referring to the way in which a computer represents the entity we call information.

We must distinguish between information and data, as the difference is important. When we speak of *data,* we conjure up images of hoards of numbers, hexadecimal dumps, or pages of letters and special symbols. In short, a computer does not store information, it stores data. *Information* is a meaning we attach to the data. At the most basic level, data are an assortment of bits and bytes and other unmentionable things. Information is a human interpretation of it. A problem exists because different computers have different ways of representing the same information. Thus, it is not enough to define effective data communications. We must define effective communication of information. The presentation layer does this.

For example, consider a network that transmits data between two computers (Figure 1.25). One stores information using ASCII and the other uses EBCDIC, which represent two different ways of storing data (Chapter 2 discusses ASCII and EBCDIC further). When the ASCII-based computer says "HELLO," the network transmits the ASCII message. The EBCDIC-based computer receives and stores the data. Unfortunately, anyone interpreting it will see it as "≪! " because of the different interpretation placed on the bits received.

Figure 1.25   Data Exchange between Two Computers

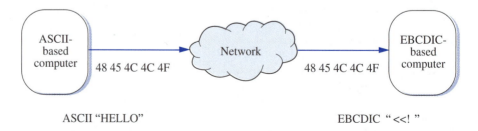

ASCII "HELLO"   EBCDIC "<<! "

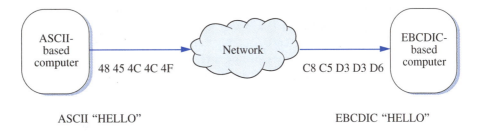

Figure 1.26   Information Exchange between Two Computers

What we really want is communication of information, as shown in Figure 1.26. The ASCII version of "HELLO" is transmitted. Because the receiver uses EBCDIC, the data must be converted. In this case, the hexadecimal characters 48 45 4C 4C 4F are transmitted, but C8 C5 D3 D3 D6 are received. The two computers have not exchanged data; instead, and more important, they have exchanged information in the form of the word "HELLO."

The problem involves more than just code conversion. We may also have problems transmitting numbers. For example, computers may store integers using either a two's complement or a one's complement format. The difference is minor, but it must be considered. In addition, the number of bits used to represent an integer varies. Common formats use 16, 32, 64, or 80 bits. Bits must be added or removed to allow for the different sizes. Sometimes a translation is impossible. For example, the maximum integer in a 16-bit format is 32,767. What happens if a computer that uses 32-bit integers tries to transfer an integer value of 50,000 to a computer limited to 16-bit integers?

Floating-point numbers also present problems. Figure 1.27 shows a common format, although many variations exist. The number of bits used for the mantissa and exponent vary. The number of bits may even vary within a machine, because numbers may be either single or double precision. The exponent may also be interpreted in different ways. Sometimes it is a power of 2; in other cases, it is a power of 16. Sometimes the mantissa is not stored in contiguous bits. When one considers the range of differences, it is amazing that computers can share numeric information at all.

The problem increases with more sophisticated data structures such as arrays, records, and linked lists. The presentation layer must consider how the fields of a

Figure 1.27   Generic Format for Floating-Point Numbers

record are stored. For example, does each one begin on a word boundary or a byte boundary? Where are link fields stored? How many bytes do they occupy? Is a multidimensional array stored by row or by column?

The presentation layer must know the system it serves. It must also know the format of data it receives from other sources. It must ensure the proper transfer of information throughout the network.

Another function of the presentation layer is **data compression,** * which is a way of reducing the number of bits while retaining their meaning. If transmission is expensive, compression can lower costs significantly and increase the amount of information that can be sent per unit of time. For example, suppose the data in a large file consist entirely of strings of capital letters. For example, it might be a list of keywords or employees' last names. How many data bits must be transferred? If the characters are ASCII coded, the number is $8n$, where n is the number of characters. If the presentation layer redefined the code by assigning 0 to A, 1 to B, and so on up to 25 to Z, each character of the alphabet can be represented using 5 bits (the fewest number of bits required to store numbers up to 25). Thus, about 38% fewer bits are actually sent. There are many other methods for data compression; Chapter 5 discusses them in more detail.

Security is another reason to change the bits (or encrypt them) before sending them. If an unauthorized person intercepts the transmitted message, its encrypted form makes the message unintelligible. To understand its meaning, the data must be decrypted. Chapter 7 deals with the important issue of encryption in detail.

APPLICATION LAYER

The application layer, the highest layer in the OSI model, communicates with the user and the application programs. It is called the application layer because it contains network applications, which differ from user applications such as payroll or accounting programs, graphic design packages, language translators, or database programs. Typical network applications include Web applications, electronic mail, file transfer, and virtual terminal protocols (all discussed in Chapter 11) and distributed systems.

Most colleges and major organizations are connected to the Internet, which allows the exchange of personal or professional messages by electronic mail. As an example, many of the comments the author and editor exchanged during production of this book were done by email. The lower layers of the model provide the means of expressing the message and getting it to its destination. The *email protocol* in the application layer defines the architecture of an electronic mail system. It stores mail in a mailbox (really a file) from which users can organize and read their messages and provide responses.

A **file transfer protocol** also allows users to exchange information, but in a different way. It typically allows a user to connect to a remote system, examine

---

* The most effective data compression can be done at this level because the most knowledge of the data and their usage is available. However, compression often is done at lower levels instead of or in addition to this level.

some of its directories and files, and copy them to the user's system. To the user it is almost that simple, except for a few problems. One is file structure. Some files consist of a simple sequence of bytes; others are flat files consisting of a linear sequence of records. Hashed files allow random access to a record through a key field value. Hierarchical files* may organize all occurrences of a key field in a tree structure. These differences pose a problem when transferring files.

The World Wide Web allows users to view documents stored at computers in other locations. It also allows the user to follow a link stored on one document to another document at another site. By following links, the user can hop from one location to another with a simple click of a mouse button. Common jargon for this is *Web browsing* or *Web surfing*. We discuss the Web and some applications more fully in Chapter 12.

A **virtual terminal protocol** allows a user at a workstation to log in to a remote computer across a computer network. Once connected, the user interacts as though the computer were on-site. Allowing access to different computers from different workstations presents problems because of the variety of equipment and software. One problem is that software often is written with specific equipment in mind. Full-screen text editors are examples. The editor displays text on a screen and allows the user to move the cursor and make changes. The displayed number of rows and columns, for example, may vary from one station to another. Commands to move the cursor and delete or insert text may require control sequences that also vary depending on the computer to which you are connected. Other examples include software that depends on screen formats for input (by this, we mean organized screen layouts, which preceded the more common graphical user interfaces of today). Often layouts provide a simple uncluttered view of a user's options. Spacing, tabs, and highlighting help the user work with the software. Again, such features are site dependent.

Distributed systems are another growing application of computer networks. A **distributed system** allows many devices to run the same software and to access common resources. Example resources include workstations, file servers, mainframes, and printers (Figure 1.28). In a true distributed system, a user logs on and has no knowledge of the underlying structure. The user requests a particular resource and gets it without knowing or caring where it came from or what kind of workstation he or she is using to get it. The distributed system hides the details.

Distributed systems present many challenges. Suppose a user requests a file by name. A problem is that different systems use different rules for naming files. How can we make these rules transparent to the user and still adhere to what a particular computer requires? Often the files exist on different computers. How does the distributed system know where to look for a requested file? Because different computers are used, how does the distributed system handle the problem of duplicate file names? The problems of a true distributed system are many.

---

* Be sure to distinguish between a file's structure and its implementation. For example, a file may be hierarchical, but there are many implementations of a hierarchical structure.

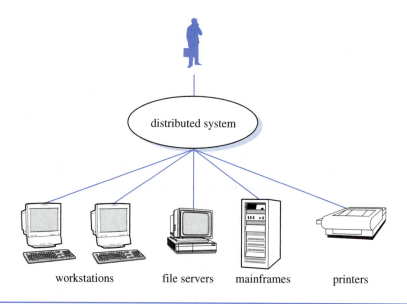

Figure 1.28   Distributed System

INTERNET LAYERS

As we stated at the beginning of this section, the OSI model has not been a commercial success. The rapid growth of email and Web applications during the 1990s pretty much ensured that the Internet and its underlying protocols would be the dominant network model.

So how does the Internet differ from OSI? One main difference is that the Internet is based on a five-layer system (Figure 1.29). We'll discuss the layers in much more detail throughout this book, but the first four layers correspond roughly to the first four layers of the OSI model. However, since the Internet was developed to work with many types of networks, it does not actually specify how layers 1 and 2 work. Layer 3 defines packet formats, routing procedures, types of service, and, depending on the version, some security measures. Layer 4 corresponds either to TCP (a connection-oriented end-to-end protocol) or UDP (User Datagram Protocol, a connectionless end-to-end protocol). Chapter 11 discusses both of these. The fifth layer, the application layer, corresponds to protocols such as HTTP (for Web navigation), FTP (for file transfers), email, and Telnet (virtual terminal protocols). The functionality in OSI layers 5 and 6 is either not supported in the Internet or has been incorporated into various Internet applications.

SUMMARY

This section described each of the seven layers of the OSI protocol model. Each layer defines communication protocols of computer networks and insulates the layer above from the details of the one below. Together, they insulate the user from

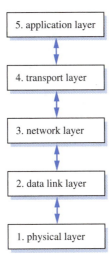

Figure 1.29   Internet Layers

bit-level details of data communications. If fully implemented, they also allow communication between incompatible devices.

The lowest three layers deal primarily with network communications. The physical layer sends and receives bit streams without regard to meaning. It does not know what the data mean or even if they are correct. There are also three connection strategies. Circuit switching creates and maintains dedicated lines between nodes. Message switching routes messages through the network. There are no dedicated lines connecting nodes. Packet switching divides a message into packets for independent routing.

The data link layer provides error detection for the physical layer. Error detection techniques include parity bits and other detection or correction codes. Some can detect single-bit errors only; others can detect when noise destroys many bits. The data link layer also contains contention strategies. Collision detection allows simultaneous transmission by multiple devices but detects any resulting collision. Each device then waits a random amount of time before retransmitting. With token passing, a token moves among the network nodes. A node can transmit only when it has the token.

The highest of the bottom three layers is the network layer. It contains routing strategies. Algorithms can determine the cheapest route between two nodes, and each node knows its successor on a route. But because the cheapest route may vary with time as network conditions change, adaptive routing strategies may be used to detect changes in the network and alter routes accordingly.

The top four layers service the user. The lowest one is the transport layer. It provides buffering, multiplexing, and connection management. Connection management ensures that delayed messages do not compromise requests to establish or release connections.

The session layer manages dialogs between users. In half-duplex communication, the session layer keeps track of who can speak and who must listen. It also allows a transfer to be resumed at the point of interruption if a problem occurs and can handle activities that must be done on an all-or-nothing basis.

The presentation layer accounts for differences in data representation. It allows two systems to exchange information even though they may have different ways of storing it. It can also compress data to decrease the number of transmitted bits. The presentation layer also implements encryption and decryption.

The last and highest layer is the application layer, which contains user services such as electronic mail, file transfer software, and virtual terminals. It communicates directly with the user or application program.

The Internet is composed of five layers: physical, data link, network, transport, and application. Elements of OSI's layers 5 and 6 have been incorporated into the Internet's applications or transport protocols.

1.5 THE FUTURE OF DATA COMMUNICATIONS

We have invested time discussing the history of communications and current technologies and models. The next logical question is: Where do we go from here? In other words, what can we expect to see in the future? Exotic and fantastic predictions are being made, but they probably are no more fantastic than today's realities appeared to people a few decades ago. To them, the concept of spacecraft circling the earth transmitting television pictures and telephone conversations was science fiction. The prospect that light could be used to transmit picture and sound was fantasy. Certainly the very idea that computers could actually "talk" to one another was absurd and maybe a little scary to people who saw too many movies about computers taking control of the world.

The fact is that much of what we will see in the future already exists. It's just that many products that are technologically feasible are not always economically feasible on a large scale. So we return to the question: What can we look forward to? Here are some possibilities.

- **Embedding Internet technology into common devices.** It may surprise some to know that 98% of all processors do *not* reside inside a traditional PC [Es00], but in fact reside in common appliances (vehicles, clocks, household appliances, factory machines, etc.). Don't be surprised if the emerging wireless technology fosters a greater communication among noncomputing devices. Imagine a thermometer inside a home capable of accessing the telephone and asking it to dial the fire department if it detects a high temperature. If the device is in an apartment instead of a home, it might contact all other apartments in the building and activate measures not only to sound an alarm inside the apartment building but also to turn on all of the lights (a potential lifesaver for the hearing impaired). In very large apartment complexes, a protocol might exist whereby one apartment calls another, which, in turn, calls still others, thus notifying all occupants in a more timely manner. Although such notification abilities already exist in the form of fire alarms, they can be tampered with. Interconnecting devices within apartments and building in some fail-safe mechanism may provide more security as well as an earlier warning system, which notifies people before problems get out of hand.

As other examples, perhaps devices embedded in automobiles could sense the position of other vehicles on the highway and force each to implement measures to prevent them from crashing. Sensors embedded in the ground might detect tremors in earthquake-prone regions and communicate with other devices in nearby buildings to sound alarms. There have even been some thoughts regarding the placement of atmospheric sensors in tornado-prone regions. When a sensor detected conditions favorable for the formation of a tornado, it would communicate with a satellite. The satellite, in response to the signal, would transmit a concentrated microwave beam in that direction that is capable of disrupting the temperature differentials that are necessary for the formation of tornados.

Another example is **telepresence,** the concept of projecting one's senses to a remote location. The basic idea is that through an Internet connection, an individual would control robotic devices at a remote site. However, there is more. Through virtual-reality-like devices, the user would see, hear, and perhaps feel events occurring at the remote site and be able to respond to them, ideally in real time. To the user, it would feel like being present in the remote location, which may in fact be many miles away. An important application would be to send in robotic devices to respond to industrial accidents in locations that are unsafe for human occupancy. Using telepresence, a user could respond to rescue or cleanup operations from a safe location.

On the entertainment front, Gibson, a leading manufacturer of guitars, has developed a technology called *MaGIC* (Media-accelerated Global Information Carrier) that allows music to be digitized and transported over an Ethernet connection on a guitar. Designed to replace the old analog jacks, it has applications for recording and editing sessions. You'll be able to play your guitar and record your own sessions on a computer at the same time.

- **Electronic telephone directories.** Although the current formats for white and yellow page telephone directories will probably be the primary source of information for a lot of people for many years, electronic telephone books are beginning to make their mark. The idea is simple: Use a PC or workstation and enter an individual's or business's name, and the telephone number is displayed. Another option is to enter a business category (restaurants, contractors, computer stores, etc.), and a list of businesses is displayed. Select any one of them to get a full listing, including telephone number and address.

  Although widely available, this service is still not widely used (but, of course, that will change). In fact, AT&T provides websites (for example, www.att.com/directory) that provide just such directory services. Through these services you can select cities, states, individual's names, or business categories, and the site will respond with the information you desire, assuming it is in the database. You can also get access to all kinds of other information not typically provided in a traditional telephone book. By clicking various links, you can download a map of the displayed location or get additional information about the site you have found, such as neighboring businesses or individuals. If it's a business, you can even conduct background checks, looking into things such as bankruptcies, lawsuits, or liens. You can find similar information (sometimes at additional cost) about individuals, such as marriage and divorce records or judgments. If you have a headset and speaker, you can click an icon that will activate software to place a call to that telephone. You can even access a link to send flowers through FTD. There's more information available at a mouse click than most people realize, and the security concerns and potential for misuse are immense.

- **Portable telephones.** Hardly new technology, cell phones have become a staple for many people, who use them for business or status purposes. Of course, many are finding other good reasons to have them. Imagine having your car break down at 2:00 A.M. on a deserted highway 10 miles from the nearest telephone booth or witnessing an accident in a remote location. The cell phone can be a lifesaver, literally. Eventually, telephone booths may be seen only in the Smithsonian. Portable telephones allow portable fax machines. If you are late for a business meeting because you are stuck in rush-hour traffic, you can fax your notes or sales charts to your office from your car. (Better yet, have a passenger who is not driving do it—another good reason for carpooling.) New wireless and satellite technologies are spawning a whole new generation of communications equipment that not only make telephone calls but also allow Internet access via a portable device. The time in which you can use such a device to turn on your lights at home or to start your dinner as you are ending your evening commute is probably not far away. Satellites will also allow cell phones to be used in locations where signals from towers will not reach, such as in mountainous regions or the middle of an ocean.

- **Electronic mail.** The Internet already allows electronic mail (email) to be exchanged worldwide. In the past, primarily companies, government agencies, and universities used this technology. However, it has now become one of the most common reasons people subscribe to Internet services. Still, there are many people who probably don't care to use such services or do not want to change lifelong habits of writing letters by hand. To them, sending greeting cards, anniversary cards, or sympathy cards electronically would not carry the same emotional content as a Hallmark card. However, as a new generation that never knew a time without personal computers begins to age, society as a whole will no doubt wonder how we ever managed without it (just as most of us now cannot imagine life without the telephone). In the future, expect to see more business done by email. For example, email use is growing rapidly as a means for physicians and their patients to communicate. Patients can email their physician for prescription refills, general diagnostic questions, appointment requests, and other things that don't require office visits. Email also provides a track record of responses that should reduce misinterpretation of what a doctor states. Even their digital signatures will be readable.

- **The digital revolution.** This concept is a little tough to describe without getting into the differences between analog and digital signals, as Chapter 3 does. For now, just think of it as communication using the same signal types a computer uses. The telephone is an example of where digital technology has made a difference. In fact, except for the signals that go directly into and out of a home, the telephone system is all digital. Although most people do not care whether their phone calls are carried by an analog or digital signal (if someone calls and tells me I won the lottery, I am not going to question the mode of transmission), digital signals have had and will have a profound impact on the services we receive. For example, digital signals carry information to a destination telephone. For users subscribing to caller ID service, the name and telephone number of the person making the call are displayed on the handset or display unit. Although many use this information to screen calls, a professional such as a doctor, lawyer, or broker might use software to route the incoming telephone number to a client or patient database, from which information can be displayed before the phone is answered. Not only do they know who is calling, but potentially relevant information is also made available before the phone is picked up. The system might even display suggested responses for when the telephone is answered, such as "Hello Mrs. Smith, how are Jack and the two boys?" This gives the customer a much more personal treatment. The 911 emergency system greatly benefits people in trouble by displaying the number of an incoherent person or small child. Displaying the caller's number also helps reduce the number of obscene phone calls. One drawback to this system is lack of privacy. Many people have unlisted phone numbers and should not have their numbers displayed whenever they make a call. Of course, caller ID can usually be disabled in such cases. The system will need to determine when a number should be displayed.

Most people are probably aware that in a few years all television broadcasts will be in digital. One of the primary benefits of this technology is improved signal quality, leading to much improved visual and sound quality. The drawback, of course, is that eventually all current televisions will become obsolete and a new generation of televisions will take over. Cable carriers will also be transmitting all-digital signals, leading to a greater integration of transmission and computer technologies. This, in turn, will open the door to many new interactive services. Consumers watching infomercials or QVC will be able to place their orders through their television sets.

- **Electronic media access.** Many people routinely make trips to their favorite video stores to rent a tape, or go to the library to borrow a book or look something up in an encyclopedia. Technology now exists to replace your television with a two-way communications device.* You will be able to use it to access a library of movies, specials, or documentaries and view them. Pay-per-view is already common in many locations, which allows you to select various movies showing at designated times (for a fee, of course). The difference here is that you'll be able to view the movies you want at the time of your choice. Similarly, you will be able to access books electronically from a library (assuming copyright issues are resolved). Electronic access probably will not replace the practice of settling down at night with a good book, but it will be useful to those who want factual information such as that found in an encyclopedia or

---

* Many cable systems already provide two-way communications, using a device available from the cable service provider.

government document. Many well-known newspapers and magazines are already available in electronic form if you have an Internet connection. Internet browsing and television technologies will merge. An advertising company will be able to design a commercial that not only tells you why you must buy a product but also lets you make the purchase instantly via the same device on which you're watching the commercial. Marketing agencies may be able to track television viewing patterns simply by accessing the channels to which you are tuned. Of course, all kinds of privacy and ethical issues assert themselves here, as many will rightfully demand their right to private viewing. We may see the day when we vote in elections from the privacy of our homes.

- **Satellite radio.** Oddly, the last significant event in radio was the creation of the FM band about 50 years ago. Since then, there has been little to change the listening habits of people. That's beginning to change. **Internet radio** allows a person at a computer to use his or her browser to connect to a radio station and listen to live broadcasts. **Satellite radio** is a technology through which companies broadcast radio by satellite. The broadcast contains multiple channels, each containing a variety of formats, such as popular or classical music, sports, and talk radio. An important advantage is that traveling users will no longer have to worry about signals fading as they move out of range. Also, they won't be restricted to just a few stations when traveling in remote areas. To facilitate satellite radio, a network of satellites must be launched into orbit and have the capability to communicate with each other and transmit to ground points. There are some issues and questions about whether people would be willing to pay for satellite radio (the current plans require a subscription to listen) when they can listen to conventional radio for free. On the other hand, this question is not much different from the analogous question about pay TV compared with broadcast TV that was asked many years ago. The real question is whether people are willing to pay for increased options; if history is a good indicator, the answer is a resounding yes.

- **Videoconferencing.** Every day millions of people spend part (often too much) of their day in meetings. Sometimes they must travel long distances at significant cost to attend meetings. Videoconferencing allows people in different locations to see and hear each other in a real-time setting. They are able to converse and display charts as though they were all in the same room. Until recently, videoconferencing had not been economical because of the enormous amount of information that multiple video images require. However, advances in desktop video technology, high-resolution graphics, PC applications, network speeds, and compression techniques have changed the field. Once considered a luxury for only the largest corporations, videoconferencing is now accessible to a wide variety of businesses. The day on which full-motion video is available at the desktop of any network user is not far away.* This technology could also be

---

* Downloading video clips from the Internet is already common, but that is not what we mean here. Such video clips are downloaded and viewed locally. We refer to the ability to view full-motion video in real time—that is, as it is actually occurring. That requires some real-time constraints that some network protocols do not provide.

used to transmit training sessions over a network. The training department could schedule broadcasts of various training programs and individuals could sit in their offices, connect to the proper channel, and watch the session on their display screen.

- **Three-dimensional imaging.** Video images are two-dimensional. The old "3-D" movies were accomplished by showing two different images of the same thing and then giving viewers special glasses. Each lens filtered out one of the images so that each eye received a slightly different image. The brain interpreted these signals differently, giving the perspective of what we call distance. Someday your television may be replaced by a holographic box in which real three-dimensional images are displayed. This development probably will not occur in the near future.

  But why stop at images? People weren't content to stop at voice transmissions. They had to figure out a way to send two-dimensional video images. Then they started talking about three-dimensional images. What about transmitting actual objects or, in the extreme case, people? Sound like science fiction? Of course it is, as anyone who has ever watched *Star Trek* knows. But so were all these other technologies at one time. But don't be too sure that's all it is. An article in reference [Ze00] discusses quantum teleportation, which is reported as a laboratory reality for photons (individual particles of light). The article describes principles in which "particles of the same type in the same quantum state are indistinguishable." This begs the logical question: Is it possible to scan an item at the atomic level, recording the types and quantum states of all the particles, and translate that information to a remote site where atoms can be extracted from matter and reassembled according to the transmitted instructions? One might argue that teleportation did not occur, but that rather a copy was made. One can counter that if the object at the remote site is truly indistinguishable down to a subatomic level, then it is, for all intents and purposes, the same object. No doubt such questions could generate many long discussions. Regardless, there's no argument that transmitting physical objects would be the ultimate in data communication.

- **Electronic locators.** Another seemingly sci-fi device allows people to wear a badge that tells a central computer their exact location. Similar devices are used today. For example, some trucking firms have installed transmitters in all of their trucks. The transmitter sends signals to a satellite, which forwards them to a company's computer and allows dispatchers to determine each truck's location. The accuracy of these systems can place a truck within several hundred feet anywhere in the country.

  These devices are starting to show up in automobiles. The car could have a small video display showing a state road map. Using the satellite tracking system, it could also display a blinking "you are here" mark showing the current location of your car. Such a system would be useful for someone lost on a lonely country road. Similar systems might be even more useful as part of a boat's navigation system on open waters (minus the road map, of course).

  This technology is also finding a place in cell phone technology. Some companies are marketing cell phones equipped with a mobile positioning service.

Imagine being out in the wilderness and getting lost or perhaps injured and unable to walk. A call to an emergency 911 service will enable rescuers to locate your position via the cell phone and provide assistance. Mobile positioning services might be used in smaller devices and placed in the collars of pets or even the clothing of small children to help locate them if they become lost.

- **Voice communications.** Currently, most data communication originates with computer devices such as workstations, scanners, display screens, or disk drives. Sophisticated processors now can be taught to recognize speech patterns. This is of great service to physically impaired people, who could control a wheelchair or a robot arm by talking to it. Current technology already allows an individual to program a VCR or create a word processing document simply by talking. Another existing technology allows a computer user to speak into a microphone connected to software that digitizes the voice and transmits it to a remote site over a network, where it can be stored in a mailbox. In effect, the PC is being used in the same fashion as the telephone.

- **NASA's Deep Space Network (DSN).** The DSN currently consists of three communication facilities located in California, Spain, and Australia. Because of the earth's rotation, these locations are needed to allow the monitoring of unmanned deep space probes at all times and can be used to return images and send commands for navigation. The network can also be used for gathering scientific data for astronomy observations, as an aid to scientific experiments, and as a backup for Earth-orbiting missions. Because the signals from deep space probes are so weak, the DSN uses sensitive reflecting antennas that are as large as a football field.

- **Mind communications.** Can a computer read a person's mind? Before you scoff at the question, remember that each person produces a brain-wave pattern that is unique and detectable by an electroencephalograph. This author once saw a documentary in which a test subject was connected to such a device while watching the projected image of a ball being moved up, down, left, and right; his brain-wave patterns were recorded and stored by a computer for later reference. Next, the person looked at the ball projected on the screen and attempted to move it himself by thinking one of the four directions. The computer compared the brain-wave patterns generated by this exercise with those stored and issued commands to move the projected ball image in the correct direction. It worked! Can a computer read a person's mind? You be the judge, but stay tuned because we're living in an exciting time.

Communications technologies will present many challenges. Perhaps the most significant ones relate to privacy and security. The tremendous amounts of information traveling through the air will invite unscrupulous people to attempt illegal reception and transmissions. How do you prevent people from getting things they should not see or have not paid for? How can you prevent people from disrupting a television network transmission and sending their own messages? These are not hypothetical situations; they have happened.

What about different governmental policies on the transmission and exchange of information? We cannot set up checkpoints at national borders to control information.

Should we restrict and filter information? If so, who defines the policies on what information is appropriate? How do we distinguish that from censorship?

The challenges are many, and we must be prepared to meet them. First, we must understand them and the technology that creates them. It is time to begin.

Review Questions

1. What is Morse code?
2. What is the difference between contention and collision?
3. Name five standards-making organizations and at least one standard for which each is responsible.
4. What is a switchboard?
5. List five communications applications and how they might be used.
6. What is an open system?
7. List five ways of organizing a local area network.
8. What is a de facto standard? Give an example of one.
9. What is meant by a layered protocol? Why are protocols layered?
10. Match the functions in the accompanying table with the OSI layer that performs them.

OSI LAYER	FUNCTION
Physical	Activity definition
Data link	Buffering
Network	Contention
Transport	Data compression
Session	Definition of a signal's electrical characteristics
Presentation	Dialog management
Application	Electronic mail
	Encryption and decryption
	Error detection
	Establishing and releasing a connection
	File transfers
	Format conversion
	Multiplexing
	Routing
	Switching
	Synchronization
	Token passing

11. Distinguish between even and odd parity.
12. Distinguish between message and packet switching.

13. Are the following statements TRUE or FALSE? Why?

    a. The first computer was developed to aid in establishing communications systems.

    b. Telstar was a satellite designed to transmit television and telephone signals across the Atlantic Ocean.

    c. An open system is one that allows free access to a variety of computing and information services.

    d. A computer network can connect many types of storage devices even if they store information in different formats.

    e. Two pairs of devices can communicate simultaneously along a common bus if each pair is at opposite ends of the bus.

    f. A fully connected LAN topology is most common because it allows direct transfer of information between any two devices.

    g. Standards eliminate the inconsistencies between computing devices.

    h. The seven-layer OSI model would, if fully implemented, allow any two computing devices to communicate provided there is a way to physically transfer the information between them.

    i. Layered protocols allow lower layers to be implemented independent of the higher layers and vice versa.

    j. Datagrams are better than virtual circuits at dealing with congestion in networks.

    k. Establishment of an OSI transport connection requires only that one side make the connection request and the other side acknowledge it.

14. Which network topologies allow token passing?

15. Which of the OSI model layers deal primarily with network operations?

16. How does the OSI model differ from the Internet model?

17. Discuss the merits and drawbacks of having a caller's telephone number displayed on a viewing screen whenever the telephone rings.

18. What is the difference between the communication of data and the communication of information?

Exercises

1. Make a sketch outlining the LAN topology at your school or place of business.

2. Which of the applications listed in Section 1.1 have you used? Why have you used them?

3. What types of devices are connected to the LAN at your school or place of business? Are they likely to be found in other LANs? Why or why not?

4. Suppose a bidirectional token ring network connects eight devices numbered 1 through 8 in clockwise order. What device failures would prevent device 1 from sending messages to device 4?

5. Suppose the network in the previous exercise had n devices. Is it possible for two devices to fail and for all the remaining devices to still be able to communicate? If so, under what conditions can this situation occur?

6. In Figure 1.19, list four routes through which A can communicate with F. How many are there all together? (Assume a route does not pass through a node more than once.)

7. Consider the following frames:

$$
\begin{aligned}
&\texttt{011010001010001}\ \ x\\
&\texttt{100111000101101}\ \ x\\
&\texttt{100001100011000}\ \ x
\end{aligned}
$$

Suppose x is the parity bit. What must x be to establish even parity? Odd parity?

8. Argue that if exactly two bits are altered during a transmission, simple parity checking will not detect the error.

9. In general, when will simple parity checking detect an error? When will errors go undetected?

10. Give examples of videoconferencing that your school or place of business has used.

11. What aspect of data communications will have the most significant impact on your personal or professional life?

12. Section 1.5 described an example in which a person gave a computer commands to move an image of a ball simply by thinking up, down, left, or right. One can argue correctly that this is a long way from reading a person's mind. How would you respond to that argument?

13. How many direct connections would there be in a fully connected topology containing n nodes?

14. List some additional applications in which non–computing devices would be required to communicate.

15. Locate your home telephone number in an online directory service such as the one found at www.att.com/directory. Can you find a map to your neighborhood?

REFERENCES

[Es00] Estrin, D., R. Govindan, and J. Heidemann. "Embedding the Internet." *Communications of the ACM,* vol. 43, no. 5 (May 2000), 39–41.

[Ho94] Holtzmann, G., and B. Pehrson. "The First Data Networks." *Scientific American,* January 1994, 124–129.

[Ze00] Zeilinger, A. "Quantum Teleportation." *Scientific American,* April 2000, 50–59.

CHAPTER 2

TRANSMISSION MEDIA AND CODES

The information links are like nerves that pervade and help to animate the human organism. The sensors and monitors are analogous to the human senses that put us in touch with the world. Databases correspond to memory; the information processors perform the function of human reasoning and comprehension. Once the postmodern infrastructure is reasonably integrated, it will greatly exceed human intelligence in reach, acuity, capacity, and precision.
—**Albert Borgman,** U.S. educator and author

data is not information
information is not knowledge
knowledge is not understanding
understanding is not wisdom
—**Cliff Stoll and Gary Schubert**

2.1 INTRODUCTION

This chapter covers some of the basics and modes of communication. It begins with a basic discussion of signals and continues with the various media used to transmit data. It then addresses the issue of why there are different ways of transmitting data. In other words, what are each method's advantages and disadvantages?

We will see that many factors help determine the best way to connect devices:

- Cost of a connection
- Amount of information that can be transmitted per unit of time (bit rate)
- Immunity to outside interference (noise)
- Susceptibility to unauthorized "listening" (security)

- Logistics (how you connect a workstation to a server differs depending on whether the server is on a different floor in the same building or in a different building across a 12-lane highway)

- Mobility (Are the communicating devices stationary? Do they move over small or large distances? Should they be unconstrained by physical connections such as wires?)

Once devices are connected, you might think the hardest part is done and the devices can easily communicate. Unfortunately, this is not correct. One major problem lies in the way information is represented and sent. For example, imagine two people stand talking to each other face to face. If they speak the same language, communication usually (but not always!) occurs. If they speak different languages and neither understands the other's language, communication usually does not occur.

Different devices may not represent or send information the same way. Thus, if one tries to communicate its information directly, the other may not understand it. The resulting problems must be dealt with by communications standards. For example, many devices transmit data using **digital signals** that may be represented electronically* by sequences of specified voltage levels. Graphically, they are often represented as a square wave (Figure 2.1a). In this figure the horizontal axis represents time and the vertical axis represents the voltage level. The alternating high and low voltage levels may be symbolically represented by 0s or 1s and constitute a sequence of 0s and 1s over a period of time. Each 0 or 1 is called a **bit,** and various codes combine such bits and use them to represent information stored in a computer. Section 2.5 discusses some of the standard ways of representing information; Section 2.2 discusses various electronic media over which such signals are sent.

Personal computers often communicate via modems over telephone lines using **analog signals** (Figure 2.1b),[†] which are formed by continuously varying voltage

Figure 2.1   Analog and Digital Signals

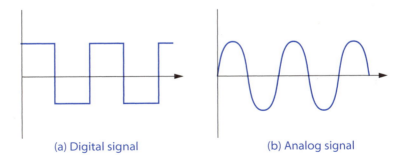

(a) Digital signal   (b) Analog signal

---

* Digital signals may also have optical representations, as we discuss in Section 2.3.

† Although much of the telephone system is digital, most telephones are devices designed to send and receive analog signals. A computer typically uses a modem to convert its digital signals to an analog format before transmitting. We discuss modems in Chapter 3.

levels. Using analog signals to represent data and converting between analog and digital signals is complex. Chapter 3 covers this issue in detail.

The next step is to determine how the signals get from one place to another. There are three types of transmission media, each with many variations. The first is a conductive metal such as copper or iron that carries an analog or digital signal as described previously. Common examples are coaxial cable and twisted wire pairs. Section 2.2 discusses their characteristics. The second medium, discussed in Section 2.3, is a transparent glass strand (optical fiber) that transmits data using light waves. The third requires no physical connection at all and relies on electromagnetic waves such as those found in broadcast television and radio. There are many options here; Section 2.4 discusses them further.

One factor to consider in choosing a communications medium is cost. For example, wires, cables, and strands all have different manufacturing costs. In addition, the devices to which they attach have various costs. Another factor to consider is the number of bits each communications medium can transmit per unit of time. Higher costs may be justified if the resulting system carries more information more quickly.

Two measures are important: bit rate and bandwidth. The **bit rate** is a measure of the number of bits that can be transmitted per unit of time. The typical unit of measure is *bits per second (bps)*. Depending on the medium and the application, bit rates commonly range from a few hundred bps to billions of bps (gigabits per second) and are pushing into the terabit (trillion bits) per second range.

Before defining bandwidth, let us take a closer look at what a signal is. Many analog signals, for example, exhibit the sine wave pattern of Figure 2.2. It is an example of a **periodic signal,** which means it repeats a pattern or cycle continuously. The **period** of a signal is the time required for it to complete one cycle. The signal in Figure 2.2 has a period of *p*.

A signal's **frequency,** *f,* is the number of cycles through which the signal can oscillate in a second. The frequency and period are related in the following manner:

$$f = \frac{1}{p}$$

Figure 2.2   Periodic Signal

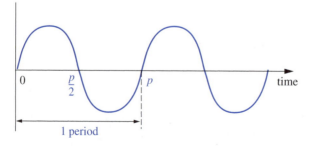

The unit of measurement is cycles per second, or **hertz (Hz).** For example, suppose p from Figure 2.2 was 0.5 microsecond (μsec). Because 0.5 μsec is the same as 0.5×10^{-6} second, the signal's frequency is $1/(0.5 \times 10^{-6})$, or $2,000,000 \text{ Hz} = 2$ megahertz (MHz).

A given transmission medium can accommodate signals within a given frequency range. The **bandwidth** is equal to the difference between the highest and lowest frequencies that can be transmitted. For example, a telephone signal can handle frequencies between 300 and approximately 3300 Hz, giving it a bandwidth of about 3000 Hz. In terms of audible sounds, this means that very high- or low-pitched sound cannot pass through the telephone. Most human speech falls within the telephone's range and consequently is easily recognizable. The loss of high- and low-frequency sounds, however, will cause a problem for someone wanting to listen to and appreciate the New York Philharmonic over the telephone.

Sometimes the term *bandwidth* is used when referring to the number of bits that can be transmitted. Technically, bandwidth and bit rates are different, but there is an important relationship between them. This complex relationship is explored in more detail in Section 3.4.

To transmit bits between two devices, there must be a way for a signal to travel between them. Typically, this requires either a physical connection or the capability to use electromagnetic waves such as those used by radio and television. The next few sections discuss several ways of making physical connections: twisted-pair wire, coaxial cable, and optical fiber. They also discuss wireless communications using infrared, microwave satellite transmission, and laser technology.

2.2   CONDUCTIVE METAL

TWISTED PAIR

One of the oldest transmission media is conducting metal, which was used to transmit information as early as 1837, when Samuel Morse invented the telegraph. Basically, it is a circuit consisting of a power source, a switch, and a sensor (Figure 2.3). The switch, at location A, can be opened or closed manually, thus controlling whether current flows. A sensor, at location B, detects current and creates the clicking sound with which you are probably familiar from TV and movie Westerns. Figure 2.3 shows a telegraph system allowing transmission in just one direction.

Figure 2.3   One-Way Telegraph

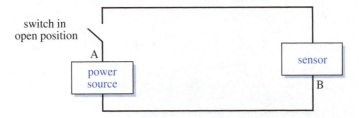

Other designs exist that allow transmissions in both directions (ref. [Sh90]). Opening and closing the switch in different patterns controls the frequency and duration of signals sent to location B. The familiar Morse code, which we present in Section 2.5, associates data with different signal patterns.

Copper wire is probably the most common way of connecting devices. Copper is used because of its electrical conductive properties. That is, electricity flows through copper with less resistance than through many other materials. In addition, copper is more resistant to corrosion than other conducting metals such as iron, a property that makes it a good choice in places where it is exposed to moisture or humidity.

One of the most common uses of copper is in the **twisted pair,** in which two insulated copper wires are twisted around each other. The insulation prevents the conductive metal in each wire from making contact and thus short-circuiting the circuit. A common use of twisted-pair wire is the transmission of a balanced signal. This means that each wire carries current but that the signals are 180° out of phase with each other.* The effects on each current from outside electromagnetic sources nearly cancel each other, resulting in a signal that degrades less rapidly. Twisting the wires helps reduce interference from external sources. If the wires were not twisted, one of the two wires might be more exposed to interference. Twisting distributes any interference more equally along both wires and, because the signal is balanced, tends to cancel interference.

Twisted pairs often are bundled together and wrapped in a protective coating that allows the bundled cable to be buried. Such cables can be rated, in part, by the number of twists per unit length of wire. A larger frequency of twists provides a greater reduction in capacitance and also helps reduce **crosstalk,** the electromagnetic interference between adjacent pairs. For a long time, this medium was the primary mode of telephone communications and is still common in connecting a home telephone to a nearby telephone exchange. It is also common in connecting computer workstations to networks.

Even though copper is a good conductor, electrical resistance still occurs, and a signal transmitted over a copper wire will eventually distort and lose strength **(attenuate).** In practice, this means there is a limit on the twisted pair's length before the transmitted signal becomes distorted beyond recognition.

If the wire must connect two points separated by a long distance, a repeater must be inserted between the two points (Figure 2.4). A **repeater** is a device that intercepts a transmitted signal before it has distorted and attenuated too badly and then regenerates the signal and retransmits it. A logical question to ask is: How far apart must repeaters be spaced? The space between repeaters depends on characteristics such as the type of signal and the bandwidth and current-carrying capacity of the wire. Many signals may be transmitted for miles before signal regeneration is necessary. With repeaters, there is no limit on how far a signal can be transmitted.

---

* By contrast, an unbalanced signal uses one wire to carry the current while the other is held at ground potential. Unbalanced signals are typically more susceptible to interference than balanced signals. We discuss this further in Section 4.4.

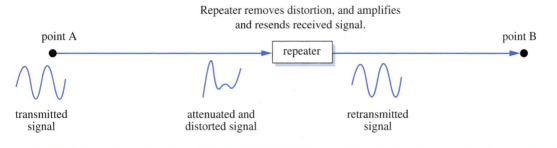

Figure 2.4   Two Points Connected Using a Repeater

There are two types of twisted-pair wires: unshielded twisted pair (UTP) and shielded twisted pair (STP). The shielded twisted pair has a braided metal sheathing over the insulation, providing better protection from outside electromagnetic interference. It also protects the signals in one pair from the electromagnetic field generated by current flowing through the other pair. The unshielded twisted pair has no such protection but is typically cheaper to produce and install. It's similar to wires that connect your telephone to a wall jack and has become common in many network environments.

Different categories of UTP are designated numerically. For example, people often use the term **Cat 5 cable** when referring to a Category 5 UTP. Typically, higher-category wire has more twists per foot to reduce interference and can accommodate higher bit rates. It also provides better resistance to **near-end crosstalk (NEXT),** a phenomenon in which the signals traveling along one wire radiate electromagnetic waves and interfere with signals traveling along another closely bundled wire. Typically, NEXT becomes more problematic with higher-frequency signals. Table 2.1 outlines the different categories of UTP and typical uses for each.

COAXIAL CABLE

Another common medium is **coaxial cable** (Figure 2.5), which consists of four components. First is the innermost conductor, such as a copper wire core. As with the twisted pair, the core carries the signal. An insulation layer surrounds the core and prevents the conductor from making contact with the third layer, typically a tightly wound wire mesh.* The wire mesh acts as a shield, protecting the core from electromagnetic interference. It also protects the core from hungry rodents looking for a free meal. The last layer is what you see on the cables connecting your VCR to your television set: a plastic protective cover.

Coaxial cable typically transmits information in either a baseband mode or a broadband mode. In **baseband mode,** the cable's bandwidth is devoted to a single stream of data. Thus, the high bandwidth capability allows high bit rates over a

---

* Sometimes a solid metal conductor is used instead of a mesh on cables that do not need much flexibility.

Table 2.1 UTP Categories

CATEGORY	USE
Cat 1	Designed for use in early telephone systems, where voice transfer was the primary need.
Cat 2	Also used in telephone systems and older local area networks with bit rates no greater than 4 Mbps.
Cat 3	Has become standard for voice-grade telephone communications and supports LAN communications of up to 10 Mbps. Must pass near-end crosstalk tests for signals up to 16 MHz.
Cat 4	Used in Ethernet and token ring networks when bit rates increased to 16 Mbps.
Cat 5	Commonly used in many networks today and can support 100 Mbps rates over distances of 100 meters or less. Also, gigabit-rate Ethernets have been designed to run over four pairs of Category 5 UTP up to a range of 100 meters (ref. [St00]). There is also an enhanced Cat 5 wire (sometimes designated as Cat 5E), which is essentially a higher grade of cable that supports bit rates of up to a gigabit per second. Some network users may recognize the Cat 5 cable as the blue cord that runs from the back of their computer to a wall jack. Must pass near-end crosstalk tests for signals up to 100 MHz.
Cat 6	The TIA has recently approved a standard for Cat 6 wire, which provides twice the bandwidth of Cat 5E wire and improved signal-to-noise characteristics.
Cat 7	Work is in progress to define Category 7 standards that would provide even higher bit rates, but as of this writing, they have not yet been completed.

cable. This is typical in local area networks, where only one data stream is present at any time. With **broadband,** the bandwidth is divided into ranges. Each range typically carries separate coded information, which allows the transmission of multiple data streams over the same cable simultaneously. Special equipment is used to combine the signals at the source and separate them at the end. Cable television is an example of multiple signals (one for each channel) traveling a single section of cable. We further discuss combining signals in Section 4.5 on multiplexing.

Figure 2.5 Coaxial Cable

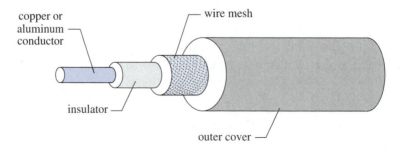

Two types of cable are sometimes called **ThickNet** and **ThinNet.*** ThinNet is a thinner, more flexible cable and was once commonly used to connect devices in a computer lab. The flexibility made it ideal when the cable had to be routed around corners and under tables. ThickNet cable was more common in older networks and may still be found in some installations. Because it is less flexible, it was restricted to connecting equipment in different buildings or for use as risers, connecting networks on different floors in a building.

For a long time, coaxial cable accommodated a higher bandwidth than twisted pair and for longer distances. It also provided more protection against electrical interference. As with the twisted pair, maximum bit rates and distances vary as emerging technologies produce more sophisticated equipment and signaling techniques. Once used as the primary carrier of signals along the main backbone in local area networks, coaxial cable is commonly being replaced by optical fiber (discussed next) and even UTP. Because of the shielding, coaxial cable does have a better error rate than UTP, but UTP is cheaper and easier to work with, an important consideration when LAN installations must meet budget constraints. However, coaxial cable might be the medium of choice when many devices are stored in small areas. In such cases, coaxial cable's shielding better protects against interference from other nearby cables.

2.3 OPTICAL FIBER

Several problems (or at least limitations) are associated with using conducting metal to transmit signals. One problem is that electrical signals are susceptible to interference coming from sources such as electric motors, lightning strikes, and other wires. We will see in Section 3.4 that this interference limits the amount of data that can be transmitted. In addition, wires and cables are heavy and bulky, especially when bundling them together. It may not seem so at first, but think about carrying several thousand feet of cable during a morning stroll. In fact, AT&T reports that a 4.5-pound spool of optical fiber can carry the same amount of information as 200 reels of copper wire weighing more than 1,600 pounds.

This weight places limitations on the installation of wire in high-traffic areas or in hard-to-reach areas such as closets or through long, narrow crawl spaces. Also, the characteristics of electrical signals and the resistance properties of conducting metal place limits on the types of signals that can be sent and the distance that signals travel before they degrade. In turn, this limits the amount of information that can be sent per unit of time.

One alternative is **optical fiber.** It uses light, not electricity, to transmit information. Telephone companies make widespread use of optical fiber, especially for long-distance service. It is impervious to electrical noise and has the capacity to transmit enormous amounts of information. In addition, optical fibers are very thin (compared with cables), which allows many of them to be bundled together in much

---

* Actually, *ThickNet* and *ThinNet* refer to types of Ethernet networks (see Chapter 9), but the terms are often used to refer to the cables used in those networks.

less space than old-fashioned cables require. For those faced with the task of routing them through conduits, above ceilings, or between walls, this is a big advantage. Optical fibers have become common in computer networks. High-capacity CDs, DVD technology, and increased integration of computers and video imaging are generating a need for networks with high bandwidth capabilities.

The principles that make optical fiber viable are grounded in physics, specifically optics and electromagnetic wave theory. We do not intend to go into a detailed discussion of these topics, but we feel it is important to cover some of the basics so you will have an idea of how it works.

To begin, consider a light source directed toward some surface (Figure 2.6). The surface represents a boundary between two media such as air and water. Let α be the angle at which the light wave intersects the boundary. Some of the light will reflect back at an angle α with the plane, and some will cross the boundary into the other medium. This is **refraction.** However, the angle the direction of light makes with the boundary changes. In other words, if β is the angle at which the light wave travels from the boundary, $\beta \neq \alpha$. Next you might ask whether β is larger or smaller than α. If you did, congratulations. That's a good question.

If $\beta > \alpha$ (as it is in Figure 2.6), we say the second medium has a higher optical density than the first (as water has a higher density than air). However, if the first medium has a higher optical density, then $\beta < \alpha$. Refraction explains why a lens in a pair of eyeglasses will distort the normal view, or why objects under water appear distorted if viewed from above the surface. The light reflected off the objects we see is distorted, making them look different.

The relation between β and α is of interest. Physicists use a measure known as the **index of refraction** (the ratio of the speed of light in a vacuum to the speed of light in a specified medium) to describe it. In addition, a well-known result in physics, Snell's law, states that the ratio of the index of refraction of the two different media in Figure 2.6 is equal to the ratio

$$\frac{\cos (\alpha)}{\cos (\beta)}$$

If this ratio is less than 1, then light is traveling into a less optically dense medium, whereas a ratio greater than 1 means it is traveling into a more optically

Figure 2.6   Light Refraction and Reflection

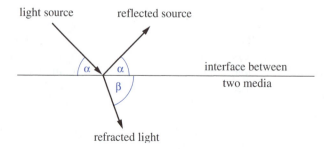

light source   reflected source

α α interface between two media

β

refracted light

dense medium. Remember, angles β and α are between 0° and 90°, so that cos (α) < cos (β) means α > β, and vice versa.

Another interesting phenomenon occurs when this ratio is less than 1 (α > β). When α is less than a certain critical angle, there is no refracted light. In other words, all the light is reflected. This is what makes fiber optics work.

The three main components of a fiber optic filament are the core, the cladding, and the protective cover. The core is made from very pure glass or plastic material. The cladding surrounds the core. It is also glass or plastic but is optically less dense than the core. How pure is the core? As we will see, an optical fiber works by allowing light to travel through the core. In some cases the fiber is up to 20 miles long. Because light travels from end to end, we can think of the core as 20 miles thick. Thus, imagine a block of glass so pure that a chunk 20 miles thick is nearly transparent.

Next question: How does light enter the fiber? A light source such as a **light-emitting diode (LED)** or a laser is placed at one end of the fiber. Each is a device that responds to an electric charge to produce a pulse of light, typically near the infrared frequency of 10^{14} Hz. The **laser** produces a very pure* and narrow beam. It also has a higher power output, allowing the light to propagate farther than that produced by an LED. The LED produces less-concentrated light consisting of more wavelengths. LEDs are less expensive and generally last longer. Lasers normally are used where a high data rate is needed over a long distance, such as in long-distance telephone lines.

The light source emits short but rapid pulses of light that enter the core at different angles. Light that hits the core/cladding boundary at less than the critical angle is totally reflected back into the core, where it eventually hits the boundary on the opposite side of the core. Because the angle of reflection is the same, it is again totally reflected back into the core. The effect is that the light bounces from boundary to boundary as it propagates down the core. Eventually, the light exits the core and is detected by a sensor. Light that hits the boundary at an angle greater than the critical one is partly refracted into the cladding and absorbed by the protective cover. This prevents light from leaking out and being absorbed by other nearby fibers.

A potential problem exists when light propagates down a core. If the core is fairly thick (relative to a wavelength of light), light enters it at many places and at many different angles. Some of the light essentially goes down the center of the core, but some hits the boundary at different angles (Figure 2.7). The study of electromagnetic waves (specifically, Maxwell's equations) tells us that some of the reflecting rays interfere with one another. Consequently, there is a finite number of angles at which the rays reflect and propagate down the length of the fiber. Each angle defines a path or a mode. Fiber that transmits light this way is called **step-index multimode fiber.**

Light that reflects at larger angles (measured relative to horizontal) reflects more often and travels a greater distance than light that reflects at smaller angles. Consequently, it takes a bit longer to get to the other end of the fiber. This phenomenon is

---

* Light often consists of many wavelengths, or colors, as indicated by the fact that light passing through a prism is divided into its component rainbow colors. A laser can produce "pure" light, or light consisting of very few wavelengths.

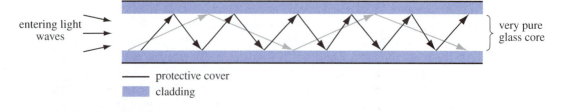

entering light
waves

protective cover
cladding

very pure
glass core

Figure 2.7   Step-Index Multimode Fiber

called **modal dispersion.** Imagine many people racing down a hallway. Some are running down the center, and others, who are blindfolded, are bouncing off the walls. We know who will win that race.

Modal dispersion is a problem if the fiber is too long. Light from one pulse (reflecting at small angles) could actually catch up with light emitted from a previous pulse (reflecting at larger angles), thus eliminating the gap in between. The sensors no longer see pulses of light; they see a steady stream of light rays, and any information that was coded in the pulses is destroyed.

One way of addressing the problem of modal dispersion is to use a **graded-index multimode fiber.** It makes use of another phenomenon related to the fact that the speed of light depends on the medium through which it travels: Specifically, light travels faster through less optically dense media.

A graded-index multimode fiber (Figure 2.8) also has a core, cladding, and protective cover. The difference is that the boundary between core and cladding is not sharply defined. In other words, moving out radially from the core, the material becomes gradually less dense. Consequently, as light travels radially outward it begins to bend back toward the center, eventually reflecting back. Because the material also becomes less dense, the light travels faster. The net result is that although some light travels a greater distance, it travels faster, and modal dispersion is reduced.

Another way of dealing with modal dispersion is to eliminate it. How? you may ask. Earlier we stated that there is a finite number of modes at which light can propagate. The exact number depends on the core's diameter and the light's wavelength. Specifically, reducing the core's diameter decreases the number of angles at which

Figure 2.8   Graded-Index Multimode Fiber

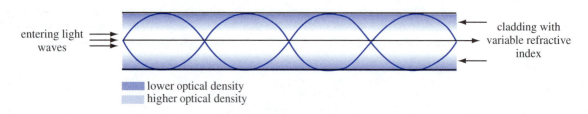

entering light
waves

cladding with
variable refractive
index

lower optical density
higher optical density

light can strike the boundary. Consequently, it also reduces the number of modes. If we reduce the diameter enough, the fiber has only one mode. Cleverly, this is called **single-mode fiber** (Figure 2.9).

How far must we reduce the diameter? Another principle of physics relates the capability to reflect an electromagnetic wave (such as light) to the size of the reflector. Specifically, it tells us that to reflect a light ray in the manner we have described, the reflector must be larger than the wavelength of the reflected light. Because the reflector here is wrapped around the core, its size depends on the core's diameter. The relation between frequency and wavelength states that

$$\text{wavelength} = \frac{\text{speed of light}}{\text{frequency}}$$

Light traveling through optical fibers has a frequency of approximately 10^{14} Hz, so its wavelength evaluates to approximately 2×10^{-6} meters, or 2 microns (1 micron = 10^{-6} meters). Thus, single-mode fibers typically have a diameter measured in microns (typically 4–8, sometimes smaller), very thin indeed (many fibers are as thin as a human hair). Its small diameter makes the fiber more fragile and difficult to splice. Consequently, it is most often used in long-distance trunk lines, an application where handling and splicing are minimal.

Optical fiber technology has many advantages over conducting metal:

- It can transmit data more quickly.
- It has very low resistance. Thus, signals can travel farther without repeaters. For example, repeaters may be placed up to 30 miles apart; cable requires them every couple of miles.
- It is unaffected by electromagnetic interference, because the signals are transmitted by light.
- It has very high resistance to environmental elements such as humidity. This property makes it well suited for coastal areas.

On the other hand, current computers are electronic devices, so the use of optical fiber requires the conversion of electrical signals to light rays and vice versa. This process adds an extra level of complexity. In addition, optical fibers are more difficult than copper wire to tap into or splice together. Components can be added relatively easily to a copper bus by tapping into it, but much more care is necessary when tapping into a glass fiber. Reference [Ro01] contains a detailed introduction to optical fiber communication.

Figure 2.9   Single-Mode Fiber

entering light waves →

2.4 WIRELESS COMMUNICATIONS

All modes of communication using conductive metal or optical fiber have one thing in common: Communicating devices must be connected physically. Physical connection is sufficient for many applications, such as connecting personal computers in an office or connecting them to a server within the same building. It is acceptable for short distances, but expensive and difficult to maintain for long distances. Imagine a coaxial cable connected to NASA flight control headquarters hanging out the back end of the space shuttle or a cable hanging between two towers in New York and London!

In many situations, a physical connection is not practical or even possible. Suppose participants in a proposed network are in two different buildings separated by an eight-lane highway. Stringing a cable over the highway or disrupting traffic to lay underground cable probably would not meet with approval by city planners. The network participants need a way of communicating without a physical connection—that is, wireless communications.

Wireless transmissions involve **electromagnetic waves.** Because they are a significant part of a physics course, we will not attempt a thorough discussion of them. For our purpose, it is sufficient to say they are oscillating electromagnetic radiation caused by inducing a current in a transmitting antenna. The waves then travel through the air or free space, where a receiving antenna may sense them. Broadcast radio and television transmit signals this way.

Figure 2.10 shows the electromagnetic wave spectrum. Radio waves are used for both radio and television transmissions. For example, television VHF (very high frequency) broadcasts range from 30 to 300 MHz, and UHF (ultra-high frequency) broadcasts range from 300 MHz to 3 GHz.* Radio waves are also used for AM and FM radio, ham radio, cellular telephones, and shortwave radio. Each of these communications is assigned a frequency band by the Federal Communications Commission (FCC). Some properties of electromagnetic radiation are important to communications. One is the previously stated relation between the wavelength and frequency:

$$\text{wavelength} = \frac{\text{speed of light}}{\text{frequency}}$$

Consequently, high frequency waves have short wavelengths, and vice versa. Table 2.2 shows some actual values.

Figure 2.10   Electromagnetic Wave Spectrum

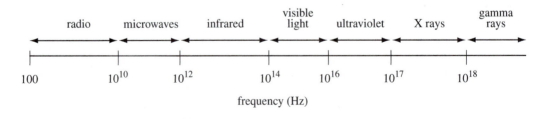

* MHz is megahertz, or 10^6 Hz. GHz is gigahertz, or 10^9 Hz.

Table 2.2   Wavelength as a Function of Frequency

FREQUENCY (HZ)	APPROXIMATE WAVELENGTH (METERS)
10^2	3×10^6
10^4	3×10^4
10^6	300
10^8	3
10^{10}	0.03
10^{12}	0.0003

Physics tells us that low-frequency waves, when broadcast from the ground, tend to reflect off the upper levels of the atmosphere with little loss. By bouncing back and forth between the atmosphere and the ground, such signals can travel far, following the curvature of the earth. Shortwave (between 3 and 30 MHz) radios, for example, have been known to receive signals from halfway around the world. Higher-frequency signals tend to reflect with more loss and typically do not travel as far (as measured across the earth's surface).

Low-frequency waves also require a very long antenna. In the 1970s and 1980s there was a controversy that involved an attempt by the Navy to install a large (more than 50 miles long) antenna in the upper peninsula of Michigan. Its purpose was submarine communication using extremely low frequency (ELF) signals in the less than 300 Hz range. The controversy over Project ELF centered on the potential health risks of people exposed to such electromagnetic radiation. Even today, there is concern over potential health risks from radiation caused by devices such as power lines and computer terminals.

Three types of wireless communication are particularly important: microwave, satellite, and infrared transmissions.

MICROWAVE TRANSMISSION

Microwave transmissions typically occur between two ground stations. Two properties of microwave transmission place restrictions on its use. First, microwaves travel in a straight line and will not follow the earth's curvature, as some lower-frequency waves will. Second, atmospheric conditions and solid objects interfere with microwaves. For example, they cannot travel through buildings.

A typical mechanism for transmitting and receiving microwave transmissions uses the parabolic dish reflector (Figure 2.11). No doubt you have seen them in backyards (for receiving satellite signals for television), on top of buildings, or mounted on a tower in the middle of nowhere (Figure 2.12). The last are commonly used for telephone communications. More recently, the 18-inch satellite dish has become popular among many consumers as a way of receiving numerous television stations and pay-per-view selections.

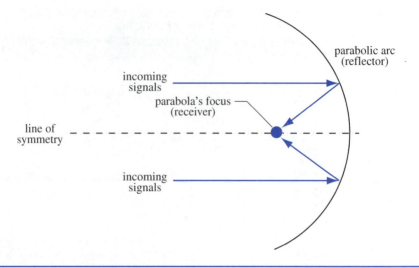

Figure 2.11   Parabolic Dish Receiving Signals

Figure 2.12   Microwave Transmission Tower

Courtesy of AT&T Archives

Parabolic dishes use a well-known but probably forgotten fact from precalculus mathematics. Given a parabolic curve, draw a straight line perpendicular to a line tangent to the curve at its vertex. This is the line of symmetry. All lines parallel to the line of symmetry reflect off the curve and intersect in a common point called the *focus*. Figure 2.11 shows how this is applicable to receiving transmissions. The actual dish is not the receiver, just a reflector. Because it has a parabolic shape, incoming signals are reflected and will intersect at the focus. Placing the actual receiver there allows the signals to be received accurately. (As a side note, parabolic reflectors are used to illustrate the whispering phenomenon at museums. Two parabolic dishes are placed at opposite ends of the room facing each other. A person at the focal point of one speaks softly, and the voice is reflected directly to the other dish. A second person listening at its focal point hears the first person's voice.)

Another type of antenna is the horn antenna (Figure 2.13). Transmitting antennas are often this type. (Figure 2.12 shows both horn and parabolic dish antennas.) The horn antenna consists of a cylindrical tube called a **waveguide.** It acts to guide the waves and transmit them directly into a concave reflector. The reflector's shape is designed to reflect the microwaves in a narrow beam. The beam travels across an unobstructed region and is eventually received by another antenna. The next time you take a leisurely drive in the countryside, look around and you may see both types of antenna mounted on towers. (But don't look too long; there are other cars on the road!)

Because there must be a direct line of sight between the transmitter and receiver, there is a limit on how far apart they can be. The limit depends on the tower's height, the earth's curvature, and the type of terrain in between. For example, antennas on tall towers separated by flat land can cover long distances, typically 20 to 30 miles, although higher towers or towers constructed on hilltops can

Figure 2.13   Horn Antenna

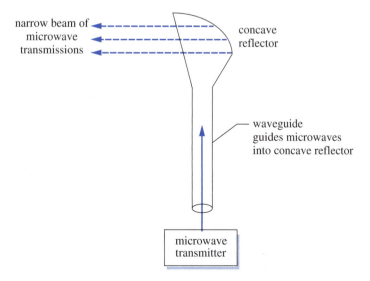

increase the distance. In some cases, antennas are separated by short distances within city limits. However, there will be a problem if someone constructs a building directly in the line of sight.

If transmissions must travel a long distance, several repeater towers may be placed in between (Figure 2.14). One antenna transmits to its neighbor, which in turn transmits to its neighbor. Proceeding this way allows transmissions between sites whose line of sight cuts through the earth.

SATELLITE TRANSMISSION

Primarily, satellite transmission is microwave transmission in which one of the stations is a satellite orbiting the earth (Figure 2.15). It is certainly one of the more common means of communication today. Applications include telephone, television, news services, weather reporting, and military use, and some foresee the day when satellites will be instrumental in extending Internet connectivity (ref. [Me00]), providing access to places where ground-based systems are not practical or even possible.

Some of you may have heard of Sir Arthur C. Clarke. He is best known as a science fiction author whose many novels include the *Space Odyssey* trilogy. Few people know that Clarke is a physicist who, in 1945, wrote about the possibility of using satellites in space for worldwide communication (ref. [Cl45]). In 1945 this idea was science fiction; today, it is common science. At the time, Clarke did not believe that satellite communications would be economically or technically feasible until the 21st century (ref. [Hu90]). Instead, it took just 20 years and the invention of the transistor for satellite communications to become a reality.

Figure 2.14   Microwave Towers Used as Repeaters

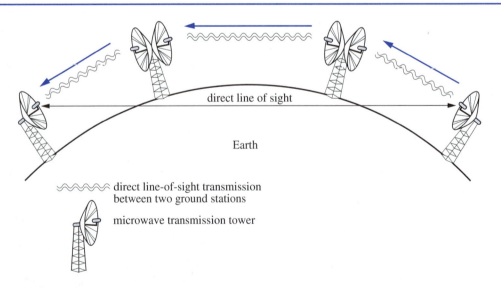

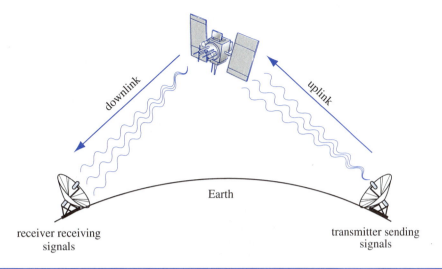

receiver receiving
signals

Earth

transmitter sending
signals

Figure 2.15   Satellite Communications

It began with a historic event on October 4, 1957, an event that shook American society and political leaders. On that day, the then Soviet Union launched the *Sputnik* satellite. *Sputnik* entered a low earth orbit (560 miles high) and sent electronic "beeps" to the ground. As it moved across the sky, the ground station had to rotate its antenna to track it. By today's standards it was not sophisticated, but then it was truly remarkable because it showed that communication between the earth and an object in space was possible.

Because the satellite moved across the sky, communication was possible for only a short time. As it dropped below the horizon, communication ceased until it later appeared above the other horizon. Such a situation is inappropriate for many of today's applications (but not all). Imagine cable TV or a telephone conversation being interrupted every time the satellite dropped below the horizon! (Of course, if it could be synchronized to occur at the start of each commercial, perhaps the concept would have merit.) Realistically, a satellite remaining in a fixed position would allow a continuous transmission, certainly an important criterion for mass media applications. The question is: How can a satellite remain in a fixed position without falling down?

Geosynchronous Satellites   Satellite orbits are predictable using mathematical models based on Kepler's laws of planetary motion. The idea is fairly simple. Given a height, a certain velocity is needed to keep an object in orbit. Higher velocities will send the object out of orbit and into space. Lower velocities will be insufficient to counteract gravitational force, and the object will fall. In other words, given a height, the orbital velocity is determined. Kepler's third law relates the time to revolve around a planet to the height of an orbit.

Specifically, suppose the period P of a satellite is the time it takes to rotate around another planetary body. Kepler's third law states that

$$P^2 = KD^3$$

where D is the distance between the satellite and the planet's center and K is a constant depending on gravitational forces. In other words, higher orbits (larger D) mean a longer period.

A logical question is: At what orbital height will a satellite have a 24-hour period? According to Kepler's law, the answer is 22,300 miles above the equator, considerably higher than *Sputnik* traveled. The answer has great significance. Because the earth takes 24 hours to rotate on its axis, an orbiting satellite at that height appears stationary to a ground observer. This is called a **geosynchronous orbit.** If the observer were a transmitter or receiver, the satellite would remain in a position that is fixed relative to the observer, and communications need not be interrupted.

Sputnik and many early satellites were in much lower orbits. Technology simply did not provide rocket engines powerful enough to boost them into higher orbits. Consequently, they rotated around the earth in less than 24 hours, which is why they appeared to move across the sky when observed from the surface. Today, powerful rockets boost communications satellites much higher into geosynchronous orbits. Three equally spaced satellites at 22,300 miles above the equator can cover almost the entire earth's surface (Figure 2.16), except some polar regions.

Satellite communication is straightforward. Each satellite has several **transponders,** devices that accept a signal within a specified frequency range and rebroadcast

Figure 2.16   Satellites in Geosynchronous Orbit above the Equator

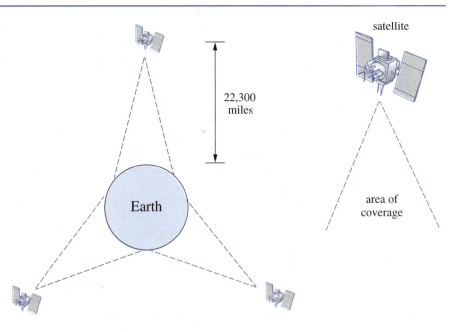

Table 2.3 Satellite Frequency Bands

BAND	UPLINK FREQUENCY RANGE (GHz)	DOWNLINK FREQUENCY RANGE (GHz)
L	1.6465–1.66	1.545–1.5585
C	5.925–6.425	3.7–4.2
Ku	14.0–14.5	11.7–12.2
Ka	27.5–30.5	17.7–21.7

it over a different frequency. A ground-based transmitter sends a signal (**uplink**) to a satellite, where one of the transponders relays the signal back down to earth (**downlink**) to a different location (see Figure 2.15). Satellite communications are now commonly used to transmit telephone and television signals. Many people have their own receivers for television reception, with increasing numbers of people using 18-inch dishes mounted on roofs and back porches.

Satellites commonly send and receive over a wide range of frequencies, with each transponder handling signals in a specified range. Typically, the uplink and downlink frequencies differ so that they do not interfere with each other. Table 2.3 shows four common bands used in commercial satellite communications and the associated uplink and downlink frequencies. Other bands are devoted solely to military and government use.

An important fact to remember about satellite transmission is that different signals in the same frequency range must not overlap. Consequently, this limits the number of satellites that can transmit within a particular band and places constraints on how close two satellites can be to each other (more about that later). The C band was the first to be used and is commonly used for broadcast television and VSAT applications (also discussed later). It is becoming saturated in part because of the explosion of worldwide media applications and in part because C band frequencies are also used in ground-based microwave transmissions.

With the world's move toward digital communications, the growth of digital satellite systems, and the migration of the broadcast television industry to high-definition television signals (HDTV), more information must be transmitted. As Section 3.4 shows, higher frequencies allow more information to be sent per unit of time. Consequently, the Ku band is also used by commercial television carriers. A problem with higher frequencies (especially those approaching the Ka band) is that atmospheric conditions such as rain or moisture cause more interference. The problem becomes worse if the ground station is farther away (measured across the earth's surface) and the signal must travel through more atmosphere (Figure 2.17). This problem can be corrected by boosting the power of a signal or by designing more sophisticated receivers to filter out noise. In fact, the stronger signals sent in the Ku band allow the use of smaller antennas or dishes. Many of you are familiar with the 18-inch dishes you can buy in many electronic stores to pick up digital television signals. But many of us old dinosaurs remember when large satellite

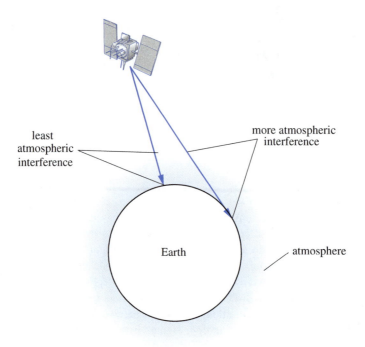

least
atmospheric
interference

more atmospheric
interference

Earth

atmosphere

Figure 2.17   Atmospheric Interference as a Function of Angle of Transmission

dishes mounted in the backyard were required. Ku signals also allow a smaller beam width, enabling transmissions to smaller geographic regions.

As signals move into the Ka range the interference problem becomes severe. Ka band satellites are still new technology but have a high priority in the policy and regulatory agendas of the United States, Europe, and Japan. There are ambitious plans to set up a global infrastructure of orbiting satellites that communicate in the Ka band; we discuss some of them shortly.

At the lower end of the frequency spectrum, the L band is used primarily for mobile satellite communications. This means that communications between cars, trucks, boats, or anything mobile are relayed through satellites. The lower frequency allows the use of equipment that is smaller, lower in cost, and requires less power. Such applications can be found in the trucking industry, where dispatchers can locate trucks within a range of just a few hundred feet (on a continental scale). Applications also exist as navigation aids: Planes, boats, and automobiles can use the system to plot their own current locations.

Geosynchronous satellites transmit a signal that can be received anywhere on earth as long as there is a direct line-of-sight path. This type of broadcasting is useful for broadcast television transmission and pay-per-view movie services, in which the receivers are widely dispersed and do not have access to cable signals. Other applications, such as for military uses, must restrict the geographic areas that can receive signals. Special antennas that provide beam shaping allow a signal to be concentrated in a smaller area such as a city. The future will provide spot beam antennas, which will allow transmissions to a single site.

Currently, there are many hundreds of satellites orbiting the planet providing communications for different applications that send and receive signals in the C and Ku bands, so how can a satellite discriminate signals that were not meant for it? For example, suppose ground stations 1 and 2 send to satellites 1 and 2, respectively, using the same frequency (Figure 2.18). The area the signal covers depends on the angle of signal dispersion. If two satellites are too close or the angle of dispersion is too large, both satellites receive both signals. Consequently, neither can tell which signal to ignore.

If the dispersion angles are smaller and satellites are sufficiently far apart, however, no two satellites will receive signals from more than one station (Figure 2.19). The FCC defines U.S. satellite positions. For example, it has defined positions at 2° increments between 67° and 143° west longitude for U.S. communications using the C band. This is closer together than the previous 4° separation allowed. Satellites transmitting signals in the Ku band may be placed at 1° increments. Increased needs require more satellites, which must be placed closer together. As a result, ground stations must have smaller dispersion angles for transmitted signals.

Satellite communications have created problems. For example, how do you prevent unauthorized reception of signals? For that matter, how do you define unauthorized reception of a signal that travels through the public airwaves? Legalities are often not clear-cut. For example, there have been different views on whether it

Figure 2.18   Satellites Receiving More Than One Signal

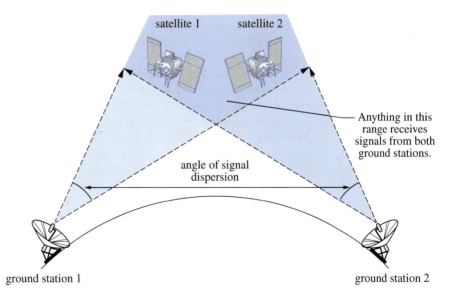

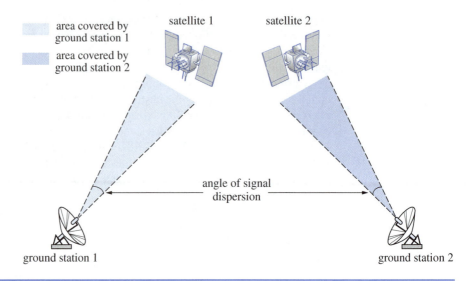

Figure 2.19   Satellites Receiving One Signal

is legal to receive cable television's pay channels such as HBO using satellite dishes. Cable companies claim they lose revenue by such access. Dish owners claim the signals travel through public airspace, and anyone should be able to receive them as they would any other television signal.

Perhaps worse, how do you prevent unauthorized transmission via satellite? There have been instances of intruders sending harmless messages via satellite. But what about an intrusion that disrupts communications? Considering how many applications rely on satellite communications, this could be disastrous. In many cases, satellite signals are scrambled or encrypted to make the signal unintelligible to unauthorized receivers. One incident, on April 27, 1986, involved a video hacker who called himself "Captain Midnight" interrupting an HBO showing of the movie *The Falcon and the Snowman.* He transmitted a signal over a satellite link that overpowered HBO's movie signal. He claimed it was done to protest the scrambling of signals. Chapter 7 deals with encryption and security in more detail.

Not all satellites are for telephones, weather forecasting, and military applications. Many private industries see satellites as an alternative to the telephone system, especially where a need exists for data transmission over a long distance. Using the phone system and going through many switches makes data transfer less reliable, and heavy usage may cause longer response times. The solution may be the **very small aperture terminal (VSAT) system,** developed in the 1980s. A VSAT system commonly connects a central location with many remote ones. For example, the central location may contain a large database to which many regional offices or users need access. Communication between two sites is via a satellite and requires the use of small antenna dishes that can be placed to allow easy access to the central location.

VSAT equipment may connect directly to user equipment such as workstations or controllers. Many applications rely on VSAT systems, especially those that require high data rates for short periods of time. Examples include the National Weather Service, news services, credit card verifications, automatic tellers, and car rental agencies.

Low Earth Orbit Satellites   Geosynchronous satellites are particularly useful for broadcast-type transmissions. Dishes can be aimed at a fixed point in the sky and can send or receive signals as needed. **Low earth orbit (LEO) satellites** offer some advantages that geosynchronous satellites do not. Applications such as military surveillance require that a satellite not remain in a fixed position. A lower orbit also allows the satellite to move relative to the earth's surface and scan different areas.

LEO satellites also require less powerful rockets and, through launch agreements with NASA or leading aerospace companies and launch providers such as Lockheed Martin, can be transported to orbit in the space shuttle or other launch vehicles such as rockets. Power requirements for devices that communicate with a LEO satellite are also less because of the reduced distance that signals must travel. LEO satellites have not been heavily used for global communications applications because the satellite is not always within range of earth-based transmitters and receivers. However, that is changing!

In theory, LEO satellites could be used for communications if there were a sufficient number of them in orbit. Figure 2.20 illustrates how. If a sufficient number of satellites were in a low earth orbit, they would all move relative to the ground. For example, in Figure 2.20a, a ground station has established communications with satellite A. Because satellite A is in low earth orbit, it is moving with respect to the ground station. As such, it will eventually fall below the horizon, making direct communication with the ground station impossible until it has revolved around the earth and appears over the opposite horizon. However, rather than waiting for satellite A, there is another satellite (B) also in low earth orbit. The two satellites are

Figure 2.20   Ground Station Communicating with LEO Satellites

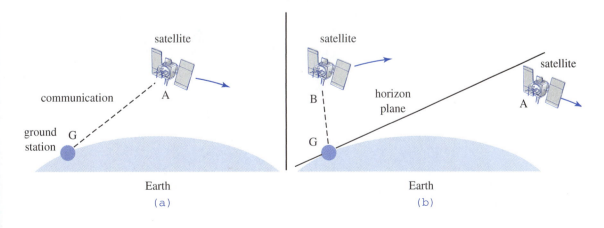

positioned so that when A falls below the horizon (Figure 2.20b), B rises above the other horizon. It can pick up the communication with the ground station that A had to abandon. When B eventually falls below the horizon, there will be yet another to take its place. If there were a sufficient number of LEO satellites, there would always be one capable of communicating with the ground station, and all points on the planet, even the most desolate ones, would be within range of a LEO satellite. This is similar to the principle on which cell phones are based. Your cell phone communicates with a single transmitter, but if you travel far enough away there is another to pick up your signal. With LEO satellites, it is the transmitters that are moving as opposed to the users.

A consequence of this is that any two locations on the planet will be connected as Figure 2.21 shows. One station (site X in Figure 2.21) communicates with the nearest available LEO satellite. The orbiting LEO satellites execute a protocol allowing them to exchange information. The protocol will allow X's message to be relayed to the LEO satellite nearest to site Y and downlinked to the site.

Although as of this writing there is no fully operational global network using LEO satellites, plans are under way to create one. In 1987 engineers at Motorola's Satellite Division conceived of a global network consisting of 77 LEO satellites. Named *Iridium* after the 77th element in the periodic table, the project was the first system of LEO satellites to be proposed. Communications with ground stations would use the L band, but intersatellite communications would be in the Ka band. Atmospheric conditions that pose an interference problem for satellite-to-ground

Figure 2.21   Two Arbitrary Stations Communicating Using LEO Satellites

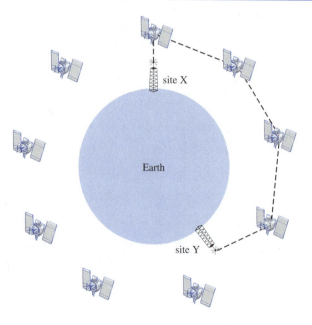

communications become less of a problem above the atmosphere. However, the Iridium consortium faced serious financial difficulties and, in the summer of 2000, Iridium LLC was officially shut down.

Another player is the Teledesic Corporation. Founded in 1990, its current primary investors are Craig McCaw, communications pioneer; William Gates, chairman and CEO of Microsoft; Saudi Prince Alwaleed Bin Talal; the Abu Dhabi Investment Company; and Boeing. Plans call for the Teledesic network to use 288 interlinked LEO satellites. An early configuration had the satellites (Figure 2.22) arranged in 12 groups of 24, with each group orbiting the earth in a polar orbit (Figure 2.23) at an altitude of approximately 1400 kilometers (about 875 miles and 1/25 the altitude of a geosynchronous orbit satellite). As the satellites move from north to south (and then from south to north), the earth rotates underneath the polar orbits. The collection of satellites is designed to cover 95% of the earth's land mass and have the capacity to support millions of users simultaneously. A more recent configuration has reduced the number of satellites to a mere 30, but more specific details were not available as of this writing.

Downlink communications are in the Ka band and operate between 18.8 and 19.3 GHz; uplink communications operate between 28.6 and 29.1 GHz. Bit rates will range from up to 100 Mbps on the uplink to 720 Mbps on the downlink. Neighboring satellites will be able to communicate with each other; together, the satellites will form a truly global communications network (Figure 2.24).

The first test satellite was launched on February 27, 1998, and Teledesic is targeting service to begin in the year 2005. In fact, Teledesic received its license from

Figure 2.22   Teledesic Satellite

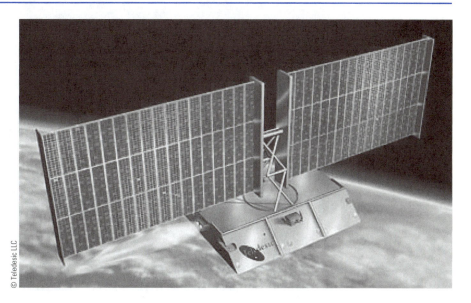

© Teledesic LLC

Figure 2.23 Constellation of Teledesic Satellites

Figure 2.24 Connecting Ground Points

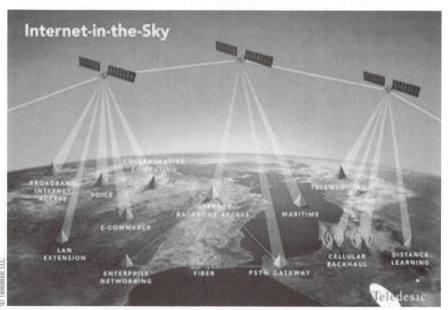

the FCC in 1997 and signed a launch contract in 1999 with Lockheed Martin for delivery of the satellites into low earth orbit. In 2002 it also signed a contract with Italian satellite manufacturer Alenia Spazio SpA to build two satellites. The global network is to provide a network for the delivery of services by others, as opposed to marketing services directly to the user. This would include computer networking, high-quality voice transmission, interactive multimedia, broadband Internet service, and a variety of other applications. Much work remains to be done in this area, especially regarding integrating the Internet with LEO satellite technology and defining appropriate routing algorithms (ref. [Ek02]).

WIRELESS LANs

One of the more interesting applications of wireless communications is the wireless LAN—a system that allows personal computers and other typical network devices to communicate without a physical connection. It promises a whole new world of applications for which cabling is impractical or for people who rarely stay in one spot. For example, medical personnel could use notebook computers or personal digital assistants connected to a wireless LAN to access medical records as they visit patients in their rooms. Executives might use a wireless LAN to access information during important meetings. An employee riding on a commuter train to or from work might access the Internet to download an important file he or she forgot before going home or to access information to prepare for an important meeting. Wireless computers can also be used in laboratories where excessive cables are a hindrance to those who need to move around frequently. Computers might access data stored on a server or print to a "connected" printer using the wireless connection. The wireless connection also allows equipment to be moved easily without worrying about disconnecting and reconnecting wires.

Two technologies used by wireless LANs are infrared and radio waves. **Infrared waves** are electromagnetic waves with frequencies just below those of visible light. Devices are equipped with LEDs or laser diodes that emit infrared light waves. These waves may be directed toward a receiver or reflected off walls and ceilings. It's similar to using a remote control to turn on the television or change the channel. There are some advantages to infrared systems. For example, infrared signals are not regulated by the FCC, unlike radio signals. Licensing is therefore not required to use infrared-based equipment. Another advantage is that infrared signals do not penetrate solid objects such as walls. That makes them more secure from outside eavesdroppers. It also allows devices in different areas of a building to use the same infrared signal without interference. Infrared signals are also impervious to radio interference. However, nonpenetration of solid objects is a disadvantage if an application calls for communication beyond solid boundaries. Another disadvantage is that infrared signals typically provide lower bit rates than other technologies. You can learn more about infrared technology in reference [We98].

Wireless LANs can also use radio transmissions up to 2.4 GHz. Figure 2.25 shows a typical configuration. A common wired network, such as an Ethernet network, forms the basic infrastructure connecting various network devices such as computers, printers, and scanners. However, another component called an

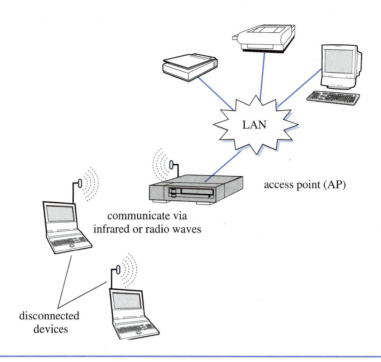

access point (AP)

communicate via
infrared or radio waves

disconnected
devices

Figure 2.25   Wireless LAN Configuration

access point (AP), connected to the wired network, acts as a bridge between the wired and wireless networks. The AP receives information from the wired network and broadcasts the information to other devices within its range.

Many different types of APs are produced by vendors such as 3Com, Cisco, Nokia, Lucent, and others (ref. [An00]); they differ based on factors such as the range of the transmitted signal, the number of users it can support, interface rates, and management abilities. They also differ on the type of radio signal transmitted. The IEEE has developed a standard for wireless networks, designated as 802.11 (http://grouper.ieee.org/groups/802/11/index.html) and, in some cases, referred to as **Wi-Fi** (for **wireless fidelity**). Various protocols are used to ensure that wireless transmission reaches the proper devices; we discuss these and other aspects of the wireless LAN more fully in Chapter 9.

BLUETOOTH

Most of the previous discussion has assumed the use of typical network devices such as personal computers, printers, and scanners. However, some developers are developing technologies that could forever change the way we view network devices. Few people would think of their wristwatch, oven timer, or VCR as being network devices, but developers of the **Bluetooth** technology hope to change that.

Bluetooth is named after Harald Blatand (Bluetooth), a Viking king who lived in the 10th century and unified Denmark and Norway. A discussion of Viking history and its relationship to current technology is a bit outside the realm of this book, but the website www.bluetooth.com has an interesting perspective on this.

The Bluetooth concept is a technology in which a microchip containing a radio transceiver is embedded in an electronic device. The intent, of course, is to allow these devices to communicate without wires or cables. It also allows them to communicate without requiring the line-of-sight path necessary for older wireless devices. Bluetooth began at Ericsson Mobile Communication in 1994 when researchers studied ways to define a low-power, low-cost interface between mobile phones and their accessories. In 1998 they formed a special interest group with IBM, Nokia, Intel, and Toshiba; today, that group has grown into an alliance of nearly 2000 companies. Although intriguing, Bluetooth has its doubters. Some see attempts to connect diverse consumer devices from many manufacturers as doomed to failure. Others claim that its 1 Mbps data rates over distances of up to 10 meters do not make it a viable technology for the 21st century.

What are the possible uses of this technology? In reference [Do00], Dornan writes: "They foresee a future where beer cans communicate with your refrigerator and your wristwatch, telling you when they're cold enough to drink. When you throw away the empties, your Bluetooth-equipped trashcan will tell the garbage truck how they can be recycled. Meanwhile, the fridge could order more beer from an online liquor store, and instruct your car not to start until you've sobered up." Although writing in jest, the author makes the point that the future will likely see devices that are not normally considered network devices communicating with one another. Because of such new technologies, the phrase **personal area network (PAN)** is beginning to appear. The idea is to allow what are normally considered consumer devices to communicate with one another. Using your wristwatch to turn on your lights and start up the coffeemaker as you head home after work is no longer beyond imagination.

FREE SPACE OPTICS

The final wireless technology we discuss is **free space optics (FSO).** Basically, it transmits data using optical technology without the fiber. It is marketed to those who want the bit rates that optical technology can provide but want to avoid the costs associated with installing optical fibers. For example, *USA Today* reported from Seattle, Washington, in April 2002 that "when LifeSpan BioSciences* sought to move its burgeoning data center last April to a new building three blocks away, it faced having to shut its research labs for a few months" because in order to make connections between labs in its old building and computers in a new building, the company would have needed to tap into the optical fibers buried in the streets. Rather than lose time and money, it elected to go another route and install a laser

---

* A company doing research in fields such as molecular pathology.

transmitter on the roof of one building and send a laser beam to a receiver on another building several blocks away. The laser transmits in the terahertz (10^{12} Hz) range, which, in contrast to satellite and microwave transmissions, is unregulated by a federal law that requires a license to transmit below 600 GHz. Of course, this could change in the future if FSO takes off and starts to use more of the terahertz spectrum.

LifeSpan BioSciences is not the only company to use FSO technology. After the September 11, 2001, attacks on the World Trade Center, *USA Today* reported that "Merrill Lynch used FSO gear from Seattle-based Terabeam to reconnect its lower Manhattan office to data centers in New Jersey and Midtown Manhattan. Law firm Mayer Brown & Pratt used equipment from San Diego-based Light-Pointe Communications to open 400 new phone lines for clients displaced by the attacks."

Proponents of FSO claim a much lower cost than optical fiber to bring systems online. Indeed, tapping into existing fiber or laying new fiber need not be done. They also claim that systems can be installed in a matter of days or weeks. Another strength is security. Although wireless technologies normally are less secure, this is not the case with FSO. Unlike satellite transmissions and microwave transmissions, which can be easily intercepted, the FSO beams are narrowly focused and hard to detect. Furthermore, if the signal were intercepted, the intended recipient would know because the transmission would be interrupted. Bit rates comparable to those found with optical fiber transmission have been reported.

This does not mean FSO is without limitations. It is a line-of-sight technology and must avoid obstructions. This can be a problem because buildings, especially tall ones, actually do sway a little and cause the narrowly focused laser to miss its mark unless sophisticated auto-tracking devices are used to adjust the transmitter's directional transmissions. Also, once the laser has traveled past a few kilometers, it becomes too wide to be properly interpreted. Some have claimed reliable service for up to 2.5 kilometers, but many tests have shown that distances of less than a kilometer are optimal. Another problem is climate. In cities where fog is common, the optimal distance drops to just a couple hundred meters because water droplets scatter light from the laser. Finally, there are social issues. Many have seen science fiction movies where lasers are used as weapons. Visions of birds flying into the line of sight and dropping cooked to the ground are not pleasant ones (dinner anyone?). Vendors claim this will not happen because the lasers they use are within approved FDA levels of intensity. Many see FSO becoming a major technology in the near future. More information on this topic can be found in reference [Al01].

SUMMARY

This section described many different transmission media. You might ask: Which one is best? The answer is not easy. In data communications, newer technologies do not necessarily make older ones obsolete. Indeed, development of fiber optics and satellite communications has not obviated the need for twisted pair or coaxial cable. Each medium has a place in the communications world. Table 2.4 compares the media discussed here.

Table 2.4 Comparison of Transmission Media

	Twisted Pair	Coaxial Cable	Optical Fiber	Microwave	Satellite	Infrared	FSO
Bit rate	Depends on the category of wire. Older Cat 3 wires have long supported 10 Mbps Ethernet rates, but newer Cat 5 wires support gigabit-rate Ethernets.	Comparable to the Cat 5 UTP for LAN environments.	Bit rates of hundreds of gigabits per second over many kilometers.	Depends on the signal's frequency. Rates can vary between approximately 10 and 300 Mbps.	Like microwaves, it depends on the frequency (10–300 Mbps).* As the Ka band becomes more commonly used, expect the rates to increase.	Up to 10 Mbps, but cannot pass through solid opaque objects such as walls.	Bit rates in the gigabit per second range at distances up to 1 kilometer.
Susceptibility to interference	Electrical interference from nearby wires or motors. Twisting the wires can reduce some noise depending on the frequency of the signal moving through the wire.	Shielding eliminates much of the electrical interference.	Immune to electrical interference.	Solid objects cause interference. Needs direct line of sight between both ends.	Interference caused by atmospheric conditions. Becomes worse at higher frequencies.	Because of the inability to pass through solid objects, infrared communications are constrained to stay within enclosed spaces.	Requires line of sight, and weather conditions such as fog can be a problem.
Distance	Depends on thickness and bit rate. Can travel up to 5–6 miles without repeaters, but the higher bit rate pairs have a limit of a couple hundred meters or less.	Also depends on bit rates. Can travel up to 5–6 miles without repeaters.	Hundreds of kilometers.	20–30 miles, but depends on height of antennas and terrain between both ends.	Worldwide.	Fairly short distances, ranging up to a couple hundred feet.	Approximately 1 kilometer, but dropping to a couple hundred meters in foggy conditions.

Table 2.4 Continued

	TWISTED PAIR	COAXIAL CABLE	OPTICAL FIBER	MICROWAVE	SATELLITE	INFRARED	FSO
Typical Uses	Particularly useful in LAN environments where connections must be made through tight spaces such as behind walls and under raised floors, or in offices, connecting workstations to wall jacks.	Once a primary medium for LANs, it is being replaced by optical fiber and UTP. It is still common for cable television service.	Commonly used in long-distance phone lines. Also popular as the primary communication medium (backbone) in a computer network.	Typically used where laying a cable is not practical, such as for telephone service in sparsely populated areas or data communications between two sites in a metropolitan area. Some potential in LAN connection.	Worldwide communication. Applications include phones, military, weather, and television.	Has applications in wireless LANs, especially in cases where restricting transmission to a confined area is important.	Used for short-range, high bit rate communications where the cost of access or laying optical fiber is prohibitive.
Comments	Can be shielded to allow higher data rates at longer distances, but shielding is more expensive and more difficult to work with.	May still be used in LAN environments to connect devices in close proximity in order to protect against electrical interference.	Difficult to splice. Adding new devices is difficult. However, optical fiber is extremely useful where very large amounts of data must be transferred over long distances.	New construction between the two sites will cause problems.	Difficult to prevent unauthorized reception. Also, a delay is caused by long distances traveled.	Wireless LANs using the same frequency can be established in different rooms.	This is a relatively new technology and some may be uncomfortable with lasers overhead (despite assurances they are safe). As the technology grows, the public will become more accepting.

Note: 1 Kbps = 2^{10} bits per second ≈ 1000 bits per second. 1 Mbps = 2^{20} bits per second ≈ 1 million bits per second. 1 Gbps = 2^{30} bits per second ≈ 1 billion bits per second.

* This figure is for each transponder. Because a satellite can contain up to two dozen transponders, the aggregate data rate for one satellite is the sum of data rates for each transponder.

2.5   CODES

The previous section described common transmission media and some of their characterics. Whether the medium uses light, electricity, or microwaves, we must answer perhaps the most basic of all communications questions: How is information coded in a format suitable for transmission? This section answers that question.

Because most data communication takes place between computers and peripheral devices, we start with the basics of computer storage. Computers are digital devices; they operate by opening and closing tiny electrical switches programmed on a chip. This explanation is an oversimplification, but it is not our intent to discuss computer and CPU architecture. Rather, we take the view that regardless of implementation, all the switches are in one of two states: open or closed. Symbolically, we represent these states by 0s or 1s expressed by bits, the smallest units of information a computer can store.

By themselves, bits are not particularly useful, because each can store only two distinct pieces of information. Grouping them, however, allows for many combinations of 0s and 1s. For example, grouping two bits allows $2^2 = 4$ unique combinations (00, 01, 10, and 11). A group of three allows $2^3 = 8$ combinations. They are formed by taking each of the four previous combinations and appending either a 0 or a 1. In general, a group of n bits allows 2^n combinations. (Can you prove this?) Grouping bits therefore allows one to associate certain combinations with specific items such as characters or numbers. We call this association a **code.** There is nothing difficult about a code. Anyone can define a code in any way. The trick is getting others to use the same code. If you get enough people to use it, you can ask IEEE or ITU to make it a standard.

Many codes exist. One of the more annoying problems in communications is to establish communications between devices that recognize different codes. It is as frustrating as trying to converse with someone who does not speak your language. To make life in communications a little easier, some standard codes have been devised. But just to make sure that life doesn't get too easy and manufacturers get too complacent, there are different, incompatible standards! (One of the more profound statements in the field of communications is, "The only problem with standards is that there are so many of them.")

The code you use depends on the type of data you are storing. Codes used for representing integers and real numbers vary widely and depend on the computer architecture. Such codes can be found in almost any book on computer organization (such as ref. [St03]). We will focus strictly on character codes.

EARLY CODES

One of the oldest codes is the **Morse code.** Developed by Samuel Morse in 1838, it was used in telegraph communications. Table 2.5 shows the code as a sequence of dots and dashes. A unique aspect of this system is that the letter codes have varying lengths; for example, the letter *E* corresponds to a single dot, and the letter *H* has four dots. The varied code length allows messages to be sent quickly. In the original telegraph, an individual sent a message by tapping a switch to open and close the

Table 2.5   Baudot, Morse, and BCD Codes

CHARACTER	BAUDOT CODE	MORSE CODE	BCD CODE	CHARACTER	BAUDOT CODE	MORSE CODE	BCD CODE
A	00011	· −	110001	S	00101	· · ·	010010
B	11001	− · · ·	110010	T	10000	−	010011
C	01110	− · − ·	110011	U	00111	· · −	010100
D	01001	− · ·	110100	V	11110	· · · −	010101
E	00001	·	110101	W	10011	· − −	010110
F	01101	· · − ·	110110	X	11101	− · · −	010111
G	11010	− − ·	110111	Y	10101	− · − −	011000
H	10100	· · · ·	111000	Z	10001	− − · ·	011001
I	00110	· ·	111001	0	10110	− − − − −	001010
J	01011	· − − −	100001	1	10111	· − − − −	000001
K	01111	− · −	100010	2	10011	· · − − −	000010
L	10010	· − · ·	100011	3	00001	· · · − −	000011
M	11100	− −	100100	4	01010	· · · · −	000100
N	01100	− ·	100101	5	10000	· · · · ·	000101
O	11000	− − −	100110	6	10101	− · · · ·	000110
P	10110	· − − ·	100111	7	00111	− − · · ·	000111
Q	10111	− − · −	101000	8	00110	− − − · ·	001000
R	01010	· − ·	101001	9	11000	− − − − ·	001001

circuit. For example, suppose each letter's code length is 5 (a code length of 4 would allow only $2^4 = 16$ possible combinations). The time it takes to send a message is proportional to five times the number of letters in the message. If some of the letters required fewer taps, the telegrapher could send the message more quickly. To take the greatest advantage of a varying-length code, the most common letters were assigned short codes. This method helped reduce the average code length.* To illustrate, consider sending the alphabet. A code length of 5 for each of 26 characters requires 130 taps to send the message. Using Morse code, the same transmission requires only 82 taps.

Another code developed by Jean-Marie-Emile Baudot was dubbed, not surprisingly, the **Baudot code.** It uses 5 bits for each character and letter (see Table 2.5) and was designed for the French telegraph. The observant reader might notice that a 5-bit code allows $2^5 = 32$ possible combinations, but that there are 36 letters and digits (not to mention other symbols not listed in Table 2.5). If you carefully scrutinize the table, you can see some duplicate codes. For example, the digit 1 and the letter *Q* have the same code. In fact, each digit's code duplicates that of some letter. (Can you find them?)

A logical question is: How can we tell a digit from a letter? The answer lies in the same principle that allows a keyboard key to represent two different characters.

---

* Some modern codes also have variable lengths, which significantly affects transmission costs. Chapter 5 discusses them in more detail.

On a keyboard, the Shift key allows the same key to generate the code for one of two characters. The Baudot code assigns the 5-bit codes 11111 (shift down) and 11011 (shift up) to determine how to interpret subsequent 5-bit codes. Upon receiving a shift down, the receiving device interprets all subsequent codes as letters. The interpretation continues until a shift up is received. Then all subsequent codes are interpreted as digits and other special symbols. Thus, sending the message "ABC123" requires the following Baudot code (read from left to right):

```
11111      00011   11001   01110   11011    10111   10011   00001
shift down    A       B       C     shift up   1       2       3
```

Another code is the **binary-coded decimal (BCD)** code, common in many early IBM mainframe computers. One of the reasons for its development was to facilitate the entry and subsequent computation of numeric data. For example, if a programmer wanted to enter the number 4385, he or she had to punch the digits 4, 3, 8, and 5 on a punched card. (Remember, we are talking about the dinosaur age of computers.) A card reader then read each digit. Instead of combining the codes for each digit and creating one representation for the precise numeric equivalent, each digit was stored using the BCD code shown in Table 2.5. This method was considered easy and efficient, especially when there was a lot of data input. The processing unit was then able to do arithmetic between numbers stored in that format. For compatibility reasons, some architectures still support computations between numbers stored in a BCD format. As computer technology evolved and new applications were found, there was a greater need to store non-numeric data. Consequently, the BCD code was expanded to include other characters. Technically, the expanded code is called the *binary-coded decimal interchange code* (BCDIC).

ASCII CODE

The most widely accepted code is the **American Standard Code for Information Interchange (ASCII).** It is a 7-bit code that assigns a unique combination to every keyboard character and to some special functions. It is used on most, if not all, personal computers and many other computers. Each code corresponds to a printable or unprintable character. Printable characters include letters, digits, and special punctuation such as commas, brackets, and question marks. *Unprintable* does not mean those that are banned from newspapers, televisions, or personalized license plates. Rather, it refers to codes that indicate a special function such as a line feed, tab, or carriage return.

Table 2.6 shows characters and their ASCII codes written in both a binary and hexadecimal format. For example, the letter *M* has the ASCII code of 1001101. Using hexadecimal notation allows us to group the bits as 100–1101 and write the code as 4D. Please note that the use of D here has no relation to the character *D*. It is simply the hexadecimal notation for the four bits 1101.

To illustrate how a transmission may work, suppose a computer sends the data in Figure 2.26 to a printer that recognizes ASCII codes. Assume the codes are sent with the leftmost one first. As the printer receives each code, it analyzes it and takes

Table 2.6   ASCII Codes

BINARY	HEX	CHAR	BINARY	HEX	CHAR	BINARY	HEX	CHAR	BINARY	HEX	CHAR
0000000	00	NUL	0010000	10	DLE	0100000	20	SP	0110000	30	0
0000001	01	SOH	0010001	11	DC1	0100001	21	!	0110001	31	1
0000010	02	STX	0010010	12	DC2	0100010	22	"	0110010	32	2
0000011	03	ETX	0010011	13	DC3	0100011	23	#	0110011	33	3
0000100	04	EOT	0010100	14	DC4	0100100	24	$	0110100	34	4
0000101	05	ENQ	0010101	15	NAK	0100101	25	%	0110101	35	5
0000110	06	ACK	0010110	16	SYN	0100110	26	&	0110110	36	6
0000111	07	BEL	0010111	17	ETB	0100111	27	'	0110111	37	7
0001000	08	BS	0011000	18	CAN	0101000	28	(	0111000	38	8
0001001	09	HT	0011001	19	EM	0101001	29	)	0111001	39	9
0001010	0A	LF	0011010	1A	SUB	0101010	2A	*	0111010	3A	:
0001011	0B	VT	0011011	1B	ESC	0101011	2B	+	0111011	3B	;
0001100	0C	FF	0011100	1C	FS	0101100	2C	,	0111100	3C	<
0001101	0D	CR	0011101	1D	GS	0101101	2D	-	0111101	3D	=
0001110	0E	SO	0011110	1E	RS	0101110	2E	.	0111110	3E	>
0001111	0F	SI	0011111	1F	US	0101111	2F	/	0111111	3F	?
1000000	40	@	1010000	50	P	1100000	60	'	1110000	70	p
1000001	41	A	1010001	51	Q	1100001	61	a	1110001	71	q
1000010	42	B	1010010	52	R	1100010	62	b	1110010	72	r
1000011	43	C	1010011	53	S	1100011	63	c	1110011	73	s
1000100	44	D	1010100	54	T	1100100	64	d	1110100	74	t
1000101	45	E	1010101	55	U	1100101	65	e	1110101	75	u
1000110	46	F	1010110	56	V	1100110	66	f	1110110	76	v
1000111	47	G	1010111	57	W	1100111	67	g	1110111	77	w
1001000	48	H	1011000	58	X	1101000	68	h	1111000	78	x
1001001	49	I	1011001	59	Y	1101001	69	i	1111001	79	y
1001010	4A	J	1011010	5A	Z	1101010	6A	j	1111010	7A	z
1001011	4B	K	1011011	5B	[	1101011	6B	k	1111011	7B	{
1001100	4C	L	1011100	5C	\	1101100	6C	l	1111100	7C		
1001101	4D	M	1011101	5D	]	1101101	6D	m	1111101	7D	}
1001110	4E	N	1011110	5E	^	1101110	6E	n	1111110	7E	~
1001111	4F	O	1011111	5F	_	1101111	6F	o	1111111	7F	DEL

some action. Thus, receiving the codes 4F, 6C, and 64 causes it to print the characters O, l, and d. The next two codes, 0A and 0D, correspond to unprintable characters. Table 2.6 shows them as LF (line feed) and CR (carriage return), respectively. When the printer receives 0A it prints nothing but activates the mechanisms to advance to the next line. The code 0D causes the print mechanism to return to its leftmost position. At this point, subsequent printable characters appear on the new line, beginning in the leftmost column (see Figure 2.26). Table 2.7 describes a few more control characters.

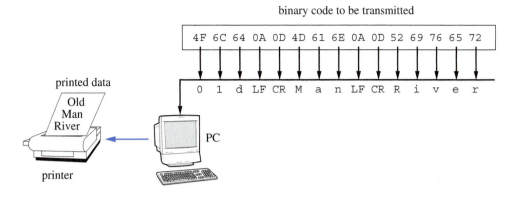

Figure 2.26 Transmitting an ASCII-Coded Message

Table 2.7 ASCII Control Characters

BEL	Bell causes the receiving device (for example a workstation) to emit an audible sound, usually heard as a "beep." This signal is commonly used to attract the user's attention when special messages are sent or when something significant is about to happen (Figure 2.27).
BS	Back Space causes the print mechanism or cursor to move backward one position. This control character can be used to print two characters in one position (useful for underlining) or to print a character in boldface (print the same character twice in the same position). On a display screen it replaces the first character with the second one.
CR	Carriage Return causes the print mechanism or cursor to return to the leftmost print position. Note: This character is independent of a line feed.
DC1, DC2, DC3, DC4	Device Controls correspond to special functions or features dependent on the device. For example, DC1 and DC3 sometimes correspond to X-ON and X-OFF characters generated by the control-Q and control-S keyboard sequences. If a device's buffers are filling up, it can send an X-OFF character to the sender, causing it to stop sending. Sending an X-ON causes transmission to continue.*
DLE	Data Link Escape acts as a toggle switch causing the device to interpret subsequently received characters differently.
FF	Form Feed is used with special forms or screens. It causes the print mechanism or cursor to advance to the beginning of the next form or screen.
HT	Horizontal Tab causes the cursor or print mechanism to advance to the next selected tab stop.
LF	Line Feed advances to the next line.
NUL	Null is used as a filler (to occupy space where there is no data) in a partially filled record.
VT	Vertical Tab causes the cursor or print mechanism to advance to the next preassigned print line.

* A student's first exposure to X-ON and X-OFF often occurs by accident. For example, suppose you enter a command from a workstation to print a file (such as one containing machine language) containing unprintable characters. The file's contents are incorrectly interpreted as ASCII-coded characters. If one of the codes corresponds to an X-OFF character, the workstation interprets it as a command to stop sending characters. Consequently, anything the user types is not transmitted, which causes the workstation to freeze up.

Figure 2.27   Significant Event Requiring Use of BEL Character

EBCDIC CODE

Another code is the **Extended Binary Coded Decimal Interchange Code (EBCDIC),** used primarily on IBM mainframes and peripherals. It is an 8-bit code, thus allowing up to 256 different characters. Like the ASCII code, there are printable and unprintable characters; however, we will not show the entire table. An Internet search engine might locate such a table for the interested reader.

UNICODE

ASCII and EBCDIC have long been in use, and those familiar with them frequently use the terms *byte* and *character* interchangeably. Both codes have been used primarily to represent common control functions, letters, and characters from the English alphabet. However, with the internationalization of networking applications, the 7- and 8-bit codes have become much too inflexible, and a new standard, **Unicode,** is being developed. Unicode supports many scripts, or collections of mathematical symbols and special characters that exist in a particular language. Examples include Arabic, Latin, Greek, Gothic, and Cyrillic scripts. The Java language also uses Unicode to support the Java *char* type.

Unicode defines a unique 16-bit number for each character independent of language and computing platform. The Unicode Consortium, a nonprofit organization that works in conjunction with ISO, defines specifications. Members include companies such as Apple, Microsoft, Oracle, IBM, Novell, and Netscape. Unicode is still evolving as new scripts are added to its definition. At the time of this writing, Unicode 3.2 had defined codes for over 90,000 characters. For this reason we have elected not to include a table of Unicode characters. Those wishing to stay current on Unicode developments can find more information at www.unicode.org.

2.6 SUMMARY

This chapter dealt mainly with communications media and equipment, applications, and communication codes. Important concepts presented in this chapter are as follows:

- Information is encoded as sequences of bits (represented by 0s and 1s) and is transmitted using electrical signals or electromagnetic waves.

- Primary communications media include twisted pair, coaxial cable, fiber optics, microwave and satellite transmission, infrared and radio waves, and free space optics.

- Electrically conducting media such as twisted pair and cable are cheaper than fiber and easier to tap into. However, they have smaller bandwidths and are subject to electrical interference.

- LAN environments often depend heavily on twisted pair for connectivity in adjacent rooms and may use optical fiber to span distances between buildings. Long-distance carriers also use optical fiber for long-distance trunk lines. Coaxial cable is used less frequently than it once was but is common for cable television service and may be used to connect LAN devices in places where protection against electrical interference is necessary. Still, the lower cost and high bit rates make UTP the choice for many.

- Microwaves and satellites communicate through free space. That is, they require no physical connection. Satellites offer worldwide communications, and microwave towers allow communication across distances where physical connections are impossible or impractical.

- Geosynchronous satellites remain in a fixed position relative to a position on the earth's surface and are useful in broadcast and communications applications. The bit rates depend on the transmission frequencies. Higher frequencies provide higher data rates but are subject to more interference in the atmosphere.

- Low earth orbit (LEO) satellites continually move across the sky. Teledesic is planning a network of them to provide a global communications network.

- Wireless LAN technology is becoming commonplace. Portable devices such as notebook computers can transmit infrared or radio waves to an access point that is connected to a LAN. This allows a device to communicate with other LAN devices despite the lack of a physical connection.

- Free space optics is a new wireless technology that offers high bit rates, comparable with those found in optical fiber. It uses a laser (highly focused beam of light) to transmit information over distances of a kilometer or less.

- To transmit data, regardless of medium, we need to use a code, a mechanism that associates bit strings with certain information. The most common codes are ASCII (American Standard Code for Information Interchange) and EBCDIC (Extended Binary Coded Decimal Interchange Code). Each associates a bit string with each keyboard character and many special control functions. Other codes of importance are Baudot, Morse, and BCD (binary-coded decimal).

- Unicode is a more recent code being used in many applications to support a much larger variety of characters and scripts than ASCII or EBCDIC can.
- Data communications is a dynamic field of study. Researchers are continually increasing the bit rates of different media and reducing their costs to make them technologically and economically feasible for more people than ever before.

Review Questions

1. What is a periodic signal?
2. List five transmission media and rank them in order of bit rate capability.
3. Distinguish between a digital and an analog signal.
4. Distinguish between bit rate and bandwidth.
5. How are a signal's period and frequency related?
6. Distinguish between baseband and broadband modes.
7. What is the difference between Cat 4 and Cat 5 twisted-wire pair?
8. Define the index of refraction.
9. What is the difference between ThickNet and ThinNet?
10. What is the difference between a laser and LED in optical fiber communications?
11. List three modes for optical fiber communication and compare them.
12. Are the following statements TRUE or FALSE? Why?
    a. Direct microwave transmission can happen between any two surface points on earth.
    b. Satellite transmission requires a stationary communication satellite.
    c. Thicker optical fiber allows a higher bit rate.
    d. Satellite transmission rates are limited only by the capability of equipment to send and receive high-frequency signals.
    e. Because LEO satellites move across the sky and fall below the horizon there are no practical uses for them in communications applications.
    f. Local area networks do not require a physical connection among their components.
    g. Light can travel through optical fiber at different speeds.
    h. Visible light and electromagnetic waves are the same.
    i. Optical fibers have a hollow center through which light passes and reflects off a reflective surface surrounding it.
    j. Free space optics requires line-of-sight transmission.
13. Distinguish between a horn and a parabolic dish antenna.
14. List three ways in which wireless devices can communicate.
15. Where was the first wireless network?
16. What is the Bluetooth technology?
17. Which transmissions are susceptible to interference?

18. Why are the wires in a twisted pair twisted (as opposed to using parallel wires)?

19. What is the purpose of the cladding in optical fiber communications?

20. What was *Sputnik?*

21. List some advantages and disadvantages of LEO satellites versus geosynchronous satellites.

22. How does free space optics differ from fiber optic communications?

23. List some advantages and disadvantages of free space optics.

24. What is the difference between a printable character and a control character?

25. What is the difference between the ASCII and the EBCDIC codes?

26. How does Unicode differ from the traditional ASCII and EBCDIC codes?

27. What was the motivation for defining Unicode?

28. The Baudot code for the character 0 (zero) is the same as that for the character *P*. How can that be?

Exercises

1. If a signal has a period of 10 nanoseconds, what is its frequency?

2. If a signal has a frequency of 500 megahertz, what is its period?

3. If a satellite's orbital height is fixed, why is it not possible to change the time required to orbit the earth by changing the speed of the satellite?

4. LANs were often connected using coaxial cable instead of twisted wires because of the better bit rates and resistance to external noise. Why is coaxial cable used much less frequently in current LAN technologies?

5. Suppose a company is trying to establish communications among several sites in different parts of a large city. Would microwave links be a good idea? Why or why not?

6. How can a satellite remain in a fixed position in the sky? Why doesn't gravity pull the satellite toward the ground?

7. Assuming that signals travel at the speed of light (186,000 miles per second), how much time does a signal require to travel from a ground station to a geosynchronous satellite? How much time is required if the satellite is in a low earth orbit of 875 miles?

8. The Teledesic Project has changed since its initial inception and has likely changed since this book's publication. Investigate the topic and write a few paragraphs on the current state of the Teledesic Project.

9. Write a program that prompts its user with a message and a bell sound to input a number and echo print it.

10. If you have access to your campus or business network, investigate the wiring (UTP, cable, optical fiber) that was chosen for connectivity.

11. What is the Baudot code for the character string SDG564FSDH65?

12. Table 2.6 shows ASCII codes for 0 through 9. Why is there no ASCII code for 10?

REFERENCES

[Al01] Allen, D. "The Second Coming of Free Space Optics." *Network,* vol. 16, no. 3 (March 2001), 55–63.

[An00] Angel, J. "Look Ma, No Cables." *Network,* vol. 15, no. 11 (November 2000), 42–52.

[Cl45] Clarke, A. C. "Extra-Terrestrial Relays: Can Rocket Stations Give World-Wide Radio Coverage?" *Wireless World* (October 1945).

[Do00] Dornan, A. "Can Bluetooth Sink Its Teeth into Networking?" *Network,* vol. 15, no. 11 (November 2000), 54–60.

[Ek02] Ekici, E., I. Akyildiz, and M. Bender. "A Multicast Routing Algorithm for LEO Satellite IP Networks." *IEEE/ACM Transactions on Networking,* vol. 10, no. 2 (April 2002), 183–192.

[Hu90] Hudson, H. *Communication Satellites.* New York: Free Press, 1990.

[Me00] Metz, C. "IP-Over-Satellite: Internet Connectivity Blasts Off." *IEEE Internet Computing,* vol. 4, no. 4 (July/August 2000), 84–89.

[Ro01] Rogers, A. *Understanding Optical Fiber Communications.* Boston: Artech House, 2001.

[Sh90] Sherman, K. *Data Communications: A User's Guide,* 3rd ed. Englewood Cliffs, NJ: Prentice-Hall, 1990.

[St00] Stallings, W. "Gigabit Ethernet." *Dr. Dobbs Journal,* vol. 25, no. 5 (May 2000).

[St03] Stallings, W. *Computer Organization and Architecture: Designing for Performance,* 6th ed. Englewood Cliffs, NJ: Prentice-Hall, 2003.

[We98] Wesel, E. *Wireless Multimedia Communications.* Reading, MA: Addison-Wesley, 1998.

CHAPTER 3

ANALOG AND DIGITAL SIGNALS

Information networks straddle the world. Nothing remains concealed. But the sheer volume of information dissolves the information. We are unable to take it all in.
—**Günther Grass,** German author

The lowest form of popular culture—lack of information, misinformation, disinformation, and a contempt for the truth or the reality of most people's lives—has overrun real journalism. Today, ordinary Americans are being stuffed with garbage.
—**Carl Bernstein,** U.S. journalist

3.1 INTRODUCTION

We have covered two primary areas of data transmission: the medium and the symbolic representation of data. Now it is time to combine them. In other words, now that we know how data may be stored symbolically, how does that relate to electrical signals, microwaves, or light waves? How do modems and cable modems transmit data? What is DSL technology? The next logical step is to relate physical signals to the symbolic representation of data. More simply put, what does a 0 or a 1 actually look like as it travels through a wire, optical fiber, or space? How many bits can a signal transmit per unit of time and are there any limitations? Can electrical interference (noise) affect the data? If so, how?

The answers depend in part on whether we use analog or digital signals. Recall from Chapter 2 that a digital signal may be represented by an alternating sequence of high and low values (0s and 1s) (Figure 3.1a). An analog signal varies continuously in a range between two values. A digital signal has a constant value for a short time and then changes to a different value. An analog signal is changing all the time and is most often represented by its characteristic sine wave (Figure 3.1b).

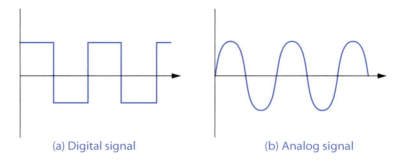

(a) Digital signal   (b) Analog signal

Figure 3.1   Analog and Digital Signals

Chapter 2 indicated that a digital signal could be used to represent data by associating a 0 or 1 with either a high or low signal. However, this approach is subject to problems. Therefore, we need to find an alternative. Section 3.2 describes various approaches. Analog signals present another problem. Because they are constantly varying, how can we associate 0s or 1s with them? We need to better understand an analog signal's characteristics. Sections 3.3 and 3.4 provide this coverage and relate the concept of bit rate to a signal's characteristics. They also discuss two famous results that specify limits on the amount of data that can be transmitted per unit of time given a signal's characteristics.

This leads to another issue: Digital and analog signals transmit data in different ways. As a result, if a computer is going to communicate over an analog phone line, we need to find a way to convert signals of one type to signals of another and back again. Sections 3.5 and 3.6 describe some techniques. Section 3.7 covers modems—common devices that convert between signal types—and conversion standards. Finally, Section 3.8 introduces DSL (Digital Subscriber Line), an alternative to conventional and cable modem technology.

3.2 DIGITAL ENCODING SCHEMES

A natural connection exists between digital signals and digitally encoded data. Data stored digitally are represented by a sequence of 0s and 1s. Because digital signals can alternate between two constant values, we simply associate 0 with one value and 1 with the other. The actual values used are not important here. With electrical signals, they are sometimes equal but opposite in sign. To keep the discussion general, we will refer to them as "high voltage" and "low voltage."

NRZ ENCODING

Perhaps the simplest encoding scheme is the **nonreturn to zero (NRZ).** A 0 is transmitted by raising the voltage level to high, and a 1 is transmitted using a low voltage. Thus, alternating appropriately between high and low voltage transmits any

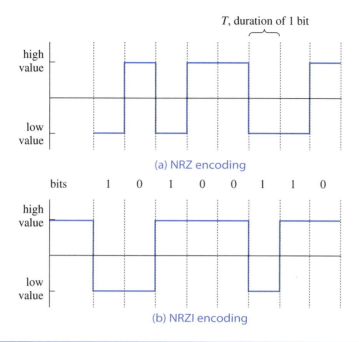

(a) NRZ encoding

(b) NRZI encoding

Figure 3.2   NRZ and NRZI Encoding

desired sequence of 0s and 1s. The name NRZ refers to the fact that the voltage level stays constant (i.e., does not return to zero) during the time a bit is transmitted. Figure 3.2a shows the NRZ transmission of the binary string 10100110.

An alternative coding scheme is *NRZI* (NRZ inverted). The difference between NRZ and NRZI is that in the latter scheme a 1 is represented by a change. If the signal was low, it becomes high. If it was high, it becomes low. Figure 3.2b shows the NRZI signal for the same bit string as represented in Figure 3.2a.

NRZ and NRZI coding are simple, but they have a problem. Look at the transmission in Figure 3.3. What is being transmitted? Your answer should be "A sequence

Figure 3.3   NRZ Encoding of a Sequence of 0s

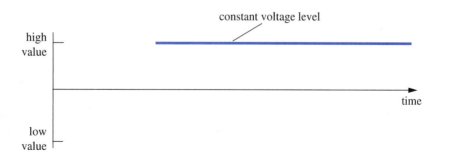

of 0s." Well, that's true, but how many 0s? To this question, you should respond that it depends on the duration of one bit. Now suppose we tell you that graphically, the duration corresponds to a line 1 millimeter long. All you have to do is measure the length of the line and convert to millimeters. This calculation will tell you the number of 1-millimeter segments there are and, consequently, the number of 0 bits. In theory this method works, but in practice it may not. Suppose one person used a ruler and constructed 1000 one-millimeter line segments end to end. How long is the resulting line? The answer should be 1 meter, but imprecision in taking measurements and actually drawing the lines will probably result in a line close to but not exactly 1 meter long. Thus, a second person measuring the line will conclude there are slightly more or less than 1000 segments. Even if the first person were lucky and measured accurately, imprecision in the second person's measurements will cause a discrepancy.

What does this have to do with data transmissions? When a device transmits a digital signal for one bit, it generates a constant signal for a certain duration, say T. An internal clock defines the timing. The receiving device must know the duration of the signal so it can sample the signal every T units. It also has an internal clock defining the timing. So all that is needed is to make sure both clocks use the same T.

Next question: Do all the clocks in your house have the same time down to the last second? Mine don't. Unfortunately, any physical device is subject to design limitations and imperfections. There will almost certainly be very small differences between the clocks that cause one's signal sampling to drift from the other's transmission. It is similar to synchronizing two clocks on New Year's Day, only to find that by the year's end they differ slightly. Similarly, musicians in an orchestra may all start playing at the same time with the same tempo, but unless they watch the conductor and listen to one another, their tempos may begin to drift. It won't take much timing drift to destroy the piece, making it sound as though the author and his colleagues played it.

Communicating devices need some mechanism for making sure their timing does not vary, much like the conductor makes sure the musicians stay synchronized. With a constant signal, there is no synchronizing mechanism. However, if the signal changes, the changes can be used to keep the devices synchronized. Some schemes force signal changes for that reason.

MANCHESTER ENCODING

The **Manchester code** uses signal changes to keep the sending and receiving devices synchronized. Some call it a **self-synchronizing code.** To avoid the situation of Figure 3.3, it distinguishes between a 0 and 1 by changing the voltage. Specifically, it represents a 0 by a change from high to low and a 1 by a change from low to high. Figure 3.4 shows the Manchester-encoded transmission of the bit string 01011001. As the figure shows, the signal will never be held constant for a time longer than a single bit interval. Even for a sequence of 0s or 1s, the signal will change in the middle of each interval. This change allows the receiving device's clock to remain consistent with the sending device's clock. A disadvantage of Manchester encoding is that twice the bandwidth is needed. That is, the signals must change twice as frequently as with NRZ encoding.

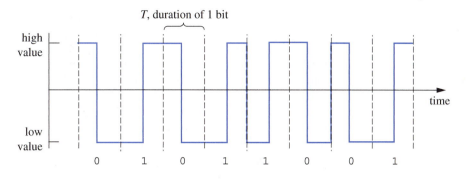

Figure 3.4   Manchester Encoding

A variation of this method is called **differential Manchester encoding.** Like Manchester encoding, there is always a signal change in the middle of each bit interval. The difference lies in what happens at the beginning of the interval. A 0 causes the signal to change at the start of the interval. A 1 causes the signal to remain where it was at the end of the previous interval. Thus, a 0 may go from low to high or high to low depending on the initial value of the signal. Figure 3.5 shows the differential Manchester encoding for the bit string 10100110. In this case, 0s and 1s are distinguished by whether there is a change in the signal at the beginning of the interval. Detecting changes is often more reliable, especially when there is noise in the channel.

3.3   ANALOG SIGNALS

Dealing with analog signals adds complexity to data communications. One problem is that digital computers are incompatible with analog transmission media. Although much of the telephone system is digital, the wires that connect directly to

Figure 3.5   Differential Manchester Encoding

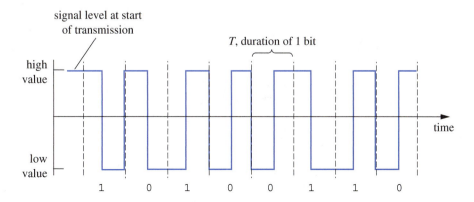

your phone transmit analog signals. As such, the device at the local switching office expects an analog signal. If you connect your computer to your telephone line, you need a device that converts a digital signal from your computer to an analog one (**modulation**) for transmission over your line. This device must also convert an analog signal received over the telephone line to a digital one (**demodulation**) for transmission back to the computer. A **modem** (short for modulation/demodulation) does both. We discuss the functions and standards of modems later in this chapter, but first we provide an important theoretical foundation for analog signals.

To start, we will define an analog signal more carefully. Earlier we stated that an analog signal is a continuously varying signal between two values, and we used a diagram similar to those in Figure 3.6 to illustrate. This definition is certainly true, but it is far from a complete description. The signal in Figure 3.6a may be represented mathematically by a simple trigonometric function $y = \sin(t)$. In other words, Figure 3.6a is the graph of $y = \sin(t)$. But we can alter sine functions in many ways and thus affect the resulting signal. In general, an analog signal is characterized by its frequency, amplitude, and phase shift.

Figure 3.6 Analog Signals

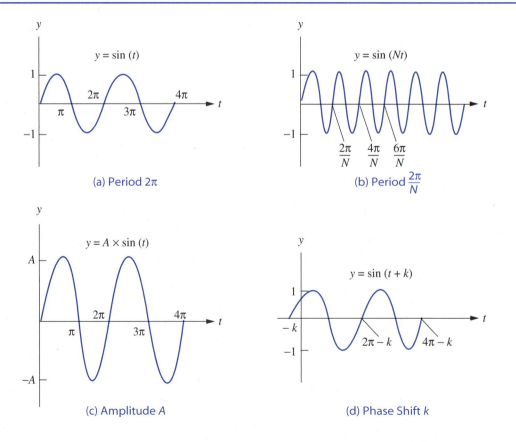

(a) Period 2π

(b) Period $\dfrac{2\pi}{N}$

(c) Amplitude A

(d) Phase Shift k

If the signal varies with time and repeats a pattern continuously, the **period** is the time it takes to complete the pattern once. Such a function is periodic. In Figure 3.6a, the period is 2π. However, by changing the function to $y = \sin(Nt)$, we change the period to $2\pi/N$ (Figure 3.6b). To see this, as t goes from 0 to $2\pi/N$, the sine function's argument (Nt) goes from 0 to 2π. In general, if $N > 1$, the period is smaller than 2π. If $N < 1$, the period is greater than 2π.

The period is related to the **frequency,** the number of times the signal oscillates per unit of time. Its units of measurement are cycles per second or, equivalently, hertz (Hz). Specifically, if f is the frequency and p is the period, then

$$f = \frac{1}{p}$$

Thus, the signal of Figure 3.6b has a frequency of $N/2\pi$ Hz.

The **amplitude** defines the values between which the signal oscillates. Because $y = \sin(t)$ oscillates between 1 and -1, $y = A \times \sin(t)$ oscillates between A and $-A$ (Figure 3.6c).

The last way to change a signal is through a **phase shift.** Graphically, this is a horizontal shift in the graph of a sine function. In general, we can achieve a horizontal shift by adding to or subtracting from the argument. For example, if $k > 0$, the graph of $y = \sin(t + k)$ (Figure 3.6d) is that of Figure 3.6a shifted to the left k units. This change is easily verified by evaluating both functions at different values of t.

FOURIER'S RESULTS

We now see that an analog signal is more complex than a simple sine wave (graph of a sine function). In general, its amplitude, frequency, and phase shift can all vary with time and thus create complex functions. Perhaps the most familiar example of an analog signal is the one produced by speaking into the telephone (Figure 3.7). As you speak, you vary the sounds you make in order to form words. Your voice also gets louder or softer depending on whether you are having an argument with your boss or speaking to your fiancé. Speaking louder or softer or in a higher or lower pitch creates sound that translates to electrical analog signals. The amplitude reflects the volume, and the frequency reflects the pitch. (At this point, there is no simple sound equivalent corresponding to a phase shift.) The result is a complex combination of signals that represents your voice.

Figure 3.7   Sound Creating an Analog Signal

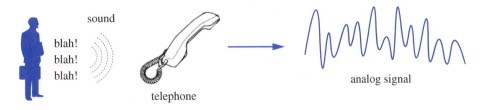

The problem now is how to transmit complex signals. There are infinitely many ways of varying the amplitude, frequency, and phase shift. Furthermore, electrical engineering tells us that different signals can experience different amounts of distortion. How do engineers design hardware to do the job? Do they design different hardware and transmission media for different signal types? Do the functions that represent different analog signals require separate analysis?

The answer to the last two questions is no. A famous mathematician, Jean Baptiste Fourier, developed a theory stating that any periodic function can be expressed as an infinite sum of sine functions of varying amplitude, frequency, and phase shift. The sum is called a **Fourier series.** Its importance is that no matter how complex periodic functions are, they all consist of the same components.

In more mathematical terms, suppose $s(t)$ is a periodic function with period P. One form for Fourier's results states that

$$s(t) = \frac{a_0}{2} + \sum_{i=1}^{\infty} \left[a_i \times \cos\left(\frac{2\pi it}{P}\right) + b_i \times \sin\left(\frac{2\pi it}{P}\right) \right]$$

(There are other forms, but this suits our needs here.)

The coefficients a_i ($i = 0, 1, 2, ...$) and b_i ($i = 1, 2, 3, ...$) are determined using

$$a_i = \frac{2}{P} \int_{-P/2}^{P/2} s(t) \times \cos\left(\frac{2\pi it}{P}\right) dt \quad \text{for } i = 0, 1, 2, 3, ...$$

and

$$b_i = \frac{2}{P} \int_{-P/2}^{P/2} s(t) \times \sin\left(\frac{2\pi it}{P}\right) dt \quad \text{for } i = 0, 1, 2, 3, ...$$

We won't derive or provide a rationale for these equations. We simply present them for the purposes of explaining the limitations of different communications media. If you are interested, you can find a more complete description of the Fourier series in references [St00], [Ge99], and [Ch02]. What is important to us is that Fourier analysis tells us that every periodic signal is a sum of analog signals with different frequencies and amplitudes. We conclude from this statement that the capability to send and analyze an analog signal depends on the range of frequencies (bandwidth) the medium is capable of handling.

Consider an example. Let $s(t)$ be defined by

$$s(t) = \begin{cases} 1 \text{ for } 0 \le t < \pi; 2\pi \le t < 3\pi; 4\pi \le t < 5\pi; \text{ etc.} \\ -1 \text{ for } \pi \le t < 2\pi; 3\pi \le t < 4\pi; 5\pi \le t < 6\pi; \text{ etc.} \end{cases}$$

Figure 3.8a shows its graph. Because it is periodic (with a period of 2π), we can write it as a Fourier series. In this case all constants a_i, for $i \ge 0$, are 0. Constants b_i are defined by

$$b_i = \begin{cases} 0 \text{ if } i \text{ is even} \\ \dfrac{4}{\pi i} \text{ if } i \text{ is odd} \end{cases}$$

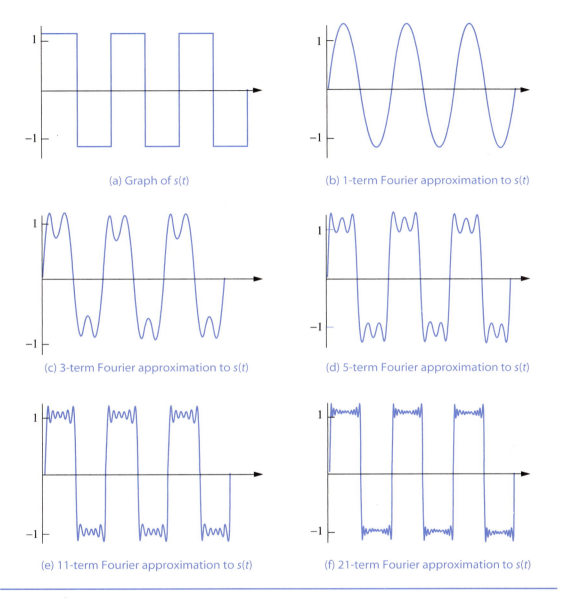

(a) Graph of s(t)

(b) 1-term Fourier approximation to s(t)

(c) 3-term Fourier approximation to s(t)

(d) 5-term Fourier approximation to s(t)

(e) 11-term Fourier approximation to s(t)

(f) 21-term Fourier approximation to s(t)

Figure 3.8   Fourier Approximations

We have used calculus to determine these values and will not duplicate the calculations here. If you are familiar with integration techniques, you should verify the results. If not, just focus on the bottom line, which is that we can write the periodic function as

$$s(t) = \sum_{i=1 \text{ and } i \text{ odd}}^{\infty} \frac{4}{\pi i} \sin(it)$$

Calculating an infinite sum is likely to take some time (probably more than you are willing and able to give). The best we can hope to do is to approximate the function using a finite number of terms—but we must accept the trade-offs. We can get an approximation quickly using few terms. Unfortunately, the approximation is not very accurate. Of course, we can easily improve the approximation by using more terms, which gives us better accuracy but takes more effort. Figures 3.8b through 3.8f show the graphs of the approximation using 1, 3, 5, 11, and 21 terms. As the graphs show, using just a few terms creates an approximation that barely resembles the original function. However, as we use more terms, the graph becomes flatter over each interval and the jumps between 1 and -1 occur more quickly.

We should also mention that it is not always necessary to use the previous equations to calculate a_i and b_i. Sometimes, the function for which we seek to find the Fourier series is actually represented by a set of data points that vary with time as opposed to a specified formula. When the data points vary with time, we say that the function is defined over the time domain. In such cases, the coefficients of the Fourier series can be approximated (often with little error) by using numerical integration techniques. Doing so constitutes calculating a *discrete Fourier transform* (sometimes called a *finite Fourier transform*). The resulting function can now be interpreted as a function of the frequencies that appear in the Fourier series. In this case we say that the function is defined over the frequency domain.

Now, if there are many data points for the function, then the calculations of the discrete Fourier transform often involve making the same calculation many times. Another technique, called the *fast Fourier transform*, recasts the previous form of a Fourier series into a sum of exponential terms with complex numbers and uses some well-known mathematical results to develop a more efficient way of making the calculation. To complicate things even further, signal analysts also depend on an *inverse fast Fourier transform*. The idea is to use fast Fourier transforms and their inverse counterparts to transform back and forth between the time and frequency domains for certain classes of functions. This is important because knowing what frequencies are most significant is useful for signal analysis and understanding how noise affects signals.

Details are obviously complex and beyond the scope of this book. However, we wanted to bring it up because our discussion of DSL later in this chapter makes reference to inverse fast Fourier transforms. If you are interested in following up on the details, references [Ge99] and [Ch02] provide excellent coverage of this topic.

APPLICATIONS OF FOURIER'S RESULTS

Again you might ask, "So what?" Well, Fourier's results are essential to the study of communications. Transmitting a complex analog signal over a medium with a limited bandwidth is the same as approximating the function using some of the Fourier series terms. We can use this principle to explain why, for example, listening to someone's CD player over a telephone is different from listening to it in person.

High-fidelity equipment is capable of producing sounds within a bandwidth of several tens of thousands of Hz. (Actual bandwidth, of course, depends on the equipment.) It can produce sounds ranging from about 30 Hz (cycles per second) to between 20,000 and 30,000 Hz. The telephone, on the other hand, can only transmit signals between approximately 300 and 3300 Hz. Consequently, the original signal loses its very low and very high frequency components. The audible effect is that low bass and high treble sounds are lost, resulting in a less than clear sound. Fourier's results also explain why a person's voice may not sound exactly the same over the phone as in person. On the other hand, a normal voice does not have the range of sounds that a musical instrument has; that is, most of the voice frequencies are within the bandwidth of a telephone. Thus, although there is some loss of tonal quality, enough is saved to recognize the voice and understand completely what is being said.

Fourier's results are also used in defining hardware. For example, a **filter** will block certain frequencies while allowing others to pass. Filters have a wide range of applications. For example, an equalizer attached to a stereo can be adjusted to bring out certain tones in music. If we want to highlight bass sounds or accentuate higher-pitched sounds such as soprano voices or a flute on the high end of the music scale, we can set the equalizer to vary the frequencies blocked by the filter.

Another example is found in cable television. A bewildered consumer may wonder how a television can receive over 100 channels. The answer lies in the capability to view a complex signal as many simple ones. Each channel is assigned a certain range of frequencies, and a signal defining the sound and pictures is created using frequencies within that range. The physical cable transmits one signal consisting of the sum of signals from all channels. This process, **multiplexing,** is discussed in more detail in Chapter 4. Selecting a channel on a television simply allows frequencies within a certain range to pass. Television circuits analyze them and produce sounds and pictures.

Still another example lies in DSL technology, which we describe later in this chapter. We will see that a common method of connecting a computer to the Internet involves generating multiple signals within specified frequency ranges, combining them, and using a fast Fourier transform to generate a result.

3.4   BIT RATE

THE NYQUIST THEOREM AND NOISELESS CHANNELS

The next step in the discussion of signals is to relate them to bit transfer. Computer networks now use all forms of transmission for this purpose. As the needs and capacities of networks continue to grow, fundamental questions must be asked. For example: Given a particular medium, how many bits can be transferred per unit of time? The **bit rate** is used to describe a medium's capacity and is measured in bits per second (bps). An important result in communications theory relates the bit rate to the bandwidth. Simply put, a higher-bandwidth medium is capable of a higher bit rate. The relation between them is so strong that many people often use the terms interchangeably.

Before describing the relation, let's make sure we understand the mechanism behind the transfer of bits. Figure 3.9 illustrates the main components. Basically, a

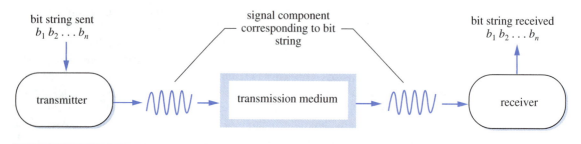

Figure 3.9   Sending Data via Signals

transmitter sends a signal representing a bit string. The receiver "listens" to the medium and creates a bit string based on the signal it receives.

Let's take a close look at the signal. First we represent the bit string by $b_1 b_2 \ldots$ b_n. The transmitter alternately analyzes each string and transmits a signal component uniquely determined by the bit values. Once the component is sent, the transmitter gets another bit string and repeats the process. The different signal components make up the actual transmitted signal. The frequency with which the components change is the **baud rate.**

Precisely how the transmitter determines each component is the topic of the next section and is not important here. If you would like something more concrete for now, just think of a unique signal amplitude for each bit combination. For example, the signal components may have up to 2^n different amplitudes, one for each unique combination of values for $b_1 b_2 \ldots b_n$.

At the receiving end, the process is reversed. The receiver alternately samples the incoming signal and generates a bit string. The bit string, of course, depends on the sample. For this process to work, the receiver must be able to sample with a frequency equal to the baud rate. (If it samples less frequently than the components can change, some can go unsampled, and the result is lost data.)

Consequently, the bit rate depends on two things: the frequency with which a component can change (baud rate) and n, the number of bits in the string. Many people often use the terms *baud rate* and *bit rate* interchangeably. Based on our discussion, we now see that this idea is not correct. In fact,

$$\text{bit rate} = \text{baud rate} \times n$$

This would seem to imply that one can always increase the bit rate by increasing either the baud rate or n. This is true, but only up to a point. Some classic results put an upper bound on the data rate.

The first result is surprisingly old, dating back to the 1920s, when Harry Nyquist developed his classic theory. References [Wa98] and [Bl99] provide a more formal treatment. We will not prove it here, but we will state it and explain its importance to data communications. First, Nyquist showed that if f is the maximum frequency the medium can transmit, the receiver can completely reconstruct a signal by sampling it $2f$ times per second. (We interject here that Nyquist assumed that absolutely no noise or distortion altered the signal. That is, he assumed a perfectly noiseless channel. We discuss noisy channels shortly.) Another way of saying this is that the receiver can reconstruct the signal by sampling it at intervals of $1/(2f)$ second, or twice each period (remember, one period $= 1/f$). For example, if the maximum frequency is 4000 Hz, the receiver need only sample the signal 8000 times per second. In other words, the signal can be recovered completely by sampling it every 1/8000th of a second.

Now, suppose the transmitter changed the signals at intervals of $1/(2f)$. In other words, the baud rate is $2f$. We then have the results of the **Nyquist theorem,** which states

$$\text{bit rate} = \text{baud rate} \times n = 2 \times f \times n$$

Some books state the Nyquist theorem using the number of different signal components instead of n. In other words, if B is the number of different components, then

$$B = 2^n$$

or, equivalently,

$$n = \log_2 (B)$$

In such cases, we can write

$$\text{bit rate} = 2 \times f \times \log_2 (B)$$

Table 3.1 summarizes some results assuming a maximum frequency of 3300 Hz, the approximate upper limit for the telephone system.

Noisy Channels

So far, this information seems to imply there is no upper bound for the bit rate given the maximum frequency. Unfortunately, this is not true for two reasons. First, more signal components mean subtler changes among them. For example, suppose a signal's amplitude must be less than or equal to 5 volts and that each component is determined by amplitude only. If we use two components defined by 2.5 and 5 volts, the signals differ by 2.5 volts. However, using 16 signal components requires a difference of about one-third volt between adjacent amplitudes. The receiver must be more sophisticated (and more expensive) to be able to detect smaller differences.

Table 3.1   Results of Nyquist's Theorem for a Maximum Frequency of 3300 Hz

N, Number of Bits per Signal Component	B, Number of Signal Components	Maximum Bit Rate (bps)
1	2	6,600
2	4	13,200
3	8	19,800
4	16	26,400

If the differences become too small, we eventually exceed the capability of a device to detect them.

The second reason occurs because many channels are subject to **noise,** which means a transmitted signal can be distorted. If the distortion is too large, the receiver cannot reconstruct the signal. For example, consider the digital signal in Figure 3.10a. (We use a digital signal simply because it is easier to illustrate. A similar discussion can certainly be made for analog signals.) The transmitter sends two signals, each of which oscillates between two voltage levels. However, the transmitted signal is subjected to some noise, and the received signal differs from it. The distortion is not too great, so the received signal still pretty clearly defines two voltage levels. Thus, it would not be too difficult to reconstruct them.

Figure 3.10b shows a similar situation, except in this case the original two voltage levels differ by less. Now when noise occurs, the two distorted signals overlap voltage levels and it is difficult, if not impossible, to reconstruct the original signal from the received one.

SHANNON'S RESULT

We have learned that noise can alter and possibly destroy information. Whether the information can be reconstructed depends on how powerful the noise is. For example, a little static electricity is not going to do much to transmissions from a 50,000-watt radio transmitting tower. However, a lightning strike can do amazing things to computer communications. The difference, of course, is the strength of the noise relative to that of the transmitted signal.

Electrical engineers use a parameter called the **signal-to-noise ratio** to quantify how much noise there is in the presence of a signal. We define it as *S/N,* where *S* is the signal power and *N* is the noise power. You may also recognize it as a specification on audio equipment to measure clarity of sound. A large ratio means a clear

Figure 3.10   Effect of Noise on Digital Signals

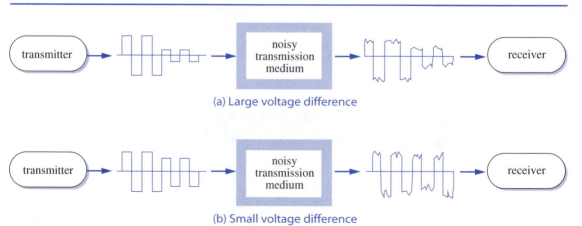

(a) Large voltage difference

(b) Small voltage difference

signal; a small one indicates more distortion. In high-fidelity equipment, high signal-to-noise ratios indicate a higher-quality sound (although in some cases the improved quality may be measurable but not audible). Because S is usually much larger than N, the ratio is often scaled down logarithmically and expressed as

$$B = \log_{10} (S/N) \text{ bels}$$

Here, bel is the unit of measurement. So, for example, if S is 10 times as large as N ($S = 10 \times N$), then $B = \log_{10} [(10 \times N)/N] = \log_{10} (10) = 1$ bel. Similarly, $S = 100N$ yields 2 bels, $S = 1000 \times N$ yields 3 bels, and so on.

Perhaps a more familiar term is the **decibel (dB).** We define it as 1 dB = 0.1 bel. To better understand what this means in terms of S and N, let's look at another example. Consider a rating of 25 dB. It is equivalent to 2.5 bels and means $B = \log_{10} (S/N) = 2.5$. This equation, in turn, forces S/N to be $10^{2.5}$ or, equivalently,

$$S = 10^{2.5} \times N = 100\sqrt{10} \times N \approx 316N$$

In the 1940s, Claude Shannon went beyond Nyquist's results and considered noisy channels. He related the maximum bit rate not only to the frequency but also to the signal-to-noise ratio. Specifically, he showed that

$$\text{bit rate} = \text{bandwidth} \times \log_2 (1 + S/N) \text{ bps}$$

The formula states that a higher bandwidth and signal-to-noise ratio allow a higher bit rate. If the noise power increases, however, the allowable bit rate decreases. The idea behind this relation is that if the signal-to-noise ratio is too small, noise can render two different signals indistinguishable.

Again, we illustrate with an example showing the practical upper limit for data transfer over telephone lines. The telephone system has a bandwidth of approximately 3000 Hz and a signal-to-noise ratio of about 35 dB, or 3.5 bels. This rating implies that $3.5 = \log_{10} (S/N)$, or $S = 10^{3.5} \times N \approx 3162N$. Using these values in Shannon's result yields the following:

$$\begin{aligned} \text{bit rate} &= \text{bandwith} \times \log_2 (1 + S/N) \\ &= 3000 \times \log_2 (1 + 3162) \text{ bps} \\ &\approx 3000 \times 11.63 \text{ bps} \\ &\approx 34{,}880 \text{ bps} \end{aligned}$$

As a final note, we stress that this is not just a theoretical result with little bearing on network users and consumers. In particular, it has a very real implication for modem users. During the 1980s, 2400 and 9600 bps modems became common. Higher-rate modems were available but rather expensive. The early and mid-1990s saw modems accommodate up to 28.8 and 33.6 Kbps, with 56 Kbps modems arriving shortly thereafter. According to Shannon's result, a bit rate of around 35,000 bps is an upper limit for conventional modems; thus, a 56 Kbps rate seems to violate Shannon's result. However, it does not because Shannon's result and the numbers we use are based on assumptions that differ from today's realities. Before Internet service providers (ISPs) were common, people often used modems to dial up and connect to another modem at a company or university site. Because of the additional analog-to-digital conversion at the remote end, noise levels were higher and a bit rate near 35 Kbps was a limit. The 56 Kbps modem can achieve the higher rates when used to connect directly with an ISP. The ISP's equipment is designed on the assumption that most of the telephone network system is digital and therefore communicates directly with it. That is, there is no analog-to-digital conversion at that end and the noise level is less. Section 3.7 discusses this issue further.

3.5   DIGITAL-TO-ANALOG CONVERSION

The previous sections described transmission using analog and digital signals. If either analog or digital signals were used exclusively, communications would be simplified and this section would not be needed. This is, of course, a motivating reason why broadcast television and cable signals are going digital. However, there is a wide mix of analog devices communicating using digital signals and digital devices communicating using analog signals. Furthermore, there are some good reasons for not converting everything to either all digital or all analog.

By now you know that computers are digital devices. In fact, most computer communications, such as workstation-to-server or computer-to-disk transmissions, use digital signals. In addition, local area networks typically rely entirely on digital signals. So where do analog signals enter the picture? The answer is remote communications. Many people use personal computers in their home to communicate with an ISP via the telephone line, cable television service, or even a satellite dish. As we have already stated, a *modem* (short for modulation/demodulation) is needed to convert between signal types. The standard modem is a device that is installed inside your computer and connects to the internal bus (Figure 3.11). Digital signals from memory or a disk file travel to the modem over the internal bus. The modem intercepts these signals, converts them to analog, and sends them to the telephone system via telephone wires plugged into a modem jack. Once in the telephone system, the signal is treated like any voice signal. The process is reversed for any information (such as downloading a file) destined for the computer. The analog signal comes through the phone line and into the modem, and the modem converts it to a digital signal and sends it to memory or a disk file via its bus.

Figure 3.11   Computer Data Transmitted over Telephone Lines

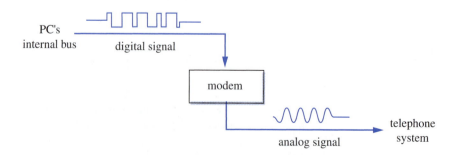

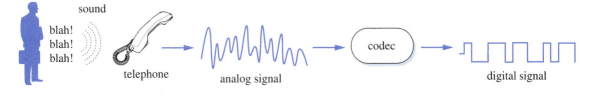

Figure 3.12 Voice Information Transmitted Digitally

Another example of analog devices communicating using digital signals is found in the telephone system itself. We know that a telephone is a device that converts voice sounds to analog signals. In the old days of the telephone system, the analog signals were transmitted over wire or cable to the receiving telephone, where they were converted into sound. Today's fiber technology has changed completely the way a voice is transmitted. Because optical fibers transmit digital signals, a device called a **codec** (short for coder/decoder) translates the analog voice signal into a digital equivalent (Figure 3.12). The digital signal is then transmitted. At some point it is converted back to an analog signal so it can be converted to sound by the telephone's receiver.

The purpose of this and the next section is to explain how digital signals are converted to analog and vice versa. Section 3.7 discusses modem operations and modem standards.

FREQUENCY MODULATION

Converting a digital signal to an analog one is not difficult. Basically, all you need to do is assign a group of one or more bit values to a particular analog signal. Section 3.3 described three ways of varying an analog signal: by frequency, amplitude, and phase shift.

One simple conversion method, **frequency shift keying (FSK),** also called **frequency modulation (FM),** assigns a digital 0 to one analog frequency and a 1 to another. For example, if 0 corresponds to a higher frequency and 1 to a lower one, Figure 3.13 shows the analog signal resulting from the bit string 01001. For each

Figure 3.13 Frequency Shift Keying (Two Frequencies), One Bit per Baud

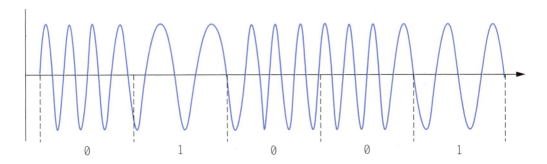

bit, a modem can transmit a signal of the appropriate frequency for a specified period of time. The period, and hence the number of cycles, varies. (Section 3.7 gives some specifics for particular modems.)

Using only two frequencies means that each signal change sends one bit of data. This is a case in which the baud rate (how often a signal's characteristics can change) and bit rate are similar. Alternative forms of frequency modulation could use more frequencies. For example, because two bits can have one of four combinations, we could assign each pair of bits to one of four frequencies. Thus, each frequency change conveys two bits of data; that is, the bit rate is twice the baud rate.

In general, n bits can have one of 2^n combinations, and each can be assigned to one of 2^n frequencies. In this case, the bit rate is n times the baud rate.

AMPLITUDE MODULATION

Amplitude shift keying (ASK), also called **amplitude modulation (AM),** is similar to frequency shift keying. The difference, as you might suspect, is that each bit group is assigned to an analog signal of a given magnitude. Also, as with FSK, a bit group may have one, two, or more bits, again defining a relation between the bit rate and baud rate.

To illustrate, suppose we designate four magnitudes as A_1, A_2, A_3, and A_4. Using these designations, Table 3.2 shows how two bits are associated with each magnitude. Figure 3.14 shows the analog signal for the bit string 00110110. In this case, the bit rate is twice the baud rate. Each of the two bits (starting from the leftmost ones) defines a signal with the appropriate magnitude. As with frequency shift keying, the signal is transmitted for a fixed period of time.

PHASE MODULATION

Phase shift keying (PSK), also called **phase modulation (PM),** is similar to the previous techniques. The signals differ by phase shift instead of frequency or amplitude. Typically, a signal's phase shift is measured relative to the previous signal. In such cases, the term **differential phase shift keying (DPSK)** is often used. As before, n bits can be assigned a signal having one of 2^n phase shifts, giving a technique in which the bit rate is n times the baud rate.

Table 3.2   Signal Association for Amplitude Modulation

BIT VALUES	AMPLITUDE OF GENERATED SIGNAL
00	A_1
01	A_2
10	A_3
11	A_4

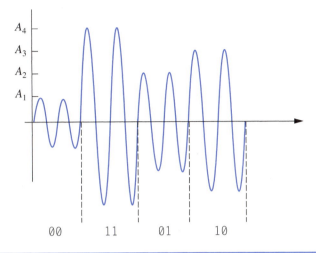

Figure 3.14   Amplitude Shift Keying (Four Amplitudes), Two Bits per Baud

QUADRATURE AMPLITUDE MODULATION

Any of the previous simple techniques can be used with any number of different signals. A greater variety in signal characteristics means a greater bit rate with a given baud rate. The problem is that a higher bit rate requires more legitimate signals and thus reduces the differences among them. As the previous section discussed, this creates difficulties because we need equipment that can differentiate between signals whose frequencies, magnitudes, or phase shifts differ by just a little. In addition, noise may distort signals so that one legitimate signal is transformed into a different legitimate one, causing an incorrect bit string to be transmitted.

One common approach is to use a combination of frequencies, amplitudes, or phase shifts, which allows us to use a larger group of legitimate signals while maintaining larger differences among them. A common technique is **quadrature amplitude modulation (QAM),** in which a group of bits is assigned a signal defined by its amplitude and phase shift.*

For example, suppose we use two different amplitudes and four different phase shifts. Combining them allows us to define eight different signals. Table 3.3 shows the relation between three-bit values and the signal. We define the amplitudes as

---

* An electrical engineer may disagree with this definition. Quadrature amplitude modulated signals are created by adding two analog signals with the same frequency. One signal corresponds to a sine function and the other to a cosine. (Sine and cosine functions differ by a 90° angle, hence the term quadrature.) This means the signal has the form $C \times \sin(x) + D \times \cos(x)$. Variable x varies with time depending on the signal's frequency, and C and D depend on the initial signal. However, trigonometry shows that $C \times \sin(x) + D \times \cos(x)$ may also be written as $A \times \sin(x + P)$, where $A = \sqrt{C^2 + D^2}$ and $P = \arcsin(C/\sqrt{C^2 + D^2})$. Thus, for our purposes, we can think of the signal as one with a varying amplitude and phase shift.

Table 3.3 Signal Association for Quadrature Amplitude Modulation

BIT VALUES	AMPLITUDE OF GENERATED SIGNAL	PHASE SHIFT OF GENERATED SIGNAL
000	A_1	0
001	A_2	0
010	A_1	$1/(4f)$
011	A_2	$1/(4f)$
100	A_1	$2/(4f)$
101	A_2	$2/(4f)$
110	A_1	$3/(4f)$
111	A_2	$3/(4f)$

A_1 and A_2 and the phase shifts as 0, $1/(4f)$, $2/(4f)$, and $3/(4f)$, where f is the frequency. The shifts correspond to one-fourth, two-fourths, and three-fourths of a period, respectively.

Figure 3.15 shows the changing signal resulting from the transmission of the bit string 001-010-100-011-101-000-011-110. (The hyphens are inserted for readability only and are not part of the transmission.) To understand why the signal looks this way, let's proceed carefully. The first three bits, 001, define a signal with amplitude A_2 and phase shift 0. Consequently, as discussed in the previous section, the signal starts at 0 volts and oscillates between A_2 and $-A_2$. As before, the number

Figure 3.15 Quadrature Amplitude Modulation (Two Amplitudes and Four Phases), Three Bits per Baud

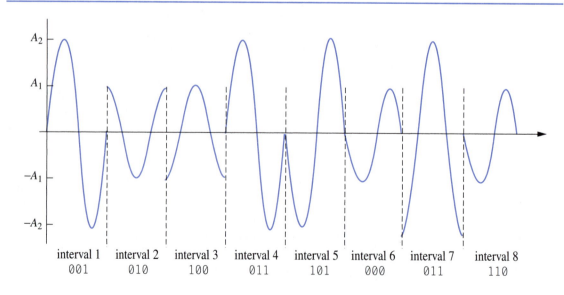

| interval 1 | interval 2 | interval 3 | interval 4 | interval 5 | interval 6 | interval 7 | interval 8 |
| 001 | 010 | 100 | 011 | 101 | 000 | 011 | 110 |

of cycles depends on the frequency and the length of time the signal is transmitted. We have drawn one cycle for convenience.

The next three bits, 010, define a signal with amplitude A_1 and phase shift $1/(4f)$. Thus, as Figure 3.15 shows, the signal oscillates between A_1 and $-A_1$. Now, with no phase shift, the signal would start at 0 and increase to A_1. However, as the previous section discussed, a positive phase shift corresponds to a left horizontal shift in the graph. To help illustrate, Figure 3.16 shows (a) a graph with no phase shift and (b) one with a phase shift of $1/(4f)$.

To understand the graph in Figure 3.16b, recall that $p = 1/f$, where p is the period. In other words, $1/(4f)$ corresponds to one-fourth of a period, and the graph in Figure 3.16b is that of Figure 3.16a shifted left one-fourth of a period. Therefore, it can be viewed as starting at its maximum, decreasing to its minimum, and rising again to its maximum. In effect, we can view the first one-fourth of a period, the part where it goes from 0 to its maximum, as being cut out. This phenomenon is exactly what the second interval in Figure 3.15 shows.

The third set of three bits, 100, defines a signal with amplitude A_1 and phase shift $2/(4f)$. Before we explain its effect, examine the signal at the end of the second interval. It is currently at its maximum of A_1. Now if there were no phase shift, the signal would just continue starting at A_1 and decrease to $-A_1$. But a phase shift of $2/(4f)$ means that half of a period is eliminated. Because the previous signal ended at its maximum, half of a period corresponds to that part of the signal that decreases from A_1 to $-A_1$. Consequently the signal begins at its minimum value at the start of the third interval.

Now let's provide a general description of how to generate a signal from a three-bit group. The signal generated by a three-bit group depends on where the previous signal ends. The phase shift is relative to that ending point. Table 3.4 defines the new signal as a function of the phase shift and the position of the previous signal. Keep in mind that the minimum or maximum in the first column refers to that of the previous signal, whereas the minimum or maximum in the second through fifth columns refers to the current signal.

Figure 3.16   Effect of Phase Shift on a Signal

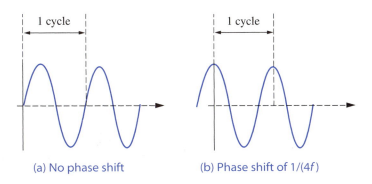

(a) No phase shift

(b) Phase shift of $1/(4f)$

Table 3.4   Rules for Signal Definition Using Quadrature Amplitude Modulation

POSITION OF PREVIOUS SIGNAL	NO PHASE SHIFT	1/4-PERIOD PHASE SHIFT	2/4-PERIOD PHASE SHIFT	3/4-PERIOD PHASE SHIFT
At 0, increasing	Start at 0, increase	Start at maximum	Start at 0, decrease	Start at minimum
At maximum	Start at maximum	Start at 0, decrease	Start at minimum	Start at 0, increase
At 0, decreasing	Start at 0, decrease	Start at minimum	Start at 0, increase	Start at maximum
At minimum	Start at minimum	Start at 0, increase	Start at maximum	Start at 0, decrease

Let's show how to apply this table in defining the signal over the fourth interval in Figure 3.15. The position of the previous signal (in interval 3) is at its minimum. Moreover, the bits 011 define a signal of amplitude A_2 and phase shift $1/(4f)$. Thus, the signal is defined by the bottom row of the third column: It starts at 0 and increases to its maximum of A_2, just as the figure shows.

Note that a three-bit value will not always define the same signal. For example, intervals 4 and 7 both correspond to 011, but the signals are different. Of course, they both have the same amplitude. However, the phase shift is relative to where the previous signal ended. As a result, even though the phase shifts are both $1/(4f)$, the two signals start at different values. Another observation worth noting is that the same signal in two different intervals may correspond to different bit values. For example, intervals 6 and 8 have the same signal but the bits are different. (Why?)

Other ways of modulating using combinations of amplitude, frequency, and phase shift are presented in Section 3.7 during its discussion of modem standards.

As the previous section discussed, higher bit rates can be achieved by associating more bits per baud and using more signal definitions. However, recall that using more signals reduces the differences among them. If too many signals are used then a small amount of noise can make one signal look like another. If this happens, the receiving modem interprets the signal incorrectly and sends the wrong bits to its device. There are ways to deal with errors; Chapter 6 discusses some error detection and correction mechanisms.

3.6 ANALOG-TO-DIGITAL CONVERSION

Some analog-to-digital conversions are nothing more than the reverse of what we have just discussed. The modem examines incoming signals for amplitudes, frequencies, and phase shifts and generates digital signals accordingly. These analog signals have constant characteristics, at least over short intervals. However, not all analog signals are like that. What about analog signals whose characteristics change continually? The most obvious example may be analog signals produced by a sound such as a voice or music. These signals are more complex than those generated by digital data and require alternative conversion techniques.

Figure 3.17 Pulse Amplitude Modulation

PULSE AMPLITUDE MODULATION

One approach to digitizing an analog signal is **pulse amplitude modulation (PAM).** In this simple process, an analog signal is sampled at regular intervals and then a pulse with amplitude equal to that of the sampled signal is generated. Figure 3.17 shows the result of sampling at regular intervals.

PULSE CODE MODULATION

PAM-generated signals look digital, but because a pulse may have any amplitude, the signal has analog characteristics. One way of making the pulses truly digital is to assign amplitudes from a predefined set to the sampled signals. This process is called **pulse code modulation (PCM).** For example, suppose we divide the amplitude range into a set of 2^n amplitudes and associate an n-bit binary number with each one. Figure 3.18 shows a division into eight values ($n = 3$).

As before, we sample the analog signal periodically. But this time we choose one of 2^n amplitudes that most closely matches the sample's amplitude. We then encode the pulse using the corresponding bit sequence. The bit sequence can then be transmitted using whatever digital transmission is in use. By sampling at regular

Figure 3.18 Pulse Code Modulation

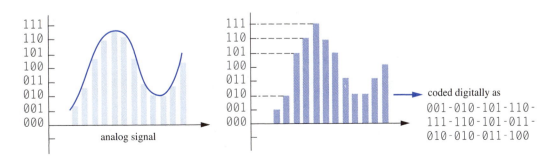

intervals at a rate of s per second, we achieve a bit rate of $n \times s$ bits per second. Figure 3.18 shows the process. The first sample corresponds to 001, the second to 010, and so on.

At the receiving end, the bit string is divided into groups of n bits, and the analog signal is reconstructed. The accuracy of the reconstruction depends on two things. The first is the sampling frequency s. Sampling at a frequency less than that of the signal can cause some oscillations to be missed completely (Figure 3.19). Consequently, the reconstructed signal can be a poor approximation to the original one. Thus, we must sample frequently enough to preserve all the characteristics of the original signal. It would seem, therefore, that more samples are better. This conclusion is true, but only up to a point. Recall the Nyquist theorem from Section 3.4. It stated that sampling a signal at a rate twice its frequency is sufficient to preserve the signal's information. Now we have a nice application for the Nyquist theorem. If the original signal's maximum frequency is f, anything larger than $s = 2f$ will not provide a better approximation than with $s = 2f$.

The second factor that affects accuracy is the number of amplitudes from which to choose. Figure 3.18 showed just eight amplitudes for simplicity. With relatively large differences between the sampled signal and the pulse, the reconstructed signal becomes distorted. This is called *quantization noise*. Reducing differences between adjacent pulse amplitudes helps reduce quantization noise; however, no matter how many amplitudes are used, some noise is unavoidable.

One more note: Higher sampling frequencies and more pulse amplitudes create higher-quality transmissions, but at a price. Each produces more bits per second, requiring a higher bit rate, which costs more.

PCM has several common applications. One is the digitizing of voice signals over long-distance telephone lines. A worldwide standard makes 8000 samples per second and uses 8 bits per sample. In accordance with the Nyquist theorem, this frequency represents a little more than twice the maximum voice frequency your

Figure 3.19   Sampling at Too Low a Frequency

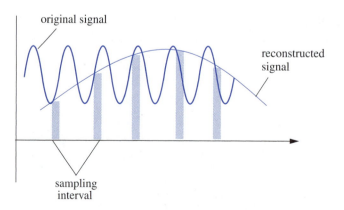

telephone can handle. It also requires a bit rate of 8×8000, or approximately 64 Kbps.*

Another application is in compact disc (CD) technology. The music on a CD is coded optically in a digital format using PCM. To preserve the high quality of sound, however, PCM coding requires a higher frequency and more bits per pulse. Actual values depend on the specific equipment. For example, we checked the owner's manual of a CD player and found the following technical specifications:

Sampling frequency: 44.1 kHz

D-A conversion: 16-bit linear

D-A, as you might guess, refers to digital-to-analog. Sixteen bits allows approximately 64,000 sample amplitudes. The sampling frequency of approximately 44,000 samples per second is slightly more than twice the listed frequency response range of 20 to 20,000 Hz. The term *linear* means the pulse amplitudes are distributed evenly.[†]

Other modulation techniques exist, but we will not elaborate here. For example, pulse duration modulation varies the duration of equal-amplitude pulses to code information. Differential pulse code modulation measures differences in consecutive samples. Delta modulation is a variation on differential pulse code modulation that uses just one bit per sample. For more information on these and other modulation techniques, consult reference [Bl99].

3.7   MODEMS

Now that we have discussed how to convert between analog and digital signals, you may think that we are done and that all you need is a modem to connect to your Internet service provider. Well, yes and no. In the early 1980s, when personal computers first became available, a lot of people rushed to be among the first to have access to these new and powerful tools. However, many overlooked one small detail. They had to learn how to use software, which was not an easy task for the novice (it wasn't always an easy task for the professional either).

In addition, many people who did manage to learn software found that their friends and colleagues bought different computers and learned different software. These differences made sharing and communicating next to impossible. The key words that apply to modems as well are *software* and *compatibility*. The modulation techniques we have described explain how digital signals are changed to analog. But to get the signals to the modem in the first place, and to retrieve digital signals

---

* In practice, optical fibers used by long-distance carriers have much higher bit rates because they are capable of carrying many phone conversations simultaneously by multiplexing. Section 4.5 discusses this in more detail.

† In some cases, such as in telephone systems, the amplitudes are not distributed evenly: There are more pulse amplitudes in a range where values are more likely to occur. This uneven distribution, called *companding*, can improve voice quality without using more bits for each sample.

that the modem creates from telephone signals, we need software. Fortunately, when consumers purchase computers with a modem installed, the modem software is included.

Now suppose you have software and a modem in your computer. When the modem receives analog signals, it must know how they were modulated. Likewise, when it modulates, it must use a scheme that the remote site can understand. If the remote site does not support the methods your modem used to modulate the digital signal, the sites will not communicate. We need compatibility to do this.

Fortunately, the standards to which modem manufacturers adhere define bit rate, baud rate, and the modulation scheme. The best-known standards, defined by ITU-T, typically are identified by V.*xx,* where *xx* is an identifying number. AT&T or Bell modems that use methods similar to certain ITU-T standards also exist.

We will start by describing a couple of the older, but simpler, standards and progress to more current ones. The ITU-T V.21 modem modulates using frequency shift keying. One bit defines the frequency; consequently its bit rate and baud rate are the same (300, very slow by today's standards).

The frequency assignment depends on whether the modem has originated (*originate mode*) or received (*answer mode*) a call. If the modem is in originate mode, it sends a 0 using 980 Hz and a 1 using 1180 Hz. In answer mode, a 0 corresponds to 1650 Hz and a 1 to 1850 Hz. Using two sets of frequency allows full-duplex communication, or two-way communication.

If the baud rate is 300, the signal's duration is $1/300 \approx 0.0033$ second. In the early days of communications, the relatively long duration made the signal less susceptible to noise. If some of it was distorted, there was enough left to be recognized by the unsophisticated (by today's standards) modems. Today's more sophisticated devices can use much shorter durations, thus increasing both baud and bit rate.

The AT&T 103 modem works similarly. It uses 1070 Hz for a 0 bit and 1270 for a 1 bit in originate mode, and 2025 Hz for a 0 bit and 2225 for a 1 bit in answer mode. Another standard is the V.22 modem. It uses phase shift keying, associating two bits with each phase shift. It has a baud rate of 600 and a bit rate of 1200. Frequency and amplitude are constant.

SIGNAL CONSTELLATION

Many modems work by changing more than just one of an analog signal's components, typically the phase shift and amplitude (QAM). This change allows more differences to be introduced into signal components and, as a result, more bits per component. QAM methods can be described visually by a **signal constellation,** a diagram that uses points plotted on a coordinate system to define all legitimate signal changes. Figure 3.20 shows how to interpret one point. It is quantified by its length (distance from the origin) and the angle it makes with the horizontal axis. Recall from the previous section that length and angle (phase shift) are defined by variables C and D, amplitudes of the sine and cosine functions that create the QAM signal. Each point defines a legitimate signal change. The signal's amplitude corresponds to the point's distance from the origin, and the phase shift corresponds to the angle with the horizontal.

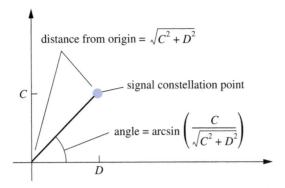

distance from origin $= \sqrt{C^2 + D^2}$

signal constellation point

angle $= \arcsin\left(\dfrac{C}{\sqrt{C^2 + D^2}}\right)$

Figure 3.20   Quantifying a Point on a Signal Constellation

In general, angles on a signal constellation measure between 0° and 360°. Previously, however, we defined phase shifts as a fraction of a period ranging between zero and one period. To interpret the signal constellation correctly, we define a linear relationship between the angles in the constellation and the fraction of a period. Specifically, an angle of $x°$ corresponds to $x/360$ of a period. So, for example, an angle of 90° corresponds to $90/360 = 1/4$ of a period.

Using this interpretation, Figure 3.21 shows the signal constellation for a V.22 modem. It shows four points all the same distance from the origin, which means the amplitude does not change with the signal. These four points also make angles of 0°, 90°, 180°, and 270° with the horizontal axis. Therefore, legitimate phase shifts are none, one-fourth, one-half, and three-fourths of a period.

A more complex standard is the V.22 bis standard. Figure 3.21 also shows its signal constellation of 16 points. The standard calls for 600 baud and 4 bits per baud, giving a data rate of 2400 bps. If you look carefully at the signal constellation,

Figure 3.21   Signal Constellations

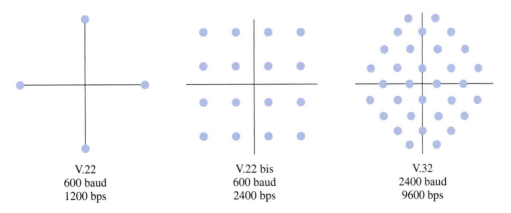

V.22
600 baud
1200 bps

V.22 bis
600 baud
2400 bps

V.32
2400 baud
9600 bps

you see there are three different amplitudes and 12 possible phase shifts. These figures should provide 36 combinations, but only 16 are used. The restriction is because of error detection mechanisms.

The last signal constellation in Figure 3.21 corresponds to the V.32 standard. It is a 32-point constellation, using 2400 baud and 5 bits per baud. However, the data rate is $4 \times 2400 = 9600$ bps. The extra bit per baud occurs because the standard uses *trellis coding*, an error detection mechanism that creates a parity bit by defining additional signal components.

By looking at these signal constellations (and others), you might notice they have one thing in common. The points all seem to be spaced evenly. This feature is not just to create pretty constellation pictures. Modems, like grumpy people who have no appreciation for art, don't care what the picture looks like. The fact remains that most communications occur over noisy lines. To say that two signals differ by a 45° phase or that one's amplitude is twice the other is legitimate only in the absence of noise. The truth is, the phases may differ by $45° \pm x°$, where x corresponds to noise. Similarly, a signal's amplitude will actually be measured as $A \pm y$, where y corresponds to noise.

Figure 3.22 shows the effect of some noise on a signal constellation. A change in amplitude moves a constellation point farther from or closer to the origin. As a result, the point for the actual signal may be anywhere in the figure's shaded region. Similarly, a distorted phase shift can cause the point to move along a small circular arc. Worse yet, noise does not discriminate. Either type of distortion can occur independent of the other. The result is that the constellation point for a distorted signal may be anywhere within a circular region of where it should be.

If the initial points are separated enough and the noise is small enough, the noisy regions do not overlap. Consequently, a modem can recognize a distorted signal. However, if the noise is such that the regions overlap, then communication is impaired. If the point for a distorted signal lies in the intersection of two shaded regions, the modem cannot tell which one it should be in (Figure 3.23).

Figure 3.22   Distortion of Signal Constellation Points

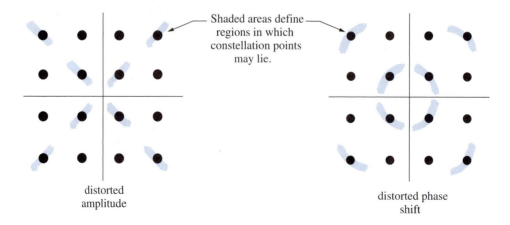

distorted amplitude

distorted phase shift

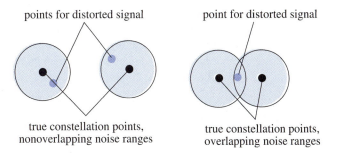

points for distorted signal

point for distorted signal

true constellation points,
nonoverlapping noise ranges

true constellation points,
overlapping noise ranges

Figure 3.23 Interpreting Constellation Points for a Distorted Signal

MODEM STANDARDS

As you probably expect, there are many modem standards. They vary in baud rate, bits per baud, and modulation technique. Newer standards also define error detection and correction methods and compression techniques. Table 3.5 summarizes some of the ITU-T standards. We must also note that many modems adhere to

Table 3.5 Some ITU-T V-Series Modem Standards

STANDARD	SUMMARY
V.21/Bell 103	300 bps bit rate using FSK.
V.22/Bell 212	1200 bps rate using PSK.
V.22 bis	2400 bps rate using QAM.
V.27	4800 bps rate using PSK.
V.29	9600 bps rate using QAM (once a common standard for facsimile transmission).
V.32	9600 bps rate using QAM and trellis coding.
V.32 bis	14,400 bps rate using QAM and trellis coding.
V.34	33,600 bps rate using QAM and trellis coding (commonly used in fax modems).
V.42	Standard for error correction techniques.
V.42 bis	Standard using Lempel-Ziv methods (discussed in Chapter 5) for compression.
V.90	56 Kbps rate (download only) that uses PCM techniques. This is viable under the assumption that there is no analog-to-digital conversion at the remote site.
V.92	Enhances V.90 by reducing the time needed to connect, increasing the upload speed, and providing better protection against accidental disconnection for those with call waiting. As of this writing, most new computers are equipped with V.92 modems.

several standards, which is useful when communicating with a site that implements several of them. Typically, the modem can dial, exchange protocols, and then automatically choose the appropriate standard. These *autobaud modems* are convenient because users do not have to remember which phone number corresponds to which standard. They also allow users to communicate using any of several standards with the same modem and computer. Users can determine the standards by looking at the technical specifications in the owner's manual. There is usually a section specifying the data encoding mechanism at several data rates.

Modem evolution continued throughout the 1990s, resulting in the V.90 standard, which provides a download rate of 56 Kbps. We stated at the end of Section 3.4 that this seemed to exceed the theoretical data rate limits imposed by Shannon's result. However, these modems are based on assumptions that differ significantly from those made by older modems.

Figure 3.24 helps explain. Older modem connections are similar to that described in Figure 3.24a. A personal computer sends a digital signal out a port to a modem, which converts the signal to the required analog format. The analog signal goes through the telephone system's local loop to the nearest central office, where it is converted back to a digital format to be compatible with the telephone company's switching equipment. From there the digital signal is routed over a carrier system to the central office that is closest to the remote site. The signal is converted back to analog and travels along another local loop to the remote site, where another modem converts the signal back to a digital format.

In Figure 3.24b, these last two conversions do not occur. An ISP has digital equipment that communicates directly with digital carrier signals that travel through the telephone network and is able to route them to the Internet without any analog-to-digital conversions. This is significant for the following reason. Suppose a user downloads information from a remote computer in Figure 3.24a. The downloaded

Figure 3.24 Connections Using a Modem

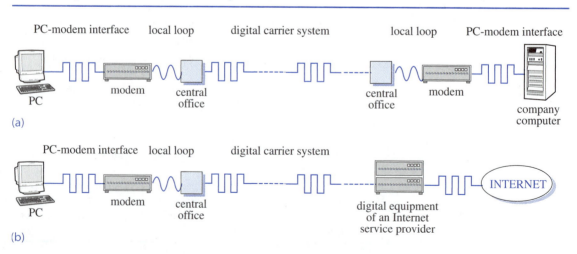

signal goes through an analog-to-digital conversion at the remote site and is converted back to an analog signal at the local site. However, quantization noise introduced at the remote site could result in the local modem receiving a different analog signal from what was sent. However, according to Shannon's result, if the bit rate is low enough, the signals are distorted less and the local analog signal is sufficiently close to the remote one so that no information is lost.

In Figure 3.24b there is no analog-to-digital conversion at the remote site; as a result, quantization noise does not occur and higher bit rates are possible. The 56 Kbps modems are designed to exploit this fact. In addition, telephone equipment uses PCM to convert between analog and digital signals; as a result, V.90 modems digitize analog signals using PCM techniques as opposed to the QAM methods of older modems.

Uploading information works a little differently. Because there is an analog-to-digital conversion at the source of an upload, quantization noise can be introduced. The V.90 standard therefore applies to downloads only, and typical 56 Kbps modems use the V.34 standard in the upstream direction. Thus, they can download information more quickly than they can upload it.

Of course, all this assumes that the local loop on the side of the modem is a line relatively free of noise, and there is often no guarantee that it is. Telephone equipment is designed to operate within certain constraints and often exceeds them. However, there is no guarantee that all phone lines will be able to support the 56 Kbps limit. In fact, some estimates suggest that just 50% of U.S. connections are clean enough to support a 56 Kbps rate.

With the world moving to digital standards for communications, a logical question to ask is: What is the future of modems? Indeed, because of noise factors and telephone equipment specifications, the 56 Kbps modem is generally considered to be the last step in modem evolution. However, despite the move to an "all-digital world," conventional telephones and the analog connection to the closest central office are not likely to change in the near future. The technology certainly exists to replace all telephones with ones that digitize sound via an embedded chip and transmit the digital signals to the central office. However, at what cost on a national or global scale? For those who still use the telephone for its original purpose (talking), the current system works just fine and the benefits derived from a mass replacement would be minimal. In other words, it's not worth the cost. For this reason, the conventional modem is likely to be in demand for the foreseeable future. It is however, receiving increasing competition from cable modems and DSL technology, our next topics.

CABLE MODEMS

Our next topic is the cable modem, a device that, in recent years, has become common in many homes. It results, in part, from the upgrade of television cable delivery systems, consumers' desire for faster Internet connections, and the inability of conventional telephone lines and modems to go beyond the 56 Kbps limit. Whereas the conventional modem we have been discussing is designed to connect with analog components of the telephone system, the **cable modem** is designed to connect with the analog components of a cable TV (CATV) provider.* Many CATV subscribers are already familiar with the cable box that typically sits on top of a television. It is connected to a wall jack through which incoming CATV signals are transmitted. The box decodes incoming scrambled signals and sends them to the television for viewing. In many areas the box can also receive commands from a remote controller and send signals back to the cable company. This capability allows subscribers to order and watch pay-per-view movies.

To some extent the cable modem is similar. Figure 3.25 shows a typical installation. A consumer subscribes to a CATV service, and a technician routes a cable

Figure 3.25   Cable Modem Placement

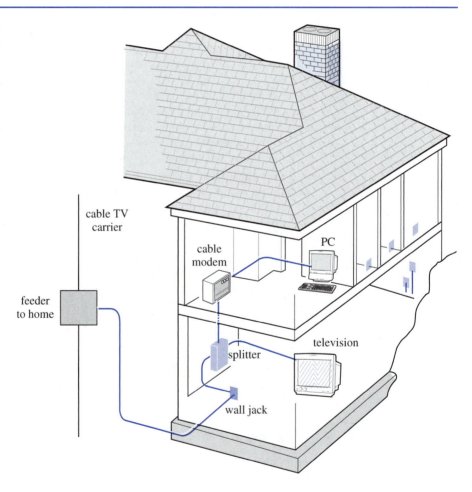

---

* In the future, all television signals will be entirely digital and current televisions will no longer be able to receive such signals without the aid of a converter. However, we're not there yet and must still contend with analog signals for a while.

from an outside feeder into a home. Inside the home, that cable plugs into the input end of a **splitter** (a device that takes a source signal and routes it over two or more output connections). Another cable connects one splitter output to a television or cable box. The signal from another output is fed to a cable modem. The consumer can then use a Cat 5 cable to connect the cable modem with the computer's network card.* Network cards are cheap and available in computer stores. In fact, most personal computers already come equipped with them.

Using a network card such as an Ethernet card (described in Chapter 9) allows the cable modem to convert analog signals to digital and send them to the computer using existing Ethernet protocols. Using an Ethernet connection allows a cable modem to use an already existing standard to connect to the computer. It also allows several computers connected by an Ethernet LAN to share the cable modem via a switch[†] (discussed in Chapter 10). In this case, each of the computers would connect to the switch, and a single cable would connect the switch and cable modem.

In effect, the cable modem is designed to give you access to the Internet via the CATV signals instead of calling an Internet service provider over the telephone. There are several advantages to this setup. One is that information can be transmitted using the high-frequency signals of CATV instead of the much lower frequencies of the telephone's local loop, resulting in much higher bit rates (measured in Mbps instead of Kbps). Another advantage is that you do not need to dial in to make a connection; the connection is always there. A disadvantage is that because CATV uses a common cable (usually optical fiber) to provide service to many homes in a neighborhood, the cable's bandwidth is shared by those users. As a result, a consumer may get one bit rate when he or she is the only one in the neighborhood downloading information. However, if neighbors start downloading information also, each individual's bit rate will be affected.

Figure 3.26 shows the basic operation of a cable modem itself. Typically, a cable signal coming into a home has a frequency range of up to about 750 MHz. This signal is divided into many 6-MHz bands, each of which carries the signal from a particular station, such as Discovery, ESPN, or CNN. Tuning in a channel effectively blocks out unwanted frequencies and allows only one 6-MHz signal to pass, enabling you to view the desired station. For Internet access, the cable company maintains a connection to the Internet through a provider. Information from the Internet can then be downloaded onto a 6-MHz band somewhere between 42 and 750 MHz.[‡]

At the user's end, the cable modem can access downloaded information by tuning into the appropriate 6-MHz band and converting those analog signals to a digital format. It then sends those signals through the appropriate port to a connected computer.

A number of techniques can be used for modulating and demodulating, but two of the more popular are quaternary phase shift keying (QPSK) and a variation of

---

* It is also possible to connect the cable modem to a computer's USB port.

[†] A hub could also be used, but switches are more common and flexible and relatively inexpensive.

[‡] Downloaded signals are typically in bands above 42 MHz because lower-frequency signals are subject to more interference from home appliances.

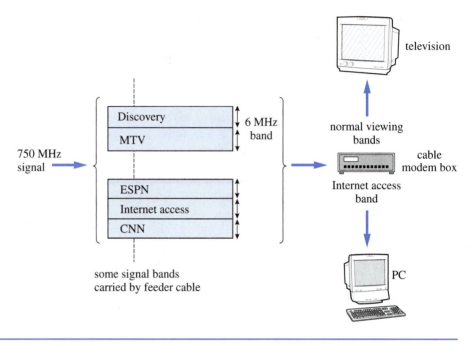

Figure 3.26   Cable Modem and Carrier Signals

QAM known as QAM64. Both are much more complex versions of similarly named techniques described earlier in the chapter. QAM64 is typical for the high-bandwidth requirements of downloading information. Some estimates have placed download data rates at up to 36 Mbps. Many personal computers are not capable of receiving data that quickly, however, so more realistic rates are between 1 and 10 Mbps.

The cable modem can also transmit information in the other direction (uploading). It can take information received from a computer and modulate it into a frequency range, usually between 5 and 40 MHz. This is the range typically used by a two-way cable network for uploading. A problem is that signals in this range are more susceptible to electrical interference from home appliances. As a result, QPSK techniques are more common for uploading because they tend to be more robust. The drawback is that they have lower bit rates. On the other hand, uploading usually has smaller bandwidth demands. For example, sending email or commands usually requires much less data than downloading a graphic or video image.

As we have indicated, there is much work yet to be done on the creation of standards for the use of cable TV networks for data transport. The IEEE 802.14 Working Group has been chartered to develop such standards, and quite a bit has been accomplished. Reference [He97] reviews some of the architectural options that are being considered for providing required services in an efficient but flexible manner.

3.8 DSL

So far, we have described two of the consumer's primary options for connecting to the Internet: modems and cable modems. Modems provide an interface between a computer and the telephone system by converting between the computer's digital signal and the telephone's analog signal. Cable modems perform a similar task, except they use a cable TV service line. Conventional modems have several important drawbacks:

- They are slow (compared with other options) and have reached their speed limits.
- They use the telephone's bandwidth, so the telephone cannot be used at the same time you're connected to the Internet.
- You have to dial an ISP each time you want to connect.

On the other hand, conventional modems are available anywhere there are telephone lines and an ISP—a major advantage. Cable modems, by contrast, are fast and always connected. However, cable TV service is not available in all areas.

This section discusses another option for the consumer: the **Digital Subscriber Line (DSL).** Like a cable modem, DSL is fast and always connected, but it does not require cable TV service or any other special wiring. It uses existing telephone lines! At first this seems to contradict what we've said previously. Connections to the Internet via telephone lines are slow. So how does DSL technology achieve its speed?

Let's start the explanation by looking at Figure 3.27. Most customer telephones connect to the telephone network using copper wires that run from the consumer premises to a local switching office. This stretch of copper is often called the **local loop** or **last mile** (a reference to the fact that it is the last part of the telephone system that is still old technology). The local loop and local office equipment process low-bandwidth signals because it has not been economically feasible to route fiber or other high-speed cables to all residences. The cost would be enormous! The configuration shown is also called **POTS** (plain old telephone service).

Figure 3.27   Local Loop

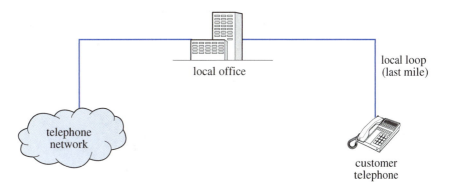

local office

local loop
(last mile)

telephone
network

customer
telephone

However, many telephone companies recognized that high-speed Internet service was a market they had not exploited. The trick was how to exploit it at reasonable cost without the high cost of replacing all the wires in the customer's local loop. The answer lies in the fact that the limited bandwidth was a function of equipment at the local office, not the actual wire in the local loop per se. Although the local loop wire was not manufactured to the specification of today's high-speed twisted pair and has serious limitations, it is still capable of transmitting higher-frequency signals (up to 1 MHz) than the telephone uses. All that is needed is special equipment at the local office to interpret the higher-frequency signals. This is the basis of DSL.

In contrast to what some believe, DSL is not a single technology. In fact, there are many flavors of DSL. Our approach here is to describe ADSL (asymmetric DSL) and then list other DSL technologies with a brief description of how they differ. For a complete discussion on DSL, Reference [Go01] contains further details.

How It Works

Asymmetric DSL is based on a couple of standards: ITU-T recommendation G.992.1 and ANSI standard T1.413 (a standard for signal modulation). The word *asymmetric* refers to the fact that download bit rates are higher than upload rates, a logical configuration because most consumers spend more time downloading large files than uploading them. Figure 3.28 shows a basic ADSL configuration.

The customer site requires special equipment: a splitter/filter and an ADSL modem. The splitter works by using two filters. One is a low-pass filter that blocks

Figure 3.28   ADSL Connection

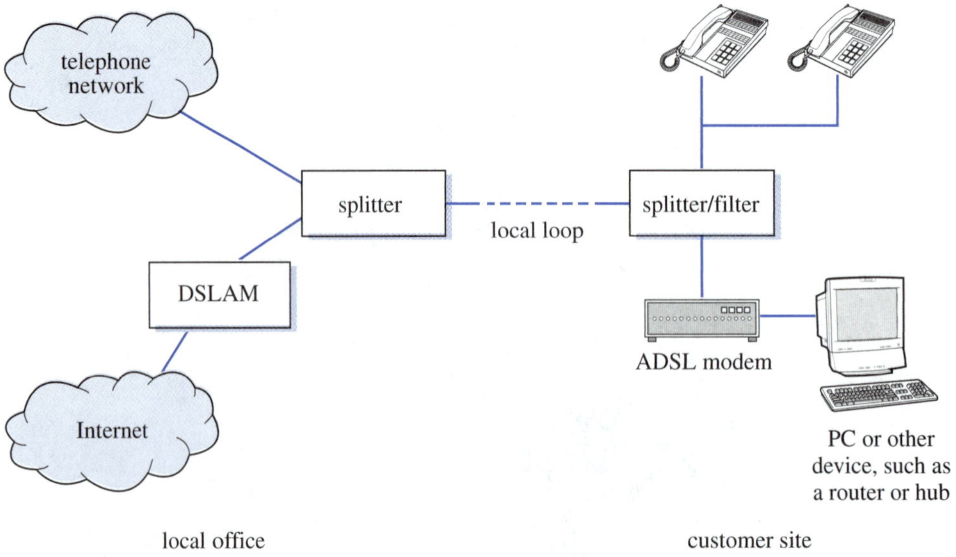

signals above 4 kHz and sends lower-frequency signals to the telephones. The other is a high-pass filter that blocks the lower-frequency signals and passes only the ADSL signals (above 4 kHz) to the ADSL modem (sometimes called an *ADSL Transmission Unit-Remote*, or ATU-R). An interesting result of this configuration is that the telephone and computer depend on signals in different ranges. Because of Fourier's results, described earlier, these signals can be combined into one and transmitted over the local loop. The advantage to the consumer is that a person using a computer can be downloading data files at the same time as someone is talking on the telephone. This overcomes one of the most significant disadvantages of conventional modems.

The local office must have equipment to deal with the different types of signals coming from a customer site. To process these signals, the local office must install a **DSL access multiplexer (DSLAM).** A splitter at the local office receives an incoming signal and sends the low-frequency signals (carrying voice) to the telephone network to complete the telephone call. It sends the higher-frequency signals (for example, from a computer) to the DSLAM, which interprets the signals that the customer's ADSL modem created and routes the data to the Internet to complete the Internet connection.

So, how does this differ from conventional modem technology? Instead of a straight modulation, ADSL modem technology is based on a technique called **discrete multitone** (ANSI standard T1.413). The basic ideas are as follows:

- Divide the frequency range from 0 Hz to 1.104 MHz into 256 separate channels, each with a bandwidth of 4.3125 kHz. Sometimes the channels are called *tones*.

- Use the five lowest channels for POTS. Yes, this allocates about 21.5 kHz for POTS (far more than is needed), but the extra bandwidth provides extra separation between POTS signals and ADSL signals and provides better immunity from noise such as crosstalk.* Unused frequencies between channels are called **guard bands.**

- Use the remaining channels for upstream or downstream transmission, with more channels reserved for downstream. This provides more bandwidth and, hence, higher bit rates for downstream transmissions. This is an advantage for most customers. One might think that upstream and downstream channels do not overlap. Indeed, it is simpler to keep the frequencies of signals going in one direction distinct from signals going in another. However, the technology exists that allows some channels to be used by both upstream and downstream transfers. It's tricky because if two signals with the same frequency are traveling in opposite directions, an echo is created. This means that a device receives not only the signal sent from the remote site but also echoes from its own signals. However, **echo suppressors** can be built into the receiving device that filter out the echoes and provide a clean reception of the remotely sent data. An advantage of this technique is an expanded bandwidth in both directions even if channels overlap.

---

* Crosstalk can occur when a signal generates electromagnetic interference, which in turn, can affect another signal in adjacent wire pairs. Crosstalk can often be reduced through well-grounded systems or by manufacturing the connections according to certain specifications. Because, in this case, the signals are traveling over already existing wires, crosstalk is minimized by avoiding signals within certain frequencies.

- To transmit data, divide an incoming bit stream into smaller groups of bits, one group for each channel (Figure 3.29). The bit groups are treated concurrently and independently.

- Apply a QAM technique (recall Section 3.5) to the bits in each channel. This creates carrier signals of differing frequencies for each channel. Each channel may specify its own QAM technique, which, in part, is determined by the number of bits for that channel. We'll soon see that the number of bits may vary across channels.

- Combine the QAM-generated signals and subject the result to an inverse fast Fourier transform to modulate the signal (recall our previous discussion on Fourier series and fast Fourier transforms).

Certainly, this overview is an oversimplification, and a few additional comments are in order. For example, a unique aspect of this method is that, unlike the conventional modems described earlier, different carrier signals are used to process groups of bits simultaneously. In theory it's possible to transmit 60 Kbps for each channel; however, that rarely happens in practice because of noise levels. In fact, as part of the DMT process the ADSL modem sends test signals over each channel to determine a noise level for each. Channels with a better signal-to-noise ratio transmit more bits than those with a worse ratio. Typically, the higher-frequency channels are more susceptible to noise, so the lower-frequency channels usually accommodate more bits. The important thing here is the adaptability of DMT in determining the bit rate based on existing line conditions.

In general, each channel has its own signal constellation specifying the number of bits for that channel. Downstream bit rates for ADSL can range from 1.5 to 6 Mbps, and much depends on the quality of the local loop. For example, wires that have been spliced or otherwise repaired can create signal echoes and distortion and reduce bit rates. Even the wire's gauge (thickness) can have an effect.

The loop length is also an issue because signals degrade over long distances. Bit rates may be lower for customers who reside farther from the local office. In fact, most resources indicate that DSL connections are not available for customers whose residences are more than about 3.5 miles from the local office.

Figure 3.29 Discrete Multitone

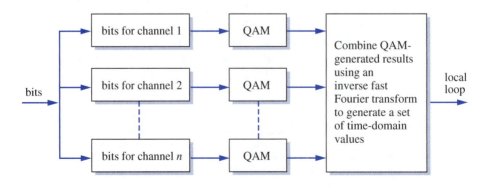

Another unique aspect is the use of an inverse fast Fourier transform. Although we mentioned inverse fast Fourier transforms in Section 3.3, going into detail is beyond the scope of this book. Suffice it to say that the collection of QAM signals defines a function over the frequency domain. By routing them into an inverse fast Fourier transform, the result is a collection of time-domain values (i.e., a discrete representation) of the function. Eventually, the discrete values are converted to analog and transmitted over the local loop. At the local office the process is reversed.

Like cable modems, ADSL modems are always on. There is no need to dial an ISP, and ADSL communications can be used in parallel with POTS conversations. Furthermore, ADSL services are sometimes available where cable TV service is not. On the other hand, cable modems use a larger bandwidth than ADSL modems and typically have higher bit rates for the average consumer.

Because ADSL technology uses existing wiring, each customer has a point-to-point link with the local office. This is in contrast to customers in the same neighborhood who use cable TV services for their Internet connections. Cable companies route cable through neighborhoods, and neighbors share the bandwidth. If you are the only person in your neighborhood with a cable modem, your connection speeds are maximized. However, as more of your neighbors connect, you all share the same bandwidth and each customer has an effect on the others. Consequently, bit rates are affected.

DIFFERENT DSL TECHNOLOGIES

Many variations of DSL exist. The reader can find more information at the following websites: www.dslforum.org and www.dsllite.com. The general notation for such technologies is *x*DSL, where the *x* represents one of many variations. The following are some of the available DSL technologies.

ADSL Lite (G.Lite, ITU standard ITU G.992.2)   As seen from the previous discussion, ADSL requires the use of a splitter/filter at the customer premises. This, in turn, usually requires a service call by a telephone company technician to install it. ADSL Lite (sometimes called splitterless ADSL) has no such requirement. The advantage is simplicity for the consumer; in fact, ADSL Lite is designed for residential customers. Modem and cable modem users know that their particular modem is the only hardware they need to connect to the telephone network or their cable TV line. If DSL technology is to be competitive, then it must also be easy to install.

The signal splitting is done at the local office instead of at the customer site (Figure 3.30). Conventional telephones do not respond to signals with a frequency higher than 4 kHz and thus ignore ADSL signals. The ADSL modem incorporates a high-pass filter that blocks out low-frequency signals and thus processes only ADSL-generated signals. The consumer sees the advantage of being able to connect to the current wiring from any location in the home. From the consumer's perspective, this is more of a plug-and-play technology than ADSL.

Another difference is that the downstream signals of ADSL Lite operate in the range between 25 and 500 kHz. This limits the downstream bit rate to around 1.5 Mbps. The reason for this limitation is that without the local splitter, ADSL Lite signals travel throughout the wires in the house, and higher-frequency signals could cause interference with basic telephone service, especially in places where the wiring is of poorer

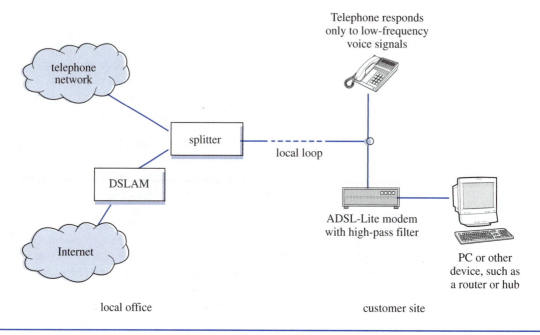

Figure 3.30 ADSL-Lite Connection

quality. By eliminating the higher-frequency signals, this problem is reduced. Although slower than ADSL, it is still around 30 times faster than conventional modems.

SDSL   In contrast to asymmetric DSL, symmetric DSL (SDSL) provides the same bit rates over a single-wire-pair local loop in both the downstream and upstream directions. *SDSL* is also used as an umbrella term that applies to other DSL technologies, such as those described in the following subsections. Sometimes *SDSL* refers to single-wire DSL, a variant on HDSL (see the next subsection). SDSL also uses a different signaling mechanism, called *two binary, one quaternary* (2B1Q). This scheme is a little like the NRZ scheme described in Section 3.2 except that instead of defining two signal levels for one bit, it defines four signal levels for each pair of bits. In other words, each of the pairs 00, 01, 10, and 11 has a specified fixed signal. The main advantage is that the bit rate is twice the baud rate (each signal change conveys two bits).

HDSL and HDSL2   High-bit-rate DSL (HDSL) is a symmetric DSL service developed in the late 1980s. It provides bit rates of 1.5 or 2.3 Mbps (both directions) and uses two or three twisted copper pairs. As stated previously, there is a variant called single-wire DSL (SDSL) that uses one pair. HDSL does not provide POTS service and was developed as an economical alternative to T1 or E1 services.* HDSL2 differs from HDSL in a couple of ways. First, the ANSI standard for HDSL2 defines a

---

* T1 refers to a common digital carrier technology that many organizations use for network connections. We discuss it in Section 4.6. E1 is a European service comparable to T1.

1.5 Mbps rate in both directions. Another difference is that that it provides that bit rate over a single wire pair (HDSL requires two for that rate). Like HDSL, it does not provide standard telephone service over that wire pair.

SHDSL   Single-pair high-speed DSL (SHDSL) is a new technology and conforms to the ITU standard G.991.2. One limitation of the previous HDSL and HDSL2 technologies was the maximum loop distance of approximately 12,000 feet. SHDSL increases the loop distance and provides services at rates up to 2.3 Mbps over a single wire pair. The standard specifies one wire pair; however, two pairs (a *four-wire mode*) can be used to extend either the loop distance or the bit rate (but not at the same time). For example, four-wire mode can be used to provide either a bit rate of 2.3 Mbps at approximately 16,000 feet or 4.6 Mbps at shorter distances. The four-wire mode spreads the bits over the two pairs equally and, from the application's point of view, provides a higher bit rate. It is targeted largely at business organizations and those users who require high upstream bit rates.

RADSL   Rate-adaptive asymmetric DSL (RADSL) does not correspond to a specific standard. It allows the ADSL modem to adapt to bit rates depending on the capacity of the local loop. There are not many references to RADSL because standard ADSL also allows the modem to adapt to the bit rate.

IDSL   Internet DSL (IDSL) is symmetric and is based on ISDN technology.* It provides bit rates of up to 128 Kbps over a loop distance of up to 18,000 feet. It provides services similar to ISDN but, in contrast to ISDN, does not provide a voice channel.

VDSL   Very high data rate DSL (VDSL) is an asymmetric service (different downstream and upstream rates) that is in the process of development. Current downstream rates are projected to be around 50 to 55 Mbps over short distances of 1,000 feet. Bit rates would decrease as the distances increase. VDSL is being developed in response to the increasing use of optical fiber in communications. The vast majority of homes are equipped with copper, and the high cost of replacing all copper wires with fiber make it unlikely that this situation will change in the near future. However, that does not mean that the entire local loop will remain copper.

Driven by competition, it has become economically and technologically practical to incorporate both fiber and copper in the local loops. Fiber may run from the local office to a neighborhood *optical network unit* (ONU) (Figure 3.31); from there, copper can provide the feed to individual homes. This will decrease the length of the local loop dependent on copper and allow higher bit rates. Another feature of VDSL is that it is being developed without using the lower spectrum of signals. It will thus be compatible with ordinary telephone service, an advantage to many consumers. The combined copper/fiber connection will also provide many advantages to places such as university campuses, business centers, or industrial parks, where there is a high concentration of users with high bit rate needs.

---

* We will cover ISDN in Chapter 13, but basically ISDN was developed and first defined as a standard by CCITT (now ITU) in 1984. It was designed to be an all-digital communications network (at a time when this idea was just emerging) and many predicted it would be the eventual successor to the telephone network.

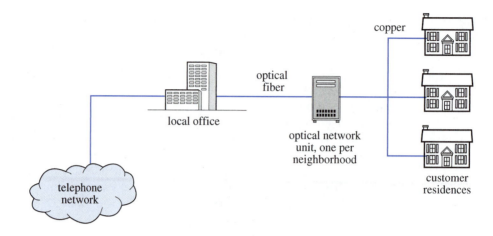

Figure 3.31   Local Loop: Fiber/Copper Hybrid

3.9 SUMMARY

This chapter dealt mainly with analog and digital signals; theoretical results relating bit rates, bandwidth, and signal-to-noise ratio; modulation techniques; and ways of connecting to the Internet. Important concepts presented in this chapter are as follows:

- Digital encoding schemes include NRZ (nonreturn to zero), Manchester, and differential Manchester. NRZ assigns a fixed voltage level to a 0 and another to a 1. Both Manchester schemes (also called self-clocking codes) distinguish between a 0 and 1 by either a high-to-low or low-to-high voltage transition. The Manchester schemes prevent long constant signals, which can cause timing problems.

- Analog signals convey information by changing amplitudes (amplitude modulation), frequencies (frequency modulation), or phase shifts (phase modulation). In general, the number of bits per change depends on the number of allowable changes.

- Fourier theory shows that complex periodic signals are made up of many signals with fixed frequencies. This has applications in the design of filters to remove unwanted frequencies and in the design of DSL technologies.

- The bit rate depends on the baud rate, frequency, and noise. The Nyquist theorem and the sampling theorem together show that over a noiseless channel the bit rate $= 2f \times \log_2 (B)$, where f is the maximum frequency and B is the number of different signals.

- Claude Shannon extended the Nyquist theorem to include noisy channels. His famous result states that the bit rate $=$ bandwidth $\times \log_2 (1 + S/N)$, where S and N are the signal and noise power, respectively. This result puts a theoretical limit on the bit rate over any noisy channel.

- A significant amount of communication involves transmitting digital data using analog signals and analog data using digital signals. Consequently, there is a need to study modulation and demodulation techniques. Digital-to-analog conversions often require changing an analog signal in response to a group of bits. Typical changes affect the amplitude (amplitude shift keying), frequency (frequency shift keying), or the phase shift (phase shift keying). Another technique known as quadrature amplitude modulation uses combinations of these changes and is used in some conventional modems.

- One way of converting from analog back to digital is to simply reverse these processes. However, if the original signal is a complex analog signal such as voice, we need a different mechanism. One approach called PCM (pulse code modulation) samples an analog signal at regular intervals. It then associates a bit string with each sample and transmits it. On the receiving end, the bits are received and the analog signal reconstructed.

- Modems are perhaps the most familiar modulation/demodulation devices. They are used to connect digital devices such as computers via the telephone system. Modems use different modulation techniques, which are defined by standards. Two devices can communicate only if the equipment on each end recognizes the same standard. Most modems are also small special-purpose computers. They can respond to commands that a user, with the help of appropriate software, enters at a personal computer.

- Cable modems are designed to provide an interface between a computer and the cable television signals that are widely available. The theory is that by having access to the much higher-frequency signals from CATV, bit rates will be much higher than telephone modems will ever be able to achieve.

- DSL technology is yet another option for consumers to connect to the Internet. Like cable modem users, DSL users are always connected. Unlike with cable modems, DSL connects via ordinary telephone lines. The technology is based on the transmission of higher-frequency signals that do not interfere with the signals that carry ordinary voice sounds. Special DSL modems implement a complex technique that uses multiple channels (tones) to transmit bit groups and complex mathematical functions (inverse fast Fourier transforms) to combine them.

Review Questions

1. What three components completely describe an analog signal?
2. Are the following statements TRUE or FALSE? Why?
   a. An arbitrary number of bits can be associated with an analog signal because the number of signal characteristics is infinite.
   b. For digital signals, using a high signal to represent a 0 and a low signal to represent a 1 is common because of its simplicity.
   c. Despite the fact that most of the world, including telephone equipment, is going digital, modems will be important devices for many years.
   d. DSL modems perform the same functions as conventional modems; they just use higher frequencies.
   e. NRZ coding requires that the medium's baud rate be twice the bit rate.

f. Because of the demand for high bit rates among consumers, the telephone companies will likely replace all copper wires with optical fibers in the near future.

g. PCM techniques, although designed for analog data, could be used for digital data as well.

h. The bit rate for an Internet connection via a cable modem depends on whether your neighbor is also using a cable modem to connect.

i. Customers can use telephone lines to connect to the Internet, but if they want to make telephone calls while another person is connected, a second phone line is needed.

j. Customers can use their cable television service to connect to the Internet, but they cannot watch television at the same time another person is connected.

3. Distinguish among NRZ, Manchester, and differential Manchester digital encoding.

4. With all the precision equipment currently available, why does a long run of 0s or 1s present a problem when using an encoding scheme such as NRZ?

5. What baud rate is required to realize a 10 Mbps data rate using NRZ encoding? Using Manchester encoding?

6. Distinguish between the Nyquist and the Shannon results.

7. Define signal-to-noise ratio.

8. Suppose a transmission were free of noise. Does this imply that there is no limit on the maximum data rate that can be achieved with current equipment?

9. Given the proliferation of computing equipment using telephone lines, why is the telephone's bandwidth only approximately 3000 Hz?

10. Shannon's result relates data rates and bandwidth in the presence of noise. However, the amount of noise varies with the medium and source. How does Shannon's result account for it?

11. What does a modem allow you to do with a personal computer?

12. What is the difference between modulation and demodulation?

13. Distinguish among frequency modulation, amplitude modulation, and phase modulation.

14. What is quadrature amplitude modulation?

15. Distinguish between pulse code modulation and pulse amplitude modulation.

16. Why are there so many different modem standards?

17. What is a signal constellation?

18. What is an intelligent modem?

19. What is quantization noise?

20. If a modem supports several different standards, how does it know which one to use when you connect to another computer over a telephone line?

21. How does DSL differ from modems and cable modems with regard to your ability to connect to an Internet service provider from home?

22. Distinguish among a conventional modem, cable modem, and DSL modem.

23. What is discrete multitone?

24. What is the difference between asymmetric DSL and symmetric DSL services? Why is there a distinction?

Exercises

1. Digital signals can be translated to analog signals by using relatively simple techniques such as varying the amplitude or frequency between two specified values. What is the advantage of using more complex schemes such as QAM?

2. Draw the digital signals for the bit string 0010100010 using each of the NRZ, Manchester, and differential Manchester digital encoding techniques. Assume the signal is "high" prior to receipt of the first bit.

3. What is the bit string associated with the following Manchester-encoded signal? What is the bit string if it is a differential Manchester-encoded signal?

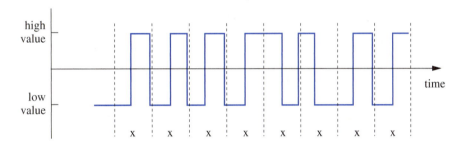

4. Draw analog signals corresponding to the following functions.

   a. $y = \sin(t)$

   b. $y = \sin(2t)$

   c. $y = 4\sin(2t)$

   d. $y = 2\sin(2t + \pi/2)$

   e. $y = 3\sin(t)$

   f. $y = \sin(t + \pi/4)$

   g. $y = \sin(2t - \pi/2)$

5. Assume the maximum analog frequency of a medium is 6000 Hz. According to the Nyquist theorem, what are the maximum bit rates for schemes that use one, two, three, and four bits per signal component?

6. According to Nyquist, what frequency is necessary to support a bit rate of 30,000 bps using only one bit per signal component? Three bits per signal component?

7. In your own words, what is the significance of Shannon's result?

8. What is the actual signal power (relative to the noise power) if the signal-to-noise ratio is given as 60 decibels?

9. What is the decibel rating if the signal power is twice the noise power?

10. Assume the maximum analog bandwidth of a medium is 6000 Hz. According to the Shannon result, what is the maximum bit rate if the signal-to-noise ratio is 40 decibels? 60 decibels?

11. According to Shannon, what bandwidth is necessary to support a bit rate of 30,000 bps assuming a signal-to-noise ratio of 40 decibels? What bandwidth is necessary if the number of decibels is doubled?

12. Suppose you want to achieve a bit rate of 64,000 bps using a maximum bandwidth of 10,000 Hz. What is the minimum allowable signal-to-noise ratio?

13. Can a phase shift of one period be used to distinguish signals?

14. Using QAM, is it possible for the same signal in two different intervals to correspond to different bit values?

15. Using QAM, do the same bits always correspond to the same analog signals?

16. Draw the QAM analog signal (carefully) that transmits the following bit string:

001011010101101010110

Assume the current analog signal is established as shown here. You need draw only one complete cycle for each modulation change.

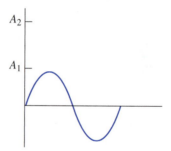

17. Suppose a modem uses quadrature amplitude modulation as described by Table 3.3. What bit sequence corresponds to the following signal (starting with the second time interval)?

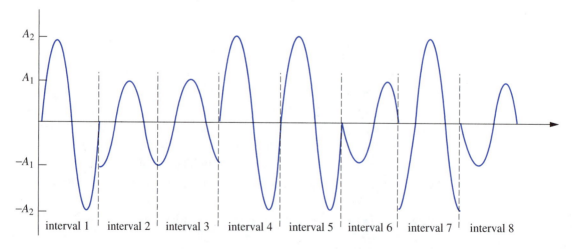

18. Design a QAM technique that uses up to eight phase shifts and two amplitudes. How many bits per baud are there?

19. Assume a QAM technique has up to m phase shifts and n amplitudes. How many bits per baud are there?

20. If you have a CD player, examine its technical specifications and relate them to the discussions on PCM.

21. Why can't professionals design modems with arbitrarily high baud rates and thus realize unlimited bit rates?

22. If you have a modem, write a short summary listing the standards it supports.

23. Draw the signal constellation for a modem that uses the QAM defined by Table 3.3. Draw another one for the QAM technique described by Exercise 18.

24. Describe the signal changes (i.e., specify the amplitude and phase changes) associated with the signal constellations in Figure 3.21.

25. How many bits correspond to one signal component using the V.21 standard? What is the duration for one signal component?

26. Repeat Exercise 25 for the V.32 standard.

27. As a consumer, articulate why you would prefer a DSL connection to the Internet over a cable modem connection.

28. As a consumer, articulate why you would prefer a cable modem connection to the Internet over a DSL connection.

REFERENCES

[Bl99] Black, U. *ATM: Foundation for Broadband Networks,* 2nd ed. Englewood Cliffs, NJ: Prentice-Hall, 1990.

[Ch02] Chapra, S., and R. Canale. *Numerical Methods for Engineers*. New York: McGraw-Hill, 2002.

[Ge99] Gerald, C., and P. Wheatley. *Applied Numerical Analysis,* 6th ed. Reading, MA: Addison-Wesley, 1999.

[Go01] Goralski, W. *ADSL and DSL Technologies*. New York: McGraw-Hill, 2001.

[He97] Hernandez-Valencia, E. J. "Architectures for Broadband Residential IP Services over CATV Networks." *IEEE Network,* vol. 11, no. 1 (January 1997).

[St00] Stallings, W. *Data and Computer Communications*. Englewood Cliffs, NJ: Prentice-Hall, 2000.

[Wa98] Walrand, J. *Communications Networks: A First Course,* 2nd ed. New York: McGraw-Hill, 1998.

CHAPTER 4

MAKING CONNECTIONS

The idea that information can be stored in a changing world without an overwhelming depreciation of its value is false. It is scarcely less false than the more plausible claim that after a war we may take our existing weapons, fill their barrels with cylinder oil, and coat their outsides with sprayed rubber film, and let them statically await the next emergency.
—**Norbert Wiener** (1894–1964), U.S. mathematician

4.1 INTRODUCTION

Chapters 2 and 3 discussed transmission fundamentals and the specific mechanisms required to transmit information. This chapter goes one step farther and discusses communication. You might ask, "What is the difference between transmission and communication?"

To answer, consider the analogy of human speech. We could discuss the mechanisms behind speech—how the vocal chords contract and expand to allow air to exit our lungs and form sound, and how the mouth manipulates these sounds to form what we call speech. We could also discuss language and the origin of many of the words we use. However, this is a long way from communicating. The words that come out must be organized to make sense. If they come out too quickly or too slowly, the speaker will not be understood. If many people speak simultaneously, no one is understood. If no one is listening to you speak or if someone speaks a language you don't understand, communication is lost. If a sentence is missing words or phrases (such as might occur when one is speaking in a second language), some meaning may be lost.

Electronic communication has similar problems. The receiver must know how message bits are organized to understand the message. The receiver must know how quickly they arrive to interpret the message. What happens if many people try to use a common medium simultaneously, as is typical in a local area network (LAN)? If all the devices try to transmit at the same time and in the same way, signals may collide and communication will not occur. Some order must be implemented that allows multiple devices to communicate with one another.

This chapter discusses these topics. Section 4.2 starts by discussing some common communication carriers and popular devices that people use frequently. Section 4.3 discusses ways of communicating using serial, parallel, synchronous, and asynchronous transmission. It also contrasts one-way and two-way communications. The best way to ensure that devices send and receive in compatible ways is to adhere to standards. Section 4.4 discusses well-established standards that are commonly used to connect devices, such as EIA-232 and EIA-449, and newer ones such as universal serial bus (USB) and FireWire that are now common on many new personal computers. Section 4.5 discusses how multiple devices can use a medium simultaneously through multiplexing techniques, and Section 4.6 discusses two common digital carrier systems: T1 and SONET. However, there are many cases where multiplexing is not an option (notably in LANs); in such cases, a device needs exclusive control of the medium to communicate. Competition among devices to gain exclusive control of a medium is contention; Section 4.7 discusses several approaches used in LAN standards.

The main thing to bear in mind throughout this chapter is that there are typically many devices that want to communicate with one another, and they must often share common transmission media. How that sharing occurs goes a long way toward establishing meaningful communications.

4.2   COMMUNICATION CARRIERS AND DEVICES

THE TELEPHONE SYSTEM

Of all the inventions in the past century, the telephone certainly has had one of the most profound effects on our lives. The ability to call almost anywhere in the world by specifying (dialing) a few numbers is absolutely incredible. But the telephone is more than just voice communications among friends and relatives; it has become indispensable to businesses using it for computer communications. The capability to transfer information across a computer network or by fax is now commonplace.

The telephone works by converting sound into electrical energy. What we perceive as sound is caused by small fluctuations in air pressure (sound waves). The waves travel through the air, causing some objects to vibrate. The same principle causes old windows or light fixtures to rattle during a thunderstorm. It also allows us to hear: The waves cause the eardrum to vibrate and send signals to the brain.

Telephones use a couple of methods to convert sound into electrical energy. The first method uses a telephone mouthpiece that consists of a chamber filled with carbon granules (Figure 4.1). Two electrical contacts are connected to the chamber. As you speak into the mouthpiece, the sound waves cause a diaphragm covering the chamber to vibrate. As it vibrates it exerts varying pressure on the carbon granules. Higher pressure causes the granules to be compacted more closely, which, in turn,

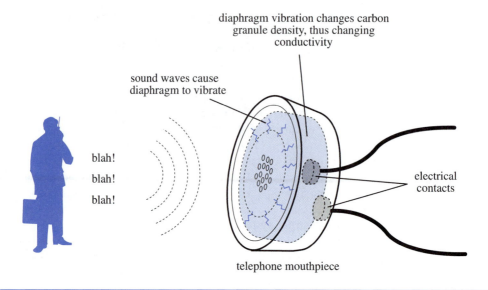

diaphragm vibration changes carbon granule density, thus changing conductivity

sound waves cause diaphragm to vibrate

blah!

blah!

blah!

electrical contacts

telephone mouthpiece

Figure 4.1 Converting Sound Waves to Electrical Signals

causes them to be a better conductor of electricity. Less pressure has the opposite effect. The net result is that varying amounts of electricity caused by the sound are conducted. On the receiving end, the electricity activates a voice coil, causing an attached speaker to vibrate. The vibrating speaker causes changes in air pressure, which we interpret as sound.

The second method uses a *foil-electret condenser microphone*. It also consists of a diaphragm that vibrates when sound waves hit it. The difference is that this diaphragm covers a hollow disk and is separated from the disk's backplate. The diaphragm is electrically charged and has a metal coating (an *electret*) on one side, although in some cases the coating may be on the backplate. When the diaphragm vibrates, the electric field between it and the backplate varies and changes the capacitance between it and the backplate. This induces a current to be generated from the backplate. This technology is also used in hearing aids and lapel microphones.

To place a phone call, the caller enters a sequence of digits by dialing or touching buttons. Each digit sends a code to a local exchange office, which interprets the sequence and determines the destination. If there is an available route to the destination and the phone is not busy, two signals are sent. The first goes to the destination and causes the phone to ring. The second goes to the source and alerts the caller that the phone is now ringing.

Because the signals are separate, it is interesting to note that a caller does not actually hear the phone ringing. In fact, because of delays in the circuits you might not hear the ring until after it occurs. Perhaps you have had the experience of having someone answer your call before you heard a ring. Common perception is that it is caused by gremlins in the line or the mystical ability of the phone system. Now you know that it happens only because someone answered the phone before the second signal got back to you.

The code for each digit depends on whether you have tone or pulse dialing. With tone dialing, each digit sends a tone consisting of a unique pair of frequencies. With pulse dialing, each digit generates from 1 to 10 pulses. Each pulse actually corresponds to opening and closing a circuit, similar to depressing the hook. In fact, if your fingers are fast enough, you can actually dial a number by rapidly depressing the hook the proper number of times for each digit.

Call Routing   The way in which phone calls are routed is an amazing feat of engineering. Remember, we are discussing a network connecting hundreds of millions of users. The first part of this network is the local loop. It consists of phones connected by copper wires running along the familiar telephone pole or in underground cables to a local exchange.* The local exchange contains switching logic and determines where to route a call. If the call is to a phone with the same exchange (first three digits of the number), the connection can be made directly to the destination. Otherwise, the routing strategy depends on the call's destination.

Figure 4.2 shows the major components (centers) of the telephone network. Class 1 regional centers are the fewest in number and cover the largest areas

Figure 4.2   Telephone Network

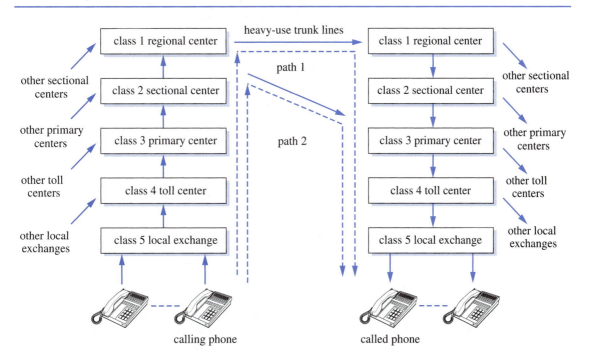

---

* Other terms used in place of *local exchange* include *end office, central office,* or *class 5 office.*

Table 4.1   Major Centers in the Telephone Network

CENTER	OWNER	AREA COVERED
Class 1 regional center	Long-distance carrier	Multistate
Class 2 sectional center	Long-distance carrier	Statewide
Class 3 primary center	Local company or long-distance carrier	Metropolitan
Class 4 toll center	Local company	One or more cities
Class 5 local exchange	Local company	Neighborhood

(typically multistate regions). Classes 2, 3, 4, and 5 are increasingly more numerous and cover smaller areas. Long-distance carriers own those covering the largest areas, and local companies own others. Table 4.1 summarizes this information. We will provide a brief discussion of the roles these centers play in the complex system of routing phone calls. For more detailed information, consult references [Le00] and [Sh90].

Class 1 centers connect to many class 2 centers. Similarly, class 2 centers connect to many class 3 centers, and so on. At the top of the hierarchy, class 1 centers are connected by high-capacity trunk lines, which are capable of transmitting many phone conversations simultaneously. In general, any two phones can connect by going up the hierarchy from the local exchange to the regional center, across a trunk to another regional center, and back down to the proper local exchange (path 1 in Figure 4.2). This is not always the best route, however. Ideally, we would like a call to go through as few centers as possible. The extreme would be to have a direct connection between every pair of phones on this network, but, of course, this is unrealistic. In some cases, many phone calls may occur between a particular sectional center and another primary center. In such cases, it is useful to place another high-capacity trunk line between them as a shortcut to bypass some of the centers and provide alternate routes (path 2 in Figure 4.2).

There are many trunk lines connecting different classes of centers. These connections, driven largely by the traffic between two areas, provide many alternate routes. In the unlikely event that all routes are operating at peak capacity, the call will not go through and the caller will receive a busy signal. However, current state-of-the-art hardware and software make this event highly unlikely.

PRIVATE BRANCH EXCHANGES

In addition to the public telephone system, there are private telephone systems, called **private branch exchanges (PBX).** Other common names are *private automatic branch exchange* (PABX) and *computer branch exchange* (CBX). A PBX is a computer designed to route telephone calls within a company or organization. This system is especially useful for larger organizations whose many employees must be able to contact one another. A PBX gives the organization complete control over its voice and data communications facilities rather than relying on the telephone company for support. As you might expect, there are advantages and disadvantages. The organization must pay for the hardware, software, and personnel to maintain the system. On the other hand, if the company is large enough and its needs great enough, this may be a cost-effective way of establishing communications.

But a PBX is more than just a telephone system. When a PBX is installed, wires connect every office, conference room, or location where a telephone may be used. Consequently, designers often elect to install additional wire pairs, cable, or optical fibers. The intent is to make them available for data traffic between computers or peripherals. In many cases, the additional wiring is installed even though there is no immediate need for data traffic. The extra cost of installing some redundant wiring is far below the cost for another installation in the future.

The PBX performs many of the same functions as a local area network, but there are important differences between them. For example, a local area network typically has a broadcast ability. This means one device can send a message to all or a group of devices connected to the network. A PBX typically is used for point-to-point communication. On the other hand, a PBX can define a circuit between communicating devices, something not typical of a LAN. This feature is an advantage if you need to exchange large amounts of data quickly between two devices. A detailed discussion of a PBX and its comparison with a LAN is beyond the purpose or scope of this book. If you are interested, reference [Sh90] contains more detail.

CELLULAR PHONES

No doubt you are familiar with another technological development embraced by many, the **cellular telephone.** Primarily, it allows its user to communicate over the telephone system when he or she is away from traditional phones. In contrast to the belief that *cellular* refers to a biological phenomenon that causes the growth of a communications device on the side on one's head, the term pertains to the way a geographic area is divided to allow communications. It is divided into multiple regions, or cells (Figure 4.3), each of which has a reception and transmission tower. A mobile telephone switching office (MTSO) has a computer that controls all the cells and connects them to the telephone system.

The cellular phone is actually a two-way radio capable of communicating with a tower. The boundaries between cells are not as well defined as Figure 4.3 indicates. Near the cell boundaries, the cellular phone is potentially within range of several towers. Each of them continuously transmits, so a phone can determine which is closest by determining which signal is strongest. When a call is made from a cellular phone, the phone communicates with the closest tower (Figure 4.4). The tower in turn communicates with the MTSO, which is capable of communicating with the regular telephone system.

Receiving a call is a little more complex, because there is no way of knowing in which cell the cellular phone is located. However, each cellular phone, like any phone, has a unique identification number. When it is called, the MTSO transmits that number to all the cell towers under its control. Each tower then broadcasts the number. Because the cellular phone is continuously monitoring broadcasts, it hears

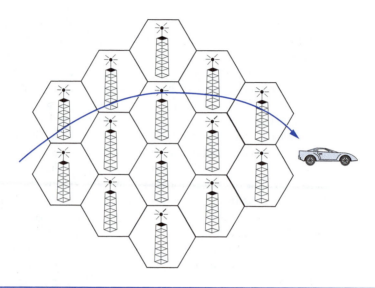

Figure 4.3   Cellular Grid

its ID broadcast and responds. The tower, hearing the response, relays the response to the MTSO, which completes the connection.

A potential problem exists when a user moves into an adjacent cell. The tower with which his or her phone is communicating eventually will be out of range. The MTSO monitors signals received from cell towers, and if it detects that a signal is becoming weak, it can reassign communication to another cell. This is called a *handoff*. The assignment occurs quickly, so there is no noticeable interruption for

Figure 4.4   Cellular Phone Communication

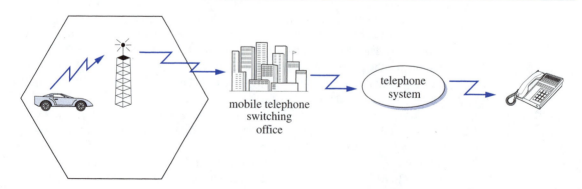

mobile telephone
switching
office

telephone
system

voice communications. If the phone is being used for data transmission, however, there may be some loss.

Of course, a logical question to ask is: What happens if the cell phone user moves to a cell under the control of a different MTSO? That is, the user moves into an area with a different cellular system. In this case, a **roaming** feature is used. Suppose a traveler moves into an area with a different cellular service. If the new service area is compatible with the traveler's home area service, calls made to the traveler can be routed into the area in which he or she is roaming. Of course, there is an extra charge for this service. It's a little like walking through the woods dropping breadcrumbs as you move along. By following the breadcrumbs, anyone who is looking for you can follow the trail and find you. The main difference between roaming and a handoff is that roaming involves a different cellular service; a handoff does not.

Using the cell phone for data communications conjures up an image of someone racing down the highway in the driver's seat with a computer or fax machine in his or her lap. If you do this or know someone who does, please let me know so I can stay off the road. But some data transfer on the highway is not as bizarre as it sounds initially. For example, an ambulance has a legitimate need for data transfer when it sends an accident victim's vital signs to the hospital. However, to discourage the use of cell phones while driving, some states are passing laws that prohibit using a cell phone while driving, except in the case of emergencies.

FAX MACHINES

Another device that became popular during the late 1980s is the **facsimile (fax) machine** (Figure 4.5). Capable of transmitting drawings, letters, or diagrams over the phone in a matter of seconds, it has become an indispensable device for many.

Fax machines are based on a principle similar to that used for displaying an image on a PC's video screen, on a television set, or in a photograph. The images that appear to be lines and colors are nothing more than dots, but they are too small to be seen individually unless you put your nose against the screen and look closely.

A fax machine works by taking a picture of the image to be sent and converting it to a binary format. You enter a sheet of paper into the fax much as you would a copier. The sheet is divided into many dots (also called **picture elements** or **pixels**), each representing a portion of the paper. We call this a *bit map representation,* because each dot may be stored as one bit of data. Each dot is black or white (binary 0 or 1), depending on what is on that part of the paper. The dots are then transmitted as binary data and reassembled at the other end. For example, Figure 4.6 shows how the letters in the word "Hello" may be represented using a bit map. For simplicity, we have shown only a few large dots; a typical bit map may use 200 dots per inch. More dots provide better-quality transmissions. Fewer dots give a grainy look to the received image.

Most fax machines do not simply take a picture and transmit the resulting dots. Proceeding that way would require long transmission times for simple documents. For example, suppose a fax recognizes 200 dots per inch. A little arithmetic shows

Figure 4.5   Fax Machine

that there are 200 × 200, or 40,000, dots for 1 square inch. But a typical sheet of paper measures 8.5 by 11 inches, or 93.5 square inches. At 40,000 dots per square inch, a typical sheet requires about 40,000 × 93.5, or 3,740,000, dots.* Using a common upload bit rate of 33.6 Kbits per second, we need 3,740,000/33.6, or nearly two minutes, to send the image on one sheet of paper. Your first reaction might be,

Figure 4.6   Bit Map Representation of "Hello"

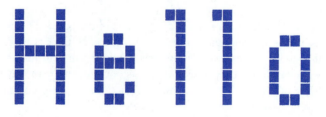

* These are only approximate numbers. We'll provide more specific information in Section 5.3.

"I have used a fax machine and it didn't take nearly that long." Well, you are correct. Most fax machines will not take that long because they use data compression. Rather than sending each dot individually, the fax groups the dots and defines an equivalent binary representation for the group using fewer bits. For example, suppose a part of the image has 800 black dots in succession. Instead of sending 800 black dots, you might send 1 black dot preceded by the number 800. Because 800 has a binary representation of 1100100000 (10 bits), the transmission requires 11 bits (don't forget 1 bit for the dot). Clearly, this is a significant reduction. There are other ways of compressing data; Chapter 5 discusses compression in more detail.

4.3 TRANSMISSION MODES

A *transmission mode* defines the way in which a bit group travels from one device to another. It also defines whether bits may travel in both directions simultaneously or whether devices must take turns sending and receiving.

SERIAL AND PARALLEL TRANSMISSION

The first distinction we make is between serial and parallel transmission. **Parallel transmission** means that a group of bits is transmitted simultaneously by using a separate line (wire) for each bit (Figure 4.7a). Typically, the lines are bundled in a cable. Parallel transmissions are common, especially where the distance between the two devices is short. For example, a PC-to-printer connection up to 25 feet is considered a safe distance. The most common example is communication between a computer and peripheral devices. Other examples include communication among a CPU, memory modules, and device controllers.

Figure 4.7 Parallel and Serial Transmission

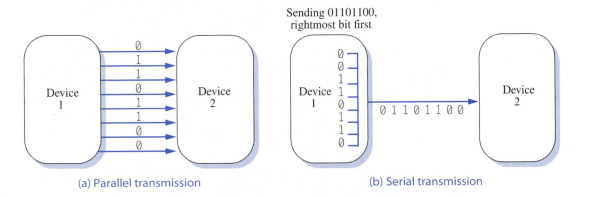

(a) Parallel transmission

(b) Serial transmission

Parallel transmission loses its advantage over longer distances. First, using multiple lines over long distances is more expensive than using a single one. Second, transmitting over longer distances requires thicker wires to reduce signal degradation. Bundling them into a single cable becomes unwieldy. A third problem involves the time required to transmit bits. Over a short distance, bits sent simultaneously will be received almost simultaneously. Over a long distance, however, wire resistance may cause the bits to drift a little and arrive at slightly different times, which can create problems at the receiving end.

Serial transmission provides an alternative to parallel transmission (Figure 4.7b). Using just one line, it transmits all the bits along it one after another. It is cheaper and more reliable than parallel transmission over long distances. It is also slower because the bits are sent one at a time.

The sending and receiving devices have an additional complexity. The sender must determine the order in which the bits are sent. For example, when sending 8 bits from 1 byte, the sender must determine whether the high-order or low-order bits are sent first. Similarly, the receiver must know where to place the first-received bit within the destination byte. It may seem like a trivial issue, but different architectures may number the bits in a byte differently; if the protocols do not agree on how to order the bits, the information will be transmitted incorrectly.

Asynchronous, Synchronous, and Isochronous Transmission

There are three ways to provide serial communication: asynchronous, synchronous, and isochronous transmission. **Asynchronous transmission** means that bits are divided into small groups (usually bytes) and sent independently. The sender can send the groups at any time, and the receiver never knows when they will arrive (somewhat like a visit from a long-lost relative).

One example (once common) is using a terminal to communicate with a computer. Pressing a key containing a letter, number, or special character sends an 8-bit ASCII code.* The terminal sends the codes at any time, depending on how well or fast you type. Internally, the hardware must be able to accept a typed character at any time. (We should note that not all keyboard entries are transmitted asynchronously. Many PCs can run terminal emulation software to connect to remote computers and can buffer entries and transmit an entire line or screen to the computer. This is synchronous transmission, which we discuss shortly.)

Terminal input is not the only example of asynchronous transmission. In some cases, data are sent to a line printer one byte at a time. Asynchronous transmission is typical of *byte-oriented input-output* (I/O), an operating system term meaning that data are transferred a byte at a time.

There is a potential problem with asynchronous transmission. Remember that the receiver does not know when data will arrive until it gets there. By the time the receiver detects it and can react, the first bit has come and gone. It is similar to

---

* We haven't forgotten that we defined the ASCII code as a 7-bit code. However, you can think of a 7-bit code as an 8-bit code in which the leading bit is always 0.

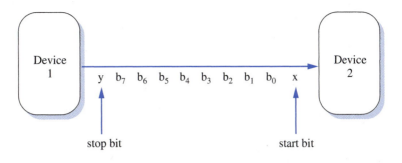

Figure 4.8   Asynchronous Communication

someone coming up behind you unexpectedly and starting to talk. By the time you react and start listening, the first few words have been missed. Consequently, each asynchronous transmission is preceded by a start bit (Figure 4.8), which alerts the receiver to the fact that data are arriving. This gives the receiver time to respond and accept and buffer the data bits. At the end of the transmission, a stop bit indicates the transmission's end. By convention an idle line (one that is transmitting no data) actually carries a signal defining a binary 1. The start bit then causes the signal to change, corresponding to a 0. The remaining bits cause the signal to change depending on bit values. Finally, the stop bit brings the signal back to the equivalent of a 1, where it stays until the next start bit arrives.

For example, suppose you enter the digits 321 at a terminal. Using an 8-bit extended ASCII code (with a leading 0) defines the following bits to be sent:

00110001 for the digit 1

00110010 for the digit 2

00110011 for the digit 3

Suppose we send each digit (leftmost bit first) separately using NRZ coding. Figure 4.9 shows the transmitted signal. In each case the start bit raises the signal, alerting the

Figure 4.9   Asynchronous Transmission of the Digits 1, 2, and 3 Using NRZ Coding

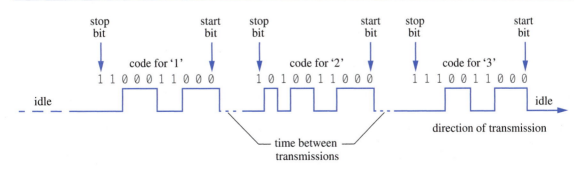

receiver that other bits will follow. When they have all arrived for that digit, the stop bit lowers the signal. It remains low until the next start bit raises it.

Asynchronous transmission is designed for use with slow devices such as keyboards and some printers. It has a high overhead. In the example just given, two extra bits are transmitted for every eight. This represents a 25% increase in the total transmission load. For slow devices that transmit little data, this is a small problem. However, for fast devices that transfer a lot of data, a 25% increase in load is significant.

Usually with **synchronous transmission,** much larger bit groups are sent. Instead of sending many characters separately, each with its own start and stop bit, characters are grouped together and then transmitted as a whole. We call this group a **data frame** or simply a **frame.** The precise organization of a data frame varies with the protocol. However, data frames do have many common characteristics. Figure 4.10 shows the organization of a generic data frame. The orientation is rightmost bits first.

The first part of the frame contains **SYN characters,** unique bit patterns that alert the receiver that a frame is arriving. A SYN character is similar to the start bit discussed previously, except that here the pattern also ensures the receiver's sampling rate and the consistency of the rate at which the bits arrive. In other words, the receiver can synchronize itself to the rate at which the bits arrive.

Next are control bits, which may include the following elements:

- Source address: Specifies where the frame originated.
- Destination address: Specifies where the frame should go. This is important in networks in which a frame may go through several nodes to get to its destination. Each intermediate node uses the destination to determine where to route the frame. Chapter 10 discusses routing further.
- Actual number of data bytes.

Figure 4.10   Synchronous Transmission

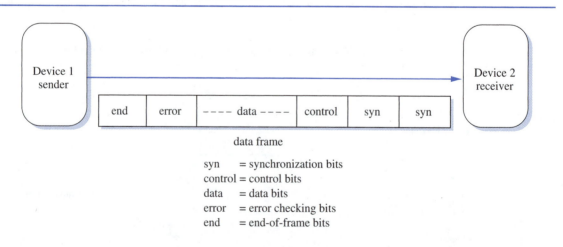

- Sequence number: Useful when many frames are sent and, for some reason, arrive out of order. The receiver uses the sequence numbers to reassemble them. Chapter 8 discusses this further.

- Frame type: Distinguished by some protocols. Chapter 8 discusses some of these.

The data bits define the information being sent. There are no start and stop bits between the characters. The error checking bits are used to detect or correct transmission errors. We know from Chapters 2 and 3 that electrical interference can distort signals. But how does the receiver know when this happens? Typically, the sender transmits extra bits that depend on the data. If the data are altered, the extra bits are not consistent with the data. Chapter 6 discusses error detection and correction techniques.

The last part of the frame is an end-of-frame marker. Like the SYN characters, it is a unique bit string indicating that no more bits will be arriving (at least until the start of the next frame).

Synchronous transmission generally is much faster than asynchronous. The receiver does not start and stop for each character. Once it detects the SYN characters, it receives all the others as quickly as they arrive. In addition, there is less overhead. For example, a typical frame may have 500 bytes (4000 bits) of data containing 100 bits of overhead (specifics will vary). In this case, the added bits mean a 2.5% increase in the total bits transferred. Compare that with the 25% increase with asynchronous transmission.

It should be noted that as the number of data bits increases, the percentage of overhead bits decreases. On the other hand, larger data fields require larger buffers in which to store them, putting a limit on the size of a frame. In addition, larger frames occupy a transmission medium for a longer uninterrupted amount of time. In an extreme case, this could cause excessive waiting by other users. Despite the synchronous nature of bits within a frame, there is also an asynchronous feature in sending frames.

A third transmission mode that has become common is **isochronous transmission.** Both asynchronous and synchronous transmission shared one feature: Over longer periods of time, the data do *not* necessarily arrive at a fixed rate. Even though data within one frame arrive at a fixed rate, there may be arbitrary gaps between frames, giving an asynchronous flavor to transmission using frames. Thus, over long periods of time, the arrival rate may be bursty. In addition, if error detection methods find an error, the frame is usually resent, further affecting the overall rate of transfer. For many applications, such as file transfers and Web applications, this is fine. It's far more important to transfer the information correctly than to worry about small delays.

However, real-time applications require a different quality of service (QoS). Examples include real-time viewing of images or listening to radio (e.g., Internet radio) from a downloading bit stream. For example, standards for television viewing require that TV images appear at a rate of 30 images per second—no more and no less. The signals must arrive at a fixed rate; there are no other options. Another example is a Web cam. A video camera is placed in a location, digitizes the images it records, and transfers the data over the Internet; users view the images as they occur. Again, images must arrive at a rate suitable for viewing; delays are not an option.

Isochronous transmission guarantees that data will arrive at a fixed rate so the user sees a quality image or hears quality sound with no distracting gaps. Usually there is no error detection. If a transmission error occurs, it is ignored and the user may (or may not) notice a slight disturbance in the image or sound. Such disturbances are not usually a problem and, in fact, are no worse than the effects caused by a lightning strike, a nearby electrical motor, or even turning on a light. The disturbance comes and goes and is forgotten.

In your reading you may encounter the term **bisync.** It is not a transmission mode in the same sense as asynchronous or synchronous. It is an acronym for **binary synchronous communications** (sometimes abbreviated as BSC), which is a protocol IBM introduced in the 1960s for synchronous communication between a computer and terminals. We discuss it in Chapter 9.

SIMPLEX, HALF-DUPLEX, AND FULL-DUPLEX COMMUNICATIONS

So far this chapter has dealt with ways to transmit information from one device to another, with a definite distinction between sender and receiver. This is an example of **simplex communications** (Figure 4.11). That is, communication goes only in one direction. The many examples include airport monitors, printers, television sets, or talking with an unsympathetic professor about a bad grade.

Other applications require a greater flexibility in which a device can both send and receive. The methods vary. Some use **half-duplex communications,** in which both devices can send and receive, but they must alternate. This method is used in some modems, LAN standards, and peripheral devices. For example, the previously mentioned bisync protocol is half duplex.

Figure 4.11   Simplex, Half-Duplex, and Full-Duplex Communication

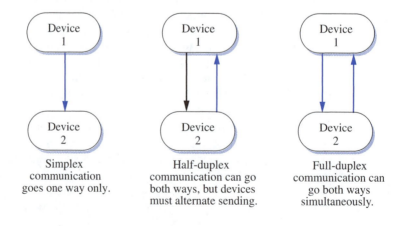

Simplex
communication
goes one way only.

Half-duplex
communication can go
both ways, but devices
must alternate sending.

Full-duplex
communication can
go both ways
simultaneously.

The most flexible method is **full-duplex communications.** Here a device can send and receive simultaneously. When a device is sending over one line, it may be receiving on another. Many PC-to-remote computer connections use full-duplex communications. This is evidenced by the ability to continue typing at the same time that information is being printed on the screen. Many modems are also full duplex.

Two-way communication becomes complex, especially over networks. Protocols must be used to make sure information is received correctly and in an orderly manner and to allow devices to communicate efficiently. These issues are discussed in the next four chapters.

4.4 INTERFACE STANDARDS

Chapter 3 and the previous section described several ways to transmit information. One might conclude that as long as two devices use the same mechanisms to send and receive, they can communicate. Communication does not necessarily occur, however. If two people speak at the same time, neither listening to the other, they are not communicating. Common sense dictates that in order to communicate, they must take turns listening and speaking. Orderly discussions require that rules (protocols) be established that recognize an individual wanting to speak. Communications among devices must be guided similarly by protocols. Sending modulated signals to a device does no good if the device is not prepared to sense the signals and interpret them.

Figure 4.12 shows a typical arrangement of connected devices. The acronym **DCE** means **data circuit-terminating equipment** (or *data communications equipment*) and **DTE** means **data terminal equipment.** The DTE (a personal computer, for example) does not connect to a network directly. It communicates through a DCE (a modem, for example). We call the connection between the DTE and DCE the **DTE–DCE interface.** This section presents some DTE–DCE interface standards and then discusses some newer connection protocols commonly found on personal computers.

Figure 4.12   DTE–DCE Interface

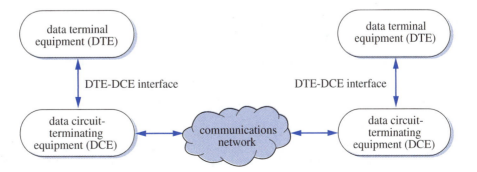

EIA-232 INTERFACE

One well-known standard is the **EIA-232 standard.*** It was developed by the Electronic Industries Association (EIA) in the early 1960s and has been revised several times, with each revision being designated by a letter. For example, perhaps the most long-lasting version, developed in the late 1960s, is known as EIA-232-C. The ITU equivalent, V.24, defines the functional aspects of operations and references another standard (V.28) that defines electrical specifications. In addition, EIA has produced several new variations, with EIA-232-F being introduced in 1997. We have no desire to differentiate among the different versions and are content to provide a discussion of basic operations common to the original EIA-232 specification. Where it relates to our discussion, we'll indicate changes made by later revisions.

The most obvious (visible) aspect of the standard is the number of lines (25) between the DTE and DCE. If the standard is fully implemented, the DTE and DCE are connected by a 25-line cable (sometimes called a DB-25 cable) that attaches to each device using a 25-pin connector (Figure 4.13). Each line has a specific function in establishing communication between the devices. Table 4.2 summarizes a few of them and specifies the signal direction (i.e., whether the line is used to transmit from the DCE to the DTE or vice versa). The table also contains the EIA designation (circuit code) for each line. We will not provide a thorough discussion of every connection, but we will describe the role some of the circuits play in a typical DTE–DCE connection. If you would like a more detailed description, reference [St00] provides it.

For purposes of discussion, suppose the DTE is a personal computer and the DCE is a modem. This was a common configuration when modems were frequently external to the PC. Chapter 3 discussed how a modem communicates with the analog world, so we now focus on a possible exchange between it and the computer. The first six circuits primarily are used to establish an exchange that ensures that neither device will send data when the other is not expecting it. Figure 4.14 shows the exchange that occurs over a period of time.

Because the DCE connects to a network on behalf of the DTE, it must know when the DTE is ready. The DTE indicates its readiness by asserting (sending a

Figure 4.13   EIA-232 Connector

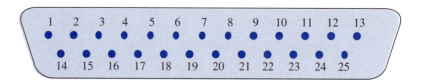

* For many years this was also known as the RS-232 serial port common on PCs. Some references also use the designation EIA/TIA-232. This reflects the fact that the EIA began working with the Telecommunications Industry Association (TIA) and in 1991 jointly released EIA/TIA-232-E.

Table 4.2   EIA-232-C Circuit Definition

CIRCUIT CODE	LINE NUMBER	SIGNAL DIRECTION	FUNCTION
AA	1		Protective ground. It is connected to the equipment frame and sometimes to external grounds.
AB	7		Electrical ground. All signal voltages are measured relative to this ground.
BA	2	DTE to DCE	Transmit data (TD). DTE transmits data to the DCE on this circuit.
BB	3	DCE to DTE	Receive data (RD). DTE receives data from the DCE on this circuit.
CA	4	DTE to DCE	Request to send (RTS). DTE uses this circuit to request permission from the DCE before it can transmit data.
CB	5	DCE to DTE	Clear to send (CTS). The DCE uses this circuit to give the DTE permission to transmit data.
CC	6	DCE to DTE	Data set ready (DSR). A signal on this line indicates the DCE has connected to a communications medium and is ready to operate. For example, if the DCE is a modem, this circuit indicates whether it is off the hook.
CD	20	DTE to DCE	Data terminal ready (DTR). A signal on this line indicates the DTE is ready to transmit or receive. It can be used to signal a modem when to connect to a communications channel.
CE	22	DCE to DTE	Ring indicator. Indicates the DCE is receiving a ringing signal (e.g., when a modem receives a call) from the communications channel.
CF	8	DCE to DTE	Data carrier detect (DCD). Indicates the DCE is receiving a carrier signal that meets suitability criteria from the communications network. Essentially, this means the DCE understands the incoming signal.

signal on) DTR circuit number 20 (time t_1 in Figure 4.14). The DCE senses the signal and responds by connecting to the network (if it has not already done so). Once the DCE has connected and is also ready, it asserts DSR circuit number 6 (time t_2). Effectively, the DCE acknowledges the DTE's state of readiness and declares that it also is ready.

Once they are both ready, the DTE requests permission to transmit data to the DCE by asserting RTS circuit 4 (time t_3). This circuit also controls the direction of flow in half-duplex communications. On sensing RTS, the DCE enters a transmit mode, meaning it is ready to transmit data over the network. It then responds by asserting the CTS circuit number 5 (time t_4). Finally, the DTE sends data over TD circuit number 2 (between times t_5 and t_6).

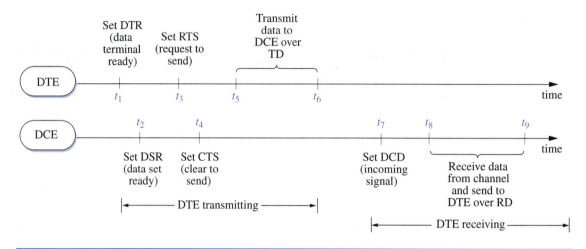

Figure 4.14   Sending and Receiving over an EIA-232 Connection

When the DCE detects an incoming signal from a network that it recognizes, it asserts DCD circuit number 8 (time t_7). As the signals come in, the DCE sends them to the DTE using RD circuit number 3. Some of the older modems had lights on the front that indicated when certain lines were asserted. This signal provided the user with a chance to see what was actually occurring. In most cases, however, the lights flashed so rapidly that it was difficult to distinguish on from off.

EIA-232 Subsets   Interestingly, many of the connectors to the EIA-232 ports of computers did not have 25 pins. Remember that we have discussed the EIA-232 *standard*. Whether a vendor chooses to implement the full standard is another matter. The fact is, many interfaces include only a subset of the EIA-232 definitions.

To illustrate, before modems were commonly installed in a personal computer, a user would purchase an external modem and connect it to the computer using a cable. A typical cable had a 25-pin connector at one end that plugged into the modem and a 9-pin connector on the other that plugged into the computer. It sounds a bit like plugging a three-pronged plug into a two-hole socket, but there is a reason for the difference. For versatility, many modems complied with the complete standard. However, many users did not need to use the full range of EIA-232 capabilities. Primarily, they needed to communicate much as we have described in the example illustrated by Figure 4.14. Consequently, PC serial ports generally required a 9-pin connector that used the seven circuits described in the example plus one or both grounds. The decision regarding how much of the standard to implement is usually driven by economics: Why implement (and pay for) the full range of capabilities when there is little chance you will ever use them? Cables with different connectors on each end connect only the needed circuits. The extra lines on the modem side were not connected to the personal computer.

One drawback to the EIA-232 standard is its limited bandwidth and distance. It is typically used for transmissions of 20,000 bits per second (bps) over a distance of up to 50 feet. In some cases, such as situations with little interference, longer distances are possible, but in those cases there are other standards, which we discuss shortly.

As a final note, we reiterate that there have been several releases of EIA-232. Although we haven't covered enough detail to explain most of the differences among releases, we will articulate one change. EIA-232-E, released in 1991, changed how RTS and CTS were interpreted. The previous example of data exchange was in half-duplex mode; however, most modems today are full duplex and often allow some form of hardware flow control.* The DTE can use RTS to indicate it can receive data from the DCE, and the DCE can use CTS for an analogous purpose. For most operations, these circuits are asserted constantly.

Null Modems   Sometimes, you may want to allow two devices (such as personal computers) to communicate directly, that is, with no network or DCEs between them. In such cases, your first reaction might be to connect their EIA-232 ports with a cable and let the protocols do their job. After all, they both send and receive from their EIA-232 ports. Using a simple cable, however, connects the same pins on each side. For example, the cable would connect pin 2 of each DTE. The problem is that both pins try to send over the same line. The first DTE sends data, and the second receives it over line 2. Because the second DTE expects to receive data over line 3, the direct connection will not work. Similarly, because the cable connects pin 3 on each end, both expect to receive on the same circuit, but neither sends over it.

One solution to this problem is to connect the DTEs but cross some circuits. Figure 4.15 shows one way to do this using a null modem. A **null modem** may be

Figure 4.15 Null Modem

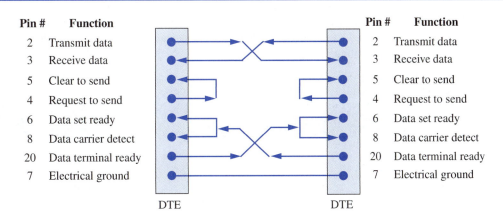

Pin #	Function
2	Transmit data
3	Receive data
5	Clear to send
4	Request to send
6	Data set ready
8	Data carrier detect
20	Data terminal ready
7	Electrical ground

DTE

Pin #	Function
2	Transmit data
3	Receive data
5	Clear to send
4	Request to send
6	Data set ready
8	Data carrier detect
20	Data terminal ready
7	Electrical ground

DTE

---

* We discuss flow control more fully in Chapter 8. For now, just think of it as a mechanism to control the rate at which data are arriving, maintaining the ability to stop and resume an incoming data flow. It's much like the handle on a faucet. Turn it one way and more water flows; turn it the other and less water flows.

either a cable connecting different pins on each connector or a device that simply crosses connections using existing cables. Either way, the result is the same. The null modem in Figure 4.15 connects pin 2 on one end to pin 3 on the other end. Consequently, when the DTE sends data using pin 2, it is routed to pin 3 on the other end, where it is received correctly.

The null modem of Figure 4.15 also connects pins 4 and 5 of the same DTE. The reason for this is found in the example discussed previously. When a DTE wants to transmit, it must request permission and wait for a Clear to Send (CTS) signal from the DCE. Since there is no DCE, the null modem routes a Request to Send (RTS) signal (pin 4) back to pin 5. The DTE, sensing its own signal on pin 5, is fooled into thinking the DCE has responded with the CTS message.

The other cross connections make sure each DTE is ready before any transmissions occur. As described previously, the DTE asserts the DTR line 20 when it is ready, expecting the DCE to respond by asserting DSR line 6. Here one DTE's line 20 is routed to the other's line 6, so that when each DTE signals it is ready, the other receives that signal. Again, this fools the DTE into thinking its DCE has connected to a network and is also ready.

Figure 4.15 shows just one example of the many variations of null modems. They vary depending on device requirements and how much of the full EIA-232 protocol they use. For other variations, see references [St00] and [Ru89].

X.21 INTERFACE

The **X.21 interface standard** is defined by ITU-T. It uses a 15-pin connector and allows balanced (electrical standard X.27) and unbalanced (X.26 standard) circuits. There are a couple of significant differences between X.21 and the EIA standard. The first is that X.21 is defined as a digital signaling interface. The second difference involves how control information is exchanged. The EIA standard defines specific circuits for control functions. More control requires more circuits, thus making connections more inconvenient. The principle behind X.21 is to put more logic circuits (intelligence) in the DTE and DCE that can interpret control sequences and reduce the number of connecting circuits.

Table 4.3   X.21 Interface Standard for a Balanced Circuit

CIRCUIT CODE	PIN NUMBER	SIGNAL DIRECTION	FUNCTION
	1		Shield
G	8		Signal ground
T	2, 9	DTE to DCE	Transmit data or control information
R	4, 11	DCE to DTE	Receive data or control information
C	3, 10	DTE to DCE	Control
I	5, 12	DCE to DTE	Indication
S	6, 13	DCE to DTE	Signal element timing
B	7, 14	DCE to DTE	Byte timing

Table 4.3 shows the X.21 circuit definitions for a balanced circuit. The DTE uses just two circuits (T and C) to transmit to the DCE. Similarly, the DCE uses two (R and I). The other circuits are used for timing signals in synchronous communications. With fewer circuits for transmission, more logic is needed to interpret the signals they carry. Typically, T and R are used to transmit bit strings, and C and I are in an ON (binary 0s) or OFF (binary 1s) state. Consequently, T and R are used for signaling and sending data and control information.

The signals on T, C, R, and I define the states (status) for the DTE and DCE. ITU-T defines many different states for X.21, but we will not elaborate on all of them here. We will, however, illustrate how the protocol works for a simple connection.

Figure 4.16 illustrates the signal exchange sequence as the DTE and DCE exchange information. To start, when both DTE and DCE are idle, the C and I circuits are both OFF and the T and R circuits transmit binary 1s. When the DTE wants to connect to a remote DTE, it begins sending 0s over T and sets C to ON (time t_1 in Figure 4.16). The DCE, sensing the change, responds by sending a sequence of + characters over R (time t_2). This is analogous to picking up the handset on a telephone and having the local switching office respond by transmitting the dial tone back to your phone.

If you were placing a phone call, your next step would be to dial the number. The DTE responds similarly by transmitting control and data information over

Figure 4.16 Sending and Receiving over an X.21 Connection

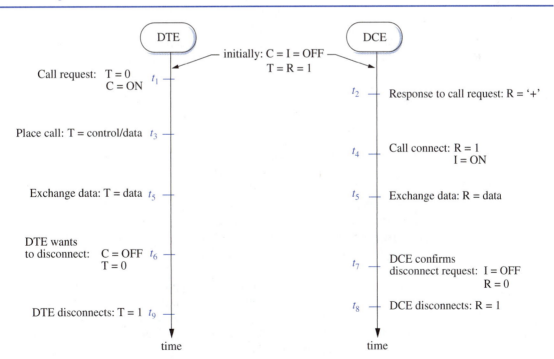

T (time t_3). This provides the DCE with necessary information, such as an address, to establish communications with a remote DTE via the network. As the DCE is trying to make the connection, it sends a series of SYN characters over R. When the connection is established, the DCE informs the DTE by sending 1s over R and setting I to ON (time t_4).

At this point (time t_5), the DTE and DCE can exchange data, with the DTE using the T circuit and the DCE using R. Eventually, the DTE will decide to terminate its activities. It indicates its intention to the DCE by transmitting 0s over T and setting C to OFF (time t_6). The DCE confirms the intention by transmitting 0s over R and setting I to OFF (time t_7). Finally, the DCE disconnects by transmitting 1s over R (time t_8), and the DTE disconnects by transmitting 1s over T (time t_9). This brings both devices to the idle state with which we began this example.

USB

One of the most common complaints from personal computer users not long ago dealt with the complexity of connecting peripheral devices. Users had to contend with serial ports, parallel ports, and special connections for game controllers, keyboards, mice, and so forth. Then, of course, the user had to install the proper drivers to make the connections work. It was all very confusing. A logical question to ask was: Why couldn't manufacturers standardize the connections and even agree on a standard across devices? After all, data transfers still boil down to sending and receiving bits. Fortunately, the correct people asked this question. Better yet, they even generated an answer: the **universal serial bus (USB).**

Initially, seven companies (Compaq, DEC, IBM, Intel, Microsoft, NEC, and Northern Telecom) collaborated to define USB. The primary motivation was to make things simpler to connect while at the same time providing higher bit rates for the newer devices hitting the market place. The result was USB version 1.0, with version 1.1 appearing shortly thereafter and version 2.0 even more recently. We're not going to articulate the many details that differentiate the versions, but we will provide an overview of how USB works. We'll see that USB provides a very flexible arrangement for connecting multiple devices, thus giving the user many options.

USB Connections   Most home computers probably use an arrangement of connections similar to that in Figure 4.17a. The computer (the host in Figure 4.17a) has a couple of USB sockets, and the user simply connects one or two USB-compatible devices, such as a scanner or digital camera. However, USB actually allows the user to connect up to 127 different devices, far more than most PC users will ever need. Of course, there are not 127 separate sockets on the back of the host computer. Instead, if the user wants to connect many devices, he or she must define an arrangement similar to that in Figure 4.17b.

A single USB device can connect directly to the host. However, to connect multiple devices the user needs a **hub,** a simple layer 1 device that regenerates and repeats signals received from one connection over other connections. The user can connect the hub to the host and then connect several other USB devices to the hub. In fact, the user may connect other hubs to the first one and other devices to the

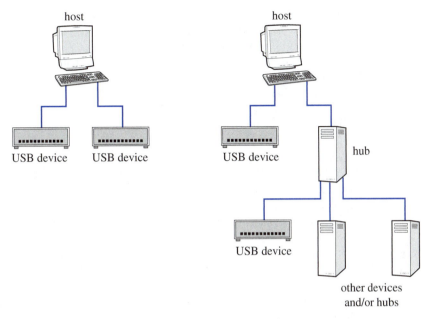

host   host

USB device   USB device   USB device   hub

USB device   other devices
and/or hubs

(a) Simple connection for most home PCs   (b) More complex connection hierarchy

Figure 4.17   Connecting USB Devices

second hub. In effect, the user is creating a hierarchical topology in which the host (the personal computer) is the root, USB devices are leaf nodes (nodes at the end of a hierarchical path), and hubs are intermediate nodes (nodes that connect something above them with something below them). Essentially, anything the host sends out along a USB connection travels to every node in the hierarchy. In theory, there is no limit to how many devices can be connected this way. However, USB uses a 7-bit addressing scheme to reference a device, which limits the total number of USB devices to 127 plus the host itself.

A USB cable connects devices. The cable contains four wires (Figure 4.18). Two of the wires (usually colored green and white) are used to carry data, using electrical signals that are equal in magnitude but opposite in polarity (i.e., a balanced signal). The wires are twisted around each other and are shielded to reduce the effect of noise. The signaling mechanism is a simple variation of the NRZ

Figure 4.18   USB Wires

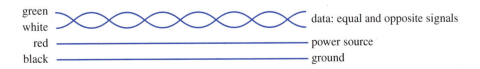

green
white   data: equal and opposite signals
red   power source
black   ground

encoding scheme (recall the previous chapter). USB defines a 0 by changing the signal at the beginning of a bit interval and a 1 by keeping the signal constant. In either case, the signal remains fixed for the bit interval (unlike Manchester encoding, which has a transition in the middle of the interval). Thus, a string of 1s represents a constant signal. The USB 1.1 standard defines a maximum bit rate of 12 Mbps; however, a newer version (USB 2.0) promises a rate of 480 Mbps. The cable also contains a black wire for ground and a red wire that delivers a low-amplitude power source to USB devices. This adds flexibility because some USB devices (e.g., mouse, keyboard) require very little power. This line provides the power they need, and manufacturers don't need to include a power source for the device.

The USB cable itself has two types of plugs, which prevents the user from connecting the wrong end of the cable to a device. Many personal computer users will recognize the small flat plug (Figure 4.19) that connects to the computer. This plug is called the standard A plug. The standard B plug (Figure 4.19) connects to a USB device and is recognized by its somewhat more square shape. Because of the different geometry, it is impossible to connect a B plug to an A socket or vice versa. Anyone who has inadvertently plugged the wrong ends of a cable into a socket and wondered why nothing was working knows the advantage of this scheme. The author can speak from experience; it *is* embarrassing. The cable length is limited to about 4.5 meters. Anything longer would not guarantee the integrity of the electrical signals.

Data Transfer   USB communication operates in a master/slave mode. Simply put, the host controls all transfers, and the devices can take action only when directed by the host. The way in which this works is rather interesting. Fundamental to transferring data over a USB connection is the concept of a **frame.** Be aware, the word *frame* is used in a specific way in the context of USB. Earlier in this chapter we defined a frame as a packaged group of bits. In USB context, a frame is a 1-millisecond slice of time. During that millisecond, information may be transferred in **packets,** the USB term for a packaged group of bits. It is unfortunate that different terms mean different things depending on the context. However, in a field that changes so rapidly, establishing universal terms across all areas is difficult.

An interesting feature of USB is that all devices are synchronized with respect to a frame. This is done not by a clock common to all devices, but through the host. At the beginning of each frame, the host sends a special packet that travels to each USB device and informs each that a new frame is beginning. What happens afterward depends on the host that controls the transfer of information, the types of devices, and what data are available for transfer. Let's see how this works.

Figure 4.19   USB Cable and Plugs

standard A plug   standard B plug

To begin, USB defines four different transmission types (sometime called frame types): control, bulk, isochronous, and interrupt. Each corresponds to a different type of exchange and is implemented by an exchange of packets. We'll see shortly how this can happen in the context of a frame, but first let's define the different transfer types.

- **Control transfer:** USB devices are **hot pluggable;** that is, new devices can be plugged in (and unplugged) without powering off the system or loading new software to make them work. Thus, the operating system running on the host must detect when a device is added or removed. At that point it enters an initialization phase, during which the host queries the new device to determine what type of device it is and what bit rates it is capable of. The device, in turn, responds to these queries, and the host eventually assigns and communicates an address to the device. This allows the host to distinguish this device from any others that are connected. After devices are connected, the host may send commands to them, request their status, or initiate an exchange of data.

- **Bulk transfer:** Some USB devices are designed to transfer large amounts of information. Examples include scanners and digital cameras. Typically, data are stored in packets and transferred with error detection mechanisms implemented on the receiving end. Chapter 6 discusses error detection and its details, but the idea is simple: Check the incoming packet for any errors that may have occurred during transmission. If an error is detected, then resend the packet. Performing error detection techniques ensures the data are transferred reliably. Remember that there may be several devices engaging in bulk transfer, and there are no guarantees as to when data will arrive. This is a quality of service that guarantees reliable transfer but not necessarily a timely one. The host coordinates the transfers.

- **Interrupt transfer:** Some computer peripherals (for example, a disk controller) operate on an interrupt system. When data are ready for transfer, the device sends a signal to the central processor. This generates an interruption in whatever the central processor is currently doing. At that point the operating system takes control, determines the reason for the interrupt, and eventually calls on a handler routine to respond. All of this requires complex protocols to enable the exchange of interrupt signals and responses.

    USB does not operate this way. When a device has data to transfer, it simply holds the data and waits to be asked by the host. It's a little like trying to extract information from two young children who got into an argument. You know the information regarding who started it is there, but neither is going to volunteer anything. You must be clever enough to extract it. Interrupt transfers are usually associated with low-volume devices. For example, when you type on the keyboard, the codes are stored until the host asks for them. Upon request from the host, the keyboard transfers a character that its user typed. The process of a host asking a device whether it has data to send is called **polling.** By having the host poll such devices with a fixed frequency, one can guarantee a smooth delivery of information. For example, if the host polled a keyboard every 50 frames (50 milliseconds), it could get up to 20 characters each second. That's a lot faster than most of us can ever hope to type. Only Superman could type faster.

- **Isochronous transfer:** Some USB devices (for example, microphones and speakers) are real-time devices that require data to be sent at a guaranteed rate. The host can reserve a part of each frame for that device and guarantee that some of the frame's time is spent on transferring data to or from that device. By transferring a certain number of bits in every frame, the host can guarantee a specified bit rate.

  In contrast to a bulk transfer, error detection does not occur. The quality of service here is timely delivery of data. Errors in the transfer are tolerated. If the data represent audio, then such an error (if it is even noticed) would show up as a small deviation (scratchy sound, click, static, gaps in sound, etc.) from the original recording, but the recording continues. The device will not request retransfer of data until the sound is perfect! Owners of old vinyl albums (particular those with scratches) know all too well the deviations from the original that can occur. Even scratched CDs can exhibit this behavior.

USB Packets   The next logical step is to describe how frames and packets relate to one another. In general, there can be several exchanges of packets during a single frame. What the exchange accomplishes depends on the types of packets that are exchanged. We will discuss three types: token, data, and handshake packets. Although the contents of these packets differ, two things are found in all packet types: a SYN field and a packet ID (PID) field. The SYN field contains a special bit pattern that forces the electrical signals to change according to the sender's clock. This allows the receiving device to synchronize its internal clock with the rate at which the bits are arriving and receive the bits correctly. The PID field contains bits that identify the packet type. Remember, a device can receive a packet at almost any time and it must have some way of identifying the type of packet it is getting.

Let's begin with the *token packet*. The host uses token packets to send information or requests to a USB device. There are several kinds of token packets. One is the SOF (Start of Frame) packet (Figure 4.20a). Previously we stated that all devices are synchronized to the start of each frame. In other words, each knows when a frame begins. However, rather than tying all devices to a common clock (difficult to do when devices are plugged and unplugged randomly), the host does the work. At the beginning of each frame (remember, this means once every millisecond), the host sends an SOF packet that gets transmitted to every USB device. The SOF packet is particularly important to real-time devices that must transfer a minimum number of bits in each frame.

Two other examples of token packets are the IN packet and OUT packet. Each of these represents a request from the host to initiate a data transfer. The difference between the two is the direction of the transfer. To illustrate, suppose the host wants to send data to a USB device (Figure 4.20b). The following occurs:

1. After sending an SOF packet, the host sends an OUT packet. The OUT packet (Figure 4.20c) contains a 7-bit address that identifies the USB device to receive the data. The appropriate device sees the OUT packet, recognizes its address within it, and prepares to receive data. In addition to the SYN and PID fields, an OUT packet also contains a Cyclic Redundancy Check (CRC) field, which

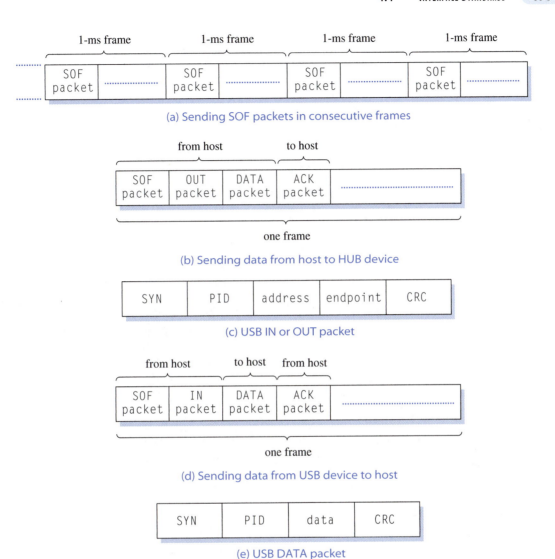

(a) Sending SOF packets in consecutive frames

(b) Sending data from host to HUB device

(c) USB IN or OUT packet

(d) Sending data from USB device to host

(e) USB DATA packet

Figure 4.20   USB Frames and Packets

is used to detect any errors that may have occurred during the transfer. We will see this field in other packets also, but since we have not yet discussed error detection details, we defer all discussions of CRC to Chapter 6. The OUT packet also has an Endpoint field, which we will discuss shortly.

2. Next, the host sends a DATA packet (Figure 4.20e) that contains the data to be transferred.

3. Finally, if there are no errors during the transfer, the USB device sends an ACK packet (actually a type of handshake packet) back to the host. If an error

was detected, then the device would send another type of handshake packet (a NAK packet) to the host. At that point the host would repeat the procedure and try to send the data again.

The host may initiate other transfers within the frame (the dotted line in Figure 4.20b), but the current transfer is complete.

If the host wanted to receive data from the device, the exchange would be as shown in Figure 4.20d:

1. The host sends an IN packet.
2. Upon receiving the IN packet, the device sends a DATA packet.
3. If no errors occurred, the host returns an ACK packet.

Note that if the device had no data to send, it would send a NAK packet. The host would recognize this as an indicator that the device had nothing to send.

An observant reader may have noticed something in the previous description: DATA packets do not contain an address. However, the DATA packet is preceded by an IN or OUT packet, which identifies the device involved in the transfer. The device, in turn, can prepare for the transfer. The observant reader may also have noticed we have glossed over the Endpoint field in the IN or OUT packet. That's because it did not relate to the previous discussion. However, a more detailed discussion of data transfers would reveal that specifying a device address is not sufficient because the address may not completely specify the source or destination of data. Some devices have multiple sources or destinations associated with them. One example is a game controller with multiple buttons, each of which may involve transfer of different information. In such cases, the Endpoint identifier is used to further refine the exact source or destination of the data.

There is much more that can be said about USB, but we must go on to other topics. The reader interested in more details can consult reference [Ax01] or the website www.usb.org.

FIREWIRE

Apple began developing **FireWire,** a technology designed to connect electronic devices, in the late 1980s. In 1995 IEEE adopted a standard, IEEE 1394, based on that design. The trademarked name is Apple FireWire. Sony also produces a version of the 1394 standard and markets it as i.Link. Purchasers of new computers will often see the spec "IEEE 1394" listed under "External Ports" along with a specification of one or two USB ports.

FireWire has much in common with USB. Both are

- Hot swappable
- Plug and play
- Serial connections
- A standard way to connect a wide variety of devices
- Relatively inexpensive to implement

However, there are also some major differences. At the time of this writing, most references cite speed as a big difference. FireWire specifications define a bit rate of

400 Mbps, whereas USB has 12 Mbps. The problem with comparing bit rates in a textbook is that by the time it goes to press, the bit rate comparisons are no longer valid. USB 2.0 specifications call for 480 Mbps, comparable to FireWire. Furthermore, work is in progress to increase the FireWire bit rate to 800 Mbps. In fact, longer-range plans call for implementing FireWire over optical fiber connections and reaching Gbps bit rates. Thus, we won't dwell on bit rates because any figures are likely to be inaccurate soon.

Connections   Like USB, FireWire is designed to connect a variety of devices, but the designers focused on support for multimedia devices (especially those that support digital video applications), such as digital camcorders or digital cameras. Many also saw it as a better alternative to SCSI (Small Computer Systems Interface), a standard high-speed interface for connecting devices. However, SCSI uses parallel communications, which means unwieldy cables and a higher cost.

FireWire supports connecting multiple devices using a **daisy chain** approach (Figure 4.21). This means you can connect several devices in sequence, with a FireWire cable (which has a maximum length of about 4.5 meters) between adjacent pairs. It is also possible for one device to mark the beginning of two daisy chains (note the two daisy chains to the left of and below the disk drive in Figure 4.21). In fact, one can actually visualize the devices as a hierarchical arrangement. The one thing that is not allowed is to connect devices so that they form a loop. For example, in Figure 4.21 you could not connect the television with the computer.

With the daisy chain approach, there's no need for a hub. Each device has one or more FireWire ports, which also act as repeaters. Any signal arriving on such a port is regenerated and resent over other ports. In fact, as we'll describe shortly, FireWire technology does not require a host computer.

One difference immediately noticeable to the consumer is that a FireWire cable contains six wires (as opposed to the four in a USB cable). There are two pairs of twisted wires, also known as TPA and TPB, and two power supplies. Like USB, the

Figure 4.21   Connecting FireWire Devices

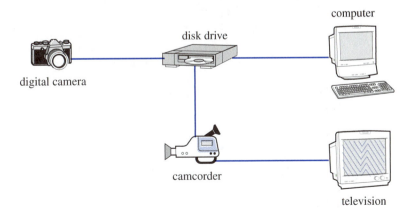

power lines can provide power to some FireWire devices, eliminating the need for a separate power source.

The use of two twisted pair for data transfer is a little different from what we have seen previously. FireWire uses an encoding method called **data strobe encoding.** Figure 4.22 shows how this works. Data to be transmitted are encoded using a form of NRZ. In this case, a 1 is a high signal and a 0 is a low signal. The receiver gets the data over TPA. However, as we have discussed before, long constant signals (long string of 1s or 0s) can cause drift between sender and receiver. With FireWire, the second pair of wires, TPB, is used to receive a **strobe signal.** The sender generates the strobe signal, which stays constant whenever the data change from 1 to 0 or vice versa. If the data do not change, then there is a transition in the strobe signal. The important detail in all of this is that with every clock cycle in the sender, either the data signal or the strobe signal changes. The receiver can detect these changes using exclusive OR logic and, in effect, recreate the sender's clock signal. It can then synchronize its own clock with the incoming bits and receive them correctly. It's a bit like Manchester encoding in that it is a self-clocking mechanism. The biggest difference is that Manchester encoding requires a baud rate that is twice the bit rate. Here, the baud and bit rates are the same. However, the technique requires an extra wire pair.

Figure 4.22   Data Strobe Encoding

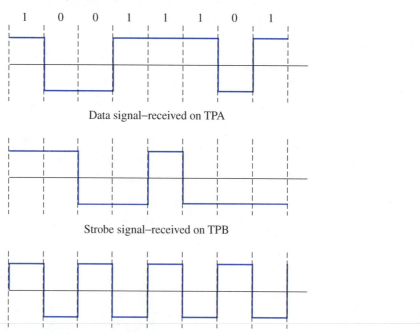

Data signal–received on TPA

Strobe signal–received on TPB

Recovered clock signal records changes in either
the data or strobe signal–at receiver

Perhaps the most fundamental difference between FireWire and USB is the type of protocol. As we saw, USB operates on a master/slave basis; FireWire is a **peer-to-peer protocol.** For our purposes here, this means that communications do not depend on a single host such as a personal computer. If there is a FireWire connection between a video camera and an external disk drive, data can be transferred from the camera directly to storage. A host computer is not necessary. Full details are complex, and we provide only an overview of the protocol. The reader interested in more detail should consult references [An99] and [St03] or www.apple.com/firewire.

The peer-to-peer design provides a wider range of connection topologies. Figure 4.22 already showed how a few devices can be connected via a daisy chain. Figure 4.23 shows a more general configuration, using 1394 bus bridges. Devices may be daisy chained together to form a **bus group.** These groups, in turn, may be connected using the bus bridges. The bridges isolate the groups from one another, allowing devices in one group to communicate independent of each device in another. That is, packets generally stay within a group. Bridges form a layer 2 connection between devices. Chapter 10 discusses types of bridges and bridge functions in much more detail. For now, just think of a bridge as a device that allows groups to function independently but will forward a packet from one group to another if the packet address specifically identifies a device in another group. There may be up to 63 devices (accessible using 6-bit IDs) in one group and up to 1023 different bus groups (identifiable using 10-bit IDs).

Communications   FireWire supports two modes of communication: asynchronous and isochronous. FireWire defines asynchronous communication as communication that involves an exchange of packets and acknowledgments. The general approach is as follows:

1. Send a packet.

2. Wait for a response.

Figure 4.23   Multiple FireWire Buses

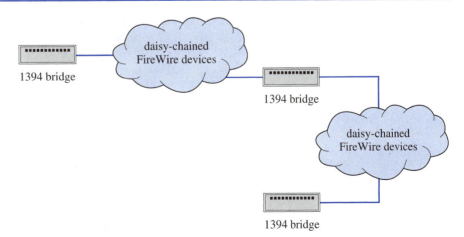

3. If the response is an acknowledgment, consider the packet received.

4. If the response is a negative acknowledgment (another packet type), then assume something happened and send the packet again.

Details of implementing such protocols can be complex; Chapter 8 deals with them in more detail. The important thing here is that packets arrive at arbitrary times and, if any have to be resent, bit rates can fluctuate.

Isochronous transfer is as we have described earlier. FireWire guarantees that packets are sent at regular intervals, thus guaranteeing a specified bit rate. There is no waiting for an acknowledgment or resending of packets.

An asynchronous packet has a header containing a 64-bit address. Sixteen bits identify a particular device via a 10-bit bus ID and a 6-bit node ID. The remaining 48 bits are used to reference memory, providing a 256-terabyte (2^{48}) memory capacity. Isochronous packets do not have an address. Instead, each has a channel number field that identifies a particular data stream that two devices have previously set up.

One reason for the channel number is to ensure that the quality of service required of an isochronous channel is met. When two devices require isochronous communication, a resource manager assigns a channel number. If two other devices also need isochronous communication, they get a different channel number. However, what happens if the resource manager assigns too many channel numbers for isochronous communication? In that case the physical bit rate is insufficient to support the requirements for all the transfers. All connections have a finite bit rate capacity, and care must be taken not to promise more than can be delivered. Thus, there must be a limit on the number of isochronous channels that are assigned.

Arbitration   As we indicated earlier, FireWire is a peer-to-peer protocol, which eliminates the dependence on a host for all transfers. Devices can thus initiate their own transfers. It sounds simple enough until you realize that a problem occurs if two devices attempt to initiate a transfer at the same time. When this occurs, **arbitration** is needed to determine which device wins. Next question: How does arbitration work?

To answer this, let's back up a bit. When a new device is connected to an existing daisy chain, all of the devices collaborate to form a hierarchical arrangement of nodes. Note that these hierarchies are contained in the groups separated by the bridges. That is, each group configures itself independent of the others.

Exactly how devices can collaborate to form a configuration is a complex process; Chapter 10 explores this topic in more detail. For now, just understand that somehow the devices can communicate and arrange themselves into a tree structure, with one of them acting as the root node. Note also that the arrangement must be a tree and that no loops are allowed. After the arrangement is defined, each node then selects an ID number based on its position in the hierarchy. Again, we won't discuss here the details of how this is done.

The device at the root acts as an arbiter. When a device wants bus access, it sends a request to the arbiter that can grant access. If two devices try at the same time, the arbiter makes a decision based on a priority assigned to each device. The priority reflects the device's distance from the root and its ID. Thus, devices closer to the root have higher priority than those farther away. The important thing here is that the arbiter can always definitively make a decision regarding which device gets the bus.

An observant reader may pose the all-important question: How can this method support isochronous communication if the sending device has a low priority? After all, *isochronous* means a guaranteed number of bits per unit of time. Devices with high priority (close to the root device) can monopolize the bus, preventing lower-priority ones from any access at all. The answer is that the arbitration we have described is only part of the process and works in conjunction with two other arbitration methods: fairness arbitration and urgent arbitration.

Fairness arbitration uses the concept of a fairness interval (amount of time). The following is a typical sequence of events:

1. At the start of a fairness interval, all devices with packets to send set a flag.

2. All competing devices send a request to the arbiter.

3. The device that gets the bus sends its packet and gets an acknowledgment from the recipient. (The device sending the acknowledgment is not required to compete for the bus, because the bus is still in control of the sending device.) It then clears its flag. The cleared flag indicates it is no longer able to request bus access during the fairness interval.

4. Eventually, all devices get the bus once during the fairness interval.

5. When no devices are cleared to request bus access, the bus remains idle for a period of time. This marks the end of the fairness interval.

6. A new fairness interval begins and the process repeats.

This procedure guarantees that no device can monopolize the bus or win arbitration decisions repeatedly.

To allow devices to be prioritized, an *urgent arbitration* method allows certain devices to be configured as urgent. Each urgent device must also set its flag at the beginning of the fairness interval, but it also sets a counter value. It competes with other devices for the bus. The difference is that when a device gets control of the bus it decrements its counter by 1. If the counter is still positive after its packet is sent and received, the device is allowed to again compete for the bus in the same fairness interval.

Note that an urgent designation is not the same as isochronous transmission. Urgent is just a way of prioritizing asynchronous packets; it still won't guarantee a specified bit rate. For isochronous transmission, the root device also acts as a *cycle master*. As cycle master, the device regularly sends out a cycle_start packet (Figure 4.24). Remember, the root device is also arbiter and has the highest priority because all others are farther from the root. Therefore, it can grant itself bus access when it needs to send the cycle_start packet. The cycle_start packet marks the start of an *isochronous cycle*. During this time, devices with an isochronous packet to send compete for the bus, and each gets a chance to send one isochronous packet. Because the cycle master starts an isochronous cycle regularly, this process meets the quality of service required of isochronous transmission.

When isochronous packets have been sent over all channels, a gap occurs, after which the fairness interval begins. At this point devices can send asynchronous

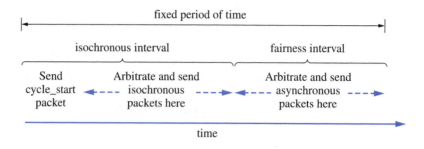

Figure 4.24 FireWire Arbitration

packets as described previously until there are none to send or until the cycle master sends another cycle_start packet. Certainly, there are details we have left out; again, the interested reader is encouraged to read about them in references [An99] and [St03] or www.apple.com/firewire.

Many other interface standards exist, but describing them all is far beyond the scope of this text. (Reference [Sh90] lists approximately 100 such standards.) We have described some of the most common or well-known standards here and will describe a couple of others later (for example, the X.25 network interface and ISDN in Chapter 13).

4.5 MULTIPLEXING

When it comes to data transmissions, it should not be hard to convince you that higher bit rates are better. If you have ever upgraded to a faster computer, disk drive, or modem, you no doubt found that the faster response times helped you work more efficiently. Some of us old-timers remember when the first 3.5-inch drives became available. The ability to get a file in just a couple of seconds was a wonderful improvement over the 5.25-inch drives. And with the hard disk drives available today, we now have to find ways to amuse ourselves while waiting for anything on a 3.5-inch disk.

The same is true of networks and communications: Faster is generally better. Speed does have its drawbacks, however. First, it is more expensive; second, it has a point of diminishing returns. That is, after a certain point many users can't make use of the increased speed. For example, LANs are now capable of gigabit per second rates, but most PC applications simply do not have the volume of data necessary to make use of that speed. Even if they did, most PC network cards don't support bit rates that high.

One response is to not worry about developing high-speed networks because most users cannot utilize their full potential. This solution has a serious flaw, however. Suppose the network shown in Figure 4.25 supports a bit rate of 10 Mbps. If the only activity involves two PCs communicating at that rate, the network serves

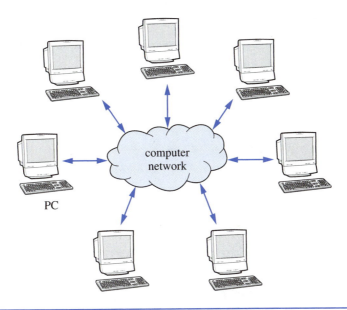

Figure 4.25   Many Users Communicating over a Network

its purpose. However, if several hundred PCs need to communicate with one another, the 10 Mbps limit will create quite a bottleneck. Increasing the bit rate will reduce that bottleneck. A good analogy is a major freeway system in a large city during rush hour. If traffic moves at 15 mph, the lines on entrance ramps will grow very long. If traffic moves at a normal speed of 55 mph, the cars will not wait as long to enter the freeway.

A second response to the problems of higher bit rates is to develop high-speed networks but somehow reduce the cost of connecting to them. In Figure 4.25, there is a cost for each PC connection. Figure 4.26 shows a common alternative using a **multiplexer** (sometimes called **mux** to minimize transmission from the larynx and movement of muscles in and around the vocal cavity known as the mouth). It is a device that routes transmissions from multiple sources to a single destination. In Figure 4.26, the sources are PCs and the destination is the network. The multiplexer also routes transmissions in the reverse direction, from the network to any of the PCs.

In general, a multiplexer's output line to the network has a much higher bit rate than any of the input lines from the PCs. This way it can utilize the network's high bit rate and, by providing a single connection for multiple users, cut the cost per connection.

This description of multiplexing is just one of several depending on the signal types and the activity of the units connected to the multiplexer. Next, we describe specific multiplexing methods and provide an example used in long-distance telephone communications.

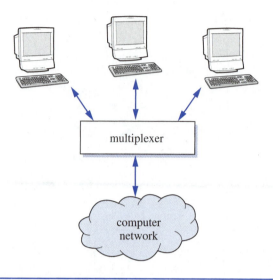

Figure 4.26   Multiplexing Low-Speed Devices

FREQUENCY-DIVISION MULTIPLEXING

Frequency-division multiplexing (FDM) is used with analog signals. Perhaps its most common use is in television and radio transmission. A multiplexer accepts analog signals from multiple sources, each of which has a specified bandwidth. The signals then are combined into another, more complex signal with a much larger bandwidth. The resulting signal is transmitted over some medium to its destination, where another mux extracts and separates the individual components.

This method of multiplexing involves several steps. First, the available bandwidth of the transmission medium is divided into separate ranges or channels. For example, the bandwidth for broadcast television (54 to 806 MHz) is divided into 68 channels of 6 MHz each. VHF channels 2 to 13 correspond to 6-MHz bands between 54 and 215 MHz. UHF channels 14 to 69 correspond to 6-MHz bands between 470 and 806 MHz. Each channel corresponds to one of the multiplexer's input signals.

Next, a **carrier signal** is defined for each channel. It is changed (modulated) by the corresponding input signal to create another signal (modulated signal). There are several ways to do this. For example, Figure 4.27 illustrates amplitude modulation. The carrier signal has a specified frequency, typically centered in a channel's bandwidth. Its amplitude is changed to alternate between values depending on the other signal's maximum and minimum values.

A complete understanding of amplitude modulation requires some knowledge of the mathematical representation of wave forms and Fourier series. Consequently, a detailed explanation is beyond the scope of this text. If you want a more rigorous discussion, see references [St00], [Wa98], and [St96]. We can, however, illustrate the process using a simple example.

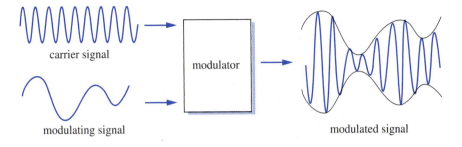

carrier signal

modulator

modulated signal

modulating signal

Figure 4.27   Amplitude Modulation

Consider an analog signal corresponding to the formula $f(t) = [\sin (2\pi t)/4] + 0.5$. Figure 4.28 shows its graph between $t = 0$ and $t = 2$. Suppose the carrier signal corresponds to $g(t) = \sin (10 \times 2\pi t)$. Figure 4.28 does not show the graph of $g(t)$ but, if drawn, its graph would oscillate 20 times between 1 and -1 as t ranged from 0 to 2. Multiplying $f(t)$ and $g(t)$ generates the modulated signal shown in Figure 4.28.

In general, signals have much higher frequencies and correspond to complex sums of sine functions. Still, the process of amplitude modulation remains essentially the same as in the example. Other modulation techniques are frequency modulation and phase modulation. As you might expect, frequency modulation alters the frequency of the carrier depending on the input signal, and phase modulation alters the signal's phase shift. Again, references [St00] and [Wa98] contain more rigorous discussions.

Figure 4.28   Graphs of Modulated Signal

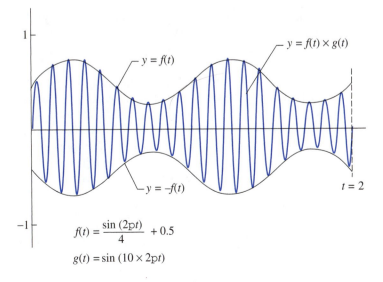

$$f(t) = \frac{\sin (2pt)}{4} + 0.5$$

$$g(t) = \sin (10 \times 2pt)$$

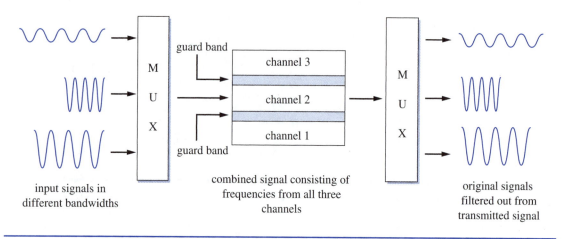

Figure 4.29 Frequency-Division Multiplexing

In the last step of frequency-division multiplexing, the modulated signals from all the inputs are combined into a single, more complex analog signal (Figure 4.29). Its frequencies lie within the ranges of all the channels. The channels themselves are separated by **guard bands** (unused parts of the frequency range) in order to prevent interference between adjacent channels. The resulting signal is transmitted and another multiplexer receives it. It then uses bandpass filters to extract the individual modulated signals. Finally, the signals are demodulated and the original signals restored. In applications such as television and radio, the channel or frequency selectors specify which of the original signals are converted to sound and picture.

TIME-DIVISION MULTIPLEXING

In **time-division multiplexing (TDM)** many input signals are combined and transmitted together, as with FDM. TDM is used with digital signals, however. As a result, TDM keeps the signals physically distinct but logically packages them together, in contrast to FDM, which combines them into a single, more complex signal.

Figure 4.30 illustrates TDM. Suppose A_i, B_i, C_i, and D_i ($i = 1, 2, 3, \ldots$) represent bit streams from distinct sources. A few bits from each source are buffered temporarily in the multiplexer. The multiplexer scans each buffer, storing the bits from each in a frame, and then sends the frame. As it does so, it begins building a new frame by again scanning the input buffers for new data that have arrived. If the timing is right, it will construct a new frame just in time to transmit it immediately following the previous one. This process keeps the output line active and makes full use of its capacity.

In Figure 4.30 the bit streams A_1, B_1, C_1, and D_1 are buffered separately. The multiplexer packages them into a single frame and transmits it. It then follows by gathering A_2, B_2, C_2, and D_2 and sending another frame. The process continues as long as the sources are providing bit streams.

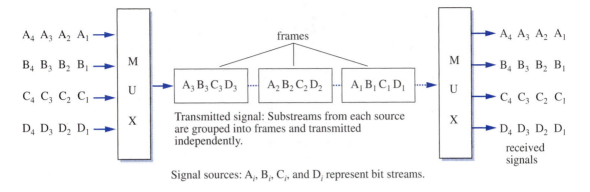

Signal sources: A_i, B_i, C_i, and D_i represent bit streams.

Figure 4.30 Time-Division Multiplexing

The multiplexer's design depends in part on the input and output transmission rates. For example, if source bits from the combined inputs arrive faster than the previous frame can be sent, frames are generated more quickly than they can be forwarded. If the multiplexer has no capacity to store the extra frames, they are lost. We must not supply the multiplexer with information faster than it can release it. On the other hand, if the source bits arrive too slowly, the previous frame will have been sent and the multiplexer either waits for enough bits to arrive or sends a frame that is only partially full. Either way, the output line is not used to its fullest capacity.

The optimal situation is when the combined input rate (the sum of rates from each source) equals the output rate. Suppose r_i is the input rate from the ith source and r_{output} is the multiplexer's transmission rate. Mathematically, we express this as

$$\sum_{i=1}^{n} r_i = r_{output}$$

For example, if data from 10 sources arrived at a rate of 10 Mbps, the multiplexer should be able to send them at a rate of 100 Mbps. (We describe an alternative shortly.)

Another part of the multiplexer's design is the size of the frame components. One design defines A_i, B_i, C_i, and D_i as 8 bits, or 1 byte. In this case the multiplexer is called a **byte multiplexer.** In other cases, A_i, B_i, C_i, and D_i are larger, containing many bytes (a block). In this case, strangely enough, it is called a *block multiplexer*.

STATISTICAL MULTIPLEXERS

Previously, we stated that an optimal design requires that the sum of input rates equals the output rate. However, sometimes this is not practical. In the previous example, we assumed that bits were arriving from each source continuously, but in many cases they arrive in bursts with periods of inactivity in between.

In such cases there are two approaches for multiplexing the data. The first is to design the multiplexer to skip empty buffers and leave part of the frame vacant. For example, in Figure 4.30, suppose the third source was inactive. That is, C_1, C_2, C_3, and C_4 do not exist. Each frame would have space reserved for those bits, but would not contain any meaningful information. This has the advantage of keeping all the frames the same size and simplifying the protocols. The obvious disadvantage is that useless information occupies the transmission medium and thus wastes bandwidth.

Another approach is to have the multiplexer scan the buffers and create a variable-size frame depending on how many buffers contain data. We call this a **statistical multiplexer.** Some also use the term *concentrator.**

Figure 4.31 shows how this works. Here all sources are active, but not at the same time. The symbol Ø indicates that no information has arrived from a source. Initially bit streams A_1 and C_1 are buffered, but the others are empty due to inactivity at the sources. Therefore, the multiplexer puts A_1 and C_1 into a frame and sends it on its way. In the meantime A_2 and C_2, along with B_1, arrive. The multiplexer puts them together in another, larger frame and sends it. At this point there is inactivity from the C source, but the D source becomes active. Now A_3, B_2, and D_1 arrive. As before, the multiplexer puts them in a frame and sends it. This process continues as long as any of the inputs are active.

A complication with this approach is that sources are no longer assigned a fixed position in the frame. For example, in Figure 4.30 bits from each source always occupied the same positions in a frame. In Figure 4.31, this is not so. For example, bits from source B sometimes occupied the second or third positions (counting from the right). In such cases the frame format is more complex and requires additional information such as destination addresses. The receiving multiplexer must have additional logic to seek out the addresses and route the information in the correct direction.

Figure 4.31   Statistical Time-Division Multiplexing

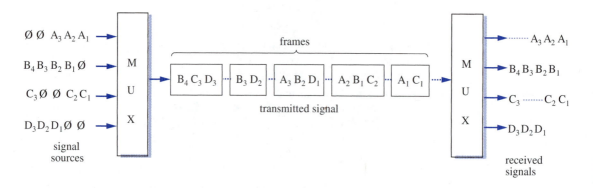

---

* Strictly speaking, the two terms are different. A *concentrator* is a more intelligent statistical multiplexer that allows us to do other things such as verify, acknowledge, and compress data. These are topics we discuss in Chapters 5 to 8. The actual definitions often depend on to whom you talk. We will not make a distinction here. In fact, sometimes the term *asynchronous time-division multiplexer* is used.

As defined, a statistical multiplexer may not fully use its output capacity. In the extreme case, if no sources are active there are no transmissions. The probability that none are active depends on how many sources there are. An astute observer may notice that we could connect additional sources to decrease this probability and keep the output line busier. If this happens, then

$$\sum_{i=1}^{n} r_i > r_{output}$$

That is, the input capacity of the multiplexer is now larger than its output capacity.

Having a higher input rate is not necessarily a problem. Remember, r_i represents the capacity of the ith source, not its actual rate. If it is inactive, the actual bit rate is 0. The design assumes that although the sum of input rates is larger than r_{output}, the sources are not all active at the same time. The ideal is when the combined input rate from active sources is equal to r_{output}. Because activity depends on the user, it is hard to predict and the ideal is difficult to achieve. There will be times when the combined input rate from active sources is smaller or even larger than r_{output}. In the latter case, additional logic and buffers must be designed to accommodate temporary surges in data. This is one reason statistical multiplexers are sometimes called concentrators: They concentrate additional data for brief periods.

An analysis of statistical multiplexers can be difficult because of the random way in which the sources send data. Many questions must be asked. How frequently will the combined input rates exceed the output rate? How often will all sources be busy? How large must the internal buffers be to handle temporary surges? How long are the delays when surges occur? One approach to the analysis is the use of *queuing theory*, a field of mathematics that defines models for studying events such as waiting in lines (queues) for events to occur. It can be applied to many areas, including communications systems in which input streams may arrive in random patterns. In such cases the events are the transmissions over the output lines. References [St00], [Wa00], and [Ma72] contain introductory discussions of queuing theory.

WAVE-DIVISION MULTIPLEXING

Another type of multiplexing is based on optics, but has similarities to frequency-division multiplexing. It is called **wave-division multiplexing** and is based on a couple of properties of visible light. Chapter 2 discussed light refraction—the change of direction that occurs when light moves from one medium to another. The angle of refraction depends not only on the optical density of the two media but also on the light's wavelength. The other property is that most light consists of many wavelengths. These two properties describe what happens when light passes through a prism (Figure 4.32) and is divided into different colors. The different wavelengths refract at different angles and hence leave the prism at different angles. The same principle creates a rainbow when the sun shines during a rainstorm.

Figure 4.33 illustrates how wave-division multiplexing works. There are several sources of electrical signals, each of which is input to a laser (or LED). As Chapter 2 discussed, the laser responds to the electrical signals and produces pulses

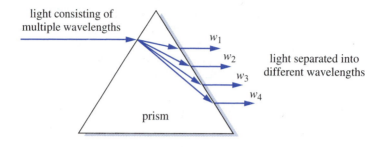

Figure 4.32   Light Refracting through a Prism

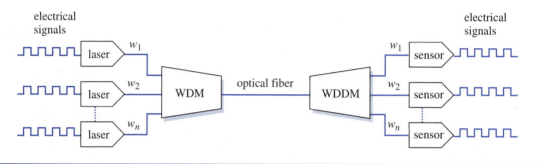

Figure 4.33   Wave-Division Multiplexing

of light. The difference here is that each laser produces light pulses of different wavelengths, w_1, w_2, . . . , w_n. Light from each wavelength is input into a wave-division multiplexer (WDM), which combines the different light sources into one. That light (consisting of several wavelengths) is then transmitted along an optical fiber as described in Chapter 2.

At the other end the process is reversed. The light from the optical fiber enters a wave-division demultiplexer (WDDM), which separates the different wavelengths much as a prism does (although a WDDM is much more complex). Light from each wavelength then proceeds to its intended destination.

Bit rates from this technology have the potential for being enormous. Standard optical fiber already has the capability of transmitting dozens of gigabits per second. As this technology develops, there is the potential for hundreds of gigabits per second, and someday we might be talking about terabits (1000 Gbps) per second.

4.6   DIGITAL CARRIERS

T1

This section describes a couple of standards used in long-distance communications. Much of what we think of as the "telephone system" was designed to transmit digitized voice signals over high-speed media such as optical fiber or microwaves.

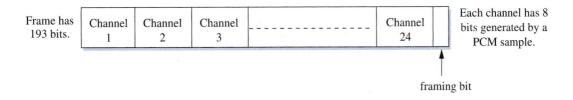

Frame has 193 bits. | Channel 1 | Channel 2 | Channel 3 | - - - - - - - - - - - - - - | Channel 24 | Each channel has 8 bits generated by a PCM sample.

framing bit

Figure 4.34 DS1 Frame

In fact, AT&T developed a complex hierarchy of communications systems used to multiplex voice signals and transmit them all over the United States. The system is also used in other countries, such as Canada and Japan. Still other countries use a similar but different system defined by ITU-T standards.

This system uses time-division multiplexing to combine many voice channels into one frame. Of the many ways to do this, one approach uses T1 transmission and DS1 signaling. The designations *T1* and *DS1* refer to the circuit and signal, respectively. For example, Figure 4.34 shows a DS1 frame in which voice data are digitized using pulse code modulation (discussed in Chapter 3). It contains 193 bits divided into 24 slots (one for each channel) of 8 bits each. This leaves one extra bit called a *framing bit,* which is used for synchronizing.

Figure 4.35 shows how a T1 carrier system works. Eight-bit voice samples are taken from each of 24 channels at a rate of 8000 per second. Each sample then occupies one slot in the DS1 frame. According to the Nyquist theorem from Chapter 3, this is sufficient to maintain all the information in the original voice analog

Figure 4.35 T1 Carrier System

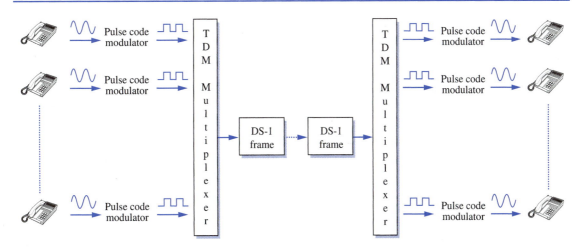

Table 4.4   North American Communication Carriers

CARRIER	FRAME FORMAT	NUMBER OF CHANNELS	DATA RATE (MBPS)
T1	DS1	24	1.544
T1c	DS1C	48	3.152
T2	DS2	96	6.312
T3	DS3	672	44.376
T4	DS4	4032	274.176

signal. Consecutive samples are stored in different DS1 frames. The voice messages are thus transmitted using many DS1 frames to another multiplexer. This multiplexer extracts the bits from each slot and routes them to their appropriate destination, where they eventually are converted back to analog signals. The result is converted into the original sound of the person's voice.

What is the bit rate of the T1 carrier system? Each 8-bit slot is generated at a rate of 8000 per second, for a rate of 64 Kbps. To support this speed, T1 must transmit a DS1 frame every 1/8000 of a second, or 8000 frames per second. In other words, it must transmit 8000×193 bits each second, for a data rate of 1.544 Mbps. This rate is slow when compared with the capabilities of optical fibers. Consequently, there are other carrier and signal designations with more channels and faster bit rates. Table 4.4 summarizes some of them. A common approach is to multiplex signals from a low-speed carrier into a high-speed one. For example, the T3 carrier can multiplex 7 DS2 frames, 14 DS1C frames, or 28 DS1 frames, giving it the ability to carry 672 channels in each frame.

Voice data is not the only type that can be transmitted. Many companies lease phone lines to transfer digital information between computers. In fact, the principle behind the fax machine is to convert images on paper to digital signals and transmit them over telephone lines.

As a final note, we mention that the number of channels in each system can be increased by using different modulation techniques. Pulse code modulation digitizes voice information at a rate of 64 Kbps. Adaptive differential pulse code modulation digitizes voice information at 32 Kbps, which allows each of the carrier systems to support twice as many channels as listed in Table 4.4.

SONET

Perhaps one of the most significant and well-known digital carrier systems is **SONET (Synchronous Optical Network).** Developed by Bellcore (Bell Communications Research), it is an ANSI-standard circuit-switching technology widely used in long-distance communication systems. It can connect high-speed workstations, Internet routers, telephone switches, and ATM (Asynchronous Transfer

Mode) switches.* In fact, many Internet queries and telephone calls travel over a SONET connection.

A similar system, **SDH (Synchronous Digital Hierarchy),** was developed shortly after SONET and is an ITU-T standard. It is perhaps more well known in European countries. There are differences between the two, but at this level of discussion they are not important. In fact, the designation SONET/SDH is common. We focus on an overview of SONET, but we encourage the reader interested in more detail to consult a reference such as [Go02].

As its name suggests, SONET is designed as a carrier using optical fiber communications. In addition, all links in a SONET network operate at the same clock rate, making it a synchronous technology. That is, all the SONET transmitters send and receive according to a common clock frequency. As a result, SONET has some features that we have not yet explored in this book. However, before we get into any detail about communications and the structure of packets and frames, we need to provide an overview.

There are many levels of SONET signaling; the primary signaling mode is STS-1 (synchronous transport signal level 1). SONET defines an STS-1 frame as an 810-byte frame. (We'll discuss its format shortly.) Because of the synchronous nature of the technology, a SONET transmitter sends one frame every 125 μsec (10^{-6} seconds). This means that SONET sends one frame containing 8×810 bits 8000 times per second. Multiplying the numbers yields a bit rate of 51.84 Mbps, the STS-1 base rate. Other signal designations are STS-3, STS-9, STS-12, STS-18, STS-24, STS-36, STS-48, STS-92, and STS-192. In general, an STS-n signal has a bit rate equal to n times the bit rate for an STS-1 signal, or $n \times 51.84$ Mbps. So, for example, an STS-3 signal has a bit rate of 155.52 Mbps. The highest level, STS-192, provides a bit rate of about 9.953 Gbps. Signaling levels will no doubt increase as technology advances. It is typical for a higher-level signal to encapsulate several lower-level ones. For example, an STS-3 frame often contains three STS-1 frames.

Depending on the context of the discussion, the designation OC-n (optical carrier n) may be used. Typically, the STS designation refers to the electrical signals of devices that have an optical connection, and the OC designation represents the actual optical signal. It's therefore not unusual to see the terms STS-n and OC-n used interchangeably. That is, an STS-3 electrical signal corresponds to an OC-3 optical signal; either way, the bit rate is 155.52 Mbps.

Device Types   Before we give an overview of the SONET technology, we first describe three primary types of devices in a SONET network and how they work together (Figure 4.36). These devices also define the layers at which SONET operates. The three device types are as follows.

- **Regenerator.** A regenerator is a device that regenerates optical signals. Such a device is needed because optical signals, like electronic signals, degrade as they travel the optical fiber. If the fiber is too long, the signal degrades to the point of not being recognizable. Thus, for long stretches of fiber (over several

---

* Chapter 13 discusses ATM.

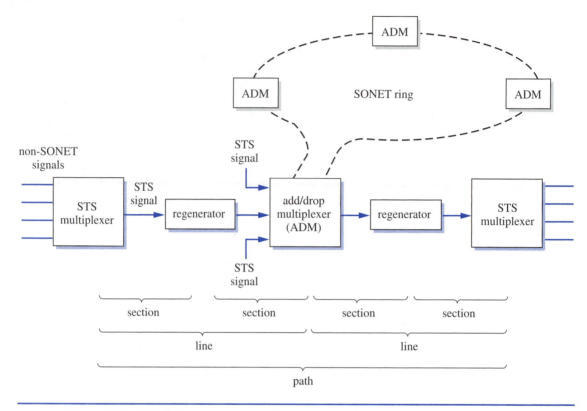

Figure 4.36   SONET Connections and Layers

dozen miles), a regenerator is needed to regenerate the bits in a SONET frame. Although Figure 4.36 shows only one regenerator between two other devices, more than one regenerator may be used in sequence. Using SONET terminology, a **section** is that part of the network between any two adjacent devices capable of regenerating a signal. We must also mention that a regenerator is not entirely a layer 1 device because it does modify a few bits in each frame that it regenerates. We'll outline the details shortly.

- **Add/drop multiplexer (ADM).** SONET ADMs may form a ring, often connecting points in large metropolitan areas, a state, or even a multistate region. SONET uses an ADM to extract traffic from outside the ring and merge it with existing traffic already on the ring. An ADM also works in reverse by providing an exit for ring traffic. Although the term *multiplexer* is used, the device is a little different from the time-division multiplexer we have described previously. In the previous case, the multiplexer combined signals from different sources into one common frame, and the demultiplexing ability extracted all the component signals and routed them to their separate destinations. In this case, the ADM need not multiplex and demultiplex all the signals in a common frame. A frame that already contains multiplexed data may be traveling the ring and arrive at an ADM. The ADM, in turn, may add some data to that frame. In other words, the entire frame is not multiplexed—just part of it is. Demultiplexing works analogously. Just some of the data may be extracted from a frame; it is not necessary to demultiplex the entire frame's contents. This is analogous to a rapid transit system. At the beginning of the run all passengers board the bus and find a seat (complete multiplexing), and at the end everyone leaves (complete demultiplexing). However, along the route passengers can board or depart at designated stops (add/drop multiplexing). The bus driver does not make everyone get off and then get back on.

The part of the network connecting an ADM to another ADM or STS multiplexer is a *line*. ADMs are sometimes referred to as *line terminating equipment*.

- **STS multiplexer.** The STS multiplexer takes signals from many different sources and generates an STS frame as output. That part of the network that connects two STS multiplexers is a *path,* and such devices are sometimes called *path terminating equipment* or *SONET terminals*. A signal from an external source that is multiplexed into an STS frame is called a *tributary*. A tributary may represent external sources such as an ATM stream, DS1 service, or any of a variety of different protocols.

These device types define three layers of SONET operations, each of which is comparable to functions found in a layer 2 data link protocol. The *section layer* is implemented in all devices and handles traffic along a physical section (direct optical link) of the network and is the lowest of the three layers. It provides framing (generation of special bit patterns to designate the start of a frame) and some parity checking to look for errors in transmissions. Chapter 6 discusses parity checking in more detail. The *line layer* is implemented in an ADM or STS multiplexer and deals with STS transmission. It locates payloads in a frame, checks for errors across a line, and provides for maintenance, synchronization, and line monitoring. Simple regeneration of frames is transparent to the line layer. The *path layer* is implemented only in an STS multiplexer and deals with end-to-end transmissions; it is responsible for multiplexing, defining the types and structure of payloads, and storing them in a frame. It also provides some maintenance and performance monitoring.

Payloads and Frames   The next step is to discuss SONET frames and their payloads. As stated previously, a SONET STS-1 frame contains 810 bytes, and frames are transmitted at 125-μsec intervals. In other words, a SONET transmitter produces a constant stream of STS-1 frames at the rate of 8000 per second. This poses a bit of a dilemma because information does not always arrive from external sources in such a synchronous fashion. In other words, although the SONET transmitters are synchronized, the external devices that provide them information are not. Thus, a logical question to ask is: How do we get data that arrive asynchronously to be encapsulated in frames that are transmitted synchronously?

One option might be to try to synchronize all the devices, but the range and scope of such devices make this impractical. Another option is to receive and buffer incoming data and drop it into frames as they are transmitted. However, if data arrive shortly after a transmitter begins sending a frame, the data must wait for the next outgoing frame, leaving the currently departing frame empty. This introduces delays into the transmission of data.

Figure 4.37 shows the approach that SONET uses. Data to be stored in a frame are called a **synchronous payload envelope (SPE)** and are defined at the path layer. Since the SPE and outgoing frame may not be synchronized, the SPE may be stored in two consecutive frames. How this is done is a function of both the SPE and frame formats. Figure 4.38a shows the structure of an STS-1 frame. The 810 bytes are organized in 90 columns and nine rows. The first 3 bytes in each of the first three rows are *section overhead* and are used for section layer activities. The first 3 bytes in each of the last six rows are *line overhead* and are used for line layer functions.

Figure 4.38b shows the relationship between an SPE and two consecutive STS-1 frames. In general, the SPE bytes (shaded region) are organized as nine rows of 87 columns and can fit entirely within a frame. However, this is not necessarily the case, because the SPE may be divided among two consecutive frames, with each SPE row split across two rows in a frame (or the first and last rows of consecutive frames). Remember, because the frames are sent at regular intervals, the SPE bytes are still transmitted in a consistent stream. It's just that the SONET layers recognize them as possibly distributed across two consecutive frames. Note also that each SPE has some overhead for path layer operations. This process is a bit like waiting for a bus at a designated location. However, instead of a bus stopping to pick up passengers, a stream of buses travel at a constant rate of speed, and people wait in line to jump on the buses as they go by. If a group were taking a bus to a ball game, then some in the group would get on the first bus. Because the bus never stopped, however, others in the group would not be able to board. They would have to wait for the next bus before jumping on. When they all jump off the moving buses at the ball park, the group would be reunited. (Please note that we are not recommending this procedure for rapid transit operations in any major city.)

Our final comments relate to the overhead bytes in the SONET frames and SPEs. Each overhead byte relates to actions performed in one of the three layers. For example, section overhead contains the following:

- **Channel ID.** This is particularly useful if several STS-1 frame bytes are combined into an STS-*n* frame. The channel ID distinguishes the bytes.

- **Framing pattern.** Two of the overhead bytes contain a framing pattern. This pattern indicates the start of the frame and allows the receiver to be

Figure 4.37   Relationship between a Frame and a Synchronous Payload Envelope

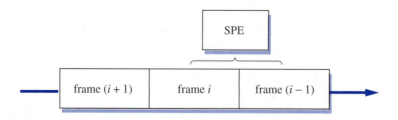

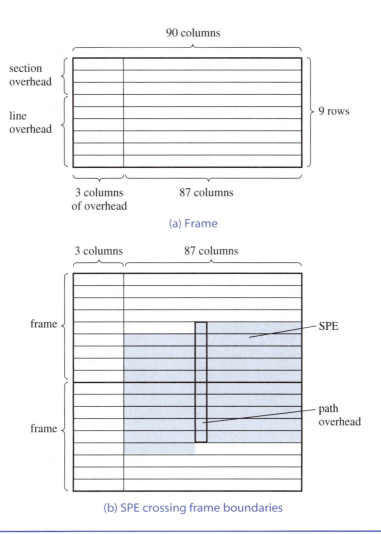

Figure 4.38   STS-1 Frames and an SPE

synchronized with the incoming bits. Because each frame is transmitted at regular intervals, the receiver knows that framing bytes arrive at regular intervals. It can also use this to detect a problem in the section. If several intervals pass without the arrival of framing patterns, then the section layer declares that a problem has occurred.

- **Parity byte.** Chapter 6 discusses parity in detail. Essentially, a parity byte can be used to determine whether any bits were damaged as they traveled along the section. The parity byte actually checks for errors in the previous frame.

- **Orderwire byte.** One byte in each frame (or 1 byte every 125 μsec) is used to provide a 64 Kbps voice communication channel to be used in maintenance activities. It is also called a *service channel;* technicians or engineers can use it for troubleshooting or for maintenance between two adjacent devices in the network without interrupting other traffic.

- **User channel.** This provides a 64 Kbps channel that local applications can use.
- **OAM communication.** OAM stands for operations, administration, and maintenance. Three bytes per frame provide a 192 Kbps channel that is used to maintain, monitor, and troubleshoot section-level communications, again without interrupting other traffic. In an oversimplification, these bytes make sure things run smoothly.

Line overhead contains the following:

- **SPE locator.** Because an SPE can begin anywhere in a frame, there are three overhead bytes that locate the byte in the frame where the SPE starts.
- **Parity byte.** This parity check is for errors that might occur across a line.
- **Automatic protection switching.** Two bytes are used to detect any problems that may occur in a multiplexer and are designed to protect all connections within a line. Details are complex, but automatic protection switching is designed to provide a measure of fault tolerance so that if a line fails, there is a backup line that can take its place.
- **OAM communication.** This is essentially the same as the OAM mentioned previously, but at a different layer.
- **Orderwire byte.** Again, this is the same as the orderwire mentioned previously, but at a different layer.

Path overhead contains the following:

- **STS path trace.** The sender uses 1 byte in each frame to send a predetermined sequence of bytes repeatedly. The receiver compares the incoming bytes with the known pattern; if any deviation from the pattern occurs, it knows there is a problem with the connection.
- **Parity byte.** Parity again, but across a path.
- **STS path signal label.** Recall that SONET can be a carrier for many other technologies. This byte identifies the protocol at a higher layer and, in effect, indicates the contents of the SPE.
- **Path status.** Allows the receiving entity to indicate the path-terminating status to the sender (the originator of the path).
- **User channel.** Same as the previous user channel, but operates between path elements.
- **Virtual tributary indicator.** We had indicated previously that a tributary represents a signal from an external source (usually one that is slower than STS-1 speeds). SONET allows data from more than one source to be included in an SPE. Thus, an SPE contains information from multiple sources, each of which is a *virtual tributary*. There are different ways to structure an SPE depending on the sources of data. This indicator specifies which way is used.

4.7 CONTENTION PROTOCOLS

Multiplexing (particularly TDM) goes a long way toward making a medium available to many users, but it is not enough. To route all users through a multiplexer onto a medium is unrealistic for two reasons. First, there may be too many users for a single multiplexer. Second, the logistics may prohibit a user from using a particular multiplexer.

A highway system provides a nice analogy. Interstate highway 94 connects Chicago and Seattle. In Chicago, many interchanges (the automobile's multiplexer) allow a driver access to the highway. But what if someone in Fargo, North Dakota, wants access to the highway in order to drive to Seattle? Would we expect her to first drive to Chicago, some 600 miles in the wrong direction? Of course not. She simply uses another access point to the interstate.

Communications media are similar. The multiplexer provides access for many users to one access point, but a large network requires many access points, just as the interstate highway system does. Access to the medium from many entry points is called **contention.** It is controlled with a **contention protocol.** Figure 4.39 shows what happens with no contention protocol in the highway system. Vehicles enter randomly and collisions occur periodically. At best they are unpleasant; at worst they are fatal. Fortunately, the highway system is not set up this way (although, with some drivers, you'd never know it). Figure 4.40 shows a common and simple contention strategy for traffic. This stop-and-go protocol uses traffic lights to control access. As long as motorists abide by the protocol, they can avoid the situation

Figure 4.39   No Contention Protocol

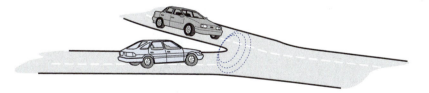

Figure 4.40   Stop-and-Go Access Protocol

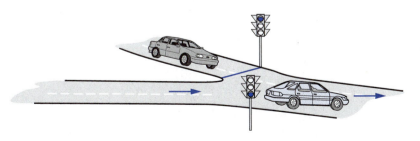

shown in Figure 4.39. We assume that unless you are from a remote area in the Himalayas you are familiar with the details of this protocol.

Communications require some protocol to ensure that transmitted data reach their destination. This section explores some of the protocols used. Perhaps not surprisingly, there are many options, depending on the actual medium, the amount of traffic, and the sophistication of the users' needs (which has a direct correlation to cost).

ALOHA PROTOCOLS

One of the earliest contention protocols was developed in an area quite different from the remote area of the Himalayas. The **Aloha protocol** was developed at the University of Hawaii in the early 1970s. We also call it **pure Aloha,** in contrast to another protocol we discuss shortly. The Aloha system was designed to establish communication among the islands using a packet radio system. The word *packet* or *frame** refers to the information broadcast during a single transmission. Terminals (Figure 4.41) were connected to a radio channel, which in turn broadcast information from the terminal to a central facility called the Menehune. Devices broadcast frames at the same frequency. Consequently, the medium (the airspace) was truly shared. Any attempt to broadcast two different frames simultaneously using the

Figure 4.41   Aloha System

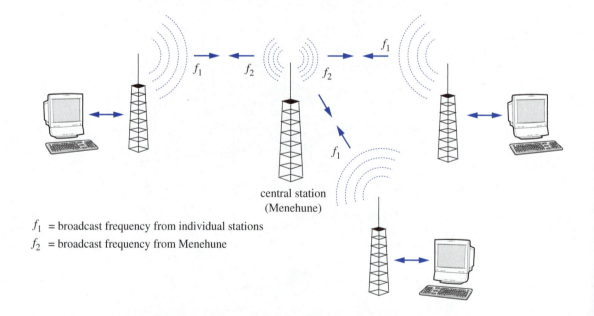

central station
(Menehune)

f_1 = broadcast frequency from individual stations
f_2 = broadcast frequency from Menehune

---

* Depending on the protocol, the term *packet* or *frame* may be used to indicate the contents of a single transmission. For now we continue to use the term *frame*.

same frequency disrupted both signals. The end result, of course, was that neither transmission was successful.

The Aloha protocol worked on a very simple principle. Essentially, it allowed for any device to broadcast at any time. If two signals collided, so be it. Each device would simply wait a random time and try again. The highway analogy would be to enter the freeway with your eyes closed. If you have a collision, get a new car and try again. Although it would be an expensive protocol for traffic control, it worked well for the Aloha system.

Collisions were detected quite easily. When the Menehune received a frame, it sent an acknowledgment. It used a different frequency so as not to interfere with incoming signals. If a device received an acknowledgment, it concluded that its frame was transmitted successfully. If not, it assumed a collision had occurred and waited to send again. Because each device waited a random time, the chance that two or more devices waited the same time was reduced. In turn this reduced the chances of a second collision. If they did collide a second time (perhaps even with another device), the same rules applied: Wait a random amount of time and try again.

In this type of situation, collisions occur not only when two devices send simultaneously, but also when two transmissions overlap even by the smallest amount. It does not matter if all or part of the frame is destroyed. It's like receiving a telephone call and hearing "I've got good news for you. You have just $%^#$%." If the "$%^#$%" represents static, you don't know if you won the lottery, received an inheritance, or were elected to political office (good news?). What's lost is gone, and conventional wisdom dictates the entire frame be sent again.

The advantage of the Aloha protocol is its simplicity. It works very well if there are not many transmissions, but if a device broadcasts more frequently or there are more devices, the protocol is less effective. In either case, more collisions occur—just as they do on heavily traveled roads.

When we are faced with increased transmissions, what can we do to decrease the collisions? First, let us analyze a little more closely how collisions occur. As stated, a collision occurs if any part of two transmissions overlaps. Suppose that T is the time required for one transmission and that two devices must transmit. The total time required for both devices to do so successfully is $2T$.

Next, consider an arbitrary interval of time $2T$. Unless one device begins its transmission at the start of the interval, completing both transmissions before the end of the interval is impossible. (Why?) Consequently, allowing a device to transmit at arbitrary times can waste time up to $2T$.

As an alternative, suppose we divide time into intervals (slots) of T units each and require each device to begin each transmission at the beginning of a slot. In other words, even if a device is ready to send in the middle of a slot, it must wait until the start of the next one (Figure 4.42b). This way, the only time a collision occurs is when both devices become ready in the same slot. Contrast this to the previous scenario (Figure 4.42a), where a collision occurs if the second device transmits when the frame is ready.

Requiring a device to transmit at the beginning of a time slot is the **slotted Aloha protocol.** According to the previous discussion, it would seem to perform better than the pure Aloha protocol. In fact, a rigorous analysis of both protocols

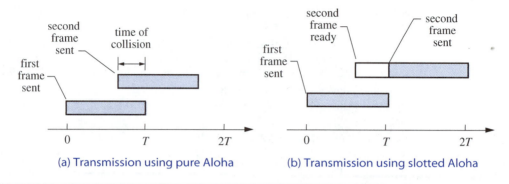

(a) Transmission using pure Aloha   (b) Transmission using slotted Aloha

Figure 4.42 Transmission Using Pure Aloha and Slotted Aloha

shows that the slotted Aloha protocol does perform better. We'll not provide a detailed description of the analysis here, but we will summarize the findings and interpret them. More rigorous discussions are found in references [Wa98], [St00], [Ro75], [Ru89], and [Mi87].

Intuitively, we know there is a relation between the number of frames sent and the number sent successfully. A mathematical model can be created that, under certain assumptions, defines the relation as follows.

Let G represent the traffic measured as the average number of frames generated per slot. Let S be the success rate measured as the average number of frames sent successfully per slot. (e is the mathematical constant 2.718. . . .) The relation between G and S for both pure and slotted Aloha is

$S = Ge^{-2G}$ (pure Aloha)

$S = Ge^{-G}$ (slotted Aloha)

Your next logical question is probably "So what? What does it mean?" For an answer, look at the graphs in Figure 4.43. The vertical axis represents S and the horizontal one represents G. Values for S range from 0 to 1. Since we have chosen the slot time to equal that required to send one frame, S can be no larger.

First note that both graphs have the same basic shape. If G is small, so is S. This makes sense because few frames will be sent successfully if there are only a few frames generated. As G increases so does S, up to a point. More transmissions means more successfully sent frames, until they start colliding. At that point, which corresponds to the high point on each graph, the success rate decreases. As G continues to increase, S approaches 0. This corresponds to the situation in which there are so many frames that they are almost always colliding. It becomes a rare event when a frame gets through without colliding.

The model shows how the pure and slotted Aloha protocols compare. Differential calculus shows how to calculate the maximum value in each case. If you are familiar with the details, just take the derivative of each function with respect to G and equate with 0. In any case, the maximum for slotted Aloha occurs at $G = 1$, for

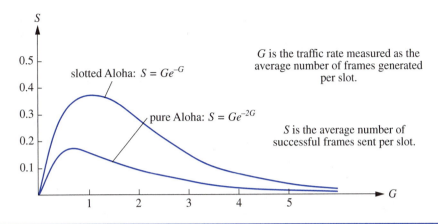

Figure 4.43   Success Rate for Slotted and Pure Aloha Protocols

which $S = 1/e \cong 0.368$. In other words, the best rate of successful transmissions is approximately 0.368 frame per slot time. Another way to say it is that about 37% of the time will be spent on successful transmissions. The rest will be spent on collisions or idle time.

For pure Aloha, the maximum occurs at $G = 0.5$, for which $S = 1/2e \cong 0.184$. Again, this means that approximately 18% of the time is spent on successful transmissions.

At first it may seem strange that slotted Aloha generally won't provide a better success rate. Providing not much more than a frame every three slots seems like underachieving. But a critical assumption the models make is that frames become ready randomly. There is no intent to coordinate transmissions beyond waiting until the beginning of the next slot. As the model shows, this important assumption degrades performance.

Another question might be, Should we try to coordinate transmissions in order to achieve better efficiency? In general, the answer is no. If you were at a personal computer connected to a network, you would probably find it inconvenient to coordinate your network access with others. Most users want access on demand and expect the protocols and hardware to provide good response.

CARRIER SENSE MULTIPLE ACCESS

An observant person might ask, "Couldn't we improve on the success rate if the devices listened to the medium* for existing transmissions before sending its own?" The devices certainly have the capability to determine when frames are in transit.

---

* Although the Aloha system was developed for packet radio, we use the term *medium* in a very general sense. Unless otherwise specified, it may be air space, fiber, cable, or twisted pair.

Why not hold a frame until another has finished? This way a device would not destroy a frame currently being sent, and the success rate should improve.

The idea of listening makes sense and is used in many networks today, such as Ethernet. (Actually, Ethernet uses a variation of it that we describe later.) We call this approach **Carrier Sense Multiple Access (CSMA).** In general, the protocol is described simply. If a device has a frame to send, it follows these steps:

1. Listen to the medium for any activity.

2. If there is no activity, transmit; otherwise, wait.

Does this system eliminate collisions? It will eliminate some but not all. A collision still can occur if two (or more) devices want to transmit at nearly the same time. If there is currently no activity, both conclude that it is safe to send and do so. The result, of course, is a collision. However, such collisions generally are less common because there is a very small time delay between when a device detects no activity and when its transmitted frame reaches other devices. For a collision to occur, another device must decide to transmit within this period of time. Because the interval is small, so is the probability that the second device will send a frame in that interval.

But collisions still can occur, and variations on CSMA try to improve efficiency by reducing their number. With one type, **p-persistent CSMA,** the device continues to monitor an active medium. When it becomes quiet, the device transmits with probability $p(0 \leq p \leq 1)$. Otherwise, it waits for one time slot (probability of $1 - p$). Note that if $p = 1$ the device always transmits when the medium is quiet. If $p = 0$ it always waits. With **nonpersistent CSMA,** the device does not continue to monitor the medium. It simply waits one time slot and again checks for activity. At this point it transmits if the medium is idle; otherwise, it waits another time slot.

Collisions still can be a problem, especially with p-persistent CSMA. If two devices want to transmit at nearly the same time and the medium is idle, a collision occurs. Although collisions for this reason may not be common, they occur in other ways. For example, consider the case where $p = 1$. If two (or more) devices become ready while another is transmitting, both wait. But since $p = 1$, both devices send when the first is done, and their frames collide. As more devices transmit, this scenario occurs more frequently and collisions become more of a problem.

One way to reduce the frequency of collisions is to lower the probability that a device will send when a previous one is done. For example, suppose two devices using a 0.5-persistent protocol are waiting. When the medium is idle, each sends with a probability of 0.5. Thus, four events occur with equal probability:

- They both transmit immediately.
- They both wait.
- The first sends and the second waits.
- The second sends and the first waits.

Rather than a certain collision, there is a 0.5 probability that one will be able to send at the beginning of the next slot. (Note, however, that there is also a 0.25 probability that neither will send. This is another type of inefficiency, which we will discuss shortly.)

Figure 4.44 shows the success rates of various *p*-persistent protocols. We will not discuss the equations that generate these curves because they are somewhat complex. However, we do consider the results and what they mean. If you are interested in the actual equations or their derivations, see reference [Kl75].

In general, smaller values of *p* result in fewer collisions. However, the number of waiting devices increases and causes a proportionate increase in the chances no one will send at all. Still, as the number of devices increases, the traffic goes up. The probability that at least two will send simultaneously increases, and eventually collisions become a problem again.

With nonpersistent CSMA, no device waits for the medium to be idle. Instead, each checks periodically and waits one time slot if it is busy. Thus, the only times collisions occur are when two devices detect a quiet medium at nearly the same time. As Figure 4.44 shows, the success rate increases with *G;* for large values of *G,* it is much better than that of persistent or Aloha protocols.

The success rate is only one statistic and can be misleading, however. As we defined it, the success rate is impressive, but it isn't achieved until there is a glut of frames that devices want to send. For example, the model's equations show that a success rate of 0.9 is achieved when *G* = 9. In other words, 90% of the time is spent sending frames only when they are generated at a rate of nine per slot. This is a rate that exceeds the medium's capacity by a factor of 9. In this case we have other

Figure 4.44   Success Rate of CSMA and Aloha Protocols

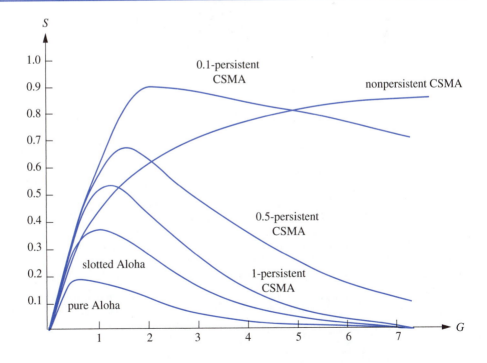

problems far exceeding those caused by the protocol. The devices are saturating the medium, thus causing delays.

A good analogy here is a bank that hires only one teller on its busiest days. Customers wait about 45 minutes to make a deposit, and they complain to the manager. The manager responds by stating that the teller is busy most of the time and therefore there is no problem. It's now time to take your money and hide it in your mattress.

For smaller values of G, the persistent protocols have higher success rates because idle time is more of a problem for the nonpersistent protocols. If a device detects another one transmitting, it waits a full slot. If the transmission ends well before that time, the medium is unnecessarily idle. For lighter traffic, the nonpersistent protocol is not aggressive enough.

COLLISION DETECTION

Another way to improve the success rate of transmissions is to reduce the time during which collisions occur. Previously, when a device had a frame, it sent the whole thing and concluded that a collision had occurred when it did not get a response. The problem is that the medium is unusable by others during the time the frame is colliding. Is there some way to have a device monitor the medium to listen for collisions? If so, it could stop transmissions immediately and decrease the time that signals are colliding.

Figure 4.45 illustrates. In Figure 4.45a, the time of collision spans from the transmission of the first frame to the end of the second one. The wasted time could extend up to two time slots. In Figure 4.45b, both devices stop transmitting when the collision occurs. Typically, each will send a jamming signal (a type of electronic scream) to ensure that all devices know a collision has occurred. In this case, the wasted time spans only part of a slot and the time required to send a short jamming signal.

Figure 4.45   Collision with and without Detection

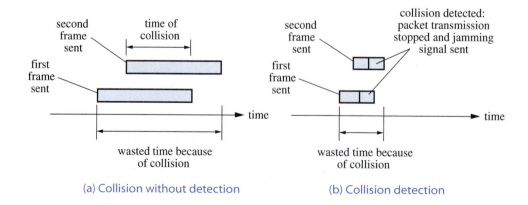

(a) Collision without detection

(b) Collision detection

Such a protocol exists and is commonly used with CSMA. We call it **Carrier Sense Multiple Access with Collision Detection (CSMA/CD).** CSMA/CD typically is used with one of the persistence algorithms. We summarize it as follows:

- If a medium is busy, the device waits per the persistence algorithm.
- If the medium is quiet, the device transmits the frame and continues to listen.
- If the device detects a collision, it immediately stops transmitting and sends a short jamming signal.
- After a collision, it waits a random amount of time before trying to send again.

The last step is important to reduce the chances that two frames will collide a second time. There is certainly no point in two devices waiting the same amount of time just to have their frames collide again.

Two issues that surface in a discussion of collision detection are frame size and transmission distance. If frames are too large, one device can monopolize the medium. On the other hand, collision detection requires that frames be at least a minimum size so that a device can detect a collision before it finishes sending the frame. If it detects a collision after the frame is sent, it does not know if its frame was involved. The frame may have reached its destination, and two other frames collided. You might respond by suggesting that we could use the method described previously that looks for an acknowledgment. We could, but we would defeat the reason for collision detection in the first place: to avoid sending the entire frame before a collision occurs.

Next question: How small should a frame be? The answer depends on the maximum time it takes to detect a collision. Sometimes a collision is detected almost immediately. In other cases, the signal may travel a very long distance only to meet another signal. Even then the noise from the collision must travel back to the sending device. Consequently, in the worst case, the time to detect a collision is twice the time it takes a signal to span the longest distance covered by the medium.

As an example, suppose the following:

- A device sends frames over a coaxial cable at a rate of 10 Mbps.
- The largest distance between two devices on the cable is 2 km.
- A signal propagates along a cable at a rate of 200 m/μsec (meters per microsecond).

In the worst case, the frame travels 2 km (taking 10 μsec) before it collides with another. The corrupted signal then travels 2 km back to the sending device. The round trip takes a total of 20 μsec. Thus, a frame should require at least 20 μsec to send. A data rate of 10 Mbps is the same as putting out 10 bits per μsec; therefore, the device could put out 200 bits in 20 μsec. This would mean that the frame should be at least 200 bits, or 200/8 = 25 bytes long. Chapter 9 discusses specific networks and protocols, and we will see that they do indeed specify minimum frame sizes.

The other problem in collision detection is distance. For example, listening and collision detection do not work well for satellite networks, in which the time required for a frame to travel from ground to satellite and back is approximately one quarter of a second. That may not sound like much, but in a world measured in microseconds it is a very long time. If a ground device listened for satellite transmissions, it could detect only what was sent one quarter of a second ago. Consequently, it may hear nothing when in reality someone else's frame is speeding up to the satellite on a collision course with anything that might be sent.

A strong advantage of the protocols discussed so far is that the protocol need not be changed when new devices are added. A device need not have knowledge of any other particular device. The ability to add new devices without changing the protocol makes growth easier. A significant disadvantage, however, is the fact that collisions do occur. We have argued that the protocols can work well, yet there is no theoretical limit on the number of collisions that can occur. There is always a small chance that unusual delays will occur. For most applications a periodic delay is not serious, but they can be disastrous in real-time applications such as chemical and nuclear plants, air traffic control systems, or factory automation.

In some cases, the wait times after collisions occur are not completely random. One common technique defines the wait time as an integral multiple of a slot time. The number of slot times must be limited so a device does not wait excessively long.

Defining the limits is not easy, however. For example, if the limit were large, random waits might also be large and cause excessive idle time. On the other hand, the larger number of slot times from which to choose would lessen the chance that two or more devices will choose the same one and collide again. If the limit were fairly small, colliding devices would not wait long; however, with fewer slot times to choose from, the chances for a second collision increase.

A technique called the **binary exponential backoff algorithm** varies the limit. It works in the following way:

- If a device's frame collides for the first time, wait 0 or 1 time slot (chosen randomly) before trying again.
- If it collides a second time, wait 0, 1, 2, or 3 slots (again, chosen randomly).
- After a third collision, wait anywhere from 0 to 7 slots.
- In general, after n collisions, wait anywhere from 0 to $2^n - 1$ slots if $n \leq 10$. If $n > 10$ wait between 0 and 1024 (2^{10}) slots.
- After 16 collisions, give up. There is probably an error somewhere, and the inability to transmit the frame is reported to the network administration. In this case, other software or a network manager must investigate in order to determine the problem.

This approach clearly tries to minimize excessive waits by keeping the number of possible time slots small. After all, if two devices collide, there is a 50% chance they will succeed on the next try (assuming that no other devices are sending).

If many devices collide, however, the chances are very small that even one will be successful on the next try. The successful one would have to choose either 0 or 1 slot, with all the others making the other choice. By increasing the number of possible slots after each collision, the chances of colliding again decrease exponentially. The only time a large number of slots is possible is when all previous attempts have failed. In this case, long waits by some may be the only solution.

COLLISION AVOIDANCE

In the wireless LAN environment, detecting collisions is not always an option. For example, suppose two devices, A and B, send to device C at the same time. It's possible that neither A nor B could see each other's signal. If they transmit via infrared, a solid barrier would prevent each from sensing the other's signal. If they transmit via low-power radio waves, they could be too far apart (even though C could be within range of both). In such cases, CSMA/CD is not an option.

The 802.11 protocol for wireless LANs adopted a **collision avoidance** scheme. Despite the name, the protocol does not avoid all collisions; however, it does significantly reduce them. It's a complicated protocol, and we will defer a discussion of it until Chapter 9.

TOKEN PASSING

The previous protocols took a somewhat anarchistic approach to sending signals by allowing devices to send whenever they wanted. A logical question at this point is whether there is some way devices can agree in advance about who sends when. In other words, is there some way they can take turns?

The difficulty with many networks is that no central control or authority makes such decisions. Still, there is a way for all participating devices to agree on a protocol for taking turns: **token passing,** a common protocol used in token ring networks. In a token ring network (Figure 4.46), the devices are commonly personal

Figure 4.46   Token Ring Network

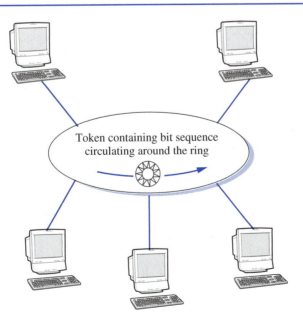

computers connected circularly to a wire or fiber medium. A **network interface card (NIC)** connects each to the network and contains the hardware and logic allowing a personal computer to communicate with the network.

The contention protocol here is an orderly one compared with the "send when you can" protocols discussed previously. The devices in a token ring execute a protocol allowing them to take turns sending. The process involves a specially formatted frame called a **token.** It contains bit codes that the NIC recognizes, and it circles the ring visiting each NIC. According to the protocol, a PC can send when its NIC has the token.*

Chapter 9 describes exactly how devices exchange frames. In general, the concept is as follows. When a device receives the token, one of two things occurs. If it has nothing to send, it simply sends the token on to its neighbor. If it does have something to send, it inserts the data and the destination address into the token. It also changes some control bits to identify the token as a data frame (one containing information). Proceeding this way allows the token to visit each device and pick up data when they are available. (It's a lot like an electronic Federal Express traveling around picking up and dropping off frames.)

When a device receives a frame, it examines the control bits. If they indicate that the frame contains no data, the device proceeds as before according to whether it has data to send. If the frame contains data, the device examines the destination address. If it is destined for some other device, it just routes it to its neighbor. Otherwise, the device copies the information. It then puts the frame back onto the ring. Eventually the frame returns to the sending device, which removes it and puts the token or another frame back onto the ring. Proceeding this way, the data eventually reach their destination.

Token ring operations can be expanded to include prioritization and a reservation system that allows a device to reserve a token that already has data for future use. We will discuss these operations in Section 9.6.

Rings have another advantage similar to that of the protocols discussed earlier: New devices can be added easily. When a device sends a frame to its neighbor, it does not know if that neighbor has been added recently or has been there a long time. Consequently, devices need not be notified of changing neighbors.

One disadvantage is that one device can hog the token. In addition, a break in the link between two consecutive devices can bring the network down because the token cannot circulate. Another problem occurs if a device fails while it is sending a token onto the ring. The result is an incomplete and invalid token circulating the ring. Devices looking for the proper token format are waiting for something that is not on the ring. Yet another problem occurs if, for some reason, the device responsible for removing a frame fails. Every device passes the frame to its neighbor, and the frame circulates forever. These problems all have solutions; we will discuss some of them in Chapter 9.

---

* In some situations this is not true. Chapter 9 provides a more detailed discussion of the token ring protocol.

Table 4.5   Summary of Contention Protocols

PROTOCOL	SIGNIFICANCE	ADVANTAGES	DISADVANTAGES
Aloha	Variations are useful in satellite communications, where listening is not practical because of the time delay.	Simple approach.	Potential delays because a device may not know its frame has collided until well after it is sent.
p-Persistent	Combined with CSMA/CD, a popular choice for Ethernet.	Tends to decrease the chances of an idle medium.	May have excessive collisions under heavy traffic, wasting bandwidth of the medium.
Nonpersistent	According to the model, the success rate does not decrease under heavy loads.	Reduces the number of collisions, especially under heavy loads.	Transmission medium may be idle even when there are devices wanting to send something.
CSMA/CD	Combined with 1-persistence, it is commonly used with Ethernet.	Reduces the time of a collision.	No theoretical upper bound on the time it takes to transmit a frame successfully.
Token ring	Once popular protocol used in office and business environments.	Upper bound on the time a device must wait before getting the token.	Unless recovery methods are built into the protocol, a malfunction at one device can destroy a token or break the ring, thus affecting the entire network.

SUMMARY OF PROTOCOLS

The contention protocols we have discussed in this section represent the most common ones. Table 4.5 summarizes them. Other protocols do exist. If you are interested in them, see references [St00] and [Ta03].

4.8   SUMMARY

This chapter dealt largely with the devices, systems, protocols, and technologies critical to making connections. The simple capability to transmit information in the form of bits is just not sufficient unless there is a way for multiple devices to interact, interface, and share transmission media. Otherwise, a device transmits bits that just end up in the netherworld. In other words, there is transmission but no communication. We need to make sure that those transmitted bits get to their intended destination and that the systems that carry those signals function according to specific protocols. Important concepts presented in this chapter are as follows:

- Communication carriers and devices include the telephone system, PBXs (private branch exchanges), cellular phones, and fax machines. The telephone system connects the largest number of people. For many years it was used primarily for voice communications, but each year finds more people using it for data communications. In fact, some organizations install a private system called a PBX for both voice and data. For internal company communication, many PBXs bypass the central office but still have trunks to the interexchange telephone system.

- Cellular telephones provide telephone users freedom from a physical connection. An area is divided into regions, or cells, each of which has a transmitter capable of communicating with the telephone system. The cellular telephone then communicates with a transmitter within the cell.

- The fax machine combines the two technologies of copying and transmission. Like a copier, it reproduces images on paper. However, it reproduces them electronically and transmits them through the telephone system. The fax on the other end receives the signals and recreates the original image.

- There are different modes of communication. Parallel transmission sends bits simultaneously using several lines, and serial transmission sends them in sequence using a single line. Simplex communication is one-way only. Half-duplex communication allows two-way communication, but the sending and receiving devices must alternate. Full-duplex communication allows both devices to send simultaneously.

- Another factor in communicating is timing. Asynchronous transmission sends each byte separately, with a start and stop bit before and after the byte. Thus, bytes arrive with random gaps of time in between. Synchronous transmission groups bytes into a frame format and sends the entire frame. Still, the data in consecutive frames may arrive in a bursty fashion, with much data arriving quickly and perhaps longer waits for the next batch. Isochronous transmission guarantees that the data from an application arrive at a consistent rate at all times. This is most suitable for real-time applications such as viewing images as they happen or listening to music as it is played.

- The EIA-232 protocol connecting a DCE and DTE is probably the most well-known interface protocol. It defines circuit definitions and rules that both devices must follow to communicate with each other. The X.21 interface was designed for digital interfaces. Compared with the EIA standards, it uses fewer lines between the DTE and DCE but requires more logic to interpret the exchanged signals.

- The universal serial bus was designed to simplify the connection of peripherals to a personal computer. Devices are hot pluggable, which means they can be connected or disconnected without turning off the machine. Using hubs, a user can connect up to 127 devices to a personal computer. USB devices communicate using serial communication and operate in a master/slave mode that dictates that all communication be coordinated by the host (usually the PC).

A typical approach is to have the host poll various devices, instructing each to send if it has data or to alert a device that the host is sending data. USB supports bulk, control, interrupt, and isochronous transfers to reflect the different types of devices it can connect.

- Like USB, FireWire was designed to simplify connecting peripherals. Unlike USB, it was designed more for devices that support multimedia applications and require a high bit rate. There are a couple of important differences between FireWire and USB. One is FireWire's use of a six-wire cable and a strobe signal that the receiver uses to synchronize itself with incoming bits. The other is that FireWire is a peer-to-peer protocol. Devices can communicate independent of a host with the aid of arbitration mechanisms that are built into the FireWire protocol.

- Many applications do not need the full power of a high-speed network, or the cost may make separate connections prohibitive. A multiplexer can serve as an interface between several devices and a single network connection. Frequency-division multiplexers combine analog signals from different channels into a single analog signal. Time-division multiplexers put bit streams from different sources into a single frame of fixed length. Statistical multiplexers also combine bit streams into a single frame, but vary the frame size depending on which sources are sending data. Wave-division multiplexing combines optical signals of different frequencies onto a common fiber and, at the other end, separates the components much like a prism separates different colors of light.

- Two common digital carriers are T1 and SONET. A T1 carrier uses time-division multiplexing to combine 8-bit groups from different sources into a common DS1 frame. A common arrangement is for a pulse code modulator at each source to generate 8000 eight-bit groups per second, for a bit rate necessary to support telephone conversations. SONET is a complex carrier service commonly used for long-distance communications. SONET transmitters generate 810-byte STS-1 frames once every 125 μsec, or 8000 frames per second. This defines a base signaling rate of 54.84 Mbps. A higher rate is STS-192, which corresponds to 9.953 Gbps. Synchronous payload envelopes that contain data are then placed into one or more frames. SONET uses regenerators to regenerate most of the bits in a frame, add/drop multiplexers to merge external data with SONET frames without multiplexing the entire contents, and STS multiplexers to perform full multiplexing of external signals into STS frames.

- Because a network is meant to service many users, it must allow them all to communicate. This means making decisions when two or more users want to send simultaneously. One approach, the Aloha protocol, was designed for packet radio communication in the Hawaiian Islands. If two frames overlap, they collide. When the sending device hears no acknowledgment, it sends again. Slotted Aloha is similar, but requires that each device send only at the start of predefined time slots.

- CSMA takes Aloha one step farther by listening to the medium before sending. It sends only if there is no traffic. If there is traffic, its next step depends on which variation is used. With *p*-persistent CSMA, the device continues to monitor the medium. When the medium becomes quiet, there is a probability of *p* that the device will send. With nonpersistent CSMA, the device does not monitor the medium. It just waits a random number of slot times and tries again. The last variation, CSMA/CD, uses a collision detection technique to stop sending if a device detects a collision. The intent is to decrease the amount of time during which frames collide.

- Another protocol is token passing, found in token ring networks. A special frame called a token circulates among the devices. A device can send only when it has the token. A token ring device is organized physically in a ring.

Review Questions

1. List the five major components of the telephone system.
2. Describe how a cellular telephone works.
3. What is a private branch exchange?
4. What is the difference between roaming and a handoff in the context of cellular telephones?
5. Distinguish between serial and parallel communication.
6. Distinguish among synchronous, asynchronous, and isochronous communication.
7. List typical fields in a data frame and what they contain.
8. Distinguish among simplex, half-duplex, and full-duplex communication.
9. Are the following statements TRUE or FALSE? Why?
   a. Parallel and serial communications require different types of cables.
   b. An EIA-232 interface requires a 25-pin connector.
   c. Two compatible PCs can communicate by installing a cable between each one's EIA-232 port.
   d. Devices using an EIA-232 interface can automatically communicate.
   e. USB devices cannot communicate independently with each other.
   f. Although most personal computers have just a couple of USB ports, it is possible to connect over 100 USB-compatible devices.
   g. Some applications can tolerate losing some data due to transmission errors.
   h. A FireWire cable has two sets of twisted wires to transmit two bit streams in parallel.
   i. FireWire-compatible devices do not need a host PC to coordinate communication.
   j. Frequency-division multiplexing is a form of parallel communication.
   k. Time-division multiplexing applies only to digital communications.
   l. SONET frames are transmitted only when there is data available.
   m. A time-division multiplexer allows its combined input capability to exceed its output capability.

    n. The nonpersistent contention protocols outperform the persistent protocols in all cases.

    o. One-persistent is optimal among the *p*-persistent protocols because a device never waits voluntarily, thus wasting time.

10. Distinguish between a DTE and DCE.

11. What is a null modem?

12. In Figure 4.15, why is each DTE's pin 20 connected to the other's pin 8?

13. In Figure 4.15, why are each DTE's pins 4 and 5 connected?

14. Distinguish between a peer-to-peer protocol and a master/slave one.

15. List the different transfer types supported by USB and describe each one.

16. Distinguish between a USB frame and packet.

17. Why do USB data packets not contain an address?

18. What is polling and why is it necessary?

19. What is a daisy chain? How does it differ from connecting devices to a common bus?

20. What is a strobe signal? What is its advantage? Disadvantage?

21. What two types of communication does FireWire support?

22. Distinguish between frequency-division multiplexing and time-division multiplexing.

23. What is a multiplexer?

24. What are guard bands?

25. What is a channel in the context of time-division multiplexing?

26. Distinguish among a carrier signal, a modulating signal, and a modulated signal.

27. What is a primary motivation for using a multiplexer?

28. Why does a DS1 frame field have 8 bits for each channel?

29. Distinguish between an add/drop multiplexer and an STS multiplexer.

30. Why does SONET not guarantee that a payload will be wholly contained in a frame?

31. Distinguish among a section, line, and path in a SONET carrier system.

32. What is a contention protocol?

33. Describe the Aloha protocol, listing its advantages and disadvantages.

34. Distinguish between slotted and pure Aloha.

35. What is the difference between 0-persistent CSMA and nonpersistent CSMA?

36. Why does collision detection improve the performance of CSMA?

37. Why does the performance of persistent contention protocols degrade as G increases, whereas the reverse is true of a nonpersistent protocol?

38. What is the binary exponential backoff algorithm?

39. What is a token?

Exercises

1. Why do asynchronous communications require additional start and stop bits? What is wrong with letting the first bit in a transmission act as a start bit and the last one act as a stop bit?

2. Since parallel communications transmit bits simultaneously, why not design parallel communications with an arbitrarily large number of parallel lines to decrease transmission time?

3. One can argue that even synchronous communications have an asynchronous component. How so?

4. What is a minimal set of circuits required to establish full-duplex communication over an EIA-232 interface?

5. Why must the DTE assert an RTS (Request to Send) circuit before sending to the DCE, but the DCE is not required to assert any RTS line prior to sending to the DTE?

6. Some null modems connect a DTE's pin 20 to its own pins 5 and 6. What purpose does this serve?

7. Some null modems connect a DTE's pin 4 to its own pin 5 and to the other DTE's pin 8. What purpose does this serve?

8. If you have a personal computer or access to a device that has an EIA-232 interface, check the manual to determine what circuits are used.

9. Write a program to produce a graph of a modulating signal and a modulated signal similar to those of Figure 4.28.

10. Suppose you could type 100 words per minute and that the average word length is six characters (including spaces). What is the minimum number of USB frames per second you would expect a USB-compatible keyboard to be polled?

11. Suppose a FireWire device sends the bits 01100011000 over the FireWire cable. Sketch both the signal corresponding to the data bits and the strobe signal.

12. Suppose five devices are connected to a statistical time-division multiplexer (similar to the situation in Figure 4.31) and that each produces output as shown here. Construct the frame that the multiplexer sends.

```
Device 1: . . . .ø    A₃    ø    A₂    A₁
Device 2: . . . .B₄   B₃    ø    B₂    B₁
Device 3: . . . .ø    C₂    ø    ø     C₁
Device 4: . . . .D₅   D₄    D₃   D₂    D₁
Device 5: . . . .ø    ø     E₂   ø     E₁
```

13. What is the purpose of adding 0.5 to the sine function to form $f(t)$ in Figure 4.28? That is, what happens if that term is eliminated?

14. Discuss the significance of the graphs in Figure 4.43.

15. Comment on the following statement:

   With 1-persistent CSMA a waiting device always transmits when the medium is clear. Why not change the protocol so that when a medium is clear the device waits the amount of time it would take for another device's transmission to reach it? If it is still clear, then transmit. This should decrease the chances of two waiting devices colliding.

16. Comment on the usefulness of a 0-persistent CSMA.

17. Suppose three devices using a 0.5-persistent protocol are waiting for an idle medium.

    a. What is the probability of a collision when the medium clears?

    b. What is the probability of a successful transmission when the medium clears?

    c. What is the probability that no device will send anything when the medium clears?

18. Repeat Exercise 17, but assume the devices use a 0.25-persistent protocol.

19. Suppose two devices using CSMA/CD and the binary exponential backoff algorithm have just sent transmissions that have collided.

    a. What is the probability that they will collide again during the next time slot?

    b. What is the probability that both devices will transmit successfully during the next two time slots?

    c. What is the probability that they will collide two more times? Three more times?

20. Suppose three devices using CSMA/CD and the binary exponential backoff algorithm have just sent transmissions that have all collided.

    a. What is the probability that they will all collide again during the next time slot?

    b. What is the probability that all three devices will transmit successfully during the next three time slots?

    c. What is the probability that any two will collide during the next time slot?

21. Suppose the binary exponential backoff algorithm is altered so that a device will always wait 0 or 1 time slots regardless of how many collisions have occurred. How is the effectiveness changed?

22. Assume n is some positive integer. Suppose the binary exponential backoff algorithm is altered so that a device will always wait anywhere between 0 and $2^n - 1$ time slots regardless of how many collisions have occurred. How is the effectiveness changed?

23. For each application below, state which transmission mode (asynchronous, synchronous, or isochronous) is best suited to it.

    a. Download a file.

    b. Connect to a printer.

    c. View images from a Web camera.

    d. Video conference.

    e. Download a multimedia file.

    f. Listen to Web radio.

    g. Connect a keyboard.

    h. Use software to make telephone calls.

    i. Watch presidential debates live online.

REFERENCES

[An99] Anderson, D. *FireWire System Architecture: IEEE 1394A,* 2nd ed. Reading, MA: Addison-Wesley, 1999.

[Ax01] Axelson, J. *USB Complete,* 2nd ed. Madison, WI: Lakeview Research, 2001.

[Go02] Goralski, W. *SONET/SDH,* 3rd ed. New York: McGraw-Hill, 2002.

[Kl75] Kleinrock, L., and F. Tobagi. "Random Access Techniques for Data Transmission over Packet-Switched Radio Channels." *AFIPS Conference Proceedings,* vol. 44 (1975), 187.

[Le00] Leon-Garcia, A., and I. Widjaja. *Communication Networks*. New York: McGraw-Hill, 2000.

[Ma72] Martin, J. *Systems Analysis for Data Transmission*. Englewood Cliffs, NJ: Prentice-Hall, 1972.

[Mi87] Mitrani, I. *Modeling of Computer and Communication Systems*. London: Cambridge University Press, 1987.

[Ro75] Roberts, L. "ALOHA Packet System with and without Slots and Capture." *Computer Communications Review,* vol. 5 (April 1975), 28–42.

[Ru89] Russell, D. *The Principles of Computer Networking*. New York: Cambridge University Press, 1989.

[Sh90] Sherman, K. *Data Communications: A User's Guide,* 3rd ed. Englewood Cliffs, NJ: Prentice-Hall, 1990.

[St00] Stallings, W. *Data and Computer Communications,* 6th ed. Englewood Cliffs, NJ: Prentice-Hall, 2000.

[St03] Stallings, W. *Computer Organization and Architecture,* 6th ed. Englewood Cliffs, NJ: Prentice-Hall, 2003.

[St96] Stanley, W. *Network Analysis with Applications,* 2nd ed. Englewood Cliffs, NJ: Prentice-Hall, 1996.

[Ta03] Tanenbaum, A. S. *Computer Networks,* 4th ed. Englewood Cliffs, NJ: Prentice-Hall, 2003.

[Wa98] Walrand, J. *Communications Networks: A First Course,* 2nd ed. Boston: Richard D. Irwin, 1991.

[Wa00] Walrand, J., and P. Varaiya. *High-Performance Communication Networks,* 2nd ed. San Francisco: Morgan Kaufmann, 1996.

CHAPTER 5

DATA COMPRESSION

A computer does not think, it feels nothing, and what it is said to "know"—bits of information all cast in the digital mode—has no fringe. Nor has it a memory, only storage room. On any point called for, the answer is all or none. Vagueness, intelligent confusion, original punning on words or ideas never occur, the internal hookups being unchangeable; they were determined once for all by the true minds that made the machine and program. When plugged in, the least elaborate computer can be relied on to work to the fullest extent of its capacity; the greatest mind cannot be relied on for the simplest thing; its variability is its superiority.
—**Jacques Barzun** (1907–), U.S. educator and author

5.1 INTRODUCTION

Did you ever listen to an MP3 audio file? Did you ever download a movie preview stored as an MPG or MPEG file? Have you ever used a fax (facsimile) machine? Almost certainly, if you're reading this book you have some technical experience and have done one or more of these actions. However, none of these would be very practical without some fairly sophisticated mathematics and compression routines. With so many new applications requiring electronic communications, the obvious trend is to build faster and less costly ways of sending data. Chapter 2 mentioned some of the current areas of development, such as optical fiber, higher-frequency microwaves, and higher grade UTP. All have their place and will certainly contribute to the field.

Some applications, however, cannot wait for new developments. Their demand has forced people to look for other ways to communicate quickly and cheaply. For example, consider one of the more significant developments of the 1980s, the fax machine. Chapter 4 described how the fax machine divides a sheet of paper into dots depending on the image on it. A typical fax uses 40,000 dots per square inch, resulting in nearly 4 million dots per page. Using a 56 Kbps modem, it would require over a minute to transmit this information. If you have ever used a fax machine, you know it does not take that long.

Another example is video. What we see as motion on a standard TV screen is actually a display of 30 pictures (frames) per second (the same principle behind motion pictures). Furthermore, each picture actually consists of approximately 200,000 dots or **pixels,** each with different intensities of the primary colors of blue, green, and red. Various combinations allow the generation of different colors in the spectrum. If 8 bits represent each of the primary colors for one pixel, then each picture requires $200,000 \times 24 = 4,800,000$ bits. A two-hour movie requires about 216,000 separate pictures, or $216,000 \times 4,800,000 = 1.0368 \times 10^{12}$ bits, far more than the capacity of any DVD. Yet DVDs do hold two-hour movies.

Both examples show that there are ways to get around the physical limits of different media. But how? The answer is **data compression,** a way to reduce the number of bits in a frame while retaining its meaning. It decreases both cost and time to send. Data compression has found uses in a variety of areas, such as fax machines, DVD technology, and the V.42 modem standards. It is also used in disk storage, and many software vendors compress programs on disks and CDs to conserve space.

The next logical question is: How do you eliminate bits and still maintain necessary information? For example, suppose the data in a large file consist entirely of strings of capital letters. If we email this file, how many bits must be transferred? If the characters are stored as 8-bit ASCII codes, the number is $8n$, where n is the number of characters. However, if the information to be sent consists of uppercase letters only, we do not need the full 8-bit ASCII code. Can we devise a code that represents just capital letters? Yes! Table 5.1 shows a 5-bit code using the numbers 0 through 25 (in binary). Using this table, the sending application can substitute each 5-bit code for the original 8-bit one. The receiving application can convert back. The result is that the information is sent and the number of data bits transferred is $5n$—a 37.5% reduction.

Again, many questions pop up (won't they ever stop?). What if there are control characters? What about lowercase letters? What if the data are not letters? These are valid questions and must be addressed. Table 5.1 is a very simple method of compression not suitable for many applications. Its main purpose is to show what

Table 5.1   Alternative Code for Capital Letters

LETTER	CODE
A	00000
B	00001
C	00010
D	00011
.	.
.	.
.	.
X	10111
Y	11000
Z	11001

compression is and what it can do. There are many other ways to compress data. However, regardless of the method used, the key is to determine whether there is redundancy in the original data and then eliminate it. For example, in the ASCII code example for the letters A through Z, redundancy exists because the first three bits of the code for each letter are the same. That redundancy suggested eliminating them and using the codes in Table 5.1. However, as we will see, there are many types of redundancy.

5.2 FREQUENCY-DEPENDENT CODES

The ASCII code and the code in Table 5.1 have one thing in common. All characters use the same number of bits. However, what if an analysis of the text showed that certain characters appeared more frequently than others? This is certainly not unusual because certain letters do, in fact, occur more frequently in writing than others. (The frequency factor is why they are worth less in a Scrabble game and, except for the vowels, which are not worth any money, why they are often chosen on the game show *Wheel of Fortune*.) Scan through the previous few paragraphs and note how often letters such as *e, s,* or *t* appear compared with letters such as *z, x,* or *j*. Would it not make sense to vary the length of the code so that frequently appearing characters correspond to shorter codes? That is, they have fewer bits. Such a code is also called a **frequency-dependent code,** and fewer bits are needed to transmit them.

HUFFMAN CODE

An example of a frequency-dependent code is the **Huffman code** (ref. [Hu52]). For example, suppose Table 5.2 shows the frequencies (percentage of time they appear) of characters in a data file. To keep the example manageable we assume just five characters. If you want, you can do a similar example with all 26 letters.

Table 5.3 shows a Huffman code for these characters. Note that we say *a* Huffman code because, as we will show, it is not unique. We will show how to develop this code shortly.

Next, suppose the bit stream 01110001110110110111 was Huffman coded. If the leftmost bits were transmitted first, how do you interpret it? Fixed-length codes have an advantage. Within a transmission, we always know where one character

Table 5.2 Frequencies for the Letters A through E

LETTER	FREQUENCY (%)
A	25
B	15
C	10
D	20
E	30

Table 5.3   Huffman Code for the Letters *A* through *E*

LETTER	CODE
A	01
B	110
C	111
D	10
E	00

ends and the next one begins. For example, in the transmission of ASCII-coded characters, every set of 8 data bits defines a new character. This is not true of Huffman codes, so how do we interpret the Huffman-coded bit stream? How do we know where one letter ends and the next one begins?

The answer lies in a property of Huffman codes called the **no-prefix property.** That is, the code for any character never appears as the prefix of another code. For example, the Huffman code for *A* is 01, so no other code starts with a 01.

Figure 5.1 shows how to interpret a Huffman-coded string. As bits are received, a device builds a substring by concatenating them. It stops when the substring corresponds to a coded character. In the example of Figure 5.1, it stops after forming the substring 01, meaning that *A* is the first character sent. To find the second character, it discards the current substring and starts building a new one with the next bit received. Again, it stops when the substring corresponds to a coded character. In this case, the next three bits (110) correspond to the character *B*. Note that the substring does not match any Huffman code until all three bits are received. This is a consequence of the no-prefix property. The device continues this approach until all bits have been received. The data in Figure 5.1 consist of the character string ABECADBC.

The following steps show how to create a Huffman code.

1. To each character, associate a binary tree consisting of just one node. To each tree, assign the character's frequency, which we call the tree's *weight*.

2. Look for the two lightest-weight trees. If there are more than two, choose any two. Merge the two into a single tree with a new root node whose left and right subtrees are the two we chose. Assign the sum of weights of the merged trees as the weight of the new tree.

3. Repeat the previous step until just one tree is left.

Figure 5.1   Receiving and Interpreting a Huffman-Coded Message

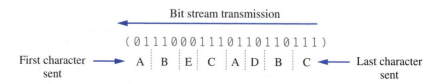

When completed, each of the original nodes is a leaf in the final binary tree. As with any binary tree, there is a unique path from the root to a leaf. For each leaf, the path to it defines the Huffman code. It is determined by assigning a 0 each time a left child pointer is followed and a 1 for each right child pointer.

Figure 5.2 (parts a through e) shows the construction of the Huffman code in Table 5.3. Figure 5.2a shows the five single-node trees with their weights. The trees for letters *B* and *C* have the smallest weights, so we merge them to give the results of Figure 5.2b. For the second merge there are two possibilities: merge the new tree with *D* or merge *A* with *D*. In this case we arbitrarily chose the first, and Figure 5.2c shows the result. Proceeding this way eventually gives the tree in Figure 5.2e. In it we see each left or right child pointer assigned a 0 or a 1. Following the pointers to a leaf node gives the Huffman code for the associated character. For example, following a left child (0) pointer and then a right child (1) pointer gets us to the leaf node for *A*. This is consistent with the Huffman code of 01 for the letter *A*.

Figure 5.2   Merging Huffman Trees

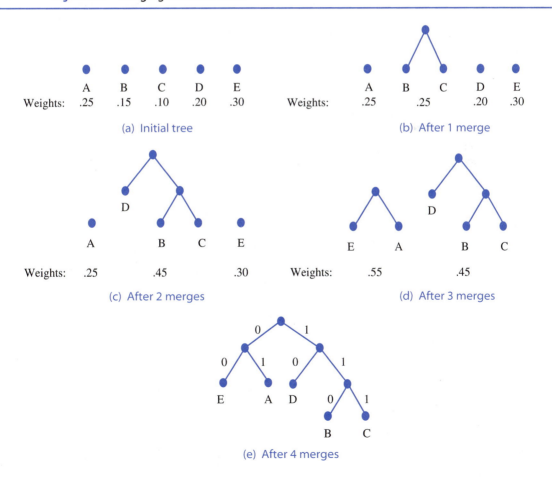

(a) Initial tree

(b) After 1 merge

(c) After 2 merges

(d) After 3 merges

(e) After 4 merges

ARITHMETIC COMPRESSION

Another example of a compression method that generates a frequency-dependent code is **arithmetic compression,** which is based on interpreting a character string as a single real number. It's not an unusual concept; for example, we could interpret the Huffman-coded 0s and 1s for a string as the bit representation for a very large integer. More characters in the string mean more bits and hence a larger number.

Arithmetic compression works by defining an association between a character string and a real number between 0 and 1. Because there are infinitely many real numbers between 0 and 1 and infinitely many character strings,* we are able to define an algorithm that associates a real number with any string.

To illustrate, we use the same letters and frequency that we used for the previous Huffman example. A difference here is that we assign a range of numbers (a subinterval of the interval [0, 1]) based on the frequency of each character. The subinterval length corresponds to the symbol's frequency. Table 5.4 shows how this works. The letter A has a frequency of 25%, and we associate the interval [0, 0.25] with A. This represents 25% of the interval and has a length of 0.25. Next, because B has a frequency of 15%, we assign the next 15% of the interval (after the subinterval [0, 0.25]) to B. Thus, the subinterval [0.25, 0.40], with a length of 0.15, corresponds to B. Because C has a frequency of 10%, we assign the next 10% of the interval to C. This is the subinterval [0.40, 0.50] and has length 0.10. Following this pattern, we assign the next 20% of the interval to D and the remaining 30% of the interval to E. Because the frequencies sum to 100%, the subinterval lengths sum to 1. Also, the collection of subintervals completely covers the original interval [0, 1].

So how does this help us? Well, assume we have a character string. The basic idea is as follows.

1. Start with the interval $[x, y] = [0, 1]$.

2. Look at the first character and determine the appropriate subinterval of $[x, y]$ based on that character's probability.

Table 5.4   Assigning Ranges to Letters Based on Frequency

LETTER	FREQUENCY (%)	SUBINTERVAL $[p, q]$
A	25	[0, 0.25]
B	15	[0.25, 0.40]
C	10	[0.4, 0.5]
D	20	[0.5, 0.7]
E	30	[0.7, 1.0]

---

* Those who have had some upper-level mathematics might know that there are different levels of infinity. In fact, by some measures there are many more values between 0 and 1 than there are character strings.

3. Redefine the interval [x, y] to be that subinterval. That is, shrink [x, y].

4. Examine the next character and again determine the appropriate subinterval of [x, y] depending on that character's probability. This is exactly what we did in step 2, except now we are working with a smaller interval [x, y] instead of [0, 1].

5. Repeat steps 3 and 4 for each character in the string.

Perhaps the most essential step is calculating a new interval from the old one, given the values for p and q (see Table 5.4). Figure 5.3 shows the basic idea. We start with interval [x, y] with width $w = y - x$. Then there exists a subinterval based on p and q that is associated with a character. Values p and q each represent a percentage of the distance from x to y. The new x value is the one associated with p, and the new y value is the one associated with q. So, for example, suppose [x, y] = [0.3, 0.9], $w = 0.9 - 0.3 = 0.6$, and [p, q] = [0.25, 0.50]. The new value for x is 25% of the distance from the current value of x toward y. In other words, the new x value = current x value + $w \times p = 0.3 + 0.6 \times 0.25 = 0.45$. The new y value = current x value + $w \times q = 0.3 + 0.6 \times 0.5 = 0.6$. Another way to think of it is that 0.45 is 25% of the distance from 0.3 to 0.9, and 0.6 is 50% of the distance from 0.3 to 0.9.

Basically, what is happening is that the process just described is generating subintervals of decreasing length. Furthermore, the subintervals depend uniquely on the string's characters and their frequencies. Also, the more characters in the string, the smaller the subinterval (remember, they decrease with each character in the string). When the last character is processed, we choose any real number in the final interval (for example, the midpoint). Choose a bit representation of that number and that is the compressed code.

It's time for an example. Let's assume the frequencies in Table 5.4 and the string CABACADA. Figure 5.4 and Table 5.5 show the first few steps of the process. Using the calculations we have outlined, we generate the following sequence of intervals: [0, 1], [0.4, 0.5], [0.4, 0.425], [0.40625, 0.41], [0.40625, 0.4071875], and [0.406625, 0.4067187]. You should match the values from each step in the figure with corresponding steps in the table and verify that they are correct. We have not gone through the entire string, leaving it as an exercise. Suppose we were to stop after the fifth step. Then we would choose any number in the interval [0.406625, 0.4067187]—say, 0.4067—to represent the string CABAC.

Now, how do we reverse the process? The basic idea is to first determine in which part of the interval [0, 1] the number is located. That determines the first character in the string. For example, suppose we are presented a number

Figure 5.3   Determining a New Interval from the Old

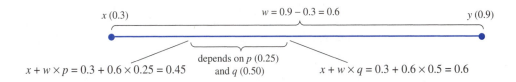

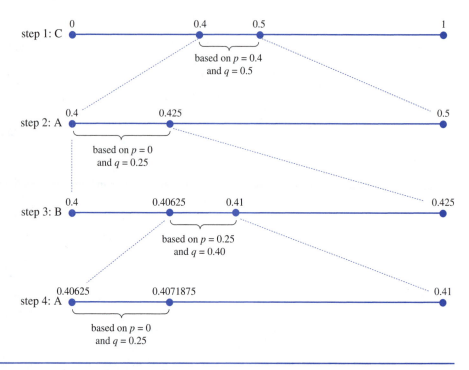

Figure 5.4   Intervals in Arithmetic Coding

$N = 0.4067$ and we know only the contents of Table 5.4. We observe that it is in the interval [0.4, 0.5]. This means the first step in the compression process had to begin with [0.4, 0.5]. This, in turn, means the first character had to be C. Any other character would have placed the number in some other subinterval. So, where do we go from there?

Table 5.6 outlines the steps of the decompression process. We next need to determine in what part of the interval [0.4, 0.5] the value N resides. This will tell us the next character. Note that N is much closer to 0.4 than to 0.5. But how much closer? To make this calculation, subtract the value of p from N to get 0.0067 (step 1 in Table 5.6) and divide by the interval width to get 0.067. This tells us that N is only about 6.7% of the distance from p to q. Again, if we compare this with possible [p, q] intervals, we see the value lies in the first quarter of the interval [0.4, 0.5]. In other words, the second step of the compression process had to use [p, q] = [0, 0.25] and the second character had to be A.

Next question: In what part of [0, 0.25] does 0.067 reside? It seems to be about a quarter of the way from 0 to 0.25, but let's be more specific. Making the same calculations as before, subtract $p = 0$ from $N = 0.067$ to get 0.067 and then divide by the interval length, 0.25. The result is 0.268, meaning that $N = 0.067$ lies about 26.8% of the distance from $p = 0$ to $q = 0.25$. Thus, the third step in the compression process had to use the interval [0.25, 0.40], and the third character was B. Continuing

Table 5.5 Steps in the Arithmetic Encoding Process

Step	String	Next Character	Current Interval [x, y]	[p, q]	Interval Width (w = y − x)	Calculation for New x (x = x + w × p)	Calculation for New y (y = x + w × q)
1	—	C	[0, 1]	[0.4, 0.5]	1.0	$0 + 1 \times 0.4 = 0.4$	$0 + 1 \times 0.5 = 0.5$
2	C	A	[0.4, 0.5]	[0, 0.25]	0.1	$0.4 + 0.1 \times 0 = 0.4$	$0.4 + 0.1 \times 0.25 = 0.425$
3	CA	B	[0.4, 0.425]	[0.25, 0.40]	0.025	$0.4 + 0.025 \times 0.25$ $= 0.40625$	$0.4 + 0.025 \times 0.4 = 0.41$
4	CAB	A	[0.40625, 0.41]	[0, 0.25]	0.00375	$0.40625 + 0.00375 \times 0$ $= 0.40625$	$0.40625 + 0.00375 \times 0.25$ $= 0.4071875$
5	CABA	C	[0.40625, 0.4071875]	[0.4, 0.5]	0.0009375	$0.40625 + 0.0009375$ $\times 0.40 = 0.406625$	$0.40625 + 0.0009375 \times 0.5$ $= 0.4067187$

Table 5.6   Extracting Characters from an Arithmetic-Encoded Number

STEP	N	INTERVAL [p, q]	WIDTH	CHARACTER	N − p	DIVIDE BY WIDTH
1	0.4067	[0.4, 0.5]	0.10	C	0.0067	0.067
2	0.067	[0, 0.25]	0.25	A	0.067	0.268
3	0.268	[0.25, 0.40]	0.15	B	0.018	0.12
4	0.12	[0, 0.25]	0.25	A	0.12	0.48
5	0.48	[0.4, 0.5]	0.10	C	0.08	0.8

in this manner, the fourth character was A and the fifth was C (see Table 5.6). Putting the characters we generate together yields the string CABAC, exactly what Table 5.5 generated.

There is one small issue with this method: How do we know when to stop? Remember, when decompressing, all we are presented with is a number and a table similar to Table 5.4. For all we know, if we had taken the compression algorithm a few steps further we'd generate a smaller interval in which the number 0.4067 resides. There's nothing there that tells us that we should stop at any particular point.

Arithmetic compression algorithms usually deal with this problem by adding one character, a terminal character, to the original character set. It is treated like the other characters. However, when it is generated during decompression, the process stops. It's a little like compressing variable-length sentences, one at a time, and stopping when a period is encountered.

There is one last point we must make. We've simply described how to associate a real number with a character string. Because we are supposed to be compressing the string, we need to ask how this relates to bit patterns. The answer lies in the methods used to store real numbers. We won't provide a discussion of the bit patterns for floating-point numbers, but for details see, for example, reference [St03]. The main idea is that any real number between 0 and 1 can be represented to within about seven digits of accuracy using a 32-bit representation. From Table 5.5, any number in the interval [0.406625, 0.4067187] could easily be represented with the desired accuracy using 32 bits. In fact, we could have processed a few more characters and still used a 32-bit representation.

However, if the character string were longer, the subintervals would become so small that we would need more than the required seven digits of accuracy. In this case, we need extended precision. Again, the details are more suitable for a book about computer organization, but it can be shown that any number between 0 and 1 can be represented to within about 16 digits of accuracy using 64 bits. If 16 digits were not sufficient, then we could go to the next level.

In general, the interval [x, y] becomes smaller as the number of characters increases. Furthermore, there are procedures that can approximate any real number to within a desired accuracy if we use a sufficient number of bits.

5.3 RUN-LENGTH ENCODING

Huffman codes reduce the number of bits to send, but they also require that frequency values be known. As described, they also assume that bits are grouped into characters or some other repeatable units. Many items that travel communications media, including binary (machine code) files, fax data, and video signals, do not fall into that category.

The fax, for example, transfers bits corresponding to light and dark space on a sheet of paper. It does not transfer the characters directly. Consequently, there is a need for a more general technique that can compress arbitrary bit strings. One approach, called **run-length encoding,** uses a simple and perhaps obvious approach: It analyzes bit strings looking for long runs of a 0 or 1. Instead of sending all the bits, it sends only how many are in the run.

This technique is especially useful for fax transmission. If you were to examine closely the space in which a character is typed, potentially 70% to 80% is white space. The exact amount, of course, depends on the font and character. The actual dark spots from typed characters make up very little of a fax transmission. For example, note the amount of white space in a magnified representation of a lowercase *f* within one print position.

RUNS OF THE SAME BIT

There are a couple of ways to implement run-length encoding. The first is especially useful in binary streams in which the same bit appears in most of the runs. In a fax example consisting primarily of characters, there will be many long runs of 0s (assuming a light spot corresponds to a 0). This approach just transmits the length of each run as a fixed-length binary integer. The receiving device receives each length and generates the proper number of bits in the run, inserting the other bit in between.

For example, suppose 4 bits are used to represent the run length. Consider the bit stream of Figure 5.5a. Figure 5.5b shows the compressed stream that is sent. The

Figure 5.5 Stream Prior to Compression and Run-Length-Encoded Stream

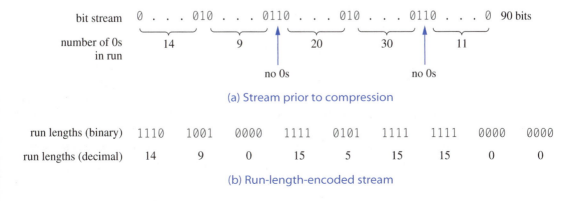

original stream starts with 14 zeros, so the first 4 bits in the compressed stream are 1110 (binary 14). The next 4 bits in the compressed stream are 1001 (binary 9 for the second run of nine 0s). After the second run there are two consecutive 1s. However, this approach sees them as two distinct 1s separated by a run of no 0s. Consequently, the third group of 4 bits is 0000.

The fourth run has 20 zeros. Unfortunately, 20 cannot be expressed using 4 bits. In this case, the run length is expressed using a second 4-bit group. The two 4-bit numbers are then added to determine the run length. In Figure 5.5b, the 1111 (binary 15) and 0101 (binary 5) groups determine a run length of 20.

If the run length is too large to be expressed as a sum of two 4-bit numbers, the method uses as many 4-bit groups as necessary. The receiving device must know that a group of all 1s means the next group corresponds to the same run. Thus, it continues summing the group values and stops after it receives something other than all 1s. Consequently, the run of length 30 is represented by 1111, 1111, and 0000. In this case the 0s are needed to tell the device that the run stops at 30 zeros.

How would the compressed stream differ if the stream in Figure 5.5a started with a 1? Similar to the case for two consecutive 1s, the method considers the stream to actually start with a run of no 0s. Thus, the first 4 bits sent would be 0000.

This technique is best suited for cases in which there are many long 0 runs. As the 1 bits increase in frequency, the technique becomes less efficient. In fact, you might try to construct a stream for which this approach actually generates a longer bit stream.

RUNS WITH DIFFERENT CHARACTERS

Knowing that the same bit is involved simplifies matters because we only need to send the run length. But what about cases with runs of different bits or even characters? In such cases, your first response is probably correct: Send the actual character along with the run length. For example, the character string

```
HHHHHHHUFFFFFFFFFFFFFFFYYYYYYYYYYYYYYYYYYYYYYDGGGGGGGGGGGG
```

might actually be sent as the alternating set of numbers and characters 7, H, 1, U, 14, F, 20, Y, 1, D, and 11, G.

FACSIMILE COMPRESSION

For years (even before WinZip and the Internet), one of the most common applications for compression was the fax machine. Section 4.2 described some basics of how a fax machine works by scanning a page and creating a bit map representation of the image on the page. In general, a black and white page image is composed of many pixels, each representing one white or black point on the page. In fact, the ITU has defined operations standards for different groups of machines. We won't articulate differences among the groups and will focus on the compression schemes used as they relate to our current discussion. Those interested in more detail should consult references [Sa00], [Ha01], [Ho97], or [He96].

Relevant to our discussion are two ITU standards, T.4 and T.6, that define compression on what they call Group 3 and Group 4 machines. Basically, these are machines that utilize digital methods for transmitting images over a telephone network. Although different page sizes are possible, we'll restrict our discussion to A4 documents, those that measure 210 by 297 mm.

An A4 document contains 1728 pixels in each line. If we sent 1 bit for each pixel, we'd need to transmit over 3 million bits for each page—a large amount of information for very simple images. The T.4 and T.6 standards exploit the fact that a typical page image contains many consecutive white or black pixels and, hence, many consecutive 0s or 1s. This would certainly suggest a run-length compression scheme. However, there are two important observations to make. First, the run lengths can vary from 0 to as large as 1728, creating many possibilities and some inefficiency in setting up a format to represent any number in this range. Second, some runs occur with high frequency. For example, most typed pages have mostly white pixels, perhaps 80% or more. The spacing between consecutive letters or before the first letter in a line is fairly consistent. In between lines, you can expect to find no black pixels at all—in other words, long runs of white pixels. For each line of text, you may find several lines (or more, depending on spacing) of 1728 white pixels.

The bottom line is that for many fax images one can predict with reasonable accuracy the probabilities that certain runs appear. This suggests some type of frequency-dependent code based on run lengths. The T.4 and T.6 standards for **facsimile compression** actually use a combination of white and black pixel runs followed by a frequency-dependent code defined by the frequency of run lengths. It's called a *modified Huffman code*. The assumptions and process are as follows:

1. Each line consists of alternating runs of white and black pixels.

2. Each line begins with a run of white pixels. Even if the page to be faxed has a black border, a process called *overscanning* adds one white pixel to the beginning and end of each line.

3. Calculate codes for the alternating white and black pixel runs and transmit the coded bits.

Table 5.7 shows a subset of the codes that define white and black pixel run lengths. The complete table defines a code for run lengths between 0 and 63, inclusive, and for run lengths of 64, 128, 192, 256, and so on. Beyond 64, the ITU defines codes only for multiples of 64. This decreases the total number of codes needed. Codes for runs of length less than 64 are *terminating codes*, and those for runs whose length is a multiple of 64 are *makeup codes*. Any run of length less than 64 is coded according to the terminating code. If the run is longer than 63 pixels, the method uses a makeup code for the longest run that is wholly contained in the original run, plus a terminating code for the remaining bits.

For example, a run length of 50 white pixels is coded as 01010011. For another example, consider a run length of 572 white pixels. It is interpreted as a run of length 512 pixels followed by another run of 60 pixels. The associated code is 01100101–01001011. In this instance 512 bits were compressed to 16 bits, almost a

Table 5.7   Some Facsimile Compression Codes

	NUMBER OF PIXELS IN RUN	CODE: WHITE PIXEL RUN	CODE: BLACK PIXEL RUN
Terminating Codes	0	00110101	0000110111
	1	000111	010
	2	0111	11
	3	1000	10
	10	00111	0000100
	20	0001000	00001101000
	30	00000011	000001101000
	40	00101001	000001101100
	50	01010011	000001010010
	60	01001011	000000101100
Makeup Codes	64	11011	0000001111
	128	10010	000011001000
	256	0110111	000001011011
	512	01100101	0000001101100
	768	011001101	000000101100
	1024	011010101	0000001110100
	1280	011011001	0000001010010
	1536	010011001	0000001011010

97% reduction. Of course, a large number of smaller runs will not compress that well, but 90% compression rates are not unusual.

A few observations about the code in Table 5.7 follow.

- Codes for white run lengths are shorter than those for black run lengths because white runs are more common.
- Both white and black run-length codes define no-prefix property codes.
- Compression is better for images that have long runs.

Although this discussion reflects both the T.4 and T.6 standards, there are differences between the standards. For example, the scheme we have described works well for typical typed pages. There are usually enough runs in each line to make use of the compression codes. If, however, the image contains complex patterns or is perhaps a photograph, there may be few long runs anywhere in the image, with most lines consisting of very short runs. Because short runs compress much less efficiently, this approach (at least as described) does not work well.

An alternative that the T.6 standard adopted makes use of the fact that two consecutive lines may not differ by much. Thus, instead of compressing each line independent of the one that preceded it, the T.6 standard establishes a base line and then determines the difference between it and the next line. If the difference is very small, then the next line can be encoded with little additional information; hence, it can be compressed very well. Because the next section discusses compression by measuring differences, we'll not elaborate here. Details of the T.6 standard are found in reference [Sa00].

5.4 RELATIVE ENCODING

The compression techniques already discussed have their applications, but in certain cases neither provides much help. A common example is video transmissions, where images may be very complex in contrast to the black and white transmission of a fax or a text file. Except perhaps for the test patterns that appear before a station goes on the air, little in a video picture is repetitive. Consequently, neither of the previous methods offers much hope of compressing the signals for a picture.

Although a single video image may contain little repetition, there is a lot of repetition over several images. Remember, a typical television signal sends 30 pictures per second. Furthermore, each picture generally varies only slightly from the previous one. Over the course of a fraction of a second not much action occurs. Therefore, rather than trying to treat each frame as a separate entity and compress it, we might think about how much a frame differs from the previous one. Encoding that information and sending it has potential when the differences are small. This method is called **relative encoding** or **differential encoding.**

The principle is fairly straightforward. The first frame is sent and stored in a receiver's buffer. The sender then compares the second frame with the first, encodes the differences, and sends them in a frame format. The receiver gets the frame and applies the differences to the frame it has, thus creating the second frame the sender had. It stores the second frame in a buffer and continues the process for each new frame.

Figure 5.6 shows how it works. Here we represent a frame using a two-dimensional array of integers. We put no interpretation on their meaning; they're just easier to draw than video signals. The first frame contains a set of integers, and the second differs very little from the first. (The colored numbers are the ones that differ.)

The figure shows another two-dimensional array below the second frame, containing 0s, 1s, and −1s. A 0 in any position means the element in that position of the frame is the same as that in the same position in the previous frame. A nonzero value indicates what the change is. Thus, a 1 means the element in that frame position is 1 larger than the one in the same position in the previous frame. A −1 means it is 1 smaller. Certainly, values other than 1 and −1 can be used. The point is that the frames to be sent contain long runs of 0s, making them candidates for run-length encoding.

5.5 LEMPEL-ZIV COMPRESSION

With run-length encoding, we compress by looking for runs of a character or a bit. The idea is to reduce repetitious or redundant transmissions. But not all redundancy occurs in the form of single-bit or single-character repetitions. In some cases, entire words or phrases may be repeated. This is especially true with large text files such

```
5 7 6 2 8 6 6 3 5 6        5 7 6 2 8 6 6 3 5 6        5 7 6 2 8 6 6 3 5 6
6 5 7 5 5 6 3 2 4 7        6 5 7 6 5 6 3 2 3 7        6 5 8 6 5 6 3 3 3 7
8 4 6 8 5 6 4 8 8 5        8 4 6 8 5 6 4 8 8 5        8 4 6 8 5 6 4 8 8 5
5 1 2 9 8 6 5 5 6 6        5 1 3 9 8 6 5 5 7 6        5 1 3 9 7 6 5 5 8 6
5 5 2 9 9 6 8 9 5 1        5 5 2 9 9 6 8 9 5 1        5 5 2 9 9 6 8 9 5 1
```

| First frame | Second frame | Third frame |

```
                           0 0 0 0 0 0 0 0 0 0        0 0 0 0 0 0 0 0 0 0
                           0 0 0 1 0 0 0 0 -1 0       0 0 1 0 0 0 0 1 0 0
                           0 0 0 0 0 0 0 0 0 0        0 0 0 0 0 0 0 0 0 0
                           0 0 1 0 0 0 0 0 1 0        0 0 0 0 -1 0 0 0 1 0
                           0 0 0 0 0 0 0 0 0 0        0 0 0 0 0 0 0 0 0 0
```

Transmitted frame contains
the encoded differences between
the first and second frames.

Transmitted frame contains
the encoded differences between
the second and third frames.

Figure 5.6   Relative Encoding

as manuscripts. An author's writing style is often characterized by a choice of words or phrases that may be repeated frequently. Program source code frequently has a single variable name (string) appearing many times.

The **Lempel-Ziv compression** method looks for often-repeated strings and stores them just once.* It then replaces multiple occurrences with a code corresponding to the original. This is one of the basic principles of database management: Store one piece of information in just one place and reference it through special codes. This technique is used by the UNIX compress command and in the V.42bis compression standard for modems. Also, GIF (Graphics Interchange Format) files use a variant of Lempel-Ziv encoding.

For example, consider the following writing sample (ref. [Cr90]):

> The tropical rain fell in drenching sheets, hammering the corrugated roof of the clinic building, roaring down the metal gutters, splashing on the ground in a torrent.

Several letter sequences are repeated. Ignoring case sensitivity, some of them are *the, ro*, and *ing*. Suppose we replace each of these strings with the special characters $\otimes$, $\oplus$, and $\varnothing$ respectively. The compressed string then becomes

> $\otimes$t$\oplus$pical rain fell in drench$\varnothing$ sheets, hammer$\varnothing$ $\otimes$corrugated $\oplus$of $\otimes$clinic build$\varnothing$, $\oplus$ar$\varnothing$ down $\otimes$metal gutters, splash$\varnothing$ on $\otimes$g$\oplus$und in a torrent.

This text did not compress the original by much, but you can't expect much repetition in a single sentence. Compression is generally not very effective (or useful, for

---

* There are actually several different Lempel-Ziv compression schemes. These variations may be called Lempel-Ziv, Lempel-Ziv-Welch, LZW, LZ77, LZ78, or even Ziv-Lempel. We will not make distinctions among the variations, but if you would like some further details you can consult reference [Ho97].

that matter) with short samples. With longer text and longer and more frequent repetitions, the compression improves because typical English text is filled with repetitions, as evidenced by words such as *the, then, them, their, there*, and *these*. However, not only text data can be subject to Lempel-Ziv compression. Any file can be considered as a sequence of ASCII-defined characters. If the file contains numerous character sequences that appear frequently, then it is a candidate for Lempel-Ziv compression.

An important characteristic of this method is that we make no assumptions about what the repeated strings look like, making the algorithm more robust and dynamic. As a consequence, however, it may at first appear there is no efficient way to implement this algorithm, because looking for repeated sequences seems to add considerable overhead. Then there is the issue of decompression. Remember, compression algorithms do not have much value if we cannot reverse the process. How can we decompress? If we received the compressed string shown previously, how could we possibly know what letter sequences correspond to the special symbols? One option would be to send a table of symbols showing the strings that they represent along with the compressed text. Of course, doing that partially counteracts the value of compressing in the first place.

It turns out that there is an efficient way to identify commonly repeated strings. Also, strange as it may seem, it is possible to determine the strings associated with the special symbols without transmitting them with the compressed text. We will show how this works by outlining both a compression and a decompression algorithm. We will, however, shorten the example by compressing text consisting of only the three characters A, B, and C. To work with a full alphabet would require a lengthy example with potentially hundreds of steps to fully realize the value of compression. This limited example will preserve the fundamental logic behind the algorithms and accomplish our task in relatively few steps.

Figure 5.7 shows both the compression and decompression algorithms (refs. [We84] and [Dr01]). These algorithms preserve the fundamental logic but are not intended to provide all the C language–specific details and declarations. We leave that as an exercise. The compression algorithm is based on the following central ideas:

1. Assign a code to each letter or character that is part of the initial text file (line 3 of the compression algorithm) and store it in a code table.

2. Set up a loop and get characters one at a time from the file. We will use a buffered string (initially the first character, line 4) built by concatenating characters from the file.

3. In each pass of a loop, read one character and append it to a buffered string to form a new temporary string (`tempstring`, line 7). If that temporary string has been encountered before (i.e., is in the code table), then move the temporary string to the buffer (line 10).

4. If the temporary string was not found in the code table, assign a code to the temporary string and store both code and string in the code table (line 14) and send the code associated with the buffered string (line 13). This code represents the compressed equivalent of the string. Last, reinitialize the buffered string to the single character that was just read (line 15).

COMPRESSION	DECOMPRESSION

```
1    void compress (FILE * fileid)
2    {
3      initialize(code table);
4      buffer=string consisting
          of first character from the file.
5      while ( (c=getc(fileid)) != EOF)
6      {
7        tempstring=concat(buffer, c);
8        search for tempstring in the
            code table;
9        if found
10       buffer = tempstring;
11       else
12       {

13          send the code associated
              with buffer;
14          assign a code to tempstring;
              store both in the code table;
15          buffer=string consisting of
              one character c;
16       }
17     } //while loop
18     send the code associated
          with buffer;
19   } //compress
20

21

22

23
24
25
```

```
1    void decompress
2    {
3      initialize(code table);
4      receive first code, call it prior;

5      print the string associated with prior;
6      while (true)
7      {
8        receive code, call it current; if no
            code then break;
9        search for current in the code table;
10       if not found
11       {
12          c=1st character of string
              associated with prior;
13          tempstring=concat(string
              associated with prior, c);
14          assign a code to tempstring;
              store both in the code table;
15          print tempstring;

16       }
17       else
18       {

19          c=1st character of string
              associated with current;
20          tempstring=concat(string
              associated with prior, c);
21          assign a code to tempstring;
              store both in the code table
22          print string associated with
              current
23       }
24     prior=current
25   } //while loop
     } //decompress
```

Figure 5.7 Lempel-Ziv Compression and Decompression Algorithms

Let's see how this algorithm works for a specific example. Suppose the characters to be read from the file are

ABABABCBABABABCBABABABCBA

Table 5.8 shows the values of relevant variables and what action is taken at each step. Table 5.9 shows the results of the code table after the compression algorithm has finished. Initially, the code table contains just three entries: A, B, and C with associated codes 0, 1, and 2, respectively. As the algorithm adds new strings to the code table, we assume it creates successive codes, starting with 3, for each new string added. As you follow through each step, remember that `tempstring` is the buffered string with c appended to it.

At step 1 the algorithm looks for AB in the code table and fails to find it. It sends the code for the buffered string A (0), stores AB (code = 3) in the code table, and defines the new buffered string as B. At step 2 the algorithm looks for BA in the code table and fails to find it. It sends the code for B (1), stores BA (code = 4) in

Table 5.8   Run-Time Results of Compression Algorithm

Loop Pass	Buffer	c	What is Sent	What is Stored in Table	New Buffer Value
1	A	B	0 (code for A)	AB (code = 3)	B
2	B	A	1 (code for B)	BA (code = 4)	A
3	A	B	—	—	AB
4	AB	A	3 (code for AB)	ABA (code = 5)	A
5	A	B	—	—	AB
6	AB	C	3 (code for AB)	ABC (code = 6)	C
7	C	B	2 (code for C)	CB (code = 7)	B
8	B	A	—	—	BA
9	BA	B	4 (code for BA)	BAB (code = 8)	B
10	B	A	—	—	BA
11	BA	B	—	—	BAB
12	BAB	A	8 (code for BAB)	BABA (code = 9)	A
13	A	B	—	—	AB
14	AB	C	—	—	ABC
15	ABC	B	6 (code for ABC)	ABCB (code = 10)	B
16	B	A	—	—	BA
17	BA	B	—	—	BAB
18	BAB	A	—	—	BABA
19	BABA	B	9 (code for BABA)	BABAB (code = 11)	B

Table 5.9 Table Produced by Compression Algorithm

String	A	B	C	AB	BA	ABA	ABC	CB	BAB	BABA	ABCB	BABAB	BABC	CBA
Code	0	1	2	3	4	5	6	7	8	9	10	11	12	13

Input string: ABABABCBABABABCBABABABCBA
Transmitted code: 0 1 3 3 2 4 8 6 9 8 7 0

the code table, and defines the new buffered string as A. At step 3 it looks for AB in the code table and this time finds it. Nothing is sent and the new buffered string is AB. At step 4 the algorithm looks for ABA in the code table and fails to find it. It sends the code for the buffered string AB (3), stores ABA (code = 5) in the code table, and defines the new buffered string as A.

This process continues and longer strings get stored in the code table. Also, the temporary strings are found in the code table more frequently and fewer transmissions occur. This causes the buffered string to become longer, and when a code table lookup does fail, the transmitted code corresponds to a longer string. The result is better compression. Table 5.8 does not show the last few steps of the algorithm; we leave it as an exercise to complete it.

The next step is to describe the decompression algorithm. Remember, all the decompression algorithm has to work with is the initial code table of characters (in our case, the code table consisting of A, B, and C with codes of 0, 1, and 2) and the incoming code values. In our example the decompression algorithm's input is the sequence 0 1 3 3 2 4 8 6 9 8 7 0. We will show its output to be the same as the original string that was input to the compression algorithm. The beauty of the decompression algorithm is its capability to reconstruct the same code table based on this limited information. Let's see how it works for the first few steps. You might want to read the next paragraph very slowly, checking and double-checking references to the algorithms and specified tables.

Initially, the decompression algorithm receives a code and calls it `prior` (line 4 of Figure 5.7). It prints the string associated with `prior` that it finds in the code table (line 5). In this case, `prior` = 0 and it prints the letter A. The algorithm then enters a loop. Table 5.10 shows relevant values with each pass of the loop and what is printed. In loop pass 1, the algorithm receives a current code of 1 (line 8 of Figure 5.7). The current code is in the code table, so the algorithm executes lines 19 through 22, storing the `tempstring`/code pair AB/3 in the code table and printing the string associated with the current code (B). Note that, as with compression, code values are assigned successively beginning with 3. In pass 2 the `prior` code is 1 and the new current code is 3. The current code is in the code table (by virtue of pass 1), so the algorithm again executes lines 19 through 22. It stores the `tempstring`/code pair BA/4 in the code table and prints the string associated with the current code (AB). In pass 3 the `prior` code is 3 and the new current code is again 3. The current code is in the code table, so the algorithm once again executes lines 19 through 22. It stores the `tempstring`/code pair ABA/5 in the code table and prints the string associated with the current code (AB).

Table 5.10   Run-Time Results of Decompression Algorithm

LOOP PASS	PRIOR (STRING)	CURRENT (STRING)	IS CURRENT CODE IN TABLE?	C	tempstring/ CODE PAIR	WHAT IS PRINTED (current or tempstring)
1	0 (A)	1 (B)	Yes	B	AB/3	B (current)
2	1 (B)	3 (AB)	Yes	A	BA/4	AB (current)
3	3 (AB)	3 (AB)	Yes	A	ABA/5	AB (current)
4	3 (AB)	2 (C)	Yes	C	ABC/6	C (current)
5	2 (C)	4 (BA)	Yes	B	CB/7	BA (current)
6	4 (BA)	8	No	B	BAB/8	BAB (tempstring)
7	8 (BAB)	6 (ABC)	Yes	A	BABA/9	ABC (current)
8	6 (ABC)	9 (BABA)	Yes	B	ABCB/10	BABA (current)
9	9 (BABA)	8 (BAB)	Yes	B	BABAB/11	BAB (current)
10	8 (BAB)	7 (CB)	Yes	C	BABC/12	CB (current)
11	7 (CB)	0 (A)	Yes	A	CBA/13	A (current)

The remaining steps follow along similar lines. The important thing to note is the way the code table is being constructed. A comparison of what is being stored in the code table with what the compression algorithm stored there (Table 5.8) shows the code table being built the same way. Consequently, code table lookups produce the same strings and the code is decompressed. As you can see, the first printed letter (A) followed by the printed letters from the last column of Table 5.10 corresponds to the initial string.

As a final note, we have shown the code table as a two-dimensional table, suggesting the use of linear searches to look for codes and strings. This will generally decrease the effectiveness of both algorithms a great deal. Instead of a table, a better approach would be to use a dictionary-based data structure in which lookups can be performed much more efficiently. In fact, Lempel-Ziv algorithms are examples of a general class of algorithms called *dictionary-based compression algorithms*. We did not use a dictionary-based data structure here because such discussions belong in a data structures course and the details would have clouded our discussion of the Lempel-Ziv algorithm. If you would like further details on dictionary-based data structures, consult reference [Dr01].

5.6   IMAGE COMPRESSION

IMAGE REPRESENTATION

One of the most significant advances in recent years has been the integration of multimedia applications with computer programs and networks. With a click of a mouse we can access photographs, pictures of classic works of art on display in the Louvre, and even movie clips from the Internet or a CD-ROM. Although transmitting images may at first seem only a small step beyond the transmission of words and sentences, multimedia applications would simply not be feasible without some very sophisticated compression algorithms.

This section and Section 5.7 investigate two popular compression methods used in the transmission and storage of visual images. We examine how a single visual image such as a photograph can be compressed and follow up by looking at video, which is essentially a sequence of still images displayed at a fast rate to give the appearance of motion. However, before we get into compression methods we must first provide a little background on how visual images may be stored and why compression is necessary.

Pictures, whether they are photographs or images on a computer screen, are made up of a lot of very small dots. These dots are also called *picture elements* or *pixels*. If the picture is of high quality, you probably cannot even see them unless perhaps you squint and place the picture very close to your eyes or use a magnifying glass. They are so densely packed that the sensory nerves in your eyes cannot distinguish them. In lesser-quality pictures the dots become more evident. For example, look very closely at a newspaper photograph and you may be able to see individual dots. Pull the picture further away and the dots blend together and the picture comes into view. One might try the same with a television picture, but parental warnings from long ago of "Don't sit so close or you'll go blind" are so deeply ingrained that they prevent me from making this recommendation.

We begin by discussing how pixels may be represented in computer memory. When we discussed fax transmissions, we referred to images that are made up of black and white pixels. This allowed us to use either a 0 or a 1 for each pixel. However, a movie or picture truly made up of just black and white images would not be very satisfying to look at. In fact, the phrase *black and white* as applied to images of old movies or to photographs is really a misnomer. These images in fact consist of various shades of gray, and each pixel must be able to represent a different shade. A common scheme is to use 8 bits to represent 256 shades of gray (ranging from white to black).

Representing images becomes more complex when we add color. High-quality images allow a wide range of colors and subtle changes in color or hue. Lesser-quality images may not distinguish among various shades of red and orange. For example, personal computers allow you to adjust the resolution of the screen to provide true color or to determine the color of the desktop, screen, icons, and title bars. In some cases you can customize your colors.

Video technology is based on the fact that any color can be represented to the human eye by using a suitable combination of the primary colors red, green, and blue (RGB). Monitor screens contain three phosphors,* one for each primary color. The electronics inside a monitor use three electron beams, one for each phosphor. By varying the intensity of each beam, the amount of primary color emitted by each

---

* A *phosphor* is a substance that emits energy in the form of light when its atoms are excited by an electron beam.

phosphor can be adjusted. The result is virtually any color in the visible spectrum. The heart of the problem is in creating a data structure that represents the proper color mix for each pixel.

Just as we can use 8 bits to represent 256 shades of gray, we can use an 8-bit group to represent each of the three primary colors. The intensity of each electron beam can be adjusted according to the 8-bit value to produce the desired color. In fact, using 8 bits for each primary color means each pixel can be represented using 24 bits, which allows up to 2^{24} possible colors. Because the human eye cannot distinguish among so many colors, we think of it as true color.

We should note that there is an alternative representation for video images that also consists of three 8-bit groups. The difference is that one group represents *luminance* (brightness) and each of the other two represents *chrominance* (color). The luminance and both chrominance values are calculated from RGB values. For example, reference [Ta03] states one possible relationship as

$$Y = 0.30R + 0.59G + 0.11B$$
$$I = 0.60R - 0.28G - 0.32B$$
$$Q = 0.21R - 0.52G + 0.31B$$

The letters *R, G,* and *B* represent values for each of the primary colors. The letters *Y, I,* and *Q* are used by the National Television Standards Committee* (NTSC) to represent the luminance and two chrominance values. There are other standards and different formulas relating these quantities, but they are not relevant to our discussion. The important thing is that for each RGB value there is a YIQ value and vice versa. If you would like additional information on chrominance and luminance values, please consult reference [Pe93].

The advantage of using luminance and chrominance is based on the sensory capabilities of the human eye, which is not uniformly sensitive to all colors. Our sensory system is more sensitive to luminance than to chrominance. This means that a small loss in chrominance values during a transmission may not be visually detectable. This is useful information when it comes to compressing images.

In the ensuing discussions we will not worry about whether pixels are represented using RGB or YIQ values. We only care that each pixel can be represented by three 8-bit groups; our main concern is to reduce the number of bits for transmission or storage.

The next step is to consider the number of pixels in a typical picture. Certainly, this will vary with picture size. However, in order to have some number to work with, let us assume a picture that fills up a VGA computer screen measuring 640 pixels by 480 pixels.[†] A little arithmetic tells us that this one image requires $24 \times 640 \times 480 = 7{,}372{,}800$ bits. How does this affect Internet traffic? Considering that video often consists of 30 images per second and that there are many images being transferred simultaneously to different users, the number of bits being pushed

* The group that defines standards for broadcast television signals in the United States.

† Today's monitors can display higher-quality images than 640×480. Also common are 800×600, 1024×768, 1152×864, and 1280×1024.

through approaches gigabit levels and higher. Without some way to compress and reduce the number of bits significantly, current technology just could not handle the traffic.

JPEG COMPRESSION

JPEG is an acronym for the Joint Photographic Experts Group, which was formed as a cooperative effort by the ISO, ITU, and IEC. Their compression standard, commonly known as **JPEG compression,** is used for both grayscale and photographic-quality color images. JPEG differs from the previously discussed compression techniques in an important way. The previous methods were examples of **lossless compression.** That is, the decompression algorithm was able to recover all of the information embedded in the compressed code. JPEG is **lossy:** The image obtained after decompression may not be the same as the original.

Whereas information loss is unacceptable in cases such as the transfer of executable files, some loss may be tolerable if the file contains an image. The reason lies in the inherent limitations of the human optical system. The simple fact is that we cannot always see subtle differences in color. Thus, if a few color pixels have been changed slightly, we may never notice the difference. An analogy may be made to looking at paint samples in a store. One person may agonize for hours over several paint samples, all of which look the same to a spouse.

JPEG compression consists of three phases (Figure 5.8): the discrete cosine transform (DCT), quantization, and encoding phases. The second and third phases are fairly straightforward, but the DCT phase is rather complex. Much of the theory is based in mathematics, requiring a knowledge of topics such as calculus, Fourier transforms, and discrete cosine transforms. We will not go into the theory behind these topics, but if you have a sufficient mathematics background you might consult references [Fe92] and [Ra90]. We will, however, present some equations, go through a couple of examples, and explain how and why the equations work on images.

DCT Phase   JPEG compression begins by dividing an image into a series of blocks consisting of 8 × 8 pixels each. If the original image measured 800 × 800 pixels, the picture would consist of a series of blocks 100 across and 100 down (Figure 5.9). If the image consisted of grayscales only, then each pixel would be represented by

Figure 5.8   JPEG's Three Phases

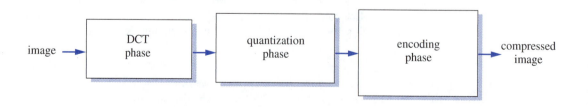

100 Blocks

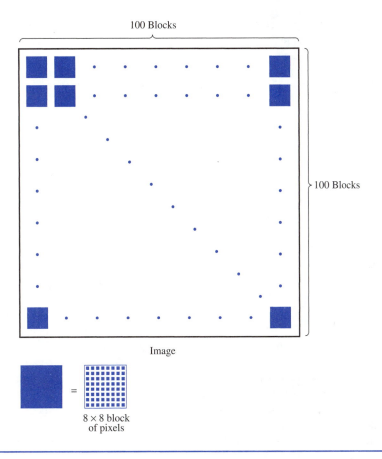

100 Blocks

Image

=

8 × 8 block
of pixels

Figure 5.9   800 × 800 VGA Screen Image Divided into 8 × 8 Pixel Blocks

an 8-bit number. We can therefore represent each block as a two-dimensional array containing eight rows and eight columns. The array's elements are 8-bit integers between 0 and 255, inclusive. The discrete cosine transform phase is applied to this array.

If the image is color, then each pixel can be represented by 24 bits or, equivalently, three 8-bit groups (representing either RGB or YIQ values; it doesn't matter here). Consequently, we can represent this 8 × 8 pixel block using three two-dimensional arrays, each with eight rows and eight columns. Each array represents pixel values from one of the three 8-bit groups. The discrete cosine transform is applied to each array.

Now we get to what the discrete cosine transform actually does. Basically, it is a function that takes a two-dimensional array with eight rows and columns and produces another two-dimensional array also with eight rows and columns. For example, if P represents the array of pixel values (with $P[x][y]$ representing the value in row x and column y), then the discrete cosine transform defines a new array, T (with $T[i][j]$ representing the value in row i and column j), as follows:*

$$T[i][j] = 0.25C(i)C(j) \sum_{x=0}^{7} \sum_{y=0}^{7} P[x][y] \cos\left(\frac{(2x+1)i\pi}{16}\right) \cos\left(\frac{(2y+1)j\pi}{16}\right) \quad \text{(5-1)}$$

for $i = 0, 1, 2, \ldots, 7$ and $j = 0, 1, 2, \ldots, 7$ and where

$$C(i) = \begin{cases} 1/\sqrt{2} \text{ if } i = 0 \\ 1 \text{ otherwise} \end{cases}$$

We'll not derive this formula. Instead let's try to understand just what this formula does to the matrix P and under what circumstances it can lead to good compression. The resulting matrix, T, contains a collection of values called **spatial frequencies.** Essentially, these spatial frequencies relate directly to how much the pixel values change as a function of their positions in the block. The value in $T[0][0]$ is called the *DC coefficient* and is related to the average of the values in the array P. (With i and j both equal to 0, the cosine functions are all 1.) The other values in T are called the *AC coefficients*. For larger values of i and j, pixel values get multiplied by cosine functions with a higher frequency.

Why is this important? Suppose that all of the P values were the same. This would correspond to an image consisting of a single color with no variation at all. In this case all of the AC coefficients correspond to sums of cosine functions that cancel each other out (since the P values could be factored out of the summations). The result is that the AC coefficients are all 0. If there is a little variation among the P values, then many, but not all, of the AC coefficients will be 0. If there is a lot of variation in the P values, few AC coefficients will be 0.

Figure 5.10 shows the results of applying the discrete cosine transform on two different arrays. The first array (Figure 5.10a) contains P values that change uniformly. This would correspond to an image with uniform color changes and little fine detail. In this case, the T array contains many AC coefficients that are 0. Note how the AC coefficients generally become smaller as they get farther away from the upper left position in the array. Values that are farther away from that position correspond to high spatial frequencies, or fine detail in the image. Because this particular image has little fine detail, these values are small and mostly 0.

In the second case (Figure 5.10b), the P values change a lot throughout the array. This would correspond to an image with large color changes over a small area. In effect, it represents an image with a lot of fine detail. In this case, the AC coefficients are all nonzero.

---

* Discrete cosine transforms have a more general definition depending on the size of the array on which they are operating. Since we are assuming an 8 × 8 array, this formula suits our purposes here.

P array
20 30 40 50 60 70 80 90
30 40 50 60 70 80 90 100
40 50 60 70 80 90 100 110
50 60 70 80 90 100 110 120
60 70 80 90 100 110 120 130
70 80 90 100 110 120 130 140
80 90 100 110 120 130 140 150
90 100 110 120 130 140 150 160

T array (values rounded to the nearest integer)

720	−182	0	−19	0	−6	0	−1
−182	0	0	0	0	0	0	0
0	0	0	0	0	0	0	0
−19	0	0	0	0	0	0	0
0	0	0	0	0	0	0	0
−6	0	0	0	0	0	0	0
0	0	0	0	0	0	0	0
−1	0	0	0	0	0	0	0

(a) *P* array representing small changes in the image

P array
100 150 50 100 100 150 200 120
200 10 110 20 200 120 30 120
10 200 130 30 200 20 150 50
100 10 90 190 120 200 10 100
10 200 200 120 90 190 20 200
150 120 20 200 150 70 10 100
200 30 150 10 10 120 190 10
120 120 50 100 10 190 10 120

T array (values rounded to the nearest integer)

835	15	−17	59	5	−56	69	−38
46	−60	−36	11	14	−60	−71	110
−32	−9	130	105	−37	81	−17	24
59	−3	27	−12	30	28	−27	−48
50	−71	−24	−56	−40	−36	67	−189
−23	−18	4	54	−66	152	−61	35
2	13	−37	−53	15	−80	−185	−62
32	−14	52	−93	−210	−48	−76	80

(b) *P* array representing large changes in the image

Figure 5.10   Discrete Cosine Transform Results on Two Different Arrays

In general, if the pixel values change more rapidly and less uniformly as a function of their position, the AC coefficients correspond to values with larger magnitudes. In addition, more of the higher spatial frequency values become nonzero. In summary, the AC coefficients are essentially a measure of pixel variation. Consequently, images with a lot of fine detail are harder to compress than images with little color variation.

The spatial frequencies are not of much use to us unless there is a way to use them to restore the original pixel values. In fact, there is an inverse formula that will convert spatial frequencies back to pixel values:

$$P[x][y] = 0.25 \sum_{i=0}^{7} \sum_{j=0}^{7} C(i)C(j)T[i][j] \cos\left(\frac{(2x+1)i\pi}{16}\right) \cos\left(\frac{(2y+1)j\pi}{16}\right) \quad (5\text{-}2)$$

We will not prove or verify this claim. We leave it as an exercise to write a program that applies Equation 5.2 to the spatial frequencies of Figure 5.10. If you do it correctly, you will calculate the original pixel values.

Quantization Phase   The second, or quantization, phase provides a way of ignoring small differences in an image that may not be perceptible. It defines yet another two-dimensional array (call it Q) by dividing each T value by some number and rounding to the nearest integer. For example, suppose that

$$T = \begin{vmatrix} 152 & 0 & -48 & 0 & -8 & 0 & -7 & 0 \\ 0 & 0 & 0 & 0 & 0 & 0 & 0 & 0 \\ -48 & -0 & 38 & 0 & -3 & 0 & 2 & 0 \\ 0 & 0 & 0 & 0 & 0 & 0 & 0 & 0 \\ -8 & 0 & -3 & 0 & 13 & 0 & -1 & 0 \\ 0 & 0 & 0 & 0 & 0 & 0 & 0 & 0 \\ -7 & 0 & 2 & 0 & -1 & 0 & 7 & 0 \\ 0 & 0 & 0 & 0 & 0 & 0 & 0 & 0 \end{vmatrix} \tag{5-3}$$

If we divided each value by 10 and rounded to the nearest integer, we would have

$$Q = \begin{vmatrix} 15 & 0 & -5 & 0 & -1 & 0 & -1 & 0 \\ 0 & 0 & 0 & 0 & 0 & 0 & 0 & 0 \\ -5 & 0 & 4 & 0 & 0 & 0 & 0 & 0 \\ 0 & 0 & 0 & 0 & 0 & 0 & 0 & 0 \\ -1 & 0 & 0 & 0 & 1 & 0 & 0 & 0 \\ 0 & 0 & 0 & 0 & 0 & 0 & 0 & 0 \\ -1 & 0 & 0 & 0 & 0 & 0 & 1 & 0 \\ 0 & 0 & 0 & 0 & 0 & 0 & 0 & 0 \end{vmatrix} \tag{5-4}$$

The reason we might do this is to create another array with fewer distinct numbers and more consistent patterns. For example, array Q has more zeros in it and would likely compress better than T. Of course, doing this prompts a logical question: How can we go from Q back to T for decompression? The answer is simple: We can't. By dividing T values and rounding we have lost information. If we tried to reverse the operation and multiply each element in Q by 10, we would end up with

$$T = \begin{vmatrix} 150 & 0 & -50 & 0 & -10 & 0 & -10 & 0 \\ 0 & 0 & 0 & 0 & 0 & 0 & 0 & 0 \\ -50 & 0 & 40 & 0 & 0 & 0 & 0 & 0 \\ 0 & 0 & 0 & 0 & 0 & 0 & 0 & 0 \\ -10 & 0 & 0 & 0 & 10 & 0 & 0 & 0 \\ 0 & 0 & 0 & 0 & 0 & 0 & 0 & 0 \\ -10 & 0 & 0 & 0 & 0 & 0 & 10 & 0 \\ 0 & 0 & 0 & 0 & 0 & 0 & 0 & 0 \end{vmatrix} \tag{5-5}$$

There's no way to know, for example, that the two -10s in column 1 should have been -8 and -7 as in the T array from Equation 5.3. Consequently, if we applied Equation 5.2 to the array in Equation 5.5 we would end up with pixel values that are approximations to the originals. In other words, we have lost some of the color. If the loss is small, however, it may not be noticed.

In practice, dividing the T values by the same constant is not practical and often results in too much loss. What we really want to do is preserve as much information in the upper left portions of the array as possible because they represent low spatial frequencies. That is, they correspond to less subtle features of the image that would be noticed if changed. Values in the lower right portion correspond to fine detail, and changes there might not be noticed as much. Consequently, the usual approach is to define a quantization array, call it U, with smaller values in the upper left portion and larger values in the lower right. Then we define Q using the formula

$$Q[i][j] = \text{Round}(T[i][j]/U[i][j]) \quad \text{for } i = 0, 1, 2, \ldots, 7 \text{ and } j = 0, 1, 2, \ldots, 7$$

where Round is a function that rounds to the nearest integer.

For example, if we use the T array from Equation 5.3 and

$$U = \begin{vmatrix} 1 & 3 & 5 & 7 & 9 & 11 & 13 & 15 \\ 3 & 5 & 7 & 9 & 11 & 13 & 15 & 17 \\ 5 & 7 & 9 & 11 & 13 & 15 & 17 & 19 \\ 7 & 9 & 11 & 13 & 15 & 17 & 19 & 21 \\ 9 & 11 & 13 & 15 & 17 & 19 & 21 & 23 \\ 11 & 13 & 15 & 17 & 19 & 21 & 23 & 25 \\ 13 & 15 & 17 & 19 & 21 & 23 & 25 & 27 \\ 15 & 17 & 19 & 21 & 23 & 25 & 27 & 29 \end{vmatrix} \tag{5-6}$$

then the quantization would yield

$$Q = \begin{vmatrix} 152 & 0 & -10 & 0 & -1 & 0 & -1 & 0 \\ 0 & 0 & 0 & 0 & 0 & 0 & 0 & 0 \\ -10 & 0 & 4 & 0 & 0 & 0 & 0 & 0 \\ 0 & 0 & 0 & 0 & 0 & 0 & 0 & 0 \\ -1 & 0 & 0 & 0 & 1 & 0 & 0 & 0 \\ 0 & 0 & 0 & 0 & 0 & 0 & 0 & 0 \\ -1 & 0 & 0 & 0 & 0 & 0 & 0 & 0 \\ 0 & 0 & 0 & 0 & 0 & 0 & 0 & 0 \end{vmatrix} \tag{5-7}$$

Reversing the process and multiplying each element in Q by the corresponding element in U would generate

$$T = \begin{vmatrix} 152 & 0 & -50 & 0 & -9 & 0 & -13 & 0 \\ 0 & 0 & 0 & 0 & 0 & 0 & 0 & 0 \\ -50 & 0 & 36 & 0 & 0 & 0 & 0 & 0 \\ 0 & 0 & 0 & 0 & 0 & 0 & 0 & 0 \\ -9 & 0 & 0 & 0 & 17 & 0 & 0 & 0 \\ 0 & 0 & 0 & 0 & 0 & 0 & 0 & 0 \\ -13 & 0 & 0 & 0 & 0 & 0 & 0 & 0 \\ 0 & 0 & 0 & 0 & 0 & 0 & 0 & 0 \end{vmatrix} \tag{5-8}$$

It is still only an approximation to the original T of Equation 5.3, but there will generally be less loss in the lower spatial frequency areas of the array, which will preserve more of the less-subtle aspects of the original image. It may come at the expense of more loss in higher spatial frequency areas but, again, the losses would be less noticeable. Furthermore, the quantized array Q still has considerable redundancy, which should lead to some good compression.

We should note that JPEG does not prescribe the contents of U. It typically depends a great deal on the application, and great efforts often go into finding a U that helps compress well with minimal loss.

Encoding Phase   Much of the discussion on JPEG so far has involved complex transformations and quantizing results. We have yet to compress anything. These steps exist primarily to transform the data into a form suitable for compression. The encoding phase finally does the compression. The main function of the encoding phase is to linearize the two-dimensional data from the Q array and compress it for transmission. A logical approach might be to linearize by transmitting Q one row at a time. With all the 0s that appear, we could use run-length coding. Although this will certainly work, there is a better way.

Figure 5.11 illustrates how we can order the elements from the array Q of Equation 5.7. If we were to order the array elements by transmitting a row at a time, starting with row 1, we would have the following runs of 0s (of length greater than 8):

- Run of length 9 from rows 1 and 2
- Run of length 13 from rows 3 and 4
- Run of length 11 from rows 5 and 6
- Run of length 15 from rows 7 and 8

If, however, we ordered the elements as indicated by the arrows in the figure, we have the following runs (of length greater than 8):

- Run of length 11
- Run of length 24

Figure 5.11   Order in which Array Elements Are Transmitted

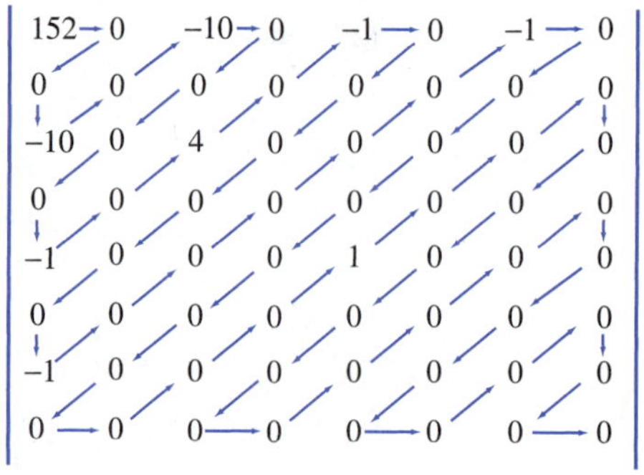

As we can see, there is a much longer run with this second order. We don't intend this to be a formal proof that this method of linearizing the elements is optimal. On the other hand, we make the argument that by following the arrows of Figure 5.11, elements representing higher spatial frequencies tend to be gathered together. That is not the case if we transmit a row or column at a time. Because the quantization array, U, often has larger values in the higher spatial frequency areas, the quantized values have a higher probability of being 0. By keeping the higher spatial frequency values together, we have a higher probability of producing long runs of 0s, which, in turn, leads to better compression.

JPEG can also use some type of Huffman code or arithmetic code for the nonzero values in cases where the DCT and quantization phases produce certain nonzero values with a higher frequency. Finally, since the 8×8 arrays represent only a small portion of an image, many arrays must be transmitted. In many images, consecutive arrays represent adjacent blocks that may differ little from each other. There is even the potential for transmitting differences among nonzero elements as opposed to the elements themselves, thus adding yet another dimension to the compression.

In summary, JPEG compression is complex and the amount of compression depends a great deal on the image and the quantization array. The quantization array is not prescribed by JPEG but rather depends on the application. Under the right conditions, JPEG is known to produce compression ratios of 20:1 and better (meaning the transmitted file is 5% the size of the original). Higher ratios are possible, but the loss in quality becomes more noticeable.

Work is also in progress on another standard, JPEG 2000, based on wavelet technology. As usual, details are complex, but wavelet technology is similar to the Fourier series in that it breaks functions down into component parts. For more information on wavelets, see reference [Sa00]. Certainly, a more detailed discussion of JPEG is possible; if you are interested in such details, you can consult references [Sa00], [Ha01], [Ho97], or [He96] or the website www.jpeg.org/.

GIF Files

We close this section with a brief reference to one other image file format: **GIF (Graphics Interchange Format).** Whereas JPEG was designed to work with full-color images (up to 2^{24} different colors), GIF reduces the number of colors to 256. Basically, it stores up to 256 colors in a table, trying to cover the range of colors in an image as closely as possible. It then replaces each 24-bit pixel value with an 8-bit index to a table entry containing the color that matches the original most closely. The resulting bit values are then subjected to a variation of Lempel-Ziv encoding for compression.

GIF files are lossy if the number of colors exceeds 256, and lossless otherwise. The format is typically best suited to graphics that contain relatively few colors and have sharply defined boundaries between colors. Such images include cartoons, charts, or line drawings. GIF will not work well on images that have a lot of variations and shading, attributes typically found in full-color photographic-quality images.

5.7   MULTIMEDIA COMPRESSION

MPEG

Having described how to compress still images, the next logical step is to discuss video or motion pictures. However, before we deal with compressing those, we must understand just how motion in a video clip is achieved. Motion, whether it is on the big screen, a television, or a video clip from a CD-ROM or the Internet on a computer monitor, is really not much more than a rapid display of still pictures. Standards for video differ worldwide, but a common standard defined by the NTSC produces motion by displaying still pictures at a rate of 30 frames per second. This is fast enough to fool your eyes, giving the perception of true motion. Images produced at rates much slower than that produce motion that appears jerky, which is reminiscent of some very old movies.

The group that defines standards for video compression is the **Moving Pictures Expert Group (MPEG).** Like JPEG, it is the result of a cooperative arrangement between the ISO, IEC, and ITU. People often use the phrase *MPEG compression* when referring to video compression. MPEG, however, is not a single standard. In fact, there are several standards.

- MPEG-1, formally known as ISO/IEC-11172, was designed for video on CD-ROM and early direct broadcast satellite systems.

- MPEG-2, formally known as ISO/IEC-13818, is used for more demanding applications, such as multimedia entertainment and high-definition television (HDTV) and was also adopted by the satellite broadcasting industry.

- MPEG-4, formally known as ISO/IEC-14496, is intended for videoconferencing over low-bandwidth channels. (Yes, there was an MPEG-3, which was originally intended for HDTV, but HDTV was added to the MPEG-2 standard instead.)

- As of this writing, work is progressing on MPEG-7, designed to support a broad range of applications and based on the assumption that multimedia data will occupy an increasing amount of bandwidth as we progress into the 21st century. MPEG-7 will provide multimedia tools for defining and accessing content and would allow, for example, searching for songs by humming a tune into a computer's microphone, searching for images by sketching a graphic known to be in the image, or scanning a company logo and searching a multimedia database of commercials to determine which ones display the logo.

- Work is also in progress on MPEG-21. There are many players in the multimedia field, and each may use its own models, rules, and procedures. MPEG-21 would define a common framework to facilitate interaction and cooperation among the different groups.

At this level we will not worry about the different MPEG variations and are content to spend some time discussing MPEG-1 (which we will, from this point on, refer to as MPEG). As before, if you would like information beyond what we present, you can consult references [Sa00], [Ho97], and [Ha01]. Also, MPEG actually compresses audio and video separately, and we will deal only with video compression. You can find a description of MPEG audio encoding in reference [Ho97].

Because video is actually a series of still pictures, it seems logical to assume that MPEG uses JPEG compression or a variation of it to compress each image. Although that is essentially true, using only JPEG compression for each still picture does not provide sufficient compression for most applications. In the last section, we stated that a still picture could contain 7,372,800 bits. At a 20:1 compression ratio, we could reduce the image to 368,640 bits. However, remember that NTSC video standards specify 30 images per second, so that we would still need to transmit $30 \times 368,640 = 11,059,200$ bits per second. That's a lot, especially if it is being sent over shared channels being used by others who also want access to video.

What makes MPEG feasible is additional redundancy (**temporal redundancy**) found in successive frames. Basically, this means that no matter how much action you see in a video, the difference between two consecutive frames is usually quite small. Even popular action heroes require a couple of seconds to get blown across a room. That's 60 frames, and the hero may only travel a few feet from one frame to another. If you consider scenes with little action, consecutive frames may be almost identical. Since JPEG compresses information found on a single image, MPEG must deal with the temporal redundancy. Actually, we addressed this issue earlier in the chapter when we discussed relative encoding. Essentially, that technique sends a base frame and then encodes successive frames by computing the difference (which will contain little information) and then compressing and transmitting it. The receiving end can reconstruct the frame based on the first base frame and the differences it receives.

To some extent this is what MPEG does, but, as you probably suspect, it is more complex than that. Calculating differences with prior frames works well to place figures that are moving across your view, since those figures are in a prior frame. But it does not work well for images that were not in a prior frame. For example, a completely new scene cannot be compressed this way. The difference between a new scene and an old one is large and you might as well just send the new scene. Another example involves objects hidden behind someone who is moving. As a person moves across a scene, objects that were hidden behind the person in a previous frame come into view in successive frames.

MPEG identifies three different types of frames:*

- **I frame (intrapicture frame).** This is a self-contained frame that is, for all intents and purposes, just a JPEG-encoded image.

- **P frame (predicted frame).** This frame is similar to what we have just discussed in that it is encoded by computing differences between a current and a previous frame.

- **B frame (bidirectional frame).** This is similar to a P frame except that it is interpolated between a previous and a future frame. (Yes, this sounds a bit peculiar, but we'll get to that).

---

* There is actually a fourth type of frame, called a DC frame, that can be used for fast searches on devices such as tape recorders. It doesn't play a role in what we are discussing here, so we won't cover it.

Two issues need to be discussed. First is how and why the different frame types appear in a frame sequence. Second is how P and B frames are constructed from other frames. We start by indicating that I frames must appear periodically in any frame sequence. There are a couple of reasons for this. As we have stated, calculating differences works well when there is little difference between frames. But small differences from a fixed frame are usually localized over a relatively short period of time. Eventually, a scene changes or new objects come into view. If we try to measure everything relative to the very first frame, we will have little success. If we use relative differencing and measure differences in consecutive frames, then any error introduced in one frame is propagated throughout subsequent frames. A second reason is appropriate in broadcast applications, where an individual can tune in at any time. If everything were encoded relative to the very first frame and you tuned in a bit late, you would have nothing to which to compare successive frames. Getting I frames periodically ensures that differences are measured to relatively current scenes. It can also eliminate the propagation of errors.

Figure 5.12 shows a typical MPEG frame sequence. Sandwiched between two I frames are four B frames and a single P frame. In general, the number of B frames can vary, but typically there will be one P frame between two groups of B frames. The P frame is essentially a difference from the prior I frame, and the B frames are interpolated from the nearest I and P frames. So, for example, the first two B frames are interpolated from the first I frame and the P frame. The last two B frames are interpolated from the last I frame and the P frame.

A logical question to ask is, How can we interpolate B frames from frames we haven't received yet? The answer is that Figure 5.12 shows the frames in the order they are to be viewed, not the order in which they are transmitted. The P frame will be sent prior to the first two B frames, and the second I frame will be sent prior to the last two B frames. The P frame and two I frames can then be buffered, and subsequently received B frames can be decoded at the viewing end.

P frames are coded using a method called *motion-compensated prediction,* which is based on concepts specified in ITU recommendation H.261. It works by dividing the image into a collection of macroblocks, each containing 256 pixels (16 horizontal and 16 vertical). Assuming each pixel has one luminescence and two chrominance values, the macroblock can be represented by three 16×16 arrays. To help speed things up, the two chrominance arrays are actually reduced to two 8×8 arrays. Figure 5.13 shows how that is done. The 16×16 array is viewed as a collection of 2×2 arrays of chrominance values. The average of each set of four chrominance values replaces the four values, and the result is an 8×8 array. Again, there is some loss in doing this, but the loss is often not perceptible.

Figure 5.12   Typical MPEG Frame Sequence

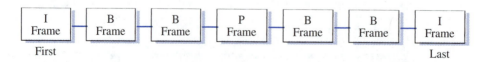

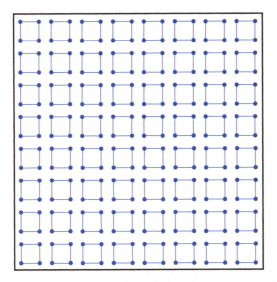

Figure 5.13 Reduction of a 16 × 16 Chrominance Array to an 8 × 8 Chrominance Array

Prior to sending a P frame, an algorithm examines each macroblock and locates the best matching macroblock in the prior I frame. It won't necessarily be in the same relative position* because we are assuming that images move from one frame to another. MPEG does not specify what constitutes a best match—this is dependent on specific applications. Once the best-match macroblock is found, the algorithm calculates differences between the matching macroblocks and also calculates a *motion vector* (essentially a vertical and horizontal pixel displacement), which it stores along with the differences. This is done for all macroblocks in a frame, and the results are encoded and transmitted in a manner similar to that specified by JPEG. At the decoding end, the differences are used to reconstruct the macroblocks, and the motion vectors are used to determine their position in the frame.

B-frame decoding is similar except macroblocks are interpolated from matching macroblocks in a prior and future frame. *Interpolation* is a way of predicting a value based on two existing values and is a common topic in numerical analysis. Figure 5.14 illustrates what we mean. If the horizontal line represents time and we know the values of some quantities (Y_P and Y_F, respectively) at some past and future times, we can estimate the value (Y_C) at the current time. One way is to draw a line connecting points corresponding to Y_P and Y_F and calculate the y-coordinate of that line at the current time. This is an example of linear interpolation. There are many other ways to interpolate, but that's another topic.

---

* This does not mean the algorithm searches the entire frame looking for a best match. Typically, it looks at the macroblock in the same relative position and at others in nearby positions. This helps speed the encoding algorithm.

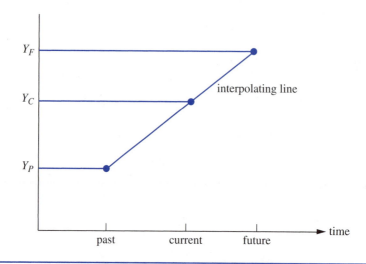

Figure 5.14 Using Interpolation to Estimate a Value

The important thing here is that both past and future frames can be searched to find matches for a macroblock, with differences and motion vectors calculated for each. The value of the macroblock and its correct placement in the current frame can then be interpolated from the matching macroblocks and the motion vectors. As previously stated, this is particularly useful when there is no good match for a macroblock in a previous frame, as can happen when new objects come into view. However, that object would likely be in a future frame, and that information can be used to calculate and place a macroblock in the current frame.

Before we finish, it is noteworthy to mention that despite the standards, MPEG encoding and decoding requires a lot of computing power. Finding matches and calculating motion vectors for a large number of bits is nontrivial. However, in many multimedia applications, video is recorded just once and stored in some medium. Because this is done well in advance of viewing, the time required for encoding is not that much of a concern. Viewing the video, however, is done frequently and in real time. Decoding must be done quickly or the motion appears jerky. Try looking at some multimedia applications using a personal computer that is a couple of years old and you will likely notice that the images do not flow with the smoothness of real video.

Faster CPUs certainly help, but the CPU does so many other things that this is not a long-term solution to the development of fast multimedia applications. One of the more significant developments a few years ago was the MMX technology built into Pentium chips for multimedia applications. It enables applications such as MPEG (actually MPEG-2) decoding, thus resulting in significant overall performance increase. Describing MMX technology belongs in a computer architecture course, but because of its impact on MPEG-2 applications it is appropriate to mention it here. Further details regarding MMX technology and its impact on multimedia performance are found in reference [Pe97].

MP3

We close this chapter on compression with an overview of a technology that's been involved in some high-profile news stories. The technology is **MP3,** a compression protocol for audio. Note that MP3 itself is not controversial. It simply defines how to compress audio files. The controversy exists in the unlicensed use and sharing of MP3-encoded music. We'll leave discussions of the controversy to others and will outline the technology behind MP3.

Before we get into this, let's provide a little background about audio bit streams. Section 3.6 described PCM (pulse code modulation), a technique for converting analog signals to digital. We discussed sampling frequencies and how they relate to the frequency range of the original audio signal. What we did not discuss was the inherent limitations of the human auditory system. Generally, most people can only hear sounds with frequencies between 20 Hz and about 20 kHz. Our auditory systems are just not capable of picking up frequencies outside that range. As a result, a common PCM technique to produce CD-quality sound uses 16-bit samples and a sampling frequency of 44.1 kHz. According to the Nyquist theorem, this is sufficient to completely reconstruct a signal within our hearing range.

A little arithmetic shows that 1 second of PCM-coded music requires $16 \times 44.1 \times 1000 \approx 700,000$ bits, and that's just for one channel. For two-channel stereo the value doubles to 1.4 megabits. Thus, a 2-minute recording would require approximately 1.4 megabits per second $\times$ 120 seconds $\approx$ 168 megabits. Not only is this a very large file, but we'd also need to deliver the bits at a bit rate of 1.4 Mbps to produce the sound. Two ways to reduce the total number of bits would be to reduce the number of bits per sample or reduce the sampling frequency. Unfortunately, both approaches correspond to a less accurate digitization of the original analog signal and result in a loss in the quality of sound. This is where compression comes in.

MP3 actually refers to MPEG layer 3 for audio compression and was adopted as an ISO/IEC standard in 1992. As this statement suggests, MPEG allows for three different layers of audio compression. The layers differ in coding complexity, compression ratios, and resulting sound quality as follows:

- Layer 1 produces about a 4-to-1 compression ratio, and sound can be produced at a bit rate of 192 Kbps for each channel.

- Layer 2 produces about an 8-to-1 compression ratio and is designed for bit rates of 128 Kbps per channel.

- Layer 3 (MP3) compresses at about a 12-to-1 ratio and is suitable for bit rates of about 64 Kbps per channel.

So how does MP3 actually work? Unfortunately, we cannot answer that question completely because there are some very sophisticated techniques involved. However, we'll provide an overview of the major concepts. Much of what is designed into MP3 is based on a **psychoacoustic model.** Psychoacoustics is basically the study of the human auditory system and can identify what we can hear and what sounds we can distinguish.

As stated previously, we can generally hear sounds in the 20 Hz to 20 kHz range. However, another issue is how well we can distinguish among different sounds in that range. Most of us can tell the difference between a bass fiddle and a flute because of the widely different frequencies that each produces. However, the model says that as two signals' frequencies become closer we really cannot distinguish between them. For example, most people could not distinguish a 2000 Hz sound from another at 2001 Hz.

Yet another issue is **auditory masking.** If sound with a certain frequency is very strong and another sound with a similar frequency is weak, we may be unable to hear the weaker sound. An optical analogy is that if you look straight into a bright light you are unable to see a small dark object that is in front of the light. Turn off the light and the small dark object appears. That's because the signal from the bright light is too strong and overpowers any reflected light from the smaller object.

An example in audio terms is that if someone plays a piano key very loudly at the same time an adjacent key is played very softly, most people are unable to hear the softer note. The louder notes overpower the softer ones. Perhaps this also explains why so few highway construction workers listen to classical music while operating a jackhammer. So, the fundamental idea behind MP3 is to capture an audio signal, determine what we cannot hear, remove those components from the audio stream, and digitize what is left. In short, it simply removes what we cannot hear.

The first step in MP3 compression is *subband coding* (Figure 5.15). This means that an audio bit stream is fed into a psychoacoustic model and a filter bank. The **filter bank** is a collection of filters, each of which creates a stream representing signal components within a specified frequency range. There is one filter for each of many frequency ranges; together, they decompose the original signal into subbands, each with a different and nonoverlapping frequency range. The theory of filter banks and subband coding is high level and requires complex calculations similar to those of the discrete cosine transforms of Section 5.6. We'll not go through them again, but if you are interested, reference [Sa00] contains a detailed description of subband coding. The main idea is to create a bit stream for each band.

However, because of auditory masking, the subbands should not all be encoded the same way. If the signals in one subband are loud, we need a good resolution of

Figure 5.15   MP3 Encoding

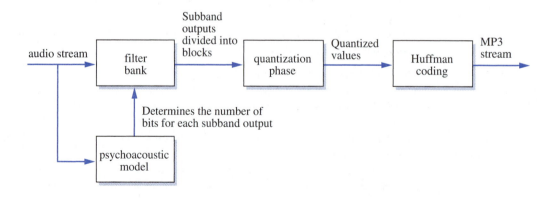

their amplitudes. That is, we need more bits. If signals in a neighboring subband are weak and are effectively masked by the louder signals, we need much less resolution for those weaker signals and can code them using fewer bits. This is where the psychoacoustic model fits into the scheme. It analyzes the audio stream and determines masking thresholds. The process is complex, because it depends on mapping the signals to a frequency domain representation and using Fourier transforms. The purpose, however, is to determine which frequencies dominate and which may not be heard. If certain frequencies will be inaudible, there is no need to completely reconstruct that part of the signal, and fewer bits are used. Thus, we have compression with no discernible loss in sound quality. The end result is that each subband is encoded using a different number of bits.

Table 5.11 Summary of Compression Techniques

COMPRESSION TECHNIQUE	TYPE OF REDUNDANCY EXPLOITED	HOW IT COMPRESSES
Huffman code	Certain characters appear more frequently than others.	Uses short bit patterns for more frequently used letters and longer ones for less frequently used letters.
Run-length encoding	Data contain long strings of the same character or bit.	Replaces a long run of a particular bit or character with its run length.
Facsimile compression	Looks for both long strings of the same bit and the frequency with which specific strings appear.	Divides a line of pixels into alternating runs of white and black pixels. Each run is encoded using a modified Huffman algorithm.
Relative encoding	Two consecutive pieces of data differ by very little.	Encodes small differences between consecutive frames instead of actual frames.
Lempel-Ziv encoding	Certain character strings appear more frequently than others.	Replaces repeated occurrences of strings with generated codes.
JPEG	Small subsets of pictures often contain little detail.	Compresses still images by applying discrete cosine transforms to 8×8 blocks of pixels, quantizing the results, and encoding the quantized frequency coefficients.
MPEG	Consecutive frames often contain nearly identical scenes.	Uses methods similar to JPEG compression but also takes advantage of redundancy between successive frames to use interframe compression by calculating differences between successive frames and using motion prediction techniques.
MP3 (MPEG layer 3 audio compression)	Signal components that are masked by other, more powerful signals or are outside the range of the human auditory system.	Uses complex psychoacoustic models and filter banks to determine which parts of an audio signal will be inaudible and seeks to remove those parts.

Finally, the subband signals go into a quantizing phase. As described in the section on JPEG compression, the quantization phase reduces the total number of values in each subband and seeks to eliminate small differences that should not be perceptible. The quantized values may then be subjected to a Huffman code, and the MP3 bit stream is created.

We realize that we have not provided a lot of detail here, but to do so requires a significant amount of mathematics along with the theory of subband coding and psychoacoustic models. If you are interested in some of this theory, we encourage you to consult reference [Sa00].

5.8 SUMMARY

The compression techniques discussed here are representative of schemes in actual use, but they by no means represent the entire spectrum of techniques. References [Sa00], [Ho97], [Fe97], and [He96] mention other techniques, and references [Ho97], [Sa00], and [He96] are devoted completely to compression techniques (and are good reading for anyone seriously interested in the topic). Remember that compression techniques are designed for different types of transmissions. Table 5.11 briefly summarizes the compression techniques discussed in this chapter.

Review Questions

1. What is a Huffman code?

2. What is the Huffman code's no-prefix property?

3. What is a frequency-dependent code?

4. What does run-length encoding mean?

5. Are the following statements TRUE or FALSE? Why?

   a. The Huffman algorithm could effectively compress a text file containing random characters.

   b. The Lempel-Ziv compression algorithm could effectively compress a large file containing source code from a program.

   c. A compression method that works well on one type of file will frequently work well on another type of file.

   d. Compression methods should always compress the file without losing any of the file's information.

   e. A compression method, when applied to a file, might actually create a larger file.

   f. Compression ratios for facsimile compression differ depending on the image being compressed.

   g. MP3 and JPEG compression are similar in that each is not capable of reconstructing the original file.

6. What is arithmetic compression?

7. What is the purpose of a terminating character in arithmetic compression?

8. What is relative encoding?

9. What is Lempel-Ziv encoding?

10. What is facsimile compression?

11. Both the Lempel-Ziv and Huffman algorithms are similar in that they take advantage of repetitions. How do they differ?

12. What are the main differences between JPEG and MPEG compression methods?

13. Distinguish among I, P, and B frames in the context of MPEG encoding.

14. What is an MP3 file?

15. What is a psychoacoustic model?

16. What does auditory masking mean? How does it help in compressing sound files?

17. Which compression techniques in this chapter are lossless? Which are lossy?

Exercises

1. Can you devise a 4-bit code similar to that in Table 5.1?

2. Devise a Huffman code for letters whose frequency of occurrence is as given in the following table.

LETTER	FREQUENCY (%)
A	15
B	25
C	20
D	10
E	10
F	20

    Without constructing them, how many different Huffman codes could you create?

3. Complete Table 5.5 and find the final interval for the string in that example.

4. Describe problems that occur if a variable-length frequency-dependent code such as Huffman does *not* have the no-prefix property.

5. Compress the following bit stream using run-length encoding. Use 5 bits to code each run length. Parenthesized expressions indicate runs.

    `1 (33 zeros) 1 (25 zeros) 1 1 1 (44 zeros) 1 (2 zeros) 1 (45 zeros)`

    Express the length of the compressed stream as a percentage of the original.

6. With run-length encoding, how many 0s must appear in a run before the code actually compresses?

7. Give an example of a situation in which run-length encoding would perform better (worse) than a Huffman code.

8. Comment on the following statement:

   > In an era of megabit and gigabit transmissions, compression schemes will save only the smallest fractions of a second. Therefore, the time saved is not worth the additional overhead of compressing bits.

9. Use the Huffman code from Table 5.3 and interpret the following bit stream (starting from the leftmost bit).

   11001110010001000011110110

10. Which of the following are Huffman codes? Why?

CHARACTER	CODE	CHARACTER	CODE	CHARACTER	CODE
A	01	A	10	A	1
B	001	B	001	B	01
C	10	C	11	C	000
D	110	D	101	D	001
E	010	E	000	E	0001

11. Complete the steps in the arithmetic encoding process in Table 5.5.

12. Apply arithmetic compression to the string DCBED using the probabilities defined in Table 5.4. What real number can be used to compress the string?

13. Repeat the previous exercise but assume the probabilities are 0.15 (A), 0.25 (B), 0.2 (C), 0.1 (D), and 0.3 (E).

14. Suppose you have 10 characters, each having equal probability. Can you suggest a simpler way to implement arithmetic encoding?

15. Using the probabilities of Table 5.4, what string corresponds to the real value 0.45734? Assume the string contains five characters.

16. One can argue that arithmetic compression is used to determine a single real number between 0 and 1. Therefore, standard storage formats for floating-point numbers may be used and the compressed code is always the same number of bits. How would you respond?

17. Using fax compression, what is the compressed code for a run of 1300 white pixels? 1300 black pixels?

18. Fill in language-specific details and implement the Lempel-Ziv algorithms of Figure 5.7.

19. How do the algorithms of Figure 5.7 change if we use a full alphabet?

20. Complete Table 5.8.

21. Run the Lempel-Ziv compression and decompression algorithms starting with the following string. Create tables similar to Tables 5.8, 5.9, and 5.10.

    BBABAABBAABACBACBACBABAAABAA

22. Write a program that applies Equation 5.2 to the spatial frequencies in each of Figures 5.10a and 5.10b.

23. Perform a discrete cosine transform (Equation 5.1) on the following pixel array. You should write a program to do the calculations.

$$
\begin{vmatrix}
10 & 10 & 10 & 10 & 10 & 10 & 10 & 10 \\
10 & 20 & 20 & 20 & 20 & 20 & 20 & 10 \\
10 & 20 & 30 & 30 & 30 & 30 & 20 & 10 \\
10 & 20 & 30 & 40 & 40 & 30 & 20 & 10 \\
10 & 20 & 30 & 40 & 40 & 30 & 20 & 10 \\
10 & 20 & 30 & 30 & 30 & 30 & 20 & 10 \\
10 & 20 & 20 & 20 & 20 & 20 & 20 & 10 \\
10 & 10 & 10 & 10 & 10 & 10 & 10 & 10
\end{vmatrix}
$$

REFERENCES

[Cr90] Crichton, M. *Jurassic Park.* New York: Ballantine Books, 1990.

[Dr01] Drozdeck, A. *Data Structures and Algorithms in C++.* Pacific Grove, CA: Brooks/Cole, 2001.

[Fe92] Feig, E., and S. Winograd. "Fast Algorithms for Discrete Cosine Transformations." *IEEE Transactions on Signal Processing,* vol. 40 (September 1992), 2174–2193.

[Fe97] Fernandez, J. *MIME, UUENCODE and ZIP: Decompressing and Decoding Internet Files.* New York: MIS Press, 1997.

[Ha01] Halsall, F. *Multimedia Communications.* Reading, MA: Addison-Wesley, 2001.

[He96] Held, G. *Data and Image Compression,* 4th ed. New York: Wiley, 1996.

[Ho97] Hoffman, R. *Data Compression in Digital Systems.* New York: Chapman and Hall, 1997.

[Hu52] Huffman, D. "A Method for the Construction of Minimum Redundancy Codes." *IRE Proceedings,* vol. 40 (September 1952), 1098–1101.

[Pe93] Pennebaker, W. B., and J. L. Mitchell. *JPEG Still Image Data Compression Standard.* New York: Van Nostrand Reinhold, 1993.

[Pe97] Peleg, A., S. Wilkie, and U. Weiser. "Intel MMX for Multimedia PCs." *Communications of the ACM,* vol. 40, no. 1 (January 1997), 25–38.

[Ra90] Rao, K. R., and P. Yip. *Discrete Cosine Transform: Algorithms, Advantages, Applications.* Boston: Academic Press, 1990.

[Sa00] Sayood, K. *Introduction to Data Compression,* 2nd ed. San Francisco: Morgan Kaufman, 2000.

[St03] Stallings, W. *Computer Organization and Architecture,* 6th ed. Englewood Cliffs, NJ: Prentice-Hall, 2003.

[Ta03] Tanenbaum, A. S. *Computer Networks,* 4th ed. Englewood Cliffs, NJ: Prentice-Hall, 2003.

[We84] Welch, T. "A Technique for High-Performance Data Compression." *Computer,* vol. 17, no. 6 (May 1984), 8–19.

CHAPTER 6

DATA INTEGRITY

So while it is true that children are exposed to more information and a greater variety of experiences than were children of the past, it does not follow that they automatically become more sophisticated. We always know much more than we understand, and with the torrent of information to which young people are exposed, the gap between knowing and understanding, between experience and learning, has become even greater than it was in the past
—**David Elkind** (1709–1784), U.S. psychologist

6.1 INTRODUCTION

Previous chapters have dealt with many of the mechanisms necessary to store and transmit information. All of these methods, no matter how sophisticated, are not sufficient to guarantee effective and safe communications. Consider an example in which you receive the following message via electronic mail:

Your brothel in New Orleans needs money.

Your reactions could be anything from confusion to shock to terror. What if your spouse got the message first? There is no way for your spouse to know that the message should have read:

Your brother in New Orleans needs money.

What happened? The person sending the message is not a practical joker or out to get you. He or she actually sent the innocuous message. The problem was in the message transmission. The letter *r* from the word *brother* was ASCII coded as 1110010. Unfortunately, some electrical interference changed the middle four bits 1001 to 0110, and the bit string received was 1101100, the code for the letter *l*.

I think we would all agree that a system that allows altered messages to be delivered is less than desirable. But the fact is that errors do occur. Any message transmitted electronically is susceptible to interference. Sunspots, electrical storms, power fluctuations, or a digger hitting a cable with a shovel can do amazing and unpredictable things to transmissions. We simply cannot allow shuttle astronauts to receive incorrect navigational instructions or Swiss banks to deposit a million dollars more than they should (unless it's into my account!). Any communications system must deliver accurate messages.

The capability to detect when a transmission has been changed is called **error detection.** In most cases, when errors are detected the message is discarded, the sender is notified, and the message is sent again. Of course, there's no guarantee the message wouldn't be corrupted again, so we must develop protocols that allow sender and receiver to exchange information regarding the message's status. In fact, there's no guarantee that the status information would not be corrupted. This requires some elaborate protocols, which we discuss in Chapter 8.

However, sometimes it is not practical to resend messages. There may not be enough time, which is often the case in real-time applications. One example is communicating with deep-space probes. It may take hours to relay important telemetry data from a remote point in space. Furthermore, if the probe is a long distance away, the signals may be very weak and highly susceptible to interference. By the time the probe gets a resend request, it may have moved to a point where the original data can no longer be recorded. Besides, over long distances the probability of the signals being corrupted is very high and chances are that the signals would never be received without some error. Another example is real-time viewing or listening to multimedia recordings. If you're watching a video and something happens to a few of the frames, it's not practical to back up and rewatch the frames. It would be like watching a movie on DVD with someone alternately pressing the rewind and play buttons. In some cases, when an error is detected it may actually be fixed without a second transmission. This is called **error correction.** The sender never knows the message was damaged and subsequently fixed. The bottom line is that the message eventually is delivered correctly.

This chapter deals with data integrity, the capability to determine when data have been corrupted. Section 6.2 discusses parity checking, a method to detect when certain bits have been corrupted. It is a simple and naïve approach and, although it is usually not implemented by itself, it does play an important role in more complex schemes. Section 6.3 discusses cyclic redundancy checks, a complicated method based on interpreting bit strings as polynomials and then doing polynomial division to determine errors. We'll see that this method is extremely accurate and, despite the complex calculations, can be implemented very efficiently. It's also commonly used.

Finally, Section 6.4 discusses one error correcting method, a Hamming code. It's a method that uses multiple parity checks in such a way that if a single bit changes then a unique combination of parity checks fails. Once the location of the damaged bit is determined, the bit can be changed and the message corrected.

6.2   SIMPLE ERROR DETECTION TECHNIQUES

PARITY CHECKS

Error detection techniques require sending additional bits whose values depend on the data that are sent. Thus, if the data are changed, the additional bit values no longer correspond to the new data (at least in theory). Probably the most common approach is *parity checking,* which involves counting all the 1 bits in the data and adding one more bit to make the total number of 1 bits even (**even parity**) or odd (**odd parity**). The extra bit is called the **parity bit.** We will base our discussions on an even parity and leave it to the reader to construct similar discussions for odd parity.

To illustrate, suppose the number of 1 bits in the data is odd. By defining the parity bit as 1, the total number of 1 bits is now even. Similarly, if the number of 1 bits in the data is already even, the parity bit is 0. Consider the bit streams in Figure 6.1. The first stream has four 1 bits. Therefore, its parity bit is 0. The second one has five 1 bits, so its parity bit is 1.

Analysis of Parity Checking   Parity checking will detect any single-bit error. The parity bit is transmitted with the data bits, and the receiver checks the parity. If the receiver finds an odd number of 1 bits, an error has occurred. Single-bit errors are very rare in electronic transmissions, however. For example, suppose an error occurs because of a brief power surge or static electricity whose duration is a hundredth of a second. In human terms, a hundredth of a second is barely noticeable. But if the data rate is 1 Mbps (megabits per second), approximately 10,000 bits may be affected in that hundredth of a second. When many bits are damaged, we call this a **burst error.**

How does parity checking work for arbitrary burst errors? Suppose two bits change during transmission. If they were both 0, they change to 1. Two extra 1s still make the total number of 1 bits even. Similarly, if they were both 1 they both change to 0 and there are two fewer 1 bits, but still an even number. If they were opposite values and both change, they are still opposite. This time the number of 1 bits remains the same. The bottom line is that parity checks do not detect double-bit errors.

In general, if an odd number of bits change, parity checking will detect the error. If an even number of bits change, parity checking will not detect the error. The conclusion is that parity checks will catch about 50% of burst errors, and a 50% accuracy rate is not good for a communications network.

Does this make parity checks useless? The answer is no, for two reasons. First, some computer memory organizations store the bits from a byte or word on different chips. Thus, when the word is accessed the bits travel different paths. In such cases the malfunction of one path can cause a single-bit error. Such architectures often use additional memory chips for parity bits. (The details are beyond the scope of this text.) The second reason is that parity checking is the basis for an error correction technique discussed in Section 6.4.

Figure 6.1   Detecting Single-Bit Errors Using Parity Checking

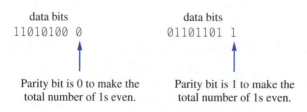

data bits
11010100 0

data bits
01101101 1

Parity bit is 0 to make the
total number of 1s even.

Parity bit is 1 to make the
total number of 1s even.

CHECKSUMS

Another approach divides all the data bits into 32-bit* groups and treats each as an integer value. These values are then added together to give a **checksum.** Any overflow that requires more than 32 bits is ignored. In effect, the process takes the modulo 2^{32} value of the sum. An extra 32 bits representing the checksum is then appended to the data before they are transmitted. The receiving device divides the data bits it gets into 32-bit groups and performs the same calculation. It then compares the result with that stored in the appended 32 bits. If the two do not match, then an error has occurred.

This approach is much more accurate than simple parity checks and detects all kinds of burst errors because randomly changing numbers usually changes the value to which they sum. However, this approach will not detect all errors. One simple example is an error that causes one of the 32-bit values to be increased by a specified amount and a different 32-bit value to be decreased by the same amount. The sum of these values and consequently of all the 32-bit values does not change, yet an error still occurred.

6.3   CYCLIC REDUNDANCY CHECKS FOR ERROR DETECTION

In this section we discuss a method called a **cyclic redundancy check (CRC)** that is much more accurate than either the parity bit or checksum method. We also show that it can be implemented efficiently.

CRC is a rather unusual but clever method that does error checking via **polynomial** division. Your first reaction is probably, "What does polynomial division have to do with transmitting bit strings?" The answer is that the method interprets each bit string as a polynomial. In general, it interprets the bit string

$$b_{n-1}b_{n-2}b_{n-3} \ldots b_2b_1b_0$$

as the polynomial

$$b_{n-1}x^{n-1} + b_{n-2}x^{n-2} + b_{n-3}x^{n-3} + \ldots + b_2x^2 + b_1x + b_0$$

For example, the bit string 10010101110 is interpreted as

$$x^{10} + x^7 + x^5 + x^3 + x^2 + x^1$$

Since each b_i is either 0 or 1, we just write x^i when b_i is 1 and do not write any term when b_i is 0.

The following steps outline the CRC method. We assume all computations are done modulo 2.

1. Given a bit string, append several 0s to the end of it (we will specify how many and why later) and call it B. Let $B(x)$ be the polynomial corresponding to B.

2. Divide $B(x)$ by some agreed-on polynomial $G(x)$ (**generator polynomial**) and determine the remainder, $R(x)$.

---

* Eight-bit or 16-bit groups could also be used.

3. Define $T(x) = B(x) - R(x)$. Later we will show that $T(x)/G(x)$ generates a 0 remainder and that the subtraction can be done by replacing the previously appended 0 bits with the bit string corresponding to $R(x)$.

4. Transmit T, the bit string corresponding to $T(x)$.

5. Let T' represent the bit stream the receiver gets and $T'(x)$ the associated polynomial. The receiver divides $T'(x)$ by $G(x)$. If there is a 0 remainder, the receiver concludes $T = T'$ and no error occurred. Otherwise, the receiver concludes an error occurred and requests a retransmission.

Before you throw your hands up in despair, we agree that questions need answering. Why do we perform each of these steps? Is there any validity to the receiver's conclusion after dividing $T'(x)$ by $G(x)$? How accurate is this method? Must a sender and receiver go through all this work each time a frame is sent? However, we cannot answer these questions until we have covered a few preliminaries. We assume you have some knowledge of polynomials and polynomial operations using real numbers, but we will provide a brief summary of modulo 2 division of polynomials.

POLYNOMIAL DIVISION

Figure 6.2 shows an example of polynomial division $T(x)/G(x)$ where

$$T(x) = x^{10} + x^9 + x^7 + x^5 + x^4$$

and

$$G(x) = x^4 + x^3 + 1$$

This is just like polynomial division from an algebra course except that the calculations use modulo 2 arithmetic. Modulo 2 addition and subtraction are defined as follows:

$$0 + 0 = 0 \qquad 1 + 0 = 1 \qquad 0 + 1 = 1 \qquad 1 + 1 = 0$$

and

$$0 - 0 = 0 \qquad 1 - 0 = 1 \qquad 0 - 1 = 1 \qquad 1 - 1 = 0$$

Figure 6.2   Calculation of $(x^{10} + x^9 + x^7 + x^5 + x^4)/(x^4 + x^3 + 1)$

$$
\require{enclose}
\begin{array}{r}
x^6 \qquad\quad + x^3 \quad + x \\
x^4 + x^3 + 1 \enclose{longdiv}{x^{10} + x^9 \qquad + x^7 \qquad + x^5 + x^4} \\
\underline{x^{10} + x^9 \qquad\quad + x^6} \\
x^7 + x^6 + x^5 + x^4 \\
\underline{x^7 + x^6 \qquad\quad + x^3} \\
x^5 + x^4 + x^3 \\
\underline{x^5 + x^4 \qquad + x} \\
x^3 \quad + x \qquad \text{remainder}
\end{array}
$$

```
                   1 0 0 1 0 1 0
              ┌─────────────────────
    1 1 0 0 1 │ 1 1 0 1 0 1 1 0 0 0 0
                1 1 0 0 1
              ─────────
                0 0 1 1 1
                0 0 0 0 0
              ─────────
                0 1 1 1 1
                0 0 0 0 0
              ─────────
                  1 1 1 1 0
                  1 1 0 0 1
                ─────────
                  0 1 1 1 0
                  0 0 0 0 0
                ─────────
                    1 1 1 0 0
                    1 1 0 0 1
                  ─────────
                    0 1 0 1 0
                    0 0 0 0 0
                  ─────────
                    1 0 1 0   remainder
```

Figure 6.3   Synthetic Division of $(x^{10} + x^9 + x^7 + x^5 + x^4)/(x^4 + x^3 + 1)$

Note that modulo 2 addition and subtraction are the same as, and in fact correspond to, the exclusive OR operation. This is an important fact we use later when we discuss CRC implementation.

Figure 6.3 shows the same division using synthetic division. You might recall from the same algebra class that it is a shortcut that uses only the coefficients of the polynomials (in this case, bit strings). Remembering to use zeros where there are no polynomial terms, the coefficient list for $x^{10} + x^9 + x^7 + x^5 + x^4$ is 11010110000 and for $x^4 + x^3 + 1$ is 11001.

How CRC Works

Let's now describe how CRC works. Suppose we want to send the bit string 1101011, and the generator polynomial is $G(x) = x^4 + x^3 + 1$. (We will discuss some criteria for choosing $G(x)$ later.)

1. Append 0s to the end of the string. The number of 0s is the same as the degree of the generator polynomial (in this case, 4). Thus, the string becomes 11010110000.

2. Divide $B(x)$ by $G(x)$. Figures 6.2 and 6.3 show the result for this example, giving a remainder of $R(x) = x^3 + x$, or its bit string equivalent of 1010. Note that we can write this algebraically as

$$\frac{B(x)}{G(x)} = Q(x) + \frac{R(x)}{G(x)}$$

where $Q(x)$ represents the quotient. Equivalently, we can write

$$B(x) = G(x) \times Q(x) + R(x)$$

3. Define $T(x) = B(x) - R(x)$. Because the subtraction takes the difference of co-efficients of like terms, we calculate the difference by subtracting the bit strings associated with each polynomial. In this case, we have

$$
\begin{array}{ll}
11010110000 & \text{bit string } B \\
\underline{-1010} & \text{bit string } R \\
11010111010 & \text{bit string } T
\end{array}
$$

Note that the string T is actually the same as string B with the appended 0s re-placed by R. Another important fact, as shown by Figure 6.4, is that if we di-vide $T(x)$ by $G(x)$, the remainder is 0.* The sender then transmits the string T.

4. If the string T arrives without damage, dividing by $G(x)$ will yield a 0 remain-der. But suppose that during transmission, string T is damaged. For example, suppose that some bits in the middle changed to 0 and the string arrives as 11000001010. The receiver synthetically divides it by $G(x)$ and the remainder is not 0 (Figure 6.5). Because the remainder is not 0, the receiver concludes

Figure 6.4   Dividing $T(x)$ by $G(x)$

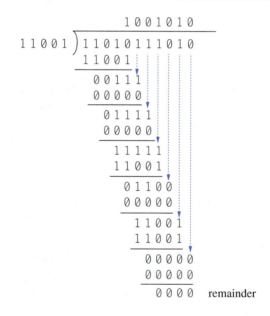

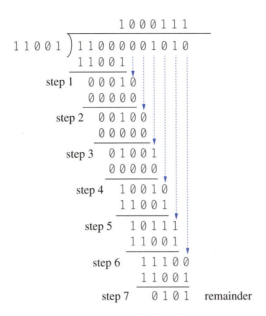

Figure 6.5   Division of Received Polynomial by $G(x)$

that an error has occurred. (*Note:* This is not the same as saying that dividing a damaged string by $G(x)$ will always yield a nonzero remainder. It can happen, but if $G(x)$ is chosen wisely, it occurs only rarely. We will discuss this topic next.)

ANALYSIS OF CRC

The mechanisms of CRC are fairly straightforward. The question we have yet to answer is whether the method is any good. Will the receiver always be able to detect a damaged frame? We relied on the proposition that a damaged frame means that dividing by $G(x)$ yields a nonzero remainder. But is this always true? Is it possible to change the bit string T in such a way that dividing by $G(x)$ does give a zero remainder?

A complete and detailed proof requires knowledge of factorization properties of polynomial rings (a field in abstract mathematics), and we will not provide one here. Instead, we will provide a brief discussion to give some sense of why it works. To begin, let's specify more accurately what we are looking for. Changing the bits in T is analogous to adding some unknown polynomial to $T(x)$. Thus, if T' represents the received string and $T'(x)$ the associated polynomial, then $T'(x) = T(x) + E(x)$, where $E(x)$ is unknown to the receiver of T'. In the previous example,

string T = 11010111010 corresponds to $T(x) = x^{10} + x^9 + x^7 + x^5 + x^4 + x^3 + x$

string E = 00010110000 corresponds to $E(x) = x^7 + x^5 + x^4$

string T' = 11000001010 corresponds to $T'(x) = x^{10} + x^9 + x^3 + x$

Don't forget that the addition is done using the exclusive OR operation. So, for example, adding the x^7 terms from $E(x)$ and $T(x)$ yields $x^7 + x^7 = (1 + 1) \times x^7 = 0$.

The question we must answer, therefore, is: When will $(T(x) + E(x))/G(x)$ generate a zero remainder? Since $(T(x) + E(x))/G(x) = T(x)/G(x) + E(x)/G(x)$ and the first term has a zero remainder, the latter term determines the remainder. Therefore, the question can be reformulated as follows: For what polynomials $E(x)$ will $E(x)/G(x)$ have a zero remainder?

We can now make the following statement:

Undetected transmission errors correspond to errors for which $G(x)$ is a factor of $E(x)$.

The next question is: Under what conditions is $G(x)$ a factor of $E(x)$? Let's examine the simplest case first, where just one bit in T changes. In this case $E(x)$ is just one term, x^k for some integer k. The only way $G(x)$ can be a factor of x^k is if $G(x)$ is x raised to some power. So as long as we choose $G(x)$ with at least two terms, it won't happen. Thus, CRC will detect all single-bit errors.

Next, consider a burst error of length $k \le r = $ degree $G(x)$.* Suppose $T(x)$ is represented by

$$t_n t_{n-1} \cdots \underbrace{t_{i+k-1} t_{i+k-2} \cdots t_i}_{k \text{ affected bits}} t_{i-1} \cdots t_1 t_0$$

and $t_{i+k-1} \ldots$ and t_i are the first and last bits to be damaged. The bits in between have been damaged arbitrarily. This means that

$$E(x) = x^{i+k-1} + \ldots + x^i = x^i \times (x^{k-1} + \ldots + 1)$$

Therefore,

$$\frac{E(x)}{G(x)} = \frac{x^i \times (x^{k-1} + \ldots + 1)}{G(x)}$$

Now, suppose we chose $G(x)$ so that x is not a factor of $G(x)$. Consequently, $G(x)$ and the x^i from the previous fraction have no common factors. Thus, if $G(x)$ is a factor of the numerator, then it must in fact be a factor of $(x^{k-1} \ldots + 1)$. Remember, however, that since we chose $k \le r$, then $k - 1 < r$, and $G(x)$ cannot be a factor of a polynomial having a smaller degree.

We therefore draw the following conclusion:

If x is not a factor of $G(x)$, then all burst errors having length less than or equal to the degree of $G(x)$ are detected.

Consider next a burst error of any length in which an odd number of bits is affected. Since $E(x)$ has a term for each damaged bit, it contains an odd number of terms. Therefore, $E(1)$ (exclusive OR of an odd number of 1s) evaluates to 1. On the other hand, suppose that $x + 1$ is a factor of $G(x)$. We can therefore write $G(x) = (x + 1) \times H(x)$, where $H(x)$ is some expression.

---

* The *degree* of a polynomial is its highest power of x.

Now look at what happens if we assume that an undetected error occurs. Recall that an undetected error means that $G(x)$ is a factor of $E(x)$. This means that $E(x) = G(x) \times K(x)$, where $K(x)$ is the other factor of $E(x)$. Replacing $G(x)$ with $(x + 1) \times H(x)$ yields $E(x) = (x + 1) \times H(x) \times K(x)$. Now, if this equation is evaluated at $x = 1$, the $x + 1$ factor makes $E(1)$ evaluate to 0. This is in direct contrast to the previous claim that $E(1)$ evaluates to 1.

Clearly both cannot occur. If we maintain our assumption that $x + 1$ is a factor of $G(x)$, then the other assumption of an undetected error damaging an odd number of bits cannot happen. In other words:

> If $x + 1$ is a factor of $G(x)$, then all burst errors damaging an odd number of bits are detected.

The last case we consider is a burst error with length greater than degree $G(x)$. From our previous discussion we have

$$\frac{E(x)}{G(x)} = \frac{x^i \times (x^{k-1} + \ldots + 1)}{G(x)}$$

But this time since we assume that $k - 1 \geq r = $ degree $G(x)$, it is possible that $G(x)$ is a factor of $(x^{k-1} + \ldots + 1)$. The question is: What are the chances this will happen? Let's first consider $k - 1 = r$. Since the degree of $G(x)$ is also r, then $G(x)$ is a factor of $(x^r + \ldots + 1)$ means that $G(x) = (x^r + \ldots + 1)$. Now, the terms between x^r and 1 define which bits are actually damaged. Since there are $r - 1$ such terms, there are 2^{r-1} possible combinations of damaged bits. If we assume all combinations can occur with equal probability, there is a probability of $1/2^{r-1}$ that the combination matches the terms of $G(x)$ exactly. In other words, the probability of an error going undetected is $1/2^{r-1}$.

The case for $k - 1 > r$ is more complex and we do not discuss it here. However, it can be shown that the probability of an undetected error is $1/2^r$. References [Pe72] and [Mo89] provide a more rigorous analysis of error detection codes.

CRC is widely used in local area networks (LANs), where there are standard polynomials for $G(x)$, such as the following:

CRC-12: $x^{12} + x^{11} + x^3 + x^2 + x + 1$

CRC-16: $x^{16} + x^{15} + x^2 + 1$

CRC-ITU: $x^{16} + x^{12} + x^5 + 1$

CRC-32: $x^{32} + x^{26} + x^{23} + x^{22} + x^{16} + x^{12} + x^{11}$
$+ x^{10} + x^8 + x^7 + x^5 + x^4 + x^2 + x + 1$

In general, CRC is very effective if $G(x)$ is chosen properly. Specifically, $G(x)$ should be chosen so that x is not a factor but $x + 1$ is a factor. In this case, CRC detects the following errors:

- All burst errors of length r less than degree $G(x)$
- All burst errors affecting an odd number of bits
- All burst errors of length equal to $r + 1$ with probability $(2^{r-1} - 1)/2^{r-1}$
- All burst errors of length greater than $r + 1$ with probability $(2^r - 1)/2^r$

For example, the CRC-32 polynomial will detect all burst errors of length greater than 33 with probability $(2^{32} - 1)/2^{32}$. This is equivalent to a 99.99999998% accuracy rate. Not bad!

CRC IMPLEMENTATION USING CIRCULAR SHIFTS

Finding an accurate error detection method is half the battle. The other half is finding a way to implement it efficiently. Considering the nearly countless number of frames that travel across networks, an efficient implementation is essential.

Having learned about CRC, your first reaction might be to write a program to do polynomial division. However, during the time it takes to run such a program, several other frames will probably arrive. As we take the time to verify each of those, even more will arrive and a real bottleneck will occur. It's like having the cashier at a grocery store call for a price check on every item in your cart. Meanwhile, the customers behind you start making nasty remarks, and the Eskimo pies in your cart are melting!

Can we divide two polynomials and get the remainder quickly? Do we even need to go through a complete division when all we really need is the remainder? The quotient was never used. Let's take a close look at Figure 6.5, which showed the synthetic division. The entire process can be visualized as nothing more than a sequence of shifts and exclusive OR operations between the divisor and parts of the dividend.

One widely used CRC implementation uses a circuit that is constructed depending on the generator polynomial $G(x)$. Because standard polynomials exist, these circuits can be mass produced. The circuit contains a shift register and does exclusive OR operations according to the following rules:

- Interpret $G(x) = b_r x^r + b_{r-1} x^{r-1} + \ldots + b_2 x^2 + b_1 x + b_0$ where b_i is either 0 or 1, $i = 0, \ldots r$. The number of bit positions in the register is r. The rightmost position corresponds to b_0 and the leftmost to $b_{r-1} x^{r-1}$.

- An exclusive OR circuit lies to the right of any position for which the associated value of b_i is 1.

- A bit string enters the register one bit at a time, starting with the rightmost position.

- As new bits enter, each bit in the register is shifted left one position. Each bit goes through exclusive OR circuits where they exist, forming one operand in the exclusive OR operation.

- The bit in the leftmost position is routed to each of the exclusive OR circuits, forming the second operand in each exclusive OR operation.

Figure 6.6 shows the register and exclusive OR circuits for the polynomial $G(x) = x^4 + x^3 + 1$. Note the exclusive OR symbol to the right of the positions corresponding to x^3 and 1, and none to the right of the positions corresponding to the missing terms x^2 and x. Initially, the register contains all 0s.

This figure shows the same computations as in Figure 6.5. At step 0, the first bit of the incoming string (the dividend from Figure 6.5) has been shifted to the leftmost register position. At step 1, the leftmost bit is routed to each exclusive OR and

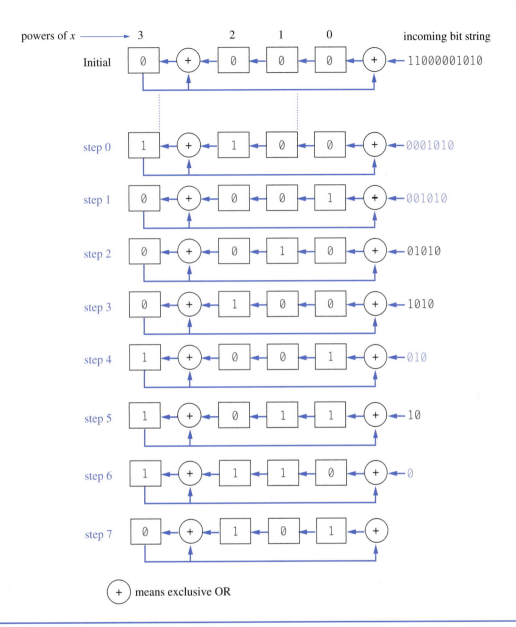

Figure 6.6   Division Using Circular Shifts

everything else shifted left. Note that the register's contents are exactly the same as the result of the first exclusive OR operation from step 1 in Figure 6.5.

Each step defines the same process of shifting left and doing exclusive OR operations. The register's contents at each step are always the same as the results of similarly labeled steps from Figure 6.5. By the time the bits from the incoming string have all been moved into the register, the register's contents are the remainder (step 7 in Figures 6.5 and 6.6).

Error detection using CRC is an accurate and widely used method. It can also be implemented efficiently, requiring time proportional to the string's length. The standard generator polynomials allow the entire method to be designed into hardware (chips), thus further enhancing its efficiency.

6.4 HAMMING CODES: ERROR CORRECTION

As stated previously, when errors are detected there are typically two choices: resend the original frame or fix the damaged frame. The latter choice requires a method to not only detect an error but also to determine precisely which bits were affected. The simple parity checks could not do this.

SINGLE-BIT ERROR CORRECTION

A method developed by R. W. Hamming involves creating special code words from data to be sent. The **Hamming code** requires the insertion of multiple parity bits in the bit string before sending. The parity bits check the parity in strategic locations. The idea is that if bits are altered, their positions determine a unique combination of parity check errors. When a frame is sent, the receiver recalculates the parity checks. If any fail, the combination of failures tells the receiver which bits were affected. The receiver then can set the bits to their correct values. This technique is quite common for memory addressing and transferring bits from registers to RAM and back.

Let's illustrate how a Hamming code works for the simplest case, the detection and correction of any single-bit error. Suppose that frames consist of 8 bits. Label them as m_1 m_2 m_3 m_4 m_5 m_6 m_7 m_8. The next step is to define parity bits for parity checks in select positions. The logical questions are: How many parity checks do we use? Which positions does each one check?

If we use one parity check, it will either fail or succeed. From this we can conclude that an error either occurs or does not occur. It says nothing about where an error might be. If we use two parity checks, one of four things can happen: They both fail; they both succeed; the first fails and the second succeeds; the second fails and the first succeeds. These four cases might be used to convey four events: no error or a bit error in one of three positions. Since there are more than three bit positions, two checks are not enough.

In general, if n parity checks are used, there are 2^n possible combinations of failures and successes. We must associate each bit position with a unique combination to allow the receiver to analyze the parity checks and conclude where an error occurred (if one occurred). However, to account for every bit position, we need an n such that 2^n is larger than the number of bits sent. We also must remember that each additional parity check requires another bit to be sent.

Table 6.1 shows the relationship between n and the number of bits sent, assuming we start with an 8-bit frame. As it shows, if we use four parity checks there are

Table 6.1   Number of Combinations of Parity Successes and Failures as a Function of n

n (NUMBER OF PARITY CHECKS)	NUMBER OF BITS SENT	2^n (NUMBER OF COMBINATIONS OF POSSIBLE PARITY SUCCESSES AND FAILURES)
1	9	2
2	10	4
3	11	8
4	12	16

16 possible combinations of parity successes and failures. The 4 additional parity bits with the 8 original bits means 12 bits are actually sent. Thus, 13 events are possible: There is no error, or there is a single-bit error in one of 12 positions.

The next step is to associate a combination with a unique event. To do this, construct four parity bits p_1, p_2, p_3, and p_4 and insert them into the frame as shown in Figure 6.7. Each parity bit establishes even parity for selected positions listed in the figure. The next questions are, Why put the parity bits in those positions? and How did we determine the positions for each parity check?

To answer these questions, let's make an observation about the positions in each parity check. The first parity check involves all the odd-numbered positions. These positions, if written in binary, all have 1 as the least significant digit. If you write the positions covered by the second parity check in binary, they all have 1 as the second least significant digit. Similarly, the positions covered by the third and fourth parity checks have 1 as the third and fourth least significant digit, respectively.

How does this help us? Create a 4-bit binary number consisting of b_4, b_3, b_2, and b_1 where $b_i = 0$ if the parity check for p_i succeeds and $b_i = 1$ otherwise ($i = 1$, 2, 3, or 4). Table 6.2 shows the relationship among erroneous bit positions, invalid

Figure 6.7   Hamming Code for Single-Bit Errors

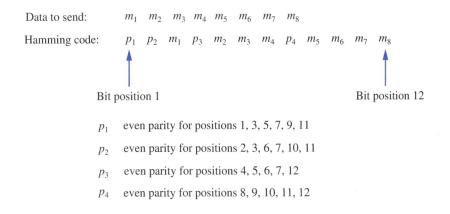

Data to send: m_1 m_2 m_3 m_4 m_5 m_6 m_7 m_8

Hamming code: p_1 p_2 m_1 p_3 m_2 m_3 m_4 p_4 m_5 m_6 m_7 m_8

Bit position 1   Bit position 12

p_1 even parity for positions 1, 3, 5, 7, 9, 11

p_2 even parity for positions 2, 3, 6, 7, 10, 11

p_3 even parity for positions 4, 5, 6, 7, 12

p_4 even parity for positions 8, 9, 10, 11, 12

Table 6.2   Bit Position Errors and Associated Parity Errors

ERRONEOUS BIT POSITION	INVALID PARITY CHECKS	$b_4, b_3, b_2,$ AND b_1
No error	None	0000
1	p_1	0001
2	p_2	0010
3	p_1 and p_2	0011
4	p_3	0100
5	p_1 and p_3	0101
6	p_2 and p_3	0110
7	$p_1, p_2,$ and p_3	0111
8	p_4	1000
9	p_1 and p_4	1001
10	p_2 and p_4	1010
11	$p_1, p_2,$ and p_4	1011
12	p_3 and p_4	1100

parity checks, and the 4-bit number. As the table shows, the 4-bit binary number and the erroneous bit position coincide.

When a receiver gets a transmitted frame, it performs each of the parity checks. The combination of failures and successes then determines whether there was no error or in which position an error occurred. Once the receiver knows where the error occurred, it changes the bit value in that position and the error is corrected.

To illustrate, consider the example in Figure 6.8. Here we see the initial frame 0110-0111 and the Hamming code 0101-1101-0111 to be transmitted. You should go through the computations to convince yourself that the parity bits establish even parity in the correct positions.

Figure 6.9 shows the received frame 0101-0101-0111. Now, if we perform each parity check, we see that the checks for p_1 and p_3 are invalid. That is, there is an odd number of 1 bits in positions 1, 3, 5, 7, 9, and 11, and in positions 4, 5, 6, 7, and 12. Thus, according to Table 6.2, the error is in bit 5. Since bit 5 is 0, the receiver changes it to 1 and the frame is corrected.

Figure 6.8   Bit Stream Before Transmission

Data:	0	1	1	0	0	1	1	1				
	m_1	m_2	m_3	m_4	m_5	m_6	m_7	m_8				

Hamming code:	0	1	0	1	1	1	0	1	0	1	1	1
	p_1	p_2	m_1	p_3	m_2	m_3	m_4	p_4	m_5	m_6	m_7	m_8

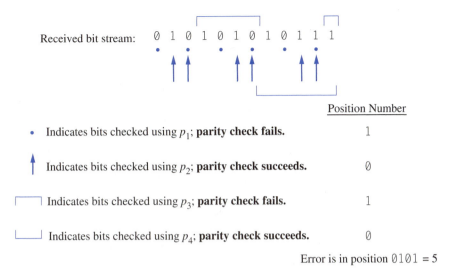

Received bit stream: 0 1 0 1 0 1 0 1 0 1 1 1

	Position Number
• Indicates bits checked using p_1; **parity check fails.**	1
↑ Indicates bits checked using p_2; **parity check succeeds.**	0
⌐ Indicates bits checked using p_3; **parity check fails.**	1
⌐⌐ Indicates bits checked using p_4; **parity check succeeds.**	0

Error is in position $0101 = 5$

Figure 6.9   Parity Checks of Frame After Transmission

MULTIPLE-BIT ERROR CORRECTION

We can make similar comments about single-bit error correcting codes that we made about single-bit error detection codes. That is, single-bit errors are not common in data communications. One response is to generalize Hamming codes for double- or multiple-bit error correction. Such codes do exist, but we will not discuss them here. The number of extra bits becomes quite large and is used in very specialized cases. If you are interested, references [Ko78] and [Ha80] discuss these codes.

There's one more class of error correction methods that we must mention: the Bose-Chaudhuri-Hocquenghem (BCH, for obvious reasons) codes and the Reed-Solomon codes, a subclass of the BCH codes. Both of these methods center on the concept of a code word, a collection of N data bits followed by M error control bits that are calculated using the data bits. The code word has $N + M$ bits, and there are 2^N possible code words. Remember, only N bits are arbitrary; the other M bits are completely determined. This means that although there are 2^{N+M} possible bit sequences in a code word, only 2^N (a small number by comparison) are legitimate code words. For example, if $N = 8$ and $M = 4$, then there are $2^8 = 256$ legitimate code words out of a possible $2^{12} = 4096$ bit arrangements.

A concept that is central to these codes is that of *distance* between two code words, or the number of bits in which two code words differ. For example, the two Hamming codes 0101-1101-0111 and 1001-1001-0111 have a distance of 3 because they differ in 3 bits (the first, second, and sixth bits). Each set of code words has a *minimum distance*. To determine it, calculate the distance between every possible pair of code words. The smallest value calculated is the minimum distance of that code word set.

Minimum distance is important because it relates directly to the number of damaged bits that can be detected and corrected. In general, if d is the minimum distance, then the method can detect any error affecting fewer than d bits (such a change would create an invalid code word) and correct any error affecting fewer than $d/2$ bits.

For example, suppose the minimum distance of a set of code words is $d = 10$. Thus, any two legitimate code words differ in at least 10 bits. Errors affecting fewer than $d/2 = 5$ bits can be corrected. To see this, suppose a code word was sent and 4 bits were damaged. Then the result would not be a valid code word (at least 10 bits must be changed to create another valid code word). Furthermore, suppose the receiver assumes that any error will affect fewer than 5 bits. The receiver of the invalid code word need only find the closest valid code word and conclude that it was the correct code word. Any other code word would have had to have at least 6 bits damaged to resemble the received word.

The trick, of course, is in selecting the code words in such a way as to maximize the minimum distance. Such a technique will maximize the number of bits that can be detected and corrected. The BCH codes and, in particular, the Reed-Solomon codes do just that. The details of those methods, however, require knowledge of Galois fields, matrix theory, and generator polynomials, and this level of mathematics motivates us to refer the reader to references [Gr01], [Wi95], and [Sw02]. However, don't let the complexity of these methods fool you into thinking they are high-level, abstract theories with few applications. Be aware that the next time you listen to music on a CD or watch a movie on DVD you're benefiting from Reed-Solomon technology.

6.5 SUMMARY

This chapter dealt primarily with two topics: detecting and correcting errors in transmitted information. Detection simply means determining whether an error has occurred and, if it has, relying on other protocols to negotiate additional exchanges to get the correct information through. Correction means making the changes after the data have been received with no extra transmission.

Three methods were discussed.

- **Parity bits.** This error detection method is geared primarily for single-bit error detection, as it is only 50% accurate for burst errors. However, it can be useful when bits are transmitted separately, such as is done in some computer memory architectures. It also is the foundation of an error correction technique.

- **Cyclic redundancy checks.** This error detection method is based on the theory of polynomial division. Bit strings are interpreted as polynomials. CRC bits are created so that a message divided by a generator polynomial yields a zero remainder. Dividing a received message by the generator polynomial and checking the remainder yields a very high probability that errors are detected. This method is commonly used and is implemented easily using circular shift circuits and a register. Certain polynomials have been declared as standards.

- **Hamming code.** This error correction code establishes a collection of parity bits for strategic positions. If any single-bit error occurs, the position will affect a unique combination of parity checks. This not only allows the error's detection but also provides its position. Knowing its position subsequently allows the bit to be corrected.

So, which is better, error detection or error correction? The answer, as you might expect, is that neither is better, at least in a general sense. Correction techniques generally require more overhead and cannot always be justified in applications where errors occur rarely. It is usually much cheaper just to ask for a retransmission. Typically, most computer networks fall into this category.

As errors occur with more frequency, the extra overhead due to increased transmissions becomes a problem. In such cases, it may be cheaper to include additional correction bits rather than clutter the media with excessive redundant transmissions.

Error rate is not the only consideration. Time may be a critical factor. Sending a frame again will take time. How much depends on many factors, such as the traffic, data rate, and distance. In most cases, a short delay in receiving an email message or a file from a LAN server is not so bad or even noticeable. However, a real-time environment in which messages must be delivered on time to avoid disaster cannot afford even small delays. Real-time applications such as viewing or listening to multimedia don't have the luxury of resending something. Data must be viewed or heard as they are sent. Deep-space probes, in which signals require many hours to reach their destination, are severely handicapped if a message must be retransmitted, especially when there is a high probability that interference will occur again. Imagine an astronaut saying, "Hello, NASA . . . can't read you. What's that about an impending collision with an alien spacecraft?"

Review Questions

1. What is a parity bit?

2. Distinguish between even and odd parity.

3. Distinguish between error correction and error detection.

4. What is a burst error?

5. Are the following statements TRUE or FALSE? Why?

   a. It is not unusual to lose a bit or two during a transmission.

   b. Although an accurate technique, CRC is time-consuming because it requires a lot of overhead.

   c. A generator polynomial can be chosen arbitrarily as long as both sender and receiver know it.

   d. CRC will detect a burst error of arbitrary length as long as the number of bits affected is odd.

   e. Error correction codes are more efficient than error detection codes because they obviate the need for retransmissions.

6. What is a cyclic redundancy check?

7. Under what conditions will CRC detect the following errors?

   a. Single-bit errors

   b. Double-bit errors

   c. Burst errors of length less than or equal to the degree of the generator polynomial

   d. Burst errors of length greater than the degree of the generator polynomial

8. What conditions should a generator polynomial satisfy? Why?

9. Classify the errors that a CRC method will always detect.

10. Classify errors that a CRC method will not detect.

11. What is a shift register?

12. What is a Hamming code?

13. Define the distance between two code words.

Exercises

1. Construct an argument showing that simple parity checking detects errors only when an odd number of bits change.

2. Suppose some static of duration 0.01 second affects the communication line for a 56 Kbps modem. How many bits could be affected?

3. Assume 128 bits of data are subjected to the checksum error detection method. Give an example that shows that it is possible to change two data bits and have the error go undetected. Give another example that shows that it is possible to change three data bits and have the error go undetected. Is it possible to have every data bit change and still have the error go undetected?

4. Why does $0 - 1 = 1$ using modulo 2 subtraction?

5. What polynomial corresponds to the following bit string?

$$0110010011010110$$

6. Calculate the remainder of the following division using the methods described by Figures 6.2 and 6.3:

$$\frac{x^{12} + x^{10} + x^7 + x^6 + x^5 + x^3 + x^2}{x^7 + x^4 + x^2 + x^1}$$

7. Suppose you want to transmit the data 100111001 and the generator polynomial is $x^6 + x^3 + 1$. What bit string is actually sent?

8. Draw the circular shift register and exclusive OR circuits for the CRC-12 and CRC-16 standard polynomials.

9. Calculate the remainder of the following division using circular shifts:

$$\frac{x^{12} + x^{10} + x^7 + x^6 + x^5 + x^3 + x^2}{x^7 + x^4 + x^2 + x^1}$$

10. Investigate the documentation for the LAN at your university or company and determine what method of error detection (if any) is used.

11. Suppose the generator polynomial had the term x as a factor. Give an example of an undetected error.

12. Suppose we want to devise a single-bit error correcting Hamming code for a 16-bit data string. How many parity bits are needed? How about for a 32-bit data string?

13. The following 12-bit Hamming-coded (single-bit correction) string was received. What ASCII-coded letter does it represent?

$$110111110010$$

14. Construct Hamming codes for each of the following characters: A, 0, and {.

15. Assume a sender has the following data frames:

FRAME NUMBER	DATA
1	0 1 1 0 1 0 0 1
2	1 0 1 0 1 0 1 1
3	1 0 0 1 1 1 0 0
4	0 1 0 1 1 1 0 0

Suppose the sender constructs a Hamming code for each frame, forms a two-dimensional bit array (each row consisting of one Hamming code), and sends it one column at a time. What does the receiver get if an error makes the fifth column all 0s? Apply error correction methods to the received data and correct it.

16. Develop a Hamming code capable of correcting any single-bit errors and detecting double-bit errors for an 8-bit data string.

17. Suppose the 4-bit number $b_4\ b_3\ b_2\ b_1$ described by Table 6.2 forms a number exceeding 12. What does that mean?

18. Write a computer program to take 8 bits of data and create a 12-bit Hamming code.

19. What is the minimum distance between two code words defined by adding an even parity bit to the data?

20. What is the minimum distance of the Hamming code defined in Section 6.4?

21. Suppose that 8 bits are added to 32 bits of data to create a 40-bit code word. What percentage of the total number of 40-bit arrangements are legitimate code words?

22. How many bits in an error can the Hamming code detect?

REFERENCES

[Gr01] Gravano, S. *Introduction to Error Control Codes*. Oxford and New York: Oxford University Press, 2001.

[Ha80] Hamming, R. W. *Coding and Information Theory*. Englewood Cliffs, NJ: Prentice-Hall, 1980.

[Ko78] Kohavi, Z. *Switching and Finite Automata Theory*, 2nd ed. New York: McGraw-Hill, 1978.

[Mo89] Moshos, G. *Data Communications: Principles and Problems*. St. Paul, MN: West, 1989.

[Pe72] Peterson, W. W., and E. J. Weldon. *Error Correcting Codes*, 2nd ed. Cambridge, MA: MIT Press, 1972.

[Sw02] Sweeney, P. *Error Control Coding: From Theory to Practice*. New York: Wiley, 2002.

[Wi95] Wicker, S. *Error Control Systems for Digital Communication and Storage*. Englewood Cliffs, NJ: Prentice-Hall, 1995.

CHAPTER 7

DATA SECURITY

> *Who could deny that privacy is a jewel? It has always been the mark of privilege, the distinguishing feature of a truly urbane culture. Out of the cave, the tribal teepee, the pueblo, the community fortress, man emerged to build himself a house of his own with a shelter in it for himself and his diversions. Every age has seen it so. The poor might have to huddle together in cities for need's sake, and the frontiersman cling to his neighbors for the sake of protection. But in each civilization, as it advanced, those who could afford it chose the luxury of a withdrawing-place.*
> —**Phyllis McGinley** (1905–1978), U.S. poet, author

7.1 INTRODUCTION

Did you ever order something over the Internet? Or look at a credit card or bank balance online? Maybe you've looked at your college transcript online. How often do you stop and think that what you are viewing is being transferred from some database to your local site and that, in theory, anyone in between can see what you can see? That includes your grades, credit account numbers, bank numbers and balances, and anything else you might consider private.

When you go to the bank, you don't normally show your deposit slips and balances to the person standing in line with you. For the same reasons, electronic funds transfers between banks must be secure so that unauthorized people cannot get access to your financial arrangements. Not just banks, but many other communications systems as well must be secure. Ideally, they should provide easy access to authorized people and no access to unauthorized people. But how can you have security when information is sent over microwaves and satellites? The information travels freely through the air, and unauthorized reception is virtually impossible to prevent. Even with cable it may be difficult to prevent someone from finding an isolated spot in a closet or basement and tapping into the cable.

One common approach to secure transmissions, strangely enough, does not worry about unauthorized reception. Why worry about what you cannot prevent? Instead, this approach alters (encrypts) messages so that even if unauthorized people intercept them they are not intelligible. Encryption is common in cable television

(CATV) transmission. Anyone with CATV can receive the premium movie stations, but the signals are scrambled so that viewing is impossible. If you pay your local cable company the appropriate fees, it will unscramble the signals for you or give you a device that does so. Only then may you watch all the available movies.

This chapter deals primarily with security issues, including protocols to ensure that information changes hands securely and methods that encrypt and decrypt sensitive data. Section 7.2 starts by describing some common encryption algorithms that use secret keys. This means that if you know the encryption key and the method used, you can reverse the process and decrypt. Some use the term *symmetric key cryptosystems* because frequently the encryption and decryption keys are the same. We'll see later that there are other possibilities. Of course, this approach means that the key must be protected. It must not fall into the wrong hands. So how can we communicate the secret key to both the sender and receiver safely and securely? Section 7.3 discusses some approaches.

Section 7.4 discusses public key encryption. Here we don't worry about the key falling into the wrong hands, because everyone knows it anyway. The idea is that even if someone knows the key and encryption method, he or she is still unable to decrypt the message. That individual must know the decryption method. Yes, this means that you could not even decrypt your own encrypted messages. Section 7.4 discusses a common public key encryption method, the RSA algorithm, and issues of verification and authentication for public key techniques.

Section 7.5 outlines Secure Sockets Layer (SSL) and Transport Layer Security, commonly implemented approaches to securing transfers over the Internet. Those who conduct such activity can recognize a secure connection when the URL begins with *https* instead of the usual *http*.

Perhaps nothing has users more worried than computer viruses and other threats to their systems. Viruses attack computers, often destroying information on them. Other threats include people who try to enter a system and look for private information. Section 7.6 discusses firewalls, which are commonly used to protect an entire infrastructure from the outside world. We discuss how firewalls work and some design approaches to firewalls. Section 7.7 discusses what a virus is, how it works, and how viruses have evolved in attempts to avoid detection procedures.

Finally, Section 7.8 deals with yet other security threats: worms and hackers. We distinguish a worm from a virus, discuss the malicious hacker, and describe the Internet worm, a well-publicized event that caused serious problems some years ago for many computers connected to the Internet.

Security is a tremendously important area, and volumes of information exist on the topic. Technical, legal, and sociological issues are involved. The issues often divide those with different political philosophies as the government and the National Security Agency (NSA) get involved with devising secure encryption schemes and ways to get around them. Even issues of academic freedom become debatable as researchers investigate ways to breach secure systems. Are they doing it for academic or illicit reasons? To be sure, there is much to be covered in this area, and we can only provide introductions to many different issues. With that in mind, let us begin.

7.2 ENCRYPTION ALGORITHMS

Error detection and correction methods help prevent people from getting incorrect information. Another potentially dangerous problem is the illegal or unauthorized reception of information. Such cases involve the usual sender and receiver, plus a third party who intercepts a transmission not intended for him or her (Figure 7.1). The worst part is that neither sender nor receiver may be aware of the unauthorized reception until the guilty party has used the intercepted information for some purpose such as blackmail, criminal fraud, or a breach of national security. By then the damage is done. Clearly, if we are going to send sensitive information over some medium, we would like some assurance of privacy.

Much effort has gone into ways to make information unintelligible to unauthorized receivers so that even if they do intercept the transmission, they won't be able to understand its contents. The rendering of information into a different, unintelligible form is called **encryption.** The authorized receiver must be able to understand the information, so he must be able to change the encrypted data to its original form. We call this **decryption.** We also use the terms **plaintext** for the original message and **ciphertext** for the encrypted one.

Figure 7.2 illustrates the process. The sender uses an **encryption key** (usually some character or numeric constant) to change the plaintext (P) into a ciphertext (C). We write this symbolically as $C = E_k(P)$, where E and k represent the encryption algorithm and key, respectively. If some unauthorized person gets C, its unintelligible form makes it useless. Eventually the receiver gets C and decrypts it to get the original message. We write this symbolically as $P = D_{k'}(C)$, where D and k' represent the decryption algorithm and key. In general, $P = D_{k'}(E_k(P))$. Also, in many cases (but not always), $k = k'$.

Figure 7.1 Sending Unsecured Messages

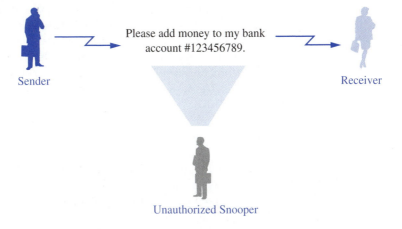

Please add money to my bank account #123456789.

Sender

Receiver

Unauthorized Snooper

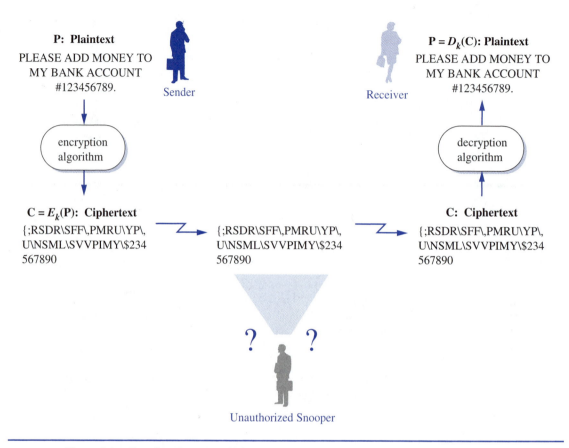

Figure 7.2   Sending Encrypted Messages

As usual, questions arise. How do the encryption and decryption algorithms work? Is an encrypted message really unintelligible to an unauthorized receiver? If an unauthorized receiver knows how the message was encrypted, can she decrypt it? Ideally, an encrypted message should be impossible to decrypt without knowing the decryption algorithm and key. Unfortunately, most completely secure codes are analogous to unsinkable ships such as the *Titanic:* As soon as you are sure it is secure, someone will prove you wrong.

CAESAR CIPHER

One of the earliest and simplest codes replaces each plaintext character with another character. The choice of a replacement depends only on the plaintext character. This method is called a **monoalphabetic cipher** or **Caesar cipher,** reputedly dating back to the days of Julius Caesar. For example, you might add 1 (the encryption key) to the ASCII code of each character. Thus, *A* becomes *B; B* becomes *C;* and so on. This approach is widely used, occurring in places such as children's television shows, decoder rings, and the backs of cereal boxes. Figure 7.2 used a Caesar cipher. Can you determine the rationale behind the letter substitutions?

The decryption algorithm normally reverses the encryption steps. In the previous example, subtracting 1 from the ASCII codes of each ciphertext character yields the original plaintext character. This is a case in which the encryption and decryption keys are equal. We should point out that the example could have changed the ASCII codes by any constant.

Although they are simple to describe and certainly seem to yield unintelligible messages, Caesar ciphers are rarely used in serious applications. They are relatively easy to decode without knowledge of the original encryption method because the code does nothing to disguise frequently used letters or combinations. For example, commonly used letters in English are *E, T, O, A,* and *N*. Thus, if a certain letter appears frequently in a ciphertext, there is a high probability it is one of these common letters rather than a *Q* or *Z*. This gives a potential codebreaker a place to start.

To illustrate, consider the following ciphertext (from Figure 7.2). Pretend you never saw the plaintext.

{;RSDR\SFF\,PMRU\YP\,U\NSML\SVVPIMY\$234567890

The most common ciphertext characters in this example are \ (seven times), S (four times), and R, P, and M (three times each). Consequently, there is a high probability they are substitutions for *E, T, O, A,* and *N*, or even a blank space.

The next step would be to try various combinations of the common plaintext characters in place of the ciphertext ones. For example, after several attempts you might come up with the following partially decrypted character string (decrypted characters are colored blue):

{;EADE\AFF\,ONEU\YO\,U\NANL\AVVOINY\$234567890

To continue, you might further observe that most messages have blanks between the words, and that the most common character (\) might represent a blank. You try it and generate

{;EADE AFF ,ONEU YO ,U NANL AVVOINY $234567890

Next you might look at the Y*O* and the A*FF* and ask how many two-letter words end in the letter *O* or how many three-letter words begin with *A* followed by a repeated letter. There are not many, so you might try replacing the *Y* with a *T* and the *F* with a *D*. Now you have

{;EADE ADD ,ONEU TO ,U NANL AVVOINT $234567890

By making some educated guesses, we have the message half decrypted. It would not be difficult to continue making educated guesses and finish decrypting. (It's really a lot like playing the game Hangman or the equivalent television show, *Wheel of Fortune*.) The important point to emphasize here is that a secure code should not preserve particular letter sequences or the frequency with which letters occur.

POLYALPHABETIC CIPHER

One way to change the frequencies and break up common sequences is to use a **polyalphabetic cipher.** Like the monoalphabetic cipher, it replaces each character with another. The difference is that a given plaintext character is not always replaced with the same ciphertext one. We can choose a replacement depending not only on the actual plaintext character but on its position in the message as well.

The following code segment illustrates a simple example. Arrays P and C represent plaintext and ciphertext characters, respectively, and K is the integer key.

```
for (int i=0; i<length of P; i++)
     C[i]=P[i]+K+(i mod 3);
```

Suppose $K = 1$. Then 1 is added to the ASCII codes of characters in positions 0, 3, 6, and so on; 2 is added to the codes in positions 1, 4, 7, and so on; and 3 is added to the codes in positions 2, 5, 8, and so on. In this case the string THEMTHENTHEY is encrypted as UJHNVKFPWIG\. This cipher seems to solve the repetition problem, but in fact it has only reduced it. Repetitions and patterns still occur. For example, the string THE is encrypted in three ways: UJH, VKF, and WIG. If there were more THE substrings, the encrypted versions would appear more frequently. You might respond by using a value greater than 3 in the code segment. This would generate more ways of encrypting THE substrings and create fewer repetitions. However, if the string is long enough, repetitions will still appear.

Besides, there are other patterns in the ciphertext. Can you see them? The first letters in each ciphertext equivalent of a THE substring (*U, V,* and *W*) are consecutive. The same is true of the second letters (*J, K,* and *I*) and the third letters (*H, F,* and *G*), although in the last two cases the letters were rearranged. Still, the patterns are there, and to a professional trying to break a code, this is a very big clue regarding the encryption method. Of course, there are other ways to disrupt patterns; we will discuss them later.

TRANSPOSITION CIPHER

A **transposition cipher** rearranges the plaintext letters of a message (rather than substituting ciphertext letters). One way to do this is to store the plaintext characters in a two-dimensional array with *m* columns. The first *m* plaintext characters are stored in the array's first row, the second *m* characters in the second row, and so on. Next we determine a permutation of the numbers 1 through *m,* and write it as p_1, $p_2, \ldots, p_m$. The permutation may be random or determined by some secret method. Either way, the final step is to transmit all the characters in column p_1, followed by those in column p_2, and so forth. The last set of characters transmitted are those in column p_m.

To illustrate, suppose the following message's characters are stored in a two-dimensional array with five columns (Table 7.1).

FOLLOW THE YELLOW BRICK ROAD

Table 7.1   Two-Dimensional Array Used for the Transposition Cipher

COLUMN NUMBERS				
1	2	3	4	5
F	O	L	L	O
W		T	H	E
	Y	E	L	L
O	W		B	R
I	C	K		R
O	A	D		

Suppose the column numbers are rearranged as 2, 4, 3, 1, 5. That is, the characters in column 2 are transmitted first, followed by the characters in columns 4, 3, 1, and 5, respectively. Therefore, the transmitted message looks like

```
O YWCALHLB LTE KDFW OIOOELRR
```

The transmitted message looks nothing like the original, but if the receiver knows the number of columns and the column number permutation, he can easily reconstruct the message. This is done by storing incoming characters in columns in the order of the permutation. In this example, the incoming characters would be stored in column 2 followed by columns 4, 3, 1, and 5. This is another example in which the decryption algorithm is defined by essentially reversing the steps of the encryption algorithm.

The problem with the transposition cipher is that it is not very secure. For one thing, letter frequencies are preserved. On reception, an unauthorized receiver could analyze the ciphertext and notice the high frequency of common letters. By itself this is an indication that letter substitutions were probably not used and that this may be a transposition cipher. The next step in breaking the code would be to group the characters and store them in different columns. The receiver would not try column arrangements randomly but would instead try arrangements that yielded commonly used sequences such as THE, ING, or IS in a row. This process would reduce the number of guesses greatly and provide a lot of help and information to the unauthorized but highly motivated receiver.

BIT-LEVEL CIPHERING

Not all transmissions are character sequences. Consequently, not all encryption methods work by manipulating or substituting characters. Some work at the bit level. One method defines the encryption key as a bit string. The choice is determined randomly and secretly. The bit string to be transmitted is divided into substrings. The length of each is the same as the length of the encryption key. Each substring is then encrypted by computing the exclusive OR between it and the encryption key.

In this case the decryption does not reverse the encryption steps, as in previous methods, but instead repeats them. In other words, to decrypt we compute the exclusive OR between the encryption key and each of the encrypted substrings. Here, the encryption and decryption alogorithms are the same.

Figure 7.3 demonstrates that doing the exclusive OR operation twice produces the original string. But does it always work this way? Yes! To see why, let p_i be any plaintext bit and $\oplus$ represent the exclusive OR operation. During the encryption/decryption process p_i is exclusively OR'd with either 0 or 1 twice. If it is 0 we have

$$(p_i \oplus 0) \oplus 0 = (p_i) \oplus 0 = p_i$$

If it is 1 we have

$$(p_i \oplus 1) \oplus 1 = p_i \oplus (1 \oplus 1) = p_i \oplus (0) = p_i$$

Either way, performing the exclusive OR twice generates the original bit p_i.

The security of this code depends partly on the length of the encryption key. A short key means the original string is divided into many substrings, with each encrypted separately. With many substrings, there is a greater chance that repetitions will occur. Because they are encrypted using the same key, the encrypted substrings are also repeated. As before, the repetitions can help an unauthorized receiver trying to break the code. Longer keys help disrupt this pattern, but there are still other patterns that occur with this method. For example, suppose you use an n-bit key and encrypt n bits of plaintext at a time. If there are two n-bit parts of the plaintext that differ in only one bit, the two generated n-bit ciphertext components will also differ by only one bit. Serious cryptologists can use this to help break codes.

In the extreme case, the length of the encryption key is the same as that of the message to be sent. In this case, each bit is encrypted using a unique bit in the key. If the key's bits are truly random, no patterns will exist in the encrypted string. Also, if the key is never used more than once, there is no opportunity to look for patterns among different ciphertexts and thus the code is truly unbreakable without trying every possible decryption key. Such unbreakable ciphers are also called **one-time pads.** The drawback is the large key that must be communicated to the receiver, thus making the method somewhat unwieldy. Another is that it can be used only once.

Figure 7.3 Encryption Using Exclusive OR Bit Operation

```
1101100101001  Plaintext
1001011001010  Encryption key
0100111100011  Ciphertext = plaintext exclusive OR'd with the encryption key
1001011001010  Decryption key (same as the encryption key)
1101100101001  Plaintext = ciphertext exclusive OR'd with the decryption key
```

DATA ENCRYPTION STANDARDS

DES   The encryption methods discussed so far are not terribly complex. In fact, when used with short keys they're not even very good because the ciphertext contains many clues that help an unauthorized person break the code. With longer keys, however, the ciphertext becomes more cryptic. In the extreme case, the code is virtually unbreakable. The difficulty is that long keys make implementation more difficult.

Approaches exist that keep the keys short (relative to the size of the message being encrypted) and use complex procedures to encrypt the data. One such method, the **Data Encryption Standard (DES),** was developed by IBM in the early 1970s based on a then experimental cryptographic system called *Lucifer*. It was adopted as a standard in 1977 by the National Bureau of Standards (now NIST) and has been used by the U.S. government for commercial and unclassified information. ANSI approved it as a private-sector standard in 1981. Applications include banking transactions and encoding PINs for automatic teller machines; users include the Department of Justice, Department of Energy, and the Federal Reserve System. The logic of this widely used method is built into hardware (VLSI chips) to make it even faster.

DES is an example of a **block cipher.** It divides a message into 64-bit blocks and encrypts each one. It uses a 56-bit key* and employs a complex combination of transpositions (rearrangement of bits), substitutions (replacing one bit group with another), exclusive OR operations, and a few other processes on a block to eventually produce 64 bits of encrypted data. In all, the 64-bit block goes through 19 successive steps, with the output of each step being input to the next step.

Figure 7.4 shows the primary steps. The first step does a transposition on the 64 data bits and the 56-bit key. The next 16 steps (labeled *encryption* in the figure) involve many operations, which we will describe shortly. Each step is the same except that it uses a different key derived from the original. The important point is that the output from one step is the input to the next. The second-to-last step (labeled *swap* in the figure) swaps the first 32 bits and the last 32 bits. The last step is another transposition. In fact, it is the reverse of the transposition done in the first step. The result is 64 bits of encrypted data.

Figure 7.5 outlines the primary operations of each of the middle 16 steps. In the figure, we represent a bit string with a letter and a numeric subscript. The subscript indicates the number of bits in the string. For example, K_{56} refers to the 56-bit string used as a key, and X_{48} is a 48-bit string resulting from some intermediate operation. When reading through the ensuing discussion, remember that even though we use the symbol X throughout the figure, it represents different strings at each stage. This method seems more sensible than using different names for each operation.

First, DES divides C_{64} (the 64 bits being encrypted) in half. The first 32 bits are L_{32} and the remaining 32 bits are R_{32}. Next, it expands R_{32} to a 48-bit string by transposing some of the bits and duplicating others. We label the result as R_{48} to reinforce the fact that it is determined completely from R_{32}. The algorithm also changes

---

* Actually, it uses a 64-bit key, but 8 bits are used for error detection. Thus, only 56 bits are used in the encryption process.

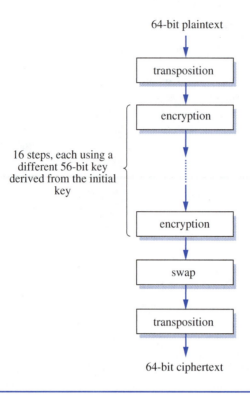

64-bit plaintext

transposition

encryption

16 steps, each using a different 56-bit key derived from the initial key

encryption

swap

transposition

64-bit ciphertext

Figure 7.4   Outline of DES

the 56-bit key by dividing it in half and doing a circular bit-shift on each half. The number of bits shifted depends on which of the 16 steps the algorithm is in. The point is that each step uses a different key. After the shifts, the key is transposed. The result is labeled K_{56}.

Next, the algorithm does an exclusive OR operation between R_{48} and the first 48 bits of K_{56}. The result is labeled X_{48}. Next, X_{48} is divided into eight 6-bit groups (X_6). Each 6-bit group goes through a substitution algorithm and is replaced by a 4-bit group X_4. The resulting eight 4-bit groups are then combined and subjected to another transposition, giving another 32-bit group X_{32}. The algorithm then does an exclusive OR operation between this string and L_{32}. Again, we call the result X_{32}. Finally, the algorithm creates a 64-bit string by using R_{32} as the first 32 bits and X_{32} as the last 32 bits. This entire process is done 16 times. Each time, the input is the result of the previous step and a different key is used.

Confusing? Well, it is supposed to be. IBM's intent was not to design a method everyone understands easily. The idea was to design a method that consists of many convoluted steps and is virtually impossible to reproduce without prior knowledge of the encryption key. We have left out many details, such as how the transpositions are done or how the 6-bit groups are substituted with 4-bit groups. The details of making substitutions depend largely on the substitution rules and tables called

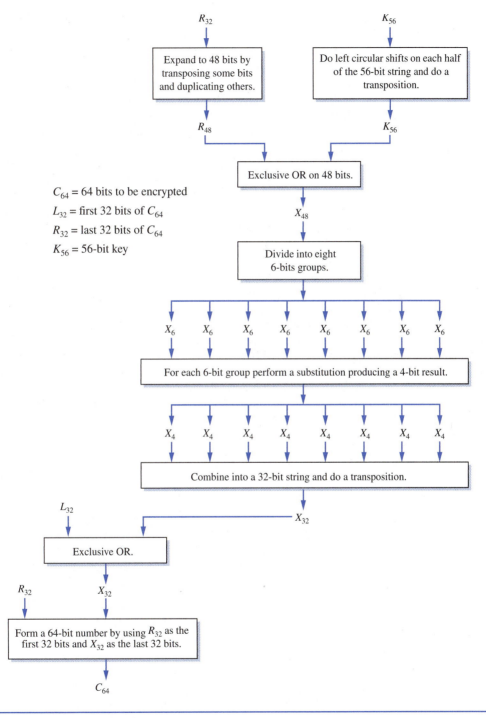

Figure 7.5 One of Sixteen Steps of the DES

S-boxes that define how a particular bit string is mapped onto another. If you are interested, reference [St95] provides a detailed description of the DES algorithm.

DES can operate in several modes, including **electronic codebook (ECB)** mode and **cipher block chaining (CBC)** mode.* In ECB mode, the algorithm simply encrypts each 64-bit plaintext block as described to produce a corresponding 64-bit ciphertext block. If the same 64-bit block occurs more than once in the original plaintext, it always generates the same 64-bit ciphertext block. Of course, this creates a pattern if the original plaintext is long enough, which can be used as a clue by someone trying to break the code.

CBC mode disrupts this pattern. Before encrypting one of the plaintext blocks, the algorithm first performs an exclusive OR operation between that block and the previously encrypted block (Figure 7.6). It then encrypts the result. For the first plaintext block, the exclusive OR operation is performed with an **initialization vector** defined at implementation. The significance is that each ciphertext block depends not only on the corresponding plaintext block, but on all previous blocks as well. Another way to think of it is that a ciphertext block depends on both the plaintext block and that block's position in the plaintext string. As a result, if the same plaintext block occurs in different positions it will likely generate different ciphertext blocks and disrupt the previously described pattern.

So how good is DES? There are many ways to attack an encryption algorithm, but the goal is invariably to determine the key and subsequently the original plaintext message. There are different techniques, often depending on patterns in the encrypted code or weaknesses in the algorithm that allow patterns to be deduced. For example, **differential cryptanalysis** involves looking at plaintext block pairs that differ in certain ways. If those differences (or similar ones) appear in the encrypted

Figure 7.6   CBC Mode for DES Encryption

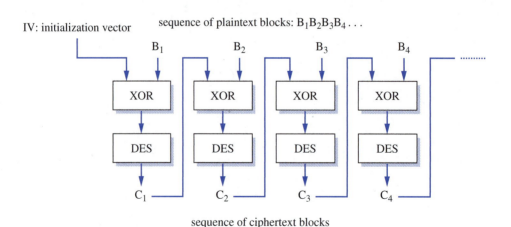

IV: initialization vector   sequence of plaintext blocks: $B_1B_2B_3B_4\ldots$

sequence of ciphertext blocks

---

* For details on other modes, see reference [Mo01].

pairs, then there is a pattern that can be exploited. Recall the polyalphabetic cipher from the previous section that exhibited such patterns. Another method of attack is simply brute force, a method in which all possible keys are tried until the correct one is found. Obviously, this is more difficult if the number of possible keys is large. Reference [Mo01] discusses other ways to attack an encryption system.

For years, many researchers studied DES trying to find weaknesses or patterns that could be used to break the code. There was little success. Furthermore, brute force attacks were considered difficult because the 56-bit key meant there existed $2^{56} \approx 7.2 \times 10^{16}$ possible key values. Unfortunately, with the gigahertz processors and parallel systems of today, this number is attainable. In fact, in 1998, the Electronic Frontier Foundation built a **DES Cracker,** a specially designed computer, at a cost of $250,000. This may be big money for you and me, but it is a pittance for organized crime, terrorist groups, or unfriendly governments with much to gain by cracking the security of high-level private or government institutions. In conjunction with a worldwide network of personal computers, the Foundation was able to try billions of keys per second and cracked the DES code in a matter of hours. That event rendered DES obsolete.

The original standardization of the DES has always been controversial (see ref. [Ko77]). Indeed, when IBM researchers began working on the problem, they used a 128-bit key. But, at the request of the NSA, it was reduced to 56 bits. The reasons behind the reduction to 56 bits haven't been made public. A 128-bit key would have meant many more possible key values ($2^{128} \approx 3 \times 10^{38}$) and would have made brute force attacks much more difficult.*

Another factor contributing to the controversy is that some people feel the rationale behind the substitutions in the DES algorithm was never fully explained. The fear was that there may be something in the substitution that could compromise the cipher's integrity. These factors have led to speculation that the NSA was uncomfortable with a code that even it would have trouble breaking. Remember, with the widespread use of electronic mail, the availability of DES chips, and the emergence of digital voice transmission, there was a lot of DES-encrypted information. The thought of being unable to decrypt when necessary would make NSA officials just a bit jittery. To make matters worse, there have been reports that the government has tried to suppress research or publication dealing with more secure ciphers.

Triple DES   The cracking of the DES code really came as no surprise, as many had been predicting for years that it would eventually happen. Consequently, many had been looking for alternatives. One is **triple DES,** which, as the name suggests, works by encrypting data three times. Based on ANSI standard X9.52, triple DES encrypts by applying three DES algorithms in succession to a plaintext message. For example, suppose $E_k(M)$ and $D_k(M)$ correspond to DES encryption and decryption

---

* How big is 3×10^{38}? Suppose a system could try 1 billion keys per microsecond (10^{15} keys per second). It would still take about 3×10^{23} seconds to try all keys. This is about 9.5×10^{15} years, longer than the time that has elapsed since the last big bang (perhaps also the one before, but no one knows).

algorithms, respectively, using a key k applied to a message M. Triple DES is calculated using $E_{k_3}(D_{k_2}(E_{k_1}(M)))$.

ANSI standard X9.52 defines three options for key values: (1) All three are independent of each other, (2) k_1 and k_2 are independent but $k_1 = k_3$, and (3) all are equal. Of course, in the last case, triple DES defaults to DES because the first two steps cancel each other. This makes triple DES backward compatible with DES and is the reason the decryption algorithm is specified as the second step.

In effect, triple DES defines a technique using a 168-bit key. Keys k_1, k_2, and k_3 simply represent the first, middle, and last 56-bit portions of that key. The method has the advantage of relying on an existing algorithm that has proved solid and has not exhibited any serious flaws. In addition, it can be phased in with existing DES systems because of its backward compatibility. Although many people predict that the 168-bit key will be immune from attack for a long time, others have criticized it for being slow, taking about three times as long as DES. Of course, *slow* is a relative term, and some believe the extra time is worth the increase in security.

AES and the Rijndael Algorithm   Recognizing that DES's days were numbered, in 1997 NIST sent out a request to the world cryptographic community for proposals on a new **Advanced Encryption Standard (AES).*** During the following year NIST received 15 such proposals and announced them at the first AES candidate conference in August 1998. It solicited comments and analyses of the candidate algorithms and, based on the results, reduced the number of candidates to five. Those algorithms were MARS, RC6, Rijndael, Serpent, and Twofish (ref. [Sc98]). Each of these algorithms was subjected to further analysis; in October 2000, NIST announced it had selected the **Rijndael algorithm** to be the new AES. Later, the secretary of commerce approved its adoption as an official government standard effective May 26, 2002.

The AES Rijndael algorithm was developed by Dr. Vincent Rijmen and Dr. Joan Daemen (which explains the algorithm's name). Like DES, it is a block cipher and specifies key sizes of 128, 192, or 256 bits. Alternative notations for AES are therefore AES-128, AES-192, and AES-256. In the latter case there are approximately 1.1×10^{77} possible keys. The magnitude of that number is so large it is difficult to comprehend. The algorithm can also encrypt block sizes of 128, 192, or 256 bits. In fact, any combination of key and block size can be used, providing nine variations. The Rijndael algorithm is projected to be at least as strong as triple DES but has the advantage of carrying out necessary operations more quickly. Because it was designed to replace DES as opposed to triple DES, many predict that AES and triple DES will coexist for some time.

Rijndael's design is based on that of another block cipher called SQUARE.[†] The details are complex, and a full understanding of Rijndael requires a substantial understanding of mathematical topics such as field theory, Galois fields, irreducible polynomials, and equivalence classes. Although it is not practical to cover these

---

* See details at http://csrc.nist.gov/encryption/aes/overview.

[†] See details at http://www.esat.kuleuven.ac.be/~rijmen/square/index.html.

128-bit block (16 bytes)

$b_0\ b_1\ b_2\ b_3\ b_4\ b_5\ b_6\ b_7\ b_8\ b_9\ b_{10}\ b_{11}\ b_{12}\ b_{13}\ b_{14}\ b_{15}$

128-bit key (16 bytes)

$k_0\ k_1\ k_2\ k_3\ k_4\ k_5\ k_6\ k_7\ k_8\ k_9\ k_{10}\ k_{11}\ k_{12}\ k_{13}\ k_{14}\ k_{15}$

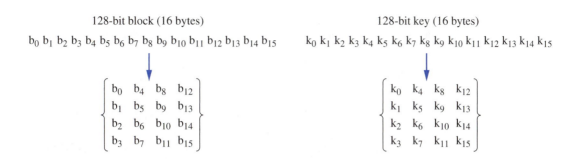

$$\begin{bmatrix} b_0 & b_4 & b_8 & b_{12} \\ b_1 & b_5 & b_9 & b_{13} \\ b_2 & b_6 & b_{10} & b_{14} \\ b_3 & b_7 & b_{11} & b_{15} \end{bmatrix} \qquad \begin{bmatrix} k_0 & k_4 & k_8 & k_{12} \\ k_1 & k_5 & k_9 & k_{13} \\ k_2 & k_6 & k_{10} & k_{14} \\ k_3 & k_7 & k_{11} & k_{15} \end{bmatrix}$$

Figure 7.7   Interpreting a Block and Key as a Matrix

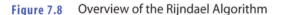

topics here, we will provide a brief overview of the Rijndael algorithm and its major steps. Several good references go into more detail, but they require that the reader have some background equivalent to one or two courses in abstract algebra. Those references are [Mo01], [Da02], http://csrc.nist.gov/encryption/aes/rijndael/Rijndael.pdf, and http://csrc.nist.gov/publications/fips/fips197/fips-197.pdf.

To begin our outline of the Rijndael algorithm we provide some preliminary concepts. Because Rijndael is a block cipher, it encrypts plaintext one block at a time. As stated previously, block and key sizes can be 128, 192, or 256 bits. However, to simplify our discussion here, we will consider the case of a 128-bit key and a 128-bit block size and comment on the other options when appropriate. Rijndael visualizes a 128-bit plaintext block as a sequence of sixteen 8-bit bytes (b_0 through b_{15}) and organizes them into a matrix (Figure 7.7) with four rows and four columns. It interprets the 128-bit key in similar fashion. For larger keys and blocks, it still uses four rows but increases the number of columns to accommodate the data.

Rijndael's first step is to perform a bitwise exclusive OR operation between the initial block and key. The result, called the *state*, is then input into the first of 10 rounds of encryption (Figure 7.8). Each round changes its input state using specified

Figure 7.8   Overview of the Rijndael Algorithm

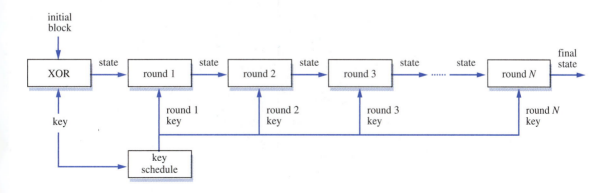

matrix operations and produces an output state (essentially another matrix), which is input to the next round of activities. At the end of the required number of rounds, encryption is complete. More rounds occur if the block or key sizes are larger, but the basic outline remains the same.

Each round uses a separate *round key* to alter the contents of the input state. The round keys are defined through a key expansion routine that starts by interpreting the initial key as a sequence of 4-byte words (one word for each column). In this discussion we start with four words, $w_0 = k_0{:}k_1{:}k_2{:}k_3$, $w_1 = k_4{:}k_5{:}k_6{:}k_7$, $w_2 = k_8{:}k_9{:}k_{10}{:}k_{11}$, and $w_3 = k_{12}{:}k_{13}{:}k_{14}{:}k_{15}$. The fifth and subsequent words are each generated from previously defined words using a recursive formula. We won't go into all of the details, but the following steps outline the approach for determining w_i, $4 \leq i < 44$. (Because there are 10 rounds and we need a key containing 4 words for each round, there are a total of 44 words, including the initial 4 words.) More rounds will require more words.

1. If i is not a multiple of 4, then define w_i as the exclusive OR between w_{i-1} and w_{i-4}. If i is a multiple of 4, do the steps that follow.

2. Perform a cyclic permutation of the bytes in w_{i-1}. If the bytes were (a, b, c, d), the permutation is (b, c, d, a).

3. Perform a substitution replacing each byte in the word from the previous step with another byte. Each substitute byte is determined by the byte that is being replaced and a table of substitution values called an *S-box*. The S-box contains rows and columns (Figure 7.9) of byte values, and each row and column is indexed by a 4-bit value. To determine the proper substitution, the Rijndael algorithm uses the first 4 bits to determine the row of the S-box and the second 4 bits to determine the column. The byte value where that row and column intersect replaces the original byte. Rijndael specifies the entire S-box contents,

Figure 7.9   S-Box Substitution

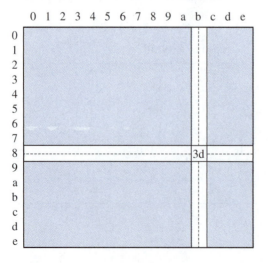

but Figure 7.9 shows that the byte value $8b$ would be replaced by the byte value $3d$ that is stored in row 8 and column d.

4. Perform an exclusive OR with a round constant that Rijndael specifies.

Once all the words are generated, the Rijndael algorithm uses the first four words in the initial exclusive OR operation and each subsequent four-word set in each subsequent round. That is, round i uses word w_i.

So, what does Rijndael do within a round? Basically, there are four steps in each round, designated by byte substitution (BSB), shift row (SR), mix column (MC), and round key addition (RKA).* Each round proceeds as follows.

1. **BSB:** Replace each byte in the current state matrix with another determined by that byte and the S-box. This is similar to the substitution in the key expansion procedure and, in fact, uses the same S-box.

2. **SR:** Shift the bytes in each row (except the first row) of the matrix a specified number of positions to the left. Elements that are shifted past the leftmost column reenter at the rightmost columns. In other words, this is a left circular shift. The number of positions to be shifted depends on the row number and the key and block sizes and is prescribed by Rijndael. In our example, rows 2, 3, and 4 are shifted left by 1, 2, and 3 byte positions, respectively. For example, the SR step would transform the matrix

$$\begin{bmatrix} 45 & 6a & 3b & 67 \\ 76 & da & d4 & 4f \\ fa & 2d & 31 & 9b \\ f5 & 4d & 33 & 78 \end{bmatrix} \text{ into the matrix } \begin{bmatrix} 45 & 6a & 3b & 67 \\ da & d4 & 4f & 76 \\ 31 & 9b & fa & 2d \\ 78 & f5 & 4d & 33 \end{bmatrix}$$

3. **MC:** This is the most difficult step to describe because of the theory underlying all of the calculations. The general idea is to interpret each column as a four-term polynomial and multiply it by another fixed polynomial $c(x) = 03x^3 + 01x^2 + 01x^1 + 02$ (prescribed by Rijndael). However, the multiplication is done modulo $x^4 + 1$, yet another Rijndael prescribed polynomial. What this means is that if $p(x)$ is the product polynomial, then the result we use is another polynomial $q(x)$ for which the degree of $q(x)$ is less than 4 and the difference $p(x) - q(x)$ is evenly divisible by $x^4 + 1$. Mathematicians say that $p(x)$ is equivalent to $q(x)$ modulo $x^4 + 1$. Another complicating factor is that the polynomials' coefficients are interpreted as 8-bit binary values and those numbers are not multiplied in the way you might think. The details are complicated, but each 8-bit value represents an element in a mathematical structure called a Galois field (a special type of finite field)† and can be interpreted as yet another polynomial whose coefficients are either 0 or 1. Furthermore, the rules for multiplying such values are complex and defined by specifics of Galois field

---

* Actually, the last round does not include the MC step.

† In general, a *field* defines a mathematical structure that contains a collection of elements and operations (addition, subtraction, multiplication, and division) that obey certain properties.

theory, an advanced branch of mathematics. Because such topics are far beyond what we can do here, we are not able to specify the details of the calculations. The main idea is that each state column (interpreted as a polynomial) is multiplied by a fixed polynomial (using advanced mathematical logic) to generate a product polynomial. That product polynomial is interpreted as a 4-byte sequence and replaces the original column.

4. **RKA:** This step performs an exclusive OR operation between the current state and the round key.

Once all 10 rounds are completed, the resulting state is the encrypted version of the initial state. To be sure, we have skipped over many details. For example, how is the S-box chosen? What are the round constants in the key expansion method? What is the significance of the polynomials $03x^3 + 01x^2 + 01x^1 + 02$ and $x^4 + 1$ in the MC step? How does Rijndael define the multiplication of polynomials? Answers to all of these questions require knowledge of mathematics typically found in an abstract algebra course and include topics such as rings, Galois fields, irreducible polynomials, polynomials with coefficients in Galois fields, and affine transformations. The bottom line is that the AES Rijndael algorithm is built on some very powerful and complex mathematical theory. The reader with some mathematical background is encouraged to explore some of the detail in references [Mo01], [Da02], http://csrc.nist.gov/encryption/aes/rijndael/Rijndael.pdf, and http://csrc.nist.gov/publications/fips/fips197/fips-197.pdf.

THE CLIPPER CHIP AND THE SKIPJACK ALGORITHM

In April 1993 the controversy surrounding encryption and alleged government intervention gained some public awareness when the Clinton administration announced plans for a new security initiative. The initiative outlined plans for a new technology called the **Clipper Chip,**[*] a government-designed and -built encryption computer chip that could be used in security devices. These devices, in turn, could be used in ordinary communications equipment such as telephones or fax machines.

The way it works is rather straightforward (Figure 7.10). The Clipper Chip contains an encryption algorithm designed into its microcircuits. Suppose you make a telephone call and want to begin a secure conversation, that is, a conversation that cannot be intercepted and understood by a third party. All you would need to do is press a button, and your security device and the remote one would exchange encryption keys.[†] The security device would then route anything you say, along with the encryption key, to the Clipper Chip, which encodes your voice signals. The telephone system then transmits your encoded message. At the other end the remote device decodes the voice transmission using its Clipper Chip (which it could do because of the encryption key exchange) and restores your original voice message. The net result is that the remote person hears your voice as in any telephone conversation.

---

[*] Although the term *Clipper* is commonly used, the official name for the technology was *Capstone*.

[†] There are various protocols to observe when exchanging encryption keys to ensure that the keys are not intercepted. We discuss one option, called the Diffie-Hellman key exchange, in the next section.

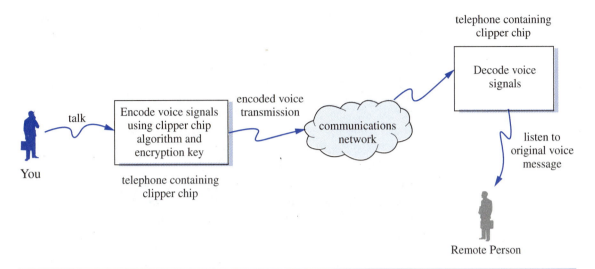

Figure 7.10   Clipper Chip Encryption

However, any third party that might tap into your conversation gets only the encoded voice signals.

The initiative was motivated by two major concerns. The first was the need for privacy of telephone conversations and for protection of any sensitive information transmitted by telephone, fax, or computer. The second was to be responsive to the needs of law enforcement individuals when sensitive information corresponds to illegal activities. These both sound like laudable goals, so why the controversy?

First, the Clipper Chip was designed by engineers in the NSA with no input from private industry (ref. [Si96]). Given the ongoing tension that exists between civil libertarians and government officials, this fact alone was sufficient fodder for controversy, but there was more. The method used for encryption is the *Skipjack algorithm,** which was developed by the NSA and whose details are classified. This caused suspicion among some, who argued that the algorithm could not be subjected to the same testing processes as other algorithms whose details were freely available. Some also saw this as a violation of the Computer Security Act, a law passed by Congress in 1987 that was intended to limit the NSA's role in the development of standards. Proponents for classifying the algorithm argued that keeping details secret had nothing to do with making the algorithm more secure. Instead, the intent was to prevent unauthorized construction of devices that were compatible with authorized ones but that did not implement certain law enforcement features.

This brings us to another controversial aspect, which involves the encryption keys themselves. Suppose someone using a telephone or other communications device were suspected of illegal activities. A common tool used by law enforcement

---

* We'll skip the details of this algorithm, but the interested reader can reference the website
http://csrc.nist.gov/encryption/skipjack/skipjack.pdf.

officials is wiretapping, or the monitoring of communications. If the suspect is encrypting all communications, the wiretap provides no useful information. Further, if the encryption method is a good one it cannot be broken in a reasonable amount of time. At the heart of the issue is whether private citizens have the right to "unbreakable" encryption techniques and whether and when law enforcement officials have the right to listen to private conversations. This is something that prompts long debates. The FBI and other law enforcement agencies urged the inclusion of a feature in the Clipper Chip that would allow them to determine the encryption key and, subsequently, to decode encrypted information.

Each Clipper Chip has the following information:

- K: An 80-bit session key used to encrypt transmitted messages. This is what law enforcement officials need to know to make the wiretap effective.

- F: An 80-bit family key. All chips in a group have the same one.

- N: A 30-bit serial number unique to each chip.

- S: An 80-bit secret key, also unique to each chip and used by law enforcement officials.

The last key, S, is the one at the center of the controversy. As stated, each Clipper Chip generates an encrypted voice message, $E_k(\text{Message})$. It also generates a law enforcement field $E_F(E_S(K) + N)$.* This last expression is important, so let's examine it closely. Essentially, the Clipper Chip produces its own session key as output, albeit in encrypted form. All you need is the method for getting it. Figure 7.11 outlines the necessary steps.

Once a wiretap has been court approved, officials apply D_F to the law enforcement field to get $E_S(K) + N$. The family key F is not secret, so that is not a problem;

Figure 7.11 Determining the Encryption Key

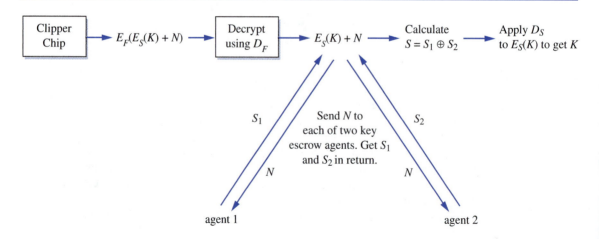

in theory, anyone could do it. At this point, officials can extract the serial number of the chip and the encrypted session key $E_S(K)$. All that remains is to apply D_S to get the session key. Since S is secret, this is not easy, but there is a way. However, let's first examine how S is created.

The secret key S is actually defined using two other keys according to the formula $S = S_1 \oplus S_2$ ($\oplus$ is the bitwise exclusive OR). The keys S_1 and S_2 are also secret and are maintained by two different **key escrow agencies.** These are agencies designed to keep and protect valuable information. When a particular Clipper Chip is constructed, one representative from each agency is present. Each representative selects a random 80-bit number, which is subjected to a series of calculations. One agent produces S_1 and the other produces S_2 for a particular chip. Neither agent knows what the other chose or ended up with. The secret key is then calculated as $S = S_1 \oplus S_2$ and is programmed into the chip. One agent records S_1 and N (chip serial number) and the other records S_2 and N. Each returns that valuable information to his or her agency, where it is kept in a secure location. The important thing here is that the secret key S is not stored in any one place. This provides an extra level of security since neither S_1 nor S_2 alone provides any useful information. In fact, the computers that calculate S and program the chip may even be destroyed as an added security measure.

Once the law enforcement officials obtain the chip's serial number, they can send a copy to each key escrow agency, along with proof that a wiretap was authorized. Each agency responds by sending its portion of the key associated with the specified serial number. The officials eventually obtain both S_1 and S_2, calculate S, and apply D_S to $E_S(K)$ to get the session key, K. At this point they are able to decrypt any messages encrypted using E_K, and the wiretap is successful.

Part of the concern centered on the key escrow agents, who were in charge of key components, and the mechanisms in place to store and protect keys. Many argued that the escrow agencies should be separate from law enforcement agencies. A major concern again is a person's right to privacy. The argument is that having one law enforcement agency getting key components from itself or another law enforcement agency has the potential for misuse. By using independent agencies with no official ties to law enforcement, a citizen's right to privacy is better protected. If you are interested in knowing more about the mechanisms for key escrow systems, you can consult reference [De96].

In concluding this section, we note that the NIST specifies cryptographic standards in its Federal Information Processing Standards (FIPS) publications. In subsequent readings about cryptographic standards, you may encounter the term *FIPS approved,* which means the standard is either in a FIPS publication or has been adopted by FIPS and is in an appendix or another document referenced by FIPS. As of this writing there are four FIPS-approved algorithms: AES, DES, triple DES, and Skipjack.

7.3 KEY DISTRIBUTION AND PROTECTION

All of the methods discussed so far assume that the decryption key is derivable from (or equal to) the encryption key. Consequently, the best encryption method in the world is no good if the key cannot be kept secret. Therefore, we face another problem: How does the sender communicate the key to the receiver (**key distribution** or *key exchange*)? For example, Clipper Chips exchange keys prior to beginning a secure conversation. Your first suggestion might be for the sender simply to send the key. But, as before, what if an unauthorized receiver gets it? Encrypt it, you might say—but what method should the sender use? How does the sender communicate that method's key to the receiver? This does not solve the problem; it merely redefines it.

Maintaining a key's secrecy is not an easy task, but there are options. For example, the two persons communicating could meet in some clandestine location (such as a local McDonald's restaurant) and agree on a key. But sometimes logistics do not allow such meetings (or maybe the principal parties are vegetarians). Another option would be to transport a key under armed guard. This conjures up images of people with attaché cases handcuffed to their wrists surrounded by people with bent noses and their hands hidden inside their suit coats.

SHAMIR'S METHOD

One method of key distribution, **Shamir's method,** is used in a scenario different from what we have described previously. Suppose the information to be encrypted is so sensitive that no one person can be trusted to send or receive it. We want to store the key in such a way that at least k people must be present to determine it. We further assume that any k people with appropriate clearance will suffice. That is, we impose no requirement that any particular person or persons be present.

Storing the key in any one spot will not work, because this violates the condition that k people must be present. We could divide the key into k distinct pieces and distribute the pieces. If each person gets one piece, we have a constraint on who may be present (only those with mutually distinct pieces). If we give several pieces to any person, fewer than $k - 1$ persons have the remaining pieces, which violates the condition that at least k persons must be present.

Shamir's method (ref. [Sh79]) is a clever one based on polynomial interpolation. Specifically, suppose that $p(x) = a_0 + a_1x + a_2x^2 + \ldots + a_{k-1}x^{k-1}$ is a polynomial of degree $k - 1$. Suppose also that $(x_1, y_1), (x_2, y_2), \ldots, (x_k, y_k)$ are known points on the graph of $p(x)$ and that $x_i \neq x_j$ whenever $i \neq j$. Then these k points determine the polynomial $p(x)$ uniquely and from them we can determine the values of $a_0, a_1, \ldots,$ and a_{k-1}.

In Shamir's method the polynomial $p(x)$ is constructed so that one of the coefficients (say a_0) is the encryption key. Each person who is cleared to send or receive information is given precisely one data point on the graph of $p(x)$, making sure that no two data points have the same x-coordinate. Any group of k persons can provide k unique data points. All of the data points allow them to determine the polynomial and consequently the key.

If there are fewer than k people, there are not enough data points to determine the polynomial uniquely. Even so, a small group of subversives could pool their data points and determine relationships among the a_i, which could yield hints to the key's value. Shamir's method avoids this possibility by doing all the computations using modular arithmetic.

DIFFIE-HELLMAN KEY EXCHANGE

Diffie-Hellman key exchange works by having a sender and receiver exchange calculated values from which an encryption key can be computed. The calculations

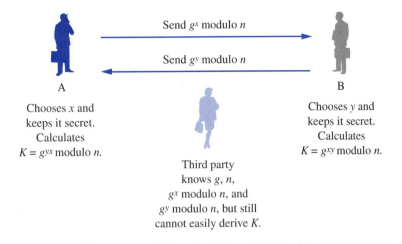

Send g^x modulo n

Send g^y modulo n

A

Chooses x and
keeps it secret.
Calculates
$K = g^{yx}$ modulo n.

B

Chooses y and
keeps it secret.
Calculates
$K = g^{xy}$ modulo n.

Third party
knows g, n,
g^x modulo n, and
g^y modulo n, but still
cannot easily derive K.

Figure 7.12   Diffie-Hellman Key Exchange

use other numbers, which do not need to be kept secret. For example, suppose two people agree to use two integers, g and n, in the calculation of the encryption key. Figure 7.12 shows an exchange between two people, A and B (their parents must have liked simple names), and illustrates who knows what.

First, A picks an integer x and calculates and sends the value of g^x modulo n to B. Similarly, B independently selects a value of y and sends g^y modulo n to A. If there is a third party listening to this conversation, we assume he knows g and n along with whatever else is being transmitted. Meanwhile, A gets g^y modulo n and raises it to the power of x, getting g^{yx} modulo n. B gets g^x modulo n and raises it to the power of y, getting g^{xy} modulo n. Using properties of modular arithmetic, g^{yx} modulo n and g^{xy} modulo n are equal. Both A and B use this as the encryption key.

What about the snooping third party? As stated, he knows both g and n and can determine the values of g^x modulo n and g^y modulo n from snooping on the communications line. But since both A and B keep the values of x and y secret, the third party cannot complete the calculations to get the encryption key. This, by itself, does not make the line secure. A logical question to ask is, If the third party knows g, n, g^x modulo n, and g^y modulo n, can he derive the values of x and y from them? In effect, the third party needs to calculate a logarithm of g^x modulo n or g^y modulo n. There are conditions that n and g can satisfy that make such derivations very difficult. At the very least, both g and n must be very large (perhaps a thousand bits). We won't provide a discussion of the conditions that must apply and why they are sufficient, as that gets us into mathematical number theory. If you are interested in this topic, reference [Sc94] has more detail.

The Diffie-Hellman exchange is susceptible to a problem known as the **man-in-the-middle attack.** In this attack, an intruder places himself in between A and B. When A sends g^x modulo n, the intruder intercepts it and replaces it with a value of $g^{x'}$ modulo n and sends it to B. Neither A nor B are aware of it. When B sends g^y

modulo n, the intruder intercepts it and replaces it with a value of $g^{y'}$ modulo n and sends it to A. Again, neither A nor B know. As far as A is concerned, she is encrypting using a key equal to $g^{xy'}$ modulo n, which the intruder also uses. Likewise, B uses a key equal to $g^{x'y}$ modulo n, which the intruder also uses to communicate with B. Both A and B think they are communicating with each other when, in reality, the intruder is intercepting all messages, decrypting them, and reencrypting them before sending them to the other side.

7.4 PUBLIC KEY ENCRYPTION

All of the previous encryption methods share one feature: If an unauthorized receiver intercepts the ciphertext and, for some reason, knows the encryption algorithm and key (E_k), then the decryption method ($D_{k'}$) is easy to determine. For example, if the ciphertext for a Caesar cipher was determined by adding k to the ASCII codes of the plaintext, we simply decrypt by subtracting k from the ASCII codes of the ciphertext. Similar comments can also be made about the other methods discussed so far.

It certainly seems reasonable that knowing E_k makes decryption trivial. Like many other reasonable things, however, it is not true. In 1976, Diffie and Hellman (ref. [Di67]) proposed the use of encryption methods for which the decryption algorithm and key are not determined easily even when both the encryption method and key are known. The rationale is that even if an unauthorized person knows the encryption algorithm and key, that knowledge is of no use in helping him or her decrypt the ciphertext.

There is another advantage to such methods. Suppose someone needs to get secret messages from many sources (Figure 7.13). Rather than having each source use a different encryption method, they can all use the same one, E_k. Only the receiver knows the decryption method $D_{k'}$. In fact, E_k could be made public. Since $D_{k'}$ cannot be derived from that knowledge, there is no danger. As long as $D_{k'}$ is kept private, even different senders cannot decrypt others' messages despite the fact they use the same encryption method.

Such systems are called **public key cryptosystems.** Typical uses include a bank receiving sensitive financial requests from many customers or a military command center receiving reports from various locations. It also is common in setting up secure websites for electronic commerce.

RSA ALGORITHM

The RSA algorithm (named after its developers, Rivest, Shamir, and Adleman, and described in reference [Ri78]), uses modular arithmetic and the factorization of very large numbers. The ciphertext is surprisingly easy to calculate and very difficult to break, even when E_k is known. Some of the theory behind this algorithm is based in mathematical number theory, specifically in notable results known as Fermat's theorem and Euler's theorem. We won't diverge into a discussion of number theory, but if you have the inclination, references [St95] and [Mo01] summarize some of the important number theoretic results.

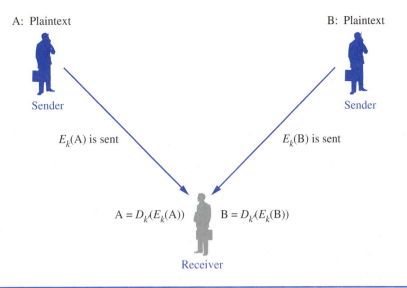

A: Plaintext

B: Plaintext

Sender

Sender

$E_k(A)$ is sent

$E_k(B)$ is sent

$A = D_k(E_k(A))$

$B = D_k(E_k(B))$

Receiver

Figure 7.13   Multiple Senders Using the Same Encryption Method

To describe how this method works, we consider messages consisting of capital letters only. However, the method can be generalized to include a larger character set. The following steps describe the RSA encryption algorithm and include an example to illustrate how it works.

1. Assign a simple code to the letters, such as 1 through 26 for A through Z, respectively.

2. Choose n to be the product of two large prime numbers p and q. (A prime number has no factors except itself and 1.) In practice, a large prime number consists of 200 or more digits. However, we will conserve space and energy by using $n = p \times q = 11 \times 7 = 77$.

3. Find a number k that is relatively prime to $(p - 1) \times (q - 1)$. Two numbers are relatively prime if they have no common factors except 1. In our example, we choose $k = 7$, which is relatively prime to $(p - 1) \times (q - 1) = 10 \times 6 = 60$. The number k is the encryption key. You might ask, Can we always find a number k with this property? The answer is yes. A well-known result in number theory proves it.

4. Divide the message into components. In general, each component will contain many letters to avoid repeated components. However, for our example, we will have just one letter per component. If the message is "HELLO," the components are H, E, L, L, and O.

5. For each component, concatenate all the binary codes of each letter in the component and interpret the resulting bit string as an integer. Here, each component has just one letter. So, the integers are 8, 5, 12, 12, and 15 (the numbers assigned to the letters originally).

6. Encrypt the message by raising each number to the power of k. However, do all arithmetic modulo n. In our example, this requires the following computations:

$$8^7 \text{ modulo } 77; \; 5^7 \text{ modulo } 77; \; 12^7 \text{ modulo } 77;$$
$$12^7 \text{ modulo } 77; \; 15^7 \text{ modulo } 77$$

The results are the encrypted message. Here the calculations evaluate to 57, 47, 12, 12, and 71, respectively. (We will show how to make this calculation shortly.) Note that here the two 12s indicate a repeated letter. This is a consequence of having one letter per component. If a component contains several letters, repetitions like this are avoided.

The receiver gets the encrypted message 57, 47, 12, 12, and 71. How does she decrypt it? The following steps show the decryption method and continue the example.

1. Find a value k' for which $k \times k' - 1 = 0$ modulo $(p - 1) \times (q - 1)$. This means that $(k \times k') - 1$ is evenly divisible by $(p - 1) \times (q - 1)$. The value for k' is the decryption key. In this example, $(p - 1) \times (q - 1) = 60$, and $k' = 43$ works nicely. That is, $7 \times 43 - 1 = 300$ is divisible by 60. Again, you might ask, Can a value k' always be found? Yes! Again, famous results in number theory by Euler and Fermat prove this.

2. Raise each encrypted number from step 6 of the encryption process to the power k', and do the arithmetic modulo n. The results are the original component numbers from step 5. In our example, this requires the following calculations:

$$57^{43} \text{ modulo } 77; \; 47^{43} \text{ modulo } 77; \; 12^{43} \text{ modulo } 77;$$
$$12^{43} \text{ modulo } 77; \; 71^{43} \text{ modulo } 77$$

The results are the original numbers: 8, 5, 12, 12, and 15.

Using previous notation, $E_k(x) = x^k$ modulo n and $D_{k'}(y) = y^{k'}$ modulo n, so we have $D_{k'}(E_k(x)) = (x^k)^{k'}$ modulo n. As long as k and k' are chosen as described, $(x^k)^{k'}$ modulo n evaluates to x. Once again, verification of this lies in the work of number theorists.

The encryption and decryption algorithms are surprisingly simple. Both involve exponentiation and modular arithmetic. But there is a potential problem: How do you calculate the exact modular value of a number such as 71^{43}? This particular number evaluates to approximately 10^{79} and is actually very small compared with numbers that occur in practice. It certainly seems to be an intimidating calculation. We are interested only in modular arithmetic, however, so we can take some shortcuts that allow you to do this on any calculator. Let's illustrate by calculating 71^{43} modulo 77.

The first step is to write the exponent as a sum of powers of 2. Doing this, we get

$$71^{43} = 71^{32+8+2+1} = 71^{32} \times 71^8 \times 71^2 \times 71^1 \qquad (7\text{-}1)$$

Now, $71^2 = 5041 = 36$ modulo 77. Again, this means 5041 and 36 have the same integer remainder on dividing by 77. Since Equation 7.1 requires only the modular value, we can replace 71^2 by 36. Furthermore, we can write 71^8 as $(71^2)^4$. Again, since we need only the modular value, this is the same as 36^4. Similarly, the modular equivalent of 71^{32} is $(71^2)^{16}$, or 36^{16}. Therefore, Equation 7.1 reduces to

$$71^{43} = 36^{16} \times 36^4 \times 36 \times 71 \text{ modulo } 77 \qquad (7\text{-}2)$$

As you can see, we have reduced the necessary calculations significantly. But we can go further. Proceeding in a similar fashion, we have $36^2 = 1296 = 64$ modulo 77. Consequently, we can write $36^4 = (36^2)^2 = 64^2$ modulo 77 and $36^{16} = (36^2)^8 = 64^8$ modulo 77. Now Equation 7.2 reduces to

$$71^{43} = 64^8 \times 64^2 \times 36 \times 71 \text{ modulo } 77 \qquad (7\text{-}3)$$

Of course, we can continue the process to get

$$\begin{aligned} 71^{43} &= 64^8 \times 64^2 \times 36 \times 71 \text{ modulo } 77 \\ &= 15^4 \times 15 \times 36 \times 71 \text{ modulo } 77 \\ &= 71^2 \times 15 \times 36 \times 71 \text{ modulo } 77 \\ &= 36 \times 15 \times 36 \times 71 \text{ modulo } 77 \\ &= 15 \text{ modulo } 77 \end{aligned}$$

There's no calculation here that cannot be verified by any calculator.

The RSA algorithm is relatively easy to implement, but is it secure? The encryption algorithm requires n and k, and the decryption algorithm requires n and k'. Now, suppose you intercept an encrypted message and that you know n and k. It doesn't seem like it should be difficult to determine k'. But remember, k' is chosen so that $(k \times k') - 1 = 0$ modulo $(p - 1) \times (q - 1)$. Therefore, all you need to do is find p and q, the factors of n. But if n is very large, say on the order of 200 digits, this is very difficult (or at least very time-consuming) to do.*

DIGITAL SIGNATURES

Another interesting use for public key cryptosystems is in verification. For example, when you make a withdrawal from a bank, you must fill out a form and sign it. Your signature verifies your identity. If you later claim you never made the withdrawal, the bank can produce the form with your signature. Of course, you can always claim the signature was forged and sue the bank. If the case goes to court, the bank can

---

* Of interest might be the RSA challenge (see www.rsasecurity.com/rsalabs/challenges/factoring/numbers.html), which provides cash awards for factoring large numbers. For example, at the time of this writing the RSA laboratories were offering a $200,000 prize for factoring the 617-digit (2048-bit) number 25195908475657893494027183240048398571429282126204032027777 13783604366202070759555626401852588078440691829064124951508218929855914 91761845028084891200728449926873928072877767359714183472702618963750149 7 18246911650776133798590957000973304597488084284017974291006424586918171951187 46 12151517265463228221686998754918242243363725908514186546204357679842338718477 44 47920739934236584823824281198163815010674810451660377306056201619676256133844 14 36038339044149526344321901146575444541784240209246165157233507787077498171257 72 46796292638635637328991215483143816789988504044536402352738195137863656439121 20 10397122822120720357. Anyone interested?

produce a handwriting expert who can verify the signature is yours. Consequently, you will lose the suit and the bank's loan officers will probably not approve your request for a mortgage on your new house.

But consider a slightly different scenario. You send a request electronically to your Swiss bank account to transfer a large sum of money to your ex-spouse's account. What can the bank do if you later claim you never made the request, especially since your ex-spouse took the money and moved to Bolivia? There is no signature on file for a handwriting expert to analyze. The bank might respond by stating a password had to be entered to authorize the request and only you knew the password. Of course, the bank's computers also have the password somewhere to verify it when you enter it. You might claim that someone got the password from the bank's records and that therefore the bank is at fault for not providing proper protection.

Is there a way for the bank to prove it was not at fault and to verify it was you who made the request? Figure 7.14 illustrates the general problem. Someone sends a message, receives a response, and then claims he never sent it. Can the receiver verify the claim is false? Verifying the identity of a sender is called **authentication.**

One method of authentication is to use a **digital signature.** Essentially, it involves encrypting a message in a way that only the sender would know. More specifically, it uses an encryption key only the sender knows. It is similar to a password except that passwords are also stored in the receiver's files for verification. The encryption key is nowhere except in the sender's possession. The sender might claim someone stole it, but since the receiver has no record of the key, the receiver is not at fault. It's like losing the key to your home. Ultimately, you are responsible.

Figure 7.15 shows how to send encrypted messages containing a digital signature. The method uses two pairs of public key encryption/decryption methods. We label them $(E_k, D_{k'})$ and $(E_j, D_{j'})$, where the public keys are j and k and the private

Figure 7.14   Sender Denying Sending a Message

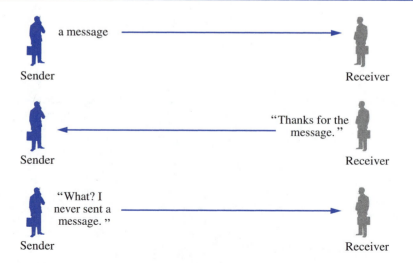

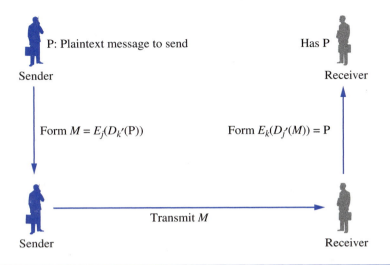

Figure 7.15   Sending a Message Using a Digital Signature

keys are k' (known only to the sender) and j' (known only to the receiver). Further-more, the pairs should have the following properties:

$$E_k(D_{k'}(P)) = D_{k'}(E_k(P)) = P \quad \text{and} \quad E_j(D_{j'}(P)) = D_{j'}(E_j(P)) = P$$

We have already stated that an encryption followed by a decryption yields the origi-nal message, but we also require the reverse to be true. That is, decrypting first and then encrypting also yields the original.

Suppose the sender wants to send an encrypted message and identify himself. If P is the plaintext message, the sender calculates $E_j(D_{k'}(P))$ and sends it.* The receiver applies $D_{j'}$ to the message. Because $D_{j'}$ and E_j are inverse operations, the result is $D_{k'}(P)$.[†] The receiver stores $D_k(P)$ in the event the sender eventually denies sending the message. Next the receiver applies E_k, giving $E_k(D_{k'}(P)) = P$, and the message is received.

Now suppose the sender denies sending the message. To authenticate the sender's identity, the receiver supplies both $D_{k'}(P)$ and P to an arbiter (someone who must decide who is lying). The arbiter applies E_k (the public key encryption method) to $D_{k'}(P)$ and gets P. This shows that the message P is derived from $D_{k'}(P)$. Furthermore, since $D_{k'}(P)$ was determined using a private key not derivable from E_k, the arbiter concludes that $D_{k'}(P)$ could have been constructed only by someone with

---

* Later in this chapter we will discuss the *message digest*, a number that is unique to a message. Fre-quently, the process calculates a message digest value and applies $D_{k'}$ to that value. If the digest is calculated properly, this is a secure way of signing and authenticating a document.

[†] If just the sender's ID was altered the first time, the receiver now has the plaintext and the ID al-tered by $D_{k'}$.

knowledge of the private key k'. Since the sender is the only person with that knowledge, the sender is guilty as charged.

As you might have guessed, this is not the only way to make a digital signature; reference [Ka01] compares and contrasts some other schemes. Also, since there are standards for most everything else, there is also one for digital signatures. The NIST FIPS publication 186-2 (http://csrc.nist.gov/publications/fips/fips186-2/fips186-2.pdf) outlines specifics for a Digital Signature Standard (DSS). The technique calls for inputting a message into a hash algorithm (discussed next) called SHA-1 (Secure Hash Algorithm 1, specified in FIPS publication 180-1, http://csrc.nist.gov/publications/fips/fips180-1/fip180-1.pdf) that determines a number unique to the message. That number, in turn, is input to a private key encryption algorithm to form the digital signature. There are, of course, reasons for this approach and details that we need to discuss. This is our next topic.

AUTHENTICATION AND MESSAGE DIGESTS

The ability to authenticate the sender of a message is certainly important in an age of electronic transfers. However, the method we have just described authenticates by encrypting the entire message. Consequently, this blurs the distinction between providing security and authentication. In some cases, we are not concerned about hiding the contents of a message but rather about ensuring that it is authentic. This is useful in cases where the message might be a contract, a letter of recommendation, or anything with legal implications. Is there a way to ensure that once a document has reached electronic form it cannot be altered without detection?

One approach uses a **hash function** H (also called a **message digest**) to associate a unique fixed-length value with a document. If M is the document, then $H(M)$ represents the **hash value** or **message digest value.** Next, apply a private key decryption algorithm represented by $D_{k'}$ to $H(M)$ and store the result, $D_{k'}(H(M))$, along with the document (Figure 7.16). If the authenticity of the document is in question, then do the following:

1. Calculate the message digest value of the document in question.

2. Apply a public key encryption algorithm to the decrypted message digest value $D_{k'}(H(M))$ stored with the document (use a public key encryption algorithm that complements the private key decryption algorithm applied to $H(M)$). The result is $E_k(D_{k'}(H(M))) = H(M)$.

3. Compare these two values. If they disagree, someone has tampered with the document.

This simple explanation raises a logical question: How hard is it to tamper with a document and not change the message digest value? For example, a simple hash function will sum the byte values (interpreted as integers) in the document. An exchange of two bytes will alter the document but leave the message digest value the same. This is an important question and is critical to the development of an authentication method.

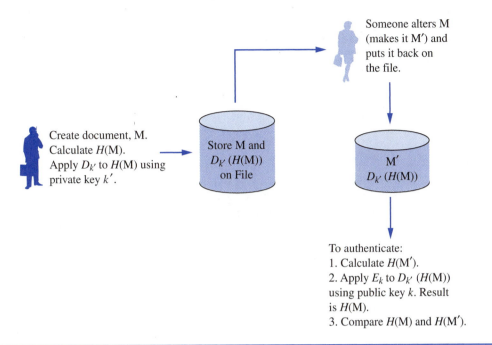

Figure 7.16   Authenticating a Document

The answer lies in the creation of one-way hash functions. A **one-way hash function** H is one that satisfies the following conditions:

- Let M be a message or document of arbitrary length. Then H is a function that associates a unique fixed-length value with M. Mathematically, we write $H(M) = V$.
- $H(M)$ is easy to calculate. This is important to develop an efficient algorithm.
- Given a value for V, it is difficult to find an M for which $H(M) = V$. This criterion is the reason for the *one-way* qualifier. A direct implication of this is that if M is a message and $V = H(M)$, then it is difficult to find another message M' for which $H(M') = V$.
- It is difficult to find two messages M_1 and M_2 for which $H(M_1) = H(M_2)$. This may seem the same as the previous criterion but, as we will soon show, there is a subtle but important difference.

One might question the need for such tight conditions on the hash function. After all, even if a message or document could be altered without changing the message digest value, wouldn't the change be noticeable? The answer is a resounding no! In 1979 a now well-known article by Yuval [Yu79] described the **birthday attack,** a technique that can be used to generate two documents with the same message digest value if the message digest is not strong enough.

The technique is so named because of its similarity to a common problem described in probability courses. The problem is stated as follows:

> Given an arbitrary collection of people in a room, how many must there be so that the probability that one of them shares your birthday is greater than 0.5?

The answer is one-half the number of days in a year, or 183.

A related problem is as follows:

> Given an arbitrary collection of people in a room, how many must there be so that the probability that any two of them share a birthday is greater than 0.5?

It is often a surprise to many to know that the answer is 23. The reason the number is lower than expected is because we don't care which birthdays match.

This is a special case of a more general problem, stated as follows:

- Let $X = \{x_1, x_2, x_3, \ldots, x_k\}$ and $Y = \{y_1, y_2, y_3, \ldots, y_k\}$ be two sets of numbers.
- Each number is random and lies between 1 and 2^m, respectively (m is some positive integer).
- Let $P(m, k)$ be the probability that X and Y have at least one number in common. In other words, $x_i = y_j$ for some i and j.
- What must k be so that $P(m, k) \geq 0.5$?

It turns out that the answer to this question is $k \approx 2^{m/2}$. We won't provide the mathematical proof of this, but if you have the background, reference [St95] has the details.

So what does this have to do with authenticating documents? Suppose an unscrupulous person, Mr. X, works for a city building inspector and is helping to publish a list of inspection reports. Mr. X prepares each report, based on input from the building inspector, and then gives it to the building inspector for approval. Upon approval the inspector runs a program that calculates a message digest value and gives the document to Mr. X for eventual publication. Suppose there is a project that does not pass inspection but for which Mr. X has been paid by the contractors to see that a positive report is published anyway. How can Mr. X achieve this?

Suppose the message digest produces a value between 1 and 2^{64}. The birthday attack has Mr. X preparing two reports. One is a valid but unfavorable report; the other is not valid but is favorable to the contractor. Mr. X can create several variations of each report, each of which has essentially the same content. For example, Mr. X might find several words for which synonyms can be substituted or places where a pronoun can be substituted for a proper noun. Even replacing two consecutive spaces with one constitutes a change. If Mr. X can identify 32 places in each report where a substitution can be made, then there are 2^{32} variations of each report. That is how many combinations of substitutions are possible.

If the message digest applied to each report generates a 64-bit number, then there is a 50-50 chance that Mr. X can find a valid and invalid report generating the same message digest value. Computationally it would not be that difficult. Granted, 2^{32} is a large number of variations for which to calculate message digest values by hand, but a computer program would not have that much trouble with it. Consequently, Mr. X can provide the proper valid report to the inspector, who, in turn, generates the message digest number for it. When Mr. X gets the validated report, he can substitute the invalid report with the same message digest number and publish the false report.

The flaw in this process is not in the scheme itself but in the size of the message digest number. For example, if the message digest value were a 128-bit number instead, then the probability of finding two matches from the 2^{32} variations of each report is extremely small. In fact, Mr. X would need 2^{64} versions of each document to have a 50-50 chance of finding a match. The sheer amount of time needed to do this makes the attempt at fraud computationally infeasible. Of course, this last statement is subject to change as computers become faster and more powerful.

The next logical question to ask is, What kinds of hashing schemes are available? One such algorithm is the *MD5 algorithm* developed by Ron Rivest at MIT (ref. [Ri92]). The algorithm produces a 128-bit message digest value. It divides the message into 512-bit blocks (some padding may be necessary to get a full 512-bit block) and operates on each block. Each block is subjected to four rounds of operations that use various bit operations and factor in values from a sine function. Eventually, a result is generated, which is used as input to encrypt the next block. As with the other block ciphers described earlier, it is a complex process and we won't go through the specifics; if you'd like to see some details, references [St95] and [Sc94] provide them. Another algorithm is the **Secure Hash Algorithm 1 (SHA-1),** which was developed by the NSA and NIST. It is more secure in that it produces a 160-bit message digest value. Like MD5, it operates on 512-bit blocks.* The process involves first dividing a 512-bit block into sixteen 32-bit words. Word groups and predefined constants are next subjected to numerous rounds of logical AND, OR, exclusive OR, and shift operations, which culminate in a 160-bit integer value. Again, more details can be found in references [St03] and [Sc94] and at http://csrc.nist.gov/publications/fips/fips180-1/fip180-1.pdf.

PRETTY GOOD PRIVACY

Certainly one of the most common (if not *the* most common) Internet applications is email. Although commonly used for informal exchanges and just staying in touch with friends, it is also critical to many business operations. As such, there is a strong need to email information securely and to authenticate the source and content of email messages. In addition, since email users rely on a wide variety of different email packages and systems, there is a need to provide encryption and authentication capabilities across platforms and packages. One such package that meets these needs is **Pretty Good Privacy (PGP).**

PGP is an email security program developed by Philip Zimmerman and is available in commercial versions or as freeware (see www.pgpi.org/ and www.pgp.com/). PGP includes public key encryption, authentication, digital signatures, and compression. It runs on many platforms and uses algorithms that have been thoroughly

---

* FIPS publication 180-1 also defines rules for padding the message if its total length is not a multiple of 512.

reviewed by many, such as RSA for public key encryption, SHA-1 and MD5 for message digests, and the IDEA algorithm (yet another block cipher, see ref. [Sc94]) for regular encryption.

When it was first developed, PGP received some notoriety. Because someone placed it on the Internet, it was freely accessible to the world community. The problem was that in the early 1990s the U.S. government considered encryption algorithms with a key size larger than 40 bits as munitions. That is, they were put into the same category as military supplies such as weapons and ammunition, items the U.S. government does not like to see exported. As such, the use of such algorithms outside the United States was considered a threat to U.S. foreign policy and national security interests and subject to strict export laws. The government concluded that PGP's availability via the Internet allowed it to be "exported" to foreign countries and that it was in violation of export laws. More recent versions were developed outside the United States to circumvent this problem. Since then, export laws and policies have been relaxed, but there are still cases in which products that use cryptographic techniques are subject to export licenses. The Bureau of Export Administration has made several policy changes to make sure that U.S. exporters are not disadvantaged by a free trade zone that allows exports to nongovernment institutions among European nations. However, there are still tight restrictions governing the export of encryption software to countries that the United States has classified as supporters of terrorism. It's a complicated issue, and policies will no doubt continue to change in response to world events. The interested reader may keep abreast of some of these changes at www.bxa.doc.gov/Encryption.

In any event, our intention here is to describe some of the major features of PGP and how it works. As previously stated, PGP can be downloaded as freeware and installed on numerous platforms such as UNIX, Windows 2000/ME/XP, and Macintosh. It is designed to be used as a plug-in for several email packages. For example, if you use Microsoft Outlook for email, the interface is modified so that you can use PGP facilities without ever leaving Outlook.

Figure 7.17 shows an example based on PGP freeware version 6.5.8 running on a Windows system; there may be small variations in other versions. Suppose you want to send a message (text: *This is a test message*) and have that message signed with a digital signature. You construct the email message as you normally do. However, if PGP is installed as a plug-in, there is a new entry, labeled PGP, available in the list of drop-down menu choices. This item was not there prior to installing PGP. By selecting the PGP item, you can see a couple of options, one of which is Sign on Send (see Figure 7.17). This means that PGP will attach a digital signature to your message after you click Send but before Outlook actually sends the message.

Now, let's suppose that's exactly what you did. When the person receiving that message opens it, he or she will see the following message, which indicates the message has been digitally signed.

```
---BEGIN PGP SIGNED MESSAGE---
Hash: SHA1

this is a test message
---BEGIN PGP SIGNATURE---
```

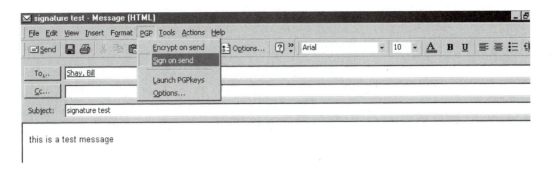

Figure 7.17   Accessing PGP Facilities from Within Microsoft Outlook

```
Version: PGPfreeware 6.5.8 for non-commercial use
<http://www.pgp.com>

iQA/AwUBPVHAkz012x9/xPKqEQL7UQCg65yJ8I4c5o7s37iMvLcqqR-
tokhAAn3E2
EzQd3vhFE41QGj308zvDSawR
= knKs

---END PGP SIGNATURE---
```

While the message is open, the receiver can select the PGP drop-down menu and select the Decrypt/Verify option (not shown in Figure 7.17). Upon selecting that option, the window containing the message changes to a form resembling the following, indicating that the signature is valid.

```
*** PGP Signature Status: good
*** Signer: William Shay <shayw@uwgb.edu>
*** Signed: 8/7/02 7:51:31 PM
*** Verified: 8/7/02 8:50:46 PM
*** BEGIN PGP VERIFIED MESSAGE ***

this is a test messáge

*** END PGP VERIFIED MESSAGE ***
```

You can encrypt your email following a similar procedure. Compose an email message and select the PGP drop-down menu, but this time select Encrypt on Send (see Figure 7.17). The person receiving the email message will see something like the following.

```
---BEGIN PGP MESSAGE---
Version: PGPfreeware 6.5.8 for non-commercial use
<http://www.pgp.com>

qANQR1DBwU4D1bHGsRJGiAYQCACzq5cJFQTYx/CgqG61KflblkBArlOYTIAE+M
xoVAuK1LsrNu1HHkUkRCrEH2eHwVw19FngHvCOxo0cniiI5GRhOE02EjOeMqeO
PYasuAWvWDGLQykNF6xqAeGWAWIt0PUr3PANUshqS5ss7TQ1mG5KgpoKMt-
```

```
szBXqDkj2nS/Dm01m/tDf+OyqRnYnS/1nZ8xHCilyQ0seDuiNSPVYpVeah550
iZfZHF7gkstd7+dSZYISuy0SeRWNUii0VW8tDfFUwpb/X0UtPH/z22waG-
wiW8id1Vz07Zm1zSM6Kw1Ma8RUf82xKM90em7pv74u/zJu8z197oGrsJBt9MQG
4/TKRgCACFAuSzyOmsUZrNWqvS1AuRYe9zY27ktXi5THt88PfB+qE855fzx0f
Axh8ovr564Cz4duKOcPcdIhIQre1guZdq71sMBGzOdReDkokXSfZ5r7snUPflAN
q4ks8K1BozB5I5irSTMs62YjUO8RRDXJ1URSRgS8t0yonXpiQjM6+eSz2QTOX
tWF29k1FQLeA6rX3q1zp2nhNwIdt3cI2xb09OTRKTrdqtbVcske2gzsKfDL3JO
FJJuK/2KZ9kcTxaiWC7WV2auLwqZ9Jrts8FwRD0B15n2hE4V+Bi0nTMn/u+XZ
MGHGVb1RqF1ZcHPOMzDrIVTa8jxhzLHQ3KHZF7K75GyS29LD8EY2RRLKb-
VZyz6odIxokEfHbqZV22sP7sC8IsydvQ9wHbsIjavXi/NeqU=
=3+11
```

```
---END PGP MESSAGE---
```

Once the receiver selects the Decrypt/Verify option from the PGP menu, the original is restored and the receiver sees the original:

```
this is a test message
```

Although this discussion shows encryption and adding a digital signature as separate examples, you can do both in the same message. You just need to select both options from the PGP menu. In addition to using PGP in email applications, encryption and signing can be applied directly to files. In a Windows operating system, you can right-click on a file name and see a PGP option. Upon selecting the PGP option, other items appear that allow you to encrypt, sign, or both. You can also *wipe* a file. This is like deleting a file. However, normal deletions only remove references to a file's data. The actual data remain and can usually be recovered using disk management utilities. This is convenient if you have accidentally deleted a file. It has also aided law enforcement officials when they recover files containing illegal material, such as child pornography, from a perpetrator's computer. When you wipe a file, the data are removed from the drive. There is no way to recover them.

PGP is certainly easy enough to use, but how does it work? First of all, both the sender and receiver have to install PGP. Second is the issue of keys. When you first install PGP, the installer gives you the option of generating a public/private key pair. After installing PGP you can also generate new public/private key pairs by running the PGPkeys utility. As the utility runs, it will prompt you for a key type (such as RSA or Diffie-Hellman/DSS), a key size, and an expiration date. This gives you some flexibility in configuring PGP to your needs. It will also ask for a *pass phrase*, a string that provides access to your private key. This is a security mechanism that allows only you to access the private key. The program requires you to enter the pass phrase any time you digitally sign a document with your private key or decrypt and encrypt messages.

Once PGP generates the key pair, it saves them in a *keyring* (particular files on your hard drive). Private keys are stored in a file named *secring.skr* and public keys in a file named *pubring.pkr*. The public key can be uploaded to a server so that others may access it. Alternatively, you can export the public key to a file and send it to whomever you wish to exchange secure emails with, or even store it on your website.

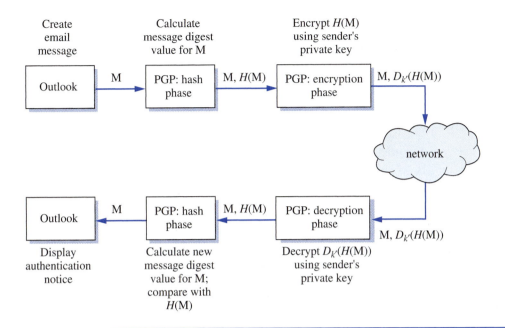

Figure 7.18   Using PGP to Authenticate a Message Created in Outlook

When PGP signs a message, it does two things (Figure 7.18): calculates a message digest value $H(M)$ from the message M using SHA-1 and encrypts the digest value using the sender's private key. This generates $D_{k'}(H(M))$ in Figure 7.18. When the message and encrypted digest value are received, two complementary actions occur. First, the digest value is decrypted using the sender's public key (which the receiver must have) and $H(M)$ is recaptured. Second, $H(M)$ is compared with the digest value calculated at the recipient's site. The two digest values must agree for the message to be authenticated.

Certainly, there is much more that one can say about PGP. How do you manage your keyrings? How do you download public keys stored on a server? What other encryption algorithms does PGP support? How can you determine whether a person who provides a public key is who he says he is? There's potential for fraud here. The list can go on. Many of these questions are specific to PGP, and we defer to sources more focused on it (references [Ga94], [Zi95], and [Op01] and the website www.pgpi.org/). However, the last question has scope far beyond PGP and is important for anyone engaging in any commercial venture using the Internet. It's also our next topic.

7.5   TRANSPORT LAYER SECURITY AND SERVER AUTHENTICATION

With so much business being conducted over the Internet these days, security has become a major concern. Perhaps you have made purchases from a website by entering your credit card number into a browser and clicking the appropriate buttons. Maybe you have made deposits and withdrawals from your bank account. Of course, you had to enter an account and PIN number first. Any time you enter private information from the supposed safety of your own home, how do you know someone is not monitoring your connection and copying information? The sites that you access must guarantee that such private information is secure or they will not remain in business for long. The question is: How can they secure what you do from the privacy of your home?

Having devoted so much space to encryption, the logical answer is to build in encryption methods. However, this generates other questions. For example, how do you get access to the proper encryption methods and keys from the privacy of your home? You need them locally before sending out private information via your Internet service provider. However, don't assume the only potential for fraud is from someone monitoring your communications. How do you know that the site to which you connect is legitimate? Just because a website has nice-looking graphics and a text box for your credit card number does not make it a legitimate business. How do you know the site operators won't take your credit card number and run?

The answers to these questions lie in protocols such as **Secure Sockets Layer (SSL)** and **Transport Layer Security (TLS),** and in X.509 certificates. An X.509 certificate provides a standard content for information used to authenticate a server; we'll discuss it shortly.

TRANSPORT LAYER SECURITY

Both SSL and TLS are protocols that lie between an application layer such as the HTTP protocol (used by browsers) and the transport layer, TCP (Transport Control Protocol of the Internet). SSL was originally developed by Netscape. Two of its main goals are to provide encryption utilities for the secure exchange of private information and to provide authentication of servers so that users can assume the server is what it claims to be. Figure 7.19 shows where TLS (or SSL) fits. Because TLS (or SSL) is inserted between the two layers, it encrypts a message M that the

Figure 7.19   Transport Layer Security (TLS)

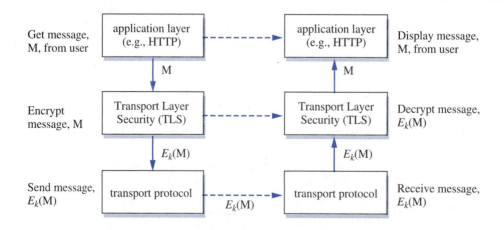

Get message, M, from user → application layer (e.g., HTTP) ⇢ application layer (e.g., HTTP) → Display message, M, from user

M ↓   M ↑

Encrypt message, M → Transport Layer Security (TLS) ⇢ Transport Layer Security (TLS) → Decrypt message, $E_k(M)$

$E_k(M)$ ↓ $E_k(M)$ ↑

Send message, $E_k(M)$ → transport protocol ⇢ $E_k(M)$ ⇢ transport protocol → Receive message, $E_k(M)$

application layer generates. It passes the result $E_k(M)$ to the transport layer, which then sends it to the transport layer on the server side. That transport layer passes $E_k(M)$ to its TLS entity, where it is decrypted back to M and passed to the server application.

Several versions of SSL have been developed, with each version providing security enhancements and more options than the previous one. In addition, TLS is being developed by the IETF for the purpose of eventually replacing SSL. According to the IETF, "The differences between this protocol and SSL 3.0 are not dramatic, but they are significant enough that TLS 1.0 and SSL 3.0 do not interoperate." We will not elaborate on those differences or on the differences between SSL versions, but will provide a few brief comments. Beyond these comments, we will not distinguish among these protocols; we refer the interested reader to references [Th00] and [Re01].

- Netscape developed SSL, and the IETF developed TLS, which is based on SSL 3.0.
- Although TLS and SSL generally do not talk to each other, TLS does have the ability to revert to SSL 3.0.
- Some low-level differences detailing how to define padding bytes to create blocks of the correct length exist between SSL and TLS.
- TLS supports additional alert codes (codes to alert the user when something is not right).
- The IETF has dropped the Fortezza* algorithms that SSL supports.

X.509 CERTIFICATE

We begin by discussing how to authenticate a server. Suppose you connect to a website and are about to enter private information such as a credit card number. How can you be sure that the site is what it claims to be? Most people feel comfortable walking into a large department store and handing the cashier their credit card, because they know who is getting their credit card number. However, suppose a traveling salesperson knocks on your door and you agree to buy something from her. How comfortable would you be providing your credit card number? She may claim she is from a reputable company, but how do you know? She may even show you an ID that shows she works for a reputable company, but how do you know it is not a forgery? There's a serious issue of trust that needs to be dealt with.

Connecting to an Internet site is very much the same. How do you know you can trust that site? The answer is in the **X.509 certificate.** It is essentially a document that the site provides to you that indicates it is what it claims. It is something like an electronic ID. Of course, there must be more, since anyone can produce a valid-looking ID.

The next piece in this puzzle is a **certificate authority (CA),** an entity that issues certificates. Consider an analogy. A company is interviewing candidates for a position. A candidate lists his qualifications and degrees on his resume, but the

---

* The Fortezza algorithms, based on Capstone, were developed by the NSA and the details are classified.

company will not make a hiring decision (at least a positive one) on that information alone. The candidate must also provide references and a transcript from an accredited college or university. The company then contacts the references and university to verify that the candidate's claims are all true. Of course, there must be a measure of trust in the references or in the university. The employer assumes their information is reliable. Over time, the employer learns whom it can trust.

So it is with a CA. As a consumer, you keep a list of CAs whom you trust on your computer. If that CA has issued a certificate for a website, then you trust that the CA has investigated that site and has, in fact, identified that site as legitimate. In other words, that CA is a trusted reference for that site.

Your next thought might be: I've ordered online before and I don't remember keeping any list of trusted CAs or checking for a certificate. That's because your browser does it for you. For example, suppose you use Netscape and connect to https://certs.netscape.com.* Note the *https* as opposed to the usual *http* in the URL. The extra *s* indicates that you have connected to a secure site that has a certificate issued by a trusted CA. That's important to know! To see who issued the certificate, select the Page Info option from the View menu. Select the Security tab; Figure 7.20 shows an example of what you might see. It identifies Thawte Consulting as a trusted CA. If you want to see the actual certificate that the CA issued, click View and you will see something similar to that in Figure 7.21.[†]

Figure 7.20   Certificate Authority Information

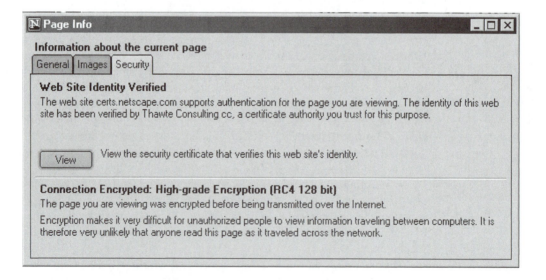

---

* Any legitimate address that starts with *https* will do.

[†] You can also see this information using Internet Explorer (IE). When you connect to a secure site, IE displays a small padlock icon at the bottom in the status bar. If you double-click that icon and select various tabs and options, you can view the certificate information.

Figure 7.21   Digital Certificate

Thawte is only one of many possible trusted CAs that your browser maintains. To see a list of other CAs in Internet Explorer (version 6), select Internet Options from the Tools menu. Next select the Content tab; click Certificates, and select one of the tabs in the resulting window. In Netscape 7.0, select Preferences from the Edit menu. Open the Privacy and Security category and select the Certificates option. Click Manage Certificates and select the Authorities tab. Verisign & Thawte are two of the largest CAs, but you should see others.

The certificate of Figure 7.21 shows the CA that issued the certificate, a range of dates during which it is valid (certificates do expire), and two fingerprints. These are digest values produced by the SHA-1 and MD5 algorithms and are used for authentication (recall our previous discussion on authenticating documents). Since anyone can create a certificate, we need a way to determine which ones are authentic.

When a user connects to a website, the browser does the following (it actually does more; we'll elaborate shortly):

- Downloads the server certificate.
- Checks the issue and expiration dates of the certificate. Is today in that range?
- Checks the fingerprints. Do they authenticate the document?
- Checks the CA. Is the CA in the trusted list?

All these questions must have affirmative answers or the user is notified of a problem. For example, if the browser cannot find the CA in the list, it will display a message similar to that shown in Figure 7.22. It's then up to the user to decide what to do next. If the user decides to proceed, she does so at her own risk.

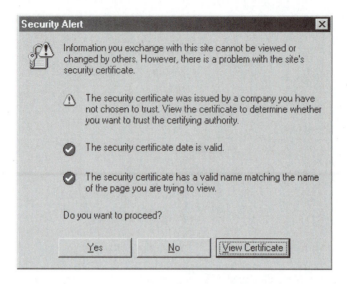

Figure 7.22   Security Alert

HANDSHAKES

The next step is to describe what TLS (or SSL) does when you attempt to connect to a secure site (designated by *https*). The initial set of exchanges between the client and server is called a **handshake** and defines cryptographic routines, key exchanges, and authentication procedures. The handshake is partly defined by the steps that follow. For a full description, see references [Th00] and [Re01].

1. The client sends information to the server. The information includes the highest SSL (or TLS) version available, a list of encryption algorithms, a list of key exchange algorithms, and a list of compression methods that the client supports. Encryption algorithms include DES, triple DES, RC2, RC4, IDEA, and Fortezza. Key exchanges include RSA, Diffie-Hellman, and Fortezza. Note that this information does not specify what *will* be done, only what can be done. The client also sends a session ID and some randomly generated data (whose purpose we'll describe shortly). The session ID can be zero or nonzero. A value of 0 means the client is requesting a new secure session. A nonzero value means the client is requesting an update of parameters on a current session. It's an extra security precaution in case there is an unauthorized person monitoring the transmissions. Changing routines periodically makes the job of snooping more difficult.

2. The server sends a version number, encryption and key exchange specification, and compression algorithm chosen from among those the client suggested. It will select the most recent (and most secure) versions that both sides support. The server also sends some randomly generated data and its certificate.

3. So far, nothing exceptional has happened because the client and server have simply exchanged information. That changes in step 3. Now that the client has received the server's certificate, it must validate the certificate and authenticate the server. Of course, part of that requires that the certificate be authenticated. The client performs the following steps. A problem in any step causes an alert to be issued to the user. All steps must be completed in order to go on.

- Compares today's date with the issue and expiration dates in the certificate. If today's date is not in that range, the certificate is not valid.
- Checks to determine whether the CA that issued the certificate is in the list of trusted CAs.
- Because the certificate could be a forgery, the client must authenticate it. The CA that issues a certificate attaches its digital signature to it. The CA uses methods described previously to determine a digest value. It then encrypts that value using its private key. Two digest algorithms, SHA-1 and MD5, are used. If a security breach is found in one, the other provides an extra measure of security.
- Accesses the CA's public key and applies it to the digital signature to get the original digest value. Performs authentication procedures similar to those we have described previously and determines whether it is the correct digest value. You might wonder where the client gets the CA's key. Remember, these keys are public knowledge and, in fact, are stored along with the list of CAs. For example, if you use previously described procedures to get a list of CAs, you can select any one of them and click View. By selecting the Details tab and selecting the Public Key Info fields, you can see a display similar to that in Figure 7.23, in which part of a public key used in

Figure 7.23   Viewing a CA's Public Key

RSA is shown (the rest of the public key can be viewed by scrolling in the Field Value field).

- Compares the domain name in the certificate with the domain name of the server. This step helps to counteract the man-in-the-middle attack in which an intruder inserts itself in between the client and server. If the insertion is done early in the handshake procedure, the intruder can then establish its own secure channels with the client and server and view information that each sends. To the client, the intruder looks like the server; to the server, the intruder looks like the client.

4. The client creates a *pre-master secret* (a 48-byte sequence), encrypts it using the server's public key,* and sends it to the server. The client will use the pre-master secret to generate a symmetric encryption key for the secure session. The server receives the pre-master secret, decrypts it using its private key, and does similar calculations to generate the key.

5. If required, the server may authenticate the client. It's a process similar to authenticating the server, and we won't go into detail here. We just note that some communications (for example, a money transfer between two financial institutions) require authentication on both sides. Most users who order items online are not authenticated this way. Once a user submits a credit card number, the server validates the number using the same methods used by any merchant, online or otherwise.

6. Both client and server use the pre-master secret to generate a *master secret*. To calculate the master secret, the client feeds its randomly generated data, the randomly generated data it received from the server (recall steps 1 and 2), and the pre-master secret into hash routines that generate a 48-byte sequence. The server proceeds analogously. Both client and server then feed the master secret into hash algorithms to eventually generate session keys used to encrypt data that they exchange later in the session.

7. The client sends the server another message confirming the creation of the session key and indicates that all future messages will be encrypted using that key and the algorithms specified earlier in the exchange. The server sends analogous information to the client. Once both the client and server receive these last messages, the secure session is established and secure communications using the encryption methods and specified key begin.

As with other topics, there is much more that can be said; we refer the interested reader to references [Th00] and [Re01] and to the websites www.ietf.org/html. charters/tls-charter.html and http://developer.netscape.com/docs/manuals/security/ sslin/ contents.htm.

---

* Using the public key is just one way to send the pre-master secret. Depending on the key exchange specifications from previous steps, one of several variations of Diffie-Hellman or Fortezza could also be used.

7.6 FIREWALLS

The security measures discussed so far are designed to protect peoples' information as they conduct business over the Internet. However, people and machines are also at risk when they are not actively doing anything. The computers you use and the machines that provide network services are all at risk from attacks by malicious people who want to disrupt activities or cause harm. This is true of the real world; it is also true in cyberspace. The question is: How can you prevent computers from being attacked? Perhaps more realistically, how can you prevent attacks from being successful?

The first step in dealing with attacks is understanding the network architecture and how attacks propagate through the network. Virtually every organization maintains its own network and allows its machines Internet access. Furthermore, each machine on the internal network has its own Internet Protocol (IP) address, making it visible to others outside the local network. Once you are visible, you are susceptible to attack.

How can we protect each machine with an IP address? Consider an analogy to a system in common use in public venues such as airports or high-profile media events. Security checkpoints are set up, and people wanting access to the venue must pass through the security checkpoint, where they are scanned or searched for items considered threatening. By forcing everyone through one or more entry points, officials can better manage security issues. If the number of entry points is small, security is easier to enforce because officials can focus their efforts on a smaller number of locations.

Many networks use a similar concept. Although each computer in an organization's network has Internet access, all Internet traffic has to pass through one or more special machines called **firewalls.** The purpose of the firewall is to examine traffic that passes and look for possible threats. Anything that looks threatening is denied passage. The rest should pass. It sounds simple, but the hard part is to decide what looks threatening, especially since many threats are disguised as legitimate traffic. We'll discuss some examples later in this chapter.

Although Chapter 11 discusses the Internet Protocol and its companion Transport Control Protocol (TCP) in detail, there are a few things we must point out before discussing how firewalls operate.

- IP and TCP correspond to layer 3 and 4 protocols, respectively.
- Internet traffic consists of many packets that travel among routers. IP packets contain data and an address that specifies where the packet came from (source) and where it is going (destination). A packet also contains a field specifying whether TCP or another layer 4 protocol, such as UDP, is using IP.
- Application data are typically divided into one or more Internet packets.
- One server on a network can provide a variety of services. A client that wants that service must specify the IP address of the server and a **port number** that identifies what service to use. There are well-known port numbers for common services such as Telnet for remote logins (port 23), FTP for file transfers (port 21), HTTP for Web activities (port 80), and SMTP for mail (port 25).

PACKET FILTERING

Perhaps the simplest approach to a firewall design is **packet filtering.** It works on a simple premise (Figure 7.24): Examine the contents of each packet's header and decide whether or not it should pass. The decision is typically made based on the contents of the packet's address fields, its port number, or which transport protocol is represented. Here are some possible examples of decisions:

• Allow any incoming packet with a TCP port designation of 23. This will allow attempts at logging on to any company machine using Telnet (a utility for remote logons).

• Allow any incoming packet with a TCP port designation of 23 whose destination address is in a list that the firewall maintains. This will allow attempts at logging in to any of a specified list of company machines using Telnet. Perhaps more important, the firewall blocks any attempt at logging in to any other machine. Network administrators determine which machines are on the list.

• Allow any incoming packet containing a destination address specified in a list the firewall maintains. This allows all service requests to pass to any server in the list.

• Allow any outgoing packet containing a destination address specified in a list the firewall maintains. This is different from the previous examples in that it applies to outgoing packets. A company may set up strict policies that states its employees can access only certain destinations to do their jobs. Such a policy would prohibit an employee from casual Web browsing or accessing any sites that are not job related.

• Allow an outgoing packet containing a source address that matches any of the IP addresses the organization maintains. This might seem a bit strange at first. After all, an outgoing packet originates at the organization, and the source would naturally match one of the organization's IP addresses. Unfortunately, this is not

Figure 7.24   Packet Filtering

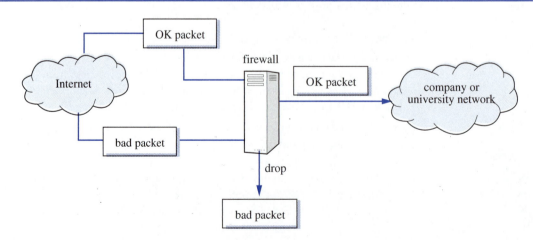

correct. Some attacks on sites are based on IP **address spoofing,** in which the IP packet contains a phony IP address in the source field in an attempt to hide the real source of the message. We discuss some types of attacks later, but the idea here is to block any outgoing packets that contain a phony source address.

Note that these examples specify which criteria are used to allow a packet. This implies a default action that states the packet should be blocked unless otherwise indicated. There is another option: By default, allow any packets unless otherwise specified. In this case, some examples of decisions to be made are as follows:

- Block any incoming packet with a TCP port designation of 23. This will prohibit any attempts at logging in to a company machine using Telnet.

- Block any incoming packet containing a source address specified in a list that the firewall maintains. If the network administrator determines that certain remote sites have been troublesome or have been sending a large amount of junk email, the firewall can block everything that originates from that site. What a great feeling to put such sites on the block list!

- Block any incoming packet containing a destination address specified in a list the firewall maintains. This allows the network administrator to provide some servers with an extra level of protection while still allowing access to other servers. It effectively makes any server in the list inaccessible to anyone on the other side of the firewall (i.e., the general Internet community).

- Block any outgoing packet containing a source and destination address specified in lists the firewall maintains. Perhaps an organization's lab manager has discovered that many are using lab computers to connect to a server that provides Internet game playing. If such activity is against the organization's policies, it can be prevented by disallowing outgoing packets from that lab to the appropriate servers.

Which default is better? If the default is to pass a packet, the network administrator must be constantly aware of where new attacks may originate or what form they may take. He or she must also be aware of what internal policies may be violated. As new possibilities occur, the firewall must be updated accordingly. Of course, the administrator might not be aware of every possibility and this approach is thus less secure.

If the default is to block a packet, then the administrator must determine how to configure legitimate needs. Nothing will pass unless it is explicitly specified in the firewall. This choice is more secure, but the administrator must be aware of legitimate user needs. If some are missed, then the firewall may block legitimate packets and cause the users to complain. Of course, the firewall can be updated, but the user perception is "They won't let us do anything unless we complain."

APPLICATION-LEVEL GATEWAY

Another type of firewall works at a higher layer. Packet filtering primarily works at layer 3, making decisions based on the packet contents (Figure 7.25a), and doesn't provide any flexibility when it comes to discriminating based on an action within a

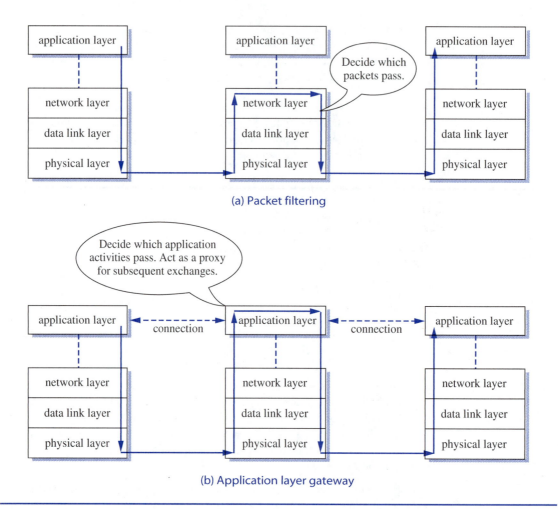

Figure 7.25 Firewall Designs

particular application. For example, you might want to allow a user to connect to a machine using a file transfer protocol in order to download files. However, you want to prohibit uploading files. This is typical of many sites that maintain repositories of files for the Internet community.

Packet filtering will not accommodate this need. It could block packets destined for port number 21 (FTP), but that would block all FTP requests, not just those for uploads. An alternative is to build more logic into a firewall that understands the applications and their abilities (Figure 7.25b). This type of firewall is called an **application-level gateway** (also called a *proxy server*). It runs special programs designed for each type of application it needs to watch. It examines specific application layer requests and then allows or denies them depending on the information provided to the firewall. It does not by default protect every application; a gateway program must be installed for each one.

For example, suppose an outside client wants an FTP connection to a server protected by the firewall. A separate program runs on that firewall and intercepts all requests from the client. If the clients sends a `get` request, that request is placed into an IP packet and routed to the firewall, where the request is extracted from the packet and examined at the firewall's application layer. If the firewall allows such requests, it sends the request through the lower layers, where it is put into another IP packet and sent to the destination. If the `get` had been a `put` instead, the firewall program would have blocked the transfer if such requests were not allowed. Of course, all of this information must be specified as a set of firewall rules defined by the organization's policies.

The main advantage of the application-level gateway over the packet filter is the increased flexibility that making decisions based on an application provides. However, there is a lot of overhead. The firewall must run the appropriate applications. In addition, the firewall breaks the connection between client and server into two separate connections: one between the client and firewall, and the other between the firewall and server. In effect, the firewall plays the role of server when talking with the client and the role of client when talking with the server. This is a lot of extra activity.

STATEFUL INSPECTION

An approach that many are embracing involves **stateful inspection.** Like the packet filter approach, it works at the network layer and avoids the extra overhead of a proxy.The packet filter makes decisions based solely on the contents of a packet. Unfortunately, clever hackers may falsify (spoof) the contents and bypass security measures. The stateful inspection approach examines the contents of a packet in the context of what has occurred previously.

Perhaps the simplest example involves the `ping` command. For example, suppose you enter the command `ping w.x.y.z` at a command-line prompt. Here, `w.x.y.z` represents some IP address. The response you receive might look like the following:

64 bytes from w.x.y.z: icmp_seq=0 ttl=109 time=106.0 ms

64 bytes from w.x.y.z: icmp_seq=1 ttl=109 time=94.3 ms

64 bytes from w.x.y.z: icmp_seq=2 ttl=109 time=109.7 ms

64 bytes from w.x.y.z: icmp_seq=3 ttl=109 time=109.6 ms

64 bytes from w.x.y.z: icmp_seq=4 ttl=109 time=109.5 ms

Basically, this response indicates that the device at the specified IP address is reachable, and the device is telling you how much time it takes for the packet to get there and back. The `ping` command is a common tool used by administrators to check whether a server is running and by some Internet sites to maintain statistics on reachability. The important thing here is that the `ping` command sends an Echo Request packet to the specified site, and the site responds by sending a series of Echo Response packets.

Of course, all of these packets must pass through the firewall. Stateful inspection says that an Echo Response packet is not allowed unless there was a previous Echo Request packet. Furthermore, the destination and source in the response must match the source and destination, respectively, in the request. The idea is that it does not make sense to allow an Echo Response packet if it was not requested in the first place. Because such packets have been used in the past in denial of service attacks (see Section 7.8), this approach provides some extra security.

In general, the firewall maintains a rulebase that contains information similar to that in Table 7.2. The Source and Destination columns represent sites, and the asterisk (*) indicates a wildcard. The Service column defines what protocols are included in the rule, and the Action column defines whether to accept or drop a packet associated with the other three columns. In general, rules can have other parameters. For example, a Time of Day field can be added to the rulebase, indicating that some packets are acceptable only at certain times. The administrator can also install *rate limiting*, which may allow services to be accessed but at reduced bit rates. This might be used for a certain user group that has no need for large file transfers. Slower bit rates would have little effect on the files they need for their work but

Table 7.2   Sample Rulebase for a Firewall

RULE NO.	SOURCE	DESTINATION	SERVICE	ACTION	COMMENT
1	*Any	ServerA.anyOrg.com ServerB.anyOrg.com ServerC.anyOrg.com	HTTP, Telnet, FTP	Accept	Allow HTTP, Telnet, and FTP access to any of the three servers A, B, or C from any outside source.
2	GroupA, GroupB	*Any	Echo reply, Echo request	Accept	GroupA and GroupB are site-specific groups (maybe a lab or classroom). Allow Echo Request and Echo Reply packets from those sites.
3	*Any	PrintServerA	*Any	Drop	Do not allow any access to PrintServerA from outside.
4	*Any	GroupA	Kazaa	Drop	Do not allow access to Kazaa on any machine in GroupA. Will disallow someone from providing files to the Internet community from any machine in GroupA.
⋮	⋮	⋮	⋮	⋮	⋮
N	*Any	*Any	*Any	Drop	If none of the other rules apply, this is the default.

would discourage them from downloading their favorite songs or movies. Of course, a real firewall will usually have many more entries than this table has.

In the absence of any other information, the firewall makes a decision on whether to accept or drop a packet depending on the rulebase. However, once packets start getting accepted, a context is defined for accepting or dropping new packets. Consider another example:

1. A remote client requests an FTP connection to server A.

2. Server A confirms the request, and an FTP control session is established. The client is now able to request an upload or download.

3. The firewall creates a state defined by the client IP address as the source of the request, the server IP address as the destination, and port number 21 (the port corresponding to the FTP connection). The state is maintained as an entry in an internal state table.

4. Subsequent packets that arrive at the firewall are examined in the context of the previous activities. For example, if the server tried to initiate a download, the packet would not automatically pass. That's because the context (state of the connection) indicates that the client has requested the connection, and only the client can initiate a data transfer.

5. Suppose, instead, that the client tries to sneak another packet through that connection that accesses another port number. That client may be trying to attack the system or to send through a packet that carries potentially damaging contents. Again, the source, destination, and port number in that packet do not match any existing state table entries. As a result, the firewall does not automatically accept the packet. Instead, it will subject that packet to the original security rules.

The main idea behind stateful inspection is to prevent a user from making a legitimate request and then using the response to that request to launch an attack. There have been many such instances of such attacks; we discuss some of them later in this chapter. With stateful inspection, all packets must be in response to a previous request or be consistent with rules specified in the security policy.

We have just scratched the surface of firewall technology, which is evolving rapidly. Sites implement a wide variety of approaches for many different reasons. What works well at one site may not be appropriate for another. This, of course, makes it impossible to state which design approach is best. All a person can do is continue to read and keep up on the technologies. Toward that end, references [Po02] and [St03] provide more in-depth coverage of firewalls, and reference [Co01a] describes many firewall products.

7.7   VIRUSES

Up to now we have considered the integrity and security of data as it travels along some medium. We answered questions about detecting data that have been damaged and disguising data so unauthorized persons cannot understand it. Other serious threats to the security and integrity of information are computer viruses and worms.

Strictly speaking, viruses and worms may be less of a computer network problem and more of an operating system or human behavior problem. Although networks certainly facilitate the spread of some viruses, just being connected to one does not mean viruses are going to jump into your computer and eat your disks. In fact, two main reasons that viruses and worms exist are security holes in operating systems and careless behavior by computer users.

On the other hand, network connections are not without danger, as victims of the Internet worm incident (discussed shortly) can testify. Access to electronic bulletin boards and connectivity among computers all over the world make the existence of worms and viruses a serious problem. Consequently, a chapter on security must at least discuss them and their capabilities.

INFECTING FILES

A **virus** is a collection of instructions attached to an executable file that does something the original executable file was not designed to do. On PCs, a virus commonly attaches to a file with the .exe or .com extension. On a Macintosh, a file's resource fork typically is infected. When a virus attaches to a file, we say the file is *infected*. **Worms** are a lot like viruses, but they usually appear as a separate program. Like a virus, they are an intrusion on the system and are potentially damaging to the system's security.

Figure 7.26 shows one way to differentiate between an infected and an uninfected file. There are other ways; if interested, you should consult references [Sp90] and [Ka94]. The uninfected file contains executable code that runs when it is referenced. In an infected file, however, the virus has placed a branch command to the virus's code. When the user calls on the infected file to do some task, the branch

Figure 7.26   Virus on an Executable File

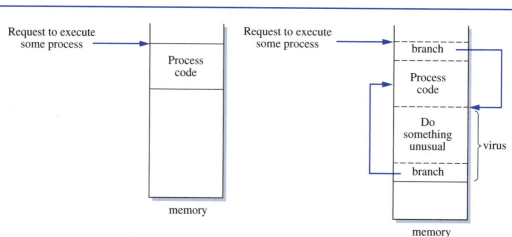

Uninfected software   Infected software

command transfers control to the virus code first. The virus does its deed and executes another branch to begin the requested task. As far as the user is concerned, the requested task is done. Unless the virus performed an obvious task such as erasing the hard disk, the user may not know the virus exists.

What is a virus capable of doing? Unfortunately, just about anything. A virus may do "harmless" tasks such as displaying Christmas trees on your computer's monitor during the holiday season.* It may be very destructive and erase your hard disk or destroy your file system. In these cases the effects usually can be minimized, but only if you have backups! If not, you're in serious trouble.

The worst viruses do not cause massive destruction immediately. Instead, they are very subtle, making small (and usually unnoticeable) changes in files as they run. Over a period of time the small changes compound and eventually are noticed. By that time, the information has been corrupted. Worse yet, if you made backups diligently, they also may be infected. Restoring the uninfected versions of the files may be difficult.

How does the virus attach itself to an executable file? The first step is to bring an infected file into your computer and run it. Once it runs, the attached virus can infect files in different ways. For example, it might probe your file system looking for other executable files (Figure 7.27). With a little knowledge of a file system, this

Figure 7.27   Virus Duplicating Itself

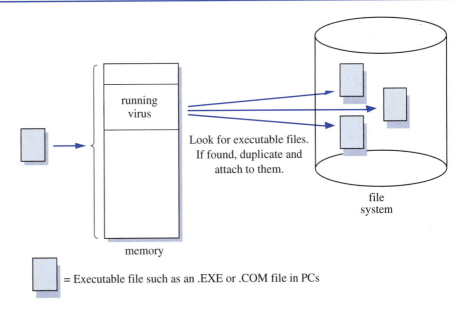

running
virus

Look for executable files.
If found, duplicate and
attach to them.

file
system

memory

= Executable file such as an .EXE or .COM file in PCs

---

* Some "harmless" viruses may actually do a great deal of harm, even if they do not explicitly destroy or damage existing information. We will see a few examples shortly.

is not difficult. Whenever it finds an executable file, the virus can execute instructions to duplicate itself and store the copy in the file, as in Figure 7.27.

Such viruses can be detected more easily than others. The process of seeking executable files and changing them requires extra disk activity. Consequently, if you notice a lot of disk activity when you do a simple task, be suspicious. Better yet, buy antivirus software that will monitor activities on your computer.

MEMORY-RESIDENT VIRUSES

Rather than scanning the disk's file system, the virus may copy itself into memory and wait for an executable file to be stored in memory. When a file enters, the virus attacks it. Picking the files off one by one as they enter memory is a much more subtle type of attack—not unlike a sly predator hiding and waiting for its prey to arrive unsuspecting, only to become the predator's next meal.

But how does a memory-resident virus become activated? It is still a program and cannot be activated until it is called. On PCs some viruses take advantage of internal interrupt mechanisms. Typically, BIOS (basic input/output system) and operating system service routines are located via an interrupt table or interrupt vector. The *interrupt table* is a collection of addresses to service routines. When a user requires a service or when some asynchronous event occurs that needs action, the operating system locates the required service by finding its address in the table and begins executing the program at that location. A memory-resident virus will change the interrupt table to create addresses that locate the virus instead (Figure 7.28).

Figure 7.28   Memory-Resident Virus

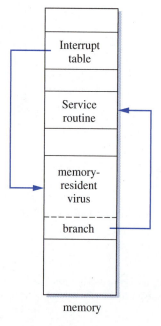

memory

Consequently, when an interrupt occurs, the routine located via the table's address is the virus, which does its deed. As before, it may try to disguise what it did by calling the intended service routine, making the user think everything is progressing normally.

VIRUS EVOLUTION

The history of the computer virus dates back to 1949, a time when most people did not even know computers existed. John Von Neumann wrote a paper entitled "Theory and Organization of Complicated Automata" describing a theory that computer programs could in fact multiply. It outlined, in effect, the model for a computer virus. Because the only computers then were just a few huge mainframes and the only programmers were engineers, there was not much interest in Von Neumann's theories. However, that has changed.

Before the mid-1980s, computer viruses were virtually nonexistent. Since then viruses have increased both in number and in complexity, as have the methods for detecting and eliminating them. Software vendors offer a range of antivirus software packages designed to locate known viruses on a personal computer. The problem is that as antivirus packages become more sophisticated so do the viruses they seek. A logical question to ask is: How do viruses become harder to detect? References [Na97] and [Ka94] explore the history and evolution of viruses and antivirus programs. We summarize the topic here.

We begin by examining how simple viruses are detected. Early viruses in the mid-1980s were quite simple and small in number. Antivirus programs worked by looking for a virus *signature,* a sequence of bytes (corresponding to machine language instructions) contained in the virus. Because there were not very many viruses, the number of signatures was small and looking for them was not a serious problem.

As time passed, two things happened to make virus detection more difficult. First, more viruses were written. Second, the proliferation of software and growth in disk capacities provided more places for viruses to hide. Simply looking for a wider variety of virus signatures throughout a disk's files became a time-consuming process. To compensate, antivirus researchers noted a couple of things: Most viruses are not lengthy programs, and viruses typically placed themselves at the beginning or end of an executable file (recall Figure 7.26). Consequently, antivirus programs concentrated their searches at the beginning and end of such files, thus significantly increasing the efficiency of their search.

Virus programmers began to realize that to be successful they had to hide the virus's signature, or at least disguise it so it would not be recognizable. Encryption is the tool they began to use. By subjecting virus code to an encryption algorithm (even a simple Caesar cipher), the signature would be altered and antivirus software would not find it. The only problem was that a program whose machine instructions are encrypted won't run.

The way around this was to insert a decryption algorithm in a file with the virus (Figure 7.29). When making a call to a process, a branch at the process's entry point transfers control to a decryption algorithm. The algorithm runs and decrypts the contents of memory containing the encrypted virus. Once decrypted, the virus can

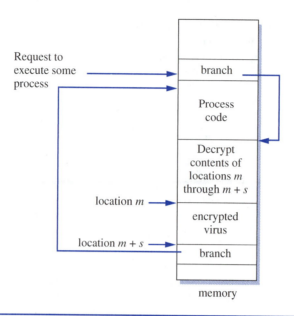

Figure 7.29   Encrypted Virus on an Executable File

execute, do its nasty deeds, and transfer control to the process. Because this happens in memory, the virus remains in encrypted form in the file and its signature remains disguised. To make things more difficult for antivirus researchers, the virus could even be written to use a different encryption key each time it infected a new file. Consequently, the same virus would look different with each file it infected.

Antivirus programmers responded by designing software to look for byte patterns common to decryption algorithms. The problem here is that code for decryption algorithms is short and often similar to code for legitimate programs. For example, does the following code represent a Caesar cipher decryption algorithm or simply a task to update information in an array?

```
for (i=0; i<s; i++)
    m[i]+=k;
```

Actually, it can be either; it's difficult to distinguish its purpose without knowing the context in which it is used.

To eliminate an inordinate number of false alarms, antivirus programs use a technique called *x-raying*. Essentially, the programs take a suspected encrypted virus and subject it to a collection of decryption algorithms known to be used with viruses. They then examine the decrypted result and look for virus signatures. This method has proved to be successful.

Not to be foiled, virus programmers responded by creating the **polymorphic virus.** Essentially, it is a virus that mutates when it infects a new file. This is similar to biological viruses (such as the AIDS virus) that often mutate, making them resistant to treatment. A polymorphic virus uses a mutation engine to change the code for the decryption algorithm each time the virus infects a file. Any experienced programmer knows that there are many ways to generate code to accomplish a specific task. The polymorphic virus just takes advantage of that fact. Consequently, each copy of a polymorphic virus is not only encrypted with a different key but uses a different decryption routine to decrypt it. For antivirus programs looking for a specific byte sequence characteristic of a virus or decryption algorithm, this is a serious problem.

How can you locate a virus when you don't know what it looks like? There has been some success at analyzing byte strings produced by mutation engines and detecting patterns. The problem is that some of the more complex engines are capable of producing well over a billion forms of decryption algorithms. The huge number of signatures that are possible make any signature-seeking detection methods impractical.

However, any computer virus must eventually decrypt and reveal itself in order to execute. This is the key that has allowed a successful response to the polymorphic virus. The difficulty is that if the antivirus programs wait until then, it is too late. Some current virus detection techniques use *generic decryption* (GD) technology. In a sense, it is a technique that fools the virus into revealing itself early, before it has a chance to do damage. More precisely, GD antivirus software contains a CPU emulator. When it examines a file, it executes software that simulates the execution of the file. If the file contains a polymorphic virus, it will decrypt itself and its signature pattern will be revealed. By periodically invoking signature-seeking routines, the virus can be detected. Even if the virus decloaked and executed before being detected, it is only a simulation and no real harm is done.

However, what if the file does not contain a virus? At some point the simulation must terminate or no real work would ever get done. The simulation might execute a specific number of instructions and then, if no virus is found, terminate. This method is not foolproof, however. A virus can contain all kinds of do-nothing instructions at the start. Examples are NOP instructions (literally instructions that do nothing) and instructions that add 0 to a register. The purpose of such instructions is to delay the real activity of the virus and to create the illusion of an innocuous program, at least for a while. Thus, if the simulation is too short, it might miss some viruses. On the other hand, if it is too long then the user gets impatient while waiting for the detection program to complete and writes to the vendor to complain about lousy responses.

The war between virus authors and everyone else continues. Current antivirus software is effective and efficient, but new viruses continue to show up, forcing many to invest significant time and money in protecting their resources.

VIRUS SOURCES

Where do viruses come from? Initially they are created by individuals who, for whatever reason, try to invade a system. Whether it is done as a prank or as an unprincipled and malicious act of destruction is usually of no consequence. What is destroyed is destroyed, and reasons are of no value to the victim.

Like any biological virus, computer viruses are spread by sharing. We saw how a file can become infected. Consider what happens if an infected file is copied to some removable medium and the medium is inserted in another computer. When the infected file is run, the other computer's files can become infected. If any of those are copied to removable media and transported to yet another computer, the virus spreads further. Obviously, you want to be very careful about where you get software.

The growing use of networks and communications has compounded the problem. What happens if an infected file gets into a Web site, commercial software, or a network file server? The virus now has the potential to spread to thousands of users in a short period of time. The growth rate of the virus can stagger the imagination.

Don't infer from this discussion that Web sites, networks, and commercially distributed software are a haven for viral infections. Reputable managers and vendors go through great effort to make sure their software is not infected. Still, in this business there are no guarantees. In 1988 there was an incident in which a commercial software package contained a virus that displayed a peace message and then erased itself. This is an example of a "harmless" virus doing damage. It may have been harmless in the sense that it neither destroyed files nor stole valuable information. The vendor, however, had to rebuild its damaged reputation and restore consumer confidence in its products. A company so affected could lose business, which in turn can force layoffs. To a vendor and its employees, such incidents are far from harmless.

Given that viruses are unavoidable, how can you deal with them? As with most illnesses, prevention is your best bet. Many virus detection packages are available. Sometimes a virus detection package scans any medium inserted into a drive, looking for viruses. If it detects one, it sounds a warning and, in some cases where the medium is a floppy disk, ejects it. The user then can request the package to remove the virus or can replace all the infected files with uninfected backups (making sure first that they are in fact uninfected).

7.8 THREATS AND ATTACKS

THE INTERNET WORM

One of the more famous instances of intrusion was the **Internet worm.** Several interesting and accessible articles describe the worm, its effects, and how it worked. Yes, it is an old story, but it's worth retelling because of its significance in providing extreme awareness that connecting computers does pose risk. We'll provide just an overview, but the interested reader should consult references [Sp89], [Ro89], [Se89], and [De90].

In November 1988 a Cornell graduate student released a worm into the Internet, which invaded thousands of Sun 3 and VAX computers running variants of the 4 BSD UNIX operating system. This worm was of the so-called harmless variety; it did not damage any information or give away any of the secret passwords it uncovered.

On the other hand, it was a serious breach of security. It replicated quickly throughout the Internet, clogging communications and forcing many systems to be shut down. It also forced many experts to spend days tracking the source of the problem and cleaning up after it. It triggered an FBI investigation to determine whether there was a violation of the 1986 Computer Fraud and Abuse Act and resulted in indictment of the perpetrator. The case went to court, and a federal jury found the defendant guilty. The defendant was sentenced to three year's probation, fined $10,000, and ordered to do 400 hours of community service [Mo90]. So much for harmless worms! (Computer worms and viruses are federal crimes and in most cases will be investigated by the FBI. Federal laws are stricter than most state laws.)

The worm itself was written in C and attacked UNIX systems through flaws in the software. It used several techniques, each of which is described in reference [Sp89]. In one approach, it used a utility called **fingerd** that allows one user to obtain information about other users. The fingerd program is designed to accept a single line of input from a remote site (a request) and send back output corresponding to the request (Figure 7.30). The flaw that was exploited was that the fingerd program's input command (the C language `gets` command) did not check for buffer overflow. Consequently, a worm running on a remote machine could connect to the fingerd program and send a specially constructed message that overflowed the fingerd program's input buffer.

Figure 7.31 shows what happened. The transmitted message overflowed the input buffer and overwrote parts of the system stack. However, the stack contains a return address (of the calling procedure) to be referenced when fingerd is finished. Because of the overflow, this address was changed to point to some instructions stored in the buffer. Consequently, when fingerd finished, control returned to the "program" located by the new return address. This "program" effectively replaced fingerd with the UNIX shell (interface or command interpreter). The result was that the worm was now connected to the shell. From that point the worm communicated with the shell and eventually sent a copy of itself, thus infecting the new machine. The worm then proceeded to inspect system files, looking for connections to other machines it could infect.

It also attacked a password file trying to decipher user passwords. Deciphering a password allowed the worm to attack other computers where that user had accounts.

Figure 7.30   The Fingerd Utility

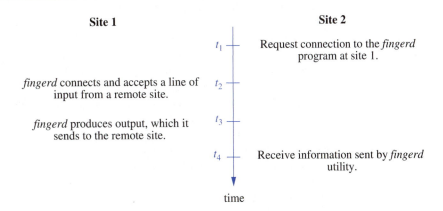

Site 1   **Site 2**

t_1 Request connection to the *fingerd* program at site 1.

fingerd connects and accepts a line of input from a remote site. t_2

fingerd produces output, which it sends to the remote site. t_3

t_4 Receive information sent by *fingerd* utility.

time

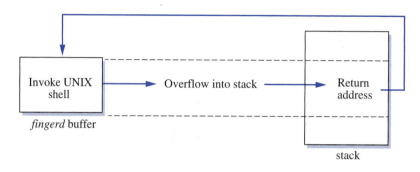

Figure 7.31 Intruding into the System

An interesting note here is that the passwords were all stored in encrypted form using DES. In theory, deciphering the passwords without the key should have been next to impossible. The worm took a rather straightforward approach, however. It simply guessed passwords, encrypted them, and looked for matches. In theory, the number of possible passwords is huge, making this an impractical method of seeking passwords. However, the worm used words from an online dictionary and in many cases found matches. In some cases, over 50% of the passwords were uncovered (ref. [Sp89]). The moral of this story is: Don't use passwords commonly found in a dictionary.

COMPUTER HACKERS

Widespread connectivity has opened many doors for another security threat, the computer hacker. Basically, a **hacker** is someone who writes programs just for the sheer enjoyment of writing them. However, some people see hackers as unprincipled people who try to gain unauthorized access to a computer system, often by exploiting security holes in operating systems and determining user passwords.

Why do unprincipled hackers do what they do? That's tough to answer. Some people believe that most hackers see breaking into a system as a challenge or a game. Such hackers either do not realize or do not care about the consequences of their actions to others. To some, looking at private information does not carry the same stigma as intruding on the privacy of a person's home. This does not necessarily make such people less dangerous, however. Some people believe the perpetrator of the Internet worm did not have malicious intent since the worm did not try to destroy information. Nevertheless, its effect was far-reaching and very disruptive. People who hack with the sole purpose of stealing or altering information do exist. They often accept the risk of getting caught or perhaps do not even care. Reference [La87] discusses the motives of some hackers and suggests that there are some very dangerous people doing the hacking.

The existence of widespread networks has created the potential for more severe and potentially dangerous problems (ref. [Na91]). For example, one hacking incident described in references [St88] and [St89] received widespread publicity. It started with a 75-cent accounting error at Lawrence Berkeley Laboratory in August 1986 and led to the arrest of a West German hacker. The hacker attacked many computers on MILNET (a military production network) and passed information to the KGB, the secret police of the former Soviet Union. In 1990 a West German court convicted the hacker of espionage for the KGB.

References [St88] and [St89] are old but still provide fascinating reading. They detail the activities of many people as they monitored the intruder's efforts and eventually tracked him to his West German location. They characterized the intruder as not particularly resourceful but very persistent, using primitive attack methods such as guessing passwords. As with the Internet worm, many of his attacks were successful simply because of the widespread use of common words as passwords.

OTHER THREATS

Attacks on computers and networks continue and in fact are increasing. High-profile sites may experience literally millions of attacks per month, most of which are repelled. One notorious type of attack is the **denial of service (DoS) attack.** One form of a DoS attack, often called the **smurf attack,** is to inundate a server and network with so much garbage that it cannot do anything else. In effect, network resources become unavailable for legitimate users, causing loss of work, time, and money. Doing this is actually quite simple and is based on the common network command `ping`. A user enters a command `ping` *IP-address* that causes an ICMP* Echo Request packet to be sent to the host. The host responds by sending a sequence of Echo Response packets back to the user. The basic idea is to learn whether the specified site is reachable and how much time it takes to send a packet there and back.

Figure 7.32 shows how this can be abused. Someone who we call the perpetrator (the G rating of this book prevents us from using the real term) sends an Echo Request packet to an unprotected network. However, this person does two things different. He puts a broadcast address into the packet's destination field, which causes the packet to be sent to every address in the network. He also puts the address of the intended victim into the packet's source address field. Each machine that gets the Echo Request packet does what it is asked—sends a series of Echo Reply packets to the source. If the number of machines that receive the Echo Request packet is large, a torrent of Echo Reply packets are sent to the victim, overwhelming its server and effectively shutting down operations.

Another type of DoS attack is the *SYN flood attack*, which is based on the protocol that TCP uses to set up a connection. Chapter 11 discusses this protocol in more detail, but its essence is as follows:

1. The client sends a TCP SYN segment requesting a connection.

2. The server sends an acknowledgment to that request.

3. The client sends a follow-up to complete the connection.

---

* This is an Internet management protocol and is discussed in Chapter 11.

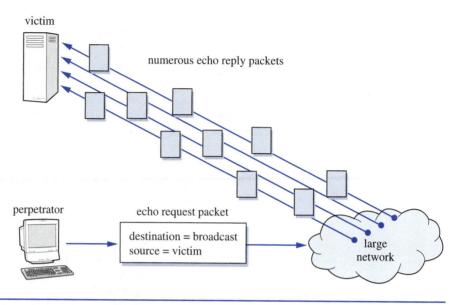

victim

numerous echo reply packets

perpetrator   echo request packet

destination = broadcast
source = victim

large
network

Figure 7.32   Denial of Service Attack

All three steps are necessary to set up the connection. In a SYN flood attack, the perpetrator sends the TCP SYN request but, as in the smurf attack, uses a phony IP address. The server then sends the acknowledgment to the spoofed address. The client at that site never sends a follow-up because it never initiated the request. This seems like the end of the story, but after the server sends its acknowledgment, it creates some data structures to prepare for what it thinks is an eventual connection. If the follow-up never arrives, a timer expires and the data structure is eventually released. However, if the perpetrator can send phony connection requests at a rate faster than the data structures expire, the victimized server may run out of memory or reach a limit that prevents it from accepting new connections from legitimate clients.

DoS attacks are not the only security problem. A **packet sniffer** is a program that looks through data packets as they travel the network. It can copy private information such as passwords and use them to launch attacks. The CERT Coordination Center (discussed shortly) reports that cable modem users have a higher risk of exposure because personal computers in the same neighborhood share the same cable line. Search engines may even pose a threat. Reference [He01] reports that some hackers have resorted to using search engines to launch attacks. Yet another threat to privacy is **spyware.** These programs are downloaded into your computer like a virus or may be part of other programs you downloaded and installed from a less than reputable site. While running, a spyware program does not affect your files or interfere with your activities in any way. However, it does log what you do (programs you run, files you access, Internet sites you visit) and reports it to the spyware program's owner. It's an insidious program that may run without you ever knowing about it.

As you've probably guessed by now, there is no shortage of attacks on systems nor, unfortunately, of people who initiate them. Network administrators must be vigilant in configuring firewalls properly and staying current on the types of attacks that develop. It's a serious problem: Some high-profile sites report over 1 million repelled attacks in just one month. With connectivity spreading to virtually every corner of the globe and people writing or acquiring programs that initiate such attacks, this is a problem that won't go away.

One approach to fighting such attacks is to develop protocols that allow both clients and servers to prove their identities to each other before establishing connections. One such product, *Kerberos,* was developed at MIT and uses cryptographic techniques. It has similarities with TLS/SSL but was developed for client/server environments, whereas TLS/SSL was developed for Web access. It's an open source security standard. Its most recent incarnation, version 5, was developed in collaboration with the IETF and is specified in RFC 1510. Reference [Co01b] discusses Kerberos in further detail.

Another security package is **IPSec.** Whereas packages such as Kerberos, TLS/SSL, and PGP were developed to work at higher layers, IPSec is designed to work at the IP layer. This makes it independent of the application and end users. IPSec allows for IP packet authentication and encryption and also provides key management facilities. We'll address issues of IP security further in Chapter 11. Reference [Pe00] also provides more detail.

Organizations exist that monitor suspicious activities. One is the CERT Coordination Center operated by Carnegie Mellon University. Originally called the Computer Emergency Response Team, it dates back to 1988 and grew out of the Defense Advanced Projects Research Agency (DARPA). CERT is funded by the U.S. Department of Defense and other federal civil agencies. CERT logs and provides much information on attacks, along with recommendations on how to combat them. Much more information can be found on their website, www.cert.org.

Although this chapter is longer than most others in this book, we've just scratched the surface with regard to security issues. The technical, social, and legal details are astounding. Some have said that the only totally secure computer is one that is not connected to a network and has been turned off. Although said partly in jest, there is much truth in this statement. Many people store private information on computers and set their own machines up as servers. It's not much different from leaving all your personal documents on a table in your front room, removing the front door, and hanging a sign outside that says "all visitors welcome."

7.9 SUMMARY

This chapter dealt with security issues, including encryption, key distribution, authentication, security packages and protocols, firewalls, viruses, and attacks. There was a heavy emphasis on encryption techniques because encryption is vital not only in disguising data that we don't want intruders to read but also in digitally signing documents and authenticating them. Encryption techniques fall into one of two categories: private key and public key encryption. The key in a private key cryptosystem

Table 7.3   Summary of Encryption and Digest Algorithms

ALGORITHM	COMMENTS
AES (Rijndael)	The newly defined standard casts 128-, 192-, or 256-bit blocks as matrices and performs multiple rounds of complex operations. Each round includes S-box substitutions, shift operations, exclusive OR operations, and other mathematical calculations based on polynomial multiplications and Galois field theory. Many expect this algorithm to be extremely difficult to break for some time.
Bit-level cipher	The key is a bit string. Exclusive OR operations between it and successive parts of the message encrypt the message. Each ciphertext block is decrypted by doing an exclusive OR with the same bit string. The method is not considered hard to break because differences between parts of the plaintext message are preserved. For example, if P1 and P2 are two different parts of the plaintext message that differ in certain bit positions, then the encrypted versions of each will differ in exactly the same bit positions.
Caesar cipher	This method substitutes one character for another. It preserves common letter sequences and is relatively easy to break. It is not suitable for any serious encryption application but is sometimes used as part of a more complex scheme.
Data Encryption Standard (DES)	Uses a complex collection of transpositions, substitutions, and exclusive or operations. The method was once controversial, as some feel that the National Security Agency weakened the standard from the original proposal. The speculation was that the NSA did not want an encryption method it would have trouble breaking. The DES algorithm was broken in 1998 by a DES Cracker machine built by the Electronic Frontier Foundation. The algorithm as it stands is now obsolete.
Polyalphabetic cipher	Like the Caesar cipher, one character is substituted for another. The difference is that the substitution choice for a common character varies depending on the letter's position in the message.
RSA algorithm	This method is an example of a public key cryptosystem that encrypts by treating a bit string as a number and raising it to a very large power using modular arithmetic. The decryption key (private key) is very difficult to determine even when the encryption key (public key) is known.
Transposition cipher	This method makes no attempt to disguise the characters but instead rearranges them. Its main use is as a component of a more complex scheme.
Triple DES	Applies the DES algorithm three consecutive times. If the three instances of the algorithm use a different key, most consider this method a difficult one to break.

must be kept secret because an intruder who determines the encryption key can then decrypt messages. Thus, a related issue is how to distribute the private key. In a public key cryptosystem, we don't care who knows the key. We assume that knowledge of it is of no use in determining the decryption routines. Table 7.3 summarizes the encryption schemes covered in this chapter.

In addition to the encryption algorithms, important concepts presented in this chapter are as follows:

- **Key distribution and escrow.** To decrypt codes, private keys must be distributed to the appropriate recipients. Shamir's method involves using a key as part of a polynomial expression. Then, points that the polynomial's graph pass through are distributed. To determine the key, a minimal number of people are needed to provide enough points to determine the original polynomial. Diffie-Hellman key exchange calls for a sender and receiver to exchange calculated values from which an encryption key can be derived. Part of the calculation is kept secret; the lack of that information makes deducing the key by a third party very difficult. However, Diffie-Hellman is susceptible to the man-in-the-middle attack. Keys for the Clipper Chip are determined by doing an exclusive OR operation between two randomly generated bit strings. Each of those bit strings is stored at different key escrow agencies, and both are needed to retrieve the key.

- **Digital signatures.** Digital signatures are a way of authenticating the author of an encrypted message. The idea is to encrypt using a private key and decrypt using a public one. If the author of a message later disputes ownership of it, the receiver can provide both the received ciphertext and the plaintext. Because the private key is known only to the author, only the author could have sent the message.

- **Authentication.** This is a means of determining whether a document is authentic or a forgery. It works by calculating a message digest, a number uniquely determined from the document's contents. That number is then signed using the private key counterpart in a public key cryptosystem. Any attempt at forging the document will almost certainly create a document whose digest value differs from the one that was signed. We mentioned two algorithms that produce message digests. The MD5 digest algorithm produces a 128-bit message digest value. It divides the message into 512-bit blocks (some padding may be necessary to get a full 512-bit block) and operates on each block. Each block is subjected to four rounds of operations that use various bit operations and factor in values from a sine function. Eventually, a result is generated, which is used as input to encrypt the next block. The Secure Hash Algorithm 1 (SHA-1), like MD5, operates on 512-bit blocks. It divides each 512-bit block into sixteen 32-bit words. Word groups and predefined constants are next subjected to numerous rounds of logical AND, OR, exclusive OR, and shift operations, producing a 160-bit integer value.

- **Clipper Chip.** The Clipper Chip was a controversial development in part because it uses algorithms designed by the NSA. It also includes a protocol allowing access to a user's private key under certain circumstances (typically when illegal activities are suspected). Because many people distrust the government, especially where privacy is concerned, the chip has inflamed the ongoing discussion between right-to-privacy groups and law enforcement officials, who argue that privacy is not a right in cases where illegal activities are happening.

- **Pretty Good Privacy.** PGP is a freeware email security program developed by Philip Zimmerman. It includes public key encryption, authentication, digital signatures, and compression. It runs on many platforms and uses algorithms that have been thoroughly reviewed, such as RSA for public key encryption, MD5 for message digests, and the IDEA algorithm for regular encryption. It received some notoriety because of its free accessibility via the Internet, which allowed it to be "exported" to foreign countries. The U.S. government argued that because cryptographic software is considered munitions, this situation was in violation of export laws. More recent versions were developed outside of the United States to circumvent this problem. Also, the rules regarding exporting such software have been relaxed somewhat.

- **Transport Layer Security.** TLS and Secure Sockets Layer (SSL) are protocols that authenticate servers (and clients, if necessary) and negotiate encryption keys and algorithms for secure transmissions. The protocol relies on an X.509 certificate issued by a certificate authority to a server's site. The certificate validates the server's claim of authenticity. Once a server is authenticated, a client may use information in the certificate, such as a public key, to send information back to the server. This information is then used by both the client and server to determine a key for subsequent encryption.

- **Firewalls.** A firewall separates an organization's computers from the Internet. Any communication between an organization's computer and a remote machine must pass through the firewall. The firewall may block transmissions based on the contents of an IP packet or on application layer actions. It may also accept or reject TCP connections between them. An increasingly common approach is to examine packets in the context of previous activities (stateful inspection). Certain packets are allowed to pass only if they are in response to a previous legitimate request.

- **Viruses, worms, and hackers.** Viruses are programs that attach themselves to other programs. What they do varies and can be very destructive. Like viruses, worms represent invasions into a system, but they are not actually part of another program. Computer hackers are individuals who attempt to break through a system's security. They may try to steal private information or plant viruses or worms in order to do damage. Two famous cases of intrusion were the Internet worm, which invaded thousands of computers on the Internet, and the West German programmer who attacked computers on MILNET and sold information to the former KGB. The number of attacks on computers worldwide is increasing; such attacks include denial of service attacks, address spoofing, packet sniffing, and spyware.

- **Legal, social, ethical, and political issues.** Developing secure codes is serious business. We have outlined some of the controversy surrounding the NSA and the development of encryption techniques. In fact, commercial encryption products were once treated as munitions, making them subject to the same rules as an F-16 fighter jet. If you were caught selling them overseas without a proper license, you were considered an international arms trafficker. In 1996, then-President Clinton issued an executive order that would transfer jurisdiction over commercial encryption exports from the State Department to the Commerce Department when the Commerce Department developed regulations to implement the order. Not all encryption algorithms are considered exportable, and information regarding some cryptographic algorithms still remains classified. In addition, the Department of Commerce may still refer export license applications to the State Department and other agencies for review.

This is a complex and very controversial issue. The debate between those arguing for the right to privacy and those opposed to privacy when it hinders law enforcement will be ongoing.

Review Questions

1. Distinguish between encryption and decryption.

2. Distinguish between ciphertext and plaintext.

3. What is a Caesar cipher?

4. Distinguish between a monoalphabetic and a polyalphabetic cipher.

5. Are the following statements TRUE or FALSE? Why?

    a. The Caesar cipher has no real value where serious security is needed.

    b. Public key encryption allows different people to use the same encryption key even when they are not supposed to know what another person is sending.

    c. Any block cipher that encrypts a block at a time is essentially a substitution cipher, replacing one block with another.

    d. An encryption method that uses a longer key is more secure than one that uses a shorter key.

    e. The most serious viruses destroy a lot of data very quickly.

    f. Encrypting by using exclusive OR operations on sections of a plaintext message is a secure method as long as the bits in the key are randomly distributed.

    g. Under certain conditions, the triple DES encryption method is no better than DES.

    h. Firewalls are commonly used to protect a network against incoming viruses.

    i. Viruses that do not destroy information or otherwise compromise a computer system are harmless.

    j. An attack on a network is not really serious unless the attack is designed to grab private information or store unlicensed programs on it.

6. What is a transposition cipher?

7. If the encryption key is long enough, encryption techniques such as bit-level ciphering are truly unbreakable. Why aren't they used more?

8. What is the Data Encryption Standard (DES)?

9. What is a DES Cracker?

10. Explain the difference between electronic codebook (ECB) mode and cipher block chaining (CBC) mode as applied to block ciphers.

11. What is an initialization vector?

12. What was the controversy surrounding DES?

13. Why has the Clipper Chip proved controversial?

14. What is the purpose of using key escrow agents to hold the keys used in the Skipjack algorithm?

15. What is Shamir's method for key distribution?

16. What is a block cipher?

17. What is the purpose of an S-box?

18. What is the man-in-the-middle attack?

19. How does public key encryption differ from regular encryption?

20. What is a digital signature?

21. What are the main features of the RSA algorithm?

22. What makes the RSA algorithm so difficult to break?

23. How do authentication and digital signatures differ?

24. What is the significance of the birthday attack?

25. What is Pretty Good Privacy?

26. Why would a cryptographic algorithm be classified as munitions and be subject to strict export laws?

27. What is the difference between wiping a file and deleting it?

28. What is an X.509 certificate?

29. Any site can create an authentic-looking certificate and claim it is from a trusted CA. How does a client determine if the certificate is a fraud?

30. What is a firewall?

31. List three types of firewalls and how they operate.

32. A firewall filters incoming data looking for possible threats to a system. It also examines outgoing data. Why does it do that?

33. What is the disadvantage of using packet filtering to screen incoming packets for possible threats to a system?

34. What does *stateful inspection* mean?

35. Distinguish between a virus and a worm.

36. What is an infected file?

37. List some ways you can help prevent the spread of computer viruses.

38. What is the UNIX fingerd utility?

39. What is a memory-resident virus?

40. What was the Internet worm?

41. What is a denial of service attack?

42. What is spyware?

43. What does a packet sniffer do?

Exercises

1. How were the letter substitutions in Figure 7.2 determined?

2. Consider two substitution ciphers. One adds a value of i to the ASCII code of the plaintext character. The other adds a value of j to the plaintext character. All

additions are modulo 256. Now consider a double-encryption method that adds i to each plaintext character and then adds j to the resulting ciphertext character to get another ciphertext character. Again, all calculations are modulo 256. How much more secure is this double encryption when compared with either single-encryption method?

3. Write a program to encrypt and decrypt using a Caesar cipher. The program should request the encryption key as input.

4. The following message was encrypted using a Caesar cipher. What is the original message?

fcvceqoowpkecvkqpucpfeqorwvgtpgvyqtmu

5. Write a decryption algorithm to decrypt ciphertext created by the polyalphabetic encryption algorithm in Section 7.2.

6. Consider the transposition cipher applied to Table 7.1. What is the transmitted message if the columns are rearranged as 5, 1, 4, 2, and 3?

7. Write a program to accept a binary string and a binary key. It should then use the key to encrypt the string using bit-level ciphering.

8. Consider the bit string 00101101010101000011111101001101 and the key 10110. Use the key to encrypt and then decrypt the string using bit-level (exclusive OR) ciphering.

9. Adapt the bit-level cipher algorithm to work in CBC (cipher block chaining) mode. Apply it using the bit string and key from Exercise 8.

10. Define a decryption algorithm for the encryption algorithm in Exercise 9.

11. Assume a plaintext message "ABCDEF" and any 8-bit key. If you encrypt by doing an exclusive OR between the ASCII code for each character in the plaintext and the key, what pattern occurs in the resulting ciphertext?

12. Suppose you were trying to crack an encryption method that used a 64-bit key. Assuming a brute force attack, how many keys per second must you try to crack the code in one month?

13. Why does triple DES specify the decryption algorithm as the second of three algorithms?

14. Construct a figure similar to Figure 7.7 for a 256-bit block.

15. Repeat the encryption process of the message "HELLO" discussed in Section 7.4 using a different encryption key but with the same value for n.

16. Suppose you intercepted the following encrypted message:

20 5 21 3 49 4 49 3 4 15

You also know that the encryption key is $k = 7$ and that it was determined using $n = 55$. Decrypt this message. Assume the letters A through Z were initially coded using 1 through 26, and a blank was initially coded using 27.

17. Using $n = 47$, $g = 5$, $x = 10$, and $y = 12$, verify that the Diffie-Hellman key exchange works. What is the encryption key?

18. Calculate 95^{91} modulo 121.

19. Write an algorithm (in the language of your choice) that will compute a^b mod n, where a, b, and n are all int types.

20. Design a largeInt class capable of storing an integer consisting of n digits (n is a positive integer). The class should include a method that multiplies two largeInt classes and produces a third one that contains the product. Record how long the multiplication algorithm takes for various values of n.

21. A simple method to calculate a message digest value is to break the message into 128-bit blocks, treat each as a 128-bit integer, and sum them. Would this be an effective digest algorithm? Why or why not?

22. Download PGP from a website and install it on your computer. Ask a friend to do the same. Use PGP to send each other both secure and signed messages.

23. Find a website that has a secure connection. What is its public key?

REFERENCES

[Co01a] Conry-Murray, A. "Firewalls for All." *Network,* vol. 16, no. 6 (June 2001), 42–47.

[Co01b] Conry-Murray, A. "Kerberos: Computer Security's Hellhound." *Network,* vol. 16, no. 7 (July 2001), 40–45.

[Da02] Daemen, J., and V. Rijmen. *The Design of Rijndael: AES, the Advanced Encryption Standard.* Heidelberg, Germany: Springer-Verlag, 2002.

[De90] Denning, P., ed. *Computers Under Attack: Intruders, Worms, and Viruses.* Reading, MA: Addison-Wesley, 1990.

[De96] Denning, D. E., and D. K. Branstad. "A Taxonomy for Key Escrow Encryption Systems." *Communications of the ACM,* vol. 39, no. 3 (March 1996), 34–40.

[Di67] Diffie, W., and M. E. Hellman. "New Directions in Cryptography." *IEEE Transactions on Information Theory,* vol. 13 (November 1967), 644–654.

[Ga94] Garfinkel, S. *PGP: Pretty Good Privacy.* Sebastopol, CA: O'Reilly & Associates, 1994.

[He01] Hernandez, J., et al. "Search Engines as a Security Threat." *Computer,* vol. 34, no. 10 (October 2001), 25–30.

[Ka94] Kane, P. *PC Security and Virus Protection Handbook.* New York: M&T Books, 1994.

[Ka01] Kaliski, B. "RSA Digital Signatures." *Dr. Dobb's Journal,* vol. 26, no. 5 (May 2001), 30–36.

[Ko77] Kolata, G. B. "Computer Encryption and the National Security Agency Connection." *Science,* vol. 197 (July 1977), 438–440.

[La87] Landreth, B., and H. Rheingold. *Out of the Inner Circle: A Hacker's Guide to Computer Security.* Bellevue, WA: Microsoft Press, 1987.

[Mo90] Montz, L. "The Worm Case: From Indictment to Verdict." In *Computers Under Attack: Intruders, Worms, and Viruses,* ed. Peter Denning. Reading, MA: Addison-Wesley, 1990.

[Mo01] Mollin, R. *An Introduction to Cryptography.* Boca Raton, FL: Chapman & Hall/CRC Press, 2001.

[Na91] National Research Council. *Computers at Risk*. Washington, DC: National Academy Press, 1991.

[Na97] Nachenberg, C. "Computer Virus-Antivirus Coevolution." *Communications of the ACM*, vol. 40, no. 1 (January 1997), 46–51.

[Op01] Oppliger, R. *Secure Messaging with PGP and S/MIME*. Norwood, MA: Artech House, 2001.

[Pe00] Perlman, R., and C. Kaufman. "Key Exchange in IPSec: Analysis of IDE." *IEEE Internet Computing,* vol. 4, no. 6 (November/December 2000), 50–56.

[Po02] Pohlmann, N., and T. Crothers. *Firewall Architecture for the Enterprise*. New York: Wiley, 2002.

[Re01] Rescorla, E. *SSL and TLS: Designing and Building Secure Systems*. Reading, MA: Addison-Wesley, 2001.

[Ri78] Rivest, R. L., A. Shamir, and L. Adleman. "On a Method for Obtaining Digital Signatures and Public Key Cryptosystems." *Communications of the ACM,* vol. 21 no. 2 (February 1978), 120–126.

[Ri92] Rivest, R. L. "The MD5 Message Digest Algorithm." RFC 1321, April 1992.

[Ro89] Rochlis, J., and M. Eichin. "With Microscope and Tweezers: The Worm from MIT's Perspective." *Communications of the ACM,* vol. 32, no. 6 (June 1989), 689–698.

[Sc94] Schneier, B. *Applied Cryptography*. New York: Wiley, 1994.

[Sc98] Schneier, B. "The Twofish Encryption Algorithm." *Dr. Dobb's Journal,* vol. 23, no. 12 (December 1998), 30–38.

[Se89] Seeley, D. "Password Cracking: A Game of Wits." *Communications of the ACM,* vol. 32, no. 6 (June 1989), 700–703.

[Sh79] Shamir, A. "How to Share a Secret." *Communications of the ACM,* vol. 22, no. 11 (November 1979), 612–613.

[Si96] Simonds, F. *Network Security: Data and Voice Communications*. New York: McGraw-Hill, 1996.

[Sp89] Spafford, E. "The Internet Worm: Crisis and Aftermath." *Communications of the ACM,* vol. 32, no. 6 (June 1989), 678–687.

[Sp90] Spafford, E., K. Heaphy, and D. Ferbrache. "A Computer Virus Primer." In *Computers Under Attack: Intruders, Worms, and Viruses,* ed. Peter Denning. Reading, MA: Addison-Wesley, 1990.

[St88] Stoll, C. "Stalking the Wily Hacker." *Communications of the ACM,* vol. 31, no. 5 (May 1988), 484–497.

[St89] Stoll, C. *The Cuckoo's Egg: Tracking a Spy Through the Maze of Computer Espionage*. New York: Doubleday, 1989.

[St95] Stinson, D. *Cryptography: Theory and Practice*. Boca Raton, FL: CRC Press, 1995.

[St03] Stallings, W. *Cryptography and Network Security: Principles and Practice,* 3rd ed. Upper Saddle River, NJ: Prentice-Hall, 2003.

[Th00] Thomas, S. *SSL and TLS Essentials: Securing the Web*. New York: Wiley, 2000.

[Yu79] Yuval, G. "How to Swindle Rabin." *Cryptologia,* vol. 3, no. 3 (July 1979), 187–190.

[Zi95] Zimmerman, P. *The Official PGP User's Guide*. Cambridge, MA: MIT Press, 1995.

CHAPTER 8

FLOW CONTROL

*Knowledge in the form of an informational commodity indispensable to
productive power is already, and will continue to be, a major—perhaps
the major—stake in the worldwide competition for power. It is conceivable
that the nation-states will one day fight for control of information, just as
they battled in the past for control over territory, and afterwards for
control over access to and exploitation of raw materials and cheap labor.*
—**Jean François Lyotard** (1924–1998), French philosopher

8.1 INTRODUCTION

Almost everything we have discussed so far has dealt with a single transmission
from a sender to a receiver. Whether we discussed digital or analog signals, compression, contention, security, or integrity, the discussion was generally aimed at a
single packet or frame. Most communications are more complex than that, and the
following issues must be addressed.

- What if the transmitted message is very long? Examples include large data files
  or a copy of a speech given at a political rally. Treating the entire message as a
  single transmission entity monopolizes the medium. This is fine for the sender
  but not so good for anyone else waiting to send.

- How do we react to damaged transmissions? Previously we stated that the receiver simply requests a retransmission. But how does the receiver do this?
  Does the sender's protocol depend entirely on the receiver's capability to notify the sender of damaged frames? Should the sender conclude that a frame
  arrived correctly if the receiver sends no such request? What happens if the
  receiver's request for a second transmission is itself damaged or lost?

- What if the sending and receiving computers work at different speeds? For example, you might download a data file from a supercomputer to a 10-year-old
  personal computer. Or perhaps the receiver is busier than the sender. In general, how do you prevent a sender from overwhelming a receiver with more
  data than the receiver can handle?

- What happens if a sender's frame gets lost? For example, the damaged part of
  a frame may include the receiver's address. If so, the frame will never be

delivered. We know the receiver can detect damaged frames. But what happens if a receiver gets nothing? Does it mean a frame was lost or that nothing was sent? How does the receiver distinguish between the two?

- In our previous examples, the distinction between sender and receiver was sharp. What if both want to send and receive simultaneously? It's a lot like talking and listening at the same time. We all do it on occasion, but some of what we hear is lost. We do not want our receivers to lose information.

This chapter discusses two important functions necessary to establish and maintain effective communications: error control and flow control. **Error control** defines how a device checks frames for errors and what it does if it finds them. Sections 6.2 and 6.3 discussed ways of detecting errors but did not address what happened afterward. A common approach is for the receiving device to send a message to the sending device indicating that an error occurred. What the sending device does next varies, and we discuss several protocols. The message is effectively a request to resend the frame, so this type of error control is often called **automatic repeat request (ARQ).**

Flow control defines the way in which many frames are sent and tracked and how the devices perform error control. It determines when frames can be sent, when they cannot be sent, and when they should be sent a second time. In general, flow control protocols ensure that all of the related frames arrive at their destination accurately and in order.

As with any topic, protocols range from simple to complex. Sections 8.2 and 8.3 discuss relatively simple flow control protocols. The protocols range from sending one frame at a time (stop-and-wait) to sending all of them at once (unrestricted flow). These sections also discuss the use of special signals or specific byte values to indicate when to send data. These are analogous to traffic signals regulating traffic flow onto a highway. As long as the light is green, traffic can enter the highway. But when the highway traffic reaches a certain saturation point the light turns red, halting any additional flow onto the highway.

Sections 8.4 and 8.5 define a more complex approach that numbers the frames and sends only a few at a time. The sender then waits for acknowledgment before sending more. The go-back-n protocol discussed in Section 8.4 assumes that frames arrive in the same order in which they were sent. The selective repeat protocol discussed in Section 8.5 allows for cases in which frames might be delayed and delivered out of order. Section 8.6 analyzes the algorithm for these approaches and defines formulas for determining effective data rates.

Discussing protocols and how they work is one thing. Verifying that they are correct is quite another. For simple algorithms, verification is often easy, but the complex ones require some special tools. Section 8.7 discusses some verification tools such as Petri nets and finite state models. Its orientation is more theoretical, and it may be skipped without loss of continuity.

This chapter is a bit more theoretical than others and does not refer to specific network protocols. That does not make it less important. In fact, it probably makes the chapter more important because it provides a foundation for the discussion of some data link and transport layer protocols in subsequent chapters. Those protocols will be much easier to understand if you already have an understanding of flow control, acknowledgments, windows, frame numbers, out-of-sequence frames, lost frames, and timers. Try to understand the concepts now, and we'll discuss implementations of them later.

8.2 SIGNALING

This section introduces relatively elementary approaches to flow control useful in simple communications systems. The first approach, *signaling,* is straightforward (Figure 8.1). The sender transmits data as long as the receiver is able to receive it. The receiver may not be able to receive data all the time, however. For example, the buffers that hold received data may be filling up, or the receiver may not be ready if it is doing other things. In such cases, the receiver sends a signal to the sender. On receipt of the signal, the sender stops transmitting. The protocol also allows for another signal to be sent when the receiver is again ready to receive more data. This approach is analogous to a nonproductive argument in which one person says, "Stop! I don't want to hear any more."

Figure 8.1   Flow Control Using Signaling

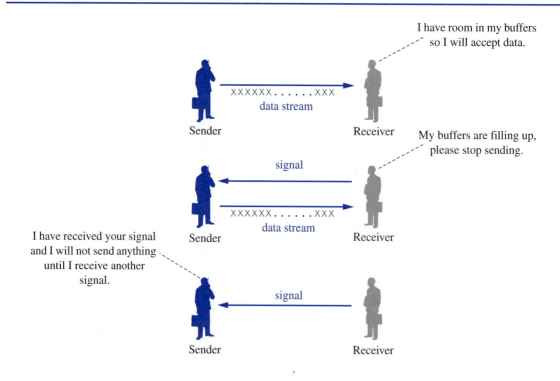

DTE–DCE FLOW CONTROL

Section 4.4 discussed one way to signal readiness to send and receive data over an EIA-232 interface. It involved sending signals over specified lines (DTR and DSR) to indicate a state of readiness. When the DTE wanted to send to the DCE, it sent another signal (RTS) requesting to send. It then waited for a Clear to Send signal (CTS) before transmitting. The details are in Section 4.4, so we won't rehash old material here.

X-ON/X-OFF

The EIA-232 interface is complex in that it requires separate lines for separate signals. Another approach is to send the signal as part of the transmitted data. This is called **in-band signaling.** In this case, the receiver has to analyze the incoming data looking for any special signals to which it must respond.

The ASCII character set defines two control characters for flow control (see Table 2.6 in Section 2.5). Symbolically, they are DC3 (hexadecimal code 13) and DC1 (hexadecimal code 11), also called X-OFF and X-ON, respectively.* They are sometimes used for flow control between a workstation and server. Figure 8.2 shows how this works.

The figure assumes full-duplex communications, so there is no distinction between a sender and receiver. A and B both send to and receive from each other. If A's buffers are starting to fill up, it can respond by inserting the X-OFF character into the data it is sending to B. When the X-OFF character arrives, B sees it and stops transmitting its data to A. (Note, however, that A is still sending to B.) If A has more room in its buffers later, A can send the X-ON character to B, which signals B that it is permissible to resume transmitting.

When one device sends the X-OFF character, it continues to receive data for a short time because of the small delay between the time the X-OFF character is sent

Figure 8.2   Flow Control Using In-Band Signaling

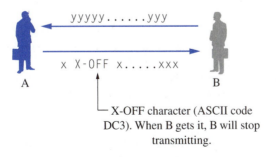

---

* They typically correspond to the control-S and control-Q keyboard sequences when using certain terminal emulators.

and the time the other device can respond to it. Consequently, a device usually will send when data in its buffers exceeds some threshold value.

Your first exposure to this protocol may have been by accident. For example, a common activity when using a terminal emulator to connect to a server is to display the contents of a text file on the screen. Occasionally, through a mistake or inattention, you might enter a command to display the contents of a binary file such as an executable file. The result usually is the appearance of strange characters on the screen, some beeping noises, and random cursor movement. In some cases, the workstation becomes unresponsive to further keyboard entries. That is, the keyboard freezes on you. Since most bytes in a binary file do not correspond to printable characters, the workstation often responds to their contents in unexpected ways. Line feed, vertical tab, or horizontal tab codes cause the cursor to move randomly. The characters may also contain the BEL code (hexadecimal code 07), causing the beeping sound. (This should destroy popular belief that the beeps are a warning that the workstation is about to self-destruct.)

The freezing problem occurs if one of the file's bytes contains an X-OFF character. Because the workstation received the X-OFF character, it responded by stopping transmission back to the server. Thus, if you make subsequent keyboard entries, they are not sent, and the workstation's screen freezes. Solutions include turning off the workstation or entering a local mode at the workstation and clearing communications.

Another common use of this protocol occurs when displaying a large file on the screen. To prevent information from scrolling off the screen, you can enter a control-S (hold the control key and enter S) from the keyboard to freeze the screen. Control-S sends an X-OFF character, which stops the transmission of the file. Later, having read what you wanted, you can enter control-Q, which sends the X-ON character and allows the file's transmission to resume.

8.3 FRAME-ORIENTED CONTROL

Protocols such as X-ON/X-OFF are byte oriented and are typical of asynchronous communications (see Section 4.3). That is, transmission can start and pause at any given byte. Synchronous communications (see Section 4.3) are frame oriented and require more organization. Information is sent and retrieved in larger pieces, not as a byte stream. Because a device must be able to buffer all the bytes in a frame it receives, different protocols are used to restrict the number of frames that can be sent. How the restrictions are applied, of course, varies.

Another consideration is that those who send and receive information usually do not care about the frames and their structure. Indeed, if you transfer a file over an Internet connection, you do not want to be bothered with these details. You simply want to enter a command or click a button to send a file and have the software worry about the details. Consequently, most protocols divide the information to be sent into frames of the appropriate format and send them. Figure 8.3 illustrates how this is done in a typical case.

Someone or something that we call a **user** has information it must send to another. Note that in this context we are not necessarily referring to a real person.

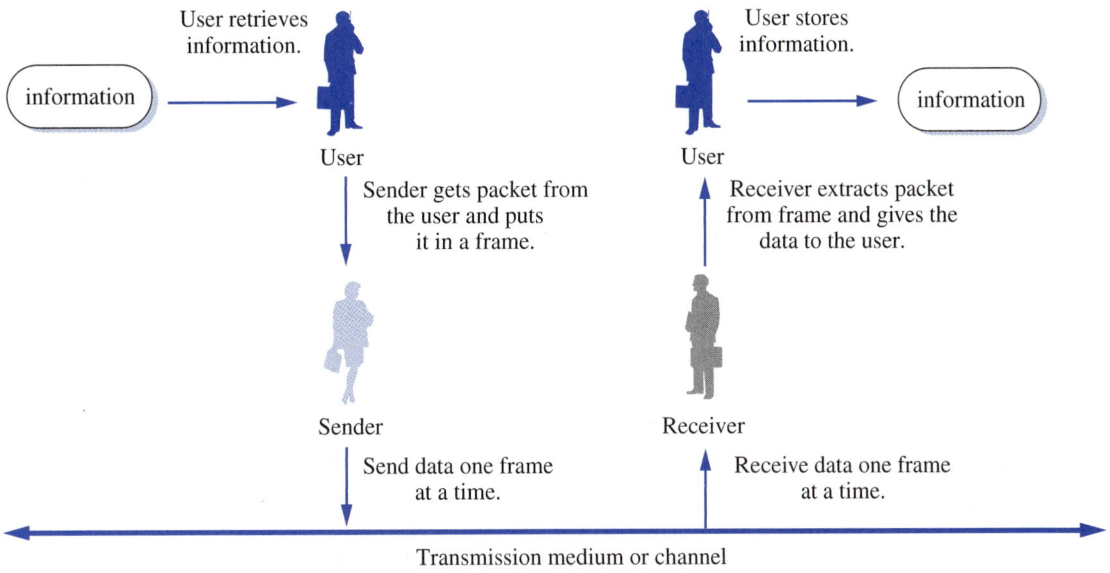

Figure 8.3   Sending and Receiving between Users

Here, the term *user* represents the next higher layer in a multilayer protocol. This makes sense because in a layered protocol, any layer is considered a user of the layer below it. For example, in the OSI model the session layer is a user of the transport layer, and the network layer is a user of the data link layer. Both of these examples are relevant because flow control protocols are an important part of both the data link and transport layers. The sender gets enough information (a **packet**) from the user to put into one frame and transmits the frame. The receiver gets the frame, extracts the packet, and gives it to the user that it serves. This process is repeated using as many frames as needed to transmit all the information.

Typically, the sender, receiver, and users of Figure 8.3 define consecutive layers in some communications software. This is typical of the interaction between the data link (sender and receiver) and network layer (user) in the OSI model. Flow control also exists in higher-layer protocols such as TCP/IP. (We describe it later in this book.) At this point, where the sender, receiver, and user exist is not important. Flow control exists in different models and in different layers. However, it is important to realize that flow control typically is part of the interaction between two consecutive layers in some protocol.

UNRESTRICTED PROTOCOL

The easiest protocol, **unrestricted protocol,** assumes the receiver either has an unlimited capacity to receive frames or processes them fast enough so that buffer space is always available. Figure 8.4 shows the sender and receiver logic written in

```
void send_data;                      Void receive_data;
{                                    {
  while there are packets to send      while there are frames to receive
  {                                    {
    get packet from the user;            wait for frame to arrive;
    put packet into a frame;             receive(frame);
    send(frame);                         Extract packet from the frame;
  }                                      Give packet to the user;
}                                      }
                                     }
            Sender code                          Receiver code
```

Figure 8.4   Unrestricted Flow Control

partial C code.* The sender and receiver use the primitive calls send and receive. Typically, they are calls to a layer below the sender and receiver that take care of details required to transmit the frame or retrieve it.

The sender executes a loop repeatedly as long as there is information to send. With each pass of the loop, it gets a packet from its user, puts it into a frame, and sends the frame. It sends frames repeatedly and makes no effort to limit the number it sends. The receiver also executes a loop repeatedly. We assume the receiver is always capable of receiving a frame. With each pass through the loop, the receiver waits (i.e., exists in a suspended or wait state) until a frame arrives. The arrival causes the receiver to wake up and receive the frame. It extracts the packet and passes it to its user and then goes back into a wait state until another frame arrives.

This approach does not consider any of the problems we have discussed previously. There is no attempt to check for damaged, lost, or delayed frames or to control the number of frames sent. It assumes that every frame will arrive without damage and in the order sent. It is much like our dependence on the post office when we mail letters.

STOP-AND-WAIT PROTOCOL

The **stop-and-wait protocol** differs from the previous protocol in two ways. First, every time the receiver gets a frame, it sends an acknowledgment back to the sender. The acknowledgment is another frame specifying whether the received frame was damaged. Second, after sending a frame, the sender waits for an acknowledgment before sending another frame. Thus, rather than sending all the frames in rapid sequence, this protocol sends one, waits for an acknowledgment, sends another, waits for an acknowledgment, and so on. In some ways the stop-and-wait protocol represents the opposite extreme of the previous method. Whereas the

---

* We make no attempt to write syntactically correct code. We will combine C syntax with informal statements to convey the program's meaning without a lot of language detail. A good exercise is to modify all the protocols we discuss into syntactically and logically correct programs.

unrestricted protocol sent the maximum number of frames per unit of time, this one sends the minimum number.

Figure 8.5 outlines the sender's and receiver's protocols. The receiver's protocol is similar to the unrestricted one. It consists of an infinite loop in which it waits for a frame to arrive. When a frame arrives, the receiver checks it for damage. Whether it uses CRC or some form of parity checking (discussed in Chapter 6) is not relevant at this level of the discussion. The important thing is that it can detect a damaged frame.

If the frame was not damaged, the receiver defines an error field in a record structure called ack as 0. It proceeds to extract the packet from the frame and give it to the user. If the frame was damaged, the error field of ack is set to 1. The receiver does not extract a packet from the frame, and the user gets nothing. In either case, the receiver sends the acknowledgment back to the sender. Because the error field specifies the status of the received frame, the sender can respond accordingly.

The sender executes a loop repeatedly, sending frames and waiting for acknowledgments. Prior to sending a frame, the sender must decide whether it should send a new one or resend the old one. It does this through a local variable called damaged whose value indicates the status of the most recently sent frame (1 means the frame was damaged; 0 means it was not). Initially, it is 0. At the beginning of the loop, the sender checks damaged. If it is 0, the sender gets a new packet from the user, puts it into a frame, and sends it. If damaged is 1, the sender sends the current frame (the one it sent earlier). Either way, it waits for an acknowledgment after sending the frame. When the acknowledgment arrives, the sender checks the error field, which the receiver defined. If the error field indicates the previous frame was damaged, the sender defines damaged $= 1$. Thus, the next time through the loop,

Figure 8.5   Stop-and-Wait Flow Control

```
void send_data;                          void receive_data;
{                                        {
   damaged=0;                               while there are packets to receive
   while there are packets to send          {
   {                                            Wait for frame to arrive;
      if (!damaged)                             receive(frame);
            /* !0 is the same as true in C */   Examine frame for transmission error;
      {                                         if no transmission error
         Get packet from the user;              {
         Put packet into a frame;                  ack.error=0;
      }                                            Extract packet from the frame;
      send(frame);                                 Give packet to the user;
      Wait for acknowledgment to arrive;        }
      receive(ack);                             else
      if ack.error                                 ack.error=1;
         damaged=1;                             send(ack);
      else                                    }
         damaged=0;                        }
   }
}

            Sender code                               Receiver code
```

the sender does not get new data from the user but resends the frame. If `damaged = 0`, the sender gets a new packet in the next pass and sends it.

As we have described it, stop-and-wait seems preferable to the unrestricted protocol. Still, it has some shortcomings:

- If the sender's frame is lost, the receiver never sends an acknowledgment, and the sender will wait forever.
- If the receiver's acknowledgment is lost, the same thing happens.
- If the acknowledgment is damaged, the sender may draw the wrong conclusion and make the protocol fail.
- The sender certainly does not overwhelm the receiver with too many frames, but perhaps it has gone to the other extreme. Both sender and receiver do a lot of waiting. It's analogous to a teacher giving an assignment one question at a time. The student takes the question home, works on it, brings it back to school, gives it to the teacher, waits for the teacher to grade it, gets another question, and does the same thing all over again. In some cases it would be far more efficient to take all the questions home, finish them, and return them the next day.

These observations need responses, and the next two sections provide them. Before discussing more complex protocols, however, let's introduce the notion of protocol efficiency.

PROTOCOL EFFICIENCY

We can measure efficiency in several ways. For example, how much buffer space does the protocol require? With the stop-and-wait protocol there is never more than one frame being sent at a time, so a buffer capacity of one frame is sufficient. With the unrestricted protocol they may arrive faster than the receiver can formally receive them. Therefore, they must be stored in the interim. The number stored depends on how fast they arrive and how quickly the receiver can dispense them. In any case, the stop-and-wait protocol requires less space and can be considered more efficient from that perspective.

Another useful measure is the **effective data rate.** It is the actual number of data bits (as opposed to the raw bit rate) sent per unit of time. To calculate the effective data rate, we divide the number of data bits sent (N) by the elapsed time between sending two frames.

Let's illustrate with an example. Assume the following definitions, with the numbers in parentheses to be used in the example:

R = bit rate (10 Mbps or 10 bits per μsec)

S = signal speed (200 meters per μsec)

D = distance between the sender and receiver (200 meters)

T = time to create one frame (1 μsec)

F = number of bits in a frame (200)

N = number of data bits in a frame (160)

A = number of bits in an acknowledgment (40)

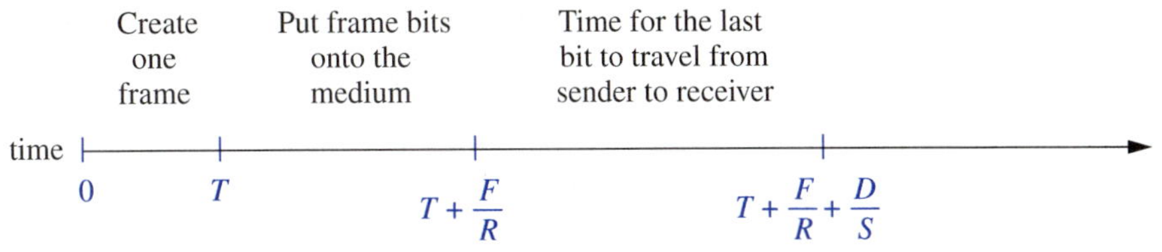

Create
one
frame

Put frame bits
onto the
medium

Time for the last
bit to travel from
sender to receiver

time

0   T $T + \dfrac{F}{R}$ $T + \dfrac{F}{R} + \dfrac{D}{S}$

Figure 8.6   Time Required to Send a Frame to Receiver

We begin by determining the amount of time needed to construct and send a frame (Figure 8.6). Assume the sender begins at time zero. The sender will have gotten information and put it into a frame at time T. The next step is to transmit the frame. Since R is the bit rate, then $1/R$ is the time needed to transmit one bit. Therefore, F/R is the time needed to transmit one frame. The total time used so far is $T + F/R$.

Once the sender has transmitted the frame, the bits require time to travel to the receiver. The travel time is D/S. Thus, after the last bit is transmitted, it requires another D/S time units to reach the receiver. Therefore, the receiver receives the last bit at time $= T + F/R + D/S$. Note that the amount of time a frame is in transit is $F/R + D/S$.

For the stop-and-wait protocol, the receiver must send an acknowledgment. A similar argument shows that the time required for the sender to receive the acknowledgment is $T + A/R + D/S$.*

Next question: How much time elapses between sending two data frames? With the unrestricted protocol, the sender starts building the next frame as soon as it has transmitted the last bit from the previous one. With stop-and-wait, the sender must wait for each acknowledgment. Therefore, the elapsed time between sending two consecutive frames is

$$\text{time} = T + \frac{F}{R} \tag{8-1}$$

for the unrestricted protocol and

$$\text{time} = \left(T + \frac{F}{R} + \frac{D}{S} \right) + \left(T + \frac{A}{R} + \frac{D}{S} \right)$$

$$= 2\left(T + \frac{D}{S} \right) + \frac{F + A}{R} \tag{8-2}$$

for the stop-and-wait protocol.[†]

---

* Strictly speaking, the amount of time needed for the receiver to construct the acknowledgment frame is different from T. However, specifics depend on CPU speed, the efficiency of the compiled code, and software scheduling. To simplify matters, we just assume both the sender and receiver can construct a frame in the same amount of time.

[†] This assumes that the receiver sends the acknowledgment as soon as it receives the frame. That is not always the case.

Thus, dividing the number of data bits by the elapsed time between two frames yields

$$\text{effective data rate (unrestricted protocol)} = \frac{N}{T + \dfrac{F}{R}}$$

$$= \frac{160 \text{ bits}}{1\ \mu\sec + \dfrac{200 \text{ bits}}{10 \text{ bits}/\mu\sec}} \tag{8-3}$$

$$\approx 7.6 \text{ bits}/\mu\sec = 7.6 \text{ Mbps}$$

and

$$\text{effective data rate (stop and wait protocol)} = \frac{N}{2\left(T + \dfrac{D}{S}\right) + \dfrac{F + A}{R}}$$

$$= \frac{160 \text{ bits}}{2\left(1\ \mu\sec + \dfrac{200 \text{ meters}}{200 \text{ meters}/\mu\sec}\right) + \dfrac{200 \text{ bits} + 40 \text{ bits}}{10 \text{ bits}/\mu\sec}} \tag{8-4}$$

$$\approx 5.7 \text{ bits}/\mu\sec = 5.7 \text{ Mbps}$$

It is important to note that raw bit rate capacity does not guarantee that much data will be moved. In this example, the stop-and-wait protocol realizes only about 57% of the raw bit rate. The effective data rate depends very much on the protocols, frame sizes, distance traveled, and so on. For example, increasing the frame size will increase the effective data rates (assuming there is a proportionate increase in the frame's data bits). This may not be obvious from the previous equations, but try it and see what happens. Can you determine what effect increases in the other variables will have on the effective data rate?

These measures provide only part of the total picture, and we make no claim that the unrestricted protocol is better just because its effective data rate is higher. Other factors to consider are the users the protocols serve, the amount of data to transfer, and the fact that others share the medium. The fact is that these two protocols represent two extremes (send everything at once and send one frame at a time), and some commonly used protocols fall somewhere in between. The next two sections discuss two of them.

8.4   GO-BACK-*n*: A SLIDING WINDOW PROTOCOL

The previous protocols work reasonably well if the number of frames and the distance between devices are not large. If the number of frames becomes large, the unrestricted protocol can flood the medium and overwhelm the receiver. Equation 8.4 shows what happens with the stop-and-wait protocol if the distance increases. The *D* in the denominator forces the effective data rate to decrease. In theory, choosing *D* large enough makes the rate arbitrarily small.

Because communications often occur over large distances and involve large amounts of data, alternative protocols are needed. One approach is a compromise between the unrestricted and stop-and-wait protocols called a **sliding window protocol.** It numbers the frames to be sent and defines a **window** as a subset of consecutive frames. If the window contains i frames numbered starting with w (w and i are integers), then the following statements are true (Figure 8.7):

- Every frame numbered less than w has been sent and acknowledged.
- No frame numbered greater than or equal to $w + i$ has been sent.
- Any frame in the window has been sent but may not yet have been acknowledged. Those not yet acknowledged are **outstanding frames.**

Initially, the window contains frames starting with frame 0. As the user provides packets, the window expands to include new frames, which then are sent. A limit on the window's size, however, limits the number of outstanding frames. When the limit is reached, the sender takes no more packets from the user. As outstanding frames are acknowledged, the window shrinks to exclude acknowledged frames. Subsequent to this the window can expand again to include more new frames to send.

As the window changes, the previous conditions must always be met and the window must always contain frames numbered consecutively. For example, if frame $w + 1$ is acknowledged but frame w is not, the window will not change until frame w is acknowledged. Even if every frame was acknowledged except frame w, the window will not change. Frames are excluded from the window in the same order in which they were included.

This approach is a compromise because it allows multiple (but not necessarily all) frames to be sent before receiving acknowledgments for each. The maximum window size defines the number of frames that may be outstanding. If the window

Figure 8.7   A Sliding Window Protocol

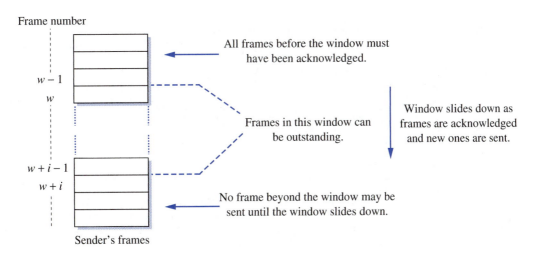

size is 1, we have essentially the stop-and-wait protocol. If the window size is greater than the total number of frames, we have essentially the unrestricted protocol. Adjusting the window size can help control the traffic on a network and change the buffering requirements.

There are two common implementations of a sliding window protocol. The **go-back-*n* protocol** requires frames to be received in the same order they are sent.* The **selective repeat protocol** (discussed in the next section) does not. Go-back-*n* is simpler because the receiver rejects every frame except the one it is supposed to receive. Selective repeat requires the receiver to be able to hold onto frames received out of order before passing them on to a higher layer in the correct order.

FRAME FORMAT

With these protocols we drop a previous assumption and eliminate the sharp distinction between sender and receiver. That is, we assume a more realistic model in which two devices (A and B) are sending to (and receiving from) each other (Figure 8.8). This is a conversational or full-duplex mode of communication. Thus the protocol must be able to not only send frames but receive them as well.

Let's review briefly what a frame actually contains. Figure 8.9 shows typical fields. We will see some specific formats in later chapters. The frame fields are as follows:

- **Source Address.** This is the address of the device sending the frame. It is often needed so that a device receiving a frame knows where to send an acknowledgment.

- **Destination Address.** This is the address where the frame should be sent. It is needed so that a device can determine which frames are destined for it.

- **Frame Number.** Each frame has a sequence number starting with 0. If this field has K bits, the largest number is $2^K - 1$. More than 2^K frames causes complications, which we discuss shortly.

Figure 8.8   Two-Way Communication between Devices A and B

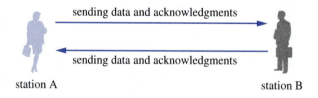

station A   station B

_____

* The reason frames can arrive out of order varies. It is a lot like the post office. The letter you mailed on Monday will probably arrive before the one you mail on Tuesday, but don't bet your retirement pension on it. Heavy traffic, hardware or software failures, and damaged frames can all contribute to delaying or even losing a frame.

- **ACK.** The integer value of this frame is the number of a frame being acknowledged. Note that because a device both sends and receives, it can avoid sending a separate acknowledgment by including the acknowledgment in a data frame. This is called **piggybacking.**

- **Type of Frame.** This field specifies the type of frame. For example, a data frame has type "data." However, there may be occasion to acknowledge a frame separately. Piggybacking can be used only when there is data to send; without data, the protocol uses separate acknowledgments using a frame of type "ACK." We also use a type "NAK" (negative acknowledgment) for problem situations. For example, the protocol sends a NAK frame when a received frame is damaged or if the wrong one has arrived. In either case, the protocol is letting the other device know something went wrong.

- **Data.** This represents the information in a data frame.

- **CRC.** This corresponds to the bits used for error checking (see Section 6.3).

FEATURES

The go-back-*n* protocol has several identifying features:

- Frame numbers must lie between 0 and $2^K - 1$ (K = number of bits in the Number field), inclusive. If there are more than 2^K frames, frame numbers are duplicated. For example, suppose $K = 6$ and there are more than 64 frames to send. Frames 0 through 63 are numbered 0 through 63. However, frames 64 through 127 are also numbered 0 through 63. In general, frames are all numbered consecutively modulo 2^K. We will see that this feature puts restrictions on the window size to allow the devices to correctly interpret the frame numbers.

    This also requires a slight adjustment in how we define a window. We still require that the window contain frames numbered consecutively.* However, we now consider 0 as the next frame number after $2^K - 1$. For example, if $K = 6$, then frames numbered 62, 63, 0, 1, 2, and so on are consecutive modulo $2^6 = 64$.

- The receiving device always expects to receive frames in order (modulo 2^K) of frame number. If it receives one out of order, it ignores the frame and sends a NAK for the frame it expected. It then waits until the correct one arrives.

Figure 8.9   Typical Frame Format

Source	Destination	Number	ACK	Type	...Data...	CRC

---

* From this point on, when we refer to a *frame number*, we mean the value that appears in the Number field of the frame.

- If a frame arrives and is damaged, the receiving device ignores it and sends a NAK for it.

- A receiving device does not acknowledge each received frame explicitly. If a sending device receives an acknowledgment for frame j and later receives one for frame k ($k > j$), it assumes all frames between j and k have been received correctly. This reduces the number of acknowledgments and lessens network traffic. Of course, the device sending the acknowledgments must make sure the assumption is valid.

- A device uses the piggyback approach whenever possible to acknowledge the most recently received frame. However, if no data frames are sent during a period of time, the device sends a separate acknowledgment frame. An **ACK timer** is set whenever a data frame arrives. The ACK timer counts down and stops only when the device sends something. The rationale is that when a data frame arrives it should be acknowledged within a period of time defined by the ACK timer. If there are no outgoing frames, the timer continues to count down to 0. If the timer reaches 0 (expires), the device sends a separate acknowledgment frame in lieu of the piggyback acknowledgment. If the device sends a frame as the timer counts down, the timer stops because an acknowledgment goes with the frame.

- The sending device buffers the packets from all frames in the window in the event it has to resend them. Packets are removed from the buffer as they are acknowledged.

- If a device does not receive an acknowledgment for a period of time, it assumes something went wrong and that one or more outstanding frames did not reach their destination. It then uses a **frame timer,** one for each frame, which is set whenever a data frame is sent. The frame timer counts down and stops only when the associated frame is acknowledged. If the frame timer expires, the protocol resends every frame in the window.

  The rationale for sending all outstanding frames is that the receiving device rejects any frame with the wrong number. If the receiving device got the first frame in the window, the sending device should have received an acknowledgment. Not getting one, the sending device assumes something happened to it. It also reasons that since the receiving device did not get the first frame, it would have rejected all subsequent frames. Thus, all frames must be resent. If there are n frames, it goes back to the beginning of the window to resend them. Hence the term go-back-n.

How many frames can the sending protocol have outstanding at one time? In other words, what is the maximum window size? If frames are numbered between 0 and $2^K - 1$, the window size can be no larger than 2^K. If it were, there would be more than 2^K frames outstanding. Consequently, there will be two different outstanding frames with the same number. When the sending device receives an acknowledgment for that number, it has no way of telling which of the two frames is actually being acknowledged. For example, suppose $K = 3$ and the first nine frames are outstanding. The first eight frames are numbered 0 through 7. The last one is numbered 0. If the sending device receives an acknowledgment for frame 0, it does not know if it corresponds to the first or the last frame.

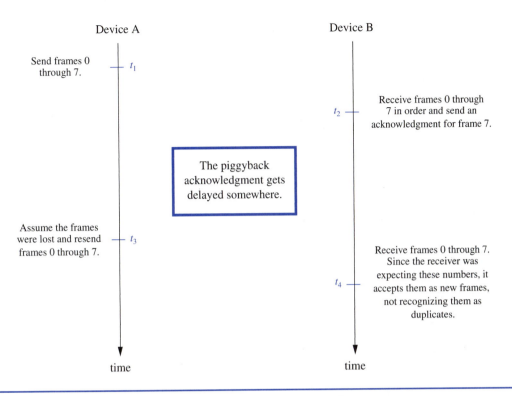

Device A   Device B

Send frames 0 —— t_1
through 7.

                                                                 Receive frames 0 through
                                                    t_2 ——   7 in order and send an
                                                                 acknowledgment for frame 7.

> The piggyback
> acknowledgment gets
> delayed somewhere.

Assume the frames
were lost and resend —— t_3
frames 0 through 7.   Receive frames 0 through 7.
                                                                 Since the receiver was
                                                                 expecting these numbers, it
                                                    t_4 ——   accepts them as new frames,
                                                                 not recognizing them as
                                                                 duplicates.

time   time

Figure 8.10   Protocol Failure when Window Size Equals 2^K

From this, we conclude that the window size must be less than or equal to 2^K. However, if the window size is equal to 2^K, an unfortunate sequence of events still can make the protocol fail. Suppose $K = 3$, and consider the events shown in Figure 8.10. Assume both devices have been exchanging frames prior to time t_1. At time t_1 device A sends frames 0 through 7 to device B. Device B receives each of them in the correct order and at time t_2 sends an acknowledgment for the most recent one received, number 7. Unfortunately, this acknowledgment gets lost because of a hardware or software error somewhere or a hungry gremlin with a voracious appetite for frames.

Device B has no way of knowing the acknowledgment was lost and is waiting for the frame after frame 7 (frame 0). Device A, on the other hand, does not receive the acknowledgment and does not know whether the frames arrived or not. Following the protocol, it resends frames 0 through 7 at time t_3. At time t_4 device B receives frame 0. The problem is that this frame 0 is a duplicate of the previous frame 0. But device B is expecting a new frame 0 and has no way of knowing it has received a duplicate. It therefore accepts the duplicate as a new frame, and the protocol fails.

The problem occurs because two consecutive windows contain the same frame numbers. Device B had no way of knowing which window frame 0 was in. Reducing the window size by 1 corrects this problem. Figure 8.11 shows what happens if similar events happen with the reduced window size. Here, device A sends frames 0 through 6

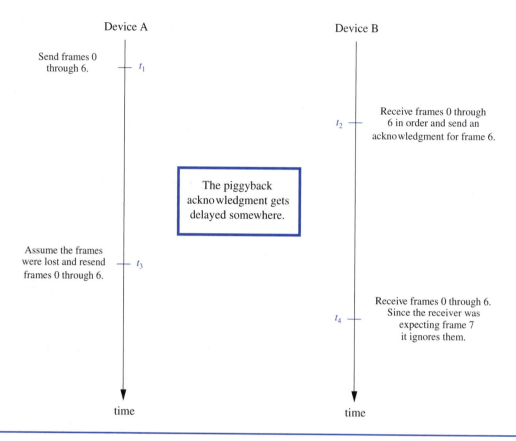

Device A

Device B

Send frames 0 through 6. — t_1

t_2 — Receive frames 0 through 6 in order and send an acknowledgment for frame 6.

The piggyback acknowledgment gets delayed somewhere.

Assume the frames were lost and resend frames 0 through 6. — t_3

t_4 — Receive frames 0 through 6. Since the receiver was expecting frame 7 it ignores them.

time

time

Figure 8.11 Protocol Success When Window Size Equals $2^K - 1$

at time t_1 and device B receives them all. At time t_2 device B acknowledges frame 6, and the acknowledgment gets lost. The difference now is that device B is expecting to receive frame 7. When device A resends frames 0 through 6 (at time t_3), they arrive at B at time t_4. Since they are not what B is expecting, B ignores them. Eventually B sends another acknowledgment, which A receives (we hope).* Device A advances its window to include frame 7, and the protocol continues. From this, we conclude that the window size must be strictly less than 2^K or the go-back-n protocol can fail.

ALGORITHM

We are finally ready to present a more detailed description of the go-back-n protocol. Figure 8.12 shows a partially coded C program containing the logic and variable names. Figure 8.7 should also help you understand the use of protocol variables w

---

* We have not yet explained how we know B sends another acknowledgment. When we discuss specifics of the algorithm, we will describe how the protocol guarantees the acknowledgment.

```
#define MAX=2ᴷ;                      /* K = number of bits in the
                                          frame.number field */

#define N=MAX−1;                      /* N is the maximum window size and largest frame
                                          number */

#define increment(x) x=(x+1) % MAX;   /* Increment x modulo MAX */
void go_back_N;
{
   int w=0;                           /* First position in the window */
   int i=0;                           /* Current size of window */
   int last=N;                        /* Frame number of last data frame received */
   packettype buffer[MAX];            /* Packet buffers */
   while (the earth rotates on its axis)
   {
      wait for an event;
      if (event is "packet from user") && (i<N)
      {                               /* If frame fits in the window, send it */
      get packet from the user and store in buffer[(w+i) % MAX];
      construct frame with frame.ack=last, frame.type=data, and frame.number=(w+i) % MAX;
      send frame;
      reset frametimer(frame.number);  /* Define timer for expected ACK of this frame*/
      stop acktimer;                   /* Stop ACK timer since an ACK is piggybacked */
      i++;                             /* Increase window size by 1 */
      continue;                        /* Skip to the end of the while loop */
      }
      if (event is "expired acktimer")
      {                                /*No frames have been sent in a while. Send a
                                          special ACK frame */
         Construct and send a frame with frame.type=ack and frame.ack=last;
         continue;
      }
      if (event is "expired frametimer")
      {                                /* Have not received an ACK in a while; resend all
                                          frames in the window */
         for (j=w; j is "between" w and (w+i−1) % MAX; increment(j) )
         {
            construct and send a data frame as before with packet from buffer [j];
            reset frametimer(j);       /* Start timer for expected ACK of this frame*/
         }
stop acktimer;                         /* Stop ACK timer; an ACK is piggybacked */
continue;
      }
      if (event is "damaged frame arrives")
      {
            Construct a frame with frame.type=nak and frame.ack=last and send it;
            stop acktimer;             /* Stop ACK timer; an ACK is being sent */
            continue;
      }
      if (event is "undamaged frame arrives")
      {                                /* Remove all frames "between" w and frame.ack
                                          from window */
            receive(frame);
            for (j=w; j is "between" w and frame.ack; increment(j) )
```

Figure 8.12 Go-back-*n* Protocol

```
{
    i--;
    stop frametimer(j);          /* Stop frame timer; the ACK has been received */
}
w=(frame.ack+1) % MAX;
if (frame.type==data) && (frame.number==((last+1) % MAX))
{                                /* If data frame is received in sequence,
                                    pass it to the patron */
                                 /* Ignore any frame received out of sequence */
    increment(last);
    extract packet from the frame and give it to the user;
    if acktimer not active then
        reset acktimer;          /* Start ACK timer for the frame being accepted */
    continue;
}
if (frame.type == nak)
{                                /* resend all buffered packets */
    for (j=w; j is "between" w and (w+i-1) % MAX; increment(j) )
    {
        construct and send a data frame as before with packet from buffer[j];
        reset frametimer(j);     /* Start timer for expected ACK of this frame*/
    }
    stop acktimer;               /* Stop ACK timer; an ACK is piggybacked */
    continue;
}
if (frame.type==data) && (frame.number!=(last+1) % MAX)
{                                /* Send a NAK for the frame that was expected */
    construct and send a frame with the frame.type=nak and frame.ack=last;
    stop acktimer;               /* Stop ACK timer; an ACK is piggybacked */
}
}                                /* end of "undamaged frame arrives" event */
}                                /* end of while loop */
}                                /* end of go_back_N */
```

Figure 8.12 Continued

and *i*. As before, we make no attempt to be syntactically correct or worry about whether the code compiles correctly. The intent is to describe how the protocol works without becoming mired in language-specific details. The important thing to remember is that both devices are running a copy of the algorithm as they exchange frames. That is, each device responds to events that correspond to it sending and receiving frames. Read the following discussion and algorithm carefully and slowly; the algorithm is complex.

The algorithm consists of a loop controlled by a condition that should remain for a very long time. If this condition becomes false, protocol failure is of little consequence by comparison. As the algorithm loops, it responds to events as they occur. If multiple events have occurred during one pass of a loop, the algorithm chooses one randomly and responds to it. We do not care how it chooses—that is system dependent. Presumably, it will respond to the other events with subsequent passes of the loop.

With each pass through the loop, the device waits for an event to occur. The five events and the protocol's responses are as follows:

1. The user has delivered a packet. If the window size (i) is its maximum value (N), nothing happens and the event remains pending until the window size decreases. If the window size is less than N, the protocol builds a data frame containing the packet. It also defines a piggyback acknowledgment of the last frame sent (`frame.ack = last`) and specifies the frame number (`frame.number = (w + i) % MAX` where `MAX` $=2^K$). The expression `(w + i) % MAX` also defines which buffer the packet is stored in. After buffering the packet and sending the frame, it increments the window size by 1 (`i++`) and resets the corresponding frame timer. It also stops the ACK timer. The ACK timer, as explained previously, detects long periods of time during which no frames are sent. Since one is sent, the ACK timer is stopped. The frame timer is meant to detect a long period of time during which the specified frame is not acknowledged. By resetting a timer, we begin the countdown.*

2. An ACK timer has expired. When no data frames are sent, the other device does not receive any piggybacked acknowledgments. In order to keep the other device aware of what the current device is receiving, the protocol sends a special acknowledgment frame when the ACK timer expires. Its sole purpose is to acknowledge the most recently received frame (`frame.ack = last`).

3. A frame timer has expired. If the protocol has not received an acknowledgment in a while, something may have gone wrong. Perhaps the acknowledgments were lost or the frames in the current window were lost. Since the protocol does not know which, it assumes the worst and resends all the frames in the window ("between"† buffer slots `w` and `(w + i - 1) %MAX`). It also resets each of the frame timers in order to provide enough time for the newly sent frames to get to their destinations and for an acknowledgment to return before assuming another error occurred. Last, it stops the ACK timer because a piggybacked acknowledgment is also being sent.

4. A damaged frame arrives. A damaged frame is ignored. If the damaged frame was the expected one, the protocol eventually will ignore all subsequently numbered frames. The protocol therefore must notify the other device that a problem occurred so it can resend all of its buffered frames. The protocol does

---

* How timers are implemented is not pertinent to our discussion. There could be an internal interrupting clock, or the protocol could just build a list of records for each timer, timestamp each record, and check the list periodically. We leave the details to someone who is willing to implement the protocol as a programming exercise.

† We define "between" w and $(w + i - 1)$ % MAX in a modulo MAX sense. If $w \leq (w + i - 1)$ % MAX, "between" has its conventional meaning. If $w \geq (w + i - 1)$ % MAX, "between" includes those numbers from w through MAX $- 1$ and 0 through $(w + i - 1)$ % MAX. For example, suppose MAX = 16. If $w = 3$ and $(w + i - 1)$ % 16 = 12, "between" means values from 3 through 12, inclusive. If $w = 12$ and $(w + i - 1)$ % 16 = 3, "between" means values 12, 13, 14, 15, 0, 1, 2, and 3.

this by sending a frame of type NAK. The device also ACKs the last frame it did receive correctly and stops the ACK timer.

5. An undamaged frame arrives. This is the most complex part of the protocol. The first thing the protocol does is receive the frame. Then it checks the piggyback acknowledgment and removes all frames that have been acknowledged from the window. It does this by decreasing the window size by 1 for each frame "between" w and `frame.ack`. It also stops the frame timers for the acknowledged frames. It then redefines the beginning of the window (w) to locate the first frame not acknowledged: `(frame.ack + 1) % MAX`.

If the frame contains data, the protocol determines whether it has the expected number, `((last + 1) % MAX)`. Remember, the variable `last` represents the most recently received frame. Thus, the number after it is the one expected. If the received frame is the expected one, the protocol extracts the packet and gives it to the user. It also increments the value of last, thus remembering the new frame most recently received. Then it sets the ACK timer, defining the time during which it should send an acknowledgment.

If the frame is a NAK frame, the protocol resends all frames in the window as it did with the expired frame timer event. If the frame is a data frame, but not the one expected, the protocol ignores it but sends a NAK frame.

8.5 SELECTIVE REPEAT: A SLIDING WINDOW PROTOCOL

The go-back-*n* protocol works well, especially over reliable media. When frames are rarely lost, damaged, or delayed, the assumption that they arrive in the order they were sent is usually valid. In the few cases where there is a problem, resending all outstanding frames loses little time. As the reliability decreases, however, the overhead of resending all frames in a window when just one is damaged or arrives out of order becomes excessive. A logical question to ask is this: Why not allow the receiving device to receive frames out of order and sort them when they all arrive? This question is answered by another sliding window protocol called *selective repeat*.

FEATURES

The selective repeat protocol is similar to go-back-*n* in the following ways:

- Frame formats are similar, and frames are numbered using a *K*-bit field (see Figure 8.9).

- The sender has a window defining the maximum number of outstanding frames.

- The selective repeat protocol uses piggybacked acknowledgments where possible and does not acknowledge every frame explicitly. If a frame is acknowledged, the sending device assumes that all prior ones have also been received.

- The protocol uses NAKs for damaged frames and frames received out of order.

- It uses timers to send special acknowledgment frames during periods of low traffic and to resend frames that have not been acknowledged for a while.

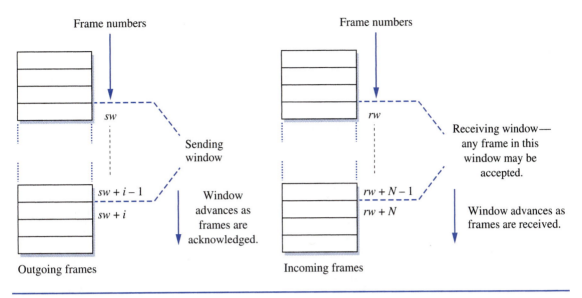

Figure 8.13   Sending and Receiving Windows for Selective Repeat Protocol

The similarities end here. Probably the most apparent difference is that the selective repeat protocol defines two windows, one each for the sending and receiving parts of the protocol (Figure 8.13). Thus, each device using a selective repeat protocol has both a sending and a receiving window. The sending window is the same as for the go-back-*n* protocol. It defines which frames may be outstanding.

The receiving window defines which frames can be received. As with the sending window, frames in the receiving window are numbered consecutively (modulo 2^K, where K = number of bits used for the frame number). Thus, the receiving device is not required to receive frames in order. A frame arriving out of order can be received as long as it is in the window. However, you will recall that part of the protocol's responsibility is to deliver packets to its user in the proper order. Thus, the protocol needs a buffer for each frame in the window. Out-of-order frames are buffered until their predecessors arrive. Then the protocol can deliver them in the correct order.

Other differences between selective repeat and go-back-*n* are listed here, along with the former protocol's responses.

- If an arriving frame is in the receiving window, it is buffered. However, it is not given to the user until all of its predecessors (within the window limits) have also arrived. Thus, whenever a frame is buffered, the protocol checks the window slots prior to the new arrival. If they all contain packets, the protocol delivers them to the user and advances the window.

- Whenever an out-of-order frame is received, the protocol sends a NAK for the frame it was expecting. The rationale is that an out-of-order frame signals that something may have happened to the one expected frame. The NAK notifies the sender of a possible loss. Remember, though, that as long as the received frame is in the window, it is still accepted.

- If a frame timer expires, only the timed-out frame is resent. With go-back-n, all outstanding frames are resent. With selective repeat, the receiving device may have received the other frames, and unless they also time out, there is no need to resend them.

- If the protocol receives a NAK, it resends just the frame specified by the NAK. Go-back-n resends all outstanding frames. The rationale for sending just one frame is the same as that for a frame timer expiration.

- A piggyback acknowledgment doesn't necessarily acknowledge the frame most recently received. Instead, it acknowledges the frame immediately prior to the one at the beginning of the receiver's window (i.e., the last one delivered to the user). The rationale is that acknowledging the most recently received frame does not allow the sending device to conclude that prior frames have also been received. Remember, the most recent frame may have arrived out of order. Effectively that would force an acknowledgment for each frame. Acknowledging the last frame delivered to the user allows the sending device to conclude that prior frames have also been delivered and thus received. Again, the result is fewer overall acknowledgments.

With the go-back-n algorithm we saw that there were constraints on the window size. Specifically, the window size had to be strictly less than 2^K or the protocol could fail with certain events. Constraints also exist with the selective repeat protocol. Suppose the maximum sending window size and receiving window size are equal. In that case, the constraint is that both must be less than or equal to one-half of 2^K (i.e., 2^{K-1}).

To see what can happen otherwise, let's consider a couple of examples. In both examples we will use $K = 3$, so that $2^K = 8$. In the first example, suppose the sending window meets the constraint and has a maximum size of 4. But consider what happens if the receiving window is larger, say 5 (Figure 8.14).

At time t_1, device A sends the maximum number of frames, frames 0 through 3. Since device B has a window size of 5, it can accept any frame numbered between 0 and 4, inclusive. At time t_2, B receives frames 0 through 3. Because they are in the window, they are accepted and passed to the user. B then advances its window to include frames 4, 5, 6, 7, and 0.

Meanwhile, the acknowledgment that B sends is lost. Eventually A gets tired of waiting and assumes something went wrong. Consequently, as dictated by the protocol, A resends frames 0 through 3 (time t_3). Because frame 0 is in the receiving window, B accepts it (time t_4), not realizing it is a duplicate of the previous frame 0. The protocol fails.

Similar problems can occur if the receiving window size meets the constraint but the sending window does not. For example, suppose this time that A's window size is 5 and B's window size is 4 (Figure 8.15). At time t_1, A sends frames 0 through 4. Since B's window size is 4, it can accept only frames 0 through 3. But

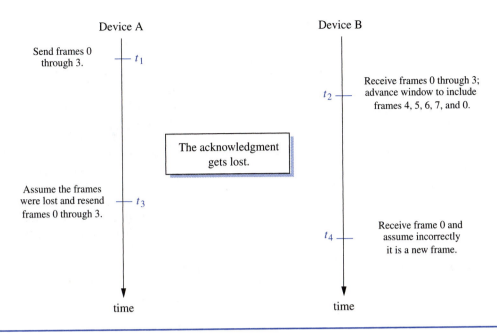

Figure 8.14 Protocol Failure: Receiving Window Size Is Greater Than 2^{K-1}

Figure 8.15 Protocol Failure: Sending Window Size Is Greater Than 2^{K-1}

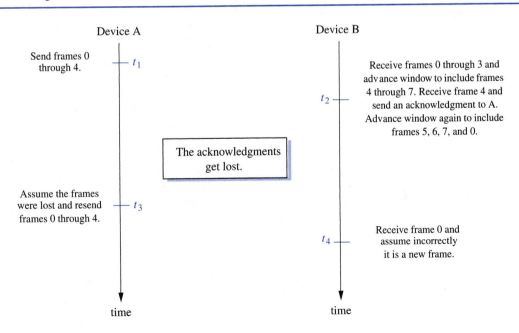

suppose frame 4 was delayed. Meanwhile frames 0 through 3 arrive and are accepted (time t_2). B advances its window to include frames 4 through 7.

When frame 4 eventually arrives, it is within the new window and is accepted. The window advances again and now includes frames 5, 6, 7, and 0. At this point B sends something to A with the acknowledgments piggybacked. The same mysterious gremlin that ate the previous acknowledgments is insatiable and gets another one. Again, A gets tired of waiting and resends frames 0 through 4 (time t_3). The frames finally get through (the gremlin is resting from its lunch) and because frame 0 is within the receiving window, it is accepted (time t_4). Again, B does not recognize that it is a duplicate of the previous frame 0, and the protocol fails.

Each of these problems can be corrected by making both window sizes equal to 4. In fact, these problems could have been eliminated by using window sizes of 5 and 3 instead of 5 and 4 (or 3 and 5 instead of 4 and 5). The problem occurs when the receiving window advances to the point of including new frame numbers still in the sending window. This can happen when the two sizes sum to a value larger than 2^K (the number of distinct frame numbers). By reducing the window sizes so that this won't happen, we eliminate that type of problem. Typically, the window sizes are the same (2^{K-1}).

ALGORITHM

Figure 8.16 contains a partially C-coded algorithm for the selective repeat protocol. It is designed similarly to the go-back-n protocol in that it loops continuously, responding to events as they occur. Both sending and receiving windows have size $N = 2^{K-1}$.

The algorithm has a few additional variables that the go-back-n algorithm does not have. In addition to the sending buffer (sbuffer) there is a receiving buffer (rbuffer). Since each window size is N, both buffers are defined as packet arrays with N elements. This generates another difference from the go-back-n algorithm. With go-back-n the packets are stored in buffer slots subscripted by the frame number. Here there are twice as many frame numbers as buffer slots. To avoid using an excessive number of buffers, the buffer subscript is equal to the frame number modulo N.

Another variable not present in the previous algorithm is the status array. Since arriving frames can be buffered in random order, we use the status array to determine whether a buffer slot is empty. A value of status[i] = 1 means buffer number i contains a packet. A value of 0 means it does not.

As the algorithm loops continuously, it responds to events. We list the events and the protocol's response here. Because of the similarities to the go-back-n protocol, we will not discuss each step in detail. We will concentrate only on those parts that differ from go-back-n.

1. The user has delivered a packet. The protocol responds much as the go-back-n protocol does. If the sending window size is its maximum value, nothing happens. Otherwise, it buffers the packet, builds a frame, and sends it. It also piggybacks an acknowledgment for the frame prior to the one in the beginning of the receiving window (frame.ack = prior(rw)). The macro named

```
#define MAX=2ᵏ;                         /* K = number of bits in the frame.number field */
#define N=MAX/2;                         /* N = maximum sending window size, actual
                                            receiving window size, and number of buffers */

#define increment(x) x=(x+1) % MAX;      /* Increment x modulo N */
#define prior (x) (x==0 ? MAX-1 : x-1)   /* Return integer prior to x modulo N */
void selective_repeat;
{
   int frame_no=0;                       /* Maintain frame numbers of outgoing frames */
   int sw=0;                             /* First position in sender's window */
   int rw=0;                             /* First position in receiver's window */
   int i=0;                              /* Current size of sender's window */
   packettype sbuffer[N];                /* Sender's packet buffers */
   packettype rbuffer [N];               /* Receiver's packet buffers */
   int status[N];                        /* Status of frame in receiving window. 1 means it
                                            arrived; 0 means it has not */

   while (Hades does not freeze over)
    {
      wait for an event;
      if (event is "packet from user") && (i<N)
       {                                 /* If frame fits in window, send it */
         Get packet from the user and store it in sbuffer[(sw+i) % N];
         construct frame with frame.ack=prior(rw), frame.type=data, and
           frame.number=frame_no;
         send frame;
         increment(frame_no);            /* Define number of next outgoing frame */
         rest frametimer(frame.number);  /* Start timer for expected ACK of this frame */
         stop acktimer;                  /* Stop ACK timer; an ACK is piggybacked */
         i++;                            /* Increase sending window size by 1 */
         continue;                       /* Skip to the end of the while loop */
       }
      if (event is "expired acktimer")
       {                                 /* No frames have been sent in a while. Send a
                                            special ACK frame */
         Construct and send a frame with frame.type=ack and frame.ack=prior(rw);
         continue;
       }
      if (event is "expired frametimer")
       {                                 /* Have not received an ACK in a while;
                                            resend frame */
         fn = frame number corresponding to the timer;
         construct and send as before a data frame with packet from sbuffer[fn % N];
         reset frametimer(fn);           /* Start timer for expected ACK of this frame */
         stop acktimer;                  /* Stop ACK timer; an ACK is being sent */
         continue;
       }
      if (event is "damaged frame arrives")
       {
         Construct a frame with frame.type=nak and with frame.ack=prior(rw); send it;
         stop acktimer;                  /* Stop ACK timer; an ACK is being sent */
         continue;
       }
      if (event is "undamaged frame arrives")
```

Figure 8.16   Selective Repeat Protocol

```
{                                     /* Remove all frames "between" sw and frame.ack from
                                         sender's windows */
    receive(frame);
    for (j=sw; j is "between" sw and frame.ack; increment(j) )
    {
      i--;
      stop frametimer(j);             /* Stop frame timer; the ACK has been received */
    }
    sw=(frame.ack+1) % MAX;
    if (frame.type==data) && (frame.number != rw)
{
    construct a frame with frame.type=nak and frame.ack=prior(rw) and send it;
    stop acktimer;                    /* Stop ACK timer; an ACK is being sent */
}
if (frame.type==data) && (frame.number is in the receiving window) &&
   (status[frame.number % N]==0)
{                                     /* If data frame is in the window and has not yet
                                         arrived, buffer it */
    extract packet from the frame and put in rbuffer[frame.number % N];
    status[frame.number % N]=1;
    for(;status[rw % N]==1; increment(rw) )
    {                                 /* Give received packets stored in consecutive
                                         window slots to the user */
      extract packet from rbuffer[rw % N] and give to user;
      status[rw % N]=0
    }
    reset acktimer;                   /* Start ACK timer for frames being accepted */
}
    if (frame.type == nak) && (framenum = (frame.ack+1) % MAX is in the sending window)
    {                                 /* Resend the frame the receiving station expected to
                                         receive */
      construct and send a frame with packet from sbuffer[framenum % N];
      reset frametimer(framenum% N); /* Start timer for expected ACK of this frame */
      stop acktimer;                  /* Stop ACK timer; an ACK is being piggybacked */
      continue;
    }
  }
 }
}
```

Figure 8.16 Continued

prior subtracts 1 modulo 2^K. Unlike the increment macro, it does not change the variable passed to it.

2. An ACK timer has expired. The protocol sends an ACK frame acknowledging the frame prior to the one in the beginning of the receiving window.

3. A frame timer has expired. Instead of resending every outstanding frame, the protocol sends only the frame corresponding to the expired timer. How the frame is determined depends on how the timers are implemented. As before, there could be an interrupt mechanism identifying the frame number or some list containing time values and frame numbers.

4. A damaged frame arrives. The protocol sends a NAK frame containing an acknowledgment for the frame prior to the one in the beginning of the receiving window.

5. An undamaged frame arrives. After receiving the frame, the protocol removes all frames that have been acknowledged from the window. If the frame contains data, the protocol checks to see if it arrived in order. In other words, is the frame number equal to the number corresponding to the beginning of the receiving window? If not, a NAK frame is sent back.

Next, the protocol checks two more conditions: Is the received frame in the window, and has its packet not yet been buffered? The packet may have been buffered already if the frame arrived previously but an ACK was late in getting back to the sending device. In that case the frame would have timed out and the protocol would have sent it again. By checking the value of `status[frame.number % N]`, we avoid the extra work of extracting a packet that is already buffered.

If both conditions are met, the packet is extracted and stored in the buffer. Next, the protocol determines whether it can advance the receiving window and deliver packets to the user. It does this by checking consecutive positions in the `status` array. It stops when it finds the first empty window slot.

Finally, if the frame is a NAK frame, the protocol examines the value in `frame.ack`. When a NAK is sent, the `frame.ack` field contains the number of the frame prior to the one in the beginning of the receiving window. This means something happened and the receiving protocol did not get the frame it expected (`(frame.ack + 1) % MAX`). If this frame is still in the sending window, the protocol must send it. (Can you construct a scenario in which this frame is not in the sending window?)

8.6   EFFICIENCY OF SLIDING WINDOW PROTOCOLS

Section 8.3 analyzed the unrestricted and stop-and-wait protocols and showed that the protocol can affect the amount of actual data transmitted per unit of time (effective data rate). We saw that the effective data rate also depended on raw bit rate, distance between devices, frame size, and other factors. A full-fledged analysis for sliding window protocols is much more difficult because other factors contribute to the effective data rate. Such factors include the rate at which frames are lost or damaged, the timer values used to determine when special ACK frames are sent, and the number of data frames in the reverse direction carrying piggybacked acknowledgments.

We will provide an analysis for sliding window protocols under certain assumptions. Specifically, we will assume that lost or damaged frames do not happen. We also assume consistent traffic in both directions to make the most use of piggybacked acknowledgments. The latter assumption allows us to ignore ACK timers because they won't be used. If you are interested in a more complete analysis of sliding window protocols, see references [Ta96] and [Wa91].

All things being equal, a sliding window's effective data rate should lie between that of the unrestricted and stop-and-wait protocols. But what effective rate can we expect from the sliding window protocols? How does the window size affect it?

Recall from Section 8.3 the following definitions and values used in the examples:

R = bit rate (10 Mbps or 10 bits per μsec)

S = signal speed (200 meters per μsec)

D = distance between the sender and receiver (200 meters)

T = time to create one frame (1 μsec)

F = number of bits in a frame (200)

N = number of data bits in a frame (160)

A = number of bits in an acknowledgment (40)

Let's add one definition to that list:

W = window size (4 frames)

To begin, we observe that two cases can occur with a sliding window protocol. The first is that the sender's window never reaches its maximum size. This will happen when the first acknowledgment arrives before all the frames in the window are sent. Once this happens, and assuming there are no delays at the other end, the sender never has to wait for an acknowledgment. In other words, old frames are removed from the window as fast as new ones are added to it. In effect, the sending protocol behaves just like the unrestricted protocol.

In the second case, when all W frames have been sent and the first acknowledgment has not yet arrived (Figure 8.17), the protocol must wait for it. When it does arrive the protocol then can send the next frame. If the acknowledgments arrive at the same rate that data frames are sent, W more frames are sent before the protocol must wait again. In other words, the protocol sends W frames, waits for the first acknowledgment, sends W more frames, waits for an acknowledgment, and so on. This protocol now resembles stop-and-wait. However, instead of sending and waiting for individual frames, it sends and waits for a window full of frames.

Mathematically, these two cases can be distinguished by comparing the time to send W frames with the time to send one frame and receive an acknowledgment. From Equation 8.1, the time to build and send one frame is $T + F/R$. Thus, the time to build and send W frames is $W \times (T + F/R)$. From Equation 8.2, the time to send a frame and receive an acknowledgment (assuming the acknowledgment comes back right away) is $2(T + D/S) + (F + A)/R = 2(T + D/S) + 2F/R = 2(T + D/S + F/R)$. In this equation we substituted F for A because acknowledgments arrive piggybacked on data frames (of size F) instead of via separate ACK frames (of size A).

Consequently, we have

$$\text{case 1 (unrestricted protocol): } W\left(T + \frac{F}{R}\right) > 2\left(T + \frac{D}{S} + \frac{F}{R}\right)$$

$$\text{case 2 (window−oriented stop−and−wait): } W\left(T + \frac{F}{R}\right) < 2\left(T + \frac{D}{S} + \frac{F}{R}\right)$$

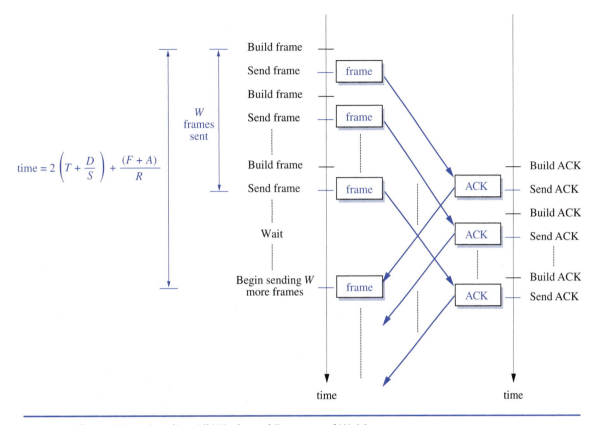

$$time = 2\left(T + \frac{D}{S}\right) + \frac{(F + A)}{R}$$

Figure 8.17   Sending All Windowed Frames and Waiting

In the first case, we have, from Equation 8.3,

$$\text{effective data rate} = \frac{N}{T + \dfrac{F}{R}} \quad \text{(unrestricted version)}$$

Because our sample values satisfy the condition of case 1, the effective data rate evaluates to

$$\frac{160 \text{ bits}}{1 \text{ μsec} + \dfrac{200 \text{ bits}}{10 \text{ bits/μsec}}} \approx 7.6 \text{ bits/μsec} = 7.6 \text{ Mbps}$$

The effective data rate for case 2 is derived from Equation 8.4. This equation was derived under the assumption that just one frame was sent. Because we now send W frames in the same amount of time, we replace N with $W \times N$. Remembering to replace A with F, we have

$$\text{effective data rate} = \frac{W \times N}{2\left(T + \dfrac{D}{S}\right) + \dfrac{2F}{R}} \quad \text{(window-oriented stop-and-wait protocol)}$$

Since our sample values do not satisfy the condition of case 2, using them in this equation would yield a nonsensical value. If we increase the distance (D) from 200 meters to 5000 meters, however, the values will satisfy the condition of case 2. Using these values, we have

$$\text{effective data rate} = \frac{4 \times 160 \text{ bits}}{2\left(1 \; \mu \text{ sec} + \dfrac{5000 \text{ meters}}{200 \text{ meters}/\mu \text{ sec}}\right) + \dfrac{2 \times 200 \text{ bits}}{10 \text{ bits}/\mu \text{ sec}}}$$

$$= 6.96 \; \mu \text{bps}$$

8.7 PROTOCOL CORRECTNESS

In the previous sections we presented some protocols and the conditions under which they seem to work correctly. Note that we say "seem to work." This uncertainty is necessary because we have not proved that they *do* work. Providing formal proof or verification that a protocol works is very difficult, and we leave such formal methods to courses in software engineering or advanced courses in protocol design. In this section we introduce two basic tools of verification.

FINITE STATE MACHINES

Much of what we perceive to be continuous or analog is, in fact, a collection of separate or discrete events. Perhaps the most common example is a motion picture. As we munch popcorn, sip sodas, or stretch our arms and yawn we view the action on the screen as a flowing or continuous movement. In reality, it is a rapid display of still pictures shown through a projector. This view allows us to see a movie in a new way as a collection of individual pictures. It is not the most desirable way to watch some of the classics, but it is precisely the way movie personnel such as special effects technicians must see a movie. They see a sequence of pictures to be spliced, cut, and altered to create the proper effect.

Computer algorithms also can be viewed as a sequence of "pictures." The computers that run them are digital devices. Their actions are controlled and synchronized by internal clocks and driven by the programs they run. Each clock pulse defines a new set of internal values and, for a brief period (the length of a clock pulse), nothing changes. In a sense, the entire architecture is frozen in time and the collection of internal values defines a picture of the **machine state.** With the next clock pulse they change, defining a new machine state. This process continues repeatedly, defining a sequence of machine states.

Similarly, we can view an algorithm as a sequence of states. Each state is defined in part by the values of program variables at an instant in time. In theory, we can categorize (list) all possible states and the events that cause a change from one state to another. The term **finite state machine** (sometimes *finite state model*) corresponds to this categorization. An event that causes a change of state is called a **state transition.**

Viewing an algorithm in this discrete way allows us to represent it through a directed graph called a **state transition diagram (STD).** Recall that a directed graph consists of a set of vertices and edges. Each vertex represents a state and usually is represented visually by a dot or circle. Each edge is an ordered pair of vertices and usually is represented visually by an arrow from the first vertex to the second. Through graph theory we can analyze the state transition diagram and draw conclusions regarding the reachability of certain states or possible sequences of events (transitions).

Figure 8.18 shows a state transition diagram. It has six different states, and the arrows show the possible transitions. For example, if the system is currently in state S_1, three different events could occur, one causing the system to move to state S_2, the others causing it to move to state S_4 or S_5.

By analyzing the graph, we can draw conclusions about the system it represents. For example, note that there are no edges pointing to S_1. This means there are no transitions to state S_1. If this graph represented an algorithm designed to respond to events, this observation could mean a flaw in the algorithm's logic. That is, the algorithm does not respond to any event that puts the system into state S_1. If this is in contrast to what we know about the system, we have detected a flaw.

This graph shows another potential problem. Suppose an event occurs that causes a transition to state S_5. It can respond only to events that cause it to move to state S_6. Once there, it can only go back to state S_5. In other words, once this model progresses to state S_5 or S_6, it will remain in one of those two states forever. This might correspond to an infinite loop or a **deadlock** (waiting for an event that will never happen). As before, this most likely represents a flaw in our algorithm.

STD FOR A SIMPLIFIED GO-BACK-*n* PROTOCOL

How can we apply this diagram to an actual protocol? First consider the go-back-*n* protocol with a sender window size of 1 and a 1-bit Frame Number field. Assume that no time-outs or transmission errors occur, all data go in one direction only (sender to receiver), and the receiver acknowledges each frame received. Essentially, it is the stop-and-wait protocol with frame numbers. The following events occur:

1. Send frame 0.

2. Receive frame 0; send ACK 0.

Figure 8.18   General State Transition Diagram

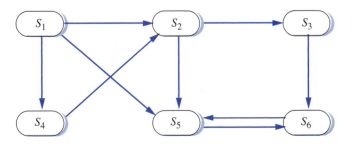

3. Receive ACK 0; send frame 1.

4. Receive frame 1; send ACK 1.

5. Receive ACK 1; send frame 0.

We can associate four distinct states with this protocol. They are labeled by ordered pairs (x, y) in Figure 8.19. The value of x is either 0 or 1 depending on the ACK number for which the sender is waiting. Similarly, y is either 0 or 1 depending on the frame number for which the receiver is waiting. Thus, state $(0, 0)$ means the sender has sent frame 0 and is expecting its acknowledgment. It also means the receiver is waiting for frame 0.

The arrival of frame 0 is an event that causes a transition from state $(0, 0)$ to $(0, 1)$. The receiver has received frame 0, sent its acknowledgment, and is now waiting for frame 1. However, the sender is still waiting for an acknowledgment to frame 0. When that acknowledgment arrives, the sender accepts it, sends frame 1 next, and begins waiting for its acknowledgment. This is state $(1, 1)$ because the receiver is still waiting for frame 1. The sending and receiving of frames and acknowledgments continues, and the states in Figure 8.19 occur in clockwise order.

An observant reader might ask: Aren't there really more states associated with this protocol? For example, there is a period of time after the sender receives the acknowledgment but before it sends its next frame. Shouldn't there be a state for which the sender is waiting for the user to provide a packet? Yes! In fact, we could go to the extreme and define a state corresponding to the execution of each step in the algorithm. But does it pay to do so?

Defining states is an important design issue. Ideally, we would like to define states that represent significant steps in a system's evolution and not worry about insignificant or trivial differences. But determining what is significant is often difficult and depends a great deal on what is being modeled. There are often many levels of refinements to which we can subject an STD. We will give an example showing how to do a refinement and how an STD can locate flaws in a system. Our purpose here, however, is only to introduce the concepts, and we will not provide elaborate STDs. If you are interested in more detail or a higher level of discussion, references [Ta96], [Wa91], [Li87], and [Ru89] can provide it.

Figure 8.19   STD for a Stop-and-Wait Protocol with Frame Numbers

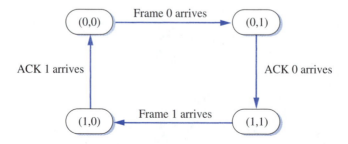

STATE TRANSITION DIAGRAM FOR A FAULTY GO-BACK-*n* PROTOCOL

Consider the previous version of the go-back-*n* protocol. This time we assume a window size of 2, which, according to Section 8.4, can fail. To help, Figure 8.20 shows the algorithm with the appropriate restrictions (e.g., the sender receives only ACKs or NAKs, the receiver receives only data, and frame numbers alternate between 0 and 1).

Figure 8.20   Go-back-*n* Protocol for One-Way Data Transfer (Window Size = 2)

```
void send_data;
{
#define increment(x) x=(x==0 ? 1 : 0);
int w=0;
int i=0;
packettype buffer[2];
while there are packets to send
{
   wait for an event;
   if (event is "packet from user") && (i<2)
   {
      get packet from the user and store in
        buffer[(w+i) % 2];
      construct and send frame with
        frame.number=(w+i) % 2;
      reset frametimer(frame.number);
      i++;
      continue;
   }

   if (event is "expired frametimer")
   {
      resend one or both frames in window;
      reset one or both frametimers;
      continue;

   }

   if (event is "undamaged frame arrives")
   {
      receive(frame);
      remove any acknowledged frames from
        window;
      decrement i by number of frames
        removed;
      stop frametimers for acknowledged
        frames;
      w=(frame.ack+1) % 2;
      if (frame.type == nak)
      {
         resend frames in the window;
         reset frametimers;
      }
   }
}
}
```

```
void receive_data;
{
#define increment(x) x=(x==0 ? 1 : 0);
int last=-1;
while there are packets to receive
{
   wait for an event;
   if (event is "damaged frame arrives")
   {
      Construct a frame with frame.type=nak
        and frame.ack=last and send it;
      stop acktimer;
      continue;

   }
   if (event is "undamaged frame arrives")
   {
      receive(frame);
      if (frame.number != last)
      {
         increment(last);
         extract packet from the frame and
           give it to the patron;
         if acktimer not active then reset
           acktimer;
         continue;
      }
   }
   if (frame.number == last)
   {
      construct and send a frame with the
        frame.type=nak and frame.ack=last;

      stop acktimer;

   }

   if (event is "expired acktimer")
   {
      Construct and send a frame with
        frame.type=ack and frame.ack=last;
      continue;
   }
}
}
```

Sender code   Receiver code

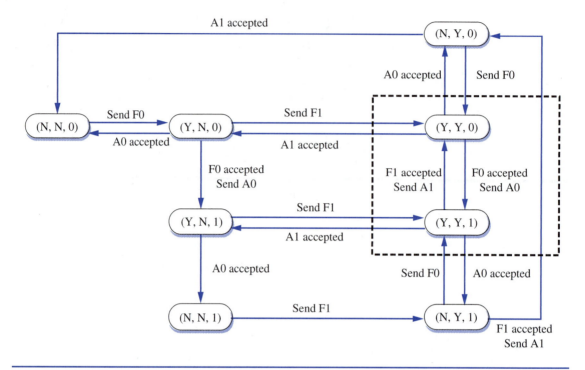

Figure 8.21   First-Approximation STD for Go-Back-*n* (Window Size = 2)

Figure 8.21 represents a first approximation to an STD showing some states and state transitions. In this case, we categorize each state by what the sender or receiver is waiting for. Specifically, we represent each state by an ordered triple (a, b, c) defined as follows:

- If the sender is waiting for an ACK to frame 0, then $a = Y$. Otherwise, $a = N$.
- If the sender is waiting for an ACK to frame 1, then $b = Y$. Otherwise, $b = N$.
- If the receiver is waiting for frame 0, then $c = 0$. Otherwise, $c = 1$.

For example, suppose the model is in state (N, N, 0). The sender is expecting no ACKs and the receiver is waiting for frame 0. If the sender sends frame 0, the model moves to state (Y, N, 0). The sender now expects an ACK for frame 0. While in this state, two other events can happen. The first is that the sender sends frame 1, in which case the model moves to state (Y, Y, 0). The other event is that frame 0 arrives and is accepted and the receiver sends an ACK. In this case the receiver now waits for the next frame and the state is (Y, N, 1).

You should take the time to follow some arrows and understand why the states change as shown. As you do so, you might find some anomalous events. For example, consider the following two ways to move from state (N, N, 0) to state (Y, Y, 0):

1. Send frames F0 and F1.
2. Send F0; F0 accepted and A0 sent; send F1; F1 accepted and A1 sent.

In the first case just one event can happen next: F0 arrives and is accepted. The other events shown (A0 and A1 accepted) cannot happen because neither acknowledgment has been sent yet. Similar reasoning shows that in the second case the only event that can occur next is that A0 or A1 is accepted. F0 cannot arrive because it has already done so. (We will assume that frames do not clone themselves as they travel, resulting in an invasion of an army of frames.) The point is that Figure 8.21 does not distinguish between cases 1 and 2 and shows events that may be impossible depending on how a state was reached.

The problem is that we have not refined our state definitions to accurately portray the system. One solution is to refine the state definitions to include the frames actually in transit, which will allow us to distinguish between the two cases (and others). It will also create additional states and state transitions and make the diagram more complex.

Figure 8.22 shows a partial refinement of the STD's boxed region from Figure 8.21. This refinement also shows how the STD can locate flaws in our design. We have further defined each state by specifying not only what the devices are waiting for but also what is actually in transit. We represent this by adding an ordered pair (x, y) to each state. Variable x defines which frames are actually in transit (0 for frame 0, 1 for frame 1, B for both, and N for neither). Similarly, y specifies which acknowledgment is in transit. For example, state $(Y, Y, 0) : (B, N)$ means the sender is waiting for an acknowledgment to frames 0 and 1 and that these frames are still in transit. The receiver is waiting for frame 0, and there are no acknowledgments in transit. We have also included additional events that cause state changes. (There are other events we have not shown, but these are sufficient for our needs.)

We next show how this refined model can expose a problem. Recall from your data structures course that a path through a graph is a list of nodes where every two adjacent nodes in the list are connected by an edge. In an STD, a path defines a sequence of events. The graph of Figure 8.22 shows a path (actually a cycle) in which

Figure 8.22   Partial Refinement of STD from Figure 8.21

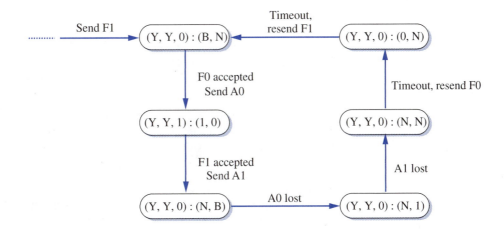

both (Y, Y, 0) and (Y, Y, 1) appear. Consider what happens if we follow the cycle repeatedly. This defines a sequence of events that causes the receiver to alternately expect and receive frames 0 and 1. However, none of the events corresponds to sending new frames (just resending old ones). This means the receiver repeatedly accepts new frames even though no new ones are being sent. That is, the receiver is accepting old frames as if they were new, just as we discussed in Section 8.4.

In general, STDs can be used to trace sequences of events and intermediate states. If a path exhibits state changes that should not occur given the events, there is a flaw in the model.

PETRI NETS

Like a finite state model, a **Petri net** uses a graph to represent states and transitions, but the way it does so is different. A Petri net consists of four parts:

1. **Places.** Represented visually by circles, places correspond to part of a state. This is one difference from the finite state model. Each vertex of an STD represents a complete state; with a Petri net, we may need several places to represent the complete state. We'll see an example shortly.

2. **Transitions.** Represented visually by a short horizontal or vertical line, transitions show movement between places.

3. **Arrows.** Arrows connect a place to a transition or vice versa. A place at the source of the arrow is called the *input place* of the transition to which the arrow points. Any place pointed to by the arrow is the *output place* of the transition at the arrow's source.

4. **Tokens.** Tokens, represented by heavy dots inside places, collectively define the current state of the system.

A Petri net can be represented by a graph. A graph vertex may be either a place or a transition, and an edge is an arrow. With STDs, state transitions are defined by moving from one vertex to another along an edge. With Petri nets, they are defined by the way tokens move from one place to another. Thus, the next step is to define the rules by which tokens can move:

- A transition is *enabled* if each of its input places contains a token.
- Any enabled transition can **fire.** That is, tokens are removed from each of the input places and tokens are stored in each of the output places. After firing, there may be more or fewer tokens, depending on the number of input places and output places.
- One transition fires at a time. If several transitions are enabled, however, the choice of transition is indeterminate. For our purposes, this means the choice is made arbitrarily. Because firing transitions will correspond to real events, we do not want rules to dictate the order in which they occur.

Figure 8.23a shows a Petri net just before firing. There are two transitions, T1 and T2, but only T1 is enabled (all of its input places have tokens). Figure 8.23b shows the Petri net after firing. The tokens are removed from each input place of

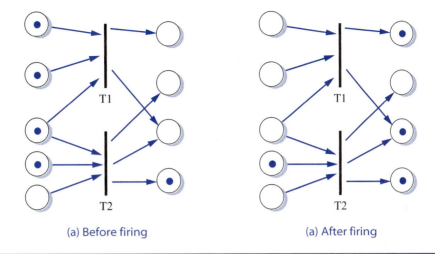

(a) Before firing   (a) After firing

Figure 8.23   Petri Net Before and After Firing

T1. Next, a token is put into each of the output places of T1. Other tokens in places associated with a different transition remain where they are.

Next, let's see how we can use a Petri net to model a protocol. The one we will use is the go-back-n protocol of Figure 8.20, changed to use a window of size 1. Figure 8.24 shows part of the Petri net for it. As before, we have left out some parts of the Petri net to simplify the diagram and our discussion.

Instead of trying to describe the state of the system in one vertex, we divide the system into its parts and represent the state of each. In this case, the system consists of a sender, receiver, and the medium between them. Thus, the system state depends on what the sender and receiver are waiting for and what is on the medium, just as with our previously refined STD. Specifically, the sender has two states, each represented by a place. The sender is waiting for an acknowledgment for frame 0 ("Wait for A0") or for frame 1 ("Wait for A1"). The receiver also has two states: waiting for frame 0 (F0) or frame 1 (F1). The four places in the middle correspond to what is on the medium. F0 and F1 are places corresponding to frame 0 or 1 being transmitted. A0 and A1 correspond to the acknowledgments for frame 0 or 1 being transmitted.

The tokens in Figure 8.24 show the current state of the system. The sender has sent frame 0, which is currently on the medium. The receiver is waiting for it, and the sender is waiting for an acknowledgment of it.

Next let's consider the transitions. Transitions correspond to events that can occur, and their input places correspond to states that must exist before the event can occur. For example, look at the first transition for the sender labeled "Receive A1, Send F0." It has two input places, "Wait for A1" for the sender and "A1" for the medium. A firing of this transition means the sender has received an ACK for frame 1 and has sent the next frame, F0. However, for this to occur the sender must be waiting for A1, and A1 must be on the way. Thus, for the transition to fire,

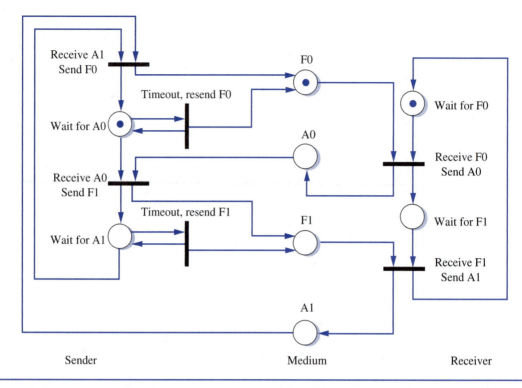

Figure 8.24   Partial Petri Net for Go-Back-*n* with Sender Window Size = 1

tokens must be in these two input places. We can make similar arguments about the other transitions for the sender and the receiver.

This Petri net also has two time-out transitions. Each has one input place corresponding to the sender waiting for an ACK. For example, suppose the sender is waiting for A0 (token in that place). The corresponding time-out transition is enabled. This does not mean it will fire, however. It means it *could* fire. If a frame timer expires, the time-out transition fires. If that happens, the token is removed from the input place, and others are placed in the two output places. One of them is the F0 place for the medium, indicating that frame 0 is being sent. The other output place is the same as the input place, meaning the sender is again waiting for A0.

Confused? Let's trace token movement for a sequence of typical events. Parts (a) through (d) of Figure 8.25 show Petri nets corresponding to successive transition firings. Places, transition, and arrows are as in Figure 8.24, but we have eliminated the labels to simplify the diagram. The token placement in Figure 8.25a is the same as in Figure 8.24. The sender is waiting for A0, the receiver is waiting for F0, and F0 is on the medium. Together they define the system state. At this point two transitions are enabled (marked with *): the first time-out transition for the sender and the transition for the receiver labeled (from Figure 8.24) "Receive F0, Send A0."

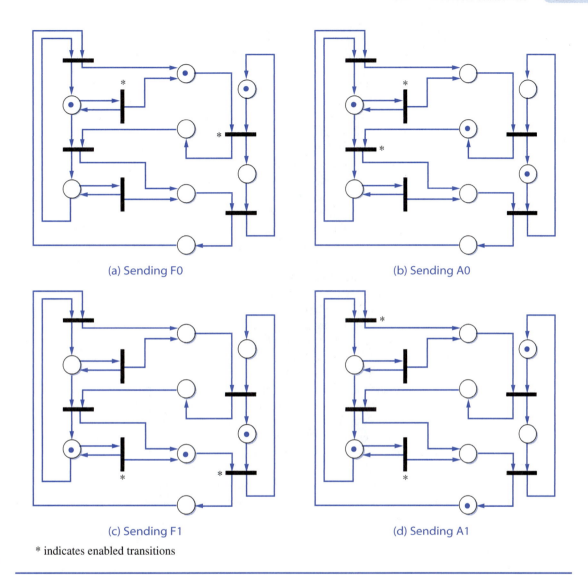

(a) Sending F0

(b) Sending A0

(c) Sending F1

(d) Sending A1

* indicates enabled transitions

Figure 8.25   Firing Sequence for Normal Exchange of Frames and Acknowledgments

Suppose the latter transition fires. The tokens are removed from the two input places and new ones put into places as shown in Figure 8.25b. The system is in a new state. The sender is still waiting for A0, which is now on the medium. The receiver is now waiting for F1. Again, two transitions in Figure 8.25b are enabled. They are the time-out and the reception of A0. Again, the latter transition fires, and the tokens are moved to their positions in Figure 8.25c. Again the system is in a new state. The sender has sent F1, which is on the medium, and is waiting for A1. Meanwhile the receiver is still waiting for F1. If the receiver gets the frame, the tokens move to their positions in Figure 8.25d. The sender is still waiting for A0, which is on its way, and the receiver is waiting for F0. If the acknowledgment arrives, the Petri net changes again and token placement is as in Figure 8.25a. Thus, if frames and acknowledgments are communicated without error, these four Petri nets describe the changing system states.

Earlier we stated that the Petri net of Figure 8.24 does not include transitions for every possible event. For example, there is always a token in one of the medium's places, implying there is always something on the medium. This, of course, is not true. A token on the medium could get lost or destroyed, resulting in a state in which the sender and receiver both are waiting but nothing is on the medium (something our Petri net doesn't show). This state is fixed easily by making each of the medium's places an input place for a new transition labeled "lost." None of these transitions would have an output place. Thus, whenever something is on the medium one of these transitions is enabled. If it fires, the token is removed from the input place. With no output place, that token disappears. Eventually a time-out transition would fire and place a token into one of the places again.

Another way we could refine the Petri net is to divide the sender's transitions into two separate ones. In our model, when the sender gets an ACK it immediately sends out the next frame. We assume there are always frames to send, but that may not be the case. We could define new sender places corresponding to situations in which the sender has to wait for a packet from its user. We encourage you to consider some of the cases and redraw the Petri nets (see the exercises at the end of the chapter).

As with STDs, Petri nets can be analyzed to look for protocol errors. For example, if tokens could never reach certain places, certain states could not be represented by the Petri net. If they are known to be possible, our model would be in error. Another error would be indicated if tokens moved through certain places without landing in places in between. For example, suppose a sequence of firings resulted in Petri nets in which a token moves alternately between the receiver's places in Figure 8.24. If, in these same Petri nets, one of the sender's places never gets a token, an error exists because the Petri nets indicate the receiver is getting frames but the sender is not sending them.

If you are interested in further study or other examples of Petri nets, see references [Ta96], [Wa91], and [Pe81].

8.8 SUMMARY

Previous chapters discussed details necessary for the transmission of a single frame, but this chapter considered multiple frames. Specifically, it discussed protocols that deal with the following issues:

- Tracking multiple frames and their acknowledgments
- Responding to frames that arrive damaged
- Responding when a frame or acknowledgment never arrives or arrives late

We discussed four flow control protocols: stop-and-wait, unrestricted, go-back-*n*, and selective repeat. The latter two are examples of a sliding window protocol. It defines a window for the sending device containing frames that can be sent but not yet acknowledged. In some ways (excluding timers, ACKs, and NAKs), all these protocols can be viewed as variations of one sliding window protocol (Table 8.1). For example, go-back-*n* is essentially selective repeat in which the receiving window has just one frame. In stop-and-wait, both windows have just one frame. The unrestricted protocol has unlimited frame sizes.

Both sliding window protocols respond to frames that arrive damaged or out of order by sending negative acknowledgments (NAKs). A device receiving a NAK must resend frames. Under the go-back-*n* protocol it resends all outstanding frames, but under the selective repeat protocol it resends only the NAK'd frame. Each protocol also relies on timers so that if an acknowledgment is not received within a period of time, the device assumes one or more frames were lost and resends them.

With both sliding window protocols there are restrictions on the window size. Generally, with the go-back-*n* protocol, if there are 2^K distinct frame numbers, the sender's window must have fewer than 2^K frames. With selective repeat, the sum of

Table 8.1 Comparison of Flow Control Protocols

	STOP-AND-WAIT PROTOCOL	UNRESTRICTED PROTOCOL	GO-BACK-*n* PROTOCOL	SELECTIVE REPEAT PROTOCOL
Sending window size	One frame	Unlimited number of frames	Less than 2^K	Less than or equal to 2^K minus receiving window size (but typically 2^{K-1})
Receiving window size	One frame	Unlimited number of frames	One frame	Less than or equal to 2^K minus sending window size (but typically 2^{K-1})
Comments	Waits for a separate acknowledgment for each frame before sending the next. This approach is slow since there is a lot of wait time.	Sends all frames regardless of how many there are. This can cause problems in network congestion and may overwhelm the receiving end. As described, we did not include any provisions for frames that are damaged or lost.	The window contains frames that have been sent but not yet acknowledged. Assumes the receiving end will only accept and deliver frames in the order they arrive. It's simpler than selective repeat and will work well if frames rarely get lost or arrive out of order. The sender will resend all frames in the window if a NAK arrives.	More complex than go-back-*n* because it may not have to resend frames that arrive late. The receiver buffers them and then delivers them in order to its user when previously numbered frames arrive. This is useful over large distances where delays and heavy traffic can easily cause frames to arrive out of order. If a NAK arrives, the sender will resend only the frame specifically requested.

the sender's and receiver's windows must not exceed 2^K. Violating these restrictions does not mean the protocol will fail, but it does mean the protocol is subject to failure if a certain sequence of events occurs.

The algorithms are complex, and providing a formal mathematical proof is outside the scope of this text. However, Section 8.7 introduced two tools that can be used for verification: state transition diagrams and Petri nets. Both use directed graphs to represent the states and state transitions of a system, but they differ in the way they do so. State transition diagrams use nodes for states and edges for state transitions. The execution of an algorithm thus can be equated to defining paths through the state transition diagram. Petri nets are more complex. They use places, transitions, arrows, and tokens. The collection of tokens corresponding to places defines the state of the system. Tokens move from place to place subject to rules that allow transitions to fire. In both cases, the models can be analyzed to detect anomalies that can occur.

Review Questions

1. What is automatic repeat request error control?
2. What is flow control?
3. What are X-ON and X-OFF characters?
4. What is unrestricted flow control?
5. What is stop-and-wait flow control?
6. Are the following statements TRUE or FALSE? Why?

   a. Unrestricted flow control generally has a better effective data rate than stop-and-wait flow control.

   b. Unrestricted flow control really amounts to no flow control.

   c. Unrestricted and stop-and-wait flow control are special cases of a sliding window protocol.

   d. Sliding window protocols can work with any size window.

   e. The go-back-n algorithm will resend several frames even if just one fails to arrive at its destination.

   f. For the selective repeat protocol, the receiving window size is independent of the sending window size.

   g. Petri nets and finite state machines represent two different ways to accomplish the same thing.

7. Distinguish between bit rate and effective data rate.
8. What important role does an acknowledgment play in a flow control protocol?
9. What is a sliding window flow control protocol?
10. What is a piggybacked acknowledgment?
11. Why are frames numbered modularly rather than being allowed to increase as large as needed?
12. List typical fields in a data frame.

13. Distinguish between a frame timer and an ACK timer.

14. What purpose does the window size play in a sliding window flow control protocol?

15. Distinguish among an ACK, a NAK, and a data frame.

16. What are the major differences between the go-back-*n* and selective repeat protocols?

17. What is the constraint on the sending window size for the selective repeat protocol?

18. For the selective repeat protocol, what is the relationship between the sending and receiving window size?

19. What is a finite state machine (or model)?

20. What is a state transition diagram?

21. What is a Petri net?

22. Define the terms *place, transition, arrow,* and *token* as applied to Petri nets.

23. What does it mean when a transition *fires?*

Exercises

1. What happens if A and B from Figure 8.2 both insert X-OFF characters into their data streams?

2. With the X-ON/X-OFF protocol, why does one device send X-OFF before the buffers are full instead of waiting until they are full?

3. Modify the unrestricted protocol in Figure 8.4 to reflect the following changes:

   a. The sender has a fixed number of frames to send.

   b. A frame could be damaged.

4. What are effective data rates for the unrestricted protocol and stop-and-wait protocol given the following values?

   R = capacity (16 Mbps)

   S = signal speed (200) meters per μsec

   D = distance between the sender and receiver (200 meters)

   T = time to create one frame (2 μsec)

   F = number of bits in a frame (500)

   N = number of data bits in a frame (450)

   A = number of bits in an acknowledgment (80)

5. For each variable (except signal speed) in Exercise 4, how will a 10-fold increase in its value affect the effective data rate for both the unrestricted and stop-and-wait protocols?

6. The scenario in Figure 8.10 shows one way the go-back-*n* protocol can fail if the window size equals the maximum number of sequence numbers. Describe another way the protocol can fail under the same assumption.

7. Consider the go-back-*n* algorithm of Figure 8.12 with a window size of 7. Describe the actions of both sending and receiving protocols, specifying variable values and

buffer contents, in the following cases. What is the current state of each protocol after responding to the events specified?

a. Device A sends frames 0 through 6. Device B receives them in order, but frame 4 was damaged.

b. Device A sends frames 0 through 6 and device B receives them in order. Device B sends one data frame to A (which A receives correctly) after receiving frame 4 but before receiving frame 5.

c. Same scenario as in (b) but the data frame sent to A is damaged.

d. Device A has 12 frames to send to B, but B has nothing to send to A.

8. How could the go-back-n algorithm of Figure 8.12 fail under each of the following conditions?

a. Remove the check for expired acktimer.

b. Remove the check for expired frametimer.

c. Remove the check for condition $(i < N)$ in the first if statement in the main loop.

d. Remove the statement w = (frame.ack+1) % MAX from the code under the last event check.

9. Reproduce the scenarios of Figures 8.14 and 8.15 with both window sizes equal to 4 and show that the protocol does not fail.

10. Consider the selective repeat algorithm of Figure 8.16 with window sizes of 4. Describe the actions of both sending and receiving protocols, specifying variable values and buffer contents, in the following cases. What is the current state of each protocol after responding to the events specified?

a. Device A sends frames 0 through 3. All except frame 2 arrive. Frame 2 is lost.

b. Device A sends frames 0 through 3. They arrive at B in the order 0, 1, 3, 2.

c. Device A sends frames 0 through 3. Device B receives frames 0 and 1 and sends a piggyback acknowledgment, which A receives.

d. Same scenario as in (c), but the acknowledgment gets lost.

11. Consider the selective repeat protocol of Figure 8.16. Construct a scenario in which the condition frame.type==nak holds, but the second condition following it does not hold.

12. How could the selective repeat algorithm of Figure 8.16 fail under each of the following conditions?

a. Remove the check for expired acktimer.

b. Remove the check for expired frametimer.

c. Remove the check for condition $(i < N)$ in the first if statement in the main loop.

d. Remove the statement sw = (frame.ack+1) % MAX from the code under the last event check.

13. Consider the analysis of the sliding window protocol in Section 8.3 and assume the following values:

R = bit rate (10 Mbps or 10 bits per μsec)

S = signal speed (200 meters per μsec)

D = distance between the sender and receiver (unknown)

T = time to create one frame (1 μsec)

F = number of bits in a frame (200)

N = number of data bits in a frame (160)

W = window size (4 frames)

At what distance will the first acknowledgment arrive precisely when the last frame in the window is sent? What is the effective data rate?

14. Consider your answer to Exercise 13. What happens to the effective data rate if the window size increases? Decreases?

15. Repeat Exercise 14 for each of the other parameters.

16. Consider the state transition diagram of Figure 8.21. Why is there no state transition from (Y, N, 1) to (Y, N, 0)?

17. Expand the boxed area of Figure 8.21 to include the states (Y, N, 0) and (Y, N, 1) and refine, resulting in an expansion of Figure 8.22.

18. Consider the Petri net of Figure 8.24. Consider the case that a sender receives an ACK but may not have the next frame to send. That is, it must wait for the user to give it a packet. What does the new Petri net look like?

19. Draw the sequence of Petri nets (similar to those in Figure 8.25) for the following sequence of events:

    a. Send F0.

    b. Time out, resend F0.

    c. Receiver gets F0 and sends A0.

    d. Sender gets A0 and sends F1.

    e. Time out, resend F1.

20. A time-out could occur after the receiver gets a frame and sends the ACK but before the sender gets the ACK. Thus, the sender would resend a frame that the receiver is not expecting. Modify the Petri net of Figure 8.24 to account for this possibility.

REFERENCES

[Li87] Lin, F., P. Chu, and M. Liu. "Protocol Verification Using Reachability Analysis: The State Space Explosion Problem and Relief Strategies." *Proceedings of the ACM SIGCOMM 1987 Workshop* (1987), 126–135.

[Pe81] Peterson, J. *Petri Net Theory and the Modeling of Systems.* Englewood Cliffs, NJ: Prentice-Hall, 1981.

[Ru89] Russel, D. *The Principles of Computer Networking.* New York: Cambridge University Press, 1989.

[Ta96] Tanenbaum, A. S. *Computer Networks,* 3rd ed. Englewood Cliffs, NJ: Prentice-Hall, 1996.

[Wa91] Walrand, J. *Communications Networks: A First Course.* Boston: Richard D. Irwin, 1991.

CHAPTER 9

LOCAL AREA NETWORKS

The more the data banks record about each one of us, the less we exist.
—**Marshall McLuhan** (1911–1980), Canadian communications theorist

9.1 INTRODUCTION

Up to this point we have focused on communication between two devices and, with the exception of multiplexing and contention in Sections 4.5 and 4.7, have not really considered the larger picture of connecting many devices. Beginning with this chapter we discuss different connection strategies and the protocols needed to maintain communication among many devices. This chapter deals primarily with layer 2 protocols that define local area network (LAN) operations. Subsequent chapters describe ways of connecting multiple LANs and discuss the protocols that define the Internet.

We begin with an overview of the different LAN topologies (configurations) shown in Figure 9.1. Historically, the two most common topologies were the bus and ring. We'll see later that new connection technologies have provided a wider range of possibilities. In the **bus topology** (Figure 9.1a), a single communication line—typically a coaxial cable or optical fiber—represents the primary medium, which we call a **segment.** Any device wanting to send to another does so over the segment. Only one device may send at a time, however, and we need some type of contention protocol. In a **ring topology** (Figure 9.1b), all the devices are arranged in a ring, with each device connected directly only to its two neighbors. If a device wants to send a frame to another, the frame must pass through all of the devices in between (either clockwise or counterclockwise). It's a little like gossip that spreads from neighbor to neighbor.

Other topologies are the star topology and a fully connected topology. In a **star topology** (Figure 9.1c), one device is a logical communication center for all others. Any two communicating devices must go through it. Finally, a **fully connected topology** (Figure 9.1d) connects every pair of devices directly. Fully connected topologies represent an extreme case and are rarely used in practice (except perhaps in small isolated cases). Therefore, we will not discuss them further.

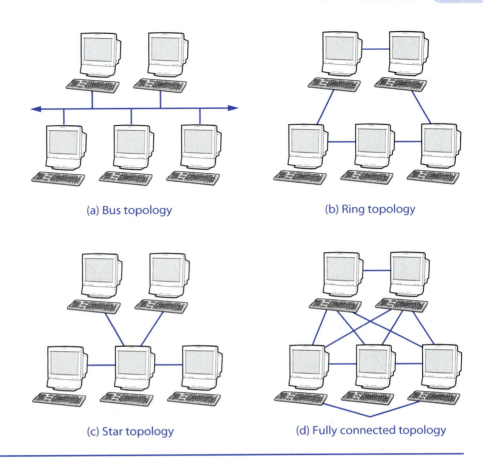

(a) Bus topology   (b) Ring topology

(c) Star topology   (d) Fully connected topology

Figure 9.1   Network Topologies

An advantage of the bus topology is its simplicity. The segment may run through one or more buildings, with feeder lines going to specific labs or classrooms (Figure 9.2) and connecting to personal computers using a switch or hub (devices that we will describe later in this chapter). It may also run the length of an assembly line in a factory, connecting devices necessary for the assembly of a product such as an automobile. Because of the linear organization, adding new devices or removing old ones is relatively easy. A disadvantage of the linear organization is that only one device can send at a time. In some cases this limitation poses no problem. However, as the number of devices increases, serious bottlenecks can occur. You might want to refresh your memory by reviewing the discussion of contention protocols in Section 4.7.

Ring topologies allow multiple devices to send using one or more tokens that circulate the ring. Recall from Section 4.7 that a *token* is a special frame that allows a device in possession of it to send. The most common ring networks use just one token, but some protocols have provisions for more. Ring topologies were once common in office environments where multiple personal computers needed to communicate among themselves or with a file server or shared printer.

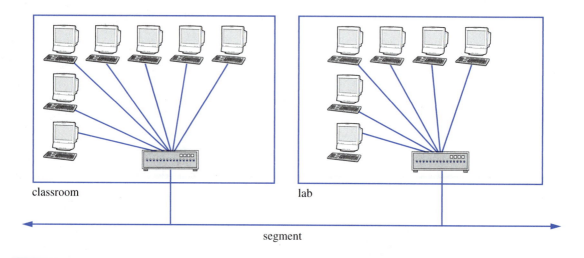

classroom lab

segment

Figure 9.2 Bus Topology Connecting Multiple Locations

The first step in discussing LAN operations is to specify the protocol that two devices use to communicate with each other. If you think this sounds a bit like what we discussed in the previous chapter, you are 100% correct. Section 9.2 builds on that material and discusses a long-time ISO data link standard from which many other data link standards evolved.

Sections 9.3 through 9.6 discuss well-established IEEE standards for bus and ring networks: several variations of Ethernet and the token ring network. Ethernet has become the dominant way to connect devices in a LAN environment and has gone through several evolutions to accommodate the increasing technologies and bit rates. Token ring, once common, is now used much less frequently. However, it does provide an excellent contrast to the ideas that define Ethernet. A third IEEE standard, called *token bus,* exists. It has a bus topology like Ethernet, but contention requires the use of a token that the devices circulate among themselves. Although it is a standard, it is rarely used any more and we have dropped coverage of it from this edition.

These LAN standards share one characteristic: They connect devices using UTP, cable, or optical fiber. However, recall from Section 2.4 that physical connections are no longer required for devices to communicate and that wireless technologies have evolved to the point where they are economical and common. This, of course, is made possible in part by developing standards such as the IEEE 802.11 wireless standard that Section 9.7 discusses.

9.2 DATA LINK CONTROL

To fully understand how LAN standards work, it is important to understand where they fit in a layered design and how they relate to other topics we have discussed thus far. Recall from Section 1.4 the seven-layer OSI reference model. The lowest three layers typically define network operations: the physical, data link, and network layers. The data link layer performs services for the network layer and assumes the existence of the physical layer. Specifically, the data link layer is responsible for accurate communication between two nodes in a network. This involves frame formats, error checking, and flow control, all of which we have discussed so far. In general, however, these topics are independent of the network topology. For example, error checking or flow control algorithms do not care whether a frame was sent via bus or ring.

As a result, the data link layer is further divided into two sublayers: the **logical link control (LLC)** and the **medium access control (MAC)** (Figure 9.3). The LLC handles logical links between the devices, whereas the MAC controls access to the transmission medium. Primarily, the LLC provides service to the network layer and calls on the MAC for tasks specific to the type of network.

The IEEE 802.3 Ethernet and IEEE 802.5 token ring standards that we discuss later are MAC protocols. Again, we see how the layering of software allows different lower-level protocols with the same higher-level ones. Many of the topics we have discussed are independent of the network topology, which gives them a great deal of flexibility and marketability.

Many different data link protocols can sit above the MAC, but interestingly, they have a common ancestor. In the early 1970s IBM developed its Synchronous Data Link Control (SDLC) protocol. Prior to that time protocols were **byte oriented.** This meant that frames were interpreted as a sequence of bytes, with each byte conveying some information as defined by the EBCDIC code (recall Section 2.5). Sometimes control bytes would appear inside a data stream, causing the data to be misinterpreted as control information. Although there were ways around this problem, IBM developed a **bit-oriented protocol,** SDLC, in which not everything had

Figure 9.3   Data Link Layer Refinement

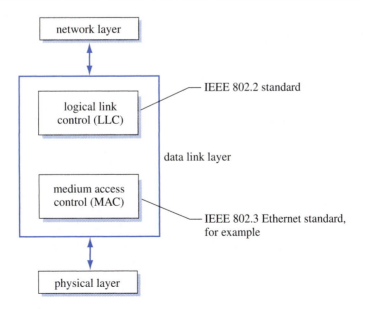

to be viewed as a sequence of bytes. This approach provided a little more flexibility in transferring increasingly diverse types of data. SDLC uses go-back-*n* flow control and was part of IBM's Systems Network Architecture (SNA), its equivalent to the OSI model. It was typically used in IBM terminal-to-computer communications.

IBM submitted its SDLC protocol to the ISO for approval as a standard. However, ISO modified it and created its own standard, known as **HDLC (High-level Data Link Control),** making it the first formal standard for bit-oriented data link control protocols. Effectively, SDLC is IBM's equivalent to HDLC. (If you sit on the other side of the fence, HDLC is ISO's equivalent to SDLC.) However, it did not end there. IBM also submitted SDLC to ANSI for acceptance. As all good standards organizations do, ANSI modified it and renamed it Advanced Data Communications Control Procedure (ADCCP).

Then, ITU adopted and modified HDLC for use in its X.25 network interface standard (discussed in Chapter 13). Originally it was labeled LAP (for Link Access Protocol), but was subsequently changed to LAPB (B for balanced). It allowed devices to be connected to packet-switched networks. A variation on LAPB is LAPD, the link control for the Integrated Services Digital Network (ISDN). ISDN is an entirely digital communications system defined by ITU. Some had predicted it would eventually replace the telephone system, but other technologies evolved and, of course, that has not happened. LAPD allows devices to communicate over the ISDN D channel (discussed in Chapter 13). IEEE also has a protocol derived from HDLC. It is called Logical Link Control (LLC) and is used in local area networks. It also allows LANs to connect to other LANs and to wide area networks.

As you can see, there is no shortage of data link control protocol standards, but they all have one thing in common. They owe much of what they are to HDLC. Because space does not allow us to cover all of the protocols (and there's probably little educational value in covering them all anyway), we will cover the granddaddy of them all, HDLC. Details about some of the other protocols can be found in references [Fo03] (for LLC) and [St99] (for LAPD).

HIGH-LEVEL DATA LINK CONTROL PROTOCOL

HDLC is a bit-oriented protocol that supports both half-duplex and full-duplex communications (see Section 4.3). As stated previously, *bit oriented* means that the protocol treats frames as bit streams. In other words, it does not recognize or interpret byte values (such as X-ON/X-OFF), as some protocols discussed previously do.

Three types of devices run the HDLC protocol:

- **Primary station** (sometimes called the *host station* or *control station*). It manages data flow by issuing commands to other devices and acting on their responses. We will see some examples later in this section. It also may establish and manage connections with multiple devices.

- **Secondary station** (sometimes called the *target station* or *guest station*). It responds to commands issued by a primary station. Furthermore, it can respond to just one primary station at a time. It does not issue commands to other devices (although it can send data).

- **Combined station.** As the name implies, it can act as both primary and secondary station. It can issue commands to and respond to commands from another combined station.

Devices running HDLC can communicate in one of three modes:

- **Normal response mode (NRM).** In NRM, the primary station controls the communication. That is, the secondary station can send only when the primary station instructs or allows it to do so. This operational mode is common in two configurations. In a **point-to-point link** (Figure 9.4a), the primary station communicates with a single secondary station. In a **multipoint link** (sometimes called a *multidrop link*), the primary station can communicate with several secondary stations (Figure 9.4b). Of course, it must manage and keep separate the different sessions it maintains with each of them.

- **Asynchronous response mode (ARM).** Like NRM, ARM involves communication between a primary station and one or more secondary stations. Here, however, the secondary station is more independent. Specifically, it can send data or control information to the primary station without explicit instructions or permission to do so. However, it cannot send commands. The responsibility for establishing, maintaining, and eventually ending the connection still resides with the primary station.

Figure 9.4   HDLC Configurations

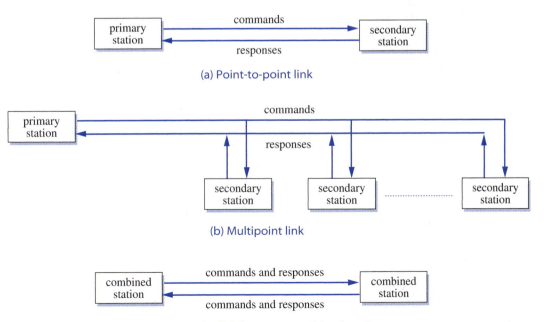

(a) Point-to-point link

(b) Multipoint link

(c) Point-to-point link between combined stations

• **Asynchronous balanced mode (ABM).** ABM is used in configurations connecting combined stations (Figure 9.4c). Either device can send data, control information, or commands. This is typical in connections between two computers and in the X.25 interface standard (discussed in Chapter 13).

Frame Format   HDLC frames are similar to the general formats discussed previously. Figure 9.5 shows the frame format. Some of the fields can occur in one of two sizes. The smaller size defines a standard format and the larger an extended format. Which format is used must be decided when the link is established.

There are three different types of frames. They differ in the contents of the Control field and whether the frame actually contains data. We will first discuss the fields common to all types and then differentiate among them.

The *Flag field* marks the beginning and end of each frame and contains the special bit pattern 01111110. A device receiving this pattern knows an HDLC frame is on its way. Because the frame size may vary, the device examines arriving bits and looks for this pattern to detect the frame's end. This pattern presents a problem: Since the protocol is bit oriented, the data fields (and others, as well) can consist of arbitrary bit patterns. If the flag pattern exists in another field, won't the device interpret it incorrectly as the end of the frame? We certainly do not want to constrain the data to disallow certain bit patterns from appearing.

Fortunately, this problem has a relatively easy solution called **bit stuffing.** The sending device monitors the bits between the flags before they are sent. If it detects five consecutive 1s (Figure 9.6), it inserts (stuffs) an extra 0 after the fifth 1. This breaks any potential flag pattern and prevents it from being sent. Now the data are no longer correct, so the receiving device must correct them. Whenever a 0 follows five consecutive 1s, it assumes the 0 was stuffed and removes it. Since the flag field is not subjected to bit stuffing by the sending device, it is the only place where the flag pattern can appear.

The *Address field* is self-explanatory. It has 8 bits for the standard format and 16 bits for the extended. The extended format allows a greater number of devices to be identified. If a primary station sends the frame, the Address field defines the identity of the secondary station where the frame is being sent. This is necessary in multipoint configurations where there are several secondary stations. If a secondary station is sending the frame, the Address field contains the sender's identity. Because there is only one primary station and secondary stations do not send to each other, the destination address is not needed. The source address is needed to let the primary station know where a frame originates.

Figure 9.5   HDLC Frame Format

number of bits:	8	8 or 16	8 or 16	variable	16 or 32	8
	Flag	Address	Control	------- Data -------	FCS	Flag

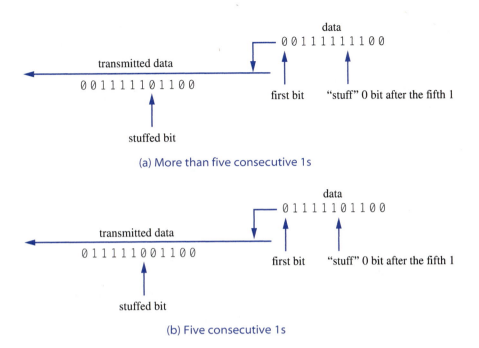

Figure 9.6   Bit Stuffing

In some cases the field may contain a **group address** or **broadcast address** (all 1s). All secondary stations in a predefined group accept a frame with a group address. Every secondary station with which the primary station has established a link accepts one with a broadcast address.

The *Data field* contains the data, and its length is variable. We will see that in some cases there are no data and this field does not exist. The **Frame Check Sequence (FCS)** is used for CRC error detection. The field may be 16 (standard format) or 32 (extended format) bits long. Most common is a 16-bit field defined as described in Section 4.3 using the CRC polynomial $x^{16} + x^{12} + x^5 + 1$.

The *Control field* is 8 (standard format) or 16 (extended format) bits long and is used to send status information or issue commands. Its contents depend on the frame's type. The three types are information frame, supervisory frame, and unnumbered frame. Figure 9.7 shows the standard format for each. With the extended format, the fields are larger or the frame contains unused bits; the differences are not important here.

The first one or two bits define the frame type. As Figure 9.7 shows, an information frame always starts with 0, a supervisory frame always starts with 10, and an unnumbered frame always starts with 11. These definitions allow the receiving devices to determine the type of an arriving frame.

Information frames are used primarily to transfer information (Data field of Figure 9.5) using either the go-back-*n* or the selective repeat sliding window

number of bits:

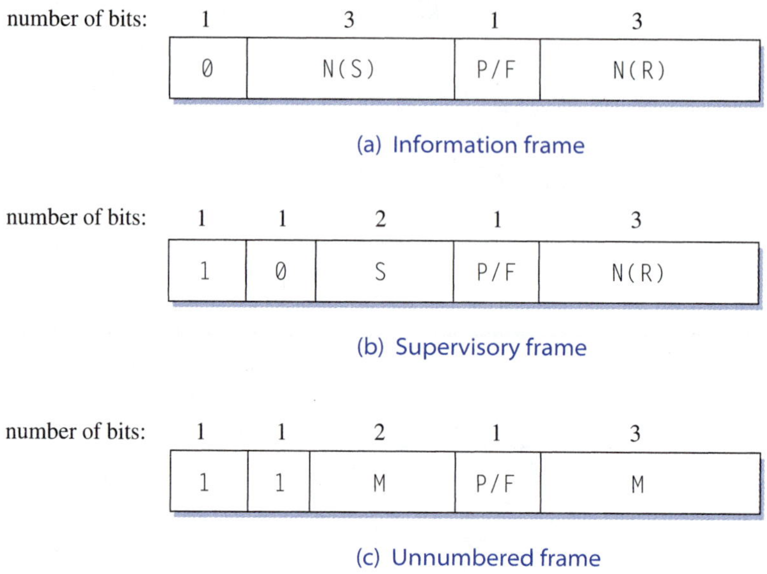

1	3	1	3
0	N(S)	P/F	N(R)

(a) Information frame

number of bits:

1	1	2	1	3
1	0	S	P/F	N(R)

(b) Supervisory frame

number of bits:

1	1	2	1	3
1	1	M	P/F	M

(c) Unnumbered frame

Figure 9.7 Control Fields for HDLC Frames

protocols. The fields N(R) and N(S) are similar to what we previously called `frame.ack` and `frame.number`, respectively. Specifically, N(R) (number of received frame) is a piggyback acknowledgment indicating that all frames up to N(R) − 1 have been received. Equivalently, the device is currently expecting a frame numbered N(R). Similarly, N(S) is the number of the frame being sent. The fields N(R) and N(S) are either 3 bits (standard frame) or 7 bits (extended frame) long. Consequently, frame numbers and arithmetic such as N(R) − 1 are modulo 8 (2^3) or modulo 128 (2^7).

The P/F bit stands for Poll/Final bit. Its meaning depends on whether the frame is being sent by a primary (Poll bit) or secondary station (Final bit). The primary station can request a response from a secondary station by sending it a frame with the P bit set to 1. For example, the primary station may want to know if the secondary station has any data to send or may request its status with regard to some ongoing process. In any case, the secondary station is expected to respond (we'll see some examples shortly). When sent by a secondary station, the F bit indicates that the current frame is the last in a sequence of frames.

Supervisory frames are used by either device to indicate its status or to NAK frames received incorrectly. The N(R) and P/F bits do the same thing as in information frames. The differences are in the 2-bit S field, which is defined as follows:

- **RR: Receive Ready** (00). When a device wants to indicate it is ready and able to receive information, it sends an RR frame. The RR frame is also used to acknowledge received frames periodically when there is no outgoing data (recall the discussion of ACK timers in the previous chapter).

- **REJ: Reject** (01). This is similar to the NAKs discussed for the go-back-*n* protocol. It requests that the other device resend all outstanding frames, starting with the one whose number is specified by N(R). This can occur if a frame arrives out of order or damaged.

- **RNR: Receive Not Ready** (10). If a device's buffers are filling or it detects an error on its side of the link, it can stop the flow of incoming frames by sending an RNR frame.

- **SREJ: Selective Reject** (11). This is similar to the NAKs discussed for the selective repeat protocol. It requests that the other device resend the frame whose number is specified by N(R).

Whereas the information and supervisory frames control and manage the transfer of frames, the *unnumbered frames* establish how the protocol will proceed. For example, we stated previously that HDLC can use go-back-*n* or selective repeat, it can use different frame sizes, and it can communicate in one of three modes. How do the devices decide when to do what?

Part (c) of Figure 9.7 shows the unnumbered frame format. The two fields marked M together define five flags whose values define the communication protocol. A primary station sends commands, and a secondary station responds to commands by setting these flags appropriately. Table 9.1 lists some of the possible commands and responses that can be coded in an unnumbered frame.

HDLC Example   The following example describes the process of establishing a link, exchanging frames, and terminating the link. Figure 9.8 shows a possible sequence of exchanges between two devices, A (primary station) and B (secondary station). We will assume a go-back-*n* protocol. Vertical arrows represent passing time. Slanted arrows between them indicate the sending of frames and their direction. Text at the arrow's source specifies the frame's contents. Text at the arrow's end specifies what happens when the frame arrives. To simplify the figure, no text appears in cases where the frame is accepted without error.

To begin, Figure 9.8a shows how a connection might be established. Device B starts by sending an unnumbered frame with the function RIM. This is a request that the primary station (A) send an unnumbered frame with function code SIM. When B receives the SIM, it begins its initialization procedure and acknowledges receipt of the SIM by sending another unnumbered frame with function UA. When A receives UA, it knows that B is initializing. In this case, A decides the response mode will be ARM and sends another unnumbered frame with that function. When B receives the frame, it again acknowledges by sending another UA frame. When A receives the acknowledgment, the stations are ready to communicate.

Figure 9.8b shows an example exchange of frames. Since the response mode is ARM, A and B both begin sending information frames (i frames). B sends its first two frames with frame numbers N(S) = 0 and 1. In both cases, N(R) is 0. Since B has not received anything yet, it is expecting the first frame (number 0). Meanwhile, A sends its first three frames with numbers N(S) = 0, 1, and 2. In the first two frames, N(R) = 0 because A has not received anything yet. However, A receives a

Table 9.1 HDLC Unnumbered Frame Functions

Function	Meaning
SNRM: Set Normal Response Mode (C)	Communicate using normal response mode and standard frame format.
SNRME: Set Normal Response Mode Extended (C)	Communicate using normal response mode and extended frame format.
SARM: Set Asynchronous Response Mode (C)	Communicate using asynchronous response mode and standard frame format.
SARME: Set Asynchronous Response Mode Extended (C)	Communicate using asynchronous response mode and extended frame format.
SABM: Set Asynchronous Balanced Mode (C)	Communicate using asynchronous balanced mode and standard frame format.
SABME: Set Asynchronous Balanced Mode Extended (C)	Communicate using asynchronous balanced mode and extended frame format.
DISC: Disconnect (C)	Initiates a disconnect between the two devices. The disconnect is completed when the other device responds with a UA function (see below).
RSET: Reset (C)	Each device tracks the values of $N(R)$ and $N(S)$ as frames come and go. If an error occurs (say at a higher level than HDLC), the data link control may have to reinitialize the frame exchange. RSET resets the tracked values of $N(R)$ and $N(S)$ to a previously established value.
SIM: Set Initialization Mode (C)	Instructs the other device to initialize its data link control functions.
UP: Unnumbered Poll (C)	A poll (request) to get status information from a specified device.
UI: Unnumbered Information (C or R)	Used to send status information. Typically sent following a UP or SIM.
XID: Exchange Identification (C or R)	Allows two devices to exchange their identification and status.
RIM: Request Initialization Mode (R)	Request from a secondary station that the primary station send SIM.
RD: Request Disconnect (R)	Request from a secondary station that the primary station initiate a disconnect by sending a DISC frame.
DM: Disconnect Mode (R)	Tells the primary station that the secondary station is not operational (i.e., is in a disconnect mode).
UA: Unnumbered Acknowledgment (R)	Used to acknowledge previously sent commands such as a set mode or disconnect.
TEST: Test (C or R)	Request to the other device to send a test response. The sending device may put something in the data field for the receiving device to return to test the link.
FRMR: Frame Reject (R)	Used to indicate an arriving frame was rejected. The REJ function rejects frames that are damaged or received out of order. FRMR is used if, for example, a control field is defined incorrectly or a frame that was never sent is acknowledged.

C = command; R = response.

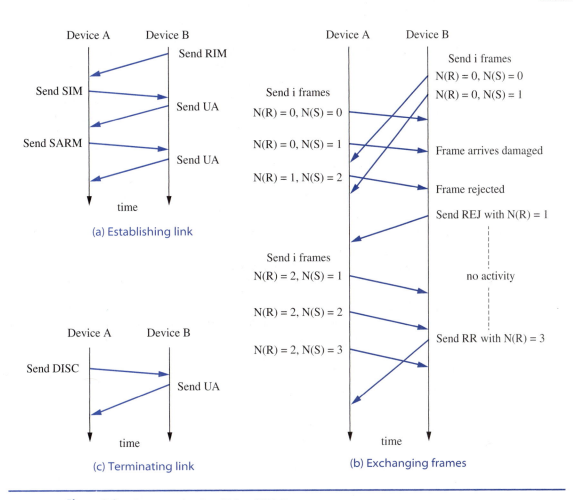

Figure 9.8   Communicating Using HDLC

frame from B after it sends its second frame. Consequently, with the third frame, A sets N(R) = 1, thus acknowledging its receipt of frame 0.

Next, suppose the second frame that A sends arrives damaged. B sends a supervisory frame containing the function code REJ and N(R) = 1. This frame does two things: It acknowledges that B received frame 0 from A and states that an error occurred and that A should resend everything beginning with frame 1. Meanwhile, B is still expecting frame 1, so when the next frame arrives, B rejects it as being out of order.

Eventually, A receives the REJ frame and resends frames beginning with the specified number. If it has three frames to send, they contain N(S) = 1, 2, and 3. Note that N(R) is now 2 in each of these frames. This is because while we were discussing what B did with the damaged frame, A received another (its second) i frame. These three frames eventually reach B. However, B has entered a period of inactivity and cannot piggyback any acknowledgments. Consequently, between the arrival of frames 1 and 2, its timer expires. It sends a supervisory frame with function code RR, which reaffirms that B is still ready to accept frames and acknowledges the receipt of frame number 2 (sets $N(R) = 3$). Using RR here is a lot like listening on the telephone to your eccentric aunt complain about her neighbors. You hold the phone by your ear while you make a batch of cookies and respond every five minutes or so with a "Yes, Aunt Mabel."

Frame exchanges like this occur until both stations have finished sending. Station A decides it is time to disconnect by sending an unnumbered frame with function code DISC (Figure 9.8c). When B receives the frame, it acknowledges it by sending a UA frame. When A receives the acknowledgment, it knows both sides have agreed to disconnect and it terminates the link. (Don't hang up on Aunt Mabel without her consent; you might be in her will!)

BINARY SYNCHRONOUS COMMUNICATIONS PROTOCOL

Before we finish, we will present a short discussion of the **binary synchronous communications protocol,** sometimes referred to as the **BSC** or **bisync protocol,** which was developed by IBM. It is used with synchronous half-duplex communications and uses stop-and-wait flow control. It is an old protocol, but we present it so we can make a contrast with a bit-oriented protocol.

Unlike the previously discussed protocols, BSC is *byte oriented.* That is, the devices interpret frames as a sequence of control and data bytes. Byte values can be interpreted using either the ASCII or EBCDIC character sets.* BSC uses several different frame formats. Figure 9.9 shows three typical ones: a control frame format

Figure 9.9   BSC Frame Formats

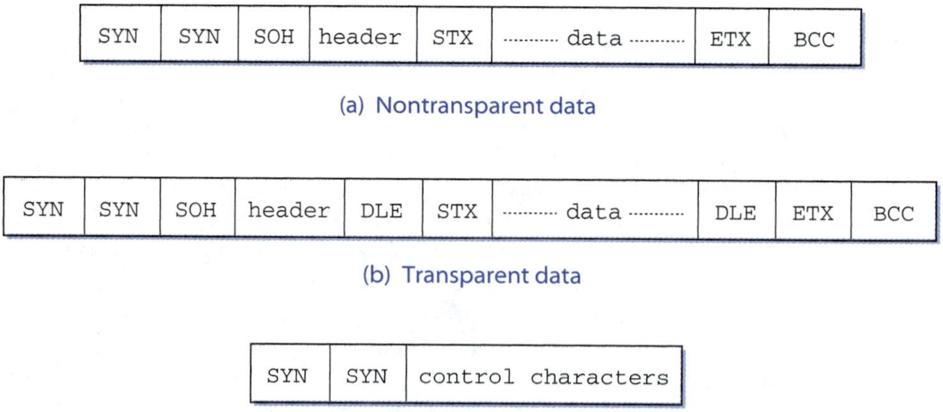

SYN	SYN	SOH	header	STX	---------- data ----------	ETX	BCC

(a) Nontransparent data

SYN	SYN	SOH	header	DLE	STX	---------- data ----------	DLE	ETX	BCC

(b) Transparent data

SYN	SYN	control characters

(c) Control frame

* It may be interesting to note that BSC can also be used with a lesser-known 6-bit code called Transcode. (Then again, maybe not.)

and two data frame formats. In each case, the frame starts with two **SYN characters.** Primarily, they allow the receiver of the frame to divide the bit stream into bytes (i.e., to note where one byte ends and the next begins).

The SYN bytes are followed by one or more control bytes. In a **control frame** (Figure 9.9c), the control bytes constitute the bulk of the information transmitted. Control information is similar to what we have discussed previously. Control bytes can acknowledge frames received correctly, NAK those received incorrectly, or request a response from another device.

In a data frame, the first control byte is SOH (Start of Header). It tells the receiving device that successive bytes in the arriving frame contain header information. Header information will vary, but typically contains the identity or address of the sending or receiving devices. For example, a destination identifier is needed when a primary device is sending something over a multipoint line, and a receiving identifier is needed when a primary device is receiving something from it.

The header information is followed by an STX (Start of Text) character (Figure 9.9a) or a DLE (Data Link Escape) and STX combination (Figure 9.9b). In the first case, STX indicates the start of text. This means that successive bytes represent data. However, since the number of data bytes can vary, the protocol needs a way to specify the end of them. It does this by using the ETX (End of Text) character. Thus, a receiving device receives and accepts the bytes as data until it encounters ETX.

For applications in which the data consist of printable character codes this is a simple way to indicate their end. But what about binary files whose data consist of bytes with random bit patterns? What happens if a frame's data contain an ETX character? What is to prevent the receiving device from interpreting it as a control byte and missing the remaining data? A device using the BSC protocol handles this by preceding the STX character with a DLE character, which acts like a toggle switch. When the receiving device sees the DLE–STX pair, it disables any checking for control bytes such as ETX. Moreover, the checking remains disabled until the receiving device encounters another DLE character. Once this DLE is encountered, the receiving device enables its checking for ETX or STX characters.

At first glance it may seem we have not solved any problems. What if the data contain a DLE character? The protocol gets around this problem by disguising DLE characters in its data. Figure 9.10 shows how. A sending device examines the

Figure 9.10   Byte Stuffing

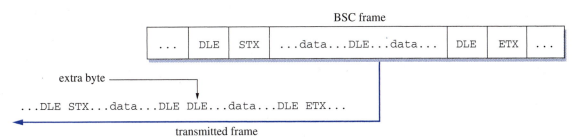

characters it sends as data. Whenever there is a DLE character, it inserts an extra DLE character. This process is called **byte stuffing** and is similar to bit stuffing, discussed previously; it just operates on a different level. Thus, when a receiving device encounters a DLE, it looks for a second one following immediately. If it finds one, it knows the second one is bogus and accepts the first as data. If not, it knows the DLE is not data and enables control character checking. Data delimited this way are called **transparent data.** That is, the Data field's contents are transparent to the receiving device. Data delimited with only STX and ETX are *nontransparent data.*

The last character from the formats shown in Figure 9.9 is **BCC, Block Check Character.** It is used in BSC's error checking method. The BCC field's contents depend on which error checking method is used. If the protocol uses the CRC check, BCC will correspond to the CRC-16 polynomial (see Section 6.3). In other cases, BSC uses a **longitudinal redundancy check.** This method visualizes the frame as a two-dimensional bit array where each row represents one byte. For each column, a parity bit is determined from the bits in that column and is stored in the BCC field.

9.3 ETHERNET: IEEE STANDARD 802.3

Now that we've discussed how two devices can exchange frames (independent of the medium to which they are connected), the next logical step is to discuss media access techniques (i.e., the MAC layer). Shortly after LANs were developed, the IEEE defined three formal standards: IEEE 802.3 for Ethernet, IEEE 802.4 for token bus, and IEEE 802.5 for token ring.

Ethernet was designed as a bus topology in which devices contend for the segment using a form of the CSMA/CD contention protocol (see Section 4.7). It is commonly used to connect workstations, servers, printers, and even old mainframe computers. Part of the Ethernet's history dates back to 1973. In his Ph.D. thesis, Robert Metcalfe described much of his research on LAN technology. After graduation, he joined the Xerox Corporation and worked with a group that eventually implemented what became known as **Ethernet.** Ethernet is named after **ether,** the imaginary substance that many once believed occupied all of space and was the medium through which light waves propagated.

Later, the concepts of the Ethernet were written up and proposed to the IEEE as a standard for LANs. The proposal had the backing of Xerox, Intel, and DEC. The IEEE eventually adopted it as a standard, and it is now referred to as IEEE standard 802.3. It is worth noting that two other proposals were made to the IEEE at about the same time. One was backed by General Motors and the other by IBM. With such influential organizations promoting particular standards, IEEE officials no doubt had difficulties deciding which of the three was most appropriate for a LAN standard. They compromised and made all three LAN standards—the other two became IEEE 802.4 (token bus) and IEEE 805.5 (token ring).

Most LANs today are based on the original Ethernet ideas, and the reader is not likely to encounter many token ring or token bus networks. For this reason, we will cover the original Ethernet concepts and the various upgrades that have occurred because of evolving technology. Also, because of its historical importance to the field and the fact that it represents a dramatically different approach to connecting devices, we will provide a discussion of the token ring network in a later section. We will not, however, cover the token bus standard.

CONCEPTS

Although Ethernet is classified as a bus topology, there are actually several ways to connect devices. Figure 9.11 shows how a connection between a personal computer and an Ethernet segment (cable)* was originally configured. Although we use the example of a personal computer, you should remember that other devices could also be connected to the cable. Electronic **terminators** were placed at both ends of the cable. They prevented electronic echoing of signals back and forth through the cable, which created false signals and caused confusion. Electronic echoing is a little like calling a radio talk show and listening to yourself as you talk. Your voice is usually delayed in order to avoid broadcasting nasty words. Thus, speaking and hearing your delayed words can be disorienting and cause you to make unintelligible sounds to the host.

A personal computer was connected to the cable via some additional hardware. First, a **transceiver** clamped onto the cable using a vampire clamp, a device with a pin that pierced the outer covering of the cable and made contact with the cable's core. The transceiver's primary purpose was to create an interface between the computer and the cable. One of its functions was to transmit bits onto the cable using CSMA/CD contention, which allowed it to determine when there was information moving along the cable and to detect collisions when they occurred. The transceiver communicated with the personal computer using a **transceiver cable.** Some called it an *attachment unit interface (AUI) cable.* The cable consisted of five twisted

Figure 9.11   Possible Ethernet Connection

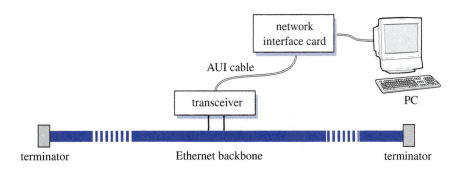

---

* This is representative of a thick Ethernet, more formally known as a 10Base5 cable. We'll discuss this and other cable specifications shortly.

pairs. Two were used to send data and control information to the computer. Two more were used for receiving data and control information. The fifth pair could be used to connect to a power source and ground. A transceiver could communicate with several devices using a multiplexer.

The transceiver cable connected to the personal computer through a **network interface card (NIC)** installed in the computer. The NIC contained the logic necessary to buffer data and move it between the transceiver cable and the computer's memory. It also did error checking, created frames, determined when to retransmit after collisions occurred, and recognized frames destined for its computer. In short, it performed those functions appropriate for the MAC layer protocol. It also relieved the personal computer's processor from these tasks and allowed it to attend to its typical activities.

To put things in perspective, let's describe and sequence the activities required for a personal computer to send data to another personal computer. The steps were as follows:

1. The sending computer executed network software that put a packet of information in the computer's memory. It then signaled the NIC via its internal bus that a packet was waiting to be sent.

2. The NIC got the packet and created the correct frame format, storing the packet in the frame's Data field. It then waited for a signal from the transceiver, which was monitoring the segment waiting for a chance to send.

3. When the transceiver detected a quiet cable, it signaled the NIC, which then sent the frame to the transceiver. The transceiver transmitted the bits onto the cable, listening for any collisions. If none occurred, it assumed the transmission was successful. If a collision did occur, the transceiver notified the NIC. The NIC executed the binary exponential backoff algorithm of Section 4.7 to determine when it should try again. If collisions continued to occur, it would signal the network software, which would provide the user with an error message or execute some algorithm in response to the error.

4. The transceiver at the receiving end monitored cable traffic. It copied frames from the cable and routed them to the NIC at that end.

5. The NIC then did a CRC error check. If there was no error, the NIC checked the destination address in the frame. If it was destined for its personal computer, the NIC buffered the frame's data (packet) in memory and generated an interrupt, thus informing the computer that a packet had arrived.

6. The personal computer executed network software and determined whether the packet could be accepted according to the flow control algorithms discussed in Chapter 8. If it could, the computer got the packet from memory for further processing. If not, the network software responded according to the protocols at the next-higher layer.

Each segment in the original standard had a maximum length of 500 meters. This was necessary because signals degrade as they propagate along the segment and, after 500 meters, may degrade too much. But what could you do if, for example, the total distance spanned by a cable exceeded that distance?

The 802.3 committee considered this problem and solved it by allowing multiple segments to be connected. Figure 9.12 shows one way to do this by using multiple segments connected by a **repeater,** a device that receives a signal, regenerates it, and retransmits it. The regeneration allows the signals to travel longer distances. In general, the original 802.3 standard allowed two computers to be separated by no more than four repeaters.*

ETHERNET FRAME FORMAT

Figure 9.13 shows the Ethernet frame format. As with previous frame formats, there are no surprises. It contains the usual information:

- **Preamble.** A 7-byte pattern consisting of alternating 0s and 1s is used for synchronization. Recall that synchronization establishes the rate at which bits are sampled. It's similar to a lead singer in a band establishing a pace by counting before beginning a song.
- **Start of Frame Delimiter.** The special pattern 10101011 indicates the start of a frame.
- **Destination Address.** If the first bit is 0, this field specifies a specific device. If it is 1, the destination address is a group address and the frame is sent to all devices in some predefined group specified by the address. Each device's interface knows its group address and responds when it sees it. If all bits are 1, the frame is broadcast to all devices.
- **Source Address.** Specifies where the frame comes from.
- **Data Length Field.** Specifies the number of bytes in the combined Data and Pad fields.

Figure 9.12   Connecting Two Segments

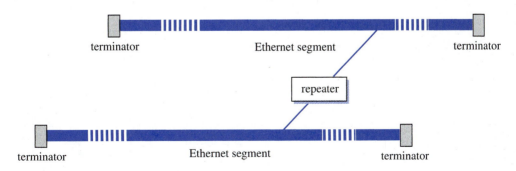

* There could be many segments in a network. The four-repeater constraint applied only to the path between two devices.

number of bytes

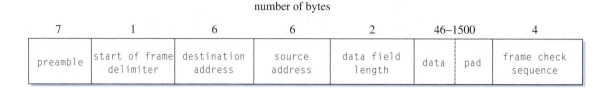

7	1	6	6	2	46–1500		4
preamble	start of frame delimiter	destination address	source address	data field length	data	pad	frame check sequence

Figure 9.13   Ethernet Frame Format

- **Data Field.** Self-explanatory.
- **Pad Field.** The Data field must be at least 46 bytes (more about this shortly). If there is not enough data, extra bytes are added (padded) to the data to make up the difference.
- **Frame Check Sequence.** Error checking using 32-bit CRC.

From Figure 9.13, we see an upper and lower limit (from 46 to 1500) on the number of data and pad bytes. The upper limit is used to prevent one transmission from monopolizing the medium for too long. The lower limit is to make sure the collision detection techniques work properly. To see why this is needed, consider the scenario of Figure 9.14. Device A transmits bits onto a segment. Those bits travel the segment and, just prior to the bits reaching B, device B starts transmitting. Both A's and B's bits collide, and the noise from that collision travels back along the segment toward A. Eventually A hears the collision and, if A is still sending, knows that its frame has collided with another. If A has finished sending its frame, then it does not know whether its frame or another has collided. It does not know whether the transmission was successful. Thus, the key to making CSMA/CD work is to make sure that if any collision occurs, the sender detects it before it is done sending its frame.

This means that the frame must be long enough so that a device is still transmitting bits when the collision is detected. So how long does it take to detect a collision?

Figure 9.14   Maximum Time to Detect a Collision

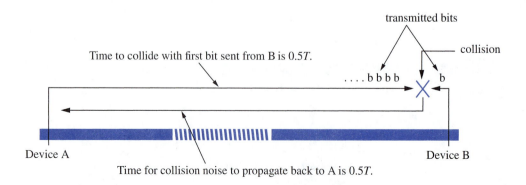

That depends, in part, on how far away from the sending device the collision occurred. Previously we had stated that each segment in the original standard had a maximum length of 500 meters and that two devices could be separated by a maximum of four repeaters. Thus, the maximum distance between two devices was 2500 meters. In addition, an electronic signal travels along copper at a rate of about 200 meters per μsec (microsecond). This means that a signal could cover 2500 meters in about 12.5 μsec. The maximum time for noise to return to the sending device is another 12.5 μsec. So in the worst case, it would take about 25 μsec for a device to detect a collision.

However, there's a complicating factor. There is a delay in each repeater as it regenerates and resends bits. The exact delay time depends on the device itself, but designers allowed for a couple of μsec delay for each repeater. Therefore, in addition to the 25 μsec travel time, there could be four delays in the data bits before the collision and four more delays in the bits resulting from the collision. Thus, the worst case was set at 50 μsec to detect a collision once a device started sending.

This means that each frame should require at least 50 μsec to transmit. At the 10 Mbps rate, a device sends 10 bits every μsec. In 50 μsec, it can send 500 bits. Add some bits for a safety margin, and the minimum frame size was set at 512 bits, or 64 bytes.

PHYSICAL IMPLEMENTATIONS OF 10 MBPS ETHERNET

After reading the previous discussion, you may look around your lab or classroom and say something like, "Except for the NIC in the personal computer, our connections don't look like that. Where are the coaxial cables and repeaters?" Of course, you're right. Evolving technology has changed the way we connect our networks. Many original implementations of the Ethernet used a 10Base5 cable, a 50-ohm, 10-millimeter diameter coaxial cable that supported a common bit rate of 10 Mbps. Some also called it **Thick Wire Ethernet** or just **ThickNet,** a clear reference to the thick, unwieldy cable. The thick 10-mm cable typically ran through basements or under floors, but it was difficult to bend and route around corners, into closets, and into other tight spaces. Consequently, it could not always be routed close to the devices that had to be connected. Thus, we had the configuration similar to that in Figure 9.11.

To allow cheaper and more flexible LANs more suited to personal computer environments, the IEEE created a modified standard, 802.3a, that used a 10Base2 cable. The cable supported the 10 Mbps bit rate but had a smaller diameter that allowed it to bend more easily, an important feature when trying to route cable around corners and into cabinets. It was also cheaper and had been dubbed **Cheapernet,** but was typically called **Thin Wire Ethernet** or **ThinNet.** The additional flexibility allowed a different connection from that shown in Figure 9.11. The thinner, more flexible 10Base2 cable could be connected directly to a personal computer using a T-connector (Figure 9.15). Done this way, the transceiver logic is built into a NIC installed in the personal computer. This method helped reduce the cost of the LAN because one 10Base2 cable could be routed to a series of personal computers, each with its own T-connector. One drawback of 10Base2 was that the thinner cable had more electronic resistance and could not span as long a distance (about 185 meters,

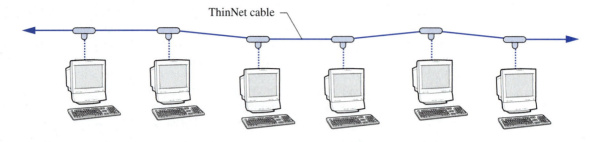

ThinNet cable

Figure 9.15 ThinNet Connections Using a T-Connector

compared with the 10Base5 maximum of 500 meters). On the other hand, the minimum distance between adjacent devices for 10Base2 cable was about half a meter, much smaller than the minimum of about 8 feet between transceivers connected to a 10Base5 cable. This made it convenient to connect multiple personal computers in a lab environment since room size often required the computers to be placed in close proximity to one another.

Figure 9.16 shows another configuration that evolved into IEEE standard 802.3i. A single device called a **hub** (sometimes called a **multiport repeater**) has many ports, each of which could connect to a device using a 10BaseT cable (a category 3, 4, or 5 UTP) that supported the 10 Mbps bit rate. The hub, in turn, was also connected to an Ethernet segment, although it was also possible to connect the hub to another hub or even to a switch or router. These last two devices deal with LAN connections; we'll discuss them in the next couple of chapters.

Figure 9.16 Connecting Personal Computers with a Hub

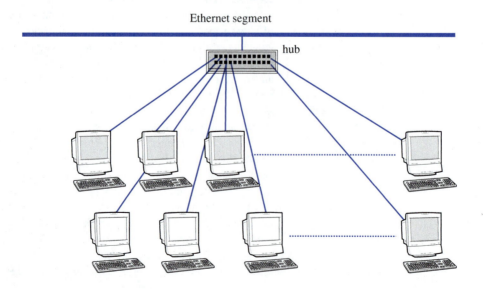

Ethernet segment

hub

Note that with this approach we no longer have a physical bus topology. So how does that affect the protocols the devices use? Oddly enough, it doesn't; the devices can still execute bus protocols, a definite convenience because the network cards don't have to be redesigned. The hub consists primarily of electronics that regenerate and route electrical signals received from one device over ports to which other devices are connected. In other words, anything a device sends is accessible by all other devices, just like a bus. Furthermore, if two devices send at the same time, their signals will collide,* again just like a bus. We say that all devices connected by a hub lie in the same **collision domain.** Thus, as far as each device is concerned, it is no different from being connected to a physical bus and it can execute the bus protocol. In effect, the bus has been downsized into a single hub.

This type of configuration has several advantages. First, it is useful in buildings where the physical configuration is not conducive to linear connections. In addition, it allows networks to be implemented using existing wiring, which is often installed when office buildings are built. Finally, the centralized communications control simplifies diagnostics and testing.

All three of these wiring standards use electric conductivity and a Manchester code for the digital signals. An optical standard is 802.3j, which specifies 10BaseF cable, a multimode optical fiber cable that, like the others, supports a 10 Mbps bit rate. Actually, 10BaseF includes three subsets: 10BaseFL (fiber link), 10BaseFB (fiber backbone), and 10BaseFP (fiber passive). 10BaseFL connects devices to a hub much like the 10BaseT cable but has a maximum length of 2000 meters. 10BaseFB is typically used to connect hubs and also has a maximum length of 2000 meters. 10BaseFP was also used to connect devices to hubs. The difference from FL was that 10BaseFP was used for small installations and used a passive coupler as a hub. The passive coupler had no external power source and could link no more than 33 devices. In addition, the maximum length was 500 meters. This approach was not common.

Table 9.2 summarizes the different connection strategies for the 10 Mbps Ethernet standard.

9.4   FAST ETHERNET (100 MBPS)

A 10 Mbps bit rate was once not only common but even considered fast. Of course, technology changes, and standards must evolve with it. User needs change as well. A 10 Mbps bit rate worked well when most applications consisted of email and small file exchanges. However, Web applications, computer-assisted design (CAD) systems, larger files such as those used for multimedia, server databases, and a larger number of users began to tax the limits of a 10 Mbps rate. Consequently, a new standard emerged that supported a 100 Mbps bit rate. It was called **Fast Ethernet,** a misnomer by today's standards but certainly a great improvement in 1995. The IEEE added Fast Ethernet to its group of 802.3 protocols and designated it 802.3u.

---

* This is not true with some later technologies, but we'll get to that.

Table 9.2 Physical Implementations of 10 Mbps Ethernet

IEEE STANDARD	CABLE STANDARD	COMMENTS
IEEE 802.3	10Base5	(ThickNet) 50-ohm coaxial cable, 10-mm diameter. Maximum segment length is 500 meters. Other maximum values are 4 repeaters, 5 segments, and 100 devices per segment. Minimum of 8 feet between transceivers. Uses Manchester coding. Used in physical bus topologies.
IEEE 802.3a	10Base2	(Cheapernet, ThinNet) 50-ohm coaxial cable, 5-mm diameter. Maximum segment length is 185 meters. Other maximum values are 4 repeaters, 5 segments, and 30 devices per segment. Minimum distance between nodes is 0.45 meter. Also uses Manchester coding. Used in physical bus topologies.
IEEE 802.3i	10BaseT	Category 3, 4, or 5 UTP. Central hub. Manchester coding. Maximum UTP length is 100 meters. Used in physical star topology.
IEEE 802.3j	10BaseFx	Multimode fiber. Maximum distance is 2000 meters for FL and FB, but 500 meters for FP. Used in physical star topology, but FP uses a passive coupler as its hub. FP is not common.

Fast Ethernet preserves most of the characteristics that we have already discussed. The Ethernet frame and address formats are the same. So are the constraints on the maximum and minimum frame size. Finally, contention is still based on CSMA/CD. In other words, the MAC layer is the same.

So, what are the main differences between Fast Ethernet and the 10 Mbps Ethernet? Well, there's the obvious—a 10-fold increase in bit rate. However, there's much more, largely because increasing the bit rate by a factor of 10 is not straightforward. It might seem easy to just develop hardware that generates bits at 10 times the rate. However, there is a problem. The media over which those bits may travel have limits.

The 10 Mbps Ethernet was designed to run over coaxial cable and, as we stated previously, was modified to make use of UTP. Fast Ethernet, however, is not designed to run over coaxial cable at all. All of its wiring standards include either UTP, STP, or optical fiber and are designed for physical star topologies. Thus, the features that distinguish Fast Ethernet from 10 Mbps Ethernet are primarily in the physical layer. We will discuss the following Fast Ethernet standards: 100BaseTX, 100BaseT4, and 100BaseFX.

100BaseTX

We start with 100BaseTX, designed to run over category 5 UTP. When developers designed Fast Ethernet to run at 100 Mbps over category 5 UTP, they faced a serious problem. Since the 10 Mbps Ethernet implementations used Manchester coding for the digital data, it would seem reasonable to just increase the frequency of the Manchester code to account for the faster bit rate. Unfortunately that does not work because the high-frequency signal needed produces too much noise (EMI, or electromagnetic interference) for the category 5 UTP. Therefore, the frequency needed to be reduced, creating an obvious problem in light of previous discussions relating bit rates and frequencies. One option was to use straight NRZI coding. Because the signal is held fixed for each bit (i.e., there is no transition in the middle of the interval), the required frequency is cut in half. The problem is a possible loss of synchronization if the signal represents a long stream of zeros (see Section 3.2).

To solve this problem, the 100BaseTX implementation uses a block encoding scheme called 4B/5B encoding. It's a scheme that replaces every half-byte (the technical term is *nibble*—honest) with 5 bits. Increasing the number of bits may seem a bit unusual and, in fact, seems to make the problem worse because now we have to transmit 25% more bits. The trick, however, is in the implementation.

Let's first examine how the code works. Table 9.3 shows how each nibble is replaced with a 5-bit counterpart. Now consider the following string of nibbles:

```
1010-0010-0000-0000-0000-0000
```

Using the entries in Table 9.3, each nibble is replaced by its 5-bit equivalent, and the resulting string is

```
10110-10100-11110-11110-11110-11110
```

Notice what happens. A long run consisting of the same bit cannot occur. No matter what string of nibbles you start with, the resulting 5-bit blocks will always contain both 0s and 1s. What's the advantage of this? Because we no longer can have a long run of the same bit value, the need for the Manchester code no longer exists. Consequently, we could use the simpler NRZI coding scheme. However, even with an NRZI code and the lower-frequency signal, there are some noise issues involved in sending it over a category 5 UTP.

To further reduce noise associated with high frequencies, a new signaling scheme was developed, called **Multilevel Line Transmission–Three Levels (MLT-3).** It

Table 9.3   Coding Using 4B/5B

DATA BITS	5B CODE	DATA BITS	5B CODE
0000	11110	1000	10010
0001	01001	1001	10011
0010	10100	1010	10110
0011	10101	1011	10111
0100	01010	1100	11010
0101	01011	1101	11011
0110	01110	1110	11100
0111	01111	1111	11101

deviates from previous coding schemes in one important way: Instead of using a two-state signal (represented by high and low, or −1 and 1), MLT-3 defines a three-state signal. We'll designate those states using −1, 0, and 1. In general, the MLT-3 signal cycles through the states in the order −1, 0, +1, 0, −1, 0, +1, 0, −1, and so on. In fact, it's much like a sequence of sine values at regularly spaced intervals.

MLT-3 responds to each bit as follows:

- If the bit is 1, the MLT-3 signal progresses to the next state in its sequence.
- If the bit is 0, the MLT-3 signal remains at its current state.

Figure 9.17 shows an example of a bit string and its associated MLT-3 signal. We assume the signal starts at 0. Since the first bit is 0, the signal remains at its current state for one interval. The second bit is 1, so the signal goes to the next state in its sequence, +1. The third bit is 0, and the signal remains where it is, at +1. The fourth bit is 1, and the signal moves to the next state in its sequence, 0. The fifth bit is 1; again, the signal changes, this time to −1. This pattern repeats for each bit in the string. For each 1 bit, the signal changes to the next state; for each 0 bit, the signal stays the same.

So how does this help? Take a good long look at Figure 9.17. It will take at least four intervals for the MLT-3 signal to go through one complete cycle (−1 → 0 → +1 → 0 → −1). By comparison, a Manchester code may go through one complete cycle (low → high → low) in one interval. This means that MLT-3 encoding requires about 25% of the maximum frequency of Manchester. It generates far less noise and works quite well over a category 5 UTP.

Figure 9.18 shows a partial layering for the Fast Ethernet protocol.* The features we have described thus far are all below the MAC layer. A **reconciliation sublayer** takes 4 bits at a time and sends them to the **physical coding sublayer (PCS)** through a **medium independent interface (MII).** The MII defines a connection between a NIC and a transceiver; if the transceiver is external to the NIC, it requires a

Figure 9.17   Multilevel Line Transmission–Three Levels (MLT-3)

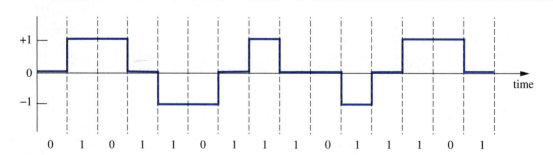

* We have left out some components, but a full description of them requires a knowledge of electronics and signaling characteristics beyond what we have covered. Reference [Fo03] contains additional details.

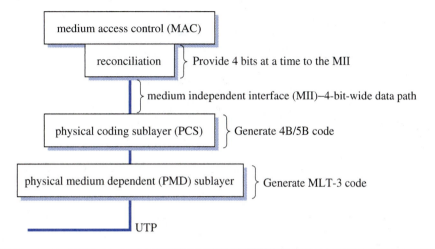

Figure 9.18 100BaseTX Physical Sublayers

cable with a 40-pin connector. If the transceiver is built into the NIC (usually the case), the MII cable is not needed. In any event, the MII provides a 4-bit-wide data path. The PCS does the block encoding, replacing each nibble with a 5-bit code. The 5-bit code is then sent to the **physical medium dependent (PMD) sublayer,** where the MLT-3 signal is generated and transmitted onto the medium.

Another feature that distinguishes 100BaseTX from earlier Ethernets is the fact that it can run in half-duplex or full-duplex mode.* Because the original Ethernet used coaxial cable and baseband Manchester encoding, only one transmission could occur at a time or collisions occurred. Thus, devices had to use half-duplex mode. The use of UTP changed that. Category 5 cable typically contains four wire pairs, and 100BaseTX uses two of them: one for sending and the other for receiving and detecting collisions. When a 100BaseTX hub connects devices, they run in half-duplex mode. That's because although there is a separate send and receive pair, two transmissions from different devices can still collide at the hub. However, devices can run in full-duplex mode (sending and receiving at the same time) if a **switch** connects them. Switches are a layer 2 type of device used to separate collision domains; we'll defer a discussion of switches and full-duplex operations until the next chapter, where we discuss switched Ethernet.

100BaseFX

Of course, running Fast Ethernet over category 5 cable is not the only option. Fiber is another, and 100BaseFX specifies Fast Ethernet over multimode optical fiber. One of fiber's advantages over copper is the segment length. 100BaseTX has a

---

* This is also true of 10BaseT.

maximum length of 100 meters, whereas 100BaseFX links can be up to 2 kilometers long if running in full-duplex mode. The implementation uses two fibers: one for transmitting and one for receiving and collision detection.

The physical layering of 100BaseFX is similar to that of 100BaseTX. It uses a 4B/5B block decoder to replace each nibble with 5 bits. However, because fiber does not have the same frequency constraints as twisted pair, it does not require the MLT-3 encoding phase. Instead, it uses NRZI.

100BaseT4

Suppose your organization made the decision to upgrade its 10 Mbps Ethernet to Fast Ethernet. Now all it needs to do is install the devices and route category 5 cable through the space in between walls, under floors, above ceiling tiles, through conduits, and who knows where else. It's a difficult and often expensive task to replace old wiring with new. Does this mean that unless you install all new category 5 wire you're doomed to live with the 10 Mbps rate? Fortunately, no.

The 100BaseT4 specification was designed for category 3 wire. This is particularly convenient for buildings that were constructed using the older voice-grade category 3 wire. It need not be replaced. The question, of course, is: How can we make it work? The frequency limitations of category 5 wiring required some innovative schemes to achieve a 100 Mbps rate. The limitations of category 3 UTP are even more severe. Using a 4B/5B decoder followed by MLT-3 encoding worked for category 5 wire but it produces too much noise for category 3 wire. For this, an entirely different approach is needed.

Like 100BaseTX, 100BaseT4 uses a three-level encoding scheme. However, its approach is quite different. Rather than use a block decoder like 4B/5B first, it uses an **8B/6T encoding** scheme. This scheme associates every byte (8 bits) value with a unique string of six ternary values, called **trits.** Symbolically we express each trit as $+$, 0, and $-$. It seems a bit strange to replace eight things with six, but keep in mind we're replacing 8 bits with 6 trits. There are $2^8 = 256$ possible 8-bit strings and $3^6 = 729$ possible 6-trit strings. Thus, the association uses only slightly more than a third of all possible trit strings.

Table 9.4 shows some of the trit codes for a small number of byte values. The entire table has 256 entries, and there's little need here to reproduce all of them. If interested, reference [Ha01] has a more complete table. Figure 9.19 shows a signal

Table 9.4 Partial 8B/6T Encoding Table

BYTE	TRIT CODE	BYTE	TRIT CODE	BYTE	TRIT CODE	BYTE	TRIT CODE
00	$-+00-+$	40	$-00+0+$	80	$-00+-+$	C0	$-+0+-+$
01	$0-+-+0$	41	$0-00++$	81	$0-0-++$	C1	$0-+-++$
02	$0-+0-+$	42	$0-0+0+$	82	$0-0+-+$	C2	$0-++-+$
03	$0-++0-$	43	$0-0++0$	83	$0-0++-$	C3	$0-+++-$
⋮	⋮	⋮	⋮	⋮	⋮	⋮	⋮

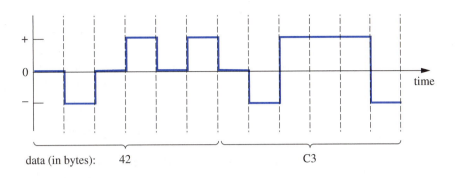

data (in bytes):   42   C3

Figure 9.19   8B/6T Encoding

associated with two consecutive byte values. Note that 16 bits are transmitted in just 12 consecutive time intervals (one for each trit), a 25% reduction compared with sending each bit using an NRZI code. Thus, since we require a 100 Mbps rate, the signal must have the capacity of changing at a baud rate of 75 million. Unfortunately, this still requires a frequency that category 3 wires cannot accommodate.

However, like the category 5 cable, category 3 cable typically has four wire pairs. What makes 100BaseT4 work is that data are transmitted through three wire pairs simultaneously. The 100BaseT4 specification states that each device uses one wire pair for transmitting and one for receiving and collision detection. It uses the other two as bidirectional media. In other words, when device A sends data to device B, it uses its transmit pair and the two bidirectional pairs to do so. If device B sends, then it uses its transmit pair (device A's receive pair) and the two bidirectional pairs to do so.

Figure 9.20 shows how this works. Device A needs to send the following sequence of bytes: B_1, B_2, B_3, B_4, and so on. Hardware at site A converts each byte to

Figure 9.20   Sending Data on 100BaseT4 over Four Wire Pairs

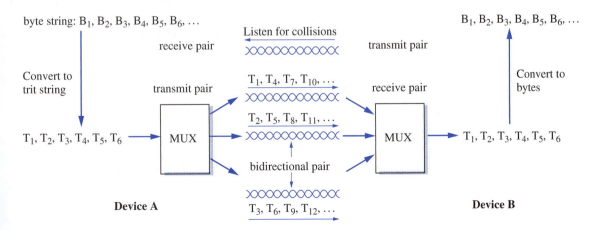

a 6-trit string, producing a sequence of trit strings, T_1, T_2, T_3, T_4, and so on, that goes into a multiplexer. The multiplexer has three outputs. Strings T_1, T_4, T_7, and so on travel along A's transmit pair (crossing over to B's receive pair). Strings T_2, T_5, T_8, and so on and T_3, T_6, T_9, and so on travel along the two bidirectional pairs. If B were sending, it would use its transmit pair and the same two bidirectional pairs.

Because transmissions occur in parallel, a smaller bit rate will suffice for each wire pair. This translates to a smaller frequency for each pair. Suppose the signal on each of the three pairs has the capacity of changing at a 25 million baud rate. This translates to a rate of 75 million trits per second. Since 6 trits expand to 8 bits, the effective bit rate is 100 Mbps. Most important, the frequency needed for a baud rate of 25 million is within the noise limits of category 3 UTP.

One drawback of 100BaseT4 is that it cannot operate in full-duplex mode because of the type of signals the physical layer uses and the fact that data transmission uses three of the four wire pairs. Thus, full-duplex operations would require at least six wire pairs or other innovative techniques.

COLLISION DOMAIN

One last issue we address is the collision domain. Both 10 Mbps and Fast Ethernet maintain the 512-bit minimum frame size. However, Fast Ethernet transmits one minimum-size frame in 5.12 μsec, 10 times faster than the 10 Mbps Ethernet. Don't forget that the signals still require time to travel the medium and that CSMA/CD requires a device to still be transmitting if a collision occurs. This is a problem for Fast Ethernet if the collision requires nearly 50 μsec to detect, because a device may have long since stopped transmitting when it detects a collision. Consequently, the collision domain size (the maximum length a signal travels) must be reduced significantly. The standard calls for just one or two hubs, depending on whether the hub is a class I or class II repeater. A class II repeater has a smaller delay and forwards bits quicker. However, it supports only one type of signal. That is, it cannot connect a 100BaseTX and 100BaseT4 cable. Two class II repeaters can be in the same collision domain as long as the link between them is 5 meters or less. A class I repeater, although slower, can connect different segment types. However, the standard specifies only one class I repeater in a collision domain.

Table 9.5 provides a final summary of the three Fast Ethernet specifications.

9.5   GIGABIT ETHERNET

The next major step in the evolution of Ethernet was another 10-fold increase in bit rate and the development of the **Gigabit Ethernet** standards. As the name indicates, they support bit rates of 1000 Mbps (1 Gbps). Not surprisingly, the motivating factors for the development of Gigabit Ethernet were similar to those for the development of Fast Ethernet: more and larger files, more multimedia applications (especially real-time applications), more users, more sophisticated Web applications, and so on. User needs continue to increase, and technology must evolve with them.

Table 9.5 Physical Implementations of the IEEE 802.3u 100 Mbps Fast Ethernet Standard

CABLE SPECIFICATION	COMMENTS
100BaseTX	Uses two wire pairs in a Cat 5 cable and 4B/5B followed by MLT-3 encoding. Maximum of two class II repeaters (if separated by 5 meters or less) or one class I repeater in a collision domain. Maximum segment length is 100 meters.
100BaseFX	Multimode optical fiber. Uses 4B/5B and NRZI encoding. Maximum of two class II repeaters or one class I repeater in a collision domain. Maximum segment length is 136 meters if both links in the collision domain are fiber and 160 meters if the other link is UTP. If fiber connects two switches, then the segment length can be 412 meters long (half duplex) or 2000 meters long (full duplex).
100BaseT4	Uses four wire pairs in a Cat 3 cable. Uses 6B/8T encoding and transmits trits simultaneously over three wire pairs. Maximum of two class II repeaters or one class I repeater between devices. Cannot be used in full-duplex mode. Maximum segment length is 100 meters.

MAC SUBLAYER

Gigabit Ethernet was designed to run over both optical fiber (1000BaseSX and 1000BaseLX) and over copper (1000BaseT and 1000BaseCX). We'll outline the physical layers shortly, but first we will focus on an important issue at the MAC layer that was not present in the Fast Ethernet standard. Gigabit Ethernet can run in both full-duplex and half-duplex modes. In full-duplex mode, collisions do not occur and CSMA/CD is disabled. However, in half-duplex mode, collisions still can occur and the collision domain size is an issue. With Fast Ethernet, we saw that a device transmitting at 100 Mbps transmits a minimum-size frame in 5.12 μsec. Consequently, the collision domain size decreased to around 200 meters for category 5 UTP. At gigabit speeds, a device transmits a minimum-size frame in 0.512 μsec. For category 5 UTP, that reduces the size of the collision domain to around 25 meters, not a very large area in which to build a network.

This is a real problem and there are a couple of ways to deal with it. The first is to eliminate collisions entirely so that a minimum frame size is not required. This can be done using switches; we discuss that in the next chapter. The second option is to increase the minimum frame size. Although many Gigabit Ethernet implementations have gone to full-duplex collision-free environments, the standard still supports CSMA/CD by increasing the minimum frame size from 512 bits to 4096 bits. This is an eightfold increase both in the size of the frame and the time needed to transmit it. In turn, this allows segment lengths of 100 meters, similar to the Fast Ethernet specifications. In full-duplex mode, the MAC frame is the same as in previous Ethernet standards. In half-duplex mode, Figure 9.21a shows how the standard increases the frame size by using a *carrier extension*.

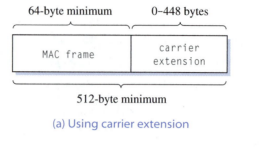

(a) Using carrier extension

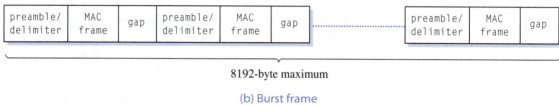

8192-byte maximum

(b) Burst frame

Figure 9.21 Gigabit Ethernet Frames

The standard Ethernet frame is as shown in Figure 9.13. If the data require fewer than 46 bytes, the Data field is padded to 46 bytes to meet the original minimum of 64 bytes. In this case, the carrier extension consists of an extra 448 bytes to meet the minimum of 512 bytes. If there are more than 46 data bytes, then the size of the carrier extension is reduced by 1 byte for every data byte over 46. If there are 494 or more data bytes, then the frame meets the minimum requirement and there is no carrier extension.

If there is a lot of data to send, this is a reasonable approach. However, if most frames have little data, the carrier extension is just a lot of extra padding and is inefficient. After all, creating a 512-byte frame to carry just a few data bytes is a lot of overhead. It's a little like taking a U-Haul to the corner store to pick up a half gallon of milk. To make the standard work a little more efficiently, Gigabit Ethernet uses *frame bursting* (Figure 9.21b). The idea is to transmit multiple frames without going through the contention protocol for each one. The standard accomplishes this by creating a *burst frame,* which consists of one MAC frame (including the carrier extension) followed by a sequence of additional MAC frames. None of the other MAC frames has the carrier extension, and a 96-bit gap separates each pair of consecutive frames.

In burst mode, the device goes through the usual CSMA protocol and, when it gets access, transmits the burst frame. The first embedded MAC frame has the carrier extension, so that the device will detect any collisions prior to transmitting the second embedded MAC frame. If no collision occurs, the device transmits the remaining MAC frames and the gaps embedded in the burst frame without going through the contention protocol for each. The gaps in between keep the medium busy; any other device trying to contend for the medium sees it as busy as long as the burst frame is occupying it.

When Gigabit Ethernet runs in full-duplex mode, the minimum frame size and burst frames are not needed because collisions do not happen. In this case Gigabit Ethernet uses the same MAC frame format as earlier versions.

1000BaseX

The first Gigabit Ethernet specification we describe is 1000BaseX, the 802.3z standard. The 1000BaseX standard actually includes three separate media: short-wavelength optical fiber (1000BaseSX), long-wavelength optical fiber (1000BaseLX), and a shielded copper cable (1000BaseCX). The latter has different electrical characteristics than category 5 UTP and allows for very fast bit rates over distances not greater than 25 meters. It is typically used to connect centralized devices in a communications rack.

The difference between short- and long-wave optical fiber is the light frequency transmitted through the fiber. Short wave uses a higher-frequency signal over multimode fiber. Long wave can use either multimode or single-mode fiber. Short-wave lasers are similar to those used in CD technology. They cost less but the signal attenuates more quickly, which means a shorter maximum distance. Long-wave lasers are more expensive but the signal maintains integrity over longer distances.

The Gigabit Ethernet physical layer stack for 1000BaseX resembles that shown in Figure 9.18. However, instead of a medium independent interface that has a 4-bit-wide data path, Gigabit Ethernet uses a Gigabit medium independent interface (GMII) that has an 8-bit-wide data path. The reconciliation layer provides 1 bit of data on each path every 8 nanoseconds to the physical coding sublayer (PCS). Each of the 8-bit paths accommodates 125 Mbps; the combined rate is 1 Gbps.

Like the PCS in Fast Ethernet, the Gigabit Ethernet PCS uses a block encoding scheme. However, it's an 8B/10B scheme that replaces 8 bits of data with 10 bits. Every 10-bit code has either four, five, or six 0s (and, of course, six, five, or four 1s). The reason for this is as before: to disrupt any long strings of 0s or 1s. The 8B/10B scheme is conceptually similar to the 4B/5B encoding scheme; however, it provides a better *DC balance*. This means that when a bit string is expanded, the result includes a similar number of 0s and 1s and frequent transitions between 0s and 1s.

There are several advantages. First is the clock synchronizing feature we have discussed previously. Second is that many more 10-bit codes exist than are needed for 8-bit data. This allows some of them to be used for control functions. Another advantage is that when used in optical fiber communications, the balance reduces data-dependent heating of lasers. This is significant because such heating can increase the error rate. Note, however, that the 8B/10B code alone does not guarantee an equal number of 0s and 1s for long bit strings—only that the frequency of 0s or 1s does not exceed 60% (since there is a maximum of six 0s or 1s in any code). To further increase DC balancing, the PCS calculates a *running disparity*. As bits are generated, the PCS keeps track of whether it generates more 1s or 0s. The running disparity is positive if more 1s have been generated, and negative otherwise. Next, the PCS converts each 8-bit byte to a 10-bit code that depends not only on the byte but also on the current running disparity value. Using two possible codes instead of one allows the PCS to generate a nearly equal number of 0s and 1s. This, in turn, reduces the data-dependent heating of the lasers and maximizes their effectiveness. Although the concept of converting 8 bits to 10 seems simple on the surface, the reasons for specific codes are quite complex.

Figure 9.22 summarizes the process. The 8B/10B encoder receives 8 bits at the rate of 1 Gbps and encodes each group of 8, producing a 10-bit code. A laser then transmits the sequence of 10-bit codes over the optical fiber at a rate of 1.25 Gbps.

1000BaseT

Gigabit Ethernet also works over category 5 UTP. However, generating gigabit rates over copper posed some serious challenges to the 802.3ab committee that was responsible for 1000BaseT specification. Section 9.4 on Fast Ethernet outlined some of the problems associated with using higher frequencies to achieve higher bit rates over UTP. The problem becomes even more difficult with the increase to gigabit speeds. Simply extending the approach used in 100BaseTX is not an option because the increased bit rate requires signal frequencies that exceed category 5 UTP ratings. In other words, it won't work!

The real problem is dealing with the noise generated by high-frequency signals over category 5 UTP. One approach is to use MLT-3 encoding for all four wire pairs instead of just one. If we could generate a 250 Mbps rate on each of four wire pairs, we'd get the desired 1 Gbps rate. Although this idea worked for 100BaseTX over three wire pairs, the bits are generated 10 times faster for 1000BaseT, and the required frequency to generate MLT-3 signals for a 250 Mbps rate over each pair is still too high. To get around this, 1000BaseT uses several very sophisticated techniques: PAM5 encoding, trellis encoding, and Viterbi decoding (Figure 9.23).

PAM5 is the acronym for *pulse amplitude modulation with five levels*. The basic idea is to take 8 bits at a time from the GMII, divide each 8-bit group into four

Figure 9.22   1000BaseX Transmission

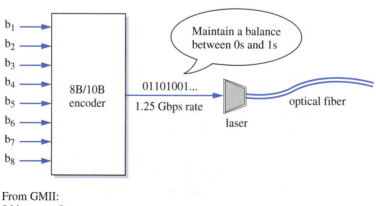

From GMII:
8 bits every 8 ns.
1000 Mbps.

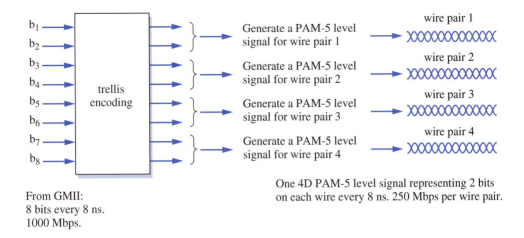

From GMII:
8 bits every 8 ns.
1000 Mbps.

One 4D PAM-5 level signal representing 2 bits
on each wire every 8 ns. 250 Mbps per wire pair.

Figure 9.23   1000BaseT Transmission

2-bit groups (one for each UTP), and then associate a particular signal level (chosen from among five possibilities) for each 2-bit group. Thus, four separate, concurrent signals convey 8 bits of information.

First question: Why use five levels in the encoding scheme? Keep in mind that four pairs are transmitting 8 bits simultaneously. Since there are $2^8 = 256$ possible values, we need at least 256 signal combinations across the four UTPs. If each wire pair could accommodate four signal levels, there would be $4^4 = 256$ possible combinations of signals over the four pairs. Although sufficient, this number does not allow any additional signals for control functions. Consequently, the standard uses five levels, which allows $5^4 = 625$ combinations of signals. The usual designation for these five levels is -2, -1, 0, $+1$, and $+2$.

To achieve gigabit rates, each wire pair must accommodate 250 Mbps. Although each signal level can accommodate 2 bits, the frequency needed to send 2 bits at a time at a rate of 125 MHz still has a signal-to-noise ratio that exceeds the specifications of category 5 UTP. To account for this, the 802ab committee built in error correction and detection techniques. This is where trellis encoding and Viterbi decoding enter the picture. *Trellis encoding* is an example of a code that uses the extra signal level in PAM5 (2 bits require only four levels) to create redundancies in the code. The redundancies, in turn, are used to increase the signal-to-noise ratio of the UTP signals. *Viterbi decoding,* on the receiving end, involves algorithms designed to look for damaged signals and recover the original. How trellis encoding and Viterbi decoding work is very complex and requires a solid knowledge of signals, voltage distributions, pulse shaping and signal equalization techniques, and signal and noise characteristics. These methods are similar to technologies used in 56 Kbps modems and are well established. However, we will not cover this material but instead refer the interested reader to other sources, such as references [Sc97], [Gr01], and [Pr01], for more detail.

One last feature that we note is the full-duplex nature of 1000BaseT. Previous standards used unidirectional transmission, in which a separate wire pair is used to transmit in each direction at any time. Transmission in 1000BaseT is bidirectional. Signals go in both directions simultaneously (Figure 9.24). As you may guess, problems arise when signals move in opposite directions at the same time. They create electronic echoes that distort the real signals. Fortunately, there is a solution to the problem: 1000BaseT implements the bidirectional mode using *hybrids,* complex devices that are capable of eliminating noise caused by echoes. Hybrids also are capable of separating locally transmitted signals from the incoming ones.

As of this writing, most workstations still use 10 Mbps or Fast Ethernet connections. The Gigabit standard is designed primarily for fiber connections used to connect switches and provide paths among Fast Ethernet groups; however, shielded copper wires can be used to connect such devices on a rack (i.e., devices in close proximity). Table 9.6 summarizes the Gigabit standards.

BEYOND GIGABIT RATES

Having discussed the evolution of Ethernet from 10 Mbps up through Gigabit Ethernet, what's next? The answer, of course, is *10 Gigabit Ethernet,* developed by the IEEE 802.3ae task force and approved as a standard in the summer of 2002. Why develop another 10-fold increase in bit rates? As before, the answer is to meet demand. Workstations are connecting to LANs at 10 and 100 Mbps rates. Home users are upgrading from 56 Kbps modems to cable modems and DSL technologies. Simply put, end users are generating and consuming more information than ever before, and the aggregate flow among all these users is increasing. Consequently, backbone technologies must keep up. The 10 Gigabit Ethernet will be used largely as a backbone, not only in LAN environments but also in metropolitan and wide area networks where the need for bandwidth is high.

Figure 9.24   UTP Full-Duplex Mode over UTP

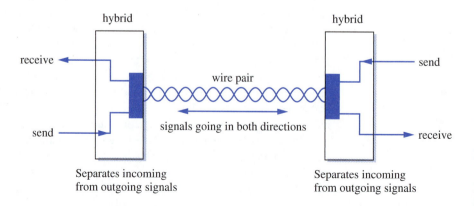

Table 9.6   Physical Implementations of the Gigabit Ethernet Standard

CABLE SPECIFICATIONS	COMMENTS
1000BaseT (IEEE 802.3ab)	Requires four pairs of category 5 UTP and runs in full-duplex mode. Signaling requires complex encoding/decoding procedures: PAM5, trellis, and Viterbi. Maximum segment length is 100 meters.
1000BaseCX (IEEE 802.3z)	Medium is a specially shielded copper cable. Maximum distance is 25 meters. Typically used for connecting rack devices in a communications center. Uses 8B/10B encoding.
1000BaseLX (IEEE 802.3z)	Long-wave optical fiber. Can be used with either multimode or single-mode fiber. Maximum lengths are 5000 meters for single-mode fiber and 550 meters for multimode. Uses 8B/10B encoding.
1000BaseSX (IEEE 802.3z)	Short-wave optical fiber. Can be used only with multimode fiber. Maximum lengths are between 220 and 550 meters, depending on the fiber's diameter. Uses 8B/10B encoding.

In developing the 10 Gigabit Ethernet, the 802.3ae task force established five criteria (see http://grouper.ieee.org/groups/802/3/ae/criteria.pdf):

- Broad market potential
- Compatibility with existing 802.3 standards
- Substantial difference from its predecessors
- Technical feasibility
- Economic feasibility

Besides the 10-fold increase over Gigabit Ethernet, 10 Gigabit Ethernet has other significant features:

- It uses the same MAC frame format as its predecessors, allowing it to remain backward compatible.
- It supports only full-duplex mode.
- It is designed to operate only over optical fiber.
- It does not include the CSMA/CD protocol of earlier Ethernets. There are no more collisions.
- It supports transmission over much longer distances (40 km over single-mode fiber).
- It can run over a SONET carrier system—specifically, over an OC-192 circuit.

The 802.3ae standard specifies two distinct physical layer types: LAN PHY and WAN PHY. The LAN PHY is designed for LAN interconnectivity and to support existing gigabit applications, but at much faster rates. As with the previous versions, the LAN PHY contains a PCS sublayer that communicates with the reconciliation sublayer. However, the 10 Gigabit Ethernet PCS layer uses a 64B/66B encoding scheme. It's similar to the 4B/5B and 8B/10B schemes discussed earlier, except it encodes 64 bits into 66 bits. Processing more bits simultaneously is quicker. Also, there are fewer overhead bits in this scheme (2 bits of every 66 as opposed to 2 bits of every 10). This allows the bit rate to more closely match the signaling frequencies needed to send the bits.

The WAN PHY is designed to extend Ethernet beyond the traditional LAN environment and to facilitate connectivity over much larger areas. Because current communications over long distances often go through multiple protocols, the use of an Ethernet technology for long-distance communications will simplify matters considerably. No longer will packets and frames have to be converted to other forms prior to transmission. Yes, the world is shrinking, and we now see the potential for worldwide information systems to be connected by LAN-based technologies.

The main difference between the WAN PHY and LAN PHY is a WAN interface sublayer (WIS) between the PCS and PMD sublayers that is designed to allow transparent communications over SONET OC-192 circuits. Because OC-192 circuit bit rates are just under 10 Gbps, it's a natural match. The WIS sublayer receives coded bits from the PCS, embeds them into a SONET frame, and outputs that frame to the PMD sublayer. This allows Ethernet to use SONET carriers for transport across wide area networks—in effect, extending the range of Ethernet networks to much larger distances.

The 802.3ae standard has optional interfaces: the 10 Gigabit media independent interface (XGMII) and XGMII attachment unit interface extension (XAUI). The XGMII allows full-duplex communication between the PCS and reconciliation sublayer and has a 74-bit-wide data path. The path includes 32 data bits in each direction as well as clocking and control functions. However, its design does not readily allow chip-to-chip or chip-to-optical-module connections because of hardware constraints that limit the distance the bus can cover. An alternative is the XAUI, which has fewer lines than the XGMII and runs at a rate two and a half times that of 1000BaseX. It also has different electrical characteristics, which extends the XGMII's reach.

The formal approval of a 10 Gigabit Ethernet standard preceded this writing by only a few months, and there are few published books and articles on it. The interested reader can get more information at the following websites: http://grouper.ieee.org/groups/802/3/ae/ and www.10gea.org/. These sites provide links to a number of white papers that provide more detailed discussion of many aspects of the 10 Gigabit standard.

Will there be a 100 Gigabit Ethernet? Probably. The first step in the standards process is the identification of a sponsor (a technical society or group within IEEE) that agrees to oversee the development process. The sponsor then puts out a Call for Interest. As of this writing, that has not yet happened for a 100 Gigabit Ethernet standard, so it will probably not be a reality soon. In addition, gigabit devices are commonly used in LAN environments; 10-gigabit devices are expensive and used primarily by telecommunications carriers. Some predict that it may be a couple of years before prices decrease to the point where 10-gigabit technology becomes more widespread and people begin feeling the pinch of a 10-gigabit rate. Still, it is dangerous to make predictions in this field; all one can do is continue reading and be aware of the changes that are occurring.

9.6 TOKEN RING: IEEE STANDARD 802.5

Token ring LAN is defined by the IEEE standard 802.5. Like Ethernet, the token ring is a MAC protocol sitting between the logical link control and the physical layer. Data rates for token ring networks are listed as 4 Mbps and 1 Mbps, although IBM token rings can run at 4, 16, or 100 Mbps. Transmission occurs using the differential Manchester coding techniques described in Section 2.4.

Devices on a token ring LAN are connected in a ring using a NIC (Figure 9.25). A device can send directly only to its neighbors, and in most cases only to one neighbor (counterclockwise in Figure 9.25). If a device wants to send to another device on the ring, the frame must go through all the intermediate interfaces. Ring contention is handled through a token (a special frame) that circulates past all the devices. The specifics of claiming tokens and sending frames are discussed later in this section. For now, we provide a very general and simple description of the process.

When a token arrives at a device, one of two things occurs. If a device does not have data to send, it routes the token to its neighbor. If a device does have something to send, it claims the token, removes it from the ring, and sends a frame in the

Figure 9.25   Token Ring Network and Circulating Token

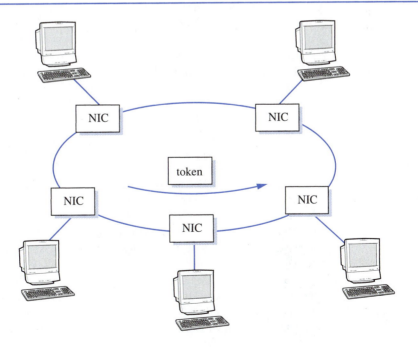

token's place. The frame then travels along the ring, and each device examines its destination address. If the destination address does not match the current device's address, the device routes the frame to its neighbor. If it does match, the destination device copies the frame, sets some status bits in it, and routes the frame to its neighbor. The frame continues along the ring until it eventually arrives at the device that created it. This device removes the frame from the ring, generates a new token, and sends the token back onto the ring.

Two observations can be made almost immediately. The first is that ring contention is more orderly than with an Ethernet. Each device knows when it can send and sends only to its neighbor. An immediate consequence is that there is no wasted bandwidth due to collisions. The second observation is that the failure of one device can cause network failure. Unlike an Ethernet, every device participates in the routing of tokens or data frames. If a device fails it may not route a received token or data frame, thus causing it to disappear from the ring.

TOKEN AND FRAME FORMATS

We already stated that a token is simply a special frame. Figure 9.26 shows both the token and frame formats. The four fields labeled "destination address," "source address," "data," and "frame check sequence" have the same meanings as those we have discussed in previous sections, so we will not elaborate again. The destination address may be an individual, group, or broadcast address. The Data field has no theoretical maximum length, but there is a limit on how long a device can transmit uninterrupted, which creates a practical limit of about 5000 data bytes.

Each frame has a **starting delimiter (SD)** and **ending delimiter (ED)** that designate a token's boundaries. The SD has the special signal pattern JK0JK000. The 0s are binary 0s as defined by the differential Manchester code. The symbols J and K correspond to special signals. To understand what they are, recall that the differential Manchester code defines a signal transition (high to low or low to high) in the middle of each signal interval. The J and K signals violate that rule. The J signal starts out like a 0 but there is no transition in the middle. Similarly, the K signal starts out like a 1 and has no transition. Sometimes these signals are referred to as **non-data-J** and **non-data-K.** Because these signals do not conform to the Manchester code for defining bits, they can never appear as part of any information. This makes them useful for indicating special conditions such as the start or end of a frame.

The ending delimiter has the signal pattern JK1JK1IE. The symbols J and K are the same as in the SD. The 1s are binary 1s. The two remaining bits correspond to an intermediate frame bit (I) and an error bit (E). As before, a communication between two devices may consist of many frames. Bit I is 0 in the last frame and 1 otherwise. Bit E is set to 1 whenever an error (such as a frame check sequence) is detected.

The second byte in each frame is the Access Control (AC) field. Its bits convey different meanings. The bit labeled t stands for *token bit* and determines the frame type. A token has $t = 0$ and a data frame has $t = 1$, thus allowing a device to determine what it is receiving. The remaining bits deal with ring maintenance and token

SD	AC	ED

(a) 3-byte token

number of bytes

1	1	1	2 or 6	2 or 6	0–5000	4	1	1
SD	AC	FC	destination address	source address	... data ...	frame check sequence	ED	FS

(b) Variable-byte frame

```
       SD (starting delimiter):  J K 0 J K 0 0 0
            AC (access control):  p p p t m r r
                                  p p p: priority bits
                                      t: token bit
                                      m: monitor bit
                                  r r r: reservation bits
         ED (ending delimiter):  J K 1 J K 1 I E
            FC (frame control):  f f z z z z z z
                                  f: frame type bits
                                  z: control bits
             FS (frame status):  a c x x a c x x
                                  a: address recognized bit
                                  c: frame copied bit
                                  x: undefined bit
```

Figure 9.26   Token and Frame Formats

reservation, discussed later. The third frame byte is the Frame Control (FC) field, which also deals with ring maintenance.

The last byte is the Frame Status (FS) field and has two copies each (in case of errors) of an Address Recognized bit (bit *a*) and a Frame Copied bit (bit *c*). The sending device initially sets bits *a* and *c* to 0. If the destination device is on the ring, it sets *a* to 1, indicating that the address has been recognized. If the destination device copies the frame, it also sets bit *c* to 1. Note that the presence of the destination does not automatically mean the frame is copied. Status set at a higher layer (such as the LLC) may temporarily prohibit receiving any frames. We have discussed such possibilities in the sections on sliding window protocols in Chapter 8.

The Frame Status field tells the sending device whether the destination device is on the ring and, if it is, whether it copied the frame. If the destination device is there but did not copy the frame, the sending device presumably can try to resend the frame later.

RESERVING AND CLAIMING TOKENS

The process of capturing tokens and sending data frames at first glance seems relatively simple. Once a device sends a frame and subsequently drains it from the ring, it creates and sends the token to its neighbor, which has the first opportunity to claim the token. Proceeding in this way allows the devices to transmit in the order in which they are connected. This process also puts an upper limit on the length of time a device must wait for a token.* But can we override this order? Are there ways to give a device a higher priority and thus allow it to send ahead of others? This certainly would be useful in cases where the token ring services high-priority or real-time devices.

To prioritize and allow devices to capture tokens in a different order, we assume that every device as well as the circulating token has a priority. The device's priority is defined locally, and the token's priority is defined by the three *Priority bits* in the AC field. A device can claim a token only if its priority is greater than or equal to the token's priority. This forces lower-priority devices to pass available tokens even if the device has something to send. Only devices with a priority higher than or equal to the token's priority can claim the token.

This system raises important questions: Who defines the token's priority? How is it done? Initially, one of the devices sends a token with priority 0. Afterward, the answer lies in the system's **reservation system,** the protocol used to reserve tokens and define priorities.

Suppose a device receives a token with a higher priority than its own priority (we'll see how this can happen shortly) or receives a data frame. Either way, the device cannot send. However, the device may be able to put in a request (reservation) for the token for the next time it arrives. To do this, a device examines the incoming *Reservation bits*. If the value stored there is smaller than the device's priority, it stores its own priority there, thus making the reservation. If the value is larger, the device cannot make a reservation at this time. Presumably some other device with a higher priority, but still lower than the token's priority, already made a reservation and it cannot be preempted by a lower-priority device. (Indeed, try booking your favorite suite at a five-star hotel when the English prime minister has already reserved that floor of the hotel.)

When a device drains a frame and creates a new token, it examines the Reservation bits of the incoming frame. If it sees that some device has made a reservation, it defines the new token's priority as the reservation value. It then stores both the old priority and the new one (which is now the current priority) locally on a stack. Afterward, it is designated as a **stacking station**—only it can restore the token to its original priority. Thus, when this token begins to travel the ring, it is claimed by the first device with a higher or equal priority. Lower-priority devices are ignored in favor of the higher-priority ones.

Figure 9.27 shows a pseudocoded algorithm that describes the priority and reservation system. Each device executes it as frames and tokens arrive. The algorithm is

---

* This statement assumes there is a limit on the length of time that a station may possess the token. In fact, a token-holding timer, with a default of 10 μsec, specifies how long a station can control a token.

```
while (Peter Pan lives in the Never Land)
{
    wait for an event;
    if (event is "frame arrives")
    {
1       if (frame originated at current station)
        {
            drain frame;
2           if (frame.res > frame.priority)
            {
                create and send token with token.priority = frame.res and token.res = 0;
                put old and new priorities on stack and designate this station as a stacking
                    station;
                continue;
            } /* end - frame.res > frame.priority */
3           if (current station is stacking station for this frame)
            {
                create and send token with token.priority = max(frame.res, old priority on stack);
                if frame.res is used replace the current priority at the top of the stack with it;
                if the old priority from the stack is used, pop the old and current priorities
                    from the stack and discontinue the stacking station designation if that
                    stack is empty;
                continue;
            } /* end - current station is stacking station for this frame */
            create and send token with token.res = frame.res and token.priority = frame.priority;
        } /* end - frame originated at current station */
        if (frame originated elsewhere)
4       {
            if (there is a frame to send) && (station priority > frame.res) store sending
5               priority in frame.res ;
            send frame;
        }
    } /* end - event is "frame arrives" */
    if (event is "token arrives")
    {
        if (current station is stacking station for this token)
6       {
            create token with token.priority = max(token.res, old priority on stack);
            if token.res is used replace the current priority at the top of the stack with it;
            if the old priority from the stack is used, pop the old and current priorities
                from the stack and discontinue the stacking station designation if that stack
                is empty;
        }
        if (there is a frame to send)
7       {
            if (station priority >= token.priority)
8               claim token, create, and send frame;
            else
                if (station priority > token.res)
9                   store sending priority in token.res;
        } /* end - frame to send */
        send frame or token;
    } /* end - event is "token arrives" */
} /* end of while loop */
```

Figure 9.27   Token Ring Protocol to Reserve and Claim a Token

simplified somewhat, as it does not show the receipt of frames destined for a device or deal with a device sending multiple frames. We intend the figure to focus only on making reservations and determining priorities, but it may be expanded as an exercise.

The algorithm refers to a frame's Reservation bits and Priority bits as `frame.res` and `frame.priority`, respectively. Similar notation is used for a token's bits. Like previous algorithms, it is event driven, where the event is the arrival of a frame or token. If a frame arrives, the device determines whether the frame originated there (condition 1) or elsewhere (condition 4). If it originated elsewhere and the current device has a frame to send, it tries to make a reservation. If the device's priority is higher than the contents of `frame.res` (condition 5), it makes the reservation. If not, it makes no reservation. Either way, it passes the frame to its neighbor.

If the frame originated at the current device, that device must drain the frame and create a new token. The question that the device must now answer is, What priority should the new token have? There are two possible answers.

First, suppose some device with a higher priority than the frame's priority has made a reservation (condition 2). The device gives the token a priority equal to that of the device making the reservation (contents of `frame.res`). It also defines `token.res = 0` to give any device a chance to make another reservation. But raising the token's priority is an awesome responsibility. Any device that does this also has the responsibility of lowering it later when the only devices with something to send have a priority lower than the token's priority. At that point the device must recognize a token whose priority it raised and lower it. To achieve this, the device (designated as a stacking station) stores the old and new (now current) priorities on a stack whenever it raises the priority.

The second possibility occurs when the reservation on the incoming frame was made by a device with a lower priority than the frame's priority. This means that as the frame travels the ring, no device that wants to send has a high enough priority to do so. Consequently, the new token's priority must be lowered. But which device has the authority to do so? If the current device did not raise the priority, it cannot lower it. Thus, it simply creates a token with the same priority and reservation value as the incoming frame's (last statement under condition 1). Presumably the token will reach the stacking station, which will lower the priority.

However, if the current device is the stacking station* (condition 3), it creates a new token with a lower priority. Next question: What is the new priority? The stacking station compares the incoming reservation value with its old stacked priority and chooses the greater value. If the reservation value is greater, it replaces the current priority on the stack. The device is still the stacking station because it has not restored the priority that existed prior to its becoming the stacking station. If the reservation value is not greater, the token gets the old stacked priority. The old and current priorities are popped from the stack and, if the stack is empty, the device is

---

* There may actually be several stacking stations because a token's priority can be raised by more than one station. What we really need here is the station that became a stacking station most recently. The station can determine this by comparing the frame's priority field with the current priority on the station's local stack. If they are the same, the current station can lower the token's priority. If not, then another station raised the priority and must subsequently lower it.

no longer a stacking station. Note that the stacking station designation is removed only when the stack is empty, because the device could be a stacking station from a previous priority increase.

Now consider what happens when a token arrives. If the device is a stacking station (condition 6), it proceeds as we have just discussed. Afterward, it determines whether there is a frame to send (condition 7). If so, it compares the token's priority with the device's priority (condition 8). If the device has a high enough priority, it claims the token. If not, it compares its priority with the value specified by the Reservation bits (condition 9). Again, if it has a high enough priority, it makes the reservation. Finally, it sends either the token or the frame (if it created one) to its neighbor.

This discussion is general and describes the major aspects of the priority and reservation system. Now it is time to see an example. Suppose four devices are ready to transmit (Figure 9.28) and that each has just one frame to send. Suppose also that device C has just captured the token and is sending its frame. We now apply the algorithm to the situation of Figure 9.28.

To help follow the algorithm, Table 9.7 summarizes what happens at each device as a frame or token travels the ring. The first column lists the steps. The second column indicates the device receiving the frame or token. The third column lists the conditions from Figure 9.27 that are true when the frame or token arrives. The fourth column specifies whether the device sends a frame or token. The last two columns specify the priority and reservation values (values 0 through 7) of the outgoing frame or token. We begin the discussion at the point where device C has just captured a token and sent its frame.

We pick up the algorithm after C sends the frame, so the first line in Table 9.7 corresponds to the arrival of a frame at D (step 1). In this case, conditions 4 and 5 are true. That is, the frame did not originate at D, D has a frame to send, and its priority is higher than that of the incoming frame. As a result, D stores its priority (2) in `frame.res` and passes the frame to its neighbor. When A receives the frame (step 2), only condition 4 is true (A's priority is too low). When B receives the frame (step 3),

Figure 9.28   Reserving Tokens on a Token Ring

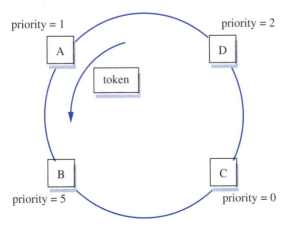

Table 9.7　Activities as Token and Frame Travel the Ring

STEP	ARRIVING AT	CONDITION	DEVICE SENDS	PRIORITY	RESERVATION
1	D (frame)	4 and 5	Frame	0	2
2	A (frame)	4	Frame	0	2
3	B (frame)	4 and 5	Frame	0	5
4	C (frame)	1 and 2	Token	5	0
5	D (token)	7 and 9	Token	5	2
6	A (token)	7	Token	5	2
7	B (token)	7 and 8	Frame	5	0
8	C (frame)	4	Frame	5	0
9	D (frame)	4 and 5	Frame	5	2
10	A (frame)	4	Frame	5	2
11	B (frame)	1	Token	5	2
12	C (token)	6	Token	2	2

it reacts as D did previously, increasing `frame.res` to 5. The frame finally arrives back at C (step 4), the originating device, where it is drained from the ring. Because conditions 1 and 2 are true, C creates and sends a token with priority equal to 5 and becomes the stacking station. D receives the token (step 5) but cannot capture it because the token's priority is too high. However, it does set the reservation value to 2 and sends the token to A (step 6). A's priority is too low, so it sends the token to B (step 7). Device B claims the token (conditions 7 and 8) and sends a frame.

The frame circulates as before and eventually comes back to B (step 11). B drains the frame and creates a token. Notice now that the token's Reservation field contains 2 and the priority is 5. Since B was not the stacking station (C was at step 4), it sends a token with the same priority and reservation values as that in the received frame. When C receives the frame (step 12), it sees condition 6 as true and lowers the token's priority to 2. The old priority is still on the stack and C still remains the stacking station. Although the remaining steps are similar to those that already have occurred, you should go through them. Note that Table 9.7 can be expanded to the point at which all devices have sent their frames and the token's priority is reduced to 0 again. We leave this as an exercise.

RING MAINTENANCE

The discussion so far suffices to describe token ring operations as long as nothing goes wrong. This is a dangerous assumption to make, however. Things can and do go wrong. For example:

- A device sends a short frame over a long ring (where the last bit is sent before the first one has come back) and subsequently crashes. It is not able to drain the frame. A frame that is not drained is an **orphan frame.**

- A device receives a frame or token and crashes before it can send it. Now there is no token circulating, and the devices waiting to send wait forever.
- Line noise damages a frame. Which device has the responsibility of fixing it?

Some problems can be handled by giving one of the devices a few additional responsibilities and designating it a **monitor station.** For example, to detect an orphan frame, a device initially creates a frame with the monitor bit in the Access Control byte (see Figure 9.26) set to 0. When the monitor receives a frame, it sets the bit to 1. An orphaned frame is not drained from the ring, causing it to arrive at the monitor a second time with the bit already equal to 1. The monitor drains the frame and generates a new token.

The monitor also can detect a lost token using a built-in timer. The timer is defined depending on the ring's length, number of devices, and maximum frame size. Whenever the monitor sends a frame or token, it starts the timer. If the monitor receives no other frame or token before the timer expires, it assumes it was lost and generates a new token.

Some problems even the monitor station cannot solve. For example, what if the malfunctioning device is the monitor station? What if a break in the ring causes a lack of tokens? Sending new ones does nothing to correct the problem.

These problems are handled using *control frames,* as shown in Table 9.8. The control bits in the FC byte (see Figure 9.29) define the frame's function. When a new device enters the ring, it sends a Duplicate Address Test frame that stores the device's own address in the Destination field. This frame ensures that the device's address is unique among those in the ring. When the frame returns, the device checks the Address Recognized bit in the frame's Status field. If it is 0, there is no other device with that address; if it is 1, the device's address is a duplicate. The device removes itself from the ring and reports the error.

If a new monitor station must be chosen, one or more devices submit bids to become the monitor station. The one with the highest address gets the job. The

Table 9.8   Token Ring Control Frames

Frame Type	Control Bits in Frame Control Octet	Meaning
Active Monitor Present	000101	Informs devices a monitor is operational and initiates the neighbor identification procedure
Beacon	000010	Locates ring faults
Claim Token	000011	Elects a new monitor
Duplicate Address Test	000000	Checks for duplicate addresses
Purge	000100	Clears the ring
Standby Monitor Present	000110	Carries out the neighbor identification procedure

problem is that none of the devices knows which one that is. To determine this, each one sends a succession of *Claim Token (CT) frames.* When a device receives a Claim Token frame, it compares the token's source address with its own. If the token's source address is higher, the device stops sending its own frames and repeats the ones it receives. If the token's source address is lower, the device drains it from the ring and continues to send its own frames. Consequently, a CT frame never makes it past another competing device with a higher address, and the only CT frames to circumnavigate the ring come from the device with the highest address. When this device receives its own CT frame, it considers itself duly elected as monitor station—after a very short campaign and without the help of contributions from special interests.

When a device is elected monitor, and periodically thereafter, it sends an *Active Monitor Present (AMP) frame* to notify the other devices that there is an active monitor station. If for some reason the monitor malfunctions, no AMP frames are sent. The other devices have timers that expire when they do not detect an AMP frame over a period of time. When this happens they make bids to become the new monitor by sending a CT frame, as discussed previously.

Before a monitor station creates and sends a new token, it first sends a *Purge frame.* Meanwhile, it drains everything it receives, including the returning Purge frame, to make sure the ring is clear before sending a new token or AMP frame.

The *Standby Monitor Present (SMP) frame* is part of the neighbor identification procedure. When the monitor sends the AMP frame, it sets the *a* bits in the Status field to 0. The first device receiving it (the downstream neighbor) records the source address and sets the *a* bits in the Status field to 1 before repeating the frame. That device now knows its immediate upstream neighbor. The *a* bits are set to 1 to inform the other devices in the ring that the arriving frame is not from their immediate neighbor. After receiving the AMP frame from its upstream neighbor, the device sends an SMP frame (also with the *a* bits equal to 0). Its downstream neighbor receives the frame, records the source address, sets the *a* bits to 1, and repeats it. After a while it sends its own SMP frame, and its downstream neighbor reacts similarly. This cascading effect causes each device to send its own SMP frame to inform its downstream neighbor of its identity. Because the *a* bits are set by the first device receiving each SMP frame, each device can distinguish a frame that its upstream neighbor originated and a frame that the upstream neighbor repeated.

A **Beacon frame** is used to inform devices that a problem has occurred and the token-passing protocol has stopped. Previously we stated that each device has a timer to detect an absence of AMP frames. When this happens, the device does not know whether the monitor malfunctioned or whether there was a break in the ring. In the latter case, sending a CT frame serves no purpose. Consequently, a device detecting a problem sends a continuous stream of Beacon frames containing the address of its upstream neighbor. If they return, the device assumes there is no break (or it has been corrected) and begins sending CT frames as before. If the beacons do not return in a specified amount of time, the device concludes there is a break somewhere and reports the error to a higher layer in the protocol. If the device receives beacons from another device, it suspends sending its own and repeats the ones it receives. Eventually, if there is a break, the only device sending Beacon frames (Figure 9.29) is the one downstream from the break.

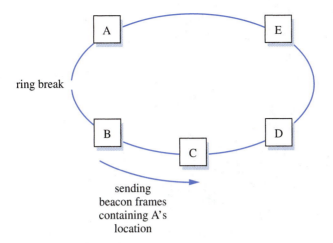

ring break

sending
beacon frames
containing A's
location

Figure 9.29   Locating a Ring Break

The maintenance protocols required of token ring networks certainly are a disadvantage when comparing token ring to Ethernet. On the other hand, controlled access to the media through tokens eliminated all collisions and made token rings a popular choice for many in the early years of networking. This was especially true where unexpected delays caused by excessive collisions caused serious problems. In addition, token rings allowed for priority transmissions—an advantage to network administrators who wanted to prioritize network traffic. However, evolving technology and network design has reduced (and in some cases eliminated) collisions in Ethernet environments. Furthermore, the bit rates at which Ethernet can operate provide sufficient bandwidth for most, if not all, traffic to reach its destination in timely fashion. As a result, although there are still a few token ring networks out there, Ethernet technologies have dominated the LAN environment in recent years.

9.7   WIRELESS NETWORKS: IEEE STANDARD 802.11

So far, this chapter has presented a lot of different ways to connect devices in a LAN, but there is one more option: Don't connect them at all, at least not physically. Of course, we are talking about wireless communications. Most people familiar with television, radio, and satellites know that it is common and that long-distance communications need it. Wireless technology has migrated to the LAN environment, and the IEEE has developed the **802.11 standard** for the **wireless LAN (WLAN).**

Conceptually, it's simple; Figure 9.30 shows a typical arrangement. Devices such as notebook computers contain a wireless network card that is capable of sending and receiving either radio or infrared waves. The waves travel through free space among the devices and allow them to communicate. It's also possible to establish

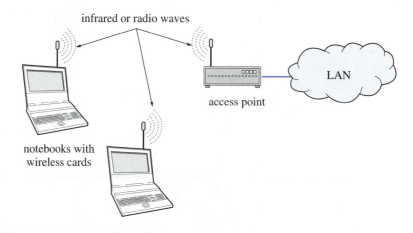

Figure 9.30   Wireless LAN Connections

communication with a wired network using a device called an **access point (AP).** It has the same capabilities to send and receive infrared or radio waves but also has a physical connection to a LAN. Through the AP, the notebooks have access to any server, printer, or other device in that LAN. The advantage is that the notebook user does not have to look for a data jack or deal with wires. She just finds a comfortable spot within range of the access point and does her work. The disadvantage of wireless LAN transmission is that bit rates are generally lower than in their wired LAN counterparts. We'll also see that there are problems with media access control that did not exist with Ethernet or token ring.

INFRARED AND RADIO WAVES

The wireless LAN uses two modes of communication: infrared waves and radio waves. As discussed in Chapter 2, infrared and radio waves are both part of the electromagnetic wave spectrum. Infrared wave frequencies lie just below those of visible light, whereas radio waves have much smaller frequencies. Infrared devices are equipped with light-emitting diodes or laser diodes that emit infrared light waves. These waves may be aimed directly toward a receiver (point-to-point) or reflected off walls and ceilings (diffused). Implementing a point-to-point infrared LAN is more difficult because the transmitting and receiving devices must be aligned. By contrast, a diffuse infrared LAN can use the reflective properties of the infrared waves. The receiver at an access point can be focused on a wall or ceiling. The device that transmits the infrared signal is aimed at a wall or ceiling, where the waves reflect and eventually reach the access point. It's similar to using a remote control to turn on the television or change the channel. You don't need to aim it at the TV but can bounce the signal off the ceiling or the wall behind you. This is particularly convenient if you like doing gymnastics while switching between reruns of *Gilligan's Island* and your favorite MTV music videos.

There are some advantages to infrared systems. For example, infrared signals are not regulated by the FCC as radio signals are. This means that licensing is not required to use infrared-based equipment. Another advantage is that because infrared signals do not penetrate solid objects, they are more secure from outside eavesdroppers. This property also allows devices in different areas of a building to use the same infrared signal without interference. Infrared signals are also impervious to radio interference, although bright sunlight or heat sources can affect them. However, nonpenetration of solid objects is a disadvantage if an application calls for communication beyond solid boundaries.

Devices that use radio waves have built-in transmitters and antennas. However, using radio waves is a little more complex than you might think. It's different from conventional radio, in which a signal is broadcast at a given carrier frequency and you tune your radio to receive it. As you may know, there are problems with using a single carrier frequency. One is interference from other devices. If you have ever listened to a radio in close proximity to a device with a motor, you know the problem. Turn on the motor and your listening pleasure is interrupted with static. On a more serious note, someone may purposely send jamming signals at the proper frequency to disrupt communications. This has serious military implications when radio communications may be used to control weapons. Another problem is that it is easier for unauthorized intruders to intercept the signals. All they need to do is tune in to the appropriate carrier frequency and listen. There's nothing you can do about it.

To deal with these problems, the 802.11 standard uses **spread spectrum,** a technology used not only in wireless LANs but also in cordless and cellular telephones. Instead of using a narrow frequency band, a spread spectrum transmission spreads the signal's spectral energy over a wider range of frequencies (i.e., larger bandwidth). This makes it less prone to interference, which usually affects just a small number of frequencies. It is also more secure. An intruder trying to listen at a particular frequency gets only a small part of the signal, which, to the intruder, looks like noise. It's an interesting concept, but the question remains: How can you spread the transmission over a wide range of frequencies? The 802.11 standard defines two types of spread spectrum technology for the WLAN physical layer: direct-sequence spread spectrum and frequency-hopping spread spectrum.

The principles behind **frequency-hopping spread spectrum (FHSS)** were developed in the early 1940s as a war effort, and patents were given to George Antheil and Hedy Keisler Markey (also known as Hedy Lamarr).* A device that uses FHSS defines a set of frequencies $f_1, f_2, f_3, \ldots, f_n$ that all lie in its broadcast range (Figure 9.31). The device transmits using frequency f_1 for a fixed period of time and

---

* If you're an old-movie or music buff you may recognize the names of Hedy Lamarr and George Antheil. She starred in many movies during the 1930s and 1940s, and he was a composer. It's an interesting trivia note that in addition to their Hollywood and music credentials, they conceived of a scheme to control armed torpedoes over long distances in such a way that the enemy could not detect or jam the transmissions. The scheme eventually evolved into a form of spread spectrum communications.

pseudo-randomly generated frequencies

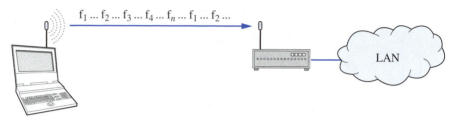

$f_1 \ldots f_2 \ldots f_3 \ldots f_4 \ldots f_n \ldots f_1 \ldots f_2 \ldots$

LAN

Figure 9.31   Frequency-Hopping Spread Spectrum Transmission

then switches to frequency f_2. It transmits on that frequency for the same amount of time and then switches to f_3. This pattern continues until the device has transmitted over each of the frequencies for a fixed period of time. When it is finished transmitting over frequency f_n, it begins again with f_1. Anyone attempting to listen on a given frequency will hear periodic bursts that are indistinguishable from noise. Unless he knows the frequency sequence and the timing for switching frequencies, an intruder is not able to intercept or jam the signal.

The device determines these frequencies using a pseudorandom number generator. That is, it uses an algorithm with an initial seed (initial value input to the algorithm) to generate the sequence of frequency values. Because a formula is used the frequencies are not truly random, but a good generator will produce numbers that have many characteristics of truly random values. The receiving device uses the same algorithm and seed to generate the same set of frequencies. Thus, it can tune into the proper frequency and switch to the next one when the frequency changes.

In contrast to conventional radio broadcasts, FHSS transmission does not require licensing by the FCC as long as the signal power is less than 1 watt, which is sufficient for close-proximity communications. FHSS communications for wireless LANs typically operate between 2.4 and 2.483 GHz, use up to 79 separate channels, and allow for 22 different patterns (order of frequencies). The rate at which the device changes frequency varies according to the communication policies in a country. In the United States, the device must switch frequencies at least 2.5 times per second.

Direct-sequence spread spectrum (DSSS) works in a very different way. Over very short times, FHSS uses narrowband transmissions, but over a long period uses a wide bandwidth. DSSS expands a single data bit into many. This forces the transmitter to operate at a higher bit rate, which, in effect, spreads a signal over a wider bandwidth. The following steps show how it works.

1. The transmitting device starts with a string of data bits.
2. For each data bit, it generates a pseudorandom bit string, called a **chipping sequence,** containing n bits.
3. It combines each data bit and the corresponding chipping sequence to create a *chip code* that is n bits long. Figure 9.32 shows how to do this using $n = 4$.

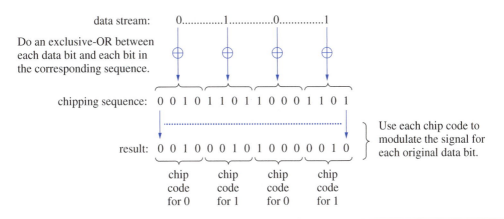

Figure 9.32   Direct-Sequence Spread Spectrum Transmission

The process does an exclusive OR operation between a data bit and each bit in the chipping sequence. The result is a sequence of 4-bit chip codes, one for each data bit. In this case, each 4-bit chip code matches the 4-bit random pattern group if the data bit was 0 and is the complement of the 4-bit random pattern group if the data bit was 1. The 802.11 standard uses an 11-bit chipping sequence called a *Barker code* to generate the chip codes.

The important thing here is that the transmitter must transmit n bits for each data bit. Thus, for example, to achieve a 1 Mbps data bit rate, the device must actually be able to transmit n Mbps. The higher bit rate, in turn, requires a larger-bandwidth signal. This is where the signal spreading occurs. The 802.11 standard applies a binary phase shift keying method to the chip code to achieve a 1 Mbps data bit rate and a quadrature phase shift keying method to achieve a 2 Mbps data bit rate. The signal is then modulated onto a carrier frequency in the 2.4 to 2.483 GHz range before transfer. Specific details depend on the modulation schemes; you can find additional details in references [Sc00] and [Du03].

CONTENTION

Now that we discussed how one wireless device communicates with another, a logical question to ask is: What happens if two or more try to do so at the same time? Because both devices share the same medium (free space), their signals will collide. This is the same problem the Ethernet developers faced, and it may seem logical to use the same solution: CSMA/CD. However, there is a problem. CSMA/CD worked in Ethernet because we could assume that a device can sense when another is transmitting and that it will hear any collisions if both send at the same time. We cannot make that assumption in a WLAN.

Figure 9.33 outlines what some call the *hidden station problem* and shows what can happen. Two devices (A and B) are sending information to an access point using infrared waves. If there is a solid barrier (a wall) between them, neither can

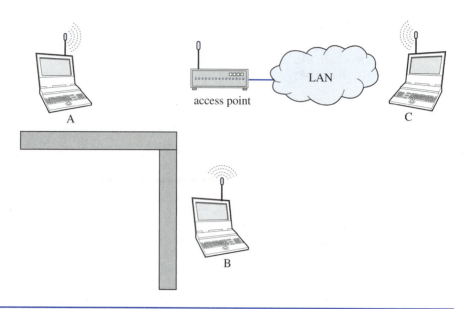

Figure 9.33 Undetected Collisions in a WLAN

sense the other's signal. Thus, CSMA/CD will not work. One possible solution to this is to not use infrared and stay with radio waves since they are impervious to solid boundaries. However, that still won't work because of another scenario that puts each device on opposite sides of the access point (devices A and C). Although the access point would be within range of A's or C's signal, devices A and C may be too far apart to see each other's signal. In that case, neither would detect a collision, and again CSMA/CD won't work.

Therefore, the WLAN needs an alternative solution. The 802.11 standard includes a MAC layer protocol called Distributed Coordination Function (DCF)* that implements **Carrier Sense Multiple Access with Collision Avoidance (CSMA/CA).** Despite the name, it does not avoid all collisions but does reduce them dramatically. The protocol works as follows:

1. A source wants to send a data frame to some destination point. First, it senses the medium. If the medium is busy, it waits until it is clear and uses a persistence strategy as described in Section 4.7. If the source senses a clear medium, it waits an additional amount of time. This extra time is used to prioritize activities. Additional wait times are defined by a short interframe space (SIFS) and a DCF interframe space (DIFS) that is longer than the SIFS. When a device is

---

* There is also another access method called Point Coordination Function (PCF), which is used when time constraints are involved. You can find further details on this in references [Fo03] and [Sc00].

contending for the medium frame, it waits for a DIFS (we'll see why soon). After the DIFS wait, if the medium is still clear, it sends a Request to Send (RTS) frame to a destination point. As the name indicates, the source is asking permission from the destination to send. The RTS frame also includes a duration value specifying how much time the device needs for sending. We'll see how that's used shortly.

2. The destination point receives the RTS frame and must respond by sending a Clear to Send (CTS) frame back to the source. However, it must also contend for the medium because other sources could be contending. Remember, other devices may not have sensed the RTS frame. The destination proceeds as described in the previous step, except that when the medium is clear, it waits for an SIFS. The idea is that if another device were trying to send an RTS, it would be forced to wait for a DIFS. Since the SIFS wait is shorter, the destination effectively gets a higher priority over some other device trying to initiate a transmission. The CTS frame also includes the duration value from the RTS frame.

3. When the source gets the CTS frame, it has received permission to send data. Now, before we continue, let's answer the logical question: What happens if two RTS frames collide? This can happen because two devices can simultaneously do what step 1 prescribed—that is, both may send an RTS frame but neither may sense the other's request or the resulting collision. However, the destination will. Consequently, it sends no CTS frame. Because neither of the requesting devices gets the CTS frame in a specified amount of time, each assumes a collision has occurred, waits a random period of time, and tries again.

   Note that although other devices may not sense the RTS frame, any device within range of the destination will sense the CTS frame and know that another device has permission to send. Therefore, each will refrain from trying to access the medium with its own RTS frame. In other words, the device that has been granted permission to send has exclusive control of the medium for a period of time. Furthermore, since the CTS frame contained the duration value, all other devices know how long to wait.

4. Once a source has received a CTS frame, it sends a data frame. This is where the collision avoidance occurs. Because other devices are aware of the impending transmission and know how long to wait, there should be no collisions.

5. When the destination receives a data frame, it returns an ACK frame. The source knows the data have been received.

6. Once the duration is over, all devices can begin contending again.

ADDRESSING

The 802.11 protocol, like other protocols, has a specified frame format. However, before we get to that, we need to have a better understanding of the 802.11 addressing mechanism, which specifies four different address fields for each frame. Why four? To answer this, we must first discuss the components that make up a wireless LAN. Figure 9.34 shows a possible configuration.

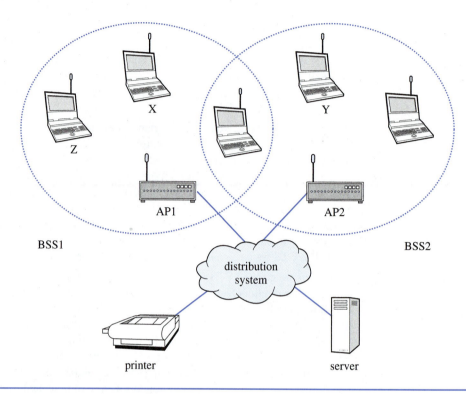

Figure 9.34   Wireless LAN Infrastructure

The set of wireless devices with which a single AP communicates defines a **basic service set (BSS).*** Because there may be multiple APs, there may also be multiple BSSs. In addition, multiple BSSs may be connected via a **distribution system (DS).** The 802.11 standard does not specify the architecture of the DS. The DS may be a LAN, a collection of LANs, or another type of network (including wireless), but in all cases it allows a device in one BSS to communicate with one in another or to gain access to servers, printers, and so forth. When a device sends a frame, there are thus four possibilities. Table 9.9 shows them in the context of Figure 9.34 and indicates how the address fields are defined.

Because of these different scenarios, the 802.11 frame has four address fields whose values depend on which scenario applies. These fields are needed to distinguish a source from a transmitter and to distinguish a receiver from a destination.

---

* Technically, the definition of a BSS is a little broader and includes all devices that contend for the same medium (i.e., the same radio frequency). However, for our purposes, this definition is sufficient.

Table 9.9   Address Fields in an 802.11 Frame

CASE	DESCRIPTION	ADDRESS1 (RECEIVER)	ADDRESS2 (TRANSMITTER)	ADDRESS3	ADDRESS4
1	X sends frame to Z, frame stays within BSS1.	Z	X	BSS1	—
2	X sends frame to Y. Frame first goes to AP1.	AP1	X	Y	—
3	AP1 sends frame originating at X to AP2 over a wireless DS. Frame is destined for Y.	AP2	AP1	Y	X
4	AP2 sends frame originating at X to Y.	Y	AP2	X	—

In the first case in our example, X sends to Z. Both are in the same BSS, and the AP is not involved. Address1 indicates the destination of the frame, and Address2 indicates the source. Here we make no distinction between source and transmitter (both are X) or destination and receiver (both are Z). Address3 just indicates the BSS ID, and Address4 is not used.

In the second case, X sends a frame destined for Y. Because X and Y are in different BSSs, the protocol is more complex. In this case, Address1 specifies AP1, and Address2, as before, indicates the source, X. The difference here is that the receiver (AP1) is not the eventual destination. The Address3 field specifies Y as the destination. This is needed so that AP1 can eventually route the frame.

The third case applies if the distribution system also follows the wireless standard. In this case, AP1 (Address2 field) is transmitting the frame, and AP2 (Address1 field) should receive it. However, neither is the original source or eventual destination. The Address4 and Address3 fields specify these as X and Y, respectively.

The last case applies when the frame leaves the DS when AP2 transmits it to Y. In this case, the destination and receiver are the same (Y), but the transmitter (AP2) and source (X) are different.

All four cases have two things in common. Address1 always specifies the device that should receive the frame. Thus, as devices monitor the radio signals containing the frame, all they need to check is the Address1 field to see if they should respond. Second, Address2 always specifies which device transmitted the frame. This is needed because of the ACK frame described previously. The receiving device must know to whom it should send the ACK frame. Thus, the main differences are in the contents of the Address3 and Address4 frames.

FRAME FORMAT

Figure 9.35 shows the contents of the 802.11 frame and the placement of the four address fields that we have just described. The Duration field indicates the time value used in the RTS/CTS frame exchange described previously. The Data field is

bytes: 2	2	6	6	6	2	6	0–2312	4
Control	Duration	address1	address2	address3	sequence control	address4	data	CRC

Figure 9.35   802.11 Frame

self evident, and the CRC field is used for error control. The Sequence Control field contains sequence numbers used for flow control. So, the only other field we need to elaborate on is the Control field.

The Control field is 2 bytes long and contains the following items:*

- **To DS bit flag.** This bit is set when a frame is going to a DS. The flag is 1 in cases 2 and 3 from Table 9.9, and 0 otherwise.

- **From DS bit flag.** This bit is set when a frame is coming from a DS. The flag is 1 in cases 3 and 4 from Table 9.9, and 0 otherwise. This and the previous flag determine how protocols interpret the address fields.

- **More Fragment bit flag.** Wireless transmission is more prone to errors than electrical or optical communications. As such, the 802.11 standard allows the maximum frame size to be decreased if the error rate is high. The reason is that damaging a smaller frame is less inefficient than damaging a larger one since less data need to be retransmitted. That poses a problem if the amount of user data requires a frame larger than a decreased maximum value. However, the protocol allows a frame to be divided into fragments. The fragments can be sent independently and reassembled at the destination to recreate the original frame. The More Fragment bit is set when the current frame is a fragment and more fragments are to follow.

- **Retry bit flag.** This flag is set when a frame is transmitted a second time (for example, because of a lack of an acknowledgment).

- **Two-bit version number.** Specifies the current version of the protocol being used.

- **Two-bit Type field and 4-bit Subtype field.** The 2-bit Type field indicates whether the current frame is a data, control, or management frame. The Subtype field further articulates the frame's purpose. For example, the 2-bit code 01 indicates a control frame. Control frames are used for media access;

---

* We have not listed every item in the Control field because some of them require more extensive coverage of the standard than we are providing. More detail can be found in references [Sc00], [Fo03], and [Be02].

examples include the previously described RTS, CTS, and ACK frames. The Subtype fields distinguish one from another. Data frames are self-explanatory. Management frames are used to configure the network.

Some examples of the use of management frames are as follows:

- **BSS configuration.** Recall from Figure 9.34 that two BSSs may overlap. This means that a device must associate with an AP if it needs access to the distribution system. To do this, a device sends an Association Request frame to the specified AP. If the AP accepts the association, it responds with an Association Response frame.

- **Finding an AP.** How does a device know what APs exist? To detect and identify APs, a device transmits a Probe Request frame. Any AP that detects the frame replies with a Probe Response frame. The originating device can then select an AP (possibly the one with the strongest signal) and associate with it as described in the previous item.

- **Roaming.** Remember, devices are mobile, which means a device may move from one BSS to another. When that happens, a device can send a Reassociate Request frame to a new AP. The AP can respond with a Reassociate Response frame. A Disassociation frame disassociates a device from a previously associated AP. However, the mobile device may no longer be within range of the old AP. As a result, it is the new AP's responsibility to send a Disassociation frame to the old AP on behalf of the device. Reassociation should be automatic. If the device is moved and detects a weakened signal from the existing AP, it needs to find an AP with a stronger signal and reassociate with it. This is analogous to how cellular telephones operate when users move from one cell to another, except on a much smaller scale.

- **Secure communications.** A device can engage in a secure communication by sending an Authenticate frame. The two devices can then exchange information regarding the nature of the secure communication and begin. When the secure communication is finished, a Deauthentication frame ends it.

WIRED EQUIVALENT PRIVACY

As one would expect, security is an issue in a wireless environment, especially when low-frequency radio waves are used. In such cases, the advantage of "connecting" devices separated by physical barriers can also become a serious security issue. Because of the low-power radio waves, a WLAN is probably safe if it lies in a farmhouse in the middle of a 10,000-acre plot. If, however, the WLAN is implemented in an apartment or office building located in a densely populated area, it is susceptible to attack. A project conducted by Peter Shipley (see www.dis.org/filez/openlans.pdf) outlined an experiment in which, using modest hardware, team members were able to locate WLANs simply by driving through neighborhoods and looking for signals. They report that it was also possible to make connections from hilltops or high-rise building to networks over 20 miles distant. Most of those networks did not implement a security protocol.

The 802.11 standard includes a security protocol called **Wired Equivalent Privacy (WEP).** We list some important points, but the interested reader should see reference [Sw03] for more details.

- WEP provides authentication and encryption between a device and an AP. The encryption algorithm uses a 40-bit secret key and appends a 24-bit initialization vector to create a 64-bit key. It uses a different initialization vector, hence a different 64-bit encryption key, for each frame. Some newer equipment allows for 128-bit encryption.

- The protocol does not specify a key exchange algorithm. The assumption is that the keys are agreed upon prior to any exchange. In Shipley's project, nearly half of those WLANs that implemented WEP used a default encryption key.

- The encryption method uses an algorithm known as RC4 (see ref. [Sc95]). The 40-bit key and 24-bit initialization vector are input to the algorithm, which generates a sequence of pseudorandom keys. Each of those keys is then exclusively OR'd with a section of plaintext from the frame. Each initialization vector is sent within the frame (in plaintext form). The receiving device uses that initialization vector and 40-bit key to generate the same key sequence and does an exclusive OR with the incoming ciphertext to recreate the original plaintext.

A group at the University of California–Berkeley has articulated several flaws in WEP encryption (see www.isaac.cs.berkeley.edu/isaac/wep-faq.html). For example, the small 24-bit initialization vector means there is a high probability that the 64-bit key, and consequently the same key sequence, will be repeated when there is heavy traffic. An intruder can intercept two or more frames encrypted with the same key and use statistical techniques (often the first step in breaking a code) to analyze patterns. Reference [Ar02] also addresses weaknesses in 802.11 security and outlines some approaches to deal with them.

VARIATIONS OF 802.11

The original 802.11 standard used one of the three physical layers: infrared, DSSS, or FHSS. All could run at 1 Mbps or 2 Mbps, very slow compared with the wired LAN protocols of today. As with the Ethernet standard, there have been several revisions of the 802.11 standard in order to provide faster communications. They are 803.11a, 803.11b, and 803.11g. All are based on CSMA/CA and differ largely in the physical layers.

For example, 802.11b, which is also known as **Wi-Fi** (short for *wireless fidelity*), uses radio frequency waves in the 2.4 GHz range and is rated at 11 Mbps. It uses only DSSS since the higher rate could not be achieved with FHSS. Another difference is in the modulating scheme. The original 802.11 standard typically uses PSK modulation, but 803.11b uses a method called *complementary code keying* (CCK).

The 803.11a standard, by comparison, transmits in the 5 GHz range and uses a form of frequency-division multiplexing in place of spread spectrum technologies. In theory, the bit rate is 54 Mbps, but in practice achievable rates are 30 Mbps or less. The faster rates, however, come at the expense of shorter distances. The 5 GHz range is significant because many devices (cell phones, Bluetooth devices, even microwave ovens) already use frequencies in the 2.4 GHz range. On the other hand, some military applications use the 5 GHz range.

Another standard is a work in progress (as of this writing): 802.11g. It is designed to operate in the 2.4 GHz range and have a bit rate of 54 Mbps. Drafts have been written that call for the use of a frequency-division multiplexing scheme for higher bit rates, and the CCK scheme to support backward compatibility with 802.11b. However, it has not yet been ratified as an official standard.

Do not be misled: This section is not a complete description of the wireless LAN protocol. It is a very complex protocol. We've presented no more than an overview of some important topics; there is much more (see references [Sc00], [Fo03], and [Be02]).

9.8   SUMMARY

This chapter dealt with local area networks and focused primarily on layer 1 and layer 2 protocols. We saw that the data link layer contains two sublayers: LLC and MAC. The LLC is independent of a specific local area network and defines point-to-point communications between two devices in a LAN. Many protocols operate at this layer, but most have evolved from the High-level Data Link Control (HDLC) protocol.

HDLC is an example of a bit-oriented protocol. That is, its frames are treated as bit streams. It is defined by the ISO for point-to-point or multipoint connections, is used for half- and full-duplex communications, and can use either the go-back-n or selective repeat protocol. It defines different frame types and uses them to exchange data, commands, or control information.

For contrast, we also described BSC, an older byte-oriented protocol in which the frames are treated as byte streams. It also is used in point-to-point or multipoint connections, but is typically used with half-duplex communications and uses a stop-and-wait flow control protocol. Like HDLC, it defines different frame types to exchange data, commands, and control information.

Most of this chapter dealt with the MAC and physical layer protocols used to implement LANs. The IEEE has defined four very different LAN standards: 802.3 Ethernet, 802.4 token bus, 802.5 token ring, and 802.11 wireless LAN. Ethernet is the dominant standard and has gone through several evolutions (Fast Ethernet, Gigabit Ethernet, 10 Gigabit Ethernet) to take advantage of new and faster technologies. Although the token bus and ring networks are no longer common, we included the token ring to provide a contrast with Ethernet. The wireless standard is relatively new and eliminates the need for physical connection, but is slower than its wired counterparts. Table 9.10 summarizes the major features of these LAN standards.

Table 9.10   Summary of LAN Standards

IEEE STANDARD	COMMENTS
IEEE 802.3	Uses a 10Base5 (ThickNet) 50-ohm coaxial cable, 10-mm diameter. Maximum segment length is 500 meters. Other maximum values are 4 repeaters, 5 segments, and 100 devices per segment. Minimum of 8 feet between transceivers. Uses Manchester coding. Used in physical bus topologies.
IEEE 802.3a	Uses a 10Base2 (Cheapernet, ThinNet) 50-ohm coaxial cable, 5-mm diameter. Maximum segment length is 185 meters. Other maximum values are 4 repeaters, 5 segments, and 30 devices per segment. Minimum distance between nodes is 0.45 meter. Also uses Manchester coding. Used in physical bus topologies.
IEEE 802.3i	Category 3, 4, or 5 UTP (10BaseT). Central hub. Manchester coding. Maximum UTP length is 100 meters. Used in physical star topology.
IEEE 802.3j	Multimode fiber (10BaseFx). Maximum distance is 2000 meters for FL and FB, but 500 meters for FP. Used in physical star topology, but FP uses a passive coupler as its hub. FP is not common.
IEEE 802.3u	Uses two wire pairs in a Cat 5 cable (100BaseTX) and 4B/5B followed by MLT-3 encoding. Maximum of two class II repeaters (if separated by 5 meters or less) or one class I repeater in a collision domain. Maximum segment length is 100 meters.
IEEE 802.3u	Multimode optical fiber (100BaseFX). Uses 4B/5B and NRZI encoding. Maximum of two class II repeaters or one class I repeater in a collision domain. Maximum segment length is 136 meters if both links in the collision domain are fiber, and 160 meters if the other link is UTP. If fiber connects two switches, then the segment length can be 412 meters long (half duplex) or 2000 meters long (full duplex).
IEEE 802.3u	Uses four wire pairs in a Cat 3 cable (100BaseT4). Uses 6B/8T encoding and transmits trits simultaneously over three wire pairs. Maximum of two class II repeaters or one class I repeater between devices. Cannot be used in full-duplex mode. Maximum segment length is 100 meters.
IEEE 802.3ab	Requires four pairs of Cat 5 UTP (1000BaseT) and runs in full-duplex mode. Signaling requires complex encoding/decoding procedures: PAM5, trellis, and Viterbi. Maximum segment length is 100 meters.
IEEE802.3z	Medium is a specially shielded copper cable (1000BaseCX). Maximum distance is 25 meters. Typically used for connecting rack devices in a communications center. Uses 8B/10B encoding.
IEEE 802.3z	Long-wave optical fiber (1000BaseLX). Can be used with either multimode or single-mode fiber. Maximum lengths are 5000 meters for single-mode fiber and 550 meters for multimode. Uses 8B/10B encoding.
IEEE 802.3z	Short-wave optical fiber (1000BaseSX). Can be used only with multimode fiber. Maximum lengths are between 220 and 550 meters, depending on the fiber's diameter. Uses 8B/10B encoding.
IEEE 802.3ae	10 Gigabit Ethernet. Full duplex only over optical fiber, and has eliminated all collisions. As of this writing, 10 Gigabit Ethernet will likely be used only by carrier services to provide connectivity among lower-bit-rate LANs.

Table 9.10   Continued

IEEE STANDARD	COMMENTS
IEEE 802.5	Token ring network. Devices are connected in a logical ring, and frames travel through them en route to their destination. A device cannot transmit anything until it has received a token (special frame that circulates the ring when no data are being transmitted). Management routines must be implemented in the event problems occur with the token.
IEEE 802.11	Wireless LAN. Uses infrared or one of two forms of spread spectrum radio waves. At 1 or 2 Mbps rates the WLAN is slower than other wired networks. Because there is no guarantee that a device will detect collisions, devices contend for the medium using CSMA/CA.
IEEE 802.11x	802.11a operates in the 5 GHz range and, in theory, can achieve bit rates of 54 Mbps. In practice, bit rates are lower. 802.11b, also called Wi-Fi, operates in the 2.4 GHz range and has a bit rate of 11 Mbps. 802.11g is still in progress, but plans call for it to also operate in the 2.4 GHz range but provide bit rates of 54 Mbps.

Review Questions

1. Distinguish between a byte-oriented and a bit-oriented protocol.
2. What are the three communication modes of HDLC? Describe each one.
3. What is bit stuffing and why is it necessary?
4. Distinguish among a primary station, secondary station, and combined station.
5. Distinguish among the main HDLC frame types.
6. Define the four status types an HDLC supervisory frame can indicate.
7. What is a broadcast address?
8. List other protocols similar to HDLC and each one's sponsoring organization.
9. List the main differences between the HDLC and BSC protocols.
10. What is a SYN character?
11. What is a Data Link Escape character?
12. Distinguish between transparent and nontransparent data.
13. What is byte stuffing?
14. Distinguish between a local area network and a wide area network.
15. List typical LAN topologies.
16. How can a physical star topology function as a logical bus topology?
17. What are the two major divisions of the data link layers, and what are their major functions?
18. What is a transceiver?

19. Are the following statements TRUE or FALSE? Why?

    a. HDLC is a byte-oriented protocol.

    b. HDLC can use either a selective repeat or go-back-*n* protocol.

    c. Ethernet is a seven-layer protocol similar to the OSI model.

    d. The Pad field in an Ethernet frame is optional.

    e. There is only one Ethernet protocol.

    f. In a token ring network, devices take turns sending frames in the order of their arrangement on the ring.

    g. Fast Ethernet and 10 Mbps Ethernet use the same MAC protocols.

    h. All three LAN protocols allow devices to be prioritized.

    i. Token ring has no central control.

    j. Any device can raise or lower the ring priority in a token ring.

    k. The only real difference between infrared and radio wave transmission in a WLAN is the bit rates that are achievable.

20. Describe each of the 802.3 cable specifications.

21. Why must an Ethernet device still be transmitting a frame that collides with another?

22. What is a T-connector used for?

23. Why are repeaters necessary in some networks?

24. What is the difference between a hub and a repeater?

25. What is a collision domain?

26. The 10 Mbps Ethernet specification used Manchester encoding. Why can't Fast Ethernet use it over category 5 UTP?

27. What is the reason for replacing 4 data bits with 5 bits in Fast Ethernet and increasing the overall number of bits to transmit?

28. Distinguish between Fast Ethernet's 100BaseTX and 100BaseT4.

29. What is MLT-3 encoding?

30. Why can't MLT-3 encoding be used for 100BaseT4?

31. Fast Ethernet has a higher bit rate than the original Ethernet, but segments must be shorter. Why?

32. Why must the Gigabit Ethernet minimum frame size be larger than the minimum frame size of its predecessors?

33. What is a burst frame?

34. For Gigabit Ethernet over fiber, why is it important to try to keep the number of 1 and 0 bits the same during a transmission?

35. What is a hybrid in Gigabit Ethernet?

36. What is the purpose of the Gigabit Ethernet's frame carrier extension?

37. How can Gigabit Ethernet work without collision detection protocols?

38. Why does an Ethernet frame have a maximum size? Minimum size?

39. What purpose does the token serve in a token ring network?

40. Discuss the content and purpose of each field in the token format (token ring network).

41. What are non-data-J and non-data-K signals?

42. What is a stacking station?

43. What is a monitor station?

44. Describe the purpose of each of the following token ring control frames:

    a. Active Monitor Present frame

    b. Beacon frame

    c. Claim Token frame

    d. Purge frame

    e. Standby Monitor Present frame

    f. Duplicate Address Test frame

45. What is an orphan frame?

46. What is an access point for a wireless LAN?

47. What are the advantages of using infrared rather than radio waves in a WLAN? Disadvantages?

48. What is spread spectrum technology?

49. Since a WLAN uses a shared medium just like the original Ethernet, why won't collision detection protocols work?

50. Describe the hidden station problem for a WLAN.

51. What is the difference between frequency-hopping spread spectrum and direct-sequence spread spectrum?

52. What is the difference between a chipping sequence and a chip code?

53. A WLAN frame contains four address fields. Furthermore, each one conveys information dependent on where it is headed and from where it was transmitted. How can the protocol interpret the contents of each address correctly?

Exercises

1. Consider a 10 Mbps 802.3 LAN (10Base5 cable). What is the longest time a device might need to detect a collision if the LAN were just a single 500-meter segment?

2. What does the MLT-3 signal look like for the bit string 01001100100110? Assume the signal is at level 0 prior to the first bit.

3. What does the 8B/6T signal look like for the two bytes 42C3?

4. Why do we seemingly complicate the token ring protocol by routing each frame bit or token bit as soon as it is received? Why not just receive all the bits for a token, examine them, and then pass them all to the next device?

5. Consider a 200-meter 4 Mbps token ring containing 20 devices, each transmitting with equal priority. Suppose no device is allowed to transmit more than 5000 data bytes before giving up the token. Once a device gives up the token, how long will it take (in the worst case) for that device to get the token again?

6. In the discussion on reserving tokens, we stated that the device that raises a token's priority has the responsibility to lower it later. Why lower it at all? Why not leave the priority as it is?

7. Finish Table 9.7 to the point at which all devices have sent their frames and a token with priority 0 is back on the ring.

8. Repeat the example described by Figure 9.28 and Table 9.7, assuming the token is traveling in a clockwise direction.

9. If a token ring is prioritized, what is the longest time a device may have to wait before it can claim a token?

10. In our discussion of SMP frames, each device receiving one repeated it and later sent its own. Why not have each device that receives an SMP frame drain it from the ring and send its own immediately? That way, each device would know its upstream neighbor in the time it takes for one SMP frame to circulate the ring.

11. Consider the algorithm of Figure 9.27. Discuss the effects of removing code associated with each of the following conditions.

    a. Condition 2

    b. Condition 4

    c. Condition 7

12. Pseudocode the logic a device uses to claim a token using the Claim Token frame.

13. What is the transmitted binary string after bit stuffing the following (leftmost bit first)?

    0101111110111101111111101111

14. Redraw Figure 9.8b, but assume that B sends SREJ (instead of REJ) when it detects the error.

15. Redraw Figure 9.8b, but assume that B has sent four information frames, which arrived at A before A sent the second batch of frames. Also assume B's third frame is damaged in transit.

16. Section 9.2 described byte stuffing by inserting an extra DLE character whenever DLE occurs in data. The intent was to avoid misinterpreting a "data DLE" as a "control DLE." Why can't we achieve the same effect simply by using STX prior to data bytes, and if ETX occurs in the data, just insert an extra ETX character?

17. Write a program that does byte stuffing on a character string. Write a complementary program that accepts a byte-stuffed character string and removes the stuffed bytes.

18. You are planning to implement a WLAN in an office environment containing many cubicles in a large space. All else being equal, would infrared or radio wave transmission be a better choice? Why?

19. You are planning to implement separate WLANs in a set of labs (one WLAN for each lab). Lab sizes vary, but all labs lie in close proximity within the same area of a building. All else being equal, would infrared or radio wave transmission be a better choice? Why?

20. Suppose in Figure 9.34 that device Y sends a frame to device Z. Show the contents of the frame's address fields as it travels from Y to AP2 to AP1 to Z.

21. A device will transmit the data bits 010010 using direct-sequence spread spectrum. The chipping sequence is the so-called Barker code 10110111000. What bits are actually transmitted?

22. You want your wireless device to be able to transmit data at a rate of 2 Mbps. If it uses the Barker code from the previous example, what is the raw bit rate that is needed?

23. Two WLAN devices are contending for the medium. One wants to request access by sending an RTS frame. Another wants to acknowledge a previous RTS request with a CTS frame. Suppose both see the medium free at the same time. Which device transmits successfully? Explain.

REFERENCES

[Ar02] Arbaugh, W., N. Shankar, Y. C. Justin Wan, and K. Zhang. "Your 802.11 Wireless Network Has No Clothes." *IEEE Wireless Communications,* vol. 9, no. 6 (December 2002), 44–51.

[Be02] Berger, R. *802.11 Unleashed.* Englewood Cliffs, NJ: Prentice-Hall, 2002.

[Du03] Dubendorf, V. *Wireless Data Technologies Reference Handbook.* New York: Wiley, 2003.

[Fo03] Forouzan, B. *Local Area Networks.* New York: McGraw-Hill, 2003.

[Gr01] Gravano, S. *Introduction to Error Control Codes.* Oxford and New York: Oxford University Press, 2001.

[Ha01] Halsall, F. *Multimedia Communications.* Reading, MA: Addison-Wesley, 2001.

[Pr01] Proakis, J. *Digital Communications.* New York: McGraw-Hill, 2001.

[Sc95] Schneier, B. *Applied Cryptography: Protocols, Algorithms, and Source Code in C,* 2nd ed. New York: Wiley, 1995.

[Sc97] Schlegel, C. *Trellis Coding.* New York: Wiley, 1997.

[Sc00] Schiller, J. *Mobile Communications.* Reading, MA: Addison-Wesley, 2000.

[St99] Stallings, W. *ISDN and Broadband ISDN with Frame Relay and ATM,* 4th ed. Englewood Cliffs, NJ: Prentice-Hall, 1999.

[Sw03] Swaminatha, T. M., and C. R. Elden. *Wireless Security and Privacy: Best Practices and Design Techniques.* Reading, MA: Addison-Wesley, 2003.

CHAPTER 10

CONNECTING NETWORKS

Information can tell us everything. It has all the answers. But they are answers to questions we have not asked, and which doubtless don't even arise.
—**Jean Baudrillard,** French semiologist

10.1 INTRODUCTION

As the need to communicate increases and the number of devices grows, the protocols described in the previous chapter become less effective. Greater needs usually require more flexibility than these topologies and protocols can provide. As the number of frames increases, the LANs become saturated and performance degrades. It's just like a city highway. At one time it may have been sufficient for the amount of traffic that traveled on it, but as the number of vehicles grows, new lanes, exit and entrance ramps, and sometimes new highways and connections among them must be built to accommodate the additional traffic flow.

One way to avoid serious bottlenecks is to divide one LAN into multiple LANs, thus reducing the number of devices per LAN. This solution helps maintain performance at an acceptable level. However, distributing all the devices to multiple LANs raises the question of which devices are assigned to which LANs. A corollary to Murphy's law states that no matter how you group them, two devices on two different LANs will need to communicate. Consequently, we must provide some way for communication across LANs while, at the same time, maintaining the LAN protocol. This invariably leads to designing ways in which to connect networks. Any two devices on a LAN communicate using the LAN's protocols. However, if they lie on two different LANs, new protocols must be developed to cross over LAN boundaries.

Different networks were designed for different people with very different goals. To assume they are isolated from one another is unrealistic, however. For example, within a large corporation different departments may have specific goals and approaches to their work. Departments of manufacturing, research and development, and marketing are very different. Different factors affect their decisions as they install computer systems or connect to networks. Consequently, they may adopt different and incompatible systems. The departments still must communicate, however, and if they use incompatible networks they have a problem. This leaves two possible solutions. The first is to force them all to adopt a specific network standard. Unfortunately, if the chosen network does not meet the goals and needs of a department, then the choice is counterproductive. The second solution is to determine some way for different networks to communicate. Because most people expect computers and networks to be servants rather than masters, the second choice is preferable.

For example, consider the scenario of Figure 10.1, which represents networks used by a large corporation with departments in New York and Texas. Two New York departments and one Texas department have each installed their own LAN. New York devices A and B access file servers on their respective LANs using protocols we have discussed in previous chapters. Texas device C does similarly. However, all three devices need access to the other LANs periodically. The two New York networks can be connected directly, but distance prohibits a direct connection with the Texas LAN. Consequently, a larger wide area network* is used to connect Texas and New York.

The ability to connect networks is certainly not new. There are standards for software and connecting devices, and any computer vendor has many such products to sell. The issue is where in the hierarchy of hardware and software these products

Figure 10.1   Interconnecting Networks

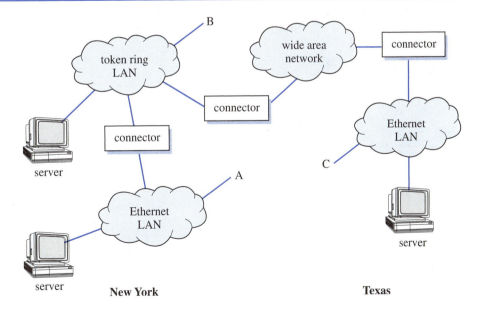

---

* We discuss wide area networks later. For now, just think of it as a network spanning a larger geographical area than a LAN and having different protocols.

fit. That is, what do they actually do? Models such as OSI provide several layers of protocols for computer networks. For example, suppose the two New York LANs of Figure 10.1 differ only in the MAC sublayer of the data link layer, but the wide area network is different at higher layers. A connection to the wide area network deals with more incompatibilities and is more complex than one connecting the two LANs.

Protocol converters, which define the logic that translates one protocol to another, are used to establish connections. In general, we can connect two identical networks at layer 1, which amounts to little more than an electronic connection to regenerate and repeat signals. We also can connect two totally incompatible networks at the highest layer using a device called a *gateway*. Such a connection requires complete knowledge of both protocols and the ability to translate one to another. We also can connect anywhere between the highest and lowest layers, depending on the degree of compatibility between the two networks.

The most common protocol converters exist at layers 1, 2, and 3 (Figure 10.2). Such devices and the protocols on which they are based form the main content of

Figure 10.2 OSI Connections

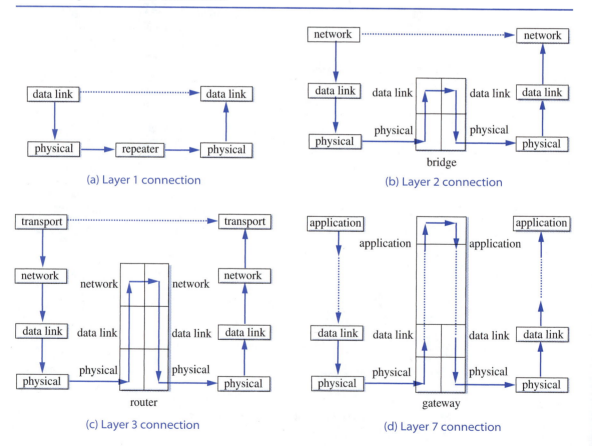

(a) Layer 1 connection

(b) Layer 2 connection

(c) Layer 3 connection

(d) Layer 7 connection

this chapter. Section 10.2 discusses layer 1 devices called hubs and repeaters. Section 10.3 discusses bridges and switches, devices that perform layer 2 translations. That section also deals with configuring connections, routing information among different LANs, and strategies on how to build tables that indicate what devices exist on what LANs. We'll start with the original layer 2 devices, bridges, and progress to current technologies, including switches, switched Ethernet, and virtual LANs. Section 10.4 discusses routers, devices used in wide area networks such as the Internet. Sections 10.5 through 10.8 describe various algorithms that routers need to determine paths to requested destinations and some of the problems caused by congestion and device failures and ways to recover from these problems. The previous chapters have dealt with individual components of a large communication system; it's now time to put these pieces together.

10.2 LAYER 1 CONNECTIONS

REPEATERS AND HUBS

Figure 10.3 shows a once common way of connecting networks using **repeaters,** devices that operate at the physical layer (layer 1). A repeater accepts a frame's bits from a LAN to which it is connected and retransmits them onto another LAN. It assumes the LANs to which it is connected use the same protocols and same frame formats. It makes no assumption as to the meaning of the bits. A repeater's primary function is to regenerate signals, thereby extending the distance covered by the LAN protocols.

Devices A, B, C, and D are each connected to a different LAN (perhaps an Ethernet segment). Each device, however, will see any frame that any other sends. For example, D sees everything A sends. Whether they accept the frame depends on to

Figure 10.3   LANs Connected with a Repeater

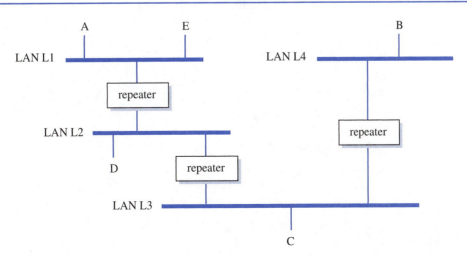

whom the frame is addressed. The devices have no knowledge of the repeater's existence; as far as they are concerned, they are all connected by a single, but larger, LAN. If the LANs are Ethernets that use CSMA/CD, then the devices all lie in the same **collision domain.** This means that if any two of A, B, C, or D send at the same time, the frames will collide.

As the previous chapter described, many devices rely on **hubs** for establishing connections. Figure 10.4 shows a typical arrangement. One hub may connect many devices, including workstations or other hubs. From the device's point of view there's little difference in being connected to a hub or a segment. If the device uses CSMA/CD for contention, it operates the same either way: send and listen for collisions. A hub functions much the same as a repeater. It accepts a signal over one port (connection), regenerates the signal, and sends it over all other ports. Sometimes a hub is called a **multiport repeater.** As with repeaters, if the devices implement CSMA/CD, they all lie in the same collision domain. Again, if any two of A, B, C, or D send at the same time, the frames will collide.

Repeaters and hubs primarily extend the reach of a network, but they can create problems. One problem is that more devices can access the medium. This leads to more traffic and can degrade LAN performance. For example, if A sends a frame to E (Figure 10.3 or 10.4), the repeaters or hubs forward the frame to all possible locations. They have no built-in logic to know that A and E are on the same LAN or connected to the same hub and that repeating the frame is pointless. The result, of course, is that none of the other devices can send until A has finished transmitting. If the devices execute CSMA/CD, extending the LAN's reach is the same as extending

Figure 10.4   Making Connections Using Hubs

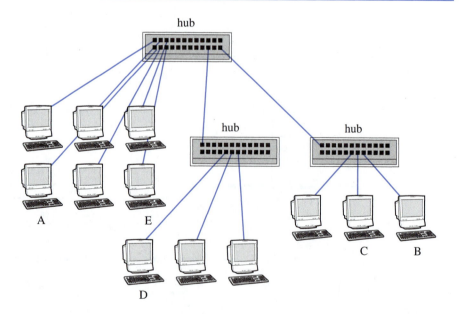

the collision domain. A second problem is security. Generally, as more people have access to information, security is more difficult to implement. If A and E are exchanging sensitive information, the frames pass by all the other devices and the potential for a security breach increases.

10.3 LAYER 2 CONNECTIONS

BRIDGES

Another way to connect LANs is to use a bridge or switch. The difference between a bridge and switch is analogous to the difference between a repeater and hub. A **bridge** traditionally connected two LANs, and a **switch** connects many devices. The important thing here is that both are connectors with the ability to execute layer 2 protocols and make decisions about when to forward any frames they receive. In fact, replace the word *repeater* with *bridge* in Figure 10.3 and *hub* with *switch* in Figure 10.4 and you have a network with the same physical topology but with a much greater ability to control, manage, and isolate traffic. Bridges were common when Ethernet devices were connected to a common segment. With the evolution of the Fast Ethernet protocol and the move to UTP as the physical medium, switches became a popular choice. We will first cover the traditional bridge functions. Dealing with bridges first provides a simpler view of things without compromising the discussion of some important tasks that both bridges and switches perform. Most of what we will say about bridges is also true of switches. We will then follow up with a discussion on switches and, in particular, switched Ethernet and virtual LANs.

A bridge is a layer 2 connector. As such, it performs data link functions such as error detection, frame formatting, and frame routing. For example, suppose device B sends a frame on LAN L2 in the network configuration of Figure 10.5. Bridge B1

Figure 10.5 LANs Connected with a Bridge

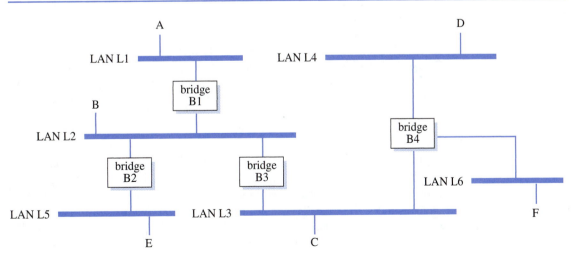

examines the destination address and, if the frame is destined for any device on LAN L1 (say A), accepts the frame and forwards it using the contention protocol of L1. (How B1 knows what is on L1 is a major issue that we discuss shortly.) If the frame is destined for a device on one of the other LANs, B1 ignores the frame. Thus, B1 acts like any other device selectively rejecting or accepting frames based on their destination.

If B1 accepts the frame, it executes error detection routines to determine whether the frame is correct. If there are no errors, it sends the frame over LAN L1. If L1's frame format is the same as L2's, the bridge sends the frame as is. If it is different, the bridge must reformat the frame it received into a format consistent with L1's standard. In some cases, reformatting is a simple matter of reorganizing the fields, adding required ones, and dropping unnecessary ones. Unfortunately, as we soon will see, in some cases the reformatting causes other problems, some of which layer 2 protocols cannot handle.

Before discussing bridge design, let's revisit an important question: What are the reasons for using bridges in the first place? One reason is to enhance efficiency. With repeaters, we saw that every frame propagates throughout each LAN, causing a lot of unnecessary traffic. To avoid this, a network manager can create a topology in which frequently communicating devices are on the same LAN. For example, each LAN of Figure 10.5 could correspond to a different department in a large company. Thus, devices within a department can communicate with each other, and the bridges do not forward any of the frames onto another LAN. For example, two devices can communicate over L1 at the same time two others communicate over L2. In general, communication within different LANs occurs in parallel, and efficiency is increased. If the LANs are Ethernets, then each bridge observes the CSMA/CD protocol when it forwards frames. An important result of this is that the bridges separate the LANs into distinct collision domains and reduce the number of collisions that would otherwise occur.

The bridges also allow interdepartmental communications when necessary. For example, if A sent a message to F, the frame would have to travel through the following sequence of bridges and LANs: L1-B1-L2-B3-L3-B4-L6. Eventually, it would reach F.

Security is another reason for using bridges. Because bridges selectively resend frames, they can prevent certain frames from propagating throughout the network. This procedure enhances security because some devices never see the transmissions of others. For example, LAN L1 might connect those devices that need to use sensitive employee information, whereas devices that have no such need are on other LANs.

BRIDGING DIFFERENT TYPES OF LANs

Bridging is more difficult when connecting different types of LANs. One problem is that different LANs may have different bit rates. For example, suppose a bridge accepts frames from a fast LAN and forwards them to a slower LAN or to one where collisions have occurred. The frames may arrive faster than they can be forwarded. Consequently, there must be sufficient buffer space in the bridge to allow a backlog of frames. Bridge delays can cause other problems, such as time-outs in the flow control protocols. Timers are set to provide a reasonable time for a frame to reach its destination and an acknowledgment to be sent. Delays at bridges can cause excessive time-outs unless the device's network software adjusts them. Now, however, timers depend on interconnection strategies and we lose some of the transparency of the topology.

Frame formatting presents another problem. Recall from Chapter 9 that each LAN standard has a different frame format. Therefore, if a bridge connects two different LANs, it must also reformat a received frame before resending it. On the surface, reformatting does not seem difficult, as it is primarily a rearrangement of information. Suppose a bridge connects an Ethernet and a token ring LAN, however. Frames on a token ring have a priority; those on an Ethernet do not. Therefore, a frame going from a token ring to an Ethernet loses its priority. Conversely, a frame going from an Ethernet to a token ring must be given a priority—but what? Usually a default is assigned. But what happens if a frame goes from a token ring to an Ethernet and then to another token ring? The frame has an initial priority, loses it when it goes on the Ethernet, and then gets another priority when it reaches the second token ring. There is no guarantee, however, that the initial and ending priorities will be the same.

ROUTING

Connecting two different LAN types brings up other issues. However, for the rest of this section, we assume that a bridge connects two similar LANs. This is more typical because Ethernet has become the dominant LAN standard. It also allows us to focus on another bridge function: forwarding frames. By itself, forwarding frames is not difficult. The hard question is, How does a bridge know when to accept and forward a frame? For example, suppose bridge B3 in Figure 10.5 detects a frame on LAN L2. If the frame's destination is device A or E, B3 should ignore it. However, suppose the destination is D, C, or F. Device C is on LAN L3, and the only way to get to devices D or F is through L3. Therefore, the bridge must accept the frame and forward it on LAN L3. But how does B3 know that D, C, and F are accessible via L3? Worse yet, what if someone moves F from L6 to L5? How does the bridge know the device is no longer accessible via L3?

These questions may seem trivial at first because you, as the reader, can see the entire network drawn in a diagram. Having a global view of a situation always makes a problem easier. But the bridges do not have this view. They connect two or more LANs and see only what arrives on them. Furthermore, a bridge certainly cannot see what happens on a LAN several bridges away. The process of deciding which frames to forward and where is called **bridge routing.** We will devote the rest of this section to discussing it.

ROUTING TABLES

Bridges make routing decisions based on information stored in a **routing table** (sometimes called a **forwarding database** or **routing directory**). Where a bridge routes a frame depends on the LAN on which the frame arrives. Each bridge has a routing table for each LAN to which it is connected. When a frame arrives on that LAN, the bridge finds the destination address in the appropriate routing table. The table's entry specifies to which LAN the bridge should forward the frame.

To illustrate, Figure 10.6 contains routing tables for the bridges in Figure 10.5. Bridge B1 has two routing tables (Figure 10.6a), one each for LANs L1 and L2. When the bridge detects a frame on L1, it determines the destination address and looks for it in the routing table for L1. If the destination address is one of B through F, the bridge forwards the frame to L2, the only way to get to those devices. If the destination is A, the bridge does not forward the frame and the frame stays on L1. Similarly, if the bridge detects a frame from L2 destined for A, it forwards the frame to L1.

The tables in bridge B3 are similar. The bridge will forward any frame from L2 to L3 that is destined for C, D, or F However, if a frame arrives on L2 and is destined for A, B, or E, the bridge will not forward it. Figure 10.5 shows that those devices cannot be reached by going from L2 to L3. You should read through the other tables and convince yourself that their entries accurately reflect the topology of Figure 10.5.

Figure 10.6   Routing Tables for Bridges in Figure 10.5

Source LAN L1		Source LAN L2	
Desti-nation	Next LAN	Desti-nation	Next LAN
A	—	A	L1
B	L2	B	—
C	L2	C	—
D	L2	D	—
E	L2	E	—
F	L2	F	—

(a) Bridge B1

Source LAN L2		Source LAN L5	
Desti-nation	Next LAN	Desti-nation	Next LAN
A	—	A	L2
B	—	B	L2
C	—	C	L2
D	—	D	L2
E	L5	E	—
F	—	F	L2

(b) Bridge B2

Source LAN L2		Source LAN L3	
Desti-nation	Next LAN	Desti-nation	Next LAN
A	—	A	L2
B	—	B	L2
C	L3	C	—
D	L3	D	—
E	—	E	L2
F	L3	F	—

(c) Bridge B3

Source LAN L3		Source LAN L4		Source LAN L6	
Desti-nation	Next LAN	Desti-nation	Next LAN	Desti-nation	Next LAN
A	—	A	L3	A	L3
B	—	B	L3	B	L3
C	—	C	L3	C	L3
D	L4	D	—	D	L4
E	—	E	L3	E	L3
F	L6	F	L6	F	—

(d) Bridge B4

How does a bridge define its routing table? One way is to program each bridge with each device's address and the LAN to which frames destined for that device should be forwarded. We call this approach **fixed routing** because we assume the tables' information does not change. In most network environments, however, this assumption is too restrictive. New devices may be added, old ones removed, and others moved to different locations. Entire LANs may be added or removed. We need correct routing regardless of a device's location and network topology. This will provide the transparency that makes a network easier to use.

If we want to use routing tables in a more dynamic environment, we have two choices. One is to reprogram the bridges every time someone adds, deletes, or moves a device. In a dynamic environment this approach is not viable, so we are left with the second choice: determine some way for the bridges to update their routing tables automatically.

TRANSPARENT BRIDGES

We call bridges that create and update their own routing tables **transparent bridges.** They have their own standard (IEEE 802.1d). They are designed so that you can plug them in and have them work immediately regardless of topology and the devices' locations. There is no need to tell them where the devices are: They will determine that automatically and initialize their routing tables, without needing special programming. If a device moves from one LAN to another, each bridge learns this and updates its routing table accordingly. This capability to update the routing table is called **route learning** or **address learning.**

Route Learning   A bridge learns what to put in its routing table by observing traffic. Whenever it receives a frame, it examines the source address. It then knows that the device sending the frame is accessible via the LAN on which the frame just arrived. The bridge examines each of its routing tables, looking for the device's address. If a table entry indicates that the device is accessible over a different LAN, the bridge changes the entry to specify the LAN on which the frame arrived. Presumably the device moved to a different LAN.

To illustrate, consider again the routing tables of Figure 10.6 and the LANs of Figure 10.5. Now suppose device D moves from LAN L4 to LAN L1. The routing tables are now incorrect, and the only devices able to send to D are those on the same LAN as D. Next, suppose D sends a frame to E on LAN L5. Bridge B1 routes the frame to L2. However, it also examines its routing tables (Figure 10.6a). Because the bridge received a frame from D on L1, it knows that D is in the direction of L1.* It therefore changes the fourth entry in each routing table and redefines them as shown in Table 10.1.

---

* Note that B1 doesn't necessarily know D is on L1. For all it knows, the frame may have gone through several bridges before getting to L1. The important thing is that the bridge knows in what direction to forward a frame.

Table 10.1 Updated Routing Table for Bridge B1 in Figure 10.5

SOURCE LAN L1		SOURCE LAN L2	
Destination	Next LAN	Destination	Next LAN
A	—	A	L1
B	L2	B	—
C	L2	C	—
D	—	D	L1
E	L2	E	—
F	L2	F	—

Bridge B1 now knows not to forward any frame from L1 that is destined for D and to forward any frame from L2 that is destined for D to L1. When bridge B2 detects D's frame from L2, it updates its tables similarly. In this case B2 realizes D is accessible via L2. However, from B2's perspective this is no different from when D was on L4. As a result, the "updated" values are the same as the original ones.

Some questions still remain. Bridges B1 and B2 learned of D's move only because D sent a frame that B1 and B2 had to forward. Bridges B3 and B4 still do not know of D's move. Must they remain ignorant until D sends something their way? What if D never does? Do they remain in the dark forever? If so, frames sent to D from LANs L3, L4, or L6 will never reach D. For that matter, what if D never sent the frame to E? Then not even bridges B1 and B2 are aware of D's move and nothing will reach D.

So far the discussion has dealt only with changing information. Another issue is how the tables are initialized. What do the bridges do at startup? Fortunately, the 802.1d specifications provide answers. Each bridge maintains a timer. Whenever the timer expires, the bridge purges the contents of the routing table. The bridge "reasons" that after a period of time, device locations may not be accurate; therefore, it removes the routing information.

This action appears to make devices inaccessible since the router maintains no information on how to reach them. However, when a bridge receives a frame destined for a device that has no entry in the routing table, the bridge uses a **flooding algorithm.** That is, it sends the frame over every LAN to which it is connected except the one on which the frame arrived. This serves two purposes: It guarantees the frame will reach its destination (assuming it exists), and it allows more bridges to see the frame and learn the direction of the sending device. This information keeps their routing tables current.

Consider the previous example in which D moves from L4 to L1 in Figure 10.5 and then sends a frame to E. If E has not sent anything for a while, its entries in each routing table are deleted. Therefore, when B1 receives D's frame, it notes that there is no entry for E and automatically forwards the frame to L2. Similarly, B2 and B3 forward the frame to L5 and L3, respectively. Finally, B4 forwards the frame to L4 and L6. The end result is that E gets the frame and each bridge forwards a frame from D and updates its routing table. Consequently, anything sent to D will be forwarded correctly (at least until the next timer expires).

The flooding algorithm also allows bridges to initialize their routing tables. Suppose a LAN is installed and all of the bridges' routing tables are empty. No bridge knows the location of any device. When a bridge receives its first frame from a LAN, it sends it along every other LAN to which it is connected. Similarly, bridges on those LANs receive the frame and also forward it using the flooding algorithm. Before long the frame has reached every bridge and every LAN. In particular, the frame has reached its destination, and every bridge knows the direction of the sending device.

As more devices send frames, the bridges forward them using routing table entries or by flooding. As the frames propagate through the network, the bridges eventually learn the direction of the sending device and can forward frames without using the flooding algorithm.

Frame Propagation   The previous approach to designing transparent bridges and route learning worked well with the examples given. However, certain topologies can cause an endless propagation of frames and glut the network. To illustrate, suppose network designers decide to add a second bridge connecting two LANs. Adding a redundant bridge between two LANs was sometimes used to protect the system in the event of failures. If the first bridge failed, the second one was already in place and there was no (or very little) delay caused by the failure. This was particularly useful in real-time systems where delays caused by equipment failure could lead to a disaster.

For example, the simple LAN connection of Figure 10.7 shows two bridges between the same two LANs. Suppose the routing tables are empty and A sends a frame to B. Since neither bridge is aware of the other, each accepts the frame and forwards it onto LAN L2. Next, bridge B1 sees B2's frame, and B2 sees B1's frame on L2. Since neither knows where B is, both bridges accept the frame and forward it onto LAN L1. Again, each will see the other's frame and forward it back to L2.

Figure 10.7   Two Bridges Connecting Two LANs

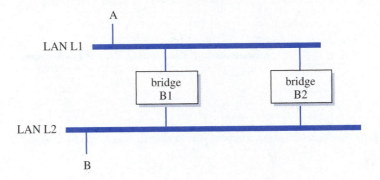

Until B identifies its location, the frames will be transferred back and forth repeatedly between both LANs.

The situation is made worse if there is a third bridge (B3) connecting the LANs. If A sends one frame along L1, each bridge forwards it to L2, putting three frames on L2. Each bridge sees two of them (one from each of the other two bridges) and forwards them onto L1, putting six frames on L1. Each bridge now sees four frames (two from each of the other two bridges) and forwards them, putting twelve frames back on L2. This process continues, causing an explosion of frames that eventually clogs the system and brings communication to a standstill.

We illustrated the problem with a simple topology showing two bridges between two LANs. The potential for endlessly circulating frames exists in other topologies as well. In particular, two distinct routes between two devices will cause a loop in the topology. This means that a frame may leave a LAN via one route only to return via another. Figure 10.8 shows a topology with multiple routes between A and B. (We'll see what the costs mean shortly.) In fact, there are at least seven routes if we ignore routes going through the same bridge twice. (Can you find them?) To see the magnitude of this problem, suppose A sends B a frame and the bridges use the flooding algorithm. Suppose a frame takes the route from L1 to L4 through bridges B1 and B2. Bridge B6 will forward the frame back to L1. Bridge B4 will forward the frame to L3. From here B5 forwards it to L1, and B3 forwards it to L2.

Figure 10.8   Multiple LANs with Loops

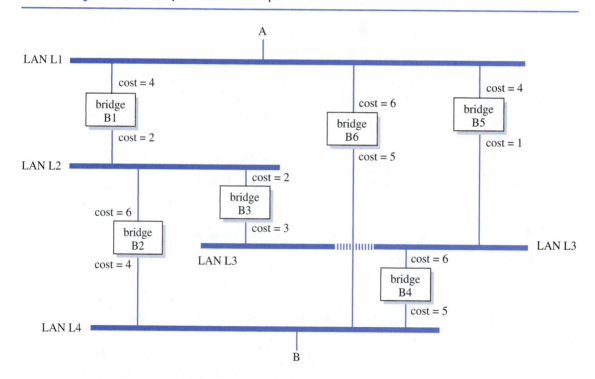

Next B1 forwards it to L1, B2 forwards it back to L4, and the process continues. As before, the single frame causes an unending increase in the number of frames moving through the network. If we consider the other routes from L1 to L4, the increase is even more rapid. The number of frames becomes excessive very quickly, and the network shuts down.

SPANNING TREE ALGORITHM

One approach to the problem of frame propagation is to eliminate the loops by not using certain bridges. We don't disconnect the bridges physically, but we prevent them from forwarding frames. Instead they are used as backups in case another bridge fails. The tricky part is determining which bridges are used and when they should automatically reconfigure if a bridge fails. As usual, we want to let the bridges do the work themselves and make the configuration transparent to the user. One solution calls for the bridges to execute a **spanning tree algorithm.** A *spanning tree,* a term from data structures, corresponds to a minimal subset of edges taken from a connected graph that connects the graph's vertices. The subset is minimal in that the spanning tree has no loops.* For more information on spanning trees, consult a reference on data structures, such as reference [Dr95] or [Pa95].

To make the algorithm work, we first associate a cost with each bridge-to-LAN connection, or **bridge port.** It may correspond to a bit rate at which a bridge port can transmit onto a LAN. Typically, lower bit rates mean a higher cost. The cost of sending a frame from one LAN to another is the sum of the costs of ports in the route. In some cases, all costs are set to 1, so that the cost of a route is simply the number of bridges in it. Figure 10.8 shows the cost of each bridge port. The cost of sending a frame from L1 to L4 via bridges B1 and B2 is 6, the sum of the costs of going from B1 to L2 (2) plus B2 to L4 (4). Note that the costs associated with the B1-to-L1 and B2-to-L2 ports are not included here. They are used for frames going in the other direction.

Next, we visualize the LAN topology as a graph. The LANs and bridges are vertices, and the connections between a LAN and a bridge are the edges. Figure 10.9 shows a graphical representation of the topology in Figure 10.8. The figure lists costs for each edge. Remember that as frames move through the graph, only costs from a bridge node to a LAN node accrue.

The spanning tree algorithm determines a set of edges that connect all the LAN nodes of Figure 10.9. Remember as we discuss the algorithm that we have the advantage of seeing the entire network topology; the bridges that execute the algorithm have no such view. They know only the LANs to which they are connected. This makes the algorithm more complex than it would be if executed by a processor that knew the entire topology.

To begin the spanning tree algorithm, the bridges elect one of their own (true partisan politics) to be a **root bridge.** It is usually the one with the lowest ID, although priorities can be used. Using data structures terminology, the root bridge

---

* In data structures, the term *cycle* is often used in place of *loop.*

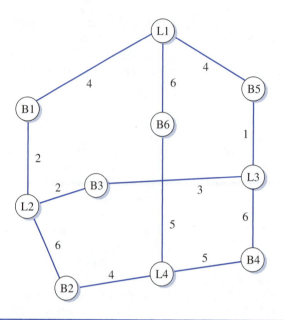

Figure 10.9 Graph Representation of the LAN Topology in Figure 10.8

will be the root of the spanning tree. The bridges elect the root bridge by first sending a series of special frames called **bridge protocol data units (BPDUs)** at regular intervals. Each BPDU contains the bridge's ID, the port ID over which the frame was first sent, and the accumulated costs of ports over which it has been received. The latter is the cost of a path from the BPDU's current location back to its source.

When a bridge receives a BPDU, it compares the source bridge's ID with its own. If its own ID is higher, it knows it will not be the root bridge. It records the sending bridge's ID and the path cost to it, increments the path cost by the cost of the receiving port, and forwards the BPDU through all its other ports. It also stops sending its own BPDUs. If the bridge's ID is lower than the one that sent the BPDU, it will not forward the frame. It reasons that the sending bridge will never be elected, so there is no point in forwarding its frames.

Eventually each bridge except the one with the lowest ID will stop sending frames because it knows it will not be the root bridge. The remaining bridge stops forwarding any frames it receives and eventually receives no more. After a time during which it receives no frames, it considers itself duly elected as root bridge. It and the other bridges then proceed to the algorithm's next step.

In the second step, each bridge determines its **root port,** the port corresponding to the cheapest path to the root bridge. Because each bridge previously recorded path costs for each BPDU received on each port, it simply looks for the cheapest. Each bridge subsequently will communicate with the root bridge using its root port.

The last step determines a **designated bridge** for each LAN. This is the bridge that eventually forwards frames from that LAN. The bridges elect a designated bridge by sending BPDUs over each LAN to which they are connected. A bridge will not send a BPDU to a LAN using a previously determined root port. Essentially, the root port determines the LAN in the direction of the root bridge. The algorithm now must determine if there are any LANs in any other direction.

Let's examine the activities from the perspective of a specific LAN. The LAN is carrying BPDUs from its bridges requesting to be the designated bridge. Each BPDU contains the cost to the root bridge from the bridge sending the BPDU. When a bridge receives a BPDU, it compares the cost in it with its own cost to the root bridge. If its own cost is larger, it knows it will not be the designated bridge and gives up its claim. Eventually the only bridge not seeing a smaller cost becomes the designated bridge for the LAN. In the event there are two or more bridges with the same smaller cost, they use their IDs to break ties. The lowest ID wins.

After selecting designated bridges for each LAN, the spanning tree algorithm is complete. Every LAN is connected to its designated bridge, and every bridge can communicate with the root bridge via its root port. This defines a unique path between any two LANs and avoids frame propagation resulting from flooding algorithms.

We now illustrate the spanning tree algorithm with an example. Consider the LAN topology of Figure 10.8 and the associated graph of Figure 10.9. The first step determines the root bridge. If we assume the bridges are numbered in increasing order from B1 through B6, then B1 is elected root bridge.

During the election process, each bridge records the cost to the root bridge through each of its ports and then selects the cheapest one. Figure 10.10 shows the root ports (designated by an arrow) and paths to the root bridge (designated by the

Figure 10.10   Graph After Determining Root Ports

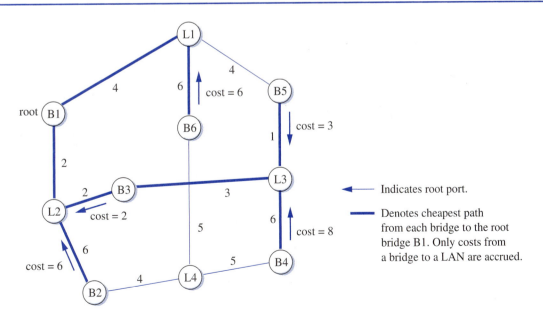

colored lines). The path costs are also listed next to the arrows. For example, bridge B2's root port is the one connected to L2. The cheapest path is B2-L2-B1, for a cost of 6. Remember, we only accrue costs from bridges to LANs. B4's root port is the one connected to L3. The path to the root bridge is B4-L3-B3-L2-B1, for a cost of 8. As the figure shows, there are other paths, but their costs are higher. You should take some time to understand why the other root ports were chosen as they were.

The last step determines the designated bridge for each LAN. The root ports connect bridges to some LANs, but there may be other LANs that are not part of the developing connection scheme. For example, in Figure 10.10 there is no root port connected to L4, and we need to determine a bridge to forward information from L4. To do this, bridges B2, B4, and B6 send BPDUs along L4 requesting to be the designated bridge. B4 states that its cost to the root bridge is 8; B2 and B6 indicate their cost to be 6. Consequently, B4 gives up its request because of its higher cost, and B6 gives up its request because of its higher ID. Thus, B2 becomes the designated bridge for L4. Proceeding similarly, B3 is the designated bridge for L3, and B1 is the designated bridge for L1 and L2 (Figure 10.11).

Figure 10.11 shows the resulting spanning tree, and Figure 10.12 relates it to the original network topology. The dotted lines indicate physical but not active connections. The bridges use these connections to send and receive BPDUs but not to forward frames in general. The tree connects all the LANs even though some of the bridges are not used. That is to be expected, however, because the bridges are redundant devices to be used in the event of a failure of another one. As long as no failure occurs, the LANs communicate using the topology of Figure 10.12.

Figure 10.11   Graph After Determining Designated Bridges

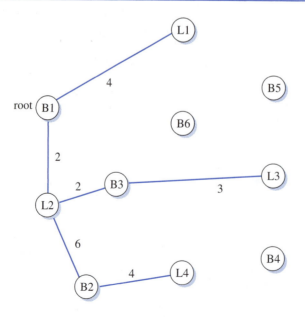

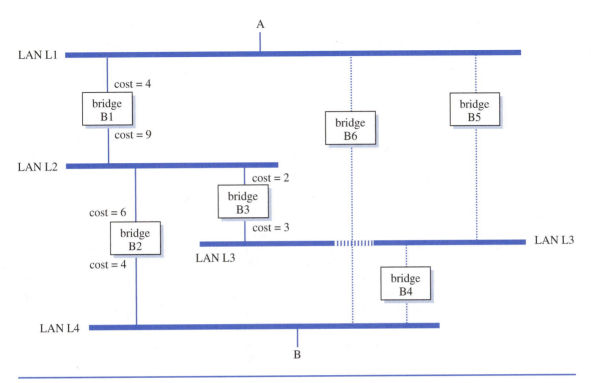

Figure 10.12 Network Topology Showing Active Bridge Connections

To detect a bridge failure and reconfigure the connection scheme, each bridge maintains a timer called a **message age timer.** During the specified time, each bridge (even the ones that are not part of the spanning tree) expects to hear from the root bridge confirming its status as root bridge. When a bridge receives this confirmation, it resets its timer. The root bridge, of course, cooperates by sending a configuration BPDU periodically to confirm its status. If a bridge malfunctions, one or more bridges do not receive a configuration BPDU and their timers expire. If a bridge other than the root bridge fails, the affected bridges exchange BPDUs to elect a new designated bridge for their LANs. If the root bridge fails, they must elect a new root bridge. Either way, they reconfigure the active topology dynamically.

SOURCE-ROUTING BRIDGES

One last approach to forwarding frames that we mention briefly puts the burden of routing on the individual devices instead of the bridges. Specifically, logic at the sending device determines a route to the destination and stores it in the frame. The route consists of a sequence of **route designators,** each consisting of a LAN and a bridge ID. When a bridge sees a frame, it determines whether there is a designator containing its ID and the ID of the LAN carrying the frame. If so, the bridge accepts the frame and forwards it to the LAN specified in the next designator.

For example, suppose A sends B (from Figure 10.8) a frame and specifies the route as L1-B5-L3-B4-L4. Both bridges connected to L1 see the frame, but since B5 follows L1 in the sequence, only B5 accepts it. B5 then forwards the frame to L3, where bridges B3 and B4 see it. Similarly, since B4 follows L3 in the sequence, only B4 accepts the frame. Finally, B4 forwards the frame to L4, where device B eventually receives the frame.

To determine the route, a device sends a frame to another device, effectively asking, "Where are you?" The receiving device gets the request and responds. When the sending device gets the response, it determines the best route. But how does the sending device know where to send the initial request when it does not know the route? It doesn't. The bridges must help by executing a variation of the flooding algorithm to make sure the request and response are received. The determination of a route to the destination is called **route discovery.**

One way to do this is to send an **all-routes broadcast frame** to the intended destination device. The frame's control field specifies the frame type and notifies the bridges that they should forward the frame onto all available LANs. An exception, of course, is made for the LAN on which the frame arrived. To avoid uncontrolled frame propagation, a device sends an all-routes broadcast frame with the route designator fields empty and the control field's routing field length equal to 0. When a bridge receives the frame, it inserts its own and the incoming LAN's IDs into the routing field and increments the routing field length. To avoid forwarding a frame it received previously, the bridge examines the existing route designators. It will not forward a frame to a LAN whose ID was part of a route designator of the incoming frame.

When a frame finally arrives at its destination, the routing field contains the route used in getting there. The destination puts this route in the routing field of a **nonbroadcast frame** and sends it back to the source device. It also sets a directional bit in the control field to notify the bridges they should interpret the route designators in reverse order. When a bridge receives a nonbroadcast frame, it forwards or drops the frame according to the information in the routing field. When the source device receives all the responses, it chooses which route to use in subsequent transmissions to B. Presumably, it would examine the costs (calculated during the broadcast) and choose the cheapest. Alternatively, it could choose the one using the fewest bridges or choose based on bridge IDs. There are other ways to determine routes, but this type of bridge is no longer common so we won't devote additional space to it.

SWITCHES AND SWITCHED ETHERNET

Since Ethernet is the dominant LAN standard we will, from this point on, assume that all our LANs are Ethernets. This will simplify our discussion and allow us to focus on relevant details. Switches perform the same functions as bridges. The primary difference is that whereas a bridge typically connects only a couple of LANs, a switch may have a couple dozen ports, thus providing many more connections. Figure 10.13 shows one configuration. One switch has many ports, each of which is

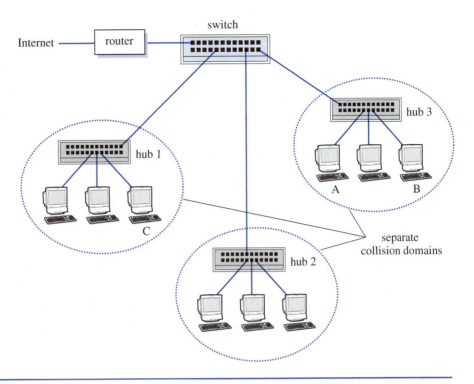

Figure 10.13   Connections Using Hubs and Switches

connected to a hub. There is also a connection to a router, which, in turn, provides Internet access. We'll discuss routers later in this chapter. Each hub connects many devices. All devices connected to a hub obey the Ethernet protocols and in effect define a single collision domain. Since switches, like bridges, selectively forward frames, each switch port leads to a different collision domain. Therefore, we really have a scenario similar to Figure 10.5, except that instead of multiple bridges we use only one switch.

Two devices connected to the same hub communicate directly through the hub. The switch ignores that traffic. However, if one device sends a frame to another that is connected to a different hub, the switch accepts that frame and forwards it over the port connecting the proper hub. In our example, the switch ignores any frame that A sends to B but accepts and forwards a frame that A sends to C. The switch, of course, must learn the locations of devices in much the same way that bridges learn their locations.

Although there are many collision domains in Figure 10.13, that topology defines a single **broadcast domain.** The 48-bit destination MAC address in an Ethernet frame can specify an individual device or it can specify a broadcast address. In the latter case, each switch will forward a broadcast frame over all outgoing ports.

Every device that sees a broadcast frame accepts it as it would a frame destined specifically for that device. In effect, a broadcast frame reaches all devices in the LAN. This is a common way for a network administrator to inform all users of important information such as problems, scheduled down times, or what happened during yesterday's soap operas.

An important fact about the topology in Figure 10.13 is that collisions still occur. Figure 10.14 shows another configuration, a fully **switched Ethernet,** that some sites are implementing. Physically it looks much like that in Figure 10.13 except all the hubs have been replaced with switches. Because switches have decreased considerably in price (as of this writing a 24-port switch can be purchased for about $800), some argue there is little need for hubs and that they have become obsolete. A major advantage of switched Ethernet is that there are no more collisions—anywhere! Because switch ports lead to separate collision domains and each device is connected to a separate switch port, each device lies in its own collision domain. Furthermore, if the connections between workstation and switch operate in full-duplex mode, devices no longer need the CSMA/CD contention protocol. Any device can still communicate with another in this configuration without fear of collisions, and the entire topology still defines one broadcast domain.

Another feature of switches is that the bit rates for ports can vary. This is especially important when a switch combines traffic from many sources onto a single

Figure 10.14   Connections Using Only Switches

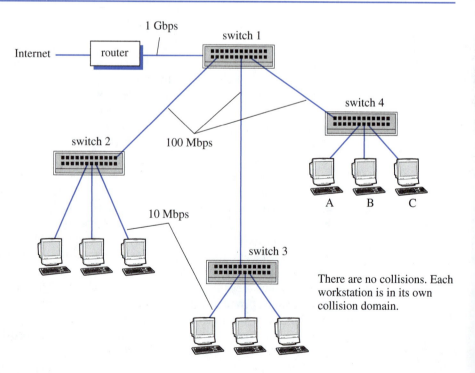

There are no collisions. Each workstation is in its own collision domain.

link. That link must support a bit rate higher than each of the feeder links or risk significant delays. Figure 10.14 shows 10 Mbps links to each workstation but 100 Mbps links between switches. It also shows a 1 Gbps link to the router. This is not the only configuration, and higher-speed links may also be established between a switch and a heavily used server. Many configurations are possible.

The topology of Figure 10.14 can be extended to multiple layers of switches (Figure 10.15). Typically, a switch at the bottom of the hierarchy is called a *private switch,* a switch for which there is no more than one Ethernet address assigned to each port. That is, each port connects directly to a single workstation. A *workgroup switch* lies above the private switch in the hierarchy. The primary difference is that multiple Ethernet addresses can be assigned to each port in a workgroup switch. In our case, the addresses for devices A, B, and C are all assigned to the same port in switch 1. Devices connected to a workgroup switch usually lie in close proximity.

The ultimate in a workgroup switch is a *backbone switch,* a switch that provides access to all devices in a broadcast domain. Although it would appear that there is no limit to how many switches can be connected, there is in fact a limit. Most switches have a maximum number of addresses that can be assigned to a port. Figure 10.15 shows that switches closer to the devices have a smaller number of addresses for each port. Switches that appear higher in the hierarchy have a larger number.

In full-duplex, fully switched Ethernets, frames will no longer collide, but frames may still be lost. For example, a switch accepts frames from many workstations and may queue them for transfer over outgoing ports. If traffic is bursty and frames arrive too fast, buffer space may fill and the switch may reject the frame. The Ethernet protocol deals with this situation using a MAC control sublayer that lies between

Figure 10.15   Private, Workgroup, and Backbone Switches

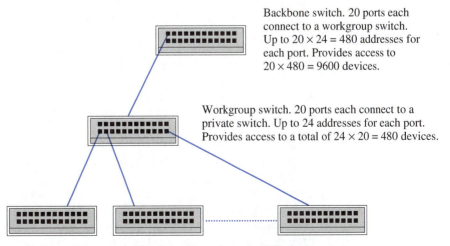

Backbone switch. 20 ports each connect to a workgroup switch. Up to $20 \times 24 = 480$ addresses for each port. Provides access to $20 \times 480 = 9600$ devices.

Workgroup switch. 20 ports each connect to a private switch. Up to 24 addresses for each port. Provides access to a total of $24 \times 20 = 480$ devices.

Private switches: One address for each of 24 ports

the original MAC and LLC sublayers of the data link layer. The MAC control sublayer defines a Pause frame to control flow as shown in the following example:

1. Device A is receiving a series of frames from device B. A's buffers are starting to fill.

2. A sends a Pause frame that contains a positive timer value to B.

3. B receives the Pause frame and refrains from sending any more frames to A until the specified time is up.

The sublayer also allows the timer value to be 0. It may seem a bit strange at first, but this setting acts to reenable the transmitting of frames. If device B was waiting because of a previous Pause frame and subsequently received a second one with a timer value of 0, it could resume sending frames immediately.

VIRTUAL LANs

Another feature that Ethernet switches allow is the creation of a **virtual LAN (VLAN).** The development of VLANs was motivated by network managers' needs to better manage traffic flow, enhance security, and separate users into workgroups. For example, it's common in many organizations to assign different employees to different projects. All the employees assigned to one project constitute a workgroup. It would be convenient if the network could be configured so that the traffic from personal computers in any one workgroup could be separated from that of another workgroup. This would spread the traffic over more links and tend to balance the overall network traffic better.

One option is to create a LAN consisting of all devices assigned to people in a workgroup. Each workgroup has its own LAN, and the network manager uses routers (layer 3 routing devices) to separate all the LANs. (We'll discuss routers later, but for now think of them as devices that separate LANs into distinct and autonomous entities.) Each LAN also corresponds to one broadcast domain. In other words, if a device sends a broadcast frame, that frame stays within the LAN and does not pass through the router.

A problem with this approach is that the employees in one workgroup may not all be in close proximity, which makes putting them all on the same LAN awkward. The group might consist of employees with different abilities from different departments located on different floors or even in different buildings. We're looking for a way to logically group together devices that may be physically distributed over larger distances but logically belong together. A VLAN is a group of devices that are logically grouped independent of their physical locations.

Figure 10.16 shows the idea. There are three groups of devices. VLAN1 contains five personal computers, a server, and a scanner. VLAN2 and VLAN3 contain three personal computers each. Logic in the switch attaches a VLAN designation to each port. Thus, the ports define what devices constitute what VLANs. Each VLAN also defines an independent broadcast domain. In other words, using layer 2 protocols, devices in VLAN1 communicate only with other devices in VLAN1. If a

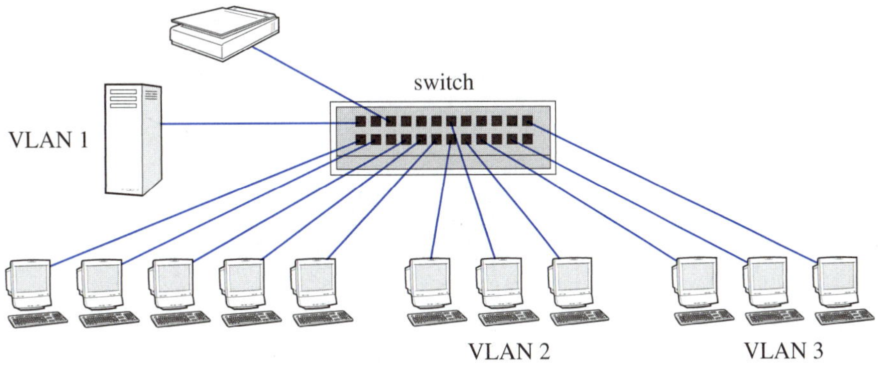

Figure 10.16   Switch Connecting Multiple VLANs

device in VLAN1 sends a broadcast frame, then the switch sends that frame out only the ports with a VLAN1 designation. Similar comments are true for VLAN2 and VLAN3.

This technique is useful for several reasons. One is that a user can send a broadcast frame only to users in the same VLAN, allowing them to communicate much more effectively among themselves and to avoid sending unnecessary data to others outside their group. Another reason is security. Layer 2 protocols will not route frames from one VLAN to another. This restricts traffic and allows the network manager to better manage traffic flow. Yet another advantage is that VLANs can be configured independent of a device's location. Although Figure 10.16 shows only one switch, there may be multiple switches having ports configured with the same VLAN designation. As a result, devices connected to different ports on different switches (and therefore in different locations) may belong to the same VLAN. The broadcast domain contains devices from a variety of locations, and devices in close proximity may or may not belong to the same broadcast domain.

The ability to create a VLAN independent of a device's physical location also provides a more robust and dynamic environment. Suppose an employee is removed from a workgroup and assigned to another. The only thing that needs to be done is to assign a new VLAN designation to the port to which the employee's device is connected. The employee does not need to move, and nothing needs to be rewired. The switch simply sees that port as part of a different VLAN, allowing the employee to communicate with an entirely new group.

So, how does a switch actually decide how to route a frame? Recall that an Ethernet frame has a destination address, but there's no mention of any VLAN designator. When a switch gets an Ethernet frame, how does it decide what to do? If routing is to be based on Ethernet addresses, where does the VLAN identifier fit in?

Figure 10.17 helps explain. Suppose that A, B, and C all lie in VLAN1 and that D lies in VLAN2. Furthermore, A and C are connected to one switch, but B and D

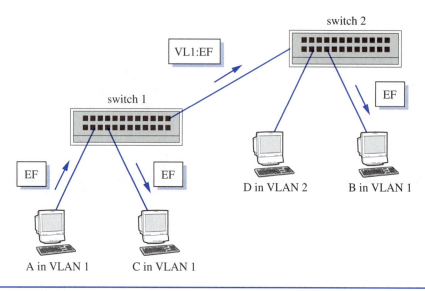

Figure 10.17   VLANs across Switches

are connected to another. When A sends an Ethernet broadcast frame, the following happens:

1. An Ethernet frame (designated by EF in the figure) is sent to switch 1. Switch 1 notes that the frame arrived over a port that has a VLAN1 designation.

2. The port connected to C also has a VLAN1 designation, so the switch sends the frame out that port.

3. Another port connects switch 1 with switch 2. Since there are VLAN1 devices in that direction, the associated port also has a VLAN1 designation. We note that other VLANs may also be associated with that same port.

4. Switch 1 adds a VLAN identifier to the Ethernet frame (shown as VL1:EF) and sends it out the port to switch 2.

5. Switch 2 receives the extended frame. The port over which switch 2 receives the frame could have several VLANs associated with it. However, because the frame contains the VLAN ID, switch 2 knows to which VLAN it belongs. Consequently, switch 2 sends the frame direct to B via the proper port. It will *not* send the frame to D, because D is not in VLAN1.

We close by noting that although the previous discussion assumed that the switch associated a VLAN with a port ID, there are other methods. For example, the switch can maintain a table that associates a set of MAC addresses with a VLAN ID. In this case, when a switch receives an Ethernet frame from a device, it looks at the frame's source address instead of the port over which it receives the frame. It uses the source address to index a table and extract the VLAN ID. An advantage here is that if a device moves, no changes need to be made to the switch because the MAC address depends on the network card in the device, not its location.

The VLAN ID may also be assigned based on layer 3 information. This is a little more complex because it requires that the switch implement some layer 3 protocols and makes the switch look more like a router. The next chapter discusses the Internet Protocol (IP), but for now we note that IP packets can be placed into the Data fields of a frame. The IP packet contains items such as an IP source address (different from the MAC address) and a specification of the protocols above IP that are being used. Thus, VLANs may be defined according to a device's IP address or even the higher-layer protocols being used. All the switch (router) needs to do is extract the packet from the frame, examine the source IP address or protocol specifier, and determine the associated VLAN designator. Reference [Fo03] provides more detail on implementing VLANs.

10.4 LAYER 3 CONNECTIONS

Local area networks (LANs) and the layer 1 and 2 connections, discussed previously, typically cover small geographic areas, usually restricted to a building or group of buildings. They are designed around relatively simple bus, ring, or star topologies. However, **wide area networks (WAN)** span the globe and need more sophisticated techniques.

Consider again the analogy of a highway system. Many cities have a single major freeway through the center (common bus) or a bypass circling them (ring). If the city is not large, this design handles most highway traffic reasonably well. But what about larger areas such as states or entire countries? It would be unreasonable to have an interstate system consisting of a single highway through America's heartland or circling the country along the coastal areas and the Canadian and Mexican borders. Instead, a complex connection strategy links major highways, bypasses, and state, county, and city roads. It is not reasonable to categorize this type of system as a bus, ring, star or a simple combination of them. It is much more complex.

Like a national highway system, the topologies of wide area networks are complex, usually somewhere between a simple bus, ring, or star structure and a fully connected one. With more complex topologies come more complex protocols for making connections and routing decisions. The fact that there are many ways to go from one point to another by itself makes the situation more complex. For example, if you live in Winona, Minnesota, and want to drive to Charleston, South Carolina, for your vacation, you will probably spend some time studying road maps to determine the best way to get there. Similarly, if you want to transfer information between computers in those two locations that are connected via a WAN, network protocols must determine how to get it there.

To add to the complexity, sometimes a link in a chosen route experiences a failure. What does the network protocol do with all the data traveling that route? In some cases, a route may prove so popular that too much data travels over it. The result is congestion and sometimes failure. Can network protocols avoid such situations? If they can't, what can they do to minimize their effects? To return to our

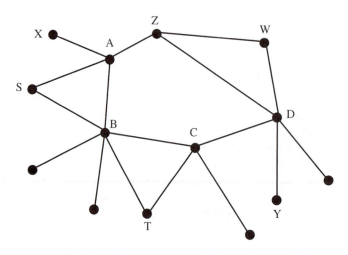

Figure 10.18   Generalized Network Topology

highway analogy, these problems are similar to major road construction preventing traffic flow or excessive traffic on the road to a popular vacation spot during a major holiday. Most of us know these problems well and understand that little can be done short of staying home.

Figure 10.18 shows a general network topology. Some devices often communicate directly with more devices than do others. Presumably they represent locations in heavily populated areas or locations with a high volume of information traffic. The devices with fewer connections might have fewer needs or correspond to more remote sites. For example, nodes A and B might represent sites in major metropolitan areas, and nodes X and Y might correspond to locations in remote parts of the country.

Suppose one device wants to communicate with another to which it is not connected directly. Network protocols must find the best path that connects them. For example, suppose X sends something to Y in Figure 10.18. Two possible paths are X-A-B-C-D-Y and X-A-Z-D-Y. Which is better? The answer typically depends on a comparison of the costs and the time required to send the information over each path.

The comparison is not always straightforward. In Figure 10.18 you might think that the path through A, Z, and D is better because it is shorter than the other alternative. Shorter is not always better, however, as anyone traveling by car knows. Many people will choose to drive a longer distance if it means using a road that has more lanes, is in better condition, or has more fast-food restaurants for the kids than a shorter alternative. Even though they drive farther, they may reach their destination more quickly and with less difficulty.

ROUTING TABLES

Similar to the bridges discussed previously, network nodes may use routing tables. Like those in Section 10.3, routing tables here do not normally specify the entire route. Instead they specify the next node in a route to a specified destination and the

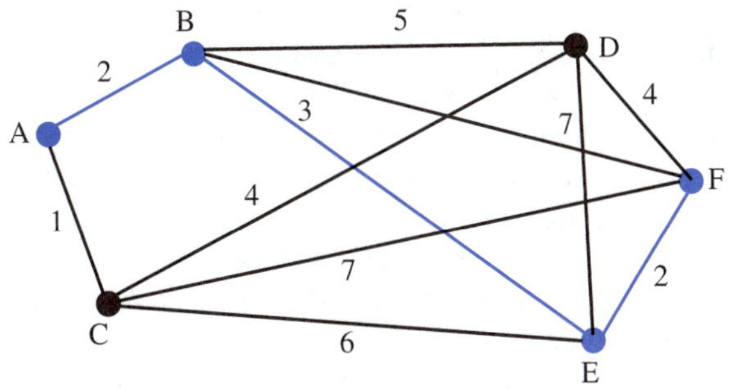

Figure 10.19   Network and Associated Connection Costs

cost to get there. For example, consider the network in Figure 10.19, where a cost is associated with the connection between two adjacent nodes. Suppose we want to find the cheapest route,* the one that minimizes the sum of the costs of the connections between adjacent nodes in the route. For example, there are several routes from A to F, but the cheapest one goes from A to B (cost of 2), B to E (cost of 3), and E to F (cost of 2) for a total route cost of 7.

Figure 10.20 shows partial routing tables of nodes A, B, and E. (We will discuss how these tables are created shortly.) Node A's table indicates that anything destined for node B, E, or F should be sent directly to B, where B's routing table will indicate the next node in the cheapest route. Similarly, anything destined for C or D should be sent to node C. From there, C's routing table indicates the next step.

Figure 10.20   Partial Routing Tables for Nodes A, B, and E

DESTINATION	NEXT NODE	COST	DESTINATION	NEXT NODE	COST	DESTINATION	NEXT NODE	COST
B	B	2	D	D	5	F	F	2
C	C	1	E	E	3			
D	C	5	F	E	5			
E	B	5						
F	B	7						

(a) Partial routing table for node A   (b) Partial routing table for node B   (c) Partial routing table for node E

---

* It's possible that all connections can be assigned a cost equal to 1. In this case the cheapest path becomes the shortest one, with the cost corresponding to the number of direct links in the path. This is sometimes called a *hop count;* we will discuss it later in this chapter.

To illustrate, suppose an application at node A wants to send data to node F. Logic at A looks for an entry in its routing table with destination F. The entry states that node B is the successor on the route, and the network protocol sends the data to B. Logic at B examines its routing table looking for an entry corresponding to destination F. The table's third entry indicates the data should go to node E next. Finally, the routing table at node E indicates that F is the next node on the route.

Who defines the routing tables and how? The process by which a routing table is defined is called a **routing algorithm.** There are several basic types, and we will discuss four of them: centralized routing, distributed routing, static routing, and adaptive routing. Then we will discuss in detail some specific routing algorithms.

CENTRALIZED ROUTING

Centralized routing means that all interconnection information is generated and maintained at a single central location. That location then broadcasts this information to all network nodes so that each may define its own routing tables. One way to maintain routing information centrally is a **routing matrix.** It consists of a row and column for each node in the network. A row corresponds to a source node, and a column corresponds to a destination node. The entry in the position specified by the row and column indicates the first node in the route from the source to the destination. From this entry the entire route can be extracted.

Figure 10.21 shows a routing matrix for the network in Figure 10.19. As before, the routes selected are the cheapest ones. In the case where two routes both have the cheapest cost, one is chosen arbitrarily. Consider again the route from A to F. According to the matrix's first row and sixth column, node B is the first one in the cheapest route. The next node is determined by considering the route from B to F. Examining the second row and sixth column indicates that node E is next. Finally, the node following E (node F) is found in the fifth row and sixth column. Thus, the route is from A to B to E to F.

Creating a routing table for a network node requires the row from the matrix corresponding to the node. For example, node A's routing table in Figure 10.20

Figure 10.21   Routing Matrix for the Network in Figure 10.19

		A	B	C	D	E	F
	A	—	B	C	C	B	B
	B	A	—	A	D	E	E
source node	C	A	A	—	D	E	F
	D	C	B	C	—	F	F
	E	B	B	C	F	—	F
	F	E	E	C	D	E	—

(minus the cost*) is the same as row 1 of the matrix. Similar statements can be made for the other nodes.

DISTRIBUTED ROUTING

Distributed routing means there is no central control. Each node must determine and maintain its routing information independently. It usually does this by knowing who its neighbors are, calculating the cost to get to a neighbor, and determining the cost for a neighbor to send data to specific destinations. Each neighbor, in turn, does the same thing. From that information each node can derive its own routing table. This method is more complex than centralized routing because it requires each node to communicate with each of its neighbors independently.

It is difficult to appreciate the complexity of this approach because examples typically show a global view of a network with its connections and their costs. This overview can bias the way we see the strategy unless we constantly remind ourselves that one node's knowledge of the entire network is very limited. To illustrate, consider the network shown in Figure 10.22. Assume that each node initially knows only the cost to its neighbors; later it can add to its information base anything its neighbors tell it. For example, A initially knows only that it can send something to B (cost = 1) or to D (cost = 2). It has no knowledge whatsoever that nodes C and E even exist. Other nodes have similar knowledge (or lack of it). However, if neighboring nodes communicate, A learns the identity of B's and D's neighbors and soon learns of nodes C and E. By learning of B's and D's costs to get there, and knowing the cost to get to B and D, node A can calculate the cost to get to C and E. By periodically exchanging information about neighboring nodes, each node learns the identity of others in the network and the cheapest paths to them. Shortly we will discuss a specific distributed algorithm to do this.

Figure 10.22 Network Example for Distributed Routing

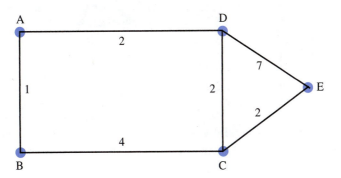

---

* We did not include costs in the routing matrix, but it is a simple matter to do so by storing the cost with each node in the matrix.

STATIC ROUTING

Static routing means that once a node determines its routing table, the node does not change it. In other words, the cheapest path is not dependent on time. The underlying assumption is that the conditions that led to the table's definition have not changed. This is sometimes a valid assumption because costs often depend on distances and the data rates between intermediate nodes. Except for major equipment upgrades and moving of equipment, these parameters do not change.

ADAPTIVE ROUTING

Static routing works well as long as network conditions do not change. In some networks, however, this is a bad assumption. For example, if the cost of each link depends on network traffic, it is time dependent. Consider the problem of sending packets from node A to node E in the network of Figure 10.22. The optimal route is A-D-C-E. Suppose that after node A transmits the packet to node D, the costs for the D-C link and the D-E link each increase to 10 because of a surge of heavy traffic. The cheapest route from A is now A-B-C-E, and the route on which the packet embarked initially is now very expensive. In this case it would actually be cheaper to send the packet back to A and start over again. An **adaptive routing** strategy allows a network node to respond to such changes and update its routing tables accordingly.

There are pitfalls to this system. For example, suppose that in our current example D does send the packet back to A and then the cost of the A-B link increases to 10. The logical choice would be to send the packet back to D. You can now see the problem: Conceivably, the packet could shuttle back and forth among several nodes, never making any progress toward its eventual destination. One technique to avoid this maintains a counter in the packet header that is incremented on each transmission. If the count exceeds some value, the packet is removed from the network. In such cases the routing logic will not guarantee delivery of the packets. However,

Table 10.2   Types of Routing

ROUTING TYPE	ADVANTAGES	DISADVANTAGES
Centralized routing	Simple method because one location assumes routing control.	The failure of the central location or any links connected to it has a severe effect on providing routing information to network nodes.
Distributed routing	Failure of a node or link has a small effect in providing accurate routing information	Exchange of information is more complex. May also take longer for a node to learn of conditions in remote locations.
Static routing	Simple method because nodes do not have to execute routing algorithms repeatedly	Insensitive to changing conditions. A good route may turn into a very bad one.
Adaptive routing	Provides the most current information regarding link costs.	High overhead because nodes must maintain current information. Transmitting information regarding changing conditions adds to network traffic.

there is usually a flow control protocol running at a higher layer, which will time out and resend the packet.

In general, adaptive routing is difficult to implement efficiently. Nodes can keep up with changing conditions only by getting reports from other nodes about link costs. These reports add to network traffic and, in turn, contribute more to the changing conditions. They also take time, so that by the time a node learns of a changing condition, that condition may no longer be in effect.

Table 10.2 provides a brief summary and comparison of the four types of routing.

10.5 DIJKSTRA'S ALGORITHM

Dijkstra's algorithm (ref. [Di59]), sometimes called the **shortest-path algorithm** or **forward search algorithm,** is a centralized, static algorithm, although it can be made adaptive by executing it periodically. It requires that a node executing it have information regarding link costs among the network nodes.

Each node executes Dijkstra's algorithm to determine the cheapest route to each network node. In cases where a route cost is simply the number of intermediate nodes, the cheapest route is also the shortest one. The algorithm is an iterative one, building a set of nodes, one by one, with each iteration. Each node in the set has the property that the cheapest route to it from the given node is known.

Figure 10.23 shows an outline of the algorithm. Initially, it defines a set S consisting of just one node, A, the node executing the algorithm. It then defines a function where, for each node X, $\text{Cost}(X) = $ the cost of the cheapest route from A to X for which intermediate nodes are in S. Initially, since S contains only node A, $\text{Cost}(X)$ is the cost of a direct link from A to X. If there is no such link, $\text{Cost}(X)$ is assigned an arbitrarily large number. The function $\text{Prior}(X)$ in the algorithm contains the node preceding X in the cheapest route.

The algorithm contains a loop. With each pass it determines a set W consisting of all nodes not in S but with a direct link to something in S (Figure 10.24). It chooses one node X in W for which $\text{Cost}(X) \leq \text{Cost}(Y)$ for any other node Y in W. It

Figure 10.23   Dijkstra's Algorithm

```
Define S as a set of nodes. Initially S contains node A.

Define Cost(X) as the cost of the cheapest route from A to X using only nodes from S
    (X excepted). Initially, Cost(X) is the cost of the link from A to X. If no such
    link exists, then Cost(X) is an arbitrarily large value (larger than any possible
    route cost). For those nodes linked to A define Prior(X) = A.

do {

    Determine the set of nodes not in S, but connected to a node in S. Call this set W.

    Choose a node X in W for which Cost(X) is a minimum. Add X to the set S.

    For each V not in S, define Cost(V) = minimum {Cost(V), Cost(X)+cost of link
        connecting X to V}. If Cost(V) is changed define Prior(V) = X.

    }
while not all nodes in S.
```

S = nodes to which cheapest route from A is known.
W = nodes connected to a node in S via a direct link.

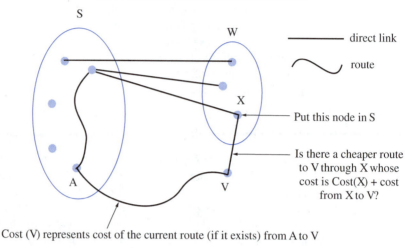

S

W

——————— direct link

~~~ route

X

Put this node in S

Is there a cheaper route
to V through X whose
cost is Cost(X) + cost
from X to V?

A

V

Cost (V) represents cost of the current route (if it exists) from A to V

Figure 10.24   Adding Nodes to S Using Dijkstra's Algorithm

then adds *X* to set *S* and updates the cost function Cost(*V*) for every *V* not yet in *S*. It compares the current Cost(*V*) with Cost(*X*) plus the cost of any direct link from *X* to *V*. If the latter value is smaller, the algorithm redefines Cost(*V*) to be that value. The intent is to determine whether the addition of *X* to *S* allows a cheaper route from *A* to *V* through nodes in *S*.

The correctness of the algorithm is not obvious, and proof that it is correct exceeds the goals of this text. For a more formal treatment, see reference [Ah83]. We will, however, apply this algorithm to the example network of Figure 10.25. Table 10.3 shows the values the algorithm generates when applied to this network. In step 1, the set *S* contains only the source node A. The only nodes connected to A are B

Figure 10.25   Network and Associated Connection Costs

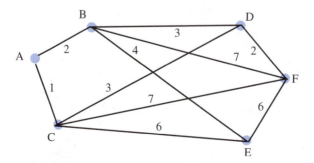

Table 10.3 Values Defined by Dijkstra's Algorithm for the Network in Figure 10.28

STEP	S	W	X	COST FUNCTION FOR B	C	D	E	F	PRIOR FUNCTION FOR B	C	D	E	F
1	{A}	{B, C}	C	2	1	∞	∞	∞	A	A	—	—	—
2	{A, C}	{B, D, E, F}	B	2	1	4	7	8	A	A	C	C	C
3	{A, B, C}	{D, E, F}	D	2	1	4	6	8	A	A	C	B	C
4	{A, B, C, D}	{E, F}	E	2	1	4	6	6	A	A	C	B	D
5	{A, B, C, D, E}	{F}	F	2	1	4	6	6	A	A	C	B	D

and C, and the costs of those edges are 2 and 1, respectively. Consequently, Cost(B) = 2 and Cost(C) = 1. Initial values for Cost(D), Cost(E), and Cost(F) are arbitrarily large and are designated by infinity (∞). Also, Prior(B) = A and Prior(C) = A. Because the algorithm has not yet found any routes to D, E, and F, the Prior function is undefined at those nodes.

As we enter the loop, the set W contains nodes B and C, because they are the only ones connected to A. Next, since Cost(C) < Cost(B), we choose X = C and add it to S. The last line in the loop now requires that we examine Cost(V) for each V not yet in S. This consists of nodes B, D, E, and F. Since the Cost function represents the cheapest path from A through nodes in S, we must ask whether the additional node in S provides a cheaper route. In other words, consider any node V not in S. If Cost(C) plus the cost of the direct link connecting C to V is less than Cost(V), then the route from A to C followed by the link from C to V represents a cheaper route. Table 10.4 shows the necessary comparisons for each node V not in S. For nodes D, E, and F, the latter values are smaller, and node C is established as their prior node. The second row of Table 10.3 reflects these changes.

The second pass through the loop proceeds similarly. Node B is added to S because Cost(B) is smallest among the nodes outside S. Furthermore, the inclusion of B in S provides a cheaper route to E (through nodes in S). Row 3 of Table 10.3 shows how the entries under E change. Node B is the new prior node for E, and Cost(E) is now 6. As an exercise, you should follow the algorithm and verify that rows 4 and 5 in Table 10.3 are correct. When the algorithm finishes, the table's

Table 10.4 Cost Comparisons for Dijkstra's Algorithm

V	COST(V)	COST(C) + COST OF LINK CONNECTING C TO V
B	2	No link from C to V
D	∞	1 + 3 = 4
E	∞	1 + 6 = 7
F	∞	1 + 7 = 8

last row shows that the cheapest routes to B, C, D, E, and F cost 2, 1, 4, 6, and 6, respectively.

The Prior function can be used to recover the actual route. For example, if you want the actual route from A to F, Prior(F) = D specifies that D precedes F on that route. Prior(D) = C specifies that C precedes D, and Prior(C) = A means A precedes C. Thus, the cheapest route from A to F is A-C-D-F.

10.6 THE BELLMAN-FORD ALGORITHM

Dijkstra's algorithm produced the cheapest path by working forward from a given source. Another approach is to work backward from a desired destination. The **Bellman-Ford algorithm** (ref. [Fo62]), sometimes called the **backward search algorithm** or the **distance-vector algorithm,** does this. It is based on the following principle. Let Cost(A, Z) be the cost of the cheapest route from node A to Z. Suppose A has a direct connection to nodes B, C, . . . , D (Figure 10.26). Then

$$
\text{Cost(A, Z)} = \text{smallest of}
\begin{cases}
\text{cost of link from A to B + cost of cheapest route} \\
\text{from B to Z} \\
\text{cost of link from A to C + cost of cheapest route} \\
\text{from C to Z} \\
\quad\vdots \\
\text{cost of link from A to D + cost of cheapest route} \\
\text{from D to Z}
\end{cases}
$$

According to this principle, node A can determine the cheapest route to Z as long as A knows the cost to each neighbor and each neighbor knows the cheapest route to Z. Node A then can perform the preceding calculation and determine the cheapest route. But how does each neighbor know the cheapest route to Z? The answer is in how the algorithm works. There are both centralized and distributed versions of the algorithm. Having already discussed a centralized algorithm, we will present the distributed version.

Figure 10.26   Cheapest Route from A to Z

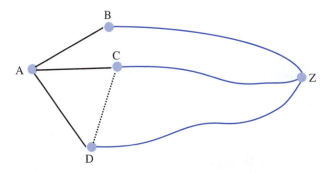

As mentioned previously, each node knows only the cost to each neighbor and any information the neighbor can provide. Thus, in the distributed algorithm each node broadcasts what it knows to each of its neighbors. Each node receives new information and updates its routing tables accordingly. As the neighbors continue to broadcast the information periodically, information about each of the network nodes and connections eventually propagates throughout the network. Information coming in to nodes may allow them to discover new nodes and new cheapest paths to other nodes.

To illustrate, we apply the algorithm to the network in Figure 10.27. Each node maintains information on the cheapest route to other nodes. It contains the route's cost and the first node on that route. Initially, each node knows only the cost to get to its neighbor. Table 10.5a shows how this information is stored. Each row corresponds to a source, and each column to a destination. Each table entry contains the first node on the route and the route's cost. In Table 10.5a the first node on a route is always the same as the node in the column heading because no routes other than those to neighbors are known yet. This situation will change as the algorithm proceeds, however.

Keep in mind that although this table lists a row and column for each node, each node knows only what is in a row corresponding to it. For example, A knows only that the costs to B and D are 1 and 2, respectively; B knows only that the costs to A and C are 1 and 4, respectively; and so on. Some nodes may not even know of others' existence. For example, A does not know nodes C and E exist. B does not know nodes D and E exist, and so on. This is indicated by *Unknown* in the table.

Figure 10.28 contains a pseudocoded version of the algorithm.* Initially, a node stores information about routes to its neighbors in its routing table. The first `while` loop indicates that the algorithm continually monitors information coming in

Figure 10.27   Network for the Bellman-Ford Algorithm

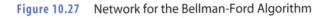

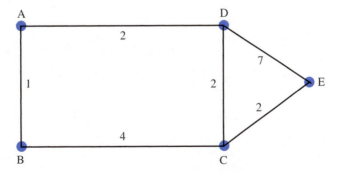

---

* This algorithm is not complete because there are cases in which it will fail. However, our intent now is to illustrate the concept of backward learning in order to find shorter paths. We will examine shortcomings of this version later.

Table 10.5 Three Iterations of the Bellman-Ford Algorithm

SOURCE	DESTINATION				
	A	B	C	D	E
(a) First Iteration					
A	—	(B, 1)	Unknown	(D, 2)	Unknown
B	(A, 1)	—	(C, 4)	Unknown	Unknown
C	Unknown	(B, 4)	—	(D, 2)	(E, 2)
D	(A, 2)	Unknown	(C, 2)	—	(E, 7)
E	Unknown	Unknown	(C, 2)	(D, 7)	—
(b) Second Iteration					
A	—	(B, 1)	(D, 4)	(D, 2)	(D, 9)
B	(A, 1)	—	(C, 4)	(A, 3)	(C, 6)
C	(D, 4)	(B, 4)	—	(D, 2)	(E, 2)
D	(A, 2)	(A, 3)	(C, 2)	—	(C, 4)
E	(D, 9)	(C, 6)	(C, 2)	(C, 4)	—
(c) Third Iteration					
A	—	(B, 1)	(D, 4)	(D, 2)	(D, 6)
B	(A, 1)	—	(C, 4)	(A, 3)	(C, 6)
C	(D, 4)	(B, 4)	—	(D, 2)	(E, 2)
D	(A, 2)	(A, 3)	(C, 2)	—	(C, 4)
E	(C, 6)	(C, 6)	(C, 2)	(C, 4)	—

Figure 10.28 Bellman-Ford Algorithm

```
For each neighbor insert the entry (neighboring node, link cost) in the current
   routing table.
while network protocols baffle me do
for each neighboring node N do
{
   receive information from N's routing table;
   for each node Z in N's routing table do
      if Z is not in the current routing table
         insert the pair (N, current cost to N + N's cost to Z) in it;
      else
         if the current cost to N + N's cost to Z < current cost to Z
            replace the current cost to Z with the current cost to N + N's cost to Z and
            specify N as the new first node along a route to Z;
}
```

from its neighbors. Inside the loop a node receives information from each of its neighbors.* From each neighbor, it learns of nodes to which the neighbor has access and the costs of the associated routes. For each node Z to which a neighbor N has access, there are two possibilities:

1. The current node has no previous knowledge of Z. The current node inserts the entry (N, current cost to N + N's cost to Z) in its routing table. The current node now knows of a route to Z via N.

2. The current node already has a route to Z. The current node compares the cost of that route with the cost of going to N plus N's cost to Z. If the latter value is smaller, the current node has found a cheaper route to Z. It replaces its current cost with the cheaper one and specifies N as the new first node along a route to Z.

Table 10.5b shows how each node's information changes as each of its neighbors tells it what it knows. B tells A it has access to C with a cost of 4. Since A knows it already has access to B with a cost of 1, it concludes it now has access to C with a cost of 5 (cost to B plus cost from B to C). Similarly, D also tells A it has access to C, but with a cost of 2. Node A now concludes that it has access to C via D with a total cost of 4. Since this is cheaper than going through B, it inserts the entry (D, 4) in its routing table (Table 10.5b). D also tells A that it has access to E with a cost of 7. Since A knows it has access to D with a cost of 2, it concludes it has access to E with a cost of 7 + 2 = 9. It then stores the entry (D, 9) in the routing table.

From our view of the network, we know there is a route from A to E through D and C that has a cost of only 6. But remember that we have a unique perspective using information that A does not yet have. Consequently, A does not yet know of this route. Don't let our view bias your interpretation of the algorithm.

Continuing in this way, B receives information from A and C about routes to other nodes.† The information from node A tells B there is a route to D with a cost of 3. Similarly, the information from C tells B there is another route to D with a cost of 6 and a route to E with a cost of 6. Assimilating this information and choosing the cheapest routes, row 2 of Table 10.5b shows B's new routing information.

After each node has heard from each neighbor once, Table 10.5b shows each node's routing table. At this point each node knows the best way to get to each neighbor and to each of its neighbor's neighbors. However, it may not yet know of any optimal routes requiring three or more links. Thus, each node goes through

---

* Although the algorithm depicts an orderly sequence of receptions from each neighbor, it will almost certainly not happen this way. The actual reception of information depends on many real-time events and is very unpredictable. Our main goal is to describe how a node responds to that information, so the algorithm serves our purposes.

† Exactly what B receives from A depends on whether A sent information before or after it received information from D. Since we cannot guarantee the timing, we will assume that each node sends what it has at the beginning of each step.

another round of gathering information from each neighbor and determining whether there are better routes. For example, A knows from Table 10.5b that the cheapest route to E is via D for a total cost of 9. However, when A hears from D again, it learns that D can now get to E with a cost of 4. Therefore, since the link cost from A to D is 2, A now concludes it can get to E via D with a total cost of 6. You should follow all the steps of the algorithm in Figure 10.28 and verify the entries in Tables 10.5b and 10.5c.

PROBLEMS WITH THE BELLMAN-FORD ALGORITHM

As long as each node continually applies the algorithm, it responds to decreases in route costs anywhere in the network. Depending on the network topology, however, it takes a little time to react to such changes. The reason is that if a link cost decreases between two nodes, only their immediate neighbors learn of it during one pass of the algorithm. Nodes two links away require up to two passes of the algorithm to learn of the changes, nodes three links away require up to three passes, and so on. In general, the time required to receive news of changing costs is proportional to the number of intermediate nodes.

However, there is a more serious problem. What happens if the cost of a link between two nodes increases? Worse yet, what happens if a link between two nodes fails? This latter case can be considered as an increase of cost to infinity. Let's take a look at an example. Row 2 in Table 10.5c indicates that the cheapest route from B to E is through C at a cost of 6. This is true partly because the cost of the C-E link is 2. What if it increased to 22? The algorithm, as described, will not change B's routing table because it only makes changes when shorter routes are found.

Fortunately, this problem has an easy solution. Unfortunately, the solution can have side effects in certain cases. In general, suppose X is a node and N is the first node on a route that X considers the cheapest to node D.

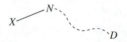

The algorithm already provides for the case where X hears from another neighbor of a cheaper route. However, suppose X hears from N that the latter's cost to D has increased. Since N was the first node on X's cheapest route to D, X must update its routing table and increase the cost of the route to D through N. It is a simple matter to modify the algorithm to do this.

For example (referring again to Table 10.5c), if the C-E link increased to 22 (an increase of 20), C tells B of the increase. B's response is to modify its routing table, changing the entry corresponding to E from (C, 6) to (C, 26). Node B now thinks the cheapest route to E is through C at a cost of 26. (Similar changes will occur at the other nodes as well.) This, of course, is incorrect, but a couple more iterations of the algorithm will establish cheaper routes through the D-E link, and the routing tables will then reflect the realities of the link costs.

This seems like a reasonable solution, but consider the following scenario:

- Assume a subset of Figure 10.27 consisting *only* of the A-B, B-C, and C-E links.
- After a couple iterations of the algorithm, C's cheapest route to E costs 2, B's cheapest route to E costs 6, and A's cheapest route to E costs 7.
- The C-E link fails (i.e., the cost of the C-E link is now ∞).

Node C sees the failure and updates its routing table to specify a cost of ∞ to reach E. Furthermore, C passes this information to B, which changes its table to indicate that the route to E through C now costs ∞. Unfortunately, B hears from A of a route to E that costs 7.* B has no idea that the route from A comes right back to B. Consequently, since the cost of the B-A link is 1, B now updates its table to indicate that the cheapest route to E goes through A at a cost of 8 (1 to get to A plus 7 for the cost of A's route to E).

Now, the following can occur:

1. A hears from B that its cheapest route to E costs 8. Consequently, A updates its routing table to indicate its cheapest route to E goes through B at a cost of 9 (1 to get to B plus 8 for the cost of B's route to E).
2. B hears from A and increases the cost of its route through A to 10.
3. A responds and increases its cost through B to 11.
4. The loop continues ad infinitum.

As A and B continue exchanging routing information, their costs continue to escalate, neither aware that the only link to E is gone. From our bird's-eye view of the network, this is ludicrous. However, each node knows only what its neighbors tell it, and this situation can occur.

This is called the *count-to-infinity problem* and can be solved by defining some threshold value. If route costs to a node go above the threshold value, then replace the cost with ∞, making the node unreachable. The problem is that the threshold must be large enough so as not to be confused with a legitimate large cost. In that case, the number of iterations needed to reach the threshold increases. As a result, the algorithm takes a much longer time to respond correctly to the problem.

You might think this problem could have been avoided entirely if A had simply not sent information to B for routes that go through B. That is, why should A tell B of a route to E that goes through B? It doesn't make sense. This brings us to another variation on the algorithm called **split horizon** (some use the term *poisoned reverse*). It is a simple modification of the information sent to a neighboring node. In general, suppose node *X* knows of a route to *D* through a neighbor *N*. The split horizon rule dictates that *X* tells *N* that its cost to *D* is ∞. (This way, *N* won't try to get to *D* through *X* and follow a route leading right back to *N*.) If this rule were

---

* This depends on timing. If A had heard first from B that the cost to E is ∞, then A would see the cost to E as ∞. The point is, we don't know what will happen first and must therefore consider all possibilities.

implemented in the previous example, A would have told B that its cost to E is ∞ (because A's route goes through B). Since B already knew the cost to E through C was ∞, B would realize that E is unreachable. In the next step A would have realized the same.

Although it solves the problem described here, there is still no guarantee this method will work in all cases. For example, again consider the network of Figure 10.27 but assume the D-E link is not present. That is, all routes to E go through the C-E link, and the routing tables reflect that. In addition,

- D's route to E goes through C first.
- B's route to E goes through C first.
- A's route to E goes through D first.

Suppose the C-E link fails at some point. C will see the cost to E as ∞. Furthermore, C will not try to go through B or D since both tell C the cost to E is ∞ (split horizon rule). Unfortunately, A and B might exchange messages (split horizon won't stop them from exchanging information), causing A to think there is a route to E through B. B will think there is a route to E through A. Now the split horizon rule no longer applies to B giving information to C. Consequently, B tells C of a route to E. C now thinks it can get to E through B.

At this point what happens becomes rather muddled because so much depends on timing. The bottom line is that the loop in the network causes A, B, C, and D to exchange messages, giving the impression of a variety of paths to E opening and closing. They begin acting senile, continually changing where they should go to get to E. This instability will continue, with costs escalating. If a threshold value is used, the loop would eventually stop. Still, it would take some time.

10.7   ADDITIONAL ROUTING METHODS

LINK STATE ROUTING

The problems we have outlined occurred because nodes were trying to exchange information about how to get to a specific destination. The nice thing about Dijkstra's algorithm is that each node executes it locally to make its own choice. The drawback is the need for a node to have information about the network's topology and link costs. If a node could get this information then it could use Dijkstra's (or any other) algorithm. The link state routing protocol is designed to do just that.

Link state routing is similar to Bellman-Ford routing in one regard: Each node communicates what it knows to its neighbors. It differs in what information it exchanges. Link state routing is designed around the following ideas:

- A node gathers information on the status of each link to each neighbor. For example, important information might include the bit rate of that link, the delay time in sending packets over that link, the number of packets queued for transmission, and the reliability of that link. These are all things that might determine the cost of a link.

- A node builds a *link state packet* for each link. The packet identifies the two nodes connected by that link and contains the information it has collected. The node then sends each packet to each neighbor.

- A node receiving link state packets forwards them to all of its neighbors (with the usual exception of the neighbor from which it received the packet).

- As link state packets are exchanged among nodes, each node eventually learns about the network topology and the cost and status of links between network nodes. Consequently, it can execute a cheapest-route algorithm such as Dijkstra's algorithm (using itself as the source) to determine its own route to a given destination (or at least determine the first node on that route). It can then build a routing table according to that information.

Like Bellman-Ford routing, this approach can take advantage of both decreasing and increasing network costs as long as each node periodically builds and sends link state packets with current information. It can also react to link failures. Furthermore, problems like the ones described previously don't occur. If a link fails, all nodes eventually hear about it via the link state packets. Consequently, they can determine new routes that avoid the absent link.

However, this doesn't mean the protocol is without problems. For example, if the network has loops, link state packets can circulate through the network forever as nodes continue to exchange them. Not only would this add to network traffic, but there would also be a problem distinguishing an old link state packet from a more recent one. A solution to this problem is to install a counter in each packet. The counter is a positive number put in the packet when it is created. Each time a node forwards a packet to a neighbor, it decrements the counter. Eventually, the counter reaches 0 and the receiving node discards it.

Another problem is that there can still be a period of time between a link failure and a remote node finding out about it. During that time packets can be routed incorrectly, which can cause delays (or even failures) in packets arriving at their destination.

As we can see, routing in a dynamic environment can be troublesome. The bad things we have described probably won't happen, but unfortunate timing can make them happen. Consequently, what you have are approaches that work most of the time but may fail every once in a while. Anyone with experience in debugging programs knows these are the toughest and nastiest problems to find. In fact, we will see later that Internet routing won't even guarantee delivery of packets. If a packet doesn't seem to be making progress, the Internet Protocol will simply throw it away. We'll discuss the Internet Protocol in Chapter 11.

HIERARCHICAL ROUTING

The routing approaches discussed so far have one thing in common: They are designed to give each node proper routing information. Sometimes, however, there are too many nodes to provide each one with routing information efficiently. Treating each node as an equal participant in a large network generates too much information to share and send throughout the network. An alternative is to have some nodes do the routing for others. A common approach is **hierarchical routing.** It has the following features:

- All nodes are divided into groups called **domains.** We can consider a domain to be a separate and independent network maintained by a company or organization. Some also use the term **autonomous system (AS).**

- Routes between two nodes in a common domain are determined using the domain's or network's protocols.

- Each domain has one or more specially designated routers that determine routes between domains. Effectively, those routers themselves form a network.

- If a domain is large it may consist of multiple subdomains, each of which contains its own designated router. These routers determine the routes between subdomains of the same domain.

Suppose node X wants to send a packet to node Y. If they are in the same domain, the route can be determined using any of the previously discussed techniques. On the other hand, suppose they are in different domains (Figure 10.29). Node X sends the packet to router A within its domain. Node A then has the responsibility of determining the best route to node Y's domain (domain 2) and sending the packet. Since node B is the designated router for domain 2, it receives the packet and then sends it to node Y. This approach applies for any pair of nodes from domains 1 and 2. Effectively, A is performing necessary routing on behalf of any node

Figure 10.29   Domains in Hierarchical Routing

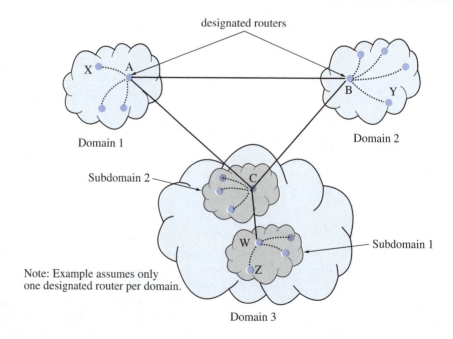

Domain 1

Domain 2

Subdomain 2

C

W

Z

Subdomain 1

Note: Example assumes only one designated router per domain.

Domain 3

designated routers

in its domain, thus reducing the total number of nodes that must perform such tasks. Node X and other nodes in domain 1 need only worry about how to get to A.

We can represent the domain concept using a hierarchical structure (Figure 10.30). All domains correspond to second-level tree nodes under a common root.* All network nodes within a domain correspond to third-level tree nodes under the domain. If the domain contains subdomains, they also are third-level tree nodes, and any network nodes in them are at the fourth level under the appropriate subdomain.

In general, network routers are defined partly by the hierarchy. Thus, suppose Z in Figure 10.29 wants to send a packet to X. Since Z is in subdomain 1, it sends the packet to W, the designated router for Z's subdomain. In turn, W routes across subdomains to C, the designated router for domain 3. C then routes across domains to A, which finally sends the packet to X.

So far we have omitted one detail. For hierarchical routing to work, the sending node specifies the destination's address, including its domain and any subdomains. By including the address, each router determines whether the destination is in the current domain (or subdomain). If it is, the router can deliver the packet. If not, the router must determine the domain to which the packet must go. This is similar to sending letters via the postal system using the typical address format

Name

Street address

City, State, Zip code

Postal workers in Hartford, Connecticut, don't care if a letter is addressed to Jane Smith at 123 Main Street unless the city and state are also specified as Hartford,

Figure 10.30 Hierarchical Arrangement of Domain Nodes

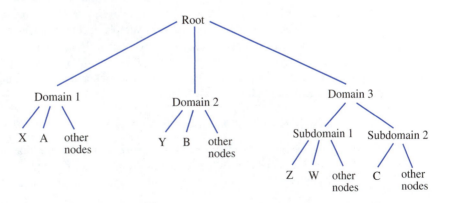

---

* Don't think of the root as an actual network node. It simply means all its dependents (domains) are connected.

Connecticut. If the city and state are different, the Hartford postal workers' routing responsibility is to make sure the letter is sent to the appropriate city, where that city's postal workers deliver letters according to address and name. Similarly, a network node specifies an address as a sequence of domain and subdomain specifiers. For example, in Figure 10.29 node X might send a packet to node Z by addressing it to Z.subdomain-1.domain-3.

The Internet is a network that uses hierarchies in its addressing scheme. The hierarchy reflects the fact that the Internet is actually a collection of networks, each with its own set of protocols. Universities, companies, and government agencies typically have a network connecting their computers. These networks, in turn, may also be part of the Internet.

An **Internet address** is a 32-bit number* represented as a sequence of four 8-bit numbers separated by dots. An example is 143.200.128.3, where each of the four numbers has an 8-bit representation. Each Internet address may also be interpreted as having two parts: an Internet Protocol (IP) network address assigned to a site network, and an address for a local device (i.e., a personal computer or server) on that network. The address given is an example of a Class B address,† meaning the first 16 bits (143.200) designate the IP network address and the other 16 bits (128.3) designate a specific device.

During routing of packets, a router first examines the IP network address. If the packet is destined for another site, it is routed based solely on that IP network address. Otherwise, the router examines the local part of the address and extracts, if necessary, the physical address identifier. After that it queues the packet for delivery to its destination along the proper physical network. From there, lower-layer network protocols handle delivery according to the type of network. This process is basically a two-level hierarchical routing technique. There are a few things that need further description; we will deal with them when we discuss the Internet in the next chapter.

Some sites may have a single IP network address assigned to them but actually have multiple physical on-site networks called **subnets.** A single IP network address allows the site to expand and develop network applications independent of its connection to the Internet. For example, local management might use part of the 16-bit local ID (perhaps the first few bits) to designate a particular subnet. This creates a three-level address hierarchy, with the first two octets designating an IP network, the next few bits designating a subnet, and the remaining bits designating the actual destination on that subnet.

ROUTING INFORMATION PROTOCOL

As we have already stated, large networks such as the Internet can, in general, be viewed as a collection of domains. Some prefer the term *autonomous system* (AS) to *domain* to reflect the fact that they can operate independently. In such networks,

---

* Some addresses have more bits, but we'll discuss that in the next chapter.

† The Internet Protocol also defines Class A addresses (8-bit network address and 24-bit local identifier) and Class C addresses (24-bit network address and 8-bit local identifier). There are also Class D and E addresses and a group of classless addresses, but we'll discuss that in Section 11.2.

we can define two main categories of routing strategies: interior and exterior proto-cols.* **Interior routing protocols** control routing among routers within an autono-mous system. **Exterior routing protocols** control routing among routers from different autonomous systems. For example, an interior protocol is used to determine a route from X to A (Figure 10.29). Exterior protocols are used to get from A to B or C.

The distinction is important because different ASs may use different metrics to calculate a best route within the AS. One might calculate a value based on bit rates, and another might depend solely on the number of routers that forward a packet. The number used to represent costs may thus be calculated differently. A route hav-ing a cost of 100 in one network may be slower than a route with a cost of 200 in another network. Consequently, finding a "best" route may be elusive because any metric used to measure the best may not apply to all of the systems. For example, the best route from X to Z in Figure 10.29 may be difficult to define because the definition of "best" may vary across domains. We'll see shortly that this can affect the protocols used.

One example of an interior protocol long used by Internet routers within an AS is the **Routing Information Protocol (RIP).** RIP is the protocol used by the routed[†] program developed at the University of California at Berkeley to perform routing on their local networks. Routers that connect multiple networks use RIP to let each other know the shortest route to a specified network. Typically, they use a **hop count,** the number of intermediate routers, to measure distance. For example, Figure 10.31 shows several networks connected by routers. The hop count from net-work N1 to N2 is 1, and the hop count from N1 to N4 is 2, using the shortest route. None of the routers knows that yet, however. The algorithm starts when each router sends a message along each of its networks. This message indicates that all of the networks to which the router is connected can be reached in one hop. When routers on that network get the message, they know which networks they can reach using two

Figure 10.31   Routers Connecting Networks

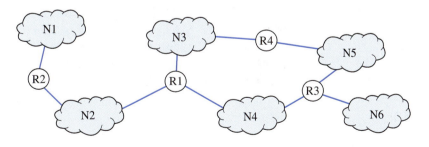

---

* These go by different names depending on who you read. For example, interior protocols may also be called *interior gateway protocols, interior router protocols, or intradomain protocols.* Exterior protocols also may be called *exterior gateway protocols, exterior router protocols, or interdomain protocols.*

[†] The program *routed* is pronounced route-dee and was named using UNIX naming conventions.

hops. They store this information in their routing tables and periodically broadcast it over the networks. By repeatedly receiving information, storing it, and broadcasting it, each router eventually knows the smallest number of hops to a given network.

Let's see how this would work on the network of Figure 10.31. Using RIP, the following events can occur:

1. R2 sends a message along N2 that it can get to N1 in one hop. (It also sends a message along N1 that it can get to N2 in one hop.)

2. Because R1 is connected to N2, it now knows it can get to N1 in two hops and stores that fact in its routing table. Subsequently, R1 broadcasts the following over N4: It can get to N2 and N3 in one hop and to N1 in two hops. (It also broadcasts similar information over N3 and N2.)

3. R3 receives and stores the information it received over N4 and broadcasts the following over N5: It can get to N4 and N6 in one hop, N2 and N3 in two hops, and N1 in three hops. It also will broadcast similar information over N4 and N6.

At this point some of the broadcast information becomes redundant. For example, because of R3's broadcast over N5, R4 learns it can get to N2 in three hops. Of course, if it previously received R1's broadcast over N3, it already knows it can get to N2 in two hops. In this case it does not store the most recent information.

What happens if a router or network along a route fails? For example, R4 knows it can get to N2 in two hops, but what if network N3 fails? When a router stores routing information, it also starts a timer. When the timer expires, the router marks the route as invalid. It depends on new routing information to reestablish a route. Of course, the routers must cooperate by sending routing information on a regular basis (typically every 30 seconds). Thus, if N3 failed, events 1 to 3 would still occur (except those involving N3). This time, when R4 learns that it can get to N2 in three hops, it stores that fact because there is no alternative.

RIP operates by exchanging *RIP packets*. Each packet represents a request to a neighbor for information or contains the number of hops to a node. Each packet contains the following fields:

- A 1-byte Command field, which indicates whether the packet represents a request or a response. A Request packet asks for information in a neighbor's routing table. The Response packet indicates the packet contains routing table information.

- A 1-byte RIP version number.

- A 4-byte Address field that contains the address of the destination node being advertised.

- A 2-byte Address Family Indicator field, which specifies what protocol the address corresponds to-for example, whether the address is an IP address or one using some other protocol.

- A 4-byte Hop Count field. This value is always between 1 and 16. RIP assumes a maximum of 15 hops to reach a node. If the node is not reachable in 15 hops, the packet contains 16. For RIP, 16 equals infinity.

- Several fields that are not used (reserved for future use).

Another version of this protocol, RIP version 2 (RIP-2), operates much the same way as RIP (version 1) but has added some capabilities, primarily to account for different ASs. It has the same packet format as RIP except that some of the unused fields from RIP contain meaningful information. A RIP-2 packet contains the following fields:

- All the specified fields of RIP. The version number, of course, is 2. The Address Family Indicator may be a special value containing all 1s, which means that the packet is used for authentication. In this case, the rest of the packet contains authentication information, although, as of this writing, password authentication is the only option.

- A 4-byte subnet mask for the specified address. Previously, we stated that the local identifier of an IP address may contain a subnet ID and another ID local to that subnet. A subnet mask helps determine which bits in an address specify the subnet ID. We'll discuss subnets and subnet masks further in Chapter 11, but basically the router must know the subnet mask in order to determine a route.

- A 2-byte Route Tag field. RIP did not recognize the existence of separate ASs. RIP-2 tries to address that shortcoming by using the Route Tag field to distinguish between internal and external routes. It does not specify the contents of this field, but allows the sender of the packet to indicate the type of route being specified. The receiving router can then respond accordingly. For example, if a value of 0 indicated an internal protocol using hop counts, the packet can be exchanged with other routers in the AS, with increments to the hop count as described previously. A nonzero value might indicate some exterior protocol, and routers must share that information as is. Of course, the routers must support the exterior protocol being advertised.

- A 4-byte Next Hop field. The RIP (version 1) packet advertises a destination, and the sender of that packet may be used as the next hop toward it. The Next Hop field explicitly specifies the address of the next node (which may be different from the packet's sender) along that route. For example, suppose A, B, and C are routers and all know that the best route to network X goes through B and the best route to network Y goes through C. In order for a fourth router D to find the best routes to X and Y using RIP, it depends on A, B, and C to execute the protocol. If RIP-2 were used, then only A would need to send RIP-2 packets to D, indicating the appropriate next hop for networks X and Y.

OPEN SHORTEST PATH FIRST

Another example of an interior routing scheme is **Open Shortest Path First (OSPF).** The "open" means that the algorithm is nonproprietary, that is, not owned by any company. Essentially, OSPF is a form of link state routing with a few additional features to jazz it up:

- OSPF includes the ability to authenticate messages.

- It provides for additional hierarchies. As explained previously, a domain may consist of subdomains.

- It can utilize multiple routes to a given destination. This is useful especially for heavily traveled routes. Sending all packets through the same route, even if it is "best," can cause congestion. Using backup routes can increase overall performance. This is called *load balancing* and is a little like being forewarned of a major traffic jam on an interstate highway. You might want to get off and travel some smaller country roads for a while.

- It can use several factors in defining link states. Example factors include the link's length, bit rate, delay, and dollar cost.

- It can better respond to the needs of the user. For example, a user might want to send a small message quickly. Since the packet is small, a high bit rate isn't critical, but following links with little or no delay is. On the other hand, a user might want to transfer a large file, which might be done best via links that support very high bit rates.

BORDER GATEWAY PROTOCOL

The **Border Gateway Protocol (BGP)** is an example of an exterior protocol. The current version is BGP-4 and is commonly used in the Internet to establish paths among routers from different autonomous systems. It shares some common features with distance-vector routing. One major difference is that instead of sharing the cost of a route to a particular destination, it shares the actual route specified as a sequence of ASs. There are several reasons for specifying actual routes instead of just the first link on a cheapest route. One is that exterior protocols such as BGP-4 are often more concerned with just getting to a destination as opposed to finding the best or cheapest way. Because routes inevitably go through one or more ASs and each AS may define link costs differently, comparing route costs through different systems may be meaningless. As a result, the very concept of a "best route" may have no meaning to an exterior protocol.

Another reason for sharing actual routes is that there may be other factors besides cost involved in finding a route. Each router might implement specific policies or constraints that any route must satisfy. This is especially important for global connections such as are found in the Internet. For example, a router in some country may have an explicit policy to avoid any route that passes through an unfriendly country. Similarly, a company router might have a policy to avoid any route going through a competitor.

Figure 10.32 illustrates the process. AS3 is an AS consisting of three subnets (SN5, SN6, and SN7) and three routers (C, D, and E). Within AS3 the routers can use an interior protocol such as RIP. However, C also runs BGP-4, which allows it to communicate with B in AS2. Router C establishes a TCP connection (discussed in Chapter 11) with B and starts by sending an Open message to B. This allows C to identify itself as a BGP-4 router. Router B, in turn, can respond with a Keep Alive message, which acknowledges C's message. This tells C that it will participate in an exchange of information regarding routes.

To update information about a route, a router sends an Update message. This message can notify a neighbor of new routes or indicate that certain routes are no

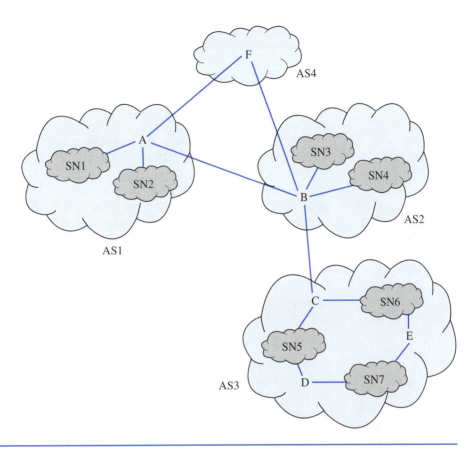

Figure 10.32   Autonomous Systems with Subnets

longer valid. In this case, C sends an Update message to B that specifies SN5, SN6, and SN7 as destination networks and AS3 as the only AS in the route. It also specifies the address of C as the way to get to AS3. Now that B has that information, it can share it with A. Specifically, it can send an Update message to A that contains SN5, SN6, and SN7 as destination networks and AS2 and AS3 as the ASs it must go through to reach them. Of course, B will also send information about SN3 and SN4. If A is connected to another AS, then the process continues and the string of ASs grows with each Update message. The important point is that when a router gets an Update message, it can determine exactly what ASs any information may travel through.

This example assumed that a router receiving the Update message will automatically update its tables. That's not necessarily the case. For example, suppose a router on the other side of AS1 gets an Update message specifying AS2 as one of the ASs. Suppose also that a high-level policy at that location prohibits sending any information along a path that includes AS2. In this case, the router does not accept the advertised route as valid and will either use what it has or wait for an Update message specifying another sequence of ASs.

An advantage of this approach is that loops in the path are easily eliminated. For example, B in Figure 10.32 may get an Update message from F specifying destinations SN5, SN6, and SN7 and ASs AS4, AS1, AS2, and AS3. Since B is part of AS2 and AS2 is already specified in the sequence, B recognizes that the route contains a loop and can ignore it.

Another possibility is that a designated route is no longer valid. For example, Router A knows it can get to SN5 through AS2 and AS3. However, suppose the link between B and C fails. Router B will send another Update message to A indicating that the paths to SN5, SN6, and SN7 through AS2 and AS3 are no longer valid. Router A then removes that information from its tables.

In conclusion, we should mention that not all routers make such complex decisions. For example, AS3 in Figure 10.32 may be in a geographic location such that the only access to the Internet is through AS2. In that case, router C uses static routing, a technique that sends all outgoing packets to the same place, namely, B. From there packets may take different routes. Incoming packets, of course, would be routed differently by C according to the internal protocols used.

SUMMARY OF ROUTING TECHNIQUES

Table 10.6 provides a brief summary of the general routing strategies discussed. They are by no means the only possibilities, but along with the routing strategies involving LAN bridges and switches, they represent a significant number of the strategies in use today. For more information on different strategies, see reference [Ta03]. In addition, references [Co99] and [Co00] devote a lot of attention to routing in the Internet.

10.8 CONGESTION AND DEADLOCK

CONGESTION

As networks grow larger and accommodate more nodes, routing strategies must deal with an ever-increasing number of packets. The increased demand can put network operations in peril. What happens when one or more network links fail? What happens if the number of packets that must be transmitted exceeds the network's ability to do so? A potentially serious consequence is **congestion,** or the excessive buildup of packets at one or more network nodes.

Once again we can draw on the useful analogy of traffic control in an urban area. Highways and roads must be designed with the anticipated amount of traffic in mind. Anyone who has driven in an urban area knows the problem. During rush hour the amount of traffic is excessive and a highway's ability to handle it diminishes. An accident or road construction can put several lanes or an entire stretch of highway out of commission. In either case traffic slows (or stops completely), causing terrible congestion. People in their cars can't reach their destinations. The transportation system has lost its usefulness temporarily.

Table 10.6 Summary of Routing Strategies

METHOD	COMMENTS
Dijkstra's algorithm	Forward learning algorithm that can be implemented as a central routing strategy. It can also be used with link state routing.
Bellman-Ford algorithm	Backward learning algorithm. Nodes learn from each neighbor the cheapest route to a node and the first node on that route. Used in the Internet or in any large network where changing link conditions require nodes to update their routing tables.
Link state routing	Nodes collaborate by exchanging link state packets providing status information on adjacent links. A node can collect all the packets it receives and determine the network topology. It can then execute its own shortest-route algorithm.
Hierarchical routing	Method of dividing nodes into domains or autonomous systems. Interior protocols perform routing within a system, whereas exterior protocols find routes across different systems. Used in the Internet or in any network where there is a large number of nodes, making it impractical for each to run the same routing strategy.
RIP	An interior routing protocol used to track the fewest number of hops to a given network. Developed by UC-Berkeley for its local networks and used in the Internet.
OSPF	An interior routing protocol similar to link state routing but which provides additional features for better performance and flexibility.
BGP	An exterior protocol that allows routers to implement specific policies or constraints that a route must meet. Routers exchange actual routes to a destination instead of just costs and the first link in a route.

Similarly, congestion in a network reduces its usefulness. Packets experience longer delays, and network users see the network as unresponsive and unable to meet their needs. What can network protocols do in such cases? One option is to do nothing and let congestion disappear naturally. Even in rush hour traffic, people eventually get home and the congestion disappears. However, this is not a practical solution for networks. (Many people probably feel it's not a practical solution to highway congestion either.) For one thing, users expect better service, and it should be provided. Second, the congestion might not disappear because it can have a compounding effect. Congestion at a node hampers the node's ability to receive packets from other nodes. Consequently, those nodes can't get rid of their packets as quickly, and incoming packets begin to accumulate there as well. This can have a chain reaction effect in which all nodes begin to experience congestion, making the problem worse.

There are several ways to handle congestion.

- **Packet elimination.** If an excessive buildup of packets occurs at a node, eliminate some of them. This reduces the number of outstanding packets waiting for transmission and reduces the network load. The drawback, of course, is that the destroyed packets do not reach their destinations. The problem of lost packets was discussed in Sections 8.4 and 8.5. Presumably, the sending node's protocol eventually will determine that a packet never reached its destination and will resend it. If the congestion was caused by a heavy burst of traffic, it may have subsided somewhat when the packet is sent the next time. Destroying packets sounds drastic, but if the congestion is sporadic, the network protocols can handle it well and the inconvenience to the unlucky user whose packets are destroyed is minimal. We do not, however, recommend this approach for automobile traffic congestion.

- **Flow control.** As Chapter 8 discussed, flow control protocols are designed to control the number of packets sent. However, they are not a true congestion control approach. The problem is that flow control limits the number of packets between two points, whereas congestion often involves packets coming into a node from many sources. Thus, even if nodes regulate the number of packets they send, congestion still can occur if too many nodes are sending them.

  You might respond by suggesting that each node regulate its traffic so that even if every node is sending, the total number of packets would still be manageable. The problem is that if many nodes are not sending, the network is underutilized. Again, you might respond by suggesting that each node reduce its outflow only if it detects other nodes sending. In a large network, however, this is not practical. Many nodes won't even see the packets sent by others. Furthermore, establishing some communication protocol among them would add to the network traffic and compound the problem we are trying to solve.

- **Buffer allocation.** This approach can be used with virtual circuits. Recall from Section 1.4 that a **virtual circuit** is an established route between network nodes that is determined before any data packets are actually sent. Once a route is established, protocols at a node on that route can reserve buffers specifically for the virtual circuit. Effectively, the establishment of a virtual circuit notifies participating nodes that packets will be forthcoming and that they should plan for them. If other requests for virtual circuit establishment come to that node, it can reject them if insufficient buffer space is available. Network protocols then would have to find a different route for the circuit or notify the source that the request for a virtual circuit has been denied. Sections 13.3 and 13.4 discuss virtual circuit protocols further.

- **Choke packets.** This approach provides a more dynamic way to deal with congestion. Each node monitors the activity on its outgoing links, tracking the utilization of each. If the utilization of the lines is small, the danger of congestion is low. However, an increasing utilization means a larger number of packets is being sent. If the utilization of any line exceeds some specified criterion, the node's protocol responds by putting itself into a special warning state. When in the warning state, the node will respond by sending a special Choke packet in response to any incoming packet destined for the outgoing line. The Choke packet goes to the source of the incoming packet. When the source receives the Choke packet, it responds by reducing the number of packets it is sending for a specified period of time.

After the period expires, one of two things can happen. If no additional Choke packets arrive, the node can increase the packet transmission rate to its original value. If more Choke packets continue to arrive, it will reduce the packet transmission rate even further. By reducing the incoming traffic, the original node has a chance to let the utilization of its outgoing lines drop below the threshold to an acceptable level.

DEADLOCK

In the worst case, congestion can become so severe that nothing moves. Figure 10.33 illustrates this problem. Three nodes, A, B, and C, have reached the point where their buffers are full and cannot accept any more packets. A's packets are all destined for B, which cannot receive any packets because its buffers are full. Thus A cannot send until B sends some of its packets and releases buffer space. B's packets are destined for C, whose buffers are also full. C's packets are destined for A, whose buffers are full. In other words, A is waiting for B's buffers to clear, B is waiting for C's buffers to clear, and C is waiting for A's buffers to clear. This situation, in which all nodes are waiting for an event that won't occur, is called **deadlock** (also called **deadly embrace** or **lock-up**).

The case just described is an example of a **store-and-forward deadlock,** so named because nodes store packets while waiting to forward them. Figure 10.34 illustrates another type, **reassembly deadlock.** In this example, the node uses common buffers for incoming packets from different sources (A and B). It also uses a selective repeat sliding window protocol for receiving packets from A and B destined for the node's host. Recall that the selective repeat protocol allows packets to

Figure 10.33   Store-and-Forward Deadlock

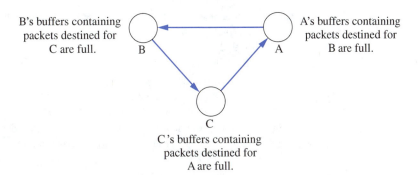

B's buffers containing packets destined for C are full.

A's buffers containing packets destined for B are full.

C's buffers containing packets destined for A are full.

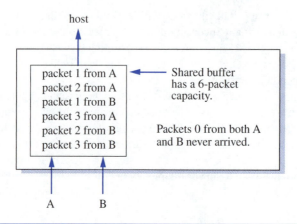

Figure 10.34   Reassembly Deadlock

arrive out of order. The receiver then reassembles them before sending them to the host.

In our example, A and B both sent a packet 0, neither of which arrived. However, subsequent packets numbered 1 through 3 from both A and B have arrived. If we assume the buffers are filled, the node cannot accept any more packets. Because both packet 0s are missing, however, the node cannot reassemble them and deliver them in order to the host. Moreover, the node will not accept either packet 0 even if it does arrive. Consequently, the node is placed in a state in which it can neither take action nor respond to an event that would allow it to take action. It is deadlocked.

Reassembly deadlock can be prevented through a handshake establishing a connection between the sending and receiving nodes. The handshake can establish the window size, and the receiver can reserve sufficient space and use it only for that connection. Store-and-forward deadlock is a bit more problematic. It can be reduced or even eliminated by using sufficient buffer space, but the problem is knowing just how much buffer space to reserve, especially in datagram services in which packets come and go randomly.

One approach to deadlock is to let it happen and then deal with it. When deadlock occurs, the typical response is to discard some packets and release the buffer space. The discarded packets, of course, never reach their destination. This is the price to be paid for breaking the deadlock. Presumably, communication protocols will determine that the packets never arrived and will send them again later. If deadlock occurs rarely, this may be the best way to deal with it.

On the other hand, for a network more susceptible to deadlock it may be less costly to take steps to prevent it from happening or at least decrease its probability of occurrence. Any of the previously mentioned congestion control techniques will decrease the chances of deadlock, but there is still no guarantee deadlock will not occur. Another approach (ref. [Me80]) maintains the number of hops (nodes through

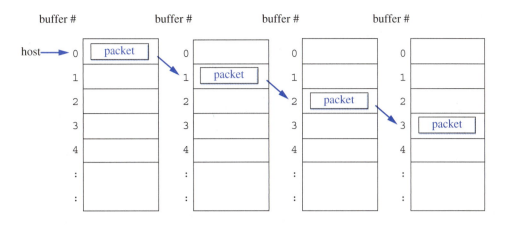

Figure 10.35   Storing Packets Depending on Hop Count

which a packet travels) in each packet. When a host first inserts a packet into the network, the hop count is 0. As the packet travels through the network, each node increments the hop count by 1. In addition, each node divides its buffers into distinct groups, each one corresponding to a hop count from 0 up to the maximum expected hops. The node then stores an incoming packet in a buffer depending on the number of hops in the packet, but only if a buffer is available. If not, the packet waits at the preceding node until it is available. Figure 10.35 shows how this works. A host submits a packet initially, and the host's node stores the packet in buffer 0. The next node to receive the packet stores it in buffer 1, the next one in buffer 2, and so on.

This method prevents deadlock because a packet always goes to (or waits for) a higher numbered buffer. Another way to state it is that a packet in one buffer will never wait for a lower or equal numbered buffer. Therefore, the circular wait condition of Figure 10.33 can never occur. The argument against this approach is that buffers may be underutilized. Preassigning a packet to a buffer prevents its transmission whenever that buffer is occupied; however, if it is the only buffer occupied, the others go unused.

10.9   SUMMARY

This chapter covered ways to connect networks and some of the devices and protocols that do so. We organized the chapter according to the layer at which networks are connected and focused on connections at layers 1, 2, and 3.

Layer 1 devices—repeaters and hubs—primarily extend the geographic distance spanned by a LAN protocol. The main difference between a repeater and hub is that a hub has more ports than a repeater. The main responsibility of either device is to accept a signal over one port, regenerate it, and transmit it over all other ports.

If the LAN protocol uses CSMA/CD, all devices connected by repeaters and hubs are in the same collision domain.

Bridges and switches operate at layer 2 and typically divide devices into separate collision domains. However, all devices connected by these devices are in the same broadcast domain. The main difference between the two is that a switch has more ports than a bridge. Both perform layer 2 routing, selectively forwarding or ignoring a frame based on its MAC address and on internal routing tables. Bridges are divided into types according to how they make routing decisions:

- Fixed-routing bridges have routing information programmed into them.
- Transparent bridges build routing tables by observing traffic and noting where devices lie by examining the source addresses in the frames.
- Source-routing bridges route according to information in the frame.

Switches have become a common way to connect Ethernet devices, leading to the development of full-duplex switched Ethernet, an Ethernet protocol that has eliminated collisions and obviated the need for CSMA/CD. Switches can also be used to create virtual LANs (VLANs), a logical group of devices that operate as a separate LAN. Each group is independent of the devices' physical location and defines a separate broadcast domain.

Layer 3 devices—routers—connect networks over much larger distances. They deal with much more complex topologies and require some sophisticated routing algorithms. We discussed four basic routing types:

- *Centralized:* Routing information is maintained in a central location.
- *Distributed:* Routing information is distributed among the nodes.
- *Static:* Routing information does not change even with varying network conditions.
- *Adaptive:* Changing network conditions alter routing information.

One way to manage routing information is to use routing tables that specify where to forward incoming packets. Maintaining them depends on the routing algorithms used. We discussed a few approaches, such as the following:

- Dijkstra's algorithm, a centralized algorithm designed to determine the cheapest path between two nodes.
- The Bellman-Ford algorithm, a distributed approach by which each node communicates information on reachable nodes to each of its neighbors.
- Link state routing, in which nodes collaborate by exchanging link state packets that provide status information on adjacent links. A node can collect all the packets it gets and determine the network topology. It can then execute its own shortest-route algorithm.
- Hierarchical routing, in which nodes are divided into groups (domains), each of which has its own routing protocol.

- The Routing Information Protocol, an interior protocol in which designated routers exchange information with each other regarding reachable networks and the number of hops required to get there.

- Open Shortest Path First protocol, an interior routing protocol similar to link state routing but which provides additional features to provide better performance and flexibility.

- Border Gateway Protocol, an exterior protocol that allows routers to implement specific policies or constraints that a route must meet. Routers exchange actual routes to a destination instead of just costs and the first link in a route.

Finally, we discussed two problems that can occur during routing. Congestion develops when a node receives more packets than it can handle efficiently, thus causing an increase in the time required to forward them. Deadlock occurs when there is a circular list of nodes, each of which cannot forward any packets to the next one in the list.

Review Questions

1. What are the differences among a repeater, bridge, and router?
2. What are the differences between a repeater and hub?
3. What are the differences between a bridge and switch?
4. What is a collision domain?
5. What is a broadcast domain?
6. List major reasons for using bridges or switches between two LANs.
7. What is a routing table?
8. What is the difference between a fixed-routing bridge and a transparent bridge?
9. What is the flooding algorithm and what purpose does it serve?
10. What problem can flooding cause when there is a loop in a LAN topology?
11. What is a spanning tree within the context of an interconnection of LANs?
12. What is a root bridge?
13. What is a bridge's root port?
14. What purpose does a LAN's designated bridge serve?
15. What is a source-routing bridge?
16. What is a bridge protocol data unit?
17. What is a protocol converter?
18. At what OSI layers can protocol converters exist? List common ones and their names.
19. What is a virtual LAN and why create one?
20. What is the difference between a private switch and workgroup switch?
21. How does a switch determine to which VLAN a device belongs?

22. List the four major routing classifications and state what is characteristic of each.

23. Are the following statements TRUE or FALSE? Why?

    a. Increasing the number of hubs used to connect Ethernet devices is always beneficial because it increases the distance spanned and the number of devices that are connected.

    b. A switch separates devices into different broadcast domains.

    c. A spanning tree algorithm eliminates loops caused by redundant bridges.

    d. Switched Ethernet has eliminated the need for cables and wires to connect devices.

    e. Distributed routing requires routing tables at each node.

    f. Adaptive routing allows a node to update its routing tables.

    g. The shortest path and the cheapest path are generally the same.

    h. Hierarchical routing organizes all network nodes into a tree structure.

    i. Congestion means that all of a network's paths have become clogged with traffic.

    j. Congestion does not always lead to deadlock.

24. Distinguish between a forward search and a backward search algorithm.

25. What is hierarchical routing?

26. Why does link state routing overcome the problem described for the Bellman-Ford algorithm?

27. Distinguish between interior and exterior protocols.

28. What do nodes that use the Routing Information Protocol maintain in their routing tables?

29. What is the difference between RIP and RIP-2?

30. Why is it difficult to determine a cheapest or best path over a long distance?

31. A router sends a packet only to the first node on a path. Why would it want to know the actual sequence of ASs that a packet it sends may go through?

32. Distinguish between network congestion and deadlock.

33. List some ways to deal with congestion.

34. What are the two types of deadlock?

35. Why does assigning packets to specific buffers, as shown in Figure 10.35, prevent store-and-forward deadlock?

Exercises

1. Consider an interconnection strategy among LANs in which the most frequently communicating LANs are connected over the fewest bridges. Assume the following LAN pairs must be no more than the specified number of bridges apart. Design an interconnection that uses the fewest number of bridges.

   • One bridge apart: L1 and L5; L2 and L3; L2 and L4

   • Two (or fewer) bridges apart: L1 and L3; L2 and L5; L1 and L2

2. Build routing tables for the following bridges.

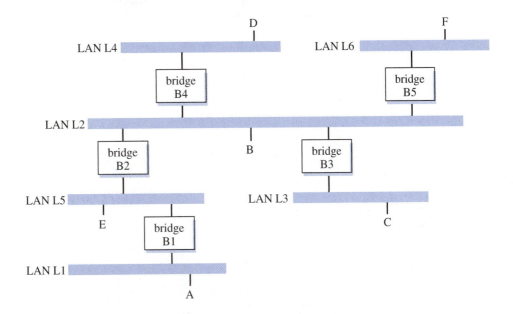

3. Consider the LANs of Figure 10.5 and assume all the routing tables are empty initially. Assume the following events occur in the order listed. Over what LANs are the specified frames transmitted? Show the routing table entries of each bridge after all frames have been sent.

    a. A sends a frame to F.

    b. E sends a frame to A.

    c. D sends a frame to E.

    d. C sends a frame to B.

4. List all routes between A and B in Figure 10.8. Ignore any route in which a frame goes through the same bridge twice. If we do not ignore those routes, how many are there?

5. Suppose bridge B1 in Figure 10.8 fails. Execute the spanning tree algorithm and show the new root bridge, cheapest bridge ports, designated bridges, and the resulting enabled bridge connections.

6. Assume the internetwork of Figure 10.8 is changed so that all listed costs are equal. Assuming that the cost of a transmission between two distinct LANs is now the number of bridges through which it must travel, determine the spanning tree.

7. Suppose A sends an all-routes broadcast frame to B in Figure 10.8. How many copies of it does B receive?

8. How many distinct routes are there from X to Y in the network of Figure 10.18?

9. Define the routing tables for all the nodes in the network in Figure 10.19.

10. Create a routing matrix for the following network. In cases where two routes have the cheapest cost, choose the one containing the fewest nodes. If both criteria are the same, then choose a route arbitrarily.

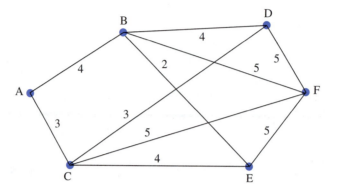

11. Apply Dijkstra's shortest-path algorithm to the following network. Create a table similar to Table 10.3 showing pertinent values at each step of the algorithm.

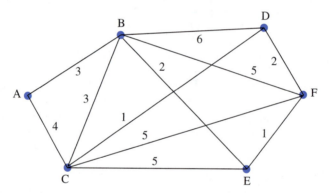

12. Design an algorithm that, when run after Dijkstra's algorithm, will list all nodes on the cheapest path to a given destination.

13. Using terminology from Dijkstra's algorithm, prove that whenever the Cost(V) function is changed, it still represents the cheapest route from A to V via nodes in S.

14. The premise of the Bellman-Ford algorithm is that if Cost(A, Z) is the cost of the cheapest route from node A to Z and A has a direct connection to nodes B, C, and D then

$$\text{Cost(A, Z)} = \text{smallest of} \begin{cases} \text{cost of link from A to B + cost of cheapest route} \\ \text{from B to Z} \\ \text{cost of link from A to C + cost of cheapest route} \\ \text{from C to Z} \\ \vdots \\ \text{cost of link from A to D + cost of cheapest route} \\ \text{from D to Z} \end{cases}$$

Why is this premise valid? That is, prove this assertion.

15. Create tables similar to Tables 10.5a through 10.5c by applying the Bellman-Ford algorithm to the following network.

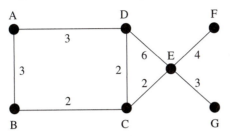

16. How is the Routing Information Protocol similar to the Bellman-Ford algorithm?

REFERENCES

[Ah83] Aho, A., J. Hopcroft, and J. Ullman. *Data Structures and Algorithms.* Reading, MA: Addison-Wesley, 1983.

[Co99] Comer, D. E., and D. Stevens. *Internetworking with TCP/IP. Vol. II. ANSI C Version: Design, Implementation, and Internals,* 3rd ed. Englewood Cliffs, NJ: Prentice-Hall, 1999.

[Co00] Comer, D. E. *Internetworking with TCP/IP. Vol.1. Principles, Protocols, and Architecture,* 4th ed. Englewood Cliffs, NJ: Prentice-Hall, 2000.

[Di59] Dijkstra, E. "A Note on Two Problems in Connection with Graphs." *Numerical Mathematics,* October 1959, 269–271.

[Dr95] Drozdek, A., and D. Simon. *Data Structures in C.* Boston: PWS, 1995.

[Fo62] Ford, L., and D. Fulkerson. *Flows in Networks.* Princeton, NJ: Princeton University Press, 1962.

[Fo03] Forouzan, B. *Local Area Networks.* New York: McGraw-Hill, 2003.

[Me80] Merlin, P. M., and P. J. Schweitzer. "Deadlock Avoidance in Store-and-Forward Networks I: Store-and-Forward Deadlock." *IEEE Transactions on Communications,* vol. COM-28 (March 1980), 345–354.

[Pa95] Parsons, T. *Introduction to Algorithms in Pascal.* New York: Wiley, 1995.

[Ta03] Tanenbaum, A. S. *Computer Networks,* 4th ed. Englewood Cliffs, NJ: Prentice-Hall, 2003.

CHAPTER 11

INTERNET PROTOCOLS AND APPLICATIONS

Among all the world's races, some obscure Bedouin tribes possibly apart, Americans are the most prone to misinformation. This is not the consequence of any special preference for mendacity, although at the higher levels of their public administration that tendency is impressive. It is rather that so much of what they themselves believe is wrong.
—**John Kenneth Galbraith,** U.S. economist

11.1 INTRODUCTION

Unless you've spent the last 10 years in remote areas of the Himalayas, you're certainly aware of the impact that the Internet has had on both our work and recreational time. Almost every business has developed websites that describe what they are about or advertise their products. Individuals also create personal websites, which can include almost anything under the sun. Fantasy football and baseball players regularly use the Internet to make trades and compete with each other. Many use it to download music and video files in addition to software updates and other types of programs. Game players compete with each other over the Internet. It would have been difficult 10 years ago to predict what has happened.

But what is the Internet exactly? Many are certainly aware of its existence, but few truly understand it. This chapter explores the Internet, what it is, how it works, and some common Internet-based applications. Section 11.2 starts with the **Internet Protocol (IP).** Actually, there are two Internet protocols. One is an ISO standard and is part of the network layer in the OSI model. We will not discuss this protocol. The other is based on an Internet protocol developed by the U.S. Defense Advanced Research Projects Agency (DARPA). It has been used in the network layer of the ARPANET and is most often used with the **Transmission Control Protocol (TCP).**

Together they are known as TCP/IP and form the layer 3 and layer 4 protocols used to connect commercial, research, military, and educational networks. Those protocols have evolved into what we today call the Internet.

Most sites run version 4 of the Internet Protocol, also called IPv4. However, it was originally designed at a time when file transfers and email were the dominant applications that had to be supported. Who, at that time, could have foreseen a global network in which video streaming (real-time transfer of video), personal websites, security threats, and authentication all had to be dealt with? Because of these considerations, IPv4 has evolved and more sites are upgrading to version 6, or IPv6. Section 11.3 discusses IPv6 and how it deals with the issues that IPv4 did not. The section also deals with the peaceful coexistence of both protocols until all IPv4 implementations are upgraded.

Section 11.4 discusses some of the layer 4 protocols of the Internet. Most of the section focuses on TCP, a connection-oriented end-to-end protocol. We'll see that both ends participate in a handshake to establish a logical connection prior to executing protocols that exchange information. Interestingly, we have already covered many of the concepts. We revisit them here in the context of TCP. In addition, we also cover the User Datagram Protocol (UDP), a connectionless layer 4 protocol, and the Real-Time Transport Protocol (RTP), a protocol developed for real-time applications. Finally, Section 11.5 discusses many of the applications that run on the Internet. We'll examine Telnet and some other, more secure, remote login protocols. We'll also look at FTP (File Transfer Protocol), mail transfer protocols, and management protocols. A notable absence is Web-based applications. That topic is too important to embed in a chapter that deals with other protocols, so we have devoted the next chapter to it.

Clearly, how the Internet works is an immense topic; this chapter just provides a glimpse of the most important aspects of the protocols. Entire books have been written about TCP/IP. The reader should understand that we only cover the fundamentals of these protocols and that there is much more to them than can be described here.

11.2   INTERNET PROTOCOL

Probably the best-known wide area network actually consists of many networks and is collectively called the **Internet.** Its history dates back to the late 1960s, when the Advanced Research Projects Agency (ARPA) of the U.S. Department of Defense (DoD) began funding universities and private organizations for the purpose of developing communications systems. The research eventually led to the development of ARPANET, a small experimental network that demonstrated the feasibility of connecting different computers by a packet-switching network. It has since grown and evolved into the Internet and connects thousands of universities, private institutions, and government agencies worldwide.

Many use the term *internet* to refer to any collection of connected networks. The network that resulted from the ARPA project is commonly referred to as the Internet (with a capital I). The Internet consists of thousands of separate networks.

It services people in probably every corner of the industrialized world, not to mention some remote areas as well. It is difficult to know just how many people use the Internet, but with networks existing in virtually every private and public organization and the proliferation of Internet service providers, users easily number in the tens of millions and, quite possibly, hundreds of millions worldwide. This section and the next present an overview of both IP and TCP. However, there are books devoted solely to these topics, and the interested reader is encouraged to consult references such as [Co99], [Co00], and [Mi99].

OVERVIEW OF TCP/IP

The Internet connects many networks, each of which runs a protocol known as TCP/IP. TCP (Transmission Control Protocol) and IP (Internet Protocol) are layer 4 and 3 protocols, respectively. They were developed along with the ARPA project and have become DoD standards. TCP/IP is probably the most widely implemented protocol in the world and runs on almost anything from personal computers to supercomputers.

The TCP/IP pair of protocols is part of a protocol collection called the *TCP/IP protocol suite* (Figure 11.1). TCP provides connection-oriented services for layer 5 Internet applications and relies on IP to route packets through the network. These applications, in turn, provide specific services for Internet users. Two ends that implement TCP execute a handshake that establishes a logical connection between them. Each side then executes flow control protocols, acknowledges segments, and responds to those that arrive damaged to provide reliable communications. TCP's predecessor in the original ARPANET was NCP (Network Control Protocol), which was designed to run on top of a reliable network. ARPANET was sufficiently reliable, but as it evolved into an internetwork, reliability was lost. Consequently, the transport protocol was forced to evolve as well. NCP, redesigned to run over unreliable networks, became TCP.

Several applications rely on TCP. For example, SMTP (Simple Mail Transfer Protocol) defines the protocol used for the delivery of mail messages over the Internet.

Figure 11.1   Internet Protocols

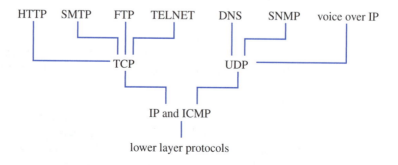

The Telnet protocol allows users to log in to remote computers via the Internet. FTP (File Transfer Protocol) allows Internet users to transfer files from remote computers. HTTP (Hypertext Transfer Protocol) is used to support Web browsers. We will discuss these protocols later.

UDP (User Datagram Protocol) is an alternative layer 4 protocol. One difference from TCP is that UDP provides a connectionless mode of communication over dissimilar networks. The overhead of establishing a connection is eliminated; a consequence of this is that data can often be transmitted more quickly. A side effect is that there is no flow control and UDP does not provide negative acknowledgments for damaged segments. That is, it does not guarantee a reliable delivery. Several applications are designed to run over UDP. For example, DNS (Domain Name System) provides a mapping of host names to addresses. SNMP (Simple Network Management Protocol) is a management protocol designed to make sure network protocols and devices are working. **Voice over IP** is an Internet telephony term that refers to protocols designed to deliver packets containing voice information.

UDP and TCP provide the transport user with the two typical modes of communication. We will discuss both TCP and UDP in more detail in the next section.

The Internet Protocol is a layer 3 protocol designed to provide a packet delivery service between two sites. It is commonly, but not exclusively, used with TCP. Figure 11.2 shows how it works with TCP. Suppose two sites (A and B) need a connection-oriented service for the transmission of some data. Common examples are email, file transfers, and most Web-based applications. TCP provides the reliable connection independent of the network architectures in between the two, and IP does the work of routing packets through different networks. It's a little like making a telephone call. At one level, you simply dial and someone at the other end answers (you hope). You have made a connection. Furthermore, you have no knowledge of how that connection was made or how many telephone switches your call

Figure 11.2   IP Transmitting over Different Networks

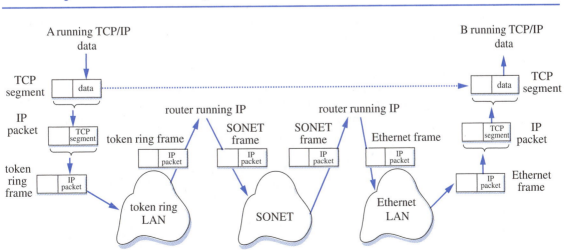

may have been routed through. The telephone companies involved handle that. Figure 11.2 shows a possible Internet connection between A and B.

To begin, the TCP at site A creates a TCP segment* containing the user's data and "sends" the segment to site B. If all goes well, B will acknowledge what it receives. From TCP's point of view, it has made a direct connection with B (dotted line). IP, however, intercepts the segment and creates an *IP packet* (whose format we discuss shortly) containing the TCP segment. Perhaps site A is a company computer and the packet needs to get to a router over a token ring LAN. In that case, data link protocols create a token ring frame, put the IP packet in the frame's Data field, and send it to the router via the token ring network. The lower-layer protocols really do not know they are transporting an IP packet and frankly do not care. They just perform their tasks as specified in the previous chapters, delivering whatever data they have.

When the frame arrives at the router, its data link layer extracts the IP packet from the token ring frame and gives it to the router's IP. IP examines the address in the packet and determines via routing tables that it should go to another router over a SONET carrier. The router's lower layers embed the IP packet into a SONET frame and send it to the other router.

The second router must also make a routing decision. In this case, it decides that the intended recipient is connected to an Ethernet network to which it has access. Consequently, the router's data link layer for that LAN creates an Ethernet frame, stores the IP packet in it, and sends it over the Ethernet. Eventually the Ethernet frame reaches its destination, where the Ethernet data link protocols extract the data (IP packet) and give it to the IP at site B. The IP interprets the packet and gives the TCP segment to TCP, which eventually extracts the data and gives it to B. This simple description serves to show IP's role in routing packets over dissimilar networks.

INTERNET ADDRESSING

Since routing is an important part of the Internet protocol, it is important to understand what an Internet address looks like and how a router interprets it. To Internet users, an Internet address has the form

server.institution.domain

That form may appear in an email address, such as user@server.institution.domain, or it may appear in a Web address, such as http://server.institution.domain.

However, this is not an actual Internet address. It is a text representation identifying a host computer or server owned by some institution that is connected to the Internet. In the case of email, the characters prior to the @ represent a user who is authorized to use the email server. In the case of a Web browser, the commonly used "www" designation represents a default server at the specified location.

---

* A TCP segment, similar to a packet, contains data and other overhead information. We discuss its format in Section 11.4.

However, an actual server name can be used in place of www (assuming that server is set up for Web use).

The periods in the text address separate its components. The rightmost component refers to an Internet domain. However, a word of caution is needed here: In this context, a **domain** is a collection of sites of a particular type. They are different from the domains described in the previous chapter and do not have any geographic significance. That is, two sites in the same domain may be in the same city or may be a thousand miles apart. These domains are used primarily for administration and organizing text addresses for eventual translation to an Internet address. As such, they are not used for routing. Table 11.1 lists some possible domain names and the types of sites to which each corresponds. Some of these domains are likely familiar, whereas others may not be. That's because some of them are recent additions to the list of possible domains and are not yet common.

The other parts of the text address can be almost anything, depending on a particular site. Typically, the names identify an organization, a department, or a specific server; we'll see later how they are handled during translation to an IP address. For example, icsa.uwgb.edu specifies a Linux-based server at the University of Wisconsin–Green Bay in the educational domain, and www.nasa.gov indicates the default Web server at the National Aeronautics and Space Administration in the government domain. If the institution is large enough, it may be divided into departments (more subdomains) and host computers (servers) within each department. For example, the author's full email address is shayw@msa.uwgb.edu. If the university

Table 11.1   Internet Domains

DOMAIN	MEANING
com	Commercial institution
edu	Educational institution
int	International organization
gov	Government agency
kids	Site suitable for children
mil	Military
net	Network service provider
org	Nonprofit organization
biz	Business
info	General use
pro	Professional
museum	Museum
coop	Business cooperative
aero	Aviation industry
name	For individuals
Country code	For example, jp for Japan or nl for the Netherlands

were large enough to warrant separate servers in different departments, a department identifier could be inserted between "msa" and "uwgb." When the site is small, there may be a default server used in applications such as email that receives all incoming messages. This obviates the need to specify the computer. In our case, a server named "msa" is the default, which allows the author's email address to be listed as shayw@uwgb.edu instead of the longer shayw@msa.uwgb.edu.

An example of a text address with more components is www.legis.state.wi.us. In this case, the top domain is *us* (for country). It's divided into subdomains, one of which is *wi* (for Wisconsin). The *wi* subdomain is further divided, using *state* to represent state offices. The remaining components indicate the legislative branch and the default Web server. If other state legislatures are needed, one can replace the state code with another. Examples include www.legis.state.ia.us (Iowa), www.legis.state.wv.us (West Virginia), www.legis.state.ak.us (Alaska), and www.legis.state.de.us (Delaware). One could also replace the *legis* subdomain with another indicating a different department. Examples here include www.dnr.state.wi.us (Department of Natural Resources) and www.dpi.state.wi.us (Department of Public Instruction).

So, how does this relate to an actual Internet address? As the previous section mentioned, the Internet is a collection of independent networks, each of which may contain many computers. Consequently, each computer can be identified by specifying two things: the participating network and a local address distinguishing it from other computers on that network. Together they define a 32-bit address* for that machine. That address is often written as a sequence of four 8-bit numbers separated by periods. For example, the previous text address msa.uwgb.edu actually has an address of 143.200.128.162. We'll see later how we know that.

Next question: Which bits represent a network number and which represent the local ID? The answer depends on the type of address. IP has long recognized several classifications of Internet addresses, which depend largely on the size of the organization's network (Table 11.2). A **Class A** network uses an 8-bit network

Table 11.2   Internet Address Classifications

	32-BIT ADDRESS				NUMBER OF POSSIBLE NETWORKS	MAXIMUM NUMBER OF NETWORK NODES
CLASSIFICATION	BYTE 1	BYTE 2	BYTE 3	BYTE 4		
Class A	0nnnnnnn	xxxxxxxx	xxxxxxxx	xxxxxxxx	$2^7 = 128$	$2^{24} = 16{,}777{,}216$
Class B	10nnnnnn	nnnnnnnn	xxxxxxxx	xxxxxxxx	$2^{14} = 16{,}384$	$2^{16} = 65{,}536$
Class C	110nnnnn	nnnnnnnn	nnnnnnnn	xxxxxxxx	$2^{21} = 2{,}097{,}152$	$2^8 = 256$
Class D	1110 followed by a 28-bit multicast address					
Class E	1111; reserved					

Note: *n*'s represent bits in the network number; *x*'s represent bits in the local identifier.

---

* This is true for IPv4. IPv6 uses 128 bits.

number whose first bit is always 0. The remaining 24 bits are assigned locally. Class A addresses are used only for very large networks. For example, the original ARPANET has a network number of 10 (binary 0000 1010). With a 24-bit local identifier, a Class A network can support up to $2^{24} = 16,777,216$ different nodes. However, with 7 variable bits in the network number, there can be no more than $2^7 = 128$ different Class A networks. **Class B** addresses use 16 bits for both the network number (the first two bits are always 10) and the local identifier. Such networks are still fairly large (up to 65,536 nodes) but nowhere near the Class A capacity. Furthermore, there can be up to $2^{14} = 16,384$ different class B networks. Finally, **Class C** addresses are for relatively small networks. They use 24 bits for the network number (the first three bits are always 110) and 8 bits for the local identifier. There can be up to $2^{21} = 2,097,152$ Class C networks.

For example, 64.37.246.3 is an Internet address for www.nasa.gov. Since 64 has a binary representation of 0100 0000, it's an example of a Class A address (first bit is 0). The server msa.uwgb.edu, on the other hand, has an Internet address of 143.200.128.162, a Class B address since 143 = <u>10</u>00 1111 (base 2). An example of a Class C address is 198.133.219.25, the address for www.cisco.com.

A **Class D** address is used for multicasting. That is, one **multicast address** defines a group of host computers. If, for example, a file is transferred to a multicast address, then every host computer in that group gets the file. It is a bit easier than explicitly sending the file to each member of that group separately. Examples where this is practical include groups that need updates to installed software or streaming a live video feed to a select group of users. We'll discuss multicast routing a little later in this section.

CLASSLESS ADDRESSES

IPv4 was designed many years ago and is showing some signs of age. One problem is address depletion, or an insufficient number of addresses to serve global needs. Because Internet addresses are 32 bits, there are only a finite number of addresses available. Your first reaction might be as follows: 32 bits allows a total of 2^{32}, or about 4.3 billion, different address. Yes, the world has more people than that, but on a global scale the majority still are not Internet users. Therefore, the problem isn't severe. That rationale is incorrect, and here's why.

As we described previously, there are different classes of Internet addresses. Suppose a medium-size organization applies for and gets a Class B network. Perhaps the organization has 1000 people, so 1000 different addresses are used. By defining a Class B network, local management has the ability to assign $2^{16} = 65,536$ different local identifiers. Since there are only 1000 users, about 64,500 Internet addresses go unused. Since they all correspond to the same Class B network number, they cannot be reclaimed by any other organization. What this particular organization does not use is lost to the general Internet population.

A logical response might be to suggest using a couple of Class C networks instead of a Class B network. Since Class C networks have 256 local identifiers for each network, it would be more efficient to assign Class C networks. In the previous example, four Class C networks would accommodate 1000 Internet users and only a few addresses would go unallocated.

There are a couple of problems with this approach. One is planning for growth. There isn't a network manager worth his or her salt who wouldn't plan for future growth in a company network. Suppose the company applies for and gets one Class C network. If the network grows beyond 256 users, it will have to apply for another Class C network. In fact, for every increment of 256 users a new application must be filed. The additional paperwork, headaches, and delays are certainly counterproductive. With a Class B network, growth up to 65,536 users can be accommodated without the formality of applications and approval processes (except the first one, of course). From the network manager's perspective this is a far simpler scenario.

Another problem is the additional routing table information. Recall that the section on hierarchical routing in Chapter 10 discussed the difference between interior and exterior routing. In the Internet, exterior routing is based on network numbers. Using Class C networks means assigning more networks. More networks means more network numbers for routers to track. Consequently, performance of exterior routing protocols suffers. Use of Class B networks reduces the number of networks the router must manage, but again, we end up with unused addresses.

Surely there must be some solution without significant side effects. There are actually a couple! One is a new version of the IP that uses more than 32 bits for an address; we'll discuss it in the next section. The other is called **classless interdomain routing,** or **CIDR,** standardized by the IETF in 1993 and currently supported by BGP-4. It specifies a group of addresses that do not fall into any of the predefined classes, yet each address in the group can still can be interpreted as a network number followed by a local identifier. In fact, the number of bits defining the network number varies to allow networks of varying size.

CIDR is commonly used to allocate multiple Class C networks. Suppose, for example, that an organization projects the need for up to 1000 different workstations with IP addresses. The CIDR approach is to allocate four consecutive class C networks. That is, the addresses that make up the four networks are all contiguous. Initially, it may not seem any different from assigning arbitrary Class C networks, but consider the following possible addresses.

Class C Network	Bit Representation	Address Range
211.195.8.0	11010011-11000011-00001000-xxxxxxxx	211.195.8.0 to 211.195.8.255
211.195.9.0	11010011-11000011-00001001-xxxxxxxx	211.195.9.0 to 211.195.9.255
211.195.10.0	11010011-11000011-00001010-xxxxxxxx	211.195.10.0 to 211.195.10.255
211.195.11.0	11010011-11000011-00001011-xxxxxxxx	211.195.11.0 to 211.195.11.255

In general, these Class C networks correspond to the contiguous set of addresses from 211.195.8.0 to 211.195.11.255. However, examine the address bits carefully and you'll see that the first 22 bits are the same for each address. Consequently, we can view an address from any of these Class C networks as a 22-bit network number followed by a 10-bit local identifier. Furthermore, a router can extract the network number (in this case, 211.195.8.0) via a logical AND operation between a 22-bit subnet mask (255.255.252.0) and an IP address.

```
         11010011-11000011-000010xx-xxxxxxxx    (IP address)
AND      11111111-11111111-11111100-00000000    (22-bit subnet mask)
         11010011-11010011-00001000-00000000    (network number)
              211      195       8       0
```

If we used eight consecutive Class C addresses, then the first 21 bits in each address would be the same. Sixteen consecutive Class C networks would share the first 20 bits, and so on.

In effect, we're grouping several smaller networks together and, for routing purposes, visualizing them as a single larger network. This is called **supernetting.** The advantage is that instead of storing multiple Class C network numbers in each router, we can store just the one network number. However, there is still an issue to deal with. We'll see later that each IP packet contains a destination IP address. By examining the first three bits, a router can determine whether an address is Class A, B, or C. It then extracts the 8-, 16-, or 24-bit network number and searches for it in the routing table. How can the router determine how many bits are in the network number when the number of bits in that number varies?

To answer this question, the router must know the number of bits in the network ID. Consequently, the usual representation of a network address *w.x.y.z* is replaced by *w.x.y.z/m*, where *m* represents the number of bits in the network ID. For example, a router can represent the four networks above using the single entry 211.195.8.0/22, where the "/22" indicates the network number is 22 bits long. When an IP packet arrives, a router tries to match the proper number of bits from a router table entry with the same number of bits in the packet's destination address. If a match is found, the packet is forwarded to the appropriate location.

OBTAINING AN ADDRESS

Perhaps the next logical question is: How do I obtain an IP address? There are several ways to answer this. For example, if you have a personal computer connected to a company or university LAN or have a computer at home connected to an ISP, you already have an IP address. The ISP or LAN manager maintains a list of IP addresses that are assigned to client machines that connect. Whenever you log on to the LAN or ISP, a typical approach is for the client machine to request an IP address from the server. The server, in turn, runs a protocol called **Dynamic Host Configuration Protocol (DHCP)** that allocates an IP address from the list it maintains. There are a couple of ways you can see what IP address your machine has. If you run a Windows operating system variant, you can choose the MS-DOS prompt from the Programs menu and enter the command ipconfig. Doing so will generate a result similar to the following:

```
1 Ethernet Adapter :
IP Address...........................24.163.137.90
Subnet Mask ......................255.255.252.0
Default Gateway ................24.163.136.1
```

You can also select the Windows Run command and enter `winipcfg`. You'll get a similar response.

Next question: How did your LAN manager or ISP get those addresses in the first place? That's a little more difficult. Just as your ISP or LAN manager manages the block of addresses it has, there must be a similar manager that manages all IP addresses. Prior to 1999 the **Internet Assigned Numbers Authority (IANA),** a federally funded organization long associated with the University of Southern California's Information Sciences Institute, was responsible for managing and allocating IP addresses. In 1999 the **Internet Corporation for Assigned Names and Numbers (ICANN),** a nonprofit organization, assumed that responsibility and some other technical functions related to DNS (described later). Its board of directors includes people from diverse companies and academic institutions worldwide. More information about this organization can be found at its website, www.icann.org.

Since most people do not like to memorize IP addresses, the next logical step is to get a host name registered. This means that the host name is stored in a distributed directory and can be referenced by client programs. For example, many people know they can access a Web search engine by using http://www.google.com. Perhaps fewer know that it can also be accessed using http://216.239.53.99. Most will agree it's far easier to remember the host name as opposed to a series of numbers. It's bad enough remembering your phone, social security, charge card, bank account, and license plate numbers. Who needs another one to memorize? The actual process of registering a domain name is done through a registrar. The usual approach is to select a registrar, fill out forms, and pay a fee. They'll do the rest of the work for you. Assuming that your host name does not conflict with an existing one, others can use it to access your site. One must be careful when selecting names because there have been instances of lawsuits against people who have used names equivalent (or even similar) to trademarked names. There are many different registrars that perform the service of registering a host name. A list of ICANN-accredited registrars can be found at www.icann.org/registrars/.

DOMAIN NAME SYSTEM

Now that we have described both the text form of an address and the 32-bit address, the next logical question is: How does one transform to the other? Each site runs a protocol that accesses a distributed database called the **Domain Name System (DNS).** The operative words here are *distributed* and *database*. As a database, DNS contains copies of text addresses and their associated 32-bit addresses. For example, the DNS contains the text address msa.uwgb.edu with its associated Internet address of 143.200.128.162.

DNS, however, is not stored in any one location. To do so would be to invite disaster should that site fail. Besides, one site would never be able to handle the hordes of requests for address translation from sites throughout the world. Instead, DNS is distributed among a collection of *DNS servers* scattered throughout the Internet. When a host computer needs an address translation, it calls on one or more of the servers to look for the specified text address and return the Internet address. In fact, if you have access to a UNIX or Linux system, you can test DNS translation using the utility nslookup. For example, entering the command `nslookup` `msa.uwgb.edu`* returns the 32-bit address 143.200.128.162. Try it on some other text addresses.

It sounds simple enough and, yes, we did oversimplify. Still, the basic idea of address lookup is correct. The difficult part is in the implementation: managing the millions of addresses among the servers and providing a quick translation of a text address. This is where the domain concept comes in. We can view DNS as a hierarchical arrangement of text addresses organized first by the domain name. Figure 11.3 shows how some text addresses are organized (space limitations dictate that we do not try to list all Internet addresses).

For example, all "edu" institutions are grouped, as are "com" institutions, and so on. Still, the edu domain is rather large, so a second-level hierarchy organizes subgroups. Universities such as UWGB (University of Wisconsin–Green Bay), UWM (University of Wisconsin–Milwaukee), MIT, and so forth are grouped under the edu domain. Similarly, other subgroupings exist under the com, org, and other domains. There may be additional hierarchies depending on whether large institutions are divided further into departments.

Now, just because we stated that text addresses are organized in a hierarchy does not mean they are stored that way. Storing and organizing are not the same. We have already mentioned the existence of servers scattered throughout the Internet and that no one server contains all of the information in DNS. The information represented by the hierarchy of Figure 11.3 is divided into *zones,* each of which is a hierarchy of one or more nodes. Furthermore, no two zones overlap. Each zone corresponds to at least two servers (primary and backups), each of which has the responsibility of managing information in that part of the hierarchy. Consequently, the hierarchy is perhaps more accurately applied to an organization of servers.

At the top of the hierarchy is a root server. Although Figure 11.3 shows just one, there are actually several root servers located throughout the world. Each root

Figure 11.3   DNS Hierarchy

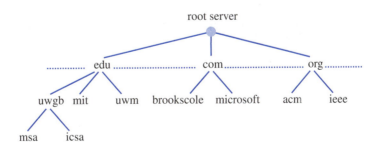

_____

* In the most recent version of Red Hat Linux, `nslookup` is deprecated. That is, the command is being phased out and users are encouraged to use a `dig` or `host` command that performs a similar function.

server knows the location of other DNS servers associated with specific domains. Those servers, in turn, locate even more DNS servers. As we progress down through the hierarchy, the servers are more specific to a particular location. Exactly how requests are handled is difficult to predict because much depends on what the servers know, who is making the request, where the requested site is located, and where the servers exist within the hierarchy. However, here is one possibility.

When a host needs an address translation, it sends a request to a local name server (same site as host). Let's call it A. If A can provide the translation, it does so and the process is complete. If not, then A sends the request to another server, B, that's one level above it in the hierarchy. If B knows the address, it sends the address back to A, which, in turn, relays it to the host. Again, the translation is complete. However, B may not know the address either. In this case, B can proceed in one of two ways. It can respond to A that it failed to do the translation and give A the address of another server, C, to try. The second option, and the one we'll assume for the rest of this discussion, is that it can send the request to C on behalf of A. Typically, C corresponds to yet another server at the next level up. Server C proceeds much the same as B.

Eventually, a server is found that knows the address, or the request filters up to the root server. However, there's virtually no way that the root server will know all possible addresses. If it gets an address it cannot resolve, it does know of another server that can help. Depending on the domain of the original request, the root server forwards the request to one of the DNS servers represented at the next level of the hierarchy. We'll call it server D. For example, text addresses that end in *com* and *edu* go to different servers. If D has access to the information represented by the text address specified, it returns the Internet address to the root server. The information eventually gets back to the host through C, B, and A. If not, then D knows of another name server that should be able to provide more information. This forwarding of requests continues until a name server is found that can do the translation. Once the address is found, it goes back to the original host through all the name servers (in reverse order) that handled and forwarded the request.

Figure 11.4 shows how this works for one case. This figure shows one small fictitious branch coming off the com domain. The ACME company maintains two

Figure 11.4   Zones in a DNS Hierarchy

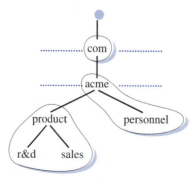

networks, one each for the products and personnel departments. The products department, in turn, consists of two divisions: research and development and sales. Circles around the nodes define zones.

Suppose an outsider specifies the text address hercules.products.acme.com. "hercules" is a computer in the research and development division of the products department of the ACME company. Assume the address cannot be translated locally and that the request goes to the root and then to the com domain name server. The name server for the com domain cannot be expected to know the full address of every host computer in every commercial network (there are just too many). However, the "acme" part of the text address tells the server that another server at the ACME site can provide more information. The text address is then sent to the ACME site.

A possible scenario is that the personnel department is fairly small but the products department is larger; consequently, management at ACME decided to use a separate server for its products network. Perhaps the network managers at the products department simply did not want to bother with the personnel network. In any event, the server in the ACME zone still cannot resolve the full address because the text address indicates a zone for which it is not responsible. Note that if the text address contained "personnel.acme.com," the server could resolve it, because both the ACME and personnel nodes are in the same zone. However, since the products node is in a different zone, a request is sent to another server in the products zone. At that point, the remaining part of the text address is the responsibility of that server, which accesses and returns the corresponding Internet address.

Must this complex process occur each time a translation occurs? Fortunately, not necessarily. When addresses are translated and the results go back through the name servers, each one can store the address in a local cache. This way if another request comes to that server, it will be able to do the translation from the cache.

IP PACKETS

Having provided the basics of Internet terminology and operation, we can now discuss the packet format and some specific features of the Internet Protocol. An IP packet is similar in many ways to the packet and frame formats previously discussed. Still, there are some unique features that warrant discussion. Figure 11.5 shows the contents of an IP packet.

The following list explains the IP packet fields.

- **Version.** Specifies the version of IP that created the packet. This allows different versions of IP to work together.

- **Header Length.** Specifies the number of 32-bit words in the **packet header** (the fields preceding the data).

- **Type of Service.** This 8-bit field was originally designed to specify transport layer requests regarding handling of the packet. It allowed different request options such as precedence, low delay, high throughput, and high reliability. A 3-bit Precedence field allowed packets to be prioritized (0 for low and 7 for high priority) and was especially useful for meeting quality of service (QoS)

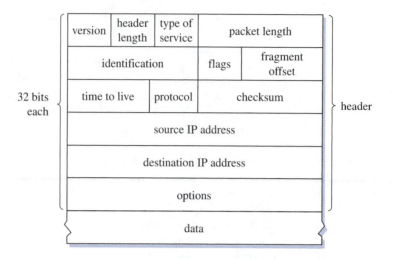

Figure 11.5   Internet Packet

requirements. A transport protocol could request a *low-delay* transmission, useful when the transport user had logged into a remote computer and wanted quick responses. A *high-throughput* request was useful in transferring large files, and the *high-reliability* request would look for networks that had a track record of providing more reliable service.

More recently the QoS issues have been addressed through complex protocols such as RSVP and RTP (both discussed later). Also, the IETF has defined a **Differentiated Services** (also known as **Diffserv**) architecture to differentiate among the different types of traffic that travel the Internet. Routers that implement the Diffserv architecture use an 8-bit Differentiated Services (DS) field to label packets for different QoS treatment. In order for the architecture to be consistent with the current IP protocol, it uses the Type of Service field for the DS field. The leftmost 6 bits define a code point that, in theory, can provide 64 different classes of traffic. The rightmost 2 bits are currently unused. The basic idea is that when a packet enters the Internet, it is labeled with a particular DS value. Routers that get the packet examine the DS field and can treat the packet based on the policies that the vendor has implemented in its routers.

- **Packet Length.** Specifies the length of the entire IP packet. It is a 16-bit field, thus providing a maximum length of 65,535 bytes.

- **Identification, Flags, Fragment Offset.** These three fields are used in fragmentation (discussed shortly).

- **Time to Live.** A station sending a packet into the Internet for the first time sets the Time to Live field to specify the maximum time the packet can remain in the Internet. When another router receives the packet, it decrements the Time to Live field by the amount of time the packet spent in the router and sends the packet to the next router. If the Time to Live field reaches 0 or less, the router discards the packet and sends an error message to the sending station. This step guarantees that routing or congestion problems do not cause packets to circulate endlessly within the Internet.

- **Protocol.** Specifies the higher-layer protocol using IP. It allows the destination IP to give the data to the appropriate entity at its end. For example, if the IP packet contains a TCP segment, the Protocol value is 6. Packets containing UDP or ICMP segments have Protocol values of 17 or 1, respectively. IGMP (a protocol used in multicasting) uses 2, and RSVP (a protocol to provide quality of service guarantees) uses 46.

- **Checksum.** Used for error detection of packet headers. Since the data corresponds to a TCP or other protocol segment, it has its own error detection, which is done at a higher layer. Thus, IP needs to worry only about detecting errors in the header. An advantage of this is that error checking fewer bits allows each router to service the packet more quickly. To calculate the checksum, the header is interpreted as a sequence of 16-bit integers. The values are added using 1's complement arithmetic, and the result is complemented and stored in the Checksum field. On the receiving end, the checksum is recalculated from the arriving information. If it disagrees with the value stored in the Checksum field, the receiver knows an error has affected the header. Note that the checksum must be recalculated with each transmission because the header changes (i.e., the Time to Live field changes).

- **Source IP Address and Destination IP Address.** These fields contain the addresses of the sending and receiving sites.

- **Options.** This field is not required in every packet but can be used to request special treatment for the packet. It consists of a series of entries, each corresponding to a requested option.

  The *Record Route option* traces the route a packet takes. The sending station reserves space for a list of IP addresses in the Options field. Each router routing the packet inserts its own address in the list (space permitting), thus allowing the receiving station to determine which ones handled the packet.

  The *Timestamp option* is similar to the Record Route option. In addition to storing its address, each router stores the time at which it routed the packet.

  The *Source Route option* allows the sender to specify the route to be taken by storing a sequence of IP addresses in the Options field. Each router uses this information instead of its own routing tables. This is not the normal mode of routing because it requires knowledge of the physical topology. It can be useful if network administrators suspect there is a problem with a router and want to test a specific route.

  The *Loose Source Route option* does not provide the exact route but does provide a list of routers through which the packet must travel.

  The *Security option* can list certain routers or locations that should be avoided during routing.

  More extensive discussions of these options and their execution are found in reference [Co00].

- **Data.** Contains the data provided by the next-higher layer.

FRAGMENTATION

One of the problems the Internet Protocol faces is that different network architectures allow different maximum frame sizes (also called **maximum transfer units, or MTUs**). If the IP packet length is smaller than each MTU encountered in a path there is no problem, but if an MTU is smaller the packet is divided into smaller units called **fragments.** The fragments travel to their eventual destination (possibly over different routes), where they must be reassembled. For fragmentation to work, the destination IP must be able to distinguish fragments from unfragmented packets and recognize which fragments correspond to the same packet, in what order they must be reassembled, and how many fragments are contained in each packet. The Identification, Flags, and Fragment Offset fields provide that information.

Suppose a router receives a packet and determines it must travel over a network with an MTU smaller than the packet length. It divides the packet into fragments, each containing part of the packet's data. Furthermore, each fragment has a **fragment header** almost identical to the packet header to allow for subsequent routing. Many fields in the fragment header perform the same roles as their counterparts in the packet header. The following fields are relevant to the current discussion:

- The router puts the packet's identification value into each fragment's *Identification field.*

- The *Flag field* contains a *More Fragments bit* (mfb). The router sets the mfb to 1 in each fragment except the last one. There is also a *Do Not Fragment bit* that, if set, does not allow fragmentation. If a router receives such a packet, it discards the packet and sends an error message to the sending station. The sending station uses the message to determine threshold values at which fragmentation occurs. That is, if the current packet size is too large, the sender could repeat with smaller packet sizes to eventually determine when fragmentation occurs.

- Because a fragment contains part of a packet's data, the router also determines the offset in the packet's Data field from where the data was extracted and stores it in the *Fragment Offset field.* It measures offsets in units of 8 bytes each. Thus, offset 1 corresponds to byte number 8, offset 2 to byte 16, and so on.

Figure 11.6 shows a packet being divided into three fragments. It assumes the network has an MTU that allows no more than 1400 bytes of data. Consequently, the router divides an incoming packet with 4000 data bytes into three fragments. Each of the first two fragments has 1400 data bytes. The first one's Fragment Offset field is 0, indicating its data begins at offset 0 in the packet. The second one's Fragment Offset field is 175, indicating its data begins at byte 1400 (8×175) of the packet. The third has 1200 bytes of data and an offset of 350. The More Fragments bits in the first two fragments are 1, indicating that each is a fragment and that more fragments exist. The last fragment's mfb is 0, indicating that it is the last fragment. The fact that it is a fragment at all is deduced from the value in the Offset field.

When the destination IP sees two different fragments with the same identification, source, and destination address, it knows they came from the same packet. It reassembles all such packets in the order indicated by the values in their respective

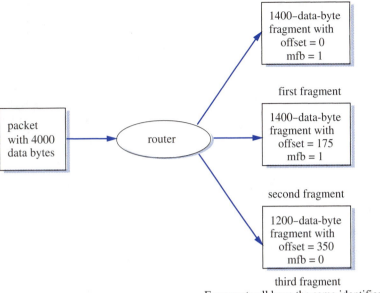

Figure 11.6   Packet Fragmentation

Offset fields. It recognizes the last fragment as the one with the mfb equal to 0 and a nonzero offset. As part of the reassembly process, it also sets a **reassembly timer** on receipt of the first fragment. If it does not receive all the fragments before the timer expires, it assumes that one or more were lost. In that case, it discards the currently held fragments and sends an error message to the sending station. The result is that it gets all the fragments or none at all.

IP ROUTING

Much of the groundwork has been set to discuss routing in the Internet. In fact, most of the ideas have already been presented in the previous chapter. IP routing is based on routing tables stored at routers and the interpretation of IP addresses and relies on the RIP-2 and BGP protocols heavily. Previous sections have already dealt with these topics, and we will not reproduce those discussions here. Still, there are a couple of routing details that should be addressed while we are on the topic of the Internet. Recall from earlier discussions that to an Internet user, an email address may have the form

user@host.department.institution.domain

Domain name servers translate the characters after the @ to a 32-bit number that is typically expressed as a sequence of four 8-bit numbers separated by decimal points (dotted notation). For example, the IP address of the host computer specified in shayw@msa.uwgb.edu corresponds to the 32-bit number 10001111-11001000-10000000-00111110 or, using the equivalent dotted notation, 143.200.128.62.

One issue we have not dealt with yet is the distinction between an IP address and a physical address. A unique 32-bit IP address is assigned to each computer on the Internet. Its *physical address* is the one used by the underlying physical network. For example, devices connected to an Ethernet sense addresses stored in IEEE 802.3 frames to determine which ones are destined for it. However, these addresses are Ethernet addresses (48-bit numbers assigned to the network interface card). They have local significance but none on a global IP scale. How will such a device recognize a packet containing an IP address?

The answer is that it doesn't. Recall from Figure 11.2 that IP packets (IP address and all) are stored in frames if they travel through a LAN. Frames contain addresses depending on the data link control protocols. Within a LAN, the frame's address specifies the frame's destination. If the frame goes to a router, the IP there extracts the packet, examines the address, and determines where to send it next. On the other hand, if the router must send the packet to a personal computer on an attached LAN, it must put the packet into a LAN frame and send it. The next question must be, If the packet is embedded in a LAN frame, what physical address is used? In other words, how does the router determine the physical address given the IP address? There are several ways, depending on specifics of the lower layers.

When a router receives an IP packet, there are two possibilities. Either the packet's destination is attached to a network to which the router is also attached, or it is not. The router recognizes the first case because the first part of each IP address specifies the network where the destination exists. If it recognizes the network as one to which it is attached, it knows it can send the packet directly to its destination. This is called *direct routing*. It puts the destination's physical address in the frame and sends it. So again the question arises: How does the router determine the physical address given the IP address?

One approach, **dynamic binding** (also called **Address Resolution Protocol**), has the router transmit a broadcast Request frame containing an IP address to all stations on the LAN. The broadcast requests that the device with that IP address respond with its physical address. That device sends its physical address back to the router, and the router stores it and the IP address in a local cache. It then sends the frame to the appropriate device using the physical address it just retrieved. By storing the IP and physical address in a local cache, the router can avoid another broadcast Request if it must send another packet to the same device. At least that is true for a while because the cache is purged periodically. The reason for the purging is to make sure the cache is current and contains correct information. Of course, a logical question is, How can information become incorrect? Isn't the physical address for a computer constant? The answer is no. If an Ethernet card in a personal computer failed, then a new one would need to be installed. Since each physical card has a unique address, any information relating the computer's IP address and old physical address would now be incorrect.

Next, suppose the destination is not reachable directly through one of the router's networks. In that case the router uses hierarchical routing as discussed in the previous chapter to determine another router and send the packet there. The packet then travels from router to router until it reaches one connected to the destination's actual network and proceeds as just described.

Let's go through an example and put this all together. The following steps summarize a router's actions:

1. Receive an IP packet and extract the IP address.
2. If the packet's Source Route option is marked, route the packet according to the route indicated. Skip the remaining steps.
3. Determine the network number contained in the IP address.
4. Does the network number match any network to which the router is connected?
5. If yes, determine the physical address of the destination (either by cache lookup or dynamic binding) and send a frame containing the IP packet to that destination.
6. If no, find the network number in the routing table and forward the packet to the specified router.
7. If, for some reason, the network is not in the routing table, forward the packet to a default router.

Assume the example topology of Figure 11.7. Router 1 is connected to a network whose number is 143.200 (i.e., every node on that network has an IP address of 143.200.*x*.*y*). Similarly, router 2 is connected to a network whose number is 143.100. Suppose router 1 receives a packet with an IP address of 143.200.10.5. It examines the network number, 143.200, and knows it can deliver the packet to the destination directly. It sends a broadcast Request frame containing the number 143.200.10.5. Since it is a broadcast frame, each device on the LAN gets it, but only device A responds by returning a frame to the router containing A's physical address.

Figure 11.7   IP Routing

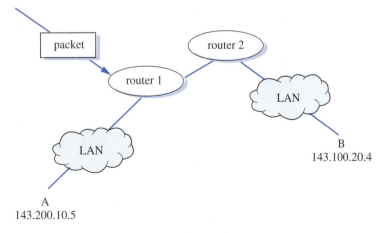

The router then stores the IP packet into a frame containing A's physical address and sends it.

On the other hand, suppose router 1 receives a packet containing address 143.100.20.4. Router 1 knows it is not connected to network 143.100 and that it must route the packet to another router. It examines its routing table and finds it should forward the packet to router 2. When router 2 gets the packet, it performs tasks similar to those we just described for router 1. Of course, the packet may have traveled through several routers, but the steps are all similar to those we have just outlined.

We close this section by posing the following question: Did you ever wonder just what route your email takes when you send it? There is a way to determine the route that is taken to a specified destination. On UNIX and Linux systems, the command `traceroute` will display the route (i.e., intermediate routers) between that system and a specified destination. In Red Hat Linux, you can enter the command by typing

```
/usr/sbin/traceroute www.alaska.org
```

Of course, you can enter any destination. The response you get will display the IP addresses of intermediate routers and the round trip time it takes for a packet to get there and back. Entering this command from a Linux server in Green Bay, Wisconsin, generated the following results.

```
 1  143.200.128.1 (143.200.128.1) 0.492 ms 0.459 ms 0.426 ms
 2  fwalla1 (143.200.208.11) 19.270 ms 30.757 ms 31.306 ms
 3  c7204vxr (143.200.225.4) 62.370 ms 62.225 ms 62.236 ms
 4  uwgreenbay-atm6-0-252.core.wiscnet.net (216.56.24.17)
    46.954 ms 52.289 ms 56.635 ms
 5  uwmilwaukee-atm1-0-4.core.wiscnet.net (140.189.8.217)
    52.952 ms 55.939 ms 53.458 ms
 6  p7-2.chcgil1-cr4.bbnplanet.net (4.24.164.101) 55.849 ms
    54.659 ms 54.359 ms
 7  p6-0.chcgil1-br2.bbnplanet.net (4.24.5.245) 53.241 ms
    55.618 ms 62.713 ms
 8  so-3-0-0.chcgil2-br2.bbnplanet.net (4.0.1.197) 77.895 ms
    62.004 ms 54.161 ms
 9  so-7-0-0.chcgil3-hcr1.bbnplanet.net (4.0.1.185) 55.233 ms
    62.002 ms 46.912 ms
10  p1-3.xchcgil4-uunet.bbnplanet.net (4.24.95.10) 68.787 ms
    71.272 ms 63.828 ms
11  0.so-5-0-0.xl2.chi13.alter.net (152.63.73.21) 76.797 ms
    69.014 ms 71.139 ms
12  0.so-2-2-0.xl2.chi2.alter.net (152.63.70.106) 62.488 ms
    70.069 ms 54.447 ms
13  0.so-1-0-0.tl2.chi2.alter.net (152.63.67.121) 70.295 ms
    54.236 ms 62.613 ms
14  0.so-5-3-0.tl2.sea1.alter.net (152.63.136.62) 109.052 ms
    109.310 ms 109.175 ms
15  0.so-1-0-0.xl2.sea1.alter.net (152.63.2.133) 109.536 ms
    108.712 ms 109.495 ms
```

```
16   pos5-0.xr2.sea1.alter.net (152.63.106.234) 93.678 ms
     108.724 ms 118.475 ms
17   194.atm7-0.gw8.sea1.alter.net (152.63.105.221) 100.296 ms
     115.843 ms 102.321 ms
18   gci-gw.customer.alter.net (157.130.182.6) 102.076 ms
     116.190 ms 125.023 ms
19   inetseasdcgw-2.gci.net (209.165.129.34) 117.285 ms 116.636
     ms 124.990 ms
20   208.155.87.121 (208.155.87.121) 156.240 ms 140.107 ms
     157.259 ms
21   209.165.128.1 (209.165.128.1) 155.268 ms 154.801 ms
     156.259 ms
22   209.165.128.82 (209.165.128.82) 156.261 ms 152.754 ms
     156.600 ms
23   205.140.73.143 (205.140.73.143) 187.115 ms 155.779 ms
     131.571 ms
```

You can probably guess the locations of some of these sites by the names that appear. In this particular case, the packet appears to travel from Green Bay through Milwaukee and Chicago and on to Seattle. The host names that end in *bbnplanet.net* correspond to Genuity, Inc., a provider of enterprise IP networking services. The name *alter.net* corresponds to UUNET, a WorldCom company, and *gci.net* corresponds to an Alaska-based company that provides data communications services to a variety of customers. Sometimes names are not provided because those networks do not provide address-to name translations. Still, you get some idea of the route taken.

If you don't have access to Linux, then you can try the DOS command `tracert`. As another example, entering the command `tracert www.alaska.org` from another workstation in Green Bay, Wisconsin, generated the following:

```
1    8 ms    10 ms     7 ms    10.42.32.1
2    9 ms     8 ms    14 ms    srp-3-0.applwi2-rtr1.new.rr.com
                               [24.164.224.24]
3   11 ms     8 ms     8 ms    srp-0-0.applwi1-rtr1.new.rr.com
                               [24.164.224.17]
4    9 ms    13 ms     9 ms    srp-4-0-0.applwi3.rtr1.new.rr.com
                               [24.164.224.91]
5   12 ms    15 ms    17 ms    pop2-chi-P8-0.atdn.net
                               [66.185.141.109]
6   17 ms    13 ms    13 ms    bb1-chi-P0-2.atdn.net
                               [66.185.148.70]
7   29 ms    36 ms    26 ms    bb1-kcy-P7-0.atdn.net
                               [66.185.152.125]
8   26 ms    25 ms    27 ms    pop1-kcy-P0-0.atdn.net
                               [66.185.137.225]
9   26 ms    49 ms    27 ms    sl-gw16-kc-9-0.sprintlink.net
                               [144.232.131.65]
10  30 ms    30 ms    49 ms    sl-bb20-kc-8-0.sprintlink.net
                               [144.232.23.53]
11  80 ms    75 ms    76 ms    sl-bb21-sea-8-3.sprintlink.net
                               [144.232.18.98]
```

```
12   75 ms    80 ms    74 ms    sl-bb21-sea-15-0.sprintlink.net
                                 [144.232.6.89]
13   75 ms    77 ms    78 ms    sl-gw11-sea-7-0.sprintlink.net
                                 [144.232.6.126]
14   76 ms    88 ms    75 ms    sl-gcomm-2-0.sprintlink.net
                                 [144.228.93.234]
15   80 ms    77 ms    77 ms    InetSeaSDCgw-2.gci.net
                                 [209.165.129.34]
16  118 ms   115 ms   111 ms    209.165.170.157
17  114 ms   112 ms   119 ms    209.165.128.1
18  113 ms   109 ms   119 ms    209.165.128.82
19  112 ms   113 ms   110 ms    www.alaska.org [205.140.73.143]
```

Some of the sites are similar, but some are very different. That's interesting because the two computers in which these commands were entered are only a couple of miles apart. So why is a different route taken? Primarily because of the ISPs. The Linux server is part of the university campus network, which is also connected to a statewide SONET-based network called Wiscnet. The DOS command was entered at a machine serviced by the Roadrunner broadband ISP. Simply put, each server uses different organizations and lines to make connections.

ROUTERS

Up to this point we have grossly oversimplified how routers do their job. Figure 11.8 shows the primary router functions. A packet arrives over an input port, and router logic does the following actions:

- Extract the destination address from the packet.
- Find that address in the routing table.
- Access the next hop value and determine the proper outgoing port.
- Move the packet to a waiting queue for that port.
- Transmit the packet.

Although this is certainly accurate, the real issue is how the router works. Router design is very complex, and there are many issues dealing with timing, queuing, scheduling, and the internal workings that move a packet from an incoming port to an outgoing one. There's no way we can cover router design here, but we will touch on a couple of important ideas. If interested in exploring routers in more detail, you can consult references [Pi03] and [Ca01]. We'll take a brief look at three issues: finding the next hop value, moving the packet from an input port to an output port, and scheduling the packet for transmission.

Finding the next hop given the destination is easy—the router looks it up in the table. The problem is that the lookup must occur very quickly. Imagine that the incoming ports are optical fiber connections and that packets are arriving at 100 Mbps rates. Unless the router can dispatch these packets as quickly as they arrive, the packets will accumulate and cause delays. In extreme cases, the buffers may overflow and the packets will be dropped.

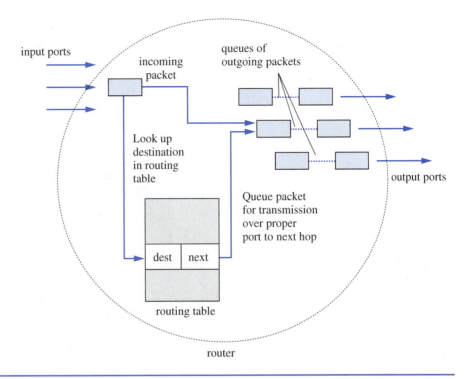

input ports

incoming packet

queues of outgoing packets

Look up destination in routing table

Queue packet for transmission over proper port to next hop

output ports

dest	next

routing table

router

Figure 11.8 Router Functions

The topic of searching is one that is covered in many programming and data structures courses. Methods include linear searches, binary searches, B-tree searches, other tree-based methods, and hash structures. Normally, linear and binary searches are far too slow for high-speed routers and are not able to process packets quickly enough. Using a hash structure, also called **content addressable memory,** is probably the fastest and most sophisticated method. The idea is fairly simple. When a router creates an entry in the table for a destination, it applies a hash function to that destination value (Figure 11.9). The function generates a location in which the next hop entry is stored. Later, when a packet arrives with the destination address, the hash function is used to determine exactly where in the table the next hop value is found. In this case, there is no searching because the proper location is calculated and the router finds the next hop value very quickly. Many issues surround the use and creation of hash functions, but those are best covered in a data structures or algorithms course. For our purposes here, it's enough to know that the next hop is found quickly.

Once the next hop is known, the router still has to move the packet from an input to an output port. It's not unlike designing the way in which multiple processors access memory. One approach is to follow the design of many microcomputers and use a *bus transport system,* in which any packet arriving over an input port is

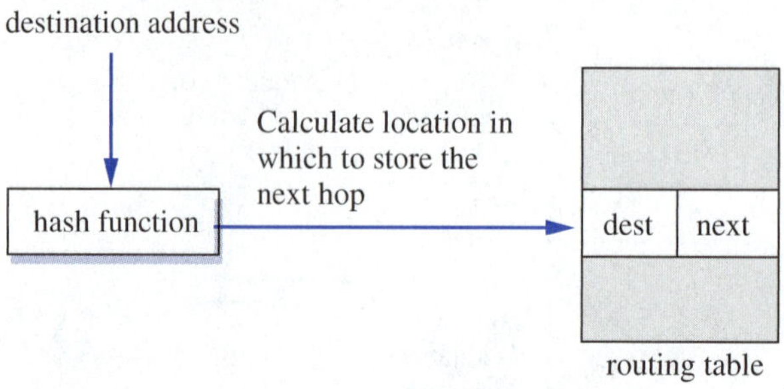

destination address

Figure 11.9   Hash Function to Update Routing Table

sent to the proper output port via the bus. It's simple, but the main drawback is the same as that of bus-based networks: Only one packet can move at a time, and that slows the process.

Another approach is to use *shared memory*. This means that multiple processors can access the same memory. The queues for each output port correspond to a designated area of the shared memory. Each input port is on a card containing a processor that finds the next hop value. That processor can then transfer the packet from one area of memory to another depending on the queue to which it is assigned. Because there are separate processors (one for each input card), there is a higher level of concurrency, which allows processing to occur more quickly. Of course, there are still issues to resolve, such as what happens if two separate processors need to move the packet to the same queue and how processors communicate with memory.

Still another approach is to design a hardware switch that connects each input port with each output port (Figure 11.10). A *switch* is a circuit that establishes connections between two endpoints. In Figure 11.10a, the packet arriving over input port A is transferred to output port Z, and the packet arriving over input port C is transferred to output port X. In Figure 11.10b, things change. The switch connects A with Y, and B with Z. Again, issues arise. What happens if all three input ports have packets destined for the same output port? How do we design the switches? As before, these are good topics for advanced study but are not discussed here.

The last issue is scheduling packets for outgoing ports. It's reasonable to assume that packets arriving over different input ports must go out through the same output port. How does the router schedule them? In what order are they transmitted? One approach is to just store packets in output port buffers in the order they arrive. That is, the buffers are really queues. Those packets that have been in the queue the longest are the ones that are transmitted. This is a simple approach and works fine for many applications. However, **quality of service (QoS)** is an issue that's become prominent in recent years. Basically, QoS defines the type of service one expects from the network.

As we've stated previously, the Internet was designed largely to handle file transfers and email. Experiencing short delays while packets sit in output queues is not an issue for these applications, and hardly anyone would notice. However, it

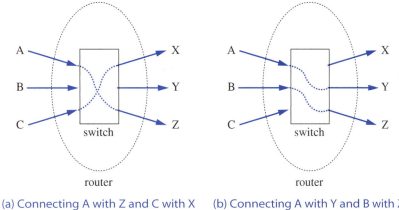

(a) Connecting A with Z and C with X   (b) Connecting A with Y and B with Z

Figure 11.10   Switch-Based Router

was not really designed for real-time audio or video streaming. In such applications the QoS expectation is that packets are delivered in timely fashion with no delays. In such cases, standard queuing of outgoing packets may run counter to the quality of service one expects of such applications. Consequently, we need other options such as a priority queue, a structure in which packets are organized by a priority that can be defined by the value in the Type of Service field in the IP packet. The highest-priority ones are closest to the front of the queue and are transmitted quickly. Somewhere between the application and the creation of the IP packet, the protocols would have to set the fields appropriate to the type of application. The important thing to note here is that some options are available for prioritizing and processing some packets faster than others. We'll revisit this issue a little later when we discuss the Resource Reservation Protocol.

MULTICAST ROUTING

All of our discussion on routing have been predicated on one assumption: Each packet has a single **unicast address,** which means that it follows a specific route from the source to a unique destination. Another option is for the packet to have a *multicast address*. As we explained earlier, a Class D IP address defines a multicast. This means that one multicast address actually defines a set of destinations, each of which must receive a copy of the packet. It's a little bit like setting up an email distribution list. Your address book has a distribution list entry that contains many email addresses. When you send out an email, you need only select the single distribution list entry. However, a separate email is sent to each individual. Multicasting works similarly except it operates at a different layer.

One example of where this is useful is multicasting a video to select users over a network. The data from a live video feed (Figure 11.11) is divided into packets

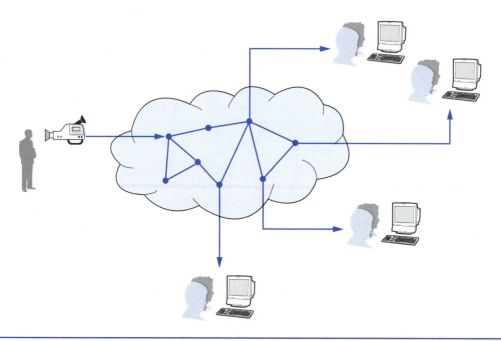

Figure 11.11   Multicasting a Video Feed

and transported across the network. However, the Class D address in each packet defines the group of people who have signed on to see the video. A copy of each packet must find its way to each person in the multicast group. At each site the data are extracted from the packets and presented in viewing form.

Multicasting has a couple of different components. First is the **Internet Group Management Protocol (IGMP),** a protocol that operates between a host and a local router and allows the host to join and leave various multicast groups. Either the host or local router can send an IGMP message embedded in an IP packet whose Protocol field value is set to 2. Examples of such exchanges follow.

- The router sends a query message to one or more hosts to find out who is in a particular multicast group. The message contains the Class D address for that group.

- A host sends a message to the local router indicating it belongs to a particular multicast group. As before, the message contains the corresponding address.

- A host sends a message to the local router indicating it no longer belongs to a particular multicast group. The message contains the corresponding address.

This part is relatively straightforward, because IGMP is used simply to indicate who is in what group. It does not specify how multicasting works. The hard part is getting this information to all routers in the network and having them implement some type of multicasting routing algorithm.

Figure 11.12 shows an example. Each of the personal computer icons represents a host that has joined a multicast group; the group consists solely of these hosts. Therefore, router A knows that three hosts are in a group, and routers C and E each know of one host in a group. The other routers are connected to networks in which no hosts have joined the group. Actually, in the context of defining a multicasting routing algorithm, there's no difference whether A knows of 3 hosts or 300 hosts in the group. Router A must be involved either way. Similarly, routers C and E must be involved. However, although routers B, D, and F have no local hosts in the group, at least one of routers B or D must also be involved. Otherwise, there's no way to get from A to C or E. In this case there's no need to involve router F.

Now that we have a diagram, this might be a good time to pose the question: Why use multicasting as opposed to just sending a separate unicast packet to each host in the group? Suppose that host X takes this approach. Therefore, in Figure 11.12, it must send four copies of every packet that originates at X. Each of those four copies must be routed through the Internet. Of course, if there were *n* members of the group, then it would have to send *n* − 1 copies of each packet. Through multicasting, X sends only one copy of each packet. When router E gets the packet, it sends one copy to C and one other copy, perhaps to B (depending on the routing algorithm

Figure 11.12   Routers Involved in Multicasting

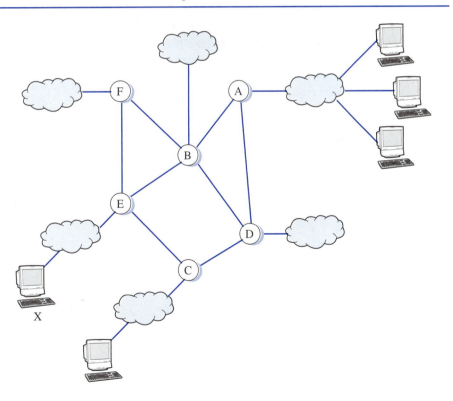

used) and eventually to A. Multicasting means fewer packets travel through the Internet; it is therefore more efficient than unicasting multiple packets. The difference here is perhaps not striking, but if each network has hundreds of hosts in the group instead of just a couple, the difference becomes significant.

Now we come to the all-important question: How does each router know what to do with a multicast packet? The oversimplified solution is to create a spanning tree of routers that reaches all hosts in the group. For the group in Figure 11.12, that tree might be A-B-E-C (Figure 11.13a) or it might be A-D-C-E (Figure 11.13b). In this case the spanning tree must contain A, E, and C and at least one node to get from A to either C or E. If some of this sounds familiar, that means you read at least that part of Chapter 9 that used the spanning tree algorithm to eliminate loops in bridged connections. In this context, the trees are typically called **multicast trees** instead of spanning trees.

The problem is right out of graph theory: Given a set of vertices and edges in a graph, create a spanning tree connecting a subset of the graph's vertices. There are several different approaches, and most fall into one of two broad categories. The first way is to create a single multicast tree connecting the proper nodes. The second is to create a single multicast tree for each possible source in a group. Once the multicast tree is created, each router in that tree simply transmits any multicast packet it receives over all outgoing links in that tree. Of course, this applies to just one multicast address. Separate trees must be created for each one.

The problem is that creating multicast trees, especially for a large number of nodes, is difficult. We described a distributed algorithm to create trees in Chapter 10; imagine the logistics on a global scale! As a result, the majority of IP routers do not support multicasting. However, this does not mean that multicasting does not

Figure 11.13 Possible Multicast Trees for the Network in Figure 11.12

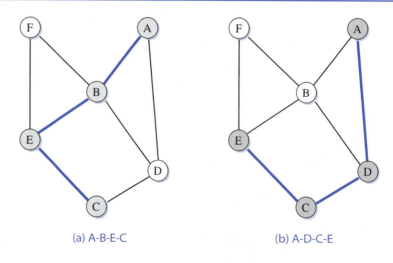

(a) A-B-E-C   (b) A-D-C-E

exists—it does. A smaller* number of IP routers make up the **Mbone,** a network within the Internet that supports Class D address routing.

The details of how the Mbone works are complex, but the idea is based on some of the routing mechanisms we have discussed to create a multicast tree. The method is the **Distance Vector Multicast Routing Protocol (DVMRP)** and uses several components. One is **reverse-path broadcasting (RPB).** A *broadcast* means that a packet should go to every possible destination. Typically, a router can implement a broadcast algorithm by forwarding a packet over each outgoing port. However, as we saw in the previous chapter, the packets travel in loops and the amount of traffic can become excessive. RPB assumes that a router knows the next link along the shortest path to a given node. Therefore, when a router gets a packet it does the following:

- Determine the source of the incoming packet and the port on which it was received.
- Look up the source in the routing table and determine the next hop in a path back to that source.
- If the next hop corresponds to the port over which the packet arrived, then send the packet over every other port.
- If the previous condition is not true, drop the packet.

For example, if router A received a packet from a source, S, via router B in Figure 11.14, it would broadcast the packet over all other ports. If it received the packet

Figure 11.14   Router Executing Reverse Broadcast Protocol

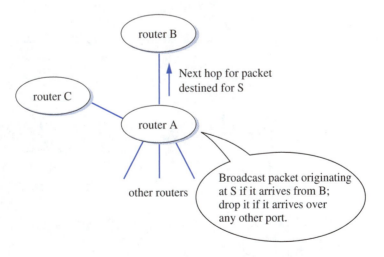

---

* *Smaller* does not mean *small*. There are still thousands of routers that run Mbone software.

over any other port, it would drop the packet. It's similar to defining a broadcast tree with source S as the root and forwarding packets only along paths that lead away from S. As long as all other routers do the same, packets will not travel in loops.

However, this method by itself does not work well for multicasting. Packets can be sent in directions where there are no hosts in the multicast group. Consequently, the broadcast tree with source S as the root must be pruned to eliminate such branches. Thus, the second component to DVMRP is a pruning algorithm that limits when a router forwards the messages.

Suppose a router gets a multicast packet. It starts by using RPB, and the initial multicast packets may go to locations do not require them. However, suppose a router gets a multicast packet but it is connected to a network that has no hosts in that multicast group. Remember, the IGMP protocol keeps the router up-to-date on who is in what group. In this case it sends a Prune message to the router from which it got the multicast message. When a router gets a Prune message associated with a multicast address, it stops multicasting in that direction. Figure 11.15a shows an example. Router A gets a multicast message from router B, but the network to which A is connected has no hosts in that group. A sends B the Prune message, and B no longer sends A multicast messages.

However, we oversimplified again! (It's getting to be a habit.) What if we have the situation of Figure 11.15b? Perhaps there are hosts past router C that *are* in the group. In that case router B must still send multicast packets to A. However, suppose that A receives a Prune packet from C and Prune packets from every other downstream router. In that case, there is no reason to send multicast packets in any of those directions, and A can send a Prune packet to B, asking B to stop sending such packets.

Figure 11.15 Pruning

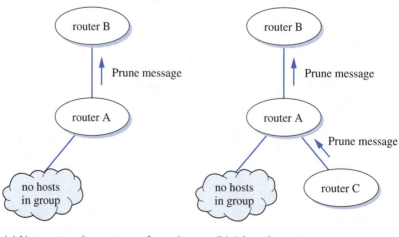

(a) No routers downstream from A   (b) A has downstream routers

What happens if A subsequently gets an IGMP message from a host indicating it is joining a group? (Won't these questions ever end?) Because A has pruned itself from the tree, it does not get multicast packets. However, A can send a Graft message to B indicating that B should resume sending multicast packets to A. (Yes, there is graft in computer science.)

Certainly, there are other issues and we, as usual, have just covered the basics. More details on multicast routing can be found in references [Ko98], [Gr02], and [Ha01]. In fact, multicast routing is even being developed for IP over LEO satellites (ref. [Ek02]).

RESOURCE RESERVATION PROTOCOL

One long-standing criticism of IP was that it did not meet the QoS needs of many newer applications. The process of updating routing tables and forwarding packets independently certainly allows the possibility that packets may arrive at variable rates. For file transfers, email, and Web surfing, that's no problem. However, applications such as multicasting live video feeds demand a QoS that defines a minimum bit rate. In turn, this means that packets must arrive at a minimum rate defined by the end user's needs.

Networks such as those in the telephone system rely on physical circuits to transfer voice data in real time. Chapter 13 will discuss Asynchronous Transfer Mode (ATM), a protocol that transfers data over virtual circuits (see Chapter 1). Both are similar in that prior to any exchange of data, there is a signaling process that establishes the circuit to be used. Once the circuit is defined, logic at each switch reserves what it needs to guarantee that it can receive and transmit data at rates quick enough to meet the QoS needs. IP does not do this.

In response, the IETF has developed a protocol, **Resource Reservation Protocol (RSVP),** that deals with QoS issues over the Internet. It's a protocol that embeds messages in IP packets. These messages contain information about a particular data flow and request that sufficient resources be reserved to meet a specified QoS. It may be used in a variety of situations, but we will describe it here in the context of a multicast to end users with different QoS needs.

Figure 11.16 defines our context. A video feed is connected to the network, and video data is to be routed to different end users. However, different users have different network connections that limit the rate at which they receive data. A has a low-speed connection that does not allow viewing of high-resolution video, whereas B has a high-speed connection that will. How can the sender send the data at both rates?

One approach to dealing with this problem is to transfer the video data in layers. This allows the sender to operate independent of the individual receiver's needs and abilities. A base layer could provide a simple, low-resolution video image. A second high-resolution layer would be used to enhance images created in the base layer. Of course, to do so requires a higher bit rate. User A could receive just the base layer at lower speeds, but user B could receive both layers at the high bit rate. Both users have a certain QoS need, and RSVP allows each of them to make requests of intermediate routers that will meet their needs.

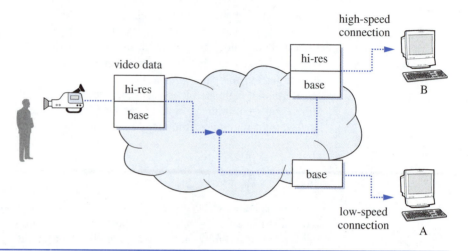

Figure 11.16   Receiving Live Video Feed at Different Rates

RSVP defines two types of messages that do this. These messages are embedded in IP packets that have a Protocol field value of 46. Routers that know RSVP can extract these messages and perform the proper actions. The first message is a Path message. The sender multicasts the Path message through the multicast tree to each receiver. When the Path message arrives at a router, it stores the address of the router from which the Path message came. This is used later when QoS requests are made. The Path message also contains a sender's Tspec (traffic specifier), a parameter that describes the traffic (for example, the bit rate) that the sender will be transmitting.

When a receiver gets the Path message, it initiates a QoS request by sending a Reserve message. The Reserve message first goes to the router that delivered the Path message. Each router, in turn, sends the Reserve message to the router that sent the previous Path message (recall, this information was stored when it got the Path message). In effect, the Reserve message is going upstream through the multicast tree.

The Reserve message contains information on the QoS the receiver expects—for example, the required bit rate. The router extracts this information and knows that it must be able to forward packets quickly enough to generate the needed bit rate. Consequently, it can reserve whatever resources are needed (perhaps buffer space) and modify its scheduling parameters so that the packets may be forwarded at the required rate. Such packets can be identified by the source and destination addresses and the value stored in the packet header's Type of Service field. RSVP does not specify how the routers do this; it only provides the required QoS needs. A router does what's needed depending on its design. The router then forwards the Reserve message to the upstream router in the multicast tree.

However, suppose a router receives several Reserve messages from downstream routers. If each specifies a different QoS for the same stream, then the router needs to send only one Reserve message to its upstream neighbor specifying the maximum rate needed. For example, suppose C and D (Figure 11.17) specify QoS

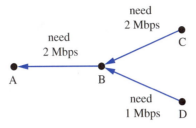

Figure 11.17   Merging Reserve Messages

needs of 1 and 2 Mbps to B. B must make sure it can meet the maximum of those needs, so it sends a Reserve message to A specifying a need of 2 Mbps.

The information in the Reserve message defines a *soft state* for the router. In contrast to a hard state (such as those defined for a virtual path), which must be explicitly changed, the soft state remains in effect only for a short time. After that time expires, the soft state disappears and the router returns to its default procedures. Thus, to maintain the soft state, the routers must receive Reserve messages periodically.

The soft state exists because routes can change in the Internet. A malfunctioning or congested router can cause routing protocols to update routing tables and divert traffic along a different route. When this happens, new routers must implement the QoS the receiver needs, and old routers should no longer reserve the required resources.

This discussion assumed only a single multicast, but of course there may be many multicasts from different sources. In addition, RSVP is not restricted to multicasts. Much more could be written about this protocol; reference [Fo03] has additional details.

INTERNET CONTROL MESSAGE PROTOCOL

Because IP does not guarantee reliable service, the **Internet Control Message Protocol (ICMP)** is used for reporting errors and for providing routers updates on conditions that can develop in the Internet. ICMP sends messages by encapsulating them in IP packets and setting the header's Protocol field to 1.

The following list explains some typical control messages sent by ICMP.

- **Destination Unreachable.** As we have stated previously, IP cannot guarantee delivery of a packet. The destination may not exist or it may be down, the sender may have made a source route request that cannot be carried out, or a packet with its Do Not Fragment bit set may be too large to be encapsulated in a frame. In such cases the router detecting the error sends an ICMP packet to the original sender. It contains the entire IP header of the undeliverable packet and the first 64 bits of its data, thus allowing the sender to recognize which packet was undeliverable.

- **Echo Request.** ICMP uses this packet to determine whether a particular destination is reachable. For example, if A wants to know whether B is reachable, it sends an Echo Request packet addressed to B. If B receives the packet, it responds by sending an Echo Reply packet back to A. The Echo Reply packet will return any data placed in the Echo Request packet. This may be simpler than committing a protocol to sending a whole series of packets to a destination only to find out it is unreachable.

- **Echo Reply.** Sent in response to an Echo Request. Users may be familiar with the `ping` utility, which uses the Echo Request/Reply combination. Users can enter `ping hostname` at a UNIX or DOS prompt to determine the reachability of a host. For example, entering `ping www.uwgb.edu -c 3` at a Linux prompt generated the following output:

```
PING weba.uwgb.edu (143.200.128.158) from 143.200.128.235
: 56(84) bytes of data.
64 bytes from weba.uwgb.edu (143.200.128.158): icmp_seq = 1
ttl = 128 time = 0.198 ms
64 bytes from weba.uwgb.edu (143.200.128.158): icmp_seq = 2
ttl = 128 time = 0.190 ms
64 bytes from weba.uwgb.edu (143.200.128.158): icmp_seq = 3
ttl = 128 time = 0.180 ms
```

Entering the `ping` command causes ICMP to send a sequence of Echo Request packets to the specified destination. The `-c 3` option specifies how many packets to send. The lines of output above represent the Echo Reply packets that are returned. The last value from each response indicates the length of the round trip.

- **Parameter Problem.** Suppose an IP packet contains an error or an illegal value in one of its header fields. A router discovering the error sends a Parameter Problem packet back to the source. This packet contains the IP header in question and a pointer to the header field that is in error.

- **Redirect.** Suppose a host station sends a packet to a router and the router knows the packet could have been delivered faster via some other router. To facilitate future routing, the router sends a Redirect packet back to the host. It informs the host where the other router is and that it should send future packets with the same destination to it. This allows the host to update its routing tables dynamically and to take advantage of changing conditions in the network. The Redirect packet is not used for router-to-router route updates because IP packets contain their source address but not the address of the most recent router that had them. When a router receives a packet from another router, it does not know which one sent it.

- **Source Quench.** If a router is receiving too many packets from a host, it can send a message requesting a reduction in the rate at which packets are sent.

- **Time Exceeded.** A Time Exceeded packet is sent when the Time to Live field in an IP packet reaches 0 or when the reassembly timer (set on receiving a packet's first fragment) expires. In either case, the packet or any unassembled fragments are dropped from the network. The guilty router then sends a Time Exceeded packet to the source indicating its packets were not delivered.

- **Timestamp Request and Reply.** Timestamp packets allow a host to estimate the time required for a round trip between it and another host. A host creates and sends a Timestamp Request packet containing the time of transmission (original timestamp). When the receiving host gets the packet, it creates a Timestamp Reply packet that contains the original timestamp, the time at which the receiving host got the packet (receive timestamp), and the time at which the receiving host sent the reply (transmit timestamp). When the original sender receives the reply, it records the time it arrived. The difference between the arrival time and the original timestamp is the time required for the round trip. By calculating the difference between the receive timestamp and transmit timestamp, the host can determine how long the other host took to respond once it got the request. By subtracting this from the round-trip time, the host can also estimate the transit time for both the request and the reply. Timestamp packets allow the host to estimate the network's efficiency in delivering packets.

- **Address Mask Request and Reply.** Previously, we mentioned subnets as a way of assigning the same IP network number to multiple physical networks. By using a few additional bits of the local ID part of an IP address, subnet numbers may be assigned to different physical networks. For example, a Class B site can manage eight separate physical networks by using 3 bits from the local ID to specify the physical network. These bits, together with the 16-bit IP network number, form the subnet number. To extract a subnet number from an IP address, an internal router uses a **subnet address mask** and performs a bitwise logical AND operation between it and the actual IP address. For example, suppose a host in the previously mentioned Class B site has an IP address of 143.200.123.78. What is the subnet number? In this case the address mask is 255.255.224.0, or

$$11111111.11111111.11100000.00000000$$

  (note the nineteen 1s because of the 16-bit IP network number and the 3 bits from the local ID). Next, do a bitwise logical AND between the mask and the IP address. The result is the 19-bit subnet number (followed by thirteen 0s), in this case 143.200.96.0. A host can send an Address Mask Request packet to a router to determine the address mask for the network to which it is attached. The router can respond with the reply.

- **Information Request and Reply.** These messages were originally designed to let a host determine its IP address when it started up. Other protocols typically do this now, and these two control messages have become obsolete.

11.3   IPv6

As we indicated at the beginning of this section, the Internet Protocol began in the late 1960s. In the field of computing, that's analogous to the Stone Age. We've stated previously that the Internet Protocol is showing signs of age; this section discusses IPv6, the heir apparent to the current Internet protocol (IPv4). Many often ask, "Was there an IPv5?" The answer is "yes, sort of." A protocol known as ST2

(Stream Protocol version 2) was developed as a connection-oriented protocol operating at layer 3. The intent was to develop a protocol for real-time data streams and to ensure that real-time packets were delivered by stated deadlines. Some saw ST2 as IPv4's successor and referred to it as IPv5. However, the development of RSVP (described earlier) dealt with real-time QoS issues, and IPv5 was subsequently dropped.

IP SHORTCOMINGS

The original purpose of the Internet was to connect computers and exchange data. Consequently, protocols were developed to accomplish this primary goal. The problem is that connecting computers will not be the only goal of a global network in the future and therefore different protocols must emerge to meet these new goals. Just as the personal computer was the phenomenon of the 1980s, multimedia and video applications are and will be the phenomena of the 1990s and the early 21st century. Entertainment and digital technology continue to blend together to create new demands on global networks. Pay-per-view service is already available on cable systems, and video on demand is becoming available. Growing numbers of people are already enjoying real-time video games over the Internet.

Mobility is another development. In the current Internet, the vast majority of host computers never change locations. They may move from one office to another, but that's a problem for local management. From the Internet Protocol's perspective they remain in fixed locations. However, this is changing. Mobile computers and satellite technology are providing the means for any two devices to communicate from anywhere in the world. The protocols must evolve to allow millions of pairs of devices to make connections from arbitrary locations.

Some see current technologies such as cell phones, pagers, PDAs, and portable computers eventually merging into a personal communication device that serves a variety of needs. Making telephone calls or being paged are obvious ones, but many see the day when such a device can do many other tasks. Homes may be equipped with computerized devices with which you can communicate. If you are getting home later than you planned, you might use a personal communication device to turn on the lights at home or start the oven. A sensor system might send a signal to you if you left without locking all the doors or turning off the lights, which, of course, you could correct using the same system. You would be able to plug the device into a portable computer and download files from any other remote computer to which you had access, all without benefit of a telephone. You might even use the system to feed your cyberpet that you left at home. All of these applications will require site-independent communications.

Security is another issue. The Internet Protocol isn't particularly secure. This is why passwords, authentication techniques, and firewalls are so important to many applications. People recognize that packets arriving on the Internet can come from virtually anywhere and that strong measures are necessary to protect their resources. The past years have seen enough examples of fraud and hacking into private computers to suggest that security will always be a concern.

Despite all of this, there is one overriding goal when developing any new protocols: the ability to coexist with current systems. The biggest impediment to any emerging technology in computing is making sure it runs concurrently with existing technologies. Then over a period of years, applications can gradually migrate from the old to the new. On a global scale there is just no other way.

People have been thinking about these ideas for many years, and the concepts are certainly not new. In 1991, the Internet Engineering Task Force (IETF) began looking at the issue of changing the existing IP and creating a next-generation IP informally referred to as IPng (IP Next Generation). In an attempt to get the computing community involved, they invited various professionals (researchers, manufacturers, vendors, programmers, etc.) to submit proposals. An appointed committee called the IPng Directorate evaluated the proposals and rejected many because they served special interests or were just too complex. However, one proposal included a design called Simple Internet Protocol (SIP) (ref. [De93]), which was extended to use ideas described in other proposals. The resulting protocol was named Simple Internet Protocol Plus (SIPP).

In 1994 the IETF met in Toronto and, based on the recommendations of the IPng Directorate, selected SIPP as the basis for the next-generation Internet Protocol, which would be formally known as **IPv6 (IP version 6).** The Internet Engineering Steering Group approved it later in the year and entered the protocols into the IETF standard process the following year. We will provide an outline of IPv6; the reader is encouraged to locate references [Hi96], [St96], [Br95], and [Co00] for additional detail.

PACKET HEADERS

We begin discussion of IPv6 by examining the packet header format. This gives us a framework in which to explain some of the options IPv6 provides and how they differ from the current version of the Internet Protocol. Figure 11.18 shows the IPv6 packet header. On comparison with the IPv4 packet of Figure 11.5, two things are immediately evident. The IPv6 addresses have more bits, and the header format has fewer options. The latter may seem to contradict the goal of providing additional capabilities, but it doesn't, as we will soon see.

Figure 11.18   IPv6 Packet Header

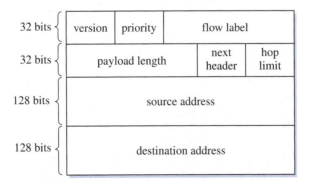

The *Version field* has 4 bits and identifies which version of IP this packet represents (value 4 for the current IP and 6 for the new one).

The *Priority field* also has 4 bits and is particularly useful in congestion control. The concept of priority is simple: Higher values indicate more important packets. It is how priorities are used that is significant. We have already discussed congestion and some ways to deal with it. IPv6 recognizes that delays in some applications such as email are often not noticeable, whereas delays in others such as multimedia applications render viewing next to impossible. The trick is identifying which packets correspond to which applications.

A site sending out IP packets can use this field to indicate importance relative to other packets the site sends. Priority values between 0 and 7, inclusive, correspond to packets that the site may hold a little longer in response to congestion. IPv6 recommends values depending on the application. For example, email has a priority of 2, FTP and HTTP have a priority of 4, Telnet has a priority of 6, and SNMP has a priority of 7. As you can see, the higher values correspond to applications for which delays are typically more noticeable. Values above 7 correspond to real-time or multimedia applications, cases where delays range from very inconvenient to unacceptable. For example, downloading sound or video files for real-time viewing requires little or no delay. (Of course, if delays could somehow be synchronized with one's need for snack breaks, then they could be tolerated.)

The 24-bit *Flow Label field* is used in conjunction with the Priority field. The idea is to identify packets that require "special handling" by routers. Normal handling requires routers to search routing tables before forwarding packets. Since tables change over time, packets with the same destination can travel different routes.

IPv6 defines a *flow* as a sequence of packets sent by a source to a single destination in response to some application. If they are packets designed to provide real-time viewing at the destination, special handling might mean to route them all the same way (and quickly) to guarantee they arrive in order. In fact, it is much like a virtual circuit. To set up a flow, the source generates a random nonzero number and stores it in the Flow Label field of each packet in that flow. A router applies a hash function to that flow number to calculate a location that contains information on how the packet should be handled. Instructions on the special handling would be set up prior to the flow. The router uses a hash function because it is generally the quickest way to find something. Random numbers are used because they result in fewer collisions when subjected to hash functions. Often, the bottom line is for the router to get the packet out as quickly as possible.

The 16-bit *Payload Length field* is the number of bytes in the packet minus 40. Since the header is 40 bytes, this field specifies how many significant bytes follow it. Do not interpret this to mean that the payload length is the number of data bytes. If there were just one header that would be true, but other headers may follow the first one.

The *Hop Limit field* is essentially the same as the Time to Live field in the IPv4 packet.

This brings us to the 8-bit *Next Header field,* an important distinction from IPv4. The current IPv4 packet header contains Options and Protocol fields to indicate when routers should take different actions. Because different options are embedded in the field of that name, each router has to parse through each packet header (specifically, the Option field) to determine whether there are options that will affect its decisions. This means additional logic and time at each router and slows the routing process.

To allow the existence of different options, IPv6 has an *extension header,* an additional header between the header of Figure 11.18 and the packet's payload (data). Each extension header also has a Next Header field that specifies the type of extension header that follows (if any). This allows several extension headers to lie between the original header and the packet payload, each indicating a different option. If there are no extension headers, then, like the Protocol field of the IPv4 header, the Next Header field specifies the transport protocol (e.g., TCP or UDP) using IPv6. Perhaps the most significant aspect of this arrangement is that some of the extension headers will be ignored by routers. Routers will therefore be able to forward packets more quickly.

The contents and format of each extension header depend on its type. At present there are six types:

- **Destination options header.** This provides information for the destination. It is not used during routing.

- **Fragmentation header.** This header provides information in the event that packet fragments must be reassembled. As such, the header contains items such as a fragment offset, a Last Fragment bit, and an identifier that is unique to the original packet. It is very similar to the fragmentation and reassembly process of IPv4. There is one significant departure from IPv4 fragmentation, however. Intermediate IPv4 routers were able to fragment an incoming packet if it was too large. IPv6 will not fragment a packet at an intermediate router. This is important because it simplifies the router logic and contributes to more efficient and quicker routing. Of course, a logical question to ask is: What happens if a router gets a packet that is too big to send over the next network? In this case, the router just throws the packet away and sends a message (via ICMP) back to the source. That message indicates that the packet was too big and specifies the maximum allowable size. The source will fragment the packet and send the fragments, each of which includes a fragmentation header. The destination will reassemble them.

- **Hop-by-hop header.** This header, if present, must be examined by each router. The idea is to specify any information that each router should have. There are a couple of options. Since the Payload Length field is 16 bits, the maximum packet size is 64 KB. This header allows *jumbo packets,* packets that exceed 64 KB in size. This is useful for transferring large amounts of data such as may be contained in a video stream. Another option is to facilitate the RSVP protocol, where packets contain information regarding bandwidth reservation that each router must process.

- **Routing header.** This provides additional routing information, such as IPv4's Loose Route option. That is, this extension header will contain the 128-bit addresses of routers through which this packet must travel.

- **Security header.** This indicates that the packet's payload has been encrypted.
- **Authentication header.** This provides for packet authentication and is used by IPSec, a security protocol at the packet level.

IPSEC

A long-standing criticism of the Internet was that it provided no security. Any security measures typically had to be implemented at higher layers and negotiated prior to any exchange of information. In response, the IETF developed **IPSec,** a protocol designed to provide secure transmission at the packet level. IPSec runs directly above IP but below any layer 4 transport protocol such as TCP. Thus, any IPSec security measures are transparent to layer 4 protocols and above.

There is an advantage to implementing security and authentication at this level. For example, suppose an application relies on SSL or TLS for authentication. At layer 4, assume that TCP exchanges segments using flow control mechanisms (it does, and we'll describe them soon). An intruder might send a bogus TCP segment into the segment stream. If the TCP segment has a valid sequence number, TCP will accept it and pass it to SSL or TLS for verification. If indeed the segment was forged, the security layer detects it. However, TCP is now looking for the next TCP segment. When the real segment arrives, TCP rejects it. If authentication occurs at a lower layer, this does not happen.

IPSec has three main components: an authentication header (AH) to provide packet authentication, an Encapsulating Security Payload (ESP) to provide packet encryption and authentication, and a key exchange protocol. This allows the use of different combinations of authentication, encryption, and key-exchange services. A specific combination along with a destination address defines a *security association* and defines the manner in which secure information is transmitted and to whom it is transmitted.

The AH may exist as one of the IPv6 extension headers or it may follow an IPv4 header. In this last case, the IPv4 header's Protocol field contains a 51 to indicate the presence of an AH. The AH contains the following fields:

- **Security Parameter Index (SPI).** This field contains a code that, along with the destination address, defines a security association. Using different SPIs allows flexibility in choosing among several security and authentication options.
- **Sequence number.** Every packet has a unique sequence number for a given SPI. The purpose is similar to that described in Chapter 8—do not accept redundant packets. This is essentially flow control for packets with a given SPI value. However, it's used for a different reason: to prevent **replay attacks.** This is when an eavesdropper observes traffic and copies packets **(packet sniffing)** that are in transit (Figure 11.19a). If those packets were sent to open a connection or provide access to some service, then resending (Figure 11.19b) allows the eavesdropper to do the same thing while bypassing normal protocols. For example, the packets might contain a user name and password sent to log in to a remote system or provide access to personal data. The eavesdropper might then try to mimic the same action later by resending the packets to get

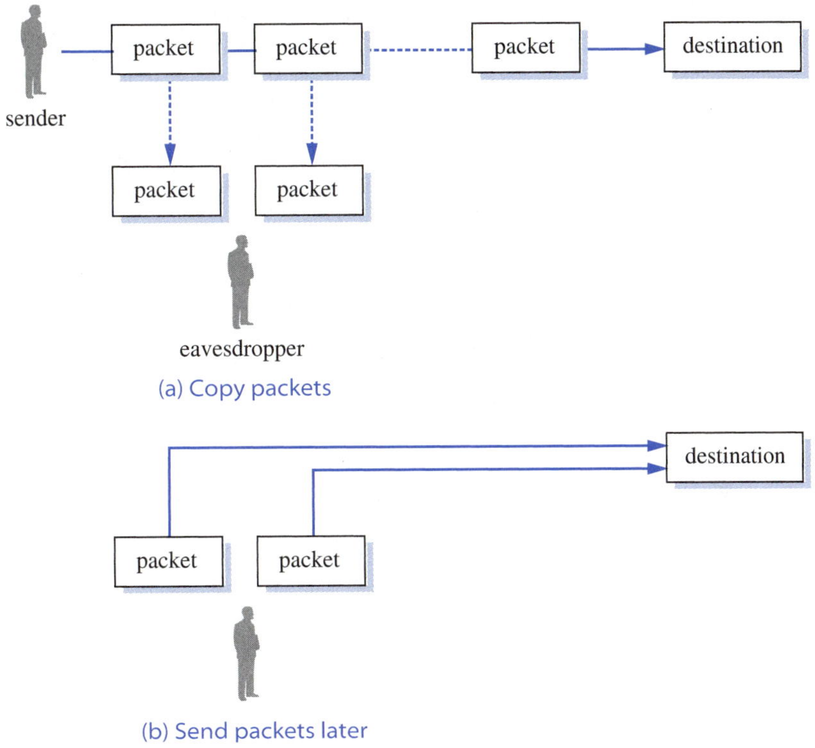

(a) Copy packets

(b) Send packets later

Figure 11.19 Replay Attack

access. If the packets are sequenced within an SPI, then any resent packets contain duplicate sequence numbers and are rejected. Of course, the perpetrator may simply try different sequence numbers, but this would be detected by the authentication mechanisms.

• **Authentication Data.** This field contains a hash value that is calculated dependent on the packet's headers and contents. Exempt from this calculation are any header fields whose contents may change during routing. Examples include IPv4's Time to Live field, checksums, and flow labels.

The ESP performs the same service as the AH but also provides confidentiality by encrypting the data. Like the AH, it may exist as an IPv6 extension header or follow the IPv4 header. It also contains an SPI, sequence number, and Authentication Data field. In addition, it contains a Payload Data field that has the encrypted data. The encryption method and key are defined by the security association and, hence, by the SPI. There is also a Pad field, because many encryption algorithms are block ciphers and require an integral number of blocks. The Pad field is used if the last of the data does not fill an entire block.

IPSec key management consists of a couple of parts and has evolved from its original incarnation. The first is the **Internet Security Association and Key Management Protocol (ISAKMP).** It does not define the actual methods used in key exchange but instead defines packet formats and the rules for exchanging packets containing key information. One key exchange algorithm that was developed for use with ISAKMP is the Oakley Key Management Protocol. Oakley is based on Diffie-Hellman but includes some authentication protocols prior to the key exchange. More recently, Oakley has evolved into the *Internet Key Exchange* (IKE) mechanism. IKE uses public or private keys to authenticate and generate session keys. The session keys are then used to encrypt the contents of the packets. Chapter 7 devoted a lot of attention to such activities and we will not go through them again. However, the interested reader can find further detail and an analysis of IKE in reference [Pe00].

IPv6 ADDRESSING

The last two fields in an IPv6 packet header are the source and destination addresses, which are self-explanatory. What is not self-explanatory are the types of addresses IPv6 defines and some issues regarding compatibility with IPv4 addressing. The most obvious difference from IPv4 is that IPv6 addresses are 128 bits, four times as long as IPv4 addresses. In theory this allows for $2^{128} \cong 10^{40}$ different addresses. One of the problems with exponential notation is that it is often difficult to understand just how large a number is. To help understand how large 2^{128} is, reference [Hi96] made some calculations and showed that if all the addresses were spread out evenly across the surface of the entire earth then there would be about 10^{24} addresses for each square meter of the earth's surface, more than enough for each person, earthworm, and insect that populates the planet. (There might even be a few left over for some viruses or bacteria.)

The three general classifications of addresses are unicast, anycast, and multicast. A *unicast address* specifies a unique interface. There are several types of unicast addresses, which we will discuss shortly. An *anycast address* specifies a group of interfaces. A packet with an anycast destination address may be delivered to any one in the group (usually the one closest to the source). A *multicast address* also specifies a group, but in this case the packet goes to each interface in the group.

Notation for 128-bit addresses differs from that used in IPv4. Using the current notation in which dots separate three-digit numbers would result in a notation containing 16 three-digit numbers separated by dots. Naturally, this becomes somewhat unwieldy. Instead, colons replace dots, and each 16 bits in an address has a four-digit hexadecimal number notation. An example IPv6 address has the form

7477:0000:0000:0000:0000:0AFF:1BDF:7FFF

Each hexadecimal digit in this representation has a unique 4-bit equivalent. The result is still unwieldy but better than the alternative.

For addresses that contain a lot of 0s (and with 2^{128} addresses, a lot of them will), a shorthand notation is used. Essentially, the 0s are not listed, and a double colon (::) indicates their presence. The actual number of 0s that are missing is calculated by subtracting the number of hexadecimal digits in the notation from 32, the number of hexadecimal digits needed for a full 128-bit representation. For example, the previous address would be written as

7477:: 0AFF:1BDF:7FFF

Since this notation contains 16 digits, we know there must be 16 missing 0s. In cases where the 0 string begins the address, the notation starts with the double colon. In other words, the address

0000:0000:0000:0000:0AFF:1BDF:000F:0077

could also be written as

:: 0AFF:1BDF:000F:0077

To further simplify addresses, leading 0s within a four-digit group need not be listed. This allows us to simplify this address's notation as follows:

::AFF:1BDF:F:77

Just as IPv4 divides its addresses into different classes depending on the leading bits, so IPv6 does something similar. There are currently 22 types of addresses, each having a unique bit prefix. The prefixes range from 3 to 10 bits. For example, an address beginning with eight 0s corresponds to an IPv4 address. (Actually, IPv4 addresses begin with many more 0s, but more about that later.) Those beginning with eight 1s are multicast addresses. Those starting with 0000 010 are compatible with Novell's IPX protocol. Most of the predefined prefixes have not been assigned and are being reserved for future growth. This leaves about 85% of the addresses reserved for the future.

Of particular interest are the unicast addresses, which are the most analogous to IPv4 addresses. Figure 11.20 shows the format of a unicast address. Like an IPv4 address, there is an implied hierarchy; it is just more complex. The first three bits of a unicast address are 010. The remaining bits define a five-level hierarchy. The example topology of Figure 11.21 illustrates how the hierarchy can be organized.

In general, an **Internet service provider (ISP)** contracts with customers to provide access to the Internet. The customers for a particular provider may all be connected through some regional network spanning a city, county, or several counties, depending on the population base. In some cases, the customers might be large companies or universities that have their own internal hierarchical structure. As Section 10.7 discussed, they may divide their network into subnets, each having a

Figure 11.20   Unicast Address Format

010	registry	provider	subscriber	subnet	interface

◄——————— 128-bit address ———————►

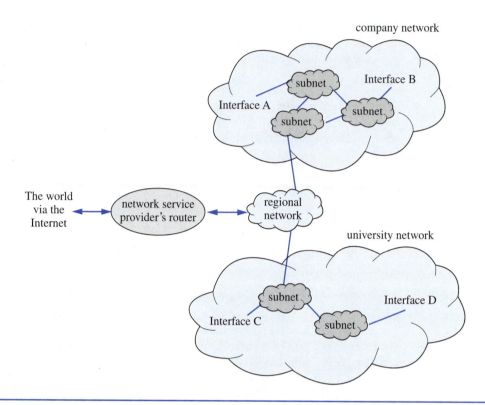

Figure 11.21   IPv6 Organization

unique identifier. These subnets would then provide eventual access to the people who use the services.

Since there are many ISPs, part of the address of Figure 11.20 identifies the provider. Thus, routing done to find the correct provider is done independent of the provider's customers. The provider then assigns subscriber IDs to its customers. Some large companies may define their own subnets. Each would have its own subnet number, and the full IPv6 addresses of each subnet would contain the same subscriber number. Finally, the subnets connect users. Each user on the same subnet has a different interface ID, but they all have the same subnet, subscriber, and provider IDs. All of this is really just an extension of the hierarchical routing strategies discussed in Section 10.7.

Finally, the *registry ID* in Figure 11.20 accounts for international or continental borders. A Canadian registry maintains a list of authorized providers in Canada. Similar registries exist in the United States, Europe, and so on. Thus, the registry ID is at the top level in the hierarchy and allows for some routing decisions to be made based on geography. This would help packets sent from Canada to the United States to avoid European routers.

COMPATIBILITY WITH IPv4

There are many millions of computers communicating using IPv4. Such a large number prohibits any possibility of converting to IPv6 overnight or during a weekend. The coordination difficulty, inevitable problems, and costs make this scenario impossible. Upgrading the world's computers to IPv6 will require many years because individual sites must define their own timetables for implementation. Consequently, both IPv4 and IPv6 routers must be able to coexist and maintain all necessary connections. IPv6 protocols are designed to recognize IPv4 protocols. On the other hand, IPv4 protocols were designed well before IPv6 and have no knowledge of it. This presents some problems that must be solved.

To help solve these problems, the IPv6 address structure allows IPv4 address types. Figure 11.22 shows two ways to put an IPv4 address into an IPv6 address structure. Since the IPv6 addresses are larger than IPv4 ones, it is not terribly difficult to find a way to store IPv4 addresses. The tricky part is to make the two protocols work together. Figure 11.22a shows an IPv4-mapped address. Suppose a packet must go through a network of IPv6 routers to get to an IPv4 destination. One option is for the routers to revert to IPv4 whenever the destination is an IPv4 node. Since the purpose of IPv6 was to improve on IPv4, that's not a good option.

If routers run IPv6, how will they know the address is that of an IPv4 node and that they should not interpret it according to the IPv6 hierarchy? Again, this is where the address type comes in. The eighty 0s and sixteen 1s designate an IPv4 address. Consequently, routers interpret addresses according to IPv4 rules as opposed to those suggested by Figure 11.20.

What about the reverse problem? Suppose two IPv6 routers need to exchange packets but the only route is through a network of IPv4 routers (Figure 11.23a). Since IPv6 addresses contain information not storable in an IPv4 packet, we seem to have a real problem here. Fortunately, there is a real solution: **tunneling.** For example, suppose A, B, C, and D in Figure 11.23a all speak IPv6 and A wants to send

Figure 11.22 IPv4 Addresses in an IPv6 Format

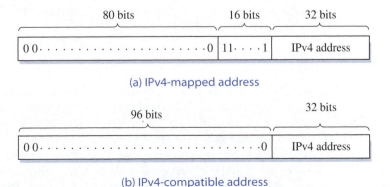

(a) IPv4-mapped address

(b) IPv4-compatible address

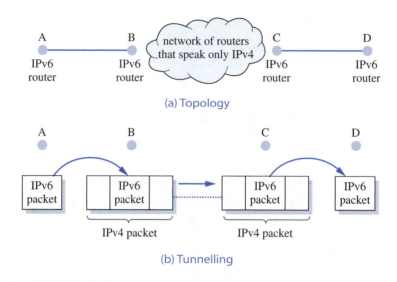

Figure 11.23   Routing IPv6 Packets over IPv4 Networks

a packet to D. Unfortunately, the only way to go from B to C is through a network of nodes that speak only IPv4. Since D's address is 128 bits, how can we push that packet through a network that has no concept of a 128-bit address?

When B gets the IPv6 packet from A, it embeds it into an IPv4 packet (Figure 11.23b) containing destination C. IPv4 protocols do what is necessary to get the IPv4 packet from B to C. When C gets the packet, it extracts the IPv6 packet from the IPv4 packet. IPv6 routing is effectively resumed when C sends the packet to D. From the perspective of IPv4, routing in this network is no different from what we have discussed before. From the perspective of IPv6, there was a single link from B to C (i.e., a *tunnel*).

Now, if you are following the details you might have one remaining question: If C is an IPv6 router, how do we get its address into the IPv4 packet? Again, this is part of the transition. Any node that is on either end of a tunnel is assigned an IPv4-compatible address as in Figure 11.22b in addition to its IPv6 address. Consequently, it is easily stored in an IPv4 packet header.

SUMMARY

IPv6 performs the same primary functions as IPv4, providing a connectionless routing capability. However, it has added capabilities such as authentication and encryption not available in IPv4. It also increases the address space dramatically and simplifies the headers to make routing more efficient. Other factors also contribute to more efficient routing with IPv6. Intermediate nodes no longer fragment and reassemble packets. There is no error detection (checksum) capability in IPv6, unlike IPv4, thus relieving routers of another time-consuming task. Removing the checksum is really no loss. Most networks are very reliable. Besides, lower-level data link protocols and, as we'll see, higher-layer protocols have error detection methods.

11.4 TRANSPORT PROTOCOLS

So far we have primarily dealt with network operations. Frame formats, routing, congestion control, and addressing are all essential to allowing one device to talk to another. But *how* they talk with each other is equally important. A *transport protocol* is the lowest-layer protocol that defines what one device can say to another on behalf of the user. The lower three layers define how a network operates; the transport layer is the first to define the end-user protocol.

There are similarities with the data link protocols we discussed previously in that we are focusing on how information is exchanged between two entities. However, data link protocols defined communications between devices with a physical connection. Connection-oriented transport protocols define communications between sites with a logical connection, often over long distances. There are also connectionless transport protocols, but for now we'll just consider a connection-oriented protocol.

The transport layer also provides the "connection" the user perceives. For example, users can log on to computers at remote sites, giving them the impression they are connected. But the connection is not a physical one as exists when connecting wires or making telephone calls. There is not necessarily a dedicated circuit devoted to transmitting information between the user and computer.

The transport layer can provide the perception of a connection by acting as an interface between the user and network protocols. It is similar to a secretary whose function is to place calls on behalf of an executive. The secretary gets the executive's request, makes the call, and reaches the desired person, thus making the connection. The executive then proceeds to have the conversation independent of any trouble the secretary may have had in finding the desired person, who may have been in an important meeting, out to lunch, or on the racquetball court. When the executive has finished talking, the secretary may end the connection by getting additional important information such as a client's address, phone number, or racquetball court location.

A transport protocol does more than make and break connections, however. The lowest three layers provide the means to connect separate devices, but the transport layer is the lowest layer that actually allows its users to communicate effectively and securely. Some transport layer functions are as follows:

- **Connection management.** This function defines the rules that allow two users to begin talking with one another as if they were connected directly. Defining and setting up the connection is also called **handshaking.**

- **Flow control.** The transport layer limits how much information one station can send to another without receiving some acknowledgment. If this sounds familiar, great! You are remembering some of the information from previous chapters. In Chapter 8 we discussed flow control and its relevance to the data link layer. To have flow control again in the transport layer may seem strange at first, but remember that the transport layer must operate independently of the lower layers. Lower layers may allow more or less (or no) flow control. To preserve independence, a transport layer may use its own flow control. It may seem redundant, but independence often introduces redundancy. Furthermore, the transport layer defines flow control between the end users. Data link protocols define flow control between two intermediate, but adjacent, entities.

- **Error detection.** This is another case that seems to duplicate lower-layer features. Some errors, however, escape lower-layer error detection. This statement seems unusual because it means that even if data link error detection provides reliable transmission along each link, there is still no guarantee of error-free transmission between the source and destination. How can this be? Consider the router in Figure 11.24 (taken from Figure 11.2). Suppose it receives the IP packet intact, but an error that affects the packet's contents occurs during reformatting of the frame containing the packet. Any number of software or hardware errors can cause such a problem. Because the checksum is calculated after the new frame is created, it includes the erroneous data. Strictly speaking, it is not a transmission error because it occurred while the packet was in the possession of the router. But try telling that to the transport user, who saw his or her data changed while in transit. A transport layer error detection mechanism would detect this error.

- **Response to users' requests.** Examples include sending and receiving data, as well as specific requests. For example, a user may request high throughput, low delays, or reliable service. As discussed in the previous section, the IP can deal with these. The transport layer passes the request from the user to the IP.

To summarize, a transport protocol must provide reliable communications between end users. This is especially important because IP does not guarantee reliable service. Transport protocols must provide acknowledgments and timers to make sure all of a user's data is sent and received. As with error detection, lower-layer protocols

Figure 11.24   Error Undetected by Lower-Layer Detection Techniques

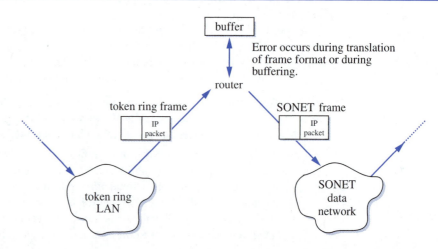

can determine when frames are lost in transit. But again, we want reliability to exist independent of lower layers. Besides, suppose an intermediate network node lost a frame after it received and acknowledged it but before it retransmitted the frame. As mentioned earlier, any number of on-site errors could cause this. Because there was no error in any point-to-point link, it would be up to an end-to-end protocol to detect the error.

TRANSMISSION CONTROL PROTOCOL

Two transport layer protocols that the DoD designed specifically to run with its ARPANET IP are the Transmission Control Protocol (TCP) and the User Datagram Protocol (UDP). TCP is a connection-oriented protocol that forms the connection management facilities of the Internet. It is the most widely used transport layer protocol in the world. UDP is a connectionless transport layer protocol. It is perhaps not used as extensively as TCP, but it does provide a transport facility for important applications such as DNS (discussed in the previous section) and SNMP (discussed in the next section). The rest of this section focuses on TCP and then discusses UDP. To be complete, we must mention that the ISO also has defined its own layer 4 transport protocol. The Internet and TCP are such dominant forces in defining connections, however, that the DoD TCP is likely to be around for a long time.

TCP provides a connection-oriented user-to-user byte stream service. This means it provides a logical connection between two sites and is capable of transmitting a sequence of bytes between them. It divides a byte steam into a sequence of segments and sends them to the destination via a variation on a sliding window flow control protocol. It provides the initial handshaking by establishing, maintaining, and releasing connections. It handles requests to deliver information to a destination reliably, an important consideration since the lower layer (usually IP) does not guarantee delivery of packets. TCP receives data or requests from its user (Figure 11.25),

Figure 11.25   TCP as a User-to-User Service

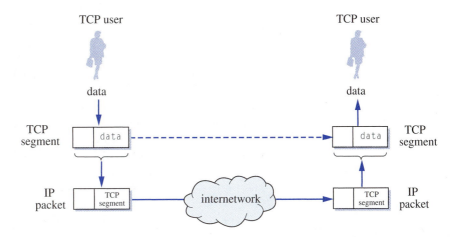

stores it in a *TCP segment* format, and gives it to the IP. It plays no role in the subsequent routing and transfer of information. The receiver's TCP gets a segment, responds to the information in it, extracts the data, and gives it to the user. From TCP's perspective, there is no network.

TCP SEGMENT

Figure 11.26 shows the contents of a TCP segment. The following list defines the fields.

- **Destination port** (16 bits). Identifies the application to which the segment is sent. This is different from the IP address, which specifies an Internet address. Since many applications can run at the same Internet node, this field identifies which application is desired. In general, TCP examines all the segments that arrive and separates (demultiplexes) them according to port number. Information in segments with the same port number is transferred to the same application. At the sending end, TCP acts as a multiplexer, taking information from different applications, creating segments for each (with appropriate port numbers), and sending them to IP for eventual routing. Port numbers below 1024 are called **well-known ports.** They are assigned by IANA and correspond to commonly used applications. For example, port 53 corresponds to a DNS name server, and ports 21 and 23 are assigned to FTP and Telnet, respectively. IANA lists ports numbered from 1024 through 49151 as registered ports. They can be used by programs run by ordinary users. As a convenience to the Internet community, IANA has already assigned many ports in this range; however, there are still many that are not assigned that people can use freely. Chapter 12

Figure 11.26   TCP Segment

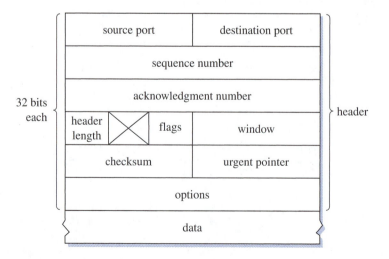

will show you how you can define your own ports to define communications between applications running at different sites. A complete list of port numbers and their assignments can be found at www.iana.org/assignments/port-numbers.

- **Source port** (16 bits). Specifies the application sending the segment.

- **Sequence number** (32 bits). Each byte in the stream that TCP sends is numbered. For example, if each data segment contained 1000 data bytes, the sequence numbers of the first bytes in consecutive segments would be x, $x + 1000$, $x + 2000$, and so on, where x is the sequence number of the first byte.* If the segment contains data, this field contains the sequence number of the segment's first data byte. In contrast to other protocols that number each packet or frame consecutively, TCP numbers the bytes. TCP also uses this field as part of the initial call connection strategy (discussed shortly). Using 32 bits allows sequence numbers up to about 4 billion. This is significant because the chances for duplicate sequence numbers are all but eliminated. In turn, this relaxes the constraints on window sizes discussed in Chapter 8 that were needed to avoid protocol errors.

- **Acknowledgment number** (32 bits). Contains the byte sequence number the receiving TCP entity expects to receive. Effectively, it acknowledges receiving all bytes prior to the one specified. This is similar to acknowledgments discussed in Chapter 8, except that here the protocol is acknowledging bytes, not packets.

- **Header length** (4 bits). Specifies the size of the TCP header as a multiple of 4 bytes. Header length can vary because of the variable-length Options field, discussed shortly, and this field allows the receiving TCP protocol to know where the data starts.

- **Flags** (6 bits). The Flag field specifies when other fields contain meaningful data or specify certain control functions. For example, two of the flags, ACK and URG (sounds like prehistoric sibling names), specify whether the Acknowledgment and Urgent Pointer fields (discussed shortly) contain meaningful data. Four other flags are as follows:

  FIN (finish): Indicates the last TCP data segment.

  PSH (push): Ordinarily, TCP decides when a segment contains enough data to warrant its transmission. In some cases an application can force TCP to send a segment earlier by issuing a Push command. For example, an interactive application might issue a Push after a user has entered a line from a keyboard. This provides a better and smoother response than allowing TCP to buffer several lines of input before sending any of them. When TCP receives a Push command, it sets the PSH field in the segment. When the PSH field is set in an incoming segment, the receiving TCP entity makes the segment's contents available to its

---

* The initial sequence number is not necessarily 1 and is negotiated when the connection is established. We discuss this in the section on connection management.

application immediately. If the application is for displaying incoming data on a video screen, this mechanism provides a quick and smooth display.

RST (reset): Indication from the sending entity that the receiving entity should break the transport connection. Used when an abnormal condition occurs, it allows both entities to terminate the connection, stop the flow of data, and release buffer space associated with the connection.

SYN (synchronize): Used in the initial connection setup, it allows the two entities to synchronize (agree on) initial sequence numbers (discussed shortly).

- **Window** (16 bits). This field tells the TCP entity that receives this segment how many more data bytes it can send beyond those that have already been acknowledged. As we will discuss shortly, this corresponds roughly to the window size of a sliding window protocol. It differs from protocols we have discussed in that a TCP entity receiving a byte stream can use this field to change the size of the window on the sending end.

- **Checksum** (16 bits). Used for transport layer error detection. The checksum algorithm interprets the contents of the TCP segment as a sequence of 16-bit integers and sums them. This is not as strong an error detection algorithm as others we have discussed in Chapter 6 and has generated some criticism.

- **Urgent Pointer** (16 bits). If the URG bit is set, the segment contains urgent data, meaning the receiving TCP entity must deliver it to the higher layers as quickly as possible. Urgent data is at the beginning of the segment, and the urgent pointer points to the first byte following the urgent data. This allows the receiving entity to distinguish urgent data from nonurgent data. Some have criticized the Urgent Pointer field as a weak implementation of urgency. True, the Urgent field generates special handling once the segment has been received, but it does not affect the flow control responsible for getting the segment there in the first place. It's a little like standing in a long line at a bank teller's window and then demanding to speak to the president once you get to the teller's window.

- **Options** (variable size). One option allows a TCP entity to specify the maximum segment size it will receive from the other entity. This value typically is specified during the initial connection setup. It is an important option because TCP may connect two computers with very different capabilities. Successful communication requires that each be aware of any limitations (such as buffer size) the other has. For example, a large mainframe would not want to overwhelm a small personal computer with segments that are too large. The personal computer would establish the maximum segment it can receive when it establishes the connection. Because the header size is a multiple of 4 bytes, the Options field is padded to make sure the header ends on a 32-bit boundary.

    Another option allows the TCP entities to agree on a 32-bit window field instead of a 16-bit one. This is particularly useful when high-bandwidth lines are used to transfer large files. A 16-bit window never allows a sending protocol to have a window larger than $2^{16} = 64$ KB.

- **Data** (variable size). User-supplied data.

CONNECTION MANAGEMENT

Connection management is the process of establishing, maintaining, and ending a connection. But what exactly is a connection? As indicated previously, a connection is more virtual than physical. (Isn't everything these days?) Basically, two TCP entities agree to exchange TCP segments and establish some parameters describing the segment exchange. Typical parameters describe the sequence numbers used for bytes and the number of bytes an entity can receive. The entities then send each other segments and do error checking, acknowledging, and flow control as if they were connected directly, leaving transmission details to the lower layers.

To begin, the two entities must agree to establish a connection. Initially, this seems straightforward: One entity makes a request to connect and the other says OK. This is a **two-way handshake.** However, it can cause problems if the first request is delayed and subsequently shows up at a much later time, thus causing an unintentional second connection.

For example, consider the timing shown in Figure 11.27. At time t_1, user A requests a connection. However, for some reason, perhaps network congestion or a problem at an intermediate site, the request is delayed. User A, thinking the message is lost, makes another connection request at time t_2. User B receives the second

Figure 11.27   Failure of a Two-Way Handshake Protocol

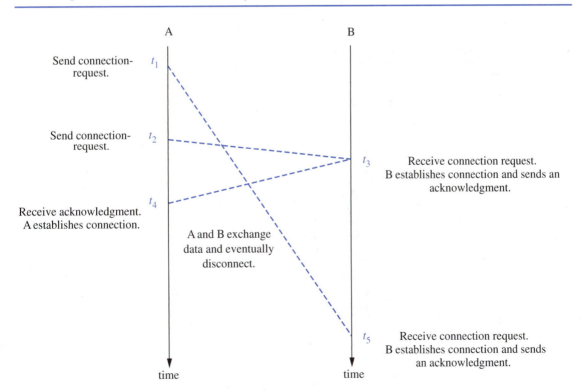

request at time t_3 and promptly acknowledges it. User A receives the acknowledgment at time t_4, and the connection is made. No problem so far.

Users A and B do whatever they are supposed to do and eventually disconnect. However, the first connection request is still floating around somewhere. Suppose it finally arrives at user B at time t_5. User B thinks it is another request and acknowledges it. As far as B is concerned there is another connection, but this time it is unintentional. Worse yet, consider what could happen if user A sent some data during the first connection that was seriously delayed. Not receiving an acknowledgment, user A would have retransmitted it. But the first request is still somewhere in the network. What happens if B finally gets it after time t_5? User B thinks it is another data segment and responds to it. How serious is this problem? Imagine if the connections were private ones to Swiss banks, and the data segments requested deposits of $5 million. Bank officials will not be happy paying interest on a bogus $5 million deposit.

More is involved than simply sending connection requests and acknowledgments. We mentioned earlier that TCP treats data as a sequence of bytes to be divided and sent in segments. Rather than numbering each segment, TCP stores the sequence number of the first data byte in the Sequence field of a segment. The Sequence field is a 32-bit field, thus allowing sequence numbers over 1 billion. To avoid the problems associated with a two-way handshake, the **three-way handshake** establishes the initial sequence numbers each TCP entity uses. The following steps of the three-way handshake are illustrated in Figure 11.28.

Figure 11.28   Three-Way Handshake Protocol

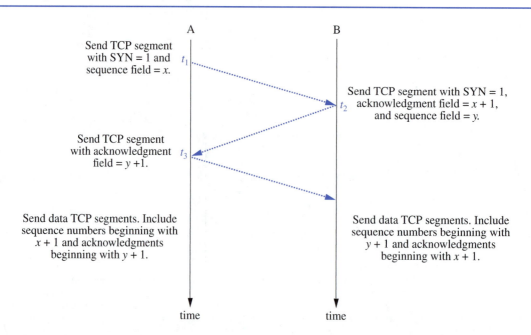

A

Send TCP segment with SYN = 1 and sequence field = x. t_1

Send TCP segment with SYN = 1, acknowledgment field = $x + 1$, and sequence field = y. t_2

Send TCP segment with acknowledgment field = $y + 1$. t_3

Send data TCP segments. Include sequence numbers beginning with $x + 1$ and acknowledgments beginning with $y + 1$.

B

Send data TCP segments. Include sequence numbers beginning with $y + 1$ and acknowledgments beginning with $x + 1$.

time   time

1. TCP entity A transmits a TCP segment requesting a connection (time t_1). It sets the SYN flag to indicate the segment represents a connection request and defines the Sequence field to be x. It may determine x using a timer or counter. Each new request is accompanied by different and larger (modulo 2^{32}) initial sequence numbers.

2. TCP entity B transmits a TCP segment acknowledging both the request and the sequence number (time t_2). It does this by setting the SYN flag and defining the Acknowledgment field $= x + 1$ and the Sequence field $= y$. B determines y in much the same way A determines x.

3. TCP entity A acknowledges the acknowledgment (time t_3). The next segment it sends contains Sequence field $= x + 1$ and Acknowledgment field $= y + 1$.

After the three segments have been sent and received, each entity knows what initial sequence number the other is using and, by way of the Acknowledgment field, has told the other what it is expecting. Subsequent data segments contain increasing (modulo 2^{32}) sequence numbers, where each increment is equal to the number of data bytes in the previous segment. We will elaborate shortly when we discuss flow control.

Terminating connections is similar to establishing them. TCP provides full-duplex communication, however, so one entity wanting to disconnect does not necessarily mean the other is ready. Basically, both parties must agree to disconnect before doing so. Consequently, another three-way handshake protocol is used to terminate a connection (Figure 11.29):

Figure 11.29   TCP Disconnect Protocol

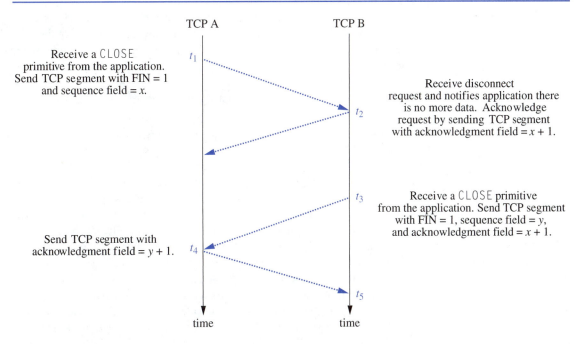

1. TCP entity A gets a CLOSE request from its application (time t_1). It responds by sending a TCP segment with the FIN flag set and Sequence field = x. The FIN flag indicates there is no more data and that the current segment represents a disconnect request. The parameter x represents the current sequence count the TCP entity had been maintaining.

2. TCP entity B receives the segment (time t_2). It responds by notifying its application of the request to disconnect, effectively telling it that no more data is on the way. It also sends a TCP segment back to A acknowledging receipt of the request. Meanwhile B's application could continue to send data or simply prepare to issue its own disconnect request.

3. TCP entity B gets a CLOSE request from its application (time t_3). It sends a TCP segment to A with the FIN flag set and Acknowledgment field = $x + 1$.

4. When TCP entity A receives the acknowledgment (time t_4), it sends an acknowledgment and disconnects. When the acknowledgment arrives at B (time t_5), it also disconnects.

FLOW CONTROL

Once the initial connection is made, the two TCP entities can exchange segments using full-duplex communication, buffering both the segments they send and those they receive. The TCP entity buffers segments it sends because there is no guarantee the segment will arrive. Therefore, it may have to retransmit it. It buffers the ones it receives because there is no guarantee segments will arrive in order. Remember, this is a logical connection as opposed to a physical one, and any number of problems in a lower layer can cause delivery problems. Effectively, the entities exchange segments using a variation of the sliding window protocols discussed in Chapter 8. We will not repeat a detailed discussion of flow control, but we do focus on a couple of differences between TCP flow control and the flow control discussed in Chapter 8:

- In TCP flow control, the sequence number refers to byte sequences instead of packet (or segment) sequences.

- Each entity can alter the size of the other's sending window dynamically using the segment's Window field.

Each entity implements flow control using a *credit mechanism,* also called a *window advertisement.* A **credit,** stored in the segment's Window field, specifies the maximum number of bytes the entity sending this segment can receive and buffer from the other entity. This number is in addition to those already received and buffered (but not yet taken by a higher layer). The TCP entity getting this segment uses the credit to determine how many more bytes it can send before it must wait for an acknowledgment or for the credit to increase.

Figure 11.30 shows an example of this mechanism. We assume that the two entities have already negotiated the initial connection, initial sequence numbers, and credits using the three-way handshake. TCP entities A and B have initial sequence

A
initial sequence number = 100

B
initial sequence number = 700

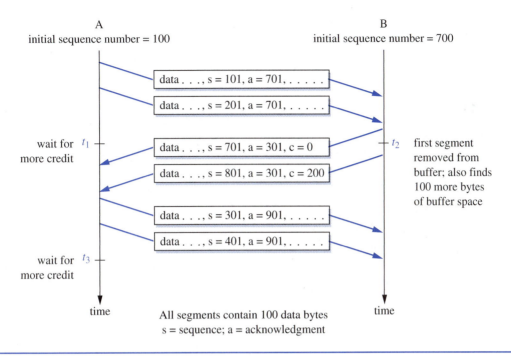

wait for t_1
more credit

data . . ., s = 101, a = 701, ...

data . . ., s = 201, a = 701, ...

data . . ., s = 701, a = 301, c = 0

data . . ., s = 801, a = 301, c = 200

data . . ., s = 301, a = 901, ...

data . . ., s = 401, a = 901, ...

wait for t_3
more credit

t_2 first segment
removed from
buffer; also finds
100 more bytes
of buffer space

time

time

All segments contain 100 data bytes
s = sequence; a = acknowledgment

Figure 11.30   Flow Control Using a Credit Mechanism

numbers 100 and 700, respectively. We also assume that each segment contains 100 bytes of data and that each entity can buffer up to 200 bytes. That is, each has a credit of 200. Entity A starts by sending two segments, one with sequence number (s) 101 and the other with sequence number 201. The acknowledgments (a) indicate what A is expecting from B. To simplify this example, we will show only the credit values in packets that B sends to A.

After sending the second frame, A has used up its credit and must wait (time t_1). Later it receives a segment from B containing a sequence number equal to 701 and an acknowledgment equal to 301. This means B has received bytes sequenced up to 300 and is expecting byte number 301 next. The segment also contains a credit (c) of 0 because the two segments that B has received are still in B's buffers. In short, B has no room for new segments and indicates this using a credit of 0. Consequently, A must still wait. At time t_2, B delivers the first segment it received to a higher layer, thus freeing up 100 bytes of buffer space. The second segment is still there, so that buffer space is still not available. However, let's assume that at this point B has also been able to increase its total buffer space to 300 bytes. Since the second segment containing the 100 bytes is still in the buffer, B now has 200 bytes of buffer space available. In the next segment it sends to A, it specifies an acknowledgment of 301 and a credit of 200.

After a while A receives that segment from B. Consequently, A sends two more segments, but at time t_3 must wait again for another acknowledgment. To simplify, this example showed only credits that B sent to A and how A was affected by them. However, be assured that credit limits apply to B also.

The main advantage of the credit mechanism is that it allows the protocol to be more robust. Rather than living with a fixed window size, the TCP entities can take advantage of changing conditions. If there is little activity at a particular site, the TCP entity may acknowledge a segment with an increased credit to make better use of otherwise unused buffer space. On the other hand, if there is a lot of activity with other connections, it may send a segment reducing the credit to keep incoming information at a manageable level.

CONGESTION CONTROL

The flow control method of the previous section seems to provide for an efficient and smooth exchange of segments. However, other problems can occur that this method does not solve. To illustrate, the previous discussion showed that the window sizes (credits) were adjusted based only on what A or B could handle. It did not take into account what might happen in between. For example, suppose both A and B are connected to 10 Mbps links and can send segments very rapidly. What happens if the only route connecting A and B goes through a 1 Mbps link? It's a little like connecting two 3-lane high-speed freeways with a 30-mph local road. The highways have a large traffic capacity, but the local road does not. The result is congestion and long backups at the exit ramps.

It's important to realize that just because a receiving entity can handle a certain number of packets does not mean the route to it can handle the same number. You may recall that the section on IP discussed some approaches to congestion, but these approaches generally deal with IP packets that are already in the network. A logical enhancement to congestion solutions would be to refine the TCP protocols to limit the amount of traffic that gets onto the network in the first place. To some extent flow control does that, but, again, it really only responds to what the receiver is capable of getting, not what is happening in between.

To enhance congestion control mechanisms, Jacobson (ref. [Ja88]) described a refinement to TCP that allows a sending entity to respond to congested links and to alter the number of segments it can send. Currently, all TCP implementations are supposed to support this technique.

To facilitate our discussion, we again use an example in which TCP entity A has established a connection with TCP entity B. We'll focus the discussion on the transmission from A to B, but be assured it works the same way for transmissions in the reverse direction. To implement this technique, A maintains a *congestion window* that specifies the number of bytes it thinks it can send without causing or adding to congestion (we'll see soon how it determines this). If the congestion window's capacity is larger than A's credit (B's capacity for receiving segments), then A will still not send more than the credit allows. In effect there is no change from previous discussions.

However, if the congestion window's capacity is smaller, then A uses that value instead of the credit to determine how many segments to send before waiting for an acknowledgment. At all times, A defines its sending window to be the smaller of the congestion window size and the credit specified by B. It then uses flow control protocols to send segments and receive acknowledgments.

At this point there are two logical questions. How can A determine when congestion exists? And how does A respond to congestion? The answer to the first question is in the time-out mechanism. Suppose A sends as many segments as its sending window allows and a time-out occurs before an acknowledgment arrives. In theory, a time-out might happen if the segment was damaged and never reached its destination. In practice, many network links are optical fiber, which is very reliable; damaged packets occur rarely in these cases. Consequently, a time-out usually means that the segment was delayed somewhere due to congestion. Thus, A interprets a time-out as the presence of congestion.

The normal response to time-outs is to resend the segments, but all this does is add to the congestion and make it worse. The approach taken here is to reduce the size of the congestion window by half, recalculate the sending window as described previously, and resend only the number of segments that the recalculated sending window allows. If another time-out occurs, the size of the congestion window is again cut in half. As long as time-outs occur, the congestion window is repeatedly reduced by half to a minimum value equivalent to one segment. If at some point the segments in the reduced window are all acknowledged, then the protocol will stop reducing the congestion window's size. By following this protocol, A rather quickly reduces the amount of information it enters onto the network. This should give the Internet protocols time to respond and alleviate the congestion.

Next, suppose A's sending window size is much smaller than the credit sent by B. If congestion is alleviated, A will have a sending window whose size was determined by conditions that no longer exist. The protocol is able to respond by increasing the window size to take advantage of the uncongested links.

To do this, whenever all of the segments in the sending window have been acknowledged and no time-outs have occurred, A will increase its congestion window by the equivalent of one segment and again recalculate the sending window size. Consequently, in the absence of time-outs A can send increasing numbers of segments, up to what B can receive, and more fully utilize the network's capacity. This pattern of reducing and increasing the congestion window continues as long as the connection is maintained.

You might have noticed that A will reduce the congestion window much more quickly than it will increase it. Largely, this reflects a philosophy that dictates that solutions to congestion must be implemented quickly because people are affected by it. On the other hand, a lack of time-outs may not mean that congestion has been eliminated. More than likely it just reflects the fact that congestion is perhaps a little less severe. Consequently, the protocol implements a more conservative approach when trying to increase the traffic. There's little point to quickly increasing the number of segments only to have congestion return.

The only remaining task is to describe how the protocol defines the congestion window initially. Actually, it works much like the recovery period after congestion, with some minor changes. Initially, the congestion window size is defined as the equivalent of one segment. If A sends one segment and gets an acknowledgment, the protocol doubles the congestion window size to the equivalent of two segments. If those segments are acknowledged, the protocol again doubles the size to four segments. In the absence of any time-outs, the congestion window size is repeatedly doubled until the credit value is reached. If at some point a time-out does occur, the protocol establishes the size as that used prior to when the time-out occurred.

As you can see, the protocol tries to increase the congestion window much more quickly in this case than it does after detecting congestion. This is logical because the protocol assumes that initially there is no congestion and tries to establish an exchange rate fairly quickly. Oddly enough, this startup procedure is called a **slow start.** The name is not in relation to the procedure followed after congestion is detected; instead, it is a slow start relative to standard flow control, in which there is no congestion window. In the latter case, A would simply send as many packets as B has indicated it can receive without any regard for how the intermediate links can handle the sudden burst in traffic.

User Datagram Protocol

We have spent most of this section on the Internet's TCP, but don't assume it is the only transport protocol in use. Although it is the most commonly used protocol, there are others. One of these is the User Datagram Protocol (UDP), a connectionless transport layer protocol. It is less complex than TCP, as indicated by the format of a UDP segment (Figure 11.31). It contains very little overhead, which suggests limited abilities. The segment includes the usual source and destination addresses, the segment length, and a checksum for error detection. Because it is connectionless, there is no handshake to establish a connection (and, of course, no disconnect protocol). When UDP has data to send, it creates a UDP segment and gives it to the IP for delivery. At the receiving end, UDP gets the data from IP and does an error check. If there is no error, UDP passes the data to its user; if there is an error, UDP discards the data. There is no formal mechanism for acknowledging errors or provisions for flow control or segment sequencing. It is little more than an interface between a higher layer and IP. Reference [Co00] discusses the protocol in more detail.

Perhaps one interesting note is that we have already described a utility that uses UDP. Earlier in this chapter we discussed a `traceroute` command that displays

Figure 11.31 UDP Segment

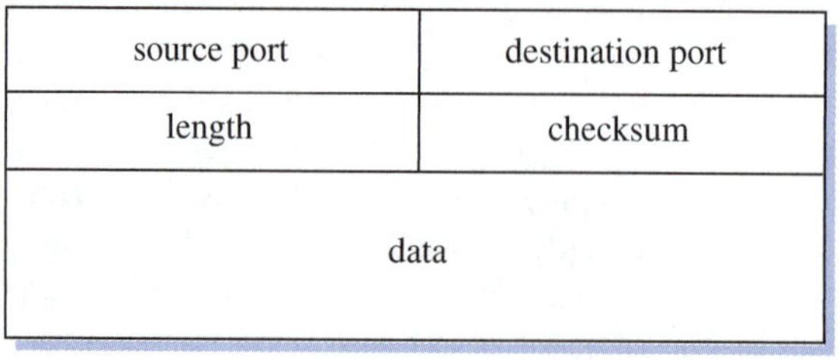

source port	destination port
length	checksum
data	

the locations along an Internet route. When a user at a source enters a `traceroute` command, the following actions occur:

1. The source creates a UDP Probe packet with an unused port number. It puts it in an IP packet with a Time to Live (TTL) value of 1 and sends it to the destination.
2. The first router decreases the TTL value and, seeing it is 0, replies with an ICMP Time Exceeded message.
3. The source gets this reply and records the router address and the round-trip time.
4. The source creates another similar UDP Probe packet and puts it in a IP packet, this time with a TTL value of 2.
5. This time the packet makes it past the first router, but the second router responds as in step 2.
6. Again, the source responds as in step 3.
7. The source repeatedly sends probes in IP packets with increasing TTL values. Each time, the packet reaches one more router on the route before it is dropped. In each case, that router responds as in step 2 and the source records the information.
8. Eventually, the TTL value is large enough so that the packet reaches the destination (if it exists and is within reach of the maximum hop value). Because the UDP Probe packet specified an unused port, the destination responds with a Port Unreachable message. The source recognizes this as the last response it will see. It logs the information and finishes.

REAL-TIME TRANSFER PROTOCOL

We've already discussed the issues surrounding the QoS demands of applications such as real-time audio or video. We've discussed some low-level approaches such as circuit-switched networks and bandwidth reservation and have indicated that we will discuss ATM, another technology based on creating virtual circuits, in Chapter 13. All have one thing in common: They reserve resources so that lower-level protocols can guarantee the QoS demanded by these applications. There is one logical question to ask: If a network does not provide such lower-level protocols, are real-time applications impossible or impractical? The answer is: not necessarily.

A transport level protocol called **Real-Time Transport Protocol (RTP)** is designed to support real-time applications such as audio or video applications. It's a little different from other protocols we have described because it is designed to work with a particular application and operates only on each end of a connection. Consequently, some think of it as an application layer protocol. On the other hand, RTP usually runs just above UDP, although it can run above other transport protocols as well. As such, some consider it a sublayer of the transport layer. However you view it is not important to our discussion here. What is important is that it typically sits between a real-time application and UDP and is an end-to-end protocol. At this layer, it sits above any routing strategies and is not going to provide any QoS guarantees. However, that's not its purpose.

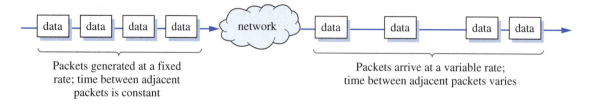

Figure 11.32   Packet Jitter

Although the Internet's low-level protocols were not designed for real-time applications, enhancements in line speed and router design have certainly allowed enormous amounts of traffic to flow through the Internet. Add in some pretty sophisticated compression algorithms, and the ability to push through data at sufficient rates to support real-time applications becomes very real despite the lack of protocols that guarantee it.

However, there are still some problems in using packet-based protocols to support real-time applications. One is **packet jitter** (Figure 11.32). Suppose you are speaking into a microphone connected to a personal computer. Local software modulates your voice using a method such as PCM and stores your voice data into consecutively generated packets. The software then sends the packets onto the network. Because this is a real-time application, local software samples your voice data at fixed intervals and generates packets at fixed rates. However, as the packets travel through the network some may experience small delays at intermediate routers. As a result, the packets (and the voice data) may arrive at the destination at variable rates. The result might be similar to playing an audio tape in which the tape speed periodically increases and decreases.

Figure 11.33 shows another problem that can occur when both audio and video are transmitted. Suppose a video camera is recording a lecture. Some protocols encode the audio and video components separately. That is, there are two data streams: one for audio and another for video. As before, both audio and video data are modulated, stored into packets, and sent onto the network. Because of delays, there's no guarantee that a video and audio packet that were generated at the same time will arrive and be played at the same time. This lack of synchronization

Figure 11.33   Unsynchronized Voice and Image Data

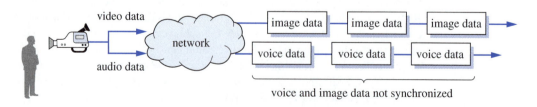

(**intermedia synchronization**) will cause the player at the destination to display the video and play the corresponding audio at slightly different times. It's a little like watching a movie in which another language was dubbed in. The words you hear don't quite match what the actors' mouths seem to be saying.

If we run real-time applications on top of TCP or UDP, these problems can appear because neither protocol was designed to deal with such issues. This is where RTP comes in. It cannot guarantee timely delivery, but it can smooth out some of the problems caused by not-too-serious delays in the data transfer.

There are actually two protocols we need to discuss. One is RTP and the other is the RTP Control Protocol (RTCP). RTP deals with data delivery, and RTCP performs some control functions. The two protocols typically correspond to consecutive port numbers, which allows them to operate independently. We'll deal with RTP first.

A typical approach puts modulated data into an RTP packet. That packet is then embedded into a UDP packet, where it is queued for transmission. So perhaps the logical place to start is to describe an RTP packet, which contains the following items:*

- **Version number.** This indicates the current version of RTP.

- **Payload type.** This is a 7-bit integer that specifies how the data was modulated and its sampling rate. There are identifiers for PCM, MPEG, JPEG, and several other modulation schemes. This allows the receiving end to use the proper decoding scheme to convert the data back to audio or video.

- **Sequence number.** Packets are sequenced to keep them in order and to determine whether any packets were lost.

- **Timestamp.** This is used to correct the packet jitter described previously. When the source generates an RTP packet, it uses a clock to store a timestamp value in the RTP packet header. This stamp corresponds to the time at which the first sample was created. It's not the value of the timestamp that is critical, but the difference between the timestamps in two consecutive RTP frames. For example, suppose the source uses PCM and takes 8-bit samples at a rate of 8000 per second and increments the timestamp value by 1 for each sample. Thus, each byte represents a sample taken every 125 μsec (or once for every timestamp value). Suppose the receiver gets two consecutive RTP packets whose timestamps differ by 100. It knows from the Payload Type field that PCM is generating samples at 125-μsec intervals. Since the timestamp difference is 100, it also knows that it must convert 100 samples to audio at the appropriate rate.[†] It also knows that it must begin playing the second packet 12.5 milliseconds (125 μsec × 100) after it started playing the first one. If the second packet arrived sooner than it needed to be played, the receiver can delay its playing in order to provide a smooth consistent sound.

---

* There are a few additional items, but they are not relevant to our discussion here.

† This is not the same as saying the packet contains 100 bytes. There may actually be fewer bytes because of compression schemes.

However, what happens if an RTP packet arrives too late to be played? One option is to simply drop it. The listener may notice a momentary gap in the sound, but that's it. More sophisticated software might even try to extrapolate the contents based on what it received in previous packets. Dropped packets aren't a problem if they happen infrequently. We'll discuss a protocol later that deals with more frequent losses.

- **Synchronization source identifier (SSRC).** This identifies the source of the data stream. If there are separate audio and video streams, each may have a different SSRC value. If there are multiple cameras at the same site, each has a different SSRC. Different SSRC values also allow a receiver to tune into different sources. The computer at the receiving end may have one window showing a lecture and another showing a Nickelodeon cartoon for when the lecture gets boring.

- **Contributing source identifier (CSRC).** Some multicasts may have multiple active participants. In other words, rather than having one speaker and everyone else listening, another option is to provide the ability for all to speak and interact. It's just like using a conference call. In this case, multiple streams may be combined (multiplexed) into one stream.* If an RTP packet contains blocks of data from multiple sources, the CSRC identifies them.

- **Number of CSRC entries.** This field is self-explanatory.

- **Data.** Modulated audio or video data.

Whereas RTP deals primarily with the transfer of data, RTCP provides some control information. An RTCP stream exists for each RTP stream. It carries information that allows both sender and receiver to provide pertinent information related to the data streams. The sender and receiver can then use this information to perform certain functions or to adapt to changing conditions. RTCP does not specify how they should respond to the information. As stated previously, RTCP operates at a different port number and runs concurrent with RTP. One thing that RTCP provides for is intermedia synchronization.

Previously, we indicated that the receiver sometimes has to synchronize data from two different media (e.g., audio and video). RTP cannot do this for a couple of reasons. First is that two different streams may have two different SSRC values. There's nothing to tie them together. However, each source has a unique identifier called the CNAME (usually of the form *username@hostaddress*), and the sender can send an RTCP packet to each receiver that associates a CNAME with one or more SSRC values. The receiver gets this information and can determine when two streams come from the same source.

Unfortunately, that's still not enough to synchronize them. Although each RTP packet has a timestamp, that value depends on the sampling rates and does not correspond to real time. In addition, different audio and video streams may have different sampling rates; therefore, comparing numbers from the two streams may not be

---

* The device that does this is called a *mixer*.

meaningful. In a sender report from RTCP, a sender can include both a timestamp value and the corresponding real time. When the receiver gets this information, it can determine which RTP streams come from the same source and then use the timestamp and real-time values to synchronize their play.

Another thing that RTCP allows is *rate adaption*. A receiver can deal with packet jitter by using timestamp values to determine appropriate play rates. However, if a packet arrives too late to be played, it may be dropped. This is not a problem if it does not happen too often. However, if the network becomes congested, more packets will arrive too late to be played. Maybe the network is not congested, but the sender is generating packets too quickly for the network to forward them. Either way, the problem of too many lost packets can be resolved if the sender generates them with less frequency or perhaps uses a better compression algorithm—but how can the sender know? The receiver can use RTCP to provide periodic reports to the sender that indicate what percentage of packets are being lost. If that percentage is too high, then the sender can adapt and use a lower sampling rate or a better compression algorithm for encoding the data. If the report indicates that no packets are being lost, the sender might even try to increase the sampling rate to provide a higher-quality stream. It can work both ways.

There's much more to dealing with real-time audio and video applications; we have just scratched the surface. If you're interested in more details related to multimedia communications, references [Ku01], [Mi02], and [Ha01] have them.

11.5   INTERNET APPLICATIONS

Since TCP/IP is such a widely used protocol, it seems logical to discuss some applications that run on TCP/IP networks. Probably the most well-known ones are Telnet, FTP, email, and, of course, the World Wide Web. There are others, of course, but space limitation dictates that we make choices regarding which to discuss. Internet applications involve interaction between programs running on different computers connected to the Internet (client/server model), and it helps to remember that all of the applications we will discuss require cooperation between two programs on different machines running a common protocol.

VIRTUAL TERMINAL PROTOCOLS

Networks provide communication between many types of equipment and software. Early applications often had users logging in to a remote computer through a local dumb terminal (devices that had little or no local computing capability). One significant problem in those days was that software was often written with specific equipment in mind. For example, an editor displayed text on a screen and allowed the user to move the cursor and make changes. But the displayed number of rows and columns varied from one terminal type to another. Commands to move the cursor and to delete and insert text required control sequences that sometimes varied by terminal type. Some terminals even had different keyboards. There was much less standardization than there is today.

Today, most dumb terminals have been replaced by personal computers, but many have software that allows them to emulate various terminals and log in to remote machines. The remote machine runs an application (server program) that provides information from a file to the user. The user then can view the information and interact locally (using client software). This interaction may involve inserting or deleting data, moving the cursor, or finding certain text. If we use the example of a full-screen text editor, one significant problem is that different editors require different keyboard sequences to perform certain actions. Anyone familiar with UNIX or Linux need only work with the vi, emacs, and pico editors to see some significant differences. When you activate an editor through a remote login, your local software must understand how your keyboard entries map to keystrokes that the editor requires. Otherwise, entering commands may have unpredictable effects on the file you are editing. As an example, when one telnets to a Linux server and calls the vi editor, the arrow keys may not function as one would expect. Instead of moving the cursor to an adjacent position, extraneous characters may actually be inserted into the file. The reason is that the codes generated by the arrow keys locally are not translated to the proper codes at the remote end that move the cursor. Terminal emulation programs allow you to map your keystrokes into different codes to make things work properly. One just has to examine what options are available in the menus.

Terminal emulation is an example of a broad classification of protocols called **virtual terminal protocols.** A *virtual terminal* is a data structure maintained by either the application software or a local site. Its contents represent the state of the local terminal. For example, the structure may include the current cursor position, reverse video indicator, cursor shape, number of rows and columns, and color. Both the user and the application can reference this structure. The application writes to the virtual terminal, and the virtual terminal software does the required translation of keyboard entries. When a user enters data, the process works in reverse: Virtual terminal protocols define the format of the data structure, software converts user input to a standard form, and the application then reads the standard "screen."

Virtual terminals may contain more data than the screen can display. This is especially useful when scrolling. For example, suppose the virtual terminal can store 200 lines in a buffer but only 24 can appear on the screen at a time. Information in the virtual terminal will specify the first and last lines of displayed data (Figure 11.34). The displayed data is the *window* and is marked by window delimiters. If the user uses the scroll bars on the side, the virtual terminal software simply changes the window delimiters. The result is that different text lines are displayed on the terminal.

Telnet   One example of a network virtual terminal protocol is **Telnet.** It was designed for the ARPANET and is one of the protocols in the TCP/IP suite. Perhaps most people know Telnet as the application that allows remote logins.

To the user, a **remote login** appears to be no different from a login to a local computer (Figure 11.35a). However, Figure 11.35b reflects the situation more accurately. A user works at a personal computer that runs protocols to connect to a network. The protocols establish a connection over the network to a remote computer. The user and remote computer exchange commands and data using network protocols.

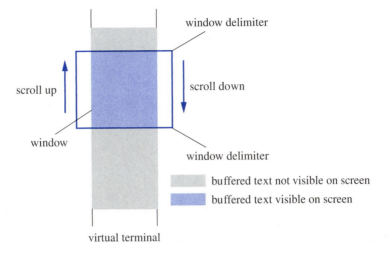

window delimiter

scroll up

scroll down

window

window delimiter

☐ buffered text not visible on screen

☐ buffered text visible on screen

virtual terminal

Figure 11.34 Windowing of Buffered Text

The user is working at a higher layer, however, so this is all transparent and the personal computer has the look and feel of a keyboard and monitor connected directly to the remote computer. The only difference may be slight delays between responses, especially if the remote computer is far away or network traffic is heavy.

Telnet works in a client/server mode (Figure 11.36). That is, a personal computer (the client) runs Telnet locally and transmits data between the user and network protocols. It also can format and send specific commands, some of which we will describe shortly. The remote computer (the server) also runs its version of

Figure 11.35 Remote Connection

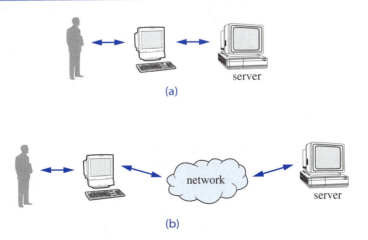

server

(a)

network

server

(b)

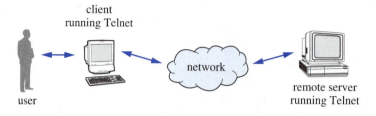

client
running Telnet

network

user

remote server
running Telnet

Figure 11.36   Telnet Client/Server Relation

Telnet. It performs similar functions, exchanging data between network protocols and the operating system and interpreting user-transmitted commands.

A user can use Telnet in several ways, depending on the client. One way is to log in to a local computer such as a UNIX or Linux system, wait for a system prompt ("$" in our example), and enter the command

$ Telnet *text-address*

The text address specifies the host computer to which the user wants to connect. Telnet then calls on the transport protocol to negotiate and establish a connection with the remote site. Once connected, the user must log in to the remote site by specifying the account number and password. It's also possible to enter the command Telnet without a text address. The local system will respond with a Telnet prompt (telnet>). You can connect to the remote site by entering a connect or open command (depending on the local system) specifying the text address.

Another option is to purchase a Telnet program and install it on your personal computer. Typically, double-clicking the application icon or selecting the application name from the menu will start the program, which produces a window similar to that in Figure 11.37. Once you enter the necessary items, the connection is made and you must enter your user name and password.

Still another way is to enter telnet://*text-address* in the address field of Internet Explorer or Netscape Navigator. How you connect is not relevant to our discussion; we will focus on what happens after you connect.

Once connected, Telnet works in the background completely transparent to the user. Everything you type goes to the server. However, sometimes you want to interact with Telnet. If you're running a Telnet program on your computer, you can do so via the drop-down menus at the top of the screen. If you are running Telnet from a Linux system, you can escape from the remote login by entering a control sequence such as control-]. This returns the Telnet prompt to the user but does not break the remote connection. Then you can enter commands directly to Telnet.

For example, suppose a user telnets from the Linux command line, logs in to the remote computer, and experiences some delays. The user may wonder if the remote server is delayed or has stopped running. The user can enter control-] and then the Telnet command send ayt. The command probes the remote server to ask whether it is running (ayt stands for "are you there"). If it is, the user sees the

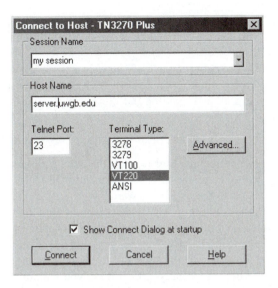

Figure 11.37   Telnet Protocol Requesting Host and Session Name

response [remote server identifier : yes]. If the user runs a program on the remote computer that enters an infinite loop, the user can escape to the Telnet prompt and enter the command send abort or send susp to either kill or suspend the running process.

The number of Telnet options is extensive, and options vary depending on the software and hardware you run. There is usually a help facility that gives you information about them. Consequently, we do not attempt a complete description of them. The best way to get detailed knowledge of how to use Telnet is through the documentation provided with your system.

Secure Shell   Telnet is perhaps the best-known remote login protocol, but it is certainly not the only one. Others are rlogin, rsh, and ssh. The rlogin (Remote Login) utility is similar to Telnet but is less flexible and was designed for UNIX systems running the rlogind daemon.* The rsh utility similarly provides remote logins but can also allow the user to specify a single command he or she wants executed on the remote machine. We won't discuss either of these utilities because the **ssh (Secure Shell)** utility is far more powerful and flexible and, for all intents and purposes, renders the others obsolete. We will give a couple of examples of how to use ssh. They

---

* A *daemon* (some pronounce it as dee-mun; some as day-mun) process is one that runs in the background waiting for some type of service request. When the request comes in, the daemon process typically creates another process to handle that request. The original continues to wait for additional requests.

were tested on a server running Red Hat Linux version 7.3. Some older versions do not support ssh, and the commands may function a little differently on other variants of UNIX.

One difference between ssh and Telnet is that ssh allows the user to easily execute a single command on a remote host. With Telnet, the user would have to log in, enter the command, and then log out. For example, in ssh the user can enter the command

ssh *user@remote_host_name* ls -l

The ssh utility prompts the user to enter the correct password. Upon doing so, the remote system executes the ls -l command to list files and attributes, and ssh returns the results to the user. Afterward, however, the user is not logged on to the remote host. The connection was made solely for the purpose of executing a single command and was terminated once the command's output was returned.

This is a simple example, but the most important difference between ssh and Telnet is that ssh will authenticate and encrypt the exchanges between the local and remote hosts. This is especially critical when you initially log in because you have to enter a password. If the password is not encrypted, you are at risk. You might as well leave your charge card in public view where anyone can copy the account number. Different versions of ssh provide encryption and authentication using different methods. We will not make distinctions here and will provide only a brief overview of some important features. The interested reader can consult references such as [Sc02], [Ma00], and [Ba01] and the website www.openssh.org for more information.

A user can initiate ssh in the same way as Telnet—just enter the appropriate command or select the appropriate button on a graphical user interface (GUI), and the connection protocol begins. The difference is in what occurs afterward. For example, one feature that ssh provides is server authentication. To understand the importance of this, suppose a user wants to establish a connection to a remote host. However, someone intercepts that request and, posing as the intended destination, returns a valid-looking response. This is called *spoofing*. When the user enters a password, it is sent to the wrong site without the user's knowledge, and the perpetrator now knows the user's password.

The ssh utility prevents this by authenticating the server to which a user connects. This authentication process is a little different from that used in SSL (see Chapter 7). To illustrate, suppose the user enters the command ssh *remote_host*. If this is the first time that ssh sees this remote host name, it cannot verify that the host is who it is supposed to be. Therefore, ssh produces a message similar to the following:

```
The authenticity of host 'remote_host (100.200.200.200)' can't
be established.
RSA key fingerprint is
a5:42:fe:ce:45:a3:7c:c4:ff:52:5f:f9:65:16:9b:4d.
Are you sure you want to continue connecting (yes/no)?
```

The secure shell is telling the user that it is not able to verify that the host is authentic and is asking the user how to proceed. It also provides a fingerprint (digest value) of the key that allows the user to determine the server's (and key's) authenticity. For example, the user could contact the remote host administrator and verify the fingerprint and key. If the user selects no, the connection is not made. If the user selects yes (and this should only be done if the user is sure the remote host is valid), the connection is made. In the latter case, a file named known_hosts is created (or updated if it already exists) in an .ssh subdirectory located in the user's home directory. That file contains the remote host's public key.

The next time the user attempts an ssh connection to that host, the ssh client gets the public key from the remote host and looks for a match in the known_hosts file. If a match is found, the client generates a random number, encrypts it using that public key, and sends it back to the remote host. If the host can decrypt the number, then it is authenticated because only the remote host knows the private key. If there is no match, then ssh produces a message similar to that shown earlier. This can happen if the host changes the public key. In that case, the user must verify again on his or her own. If there is a match but the remote host cannot decrypt the number, the authentication does not occur and there is no connection.

Once the connection is made, the client and server negotiate a session key that is used to encrypt subsequent exchanges. How the session key is determined varies with the ssh version. For example, it may be the random number that the client generates. Because the client encrypts the random number with the remote host's public key, only the host can decrypt it. The client and server may also execute a Diffie-Hellman key exchange.

The ssh program also provides for client authentication. Depending on the version, there are several ways to do this. One way, of course, is to require the user to enter a private password. Another way allows the user to log in securely without entering a password. The following steps, run on a Linux system, show one possible approach to setting up client authentication.

1. The user executes the command ssh-keygen -t dsa. This command creates a public and private key that are stored in the files id_dsa.pub and id_dsa, respectively. Those files are located in the .ssh subdirectory in the user's local home directory.

2. The user copies the id_dsa.pub file to another file, authorized_keys, in the .ssh subdirectory in the user's remote home directory. Note that the public key is now on both hosts.

3. The user initiates a connection using ssh remote_host_name. The user is connected without having to enter a password.

How did this happen? Instead of using the password for user authentication, ssh used the key pair that the user generated to authenticate the user. The following outlines the exchange:

1. During the initial setup, the ssh server gets the user's public key from the authorized_keys file. It then generates a random number and encrypts it with the user's public key.

2. The ssh server sends the encrypted key to the ssh client, challenging the client to decrypt it with the user's private key.

3. The ssh client decrypts it using the private store in id_dsa and sends the result back to the server.

4. The server determines that the client successfully decrypted the number, which confirms the authenticity of the user (only the user should know the private key).

5. The user is logged in.

The ssh utility is very powerful, and a lot happens in between the time a user enters the `ssh` command and login occurs. Many other options exist for authentication and key exchange. These include digital signature algorithms, RSA, Blowfish, triple DES, AES, and Diffie-Hellman exchanges. In fact, on Linux the user can enter `ssh` *remote_host_name* `-v`. The `-v` options makes the ssh protocol run in verbose mode. That is, it informs the user of all the interactions that occur while trying to connect and authenticate. It's interesting to follow but is very detailed and requires knowledge beyond what we can cover. Again, the interested reader should consult one of the previous references or the Linux man pages.

A freeware version of ssh called PuTTy is available. A search using an Internet search engine should reveal locations from which you can download the program. It maintains a log file that shows the exchanges, much like the verbose mode in Linux.

FILE TRANSFERS

One of the most common network applications is file transfer. It has many uses. People working on group projects or doing related research often must share files. The ability to access and transfer files is essential for information sharing. Instructors create files for students to use in programming assignments. Users may transfer files between a home computer and a file server at work in order to keep backups.

In most cases, all files are in one place, and a file server manages them. When a user wants to transfer a file, he or she makes a request to the appropriate application. It, in turn, observes the network's file transfer protocols. However, there are issues to deal with.

One is the file structure, which may vary. For example, some files consist of a simple sequence of bytes. Others are *flat files* consisting of a linear sequence of records. *Hashed files* allow random access to a record through a key field value. *Hierarchical files* may organize all occurrences of a key field in a tree structure.* These differences can pose a problem if the destination system does not support the source file's structure.

One way to simplify transfers between incompatible systems is to define a **virtual file structure,** one supported by the network for the purpose of file transfer. Figure 11.38 shows the transfer process. User A wants to transfer a file to user B, but they work on computers that support different file systems. User A's file must be translated into a network-defined structure. The file transfer protocol then handles the actual transfer, and the file finally is converted to a structure supported by user B's computer.

---

* Be sure to distinguish between a file's structure and its implementation. For example, a file may be hierarchical, but there are many implementations of a hierarchical structure.

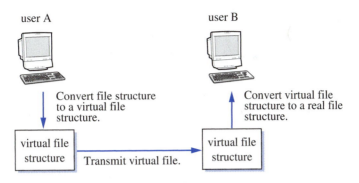

Figure 11.38   File Transfer between Computers Supporting Different File Structures

A virtual file structure must preserve the essential ingredients of a file. For example, it must contain the file's name, attributes, and coded information on the actual structure to allow for proper translation. Of course, it must also contain the data.

Another issue in file transfer is accessibility. A file transfer system should not honor every request. It must consider protection. Can files be transferred both ways? Is the requester even allowed access? Law enforcement and defense agencies would not want a system that allows access to all of their files. Multiple accesses to files also must be considered. Are they allowed? Passwords, locks, and keys are used for file protection and concurrency control.

FTP   One common file transfer protocol is called just that—*File Transfer Protocol,* or FTP (no kudos for imagination here). It is another protocol in the TCP/IP suite and is built on the same client/server paradigm as Telnet. A user, interacting with a local FTP program, connects to a remote site also running FTP. As with Telnet, this can be done in a couple of ways. One way, if running on Linux, for example, is to simply enter the command

<code>ftp text-address</code>

which will establish a connection to the specified remote computer, much as Telnet does.* The second way is to enter

<code>ftp</code>

and wait for the prompt `ftp>`. Next the user enters

<code>open text-address</code>

to establish the connection. Depending on the local system, sometimes `connect` is used instead of `open`. Once connected, the user is asked to enter a user identification

---

* As with Telnet, FTP can be run from a GUI or a Web browser. We'll proceed as if you were entering your own commands. It works the same either way.

Table 11.3   FTP Commands

COMMAND	MEANING
cd	Changes the working directory on the remote host.
close	Closes the FTP connection.
dir or ls	Provides a directory listing of the current working directory.
get	Copies the specified file from the remote host to the local system. The local file receives the same name as the one on the remote host. In the event there is incompatibility between naming conventions or the user simply wishes to give the transferred file a different name, the user can specify a second parameter indicating a local file name.
glob	Acts as a toggle allowing or disallowing the use of wildcard characters. For example, if * is a wildcard character and its use is allowed, then mget *.TXT would get all files with a .txt extension.
help	Displays a list of all client FTP commands.
mget	Copies multiple files from the remote host to the local system.
mput	Copies multiple files from the local system to the remote host, contingent on the remote host allowing the creation of new files.
put	Copies a specified file from the local system to the remote host if allowed by the remote host.
pwd	Displays the current working directory on the remote host.
quit	Quits FTP.
remotehelp	Displays a list of all server FTP commands.

followed by a password. On entering the appropriate identification and password, the user can then peruse subdirectories, get directory lists, and get copies of files.

Many sites make files available to the general Internet community. This means a user can access them without having an account on that machine. When a user connects to the site, he or she usually enters "anonymous" for the account name and either "guest" or his or her email address as the password. The latter is used to track accesses. This application is often called **anonymous FTP.** *

On the surface, FTP looks just like Telnet: Both allow a user to establish a remote connection. The difference is that Telnet allows a legitimate login, whereas FTP primarily provides access to certain files and directories.

Once the FTP connection is established, the user sees the prompt ftp >. At that point he or she has many choices. As before, we do not try to cover all the commands; instead, we summarize some of the most commonly used ones in Table 11.3. The user can get information about the commands by typing help or a question mark (?). Probably the most commonly used commands are cd, to change the working directory in the remote host, and get, which copies a file from the remote to the local site.

---

* With so many sites setting up Web servers, anonymous FTP is less common than it once was because users can access those same files using a browser and the HTTP protocol. The next chapter discusses these in more detail.

Anonymous FTP allowed files and technical reports to be made available to the Internet community before Web servers were common. Just what was available depended on what the remote site put in the anonymous FTP account. Anonymous FTP sites still exist and we present an example showing how to use FTP to get access to a wide range of network- and communications-related information through a series of documents called the **Request for Comments (RFC) series.** These are research notes that are available in electronic or printed form. They cover a wide range of topics, such as Internet protocols, network management and administration, email, network standards, and much more.

One repository for RFC documents is at ftp.ietf.org. RFCs are numbered and have the form RFC*xxxx*, where the designation *xxxx* is a four-digit number. We will not even think about providing a list of RFCs since it would require about 40 pages to do so. Table 11.4 lists a few RFCs that relate to topics covered in this book. There may be many more for a given topic.

Table 11.4   RFC Documents

TOPIC	RFC NUMBER
Border Gateway Protocol (BGP)	1105, 1266, 1265, 1771
Domain Name System (DNS)	1591, 1101
File Transfer Protocol (FTP)	114, 172, 265, 354, 542, 765, 959
Hypertext Transfer Protocol (HTTP)	2068, 2616
Internet Control Message Protocol (ICMP)	777, 792
Internet Protocol (IP)	791, 760
Internet Protocol version 6 (IPv6)	2460
Internet Protocol over ATM	1577
IPSec	2401
Open Shortest Path First (OSPF) protocol version 2	2328
Routing Information Protocol (RIP)	1387, 1388, 1721, 1723, 1058
Resource Reservation Protocol (RSVP)	2205
Simple Mail Transfer Protocol (SMTP)	788, 821
Simple Network Management Protocol (SNMP) version 2	1901–1907
Simple Network Management Protocol (SNMP) version 3	2570–2575
Telnet protocol specification	764, 854
Transmission Control Protocol (TCP)	793, 761, 675
Transmitting IP datagrams over IEEE 802 networks	1042
Transmitting IP datagrams over public data networks	877
Uniform Resource Locators (URLs) on the Web	1738
User Datagram Protocol (UDP)	768
X.25 critique	874
X.400 email standard	822, 987, 1616
X.509 certificates	2459, 2560

```
1    /home/shayw-$>ftp ftp.ietf.org
2    Connected to 4.17.168.6 (4:17.168.6).
3    220 www.ietf.org NcFTPd Server (licensed copy) ready.
4    Name (ftp.ietf.org:shayw): anonymous
5    331 Guest login ok, send your complete e-mail address as password.
6    Password: shayw@uwgb.edu
7    230-You are user #3 of 50 simultaneous users allowed.
8    230-
9    230 Logged in anonymously.
10   Remote system type is UNIX.
11   Using binary mode to transfer files.
12   ftp> ls
13   227 Entering Passive Mode (4,17,168,6,206,14)
14   150 Data connection accepted from 143.200.128.235:34548; transfer starting.
15   lrwxrwxrwx    1 ftpuser ftpusers        7  Jun 21  2001 bin-> usr/bin
16   drwxrwxr-x 250 ftpuser ftpusers     4608   May 3  2001 concluded wg-ietf-mail-archive
17   dr-xr-xr-x   2 ftpuser ftpusers      512  Jul 19  1996 dev
18   dr-xr-xr-x   2 ftpuser ftpusers      512  Aug 13  1998 etc
19   drwxr-xr-x   3 ftpuser ftpusers     6656   Sep 6 15:06 iesg
20   drwxrwxr-x 487 ftpuser ftpusers     9216  Sep 13 16:07 ietf
21   drwxr-xr-x   6 ftpuser ftpusers      512   Feb 2  1999 ietf-gopher
22   drwxrwxr-x 212 ftpuser ftpusers     4096  Sep 15 15:33 ietf-mail archive
23   drwxr-xr-x  16 ftpuser ftpusers      512  May 30  2001 ietf-online-proceedings
24   drwxrwxr-x   2 ftpuser ftpusers 184832    Oct 1 13:54 internet-drafts
25   dr-xr-xr-x   2 ftpuser ftpusers      512  Aug 29  1996 lib
26   drwxr-xr-x   2 ftpuser ftpusers      512  Apr 17  1996 lost+found
27   drwxr-xr-x   3 ftpuser ftpusers      512  Sep 13 09:47 pub
28   drwxrwxr-x   9 ftpuser ftpusers    74752   Oct 1 19:29 rfc
29   dr-xr-xr-x   5 ftpuser ftpusers      512  Apr 18  1996 usr
30   226 Listing completed.
31   ftp> cd rfc
32   250- "/rfc" is new cwd.
33   250-
34   250-* = = = = = = = = = = = = = = = = = = == == = = = = = = = *
35   250-*
36   250-* This directory is maintained by the RFC Editor. If you experience*
37   250-* any problems, please report them to rfc-editor@rfc-editor.org.    *
38   250-*
39   250-* = = = = = = = = = = = = = = = = = = = = = = = = = = = =*
40   250
41   ftp> get rfc-index.txt
42   local: rfc-index.txt remote: rfc-index.txt
43   227 Entering Passive Mode (4,17,168,6,218,101)
44   150 Data connection accepted from 143.200.128.235:34549; transfer starting
45   for rfc-index.txt (524437 bytes).
46   226 Transfer completed.
47   524437 bytes received in 4.42 sees (1.2e+02 Kbytes/sec)
48   ftp> quit
49   221 Goodbye.
50   /home/shayw-$>
```

Figure 11.39 Sample Use of FTP to Transfer a File

An RFC repository site maintains an RFC list in a file that can be accessed using FTP. Figure 11.39 shows how the file was retrieved using a Linux system. Boldface characters represent those typed by the user, and plain characters correspond to FTP responses. Line 1 shows the FTP command to connect to the remote site ftp.ietf.org. Line 4 corresponds to the login request and the entry for the anonymous login. Line 6 requests the password, which in this case is the author's email address. As with most systems, the password was not echoed and is shown here only to illustrate the interaction. Line 12 displays the contents of the current directory at the FTP site. Line 31 changes the working directory to the rfc subdirectory of the current directory. This is the subdirectory containing RFC documents. Finally, line 41 requests that a copy of a file named rfc-index.txt be transferred to the local site. This file contains a list of all RFCs available in that repository as well as the topics covered. The copied file also will be named rfc-index.txt. The remaining lines indicate the status of the file transfer as it occurs. Finally, line 48 exits FTP.

If you wanted a copy of a particular RFC, you would enter

```
get rfcxxxx.txt
```

where *xxxx* represents the four-digit RFC number.

Of course, this is not the only way to access such documents. If you have a browser and an Internet connection, you can use them to access FTP sites. Just specify ftp://*ftp-site* as the URL. Figure 11.40 shows the results of entering

Figure 11.40   Using FTP through a Browser

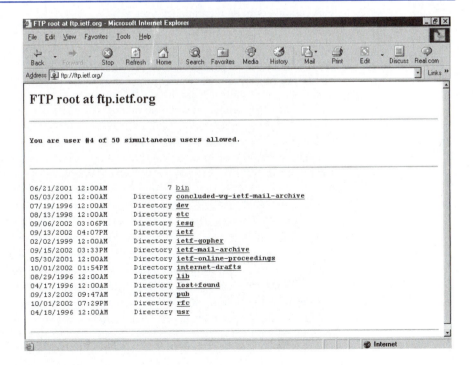

ftp://ftp.ietf.org in the address field of Internet Explorer. Compare the directories shown with those in lines 16 to 29 of Figure 11.39. Just click a directory to enter it, and click subsequent file names to view the files.

Secure Copy   Like Telnet, FTP is not secure. There is no encryption or authentication. However, the **Secure Copy (scp)** program provides those functions. It works like FTP but uses the same authentication and security as ssh. One way to copy a file using scp is to enter the following command (again, we are assuming Linux):

$$scp\ username@host:filename1\ filename2$$

It's actually quite simple: Copy a file (*filename1*) from an account (*username*) on the specified host. Store the file as *filename2* on the local host. After the user enters this command, scp prompts the user to enter a password for the account on the remote host. Of course, many options exist that allow the user to specify such things as the encryption method used and how to do authentication. In fact, if the user runs scp in verbose mode (using the −v option), the exchange between local and remote host looks very similar to that caused by running ssh.

SIMPLE MAIL TRANSFER PROTOCOL

Certainly one of the most common uses of networks is electronic mail, the ability to send a message or file to a specific user at a local or remote site. Typically, you send a message by specifying the email address of the recipient. The usual address format is *name@host-text-address*. The message is buffered at the destination site and is accessible only by the intended user.

Email has some similarities with file transfer protocols. For example, both use a client and server to negotiate transfer of data. However, email typically sends the file to a specified user, in whose account the message is buffered. Also, the email client and server work in the background. For example, if you get a file using FTP, you typically must wait until the file arrives before doing another task. If you send (or receive) a file using email, you can do other tasks while the client and server perform the mail delivery in the background. In the case of receiving mail, you need not even be logged on. You will be notified of new mail the next time you log in to the system.

The standard mail protocol in the TCP/IP suite is the **Simple Mail Transfer Protocol (SMTP).** It runs above TCP/IP and below any local mail service. Its primary responsibility is to make sure mail is transferred between different hosts. By contrast, the local service is responsible for distributing mail to specific recipients.

Figure 11.41 shows the interaction between local mail, SMTP, and TCP. When a user sends mail, the local mail facility determines whether the address is local or requires a connection to a remote site. In the latter case, the local mail facility stores the mail (much as you would put a letter in a mailbox), where it waits for the client SMTP. When the client SMTP delivers the mail, it first calls TCP to establish a connection with the remote site. When the connection is made, the client and server SMTPs exchange packets and eventually deliver the mail. At the remote end, the local mail facility gets the mail and delivers it to the intended recipient.

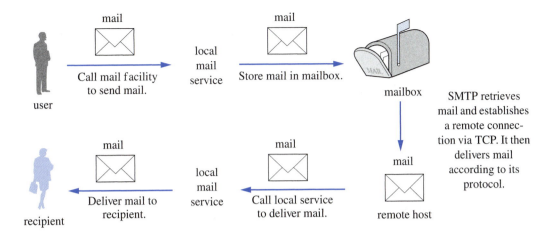

Figure 11.41   SMTP Interacting with Local Mail and TCP

Figure 11.42 shows the packet exchange between the client and server. The packets are also called SMTP *protocol data units* (PDUs) or simply *commands*. When the TCP connection is made, the server sends a 220 PDU indicating it is ready to receive mail. The number 220 serves to identify the type of packet. Afterward, the client and server exchange the identities of their respective sites. Next, the client sends a MAIL FROM PDU indicating there is mail and identifying the sender. If the server is willing to accept mail from that sender, it responds with a 250 OK PDU.

The server then sends one or more RCPT TO PDUs specifying the intended recipients to determine whether the recipients are there before sending the mail. For each recipient, the server responds with a 250 OK PDU (recipient exists) or a 550 Recipient Not Here PDU. After the recipients have all been identified, the client sends a DATA PDU indicating it will begin mail transmission. The server's response is a 354 Start Mail PDU, which gives the OK to start sending and specifies a sequence the client should use to mark the mail's end. In this case the sequence is <CR><LF>.<CR><LF>. The client sends the mail in fixed-size PDUs, placing this sequence at the mail's end. When the server gets the last PDU, it acknowledges receipt of the mail with another 250 OK PDU. Finally, the client and server exchange PDUs indicating they are ceasing mail delivery, and TCP releases the connection.

This description has outlined the basic functionality of SMTP and has not gone into the details of PDU format or issues such as forwarding mail or responding to nonexistent addresses. More information on SMTP can be found in references [Co00] and [Ru89] and in RFC documents 788 and 821.

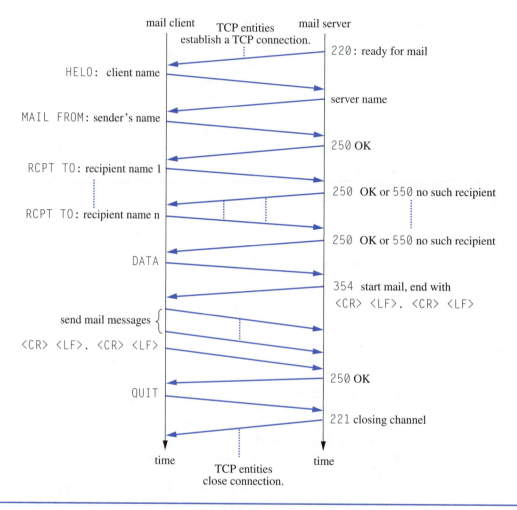

Figure 11.42 Sending Email Using SMTP

SIMPLE NETWORK MANAGEMENT PROTOCOL

The **Simple Network Management Protocol (SNMP)** is a management protocol designed to make sure network protocols and devices not only work but work well. It allows managers to locate problems and make adjustments by exchanging a sequence of commands between a client and a server. Unlike previous applications, it runs on top of UDP instead of TCP. Still, because it is an important part of Internet management, it warrants a discussion.

Figure 11.43 shows the SNMP architecture. A network manager runs a management client program at a site that communicates with a management server program at another site. Typically, the server programs are run on remote hosts and

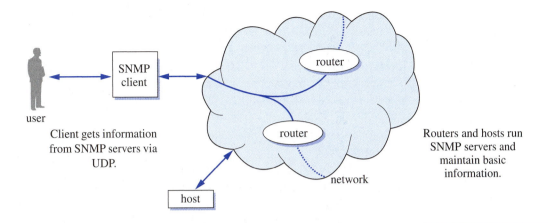

Figure 11.43   SNMP Architecture

especially on network routers. Both management programs use commands defined by the SNMP protocol. Primarily, the commands define how to request information from a server and send information to a server or client.

SNMP has several goals (described in RFC 1157). The first is to simplify management functions to reduce support costs and make SNMP easy to use. Second, it must be extensible to accommodate future updates in network operations and management. Third, the protocol must be independent of the design specifics of hosts or routers. The result is an application layer protocol that interfaces with transport services.

Because SNMP is a management application, it must know what processes it is to manage and how to refer to them. The routers and hosts that SNMP manages are called *objects*. An object has a formal definition according to **ASN.1 (Abstract Syntax Notation 1),** a formal language designed expressly for the definition of PDU formats and objects. A formal treatment of the objects and ASN.1 is far beyond the scope of this text, but you can find some additional information in references [Su00], [Co00], and [Co99].

Management Information Base   Each object's server maintains a database of information that describes its characteristics and activities. Because there are different object types, a standard defines precisely what should be maintained. This standard, the **Management Information Base (MIB),** was defined by the group that proposed SNMP. Eight categories of information are specified by the MIB. As before, a complete description of each one is very detailed, and references [Su00], [Co00], [St99], and [Mi00] have more information. Here we will specify each of the categories and some examples of the information they contain.

- **System.** Describes the host or router operating system and contains information such as when the server was booted, a description of the device it runs on, the device location, and a contact person.

- **Interface.** Describes each network interface and contains items such as MTU (see Section 11.2) size, transmission rate, the number of packets discarded for various reasons, the number of bytes transmitted and received, the number of interfaces, and an interface description.

- **Address translation.** Contains a table used to change an IP address into a network-specific one.

- **IP.** Describes information specific to the Internet Protocol. Examples of information maintained include the default Time to Live value for IP packets, the number of datagrams eliminated for various reasons, the number of datagrams forwarded and delivered to the transport protocol and received from the data link protocol, the number of fragments created, the number of datagrams reassembled, and routing tables.

- **ICMP.** Describes information specific to ICMP. Primarily, it contains many counters tracking the numbers of each type of control message (see Section 11.2) sent by ICMP.

- **TCP.** Among the items it contains are time-out lengths, the number of connections, the number of segments sent and received, the maximum number of simultaneous connections, the IP address of each entity using TCP, the IP address of the remote connection, and the number of failed connection attempts.

- **UDP.** Among the items it contains are the number of datagrams delivered, discarded, or received and the IP addresses of entities using UDP.

- **EGP (Exterior Gateway Protocol).** This is a protocol to exchange routing information between two autonomous networks in an internetwork. As with other categories, the MIB maintains counters tracking the number of EGP messages sent and received.

SNMP Commands   The management programs that use SNMP run asynchronously. That is, they send out requests but can do other things while waiting for responses. Generally, the requests, or PDUs, request information from a server, send information to a remote management program, or respond to special conditions. SNMP defines five PDU formats:

1. **GetRequest.** This command causes a GetRequest PDU* to be sent containing a command code, object name, and specification of an MIB variable. The receiving entity responds by sending a GetResponse PDU containing values of the variable requested or an error code in the event of an error.

---

* The specific PDU format and mechanism for identifying MIB variables is rather complex. References [Mi00] and [St99] contain fairly detailed discussions.

2. **GetNextRequest.** This command is similar to GetRequest except that the request is for values of variables that "follow" the ones specified in the PDU. The notion of following is based on a lexicographic order determined by the MIB design. This is especially useful for traversing tables maintained by the management server.

3. **GetResponse.** A PDU sent in response to a previously received GetRequest PDU. It contains values requested or error codes.

4. **SetRequest.** This command allows the manager to update values of MIB variables maintained by remote management programs and to remotely alter the characteristics of a particular object, which, in turn, can affect network operations. The format does not violate any security measures that prevent unauthorized updates.

5. **Trap.** This PDU is sent from a server to the manager when specific conditions or events have occurred. It allows the manager to stay abreast of changes in the operating environment. Some of the Trap PDUs and their events are listed here:

   a. **Coldstart trap.** The management program has been reinitialized, with potential changes in the object's characteristics.

   b. **Warmstart trap.** Reinitialization has occurred, but no characteristics have been altered.

   c. **Linkdown trap.** A communications link has failed.

   d. **Linkup trap.** A previously failed communication has been restored.

   e. **EgpNeighborLoss trap.** The station has lost contact with an EGP peer neighbor.

   f. **Authentication failure trap.** An SNMP PDU that failed an authentication check has been received.

A newer version of SNMP, SNMPv2, was designed to overcome some of the perceived weaknesses of SNMP. For example, one of the criticisms of SNMP is that because of its simple command format, communication requires a large number of packets. SNMPv2 provides more messaging options, thus allowing the clients and hosts to communicate more efficiently. An example is the GetBulkRequest command, which retrieves information that previously was obtained via multiple request PDUs. The number of error codes was also expanded to provide better information regarding the cause of errors. Another enhancement is increased flexibility to allow SNMPv2 to run on top of multiple protocols such as AppleTalk, IPX, and OSI.

There is also an SNMPv3, which includes three levels of security. The lowest level provides neither authentication nor security, thus making it backward compatible with previous versions. The next level uses authentication based on SHA or MD5 algorithms to make sure that a PDU is not changed or to verify a PDU's source. The highest level provides encryption using the CBC mode of DES encryption.

As with just about any protocol, the SNMP versions are not the only management protocols available. The ISO management protocol is the **Common Management Information Protocol (CMIP).** When used over a TCP connection, CMIP is known as CMOT (CMIP over TCP). CMIP is more complex than SNMP and is reputed to be more suitable for larger networks. **Remote Monitoring (RMON)** is yet another protocol. It has two separate components: an *agent station* or *probe* and a *management station.* A probe can be a specific device that is dedicated to gathering information, or it can be a software agent that runs on an existing network node such as a workstation, server, router, or switch. In the latter case the software runs in the background while the device performs its normal duties, albeit at a slower than normal pace. The purpose of a probe is to gather information about network activity, such as the number of packets sent and dropped, number of multicast packets, packet sources, LAN segment errors, and much more. In fact, the IETF defines different groups of statistics and how they should be used. The probe then sends the information it gathers to the management station for storage in an MIB. Vendor software then analyzes the data to provide information on network performance and to track network problems. Network management is a huge topic, and entire textbooks have been written on it. Those interested in more complete coverage of management can consult references [Su00], [Mi00], or [St99].

11.6 SUMMARY

This chapter dealt primarily with protocols that define what the Internet is and some of the applications that run on it. In general, the Internet is the collection of devices that support TCP/IP. IP is a layer 3 protocol, and TCP a layer 4 protocol. Some major features and issues regarding IP are as follows:

- It allows the transfer of data over dissimilar networks and makes the differences transparent to higher-layer protocols.

- It defines packet format, routing options, types of service, and ways to deal with packets that are too large to travel some networks.

- It uses hierarchical routing, thus requiring addresses to be interpreted as a network number followed by a local identifier.

- It relies on DNS (Domain Name Service), which uses a distributed database to convert addresses from a text-based notation to a numeric IP address.

- It provides multicasting via different protocols. The Internet Group Management Protocol (IGMP) operates between a host and a local router and allows the host to join and leave various multicast groups. Next, it relies on the Mbone, a collection of routers that implement Class D routing. It operates by adapting routing protocols to create a multicast tree over which Class D packets travel.

- Because IP does not provide the quality of service required of real-time applications, the Resource Reservation Protocol (RSVP) was developed. It embeds messages in IP packets that contain information about a particular data flow and request that sufficient resources be reserved. Specific details of how to do this are dependent on intermediate routers.

- One thing that IP does not do is guarantee delivery of its packets. Consequently, another protocol, the Internet Control Message Protocol (ICMP), does error reporting and provides routers with updates on conditions that develop in the Internet. It defines different control and error messages and transmits them via the IP.

- Because IP is not secure, IPSec was developed. It provides an authentication header to provide packet authentication, an Encapsulating Security Payload to provide packet encryption and authentication, and a key exchange protocol.

- Because of the tremendous growth in the number of Internet users and new technologies, IPv6 was developed. It provides a much larger address space than IPv4 that allows, in theory, up to 2^{128} unique addresses. It also uses multiple packet headers and streamlines the routing process. It will take years to incorporate IPv6 entirely into the Internet, and there are provisions that allow it to run alongside IPv4 until that happens.

Transport protocols are the lowest-layer protocols that deal with end-user communication and work independently of network operations. A common protocol used in the Internet is the Transmission Control Protocol (TCP), a connection-oriented protocol. Some of its primary functions are connection management, flow control, and error detection. Effectively, TCP guarantees the reliable exchange of information. Some important aspects of TCP are as follows:

- Definition of a single-segment format for both data and control
- A three-way handshake that requires not only an acknowledgment of a connection request but an acknowledgment of the acknowledgment
- A credit mechanism for flow control similar to sliding window protocols
- Management of a congestion window that responds to changing network conditions caused by heavy traffic

Other transport protocols also exist. One is UDP, a connectionless protocol that has less overhead than TCP and fewer abilities. Another is the Real-Time Transport Protocol (RTP), which was designed to support real-time applications such as audio or video applications. Although it does not guarantee a specific QoS, it helps reduce packet jitter to provide a more consistent play of the media; it also deals with multiple streams to make sure that video and audio streams are synchronized.

There are many applications that run on the Internet; we covered just a few of them.

- Telnet allows users to log in to a remote host computer. Telnet coordinates the exchange between local and remote hosts.

- The Secure Shell (ssh) utility performs the same functions as Telnet (and more) but also provides for encryption as well as remote host and user authentication.

- FTP allows a user to connect to a remote host for the purpose of viewing or downloading files.

- Secure Copy performs the same functions as FTP but also provides for encryption and authentication.

- SMTP (Simple Mail Transfer Protocol) defines PDUs and the sequence of exchanges necessary to provide email service.

- SNMP (Simple Network Management Protocol) gathers information on network traffic and statistics. The information can be analyzed by software to generate statistics on network performance and problem areas.

Review Questions

1. What does the Dynamic Host Configuration Protocol (DHCP) do?

2. Addresses such as 143.200.128.162 and msa.uwgb.edu refer to the same node on the Internet. What is the difference between them?

3. Distinguish among a Class A, B, C, and D IP address.

4. How does a classless address differ from one of the Class A, B, or C addresses?

5. What is the difference between a multicast and unicast address?

6. What is ICANN (Internet Corporation for Assigned Names and Numbers)?

7. What does DNS do?

8. Are the following statements TRUE or FALSE? Why?

   a. IP guarantees that all information will reach its intended destination.

   b. IP packets associated with a given application such as email may take different routes to the destination.

   c. An essential component of router design is determining how a router locates an IP address in its routing table.

   d. Both TCP and UDP operate similarly as layer 4 protocols.

   e. The Real-Time Transport Protocol guarantees a real-time quality of service at the transport layer.

   f. Telnet allows you to log in to any account on a remote machine as long as it is reachable via a network connection.

   g. The Secure Shell utility can allow a user to log in to a remote host (on which the user has an account) without entering a password.

   h. TCP and IP are OSI model layer 3 and layer 4 protocols, respectively.

   i. Sending mail over the Internet does not require a connection.

9. What is the purpose of dividing the DNS hierarchy into zones?

10. What is the reason for having a Type of Service field in an IP packet?

11. Why is IP packet fragmenting sometimes necessary?

12. List some major functions of IP.

13. What is the Time to Live field in an IP packet?

14. What is a maximum transfer unit? How does it affect the Internet Protocol?

15. Distinguish between an Internet address and a physical address.

16. What is dynamic binding?

17. What does quality of service mean?

18. What is the Internet Management Group Protocol?

19. What is a multicast tree?

20. What is the Mbone?

21. What is the purpose of a Prune packet for the Distance Vector Multicast Routing Protocol?

22. What is the Resource Reservation Protocol?

23. What is the difference between a soft and hard router state?

24. What is the Internet Control Message Protocol used for?

25. List typical control messages defined by ICMP.

26. IPv4 provides a 32-bit IP address. A 32-bit number can have one of about 4 billion different values. Since that represents more than half the population of the planet and (on a global scale) most people do not have Internet connections, why is IPv4 running out of addresses to use?

27. How does IPv4 fragmentation differ from IPv6 fragmentation?

28. What is tunneling?

29. List several factors that contribute to IPv6's ability to route more quickly.

30. Why did IPv6 eliminate the checksum in the packet header?

31. What are the different IPv6 packet headers?

32. What is IPSec?

33. How does TCP use a port number?

34. What is a timestamp request?

35. What is the difference between a two-way and three-way handshake?

36. What is an urgent pointer?

37. What is a TCP credit?

38. What is the User Datagram Protocol?

39. How does the Real-Time Transport Protocol help support real-time applications when it has no control over routing within the network?

40. What is packet jitter?

41. What is a potential problem with separating an audio and video stream from a single source?

42. What is RTCP rate adaption?

43. What is Telnet?

44. How does ssh differ from Telnet?

45. The ssh utility can authenticate a user via passwords or via a public/private key mechanism. Describe the difference.

46. What is a virtual file structure?

47. How does anonymous FTP differ from FTP?

48. What is an RFC?

49. What is SMTP?

50. What is SNMP?

51. What is SNMP's Management Information Base?

Exercises

1. Classify each of the following addresses as Class A, B, C, or D.

    a. 183.104.200.32

    b. 230.4200.104.32

    c. 210.20.34.100

    d. 115.193.23.32

2. What is the network number of the IP address 140.100.120.02 if the subnet mask is 255.255.224.0?

3. Does it make sense to have a subnet mask equal to 255.255.224.7? Why or why not?

4. Suppose an organization needs 8000 IP addresses. How many Class C addresses would be needed? If they were consecutive, describe the CIDR addressing scheme.

5. If you have an ISP or your computer is connected to a LAN, determine the IP address for your computer and the subnet mask. Next, determine the class of your address and the subnet and local IDs in your IP address.

6. Suppose a router at A in the figure shown here receives an IP packet containing 4000 data bytes, fragments the packet, and routes the fragments to B via network 1. B in turn routes all the fragments except the second one to C via network 3. However, it fragments the second one and sends the fragments to C via network 2. Show the fragments that C receives and specify relevant values in the fragment headers.

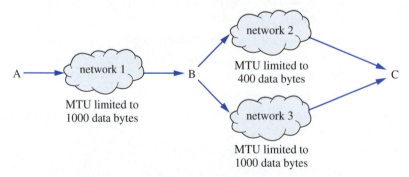

7. In IP fragmentation, why is the Identification field in the fragment header necessary? Why can't the destination simply use the source address to determine related packets and reassemble them according to the Offset field values?

8. What does the routing table for router G look like for the internetwork in the accompanying figure? For each network, specify the address of a router to which a packet must be sent. In the case of a direct connection, indicate that the packet must be delivered directly to its destination.

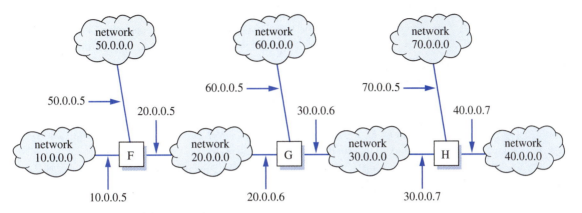

9. In the previous exercise, what do the routing tables for F and H look like?

10. Pick your favorite website and determine a route to that site from your current location.

11. Which of the following applications would you expect to require a real-time quality of service?

   a. Downloading audio files

   b. Accessing a remote host using Telnet or ssh

   c. Watching a live training session on your personal computer

   d. Downloading video files

   e. Watching a broadcast of a breaking news event

   f. Using FTP to download very large files

   g. Using FTP to download very small files

12. Why don't TCP segments contain the number of data bytes each one has? How is the receiving TCP entity supposed to know how many data bytes to extract from a segment?

13. Assume the following:

   • TCP entities A and B have initial sequence numbers 400 and 900, respectively.

   • Each segment contains 100 data bytes, and each has an initial credit of 200 bytes.

   • Each entity delivers a segment as soon as it receives it, thus freeing up the buffer space.

   • A is capable (flow control permitting) of sending TCP segments at intervals of time T (starting at $T = 0$); B is capable of sending its segments at intervals of time $3T$ (starting at time $1.5T$).

Assuming the transmission time between A and B is negligible, sketch a diagram similar to Figure 11.30 showing the segment exchange up to time $12T$.

14. Repeat the previous exercise assuming A's credit increases to 300 after it receives the second segment from B.

15. Consider TCP's flow control logic, discussed in Section 11.4. Since an entity uses the Credit field to determine when it can send new segments, what is the purpose of the acknowledgment? In other words, what would happen if we eliminated the Acknowledgment field from the segment?

16. Suppose that a route from node A to node Z goes through intermediate routers P, Q, R, and X. Describe the packets (types and relevant contents) that are sent and received by A in response to a `traceroute` command.

17. Do a remote login to some account and experiment with the Telnet commands. For example, you can do the following:

    a. Type a large file, escape to Telnet, and abort the output.

    b. Determine the response to the `send ayt` command.

    c. Run a long program, escape to Telnet, and interrupt the process.

    d. Escape to Telnet and type `help` to explore other Telnet commands.

    If you only have an account on one server, you might be able to log in to your account and access your account a second time via Telnet. It's a little like calling yourself on the telephone, but it works and allows you to become familiar with Telnet. (You will have to determine whether your site allows multiple logins to one account.)

18. Connect to a remote site via anonymous FTP, transfer a file to your account, and write a short summary of the file's contents.

19. Consider Figure 11.12 and assume that each network cloud has 50 hosts in a multicast group. If host X belongs to that group, how many copies of each packet travel through the Internet if unicasting is used? If multicasting is used, how many copies of each packet travel through the Internet?

20. If you have an account on a server, set up ssh so that when you log in, the server authenticates you via a public/private key system.

REFERENCES

[Ba01] Barrett, D., and R. Silverman. *SSH: The Secure Shell*. San Francisco: O'Reilly, 2001.

[Br95] Bradner, B., and A. Mankin. "The Recommendation for the IP Next Generation Protocol." RFC 1752, January 1995.

[Ca01] Caslow, A., and V. Pavlichenko. *Cisco Certification: Bridges, Routers and Switches for CCIEs,* 2nd ed. Englewood Cliffs, NJ: Prentice-Hall, 2001.

[Co99] Comer, D. E., and D. Stevens. *Internetworking with TCP/IP. Vol. II. ANSI C Version: Design, Implementation, and Internals,* 3rd ed. Englewood Cliffs, NJ: Prentice-Hall, 1999.

[Co00] Comer, D. E. *Internetworking with TCP/IP. Vol. 1. Principles, Protocols, and Architecture,* 4th ed. Englewood Cliffs, NJ: Prentice-Hall, 2000.

[De93] Deering, S. "SIP: Simple Internet Protocol." *IEEE Network Magazine,* vol. 7, no. 3 (May/June 1993), 16–28.

[Ek02] Ekici, E., I. Akyildiz, and M. Bender. "A Multicast Routing Algorithm for LEO Satellite IP Networks." *IEEE/ACM Transactions on Networking,* vol 10, no. 2 (April 2002), 183–192.

[Fo03] Forouzan, B. *TCP/IP Protocol Suite,* 2nd ed. New York: McGraw-Hill, 2003.

[Gr02] Gralla, P. *How the Internet Works,* 6th ed. Englewood Cliffs, NJ: Prentice-Hall, 2002.

[Ha01] Halsall, F. *Multimedia Communications.* Reading, MA: Addison-Wesley, 2001.

[Hi96] Hinden, R. "IP Next Generation Overview." *Communications of the ACM,* vol. 39, no. 6 (June 1996), 61–71.

[Ja88] Jacobson, V. "Congestion Avoidance and Control." *Proceedings of SIGCOMM Symposium,* August 1988, 314–329.

[Ko98] Kosiur, D. *IP Multicasting: The Complete Guide to Interactive Corporate Networks.* New York: Wiley, 1998.

[Ku01] Kurose, J., and K. Ross. *Computer Networking.* Reading, MA: Addison-Wesley, 2001.

[Ma00] Mann, S., and E. Mitchell. *Linux Systems Security: The Administrator's Guide to Open Source Security Tools,* 2nd ed. Englewood Cliffs, NJ: Prentice-Hall, 2000.

[Mi99] Miller, M. *Troubleshooting TCP/IP,* 3rd ed. New York: M&T Books, 1999.

[Mi00] Miller, M. *Managing Internetworks with SNMP,* 3rd ed. New York: Wiley, 2000.

[Mi02] Miller, M. *Voice over IP Technologies: Building the Converged Network,* 2nd ed. New York: Wiley, 2002.

[Pe00] Perlman, R., and C. Kaufman. "Key Exchange in IPSec: Analysis of IDE." *IEEE Internet Computing,* vol. 4, no. 6 (November/December 2000), 50–56.

[Pi03] Pink, S. *High Speed Routers and Firewalls.* Reading, MA: Addison-Wesley, 2003.

[Ru89] Russel, D. *The Principles of Computer Networking.* Cambridge, England: Cambridge University Press, 1989.

[Sc02] Schetina, E., K. Green, and J. Carlson. *Internet Site Security.* Reading, MA: Addison-Wesley, 2002.

[St96] Stallings, W. "IPv6: The New Internet Protocol." *IEEE Communications Magazine,* vol. 34, no. 7 (1996), 96–108.

[St99] Stallings, W. *SNMP, SNMPv2, SNMPv3, and RMON 1 and 2,* 3rd ed. Reading, MA: Addison-Wesley, 1999.

[Su00] Subramanian, M. *Network Management Principles and Practice.* Reading, MA: Addison-Wesley, 2000.

CHAPTER 12

INTERNET PROGRAMMING

We tend to be so bombarded with information, and we move so quickly, that there's a tendency to treat everything on the surface level and process things quickly. This is antithetical to the kind of openness and perception you have to have to be receptive to poetry. . . . Poetry seems to exist in a parallel universe outside daily life in America.
—**Rita Dove**, U.S. poet

12.1 INTRODUCTION

Have you ever used a search engine to look for something on the Internet? How about a form to order something? Maybe you've used Instant Messenger to carry on conversation with friends. Did you even stop to think that if others can write software that works in an Internet environment, then maybe you could also? Now that you have an understanding of what networks are all about, all that's needed is to apply some programming knowledge and find out how to interact with network protocols. Oddly enough, many of the technical details are not terribly difficult because we can assume that the network protocols implement all the really horrible details. Once you assume something already exists, all you have to do is build another layer on top.

The purpose of this chapter is to show some ways in which this can be done. In this chapter we develop some different applications that rely on Internet protocols. We'll write some things on the client side and some on the server side. Volumes have been written on how to program in an Internet environment, and we have selected just a couple of different approaches. As with other topics in this book, entire textbooks could be written about each of our examples. Our intent here is to provide just enough exposure to details to understand how some basic Internet programs work. From there each person can expand his or her knowledge in a wide variety of ways.

We start in Section 12.2 with an example that shows how a client and server can exchange packets for the purpose of downloading a file. We will use the UNIX socket interface to the transport layer and describe some basic functionality. We'll finish by designing code that actually downloads a file from one host to another. Once the socket concept is understood, the door is open to all kinds of other applications, such as messaging programs and client/server database searches.

In Section 12.3 we'll direct our attention to a Web-based environment. We'll provide an introduction to the Hypertext Transfer Protocol (HTTP) and the Hypertext Markup Language (HTML) and describe how to create websites that perform various functions. This section focuses on the client side and provides an introduction to JavaScript, a language capable of interacting with Web forms to perform various actions. In Section 12.4, we'll move to the server side and focus on CGI (Common Gateway Interface) programming via the C language. It's a way of writing programs on a remote host to respond to requests sent by a client. As an example, we'll illustrate how a simple Internet search engine can be set up.

The last section will describe a somewhat limited but fully functional pizza ordering system and a different approach to server-side programming. We'll cover a scripting language* called Perl and show how to write a Perl script that receives orders, verifies phone numbers, calculates order costs, and returns that information to the client. Together, these examples provide a solid base on which to learn other Internet programming tools and to build more sophisticated examples.

12.2   SOCKET PROGRAMMING

When network applications were first being generated, many of them ran under the UNIX operating system, in particular, Berkeley UNIX. To facilitate sending and receiving data over a network connection, a set of TCP primitives was designed to be used by UNIX applications. Through these primitives, UNIX applications running on different computers connected to the Internet could communicate using a mechanism called a *socket*. As networks developed and languages and operating systems grew more elaborate, the socket evolved to allow network communications from a variety of languages and operating systems. In addition to socket-based programs on UNIX, such programs have become common on personal computers and in the Java and C++ environments.

The primary goal of this section is to provide a minimal but very functional client/server model that runs on Linux (a variant of UNIX). This means we will show you how to develop two distinct programs that can talk to each other. The only assumption is that they run on two different Linux systems that have Internet access. Specifically, we will develop two programs that implement a file transfer protocol. One program will read text from a file, divide it into packets, and send them to the other program through a socket connection. The second program will

---

* A *scripting language* is one whose source code is interpreted as it is executed. This is in contrast to a *compiled language,* which is translated into machine code and then executed directly by the central processor.

accept the packets one at a time and build a file from their contents. Furthermore, these programs can run concurrently and asynchronously on different computers. At the end of the section we note possible extensions to this project that allow the client or server (or both) to be written either on a Linux system or in Java. We also reference sample code that does this.

To keep this section concise and focused, we will provide only the necessary socket details for this application and will not build a lot of options into the programs. We will also not attempt to provide an exhaustive treatment of all socket commands and all the environments in which they can be used. At this level, these details are not important because our goal is to provide functionality. As such, we will develop an actual working client/server application and you can build from there. If you have a Linux system, you should be able to run the programs we present with little or no modification. We will assume basic knowledge of Linux and the C programming language. There are many ways to expand on what we will do, and anyone interested in a detailed description of sockets, their commands, and various options should consult references [Co99] and [Co00].

SOCKETS

The **socket** is a construct that supports network input/output (I/O). An application creates a socket when it needs a connection to a network. It then establishes a connection* to a remote application via the socket and communicates with it by reading data from the socket and writing data to it.

Figure 12.1   Socket Connection to a Network

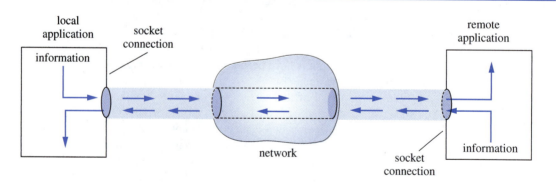

---

* We are assuming that the sockets we create use TCP and are connection oriented. There are sockets that are connectionless and rely on UDP. Because of space limitations, we will focus only on the connection-oriented sockets and refer the reader to reference [Ku03] for a treatment of UDP sockets.

Figure 12.1 illustrates the idea. A local program can direct information through a socket into the network. Once there, network protocols (which we don't worry about at this level) guide the information through the network, where it is accessed by a remote program. Similarly, the remote program can put information into its socket. From there, it goes through the network and ends up back at the local program. By defining the rules through which the local and remote programs exchange information, we can, in fact, define our own protocol.

CLIENT/SERVER MODEL

Before we try to define any kind of protocol, we begin by describing a fundamental model behind most network protocols, the **client/server model.** The essence of the client/server model (Figure 12.2) involves two distinct programs, usually running on different machines at different locations. The machines have network connections. Whether the network is a local area network, a wide area network, or something in between is not a concern at this point. The fundamental concept is the same either way.

Figure 12.2   Client/Server Model

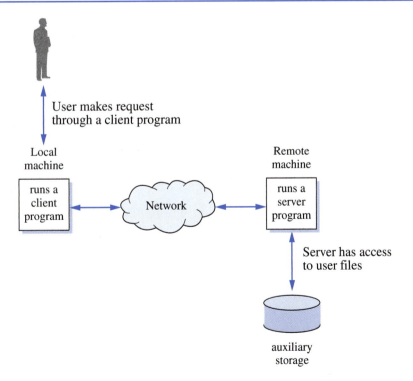

User makes request through a client program

Local machine

runs a client program

Network

Remote machine

runs a server program

Server has access to user files

auxiliary storage

Essentially, both the client and server act out certain roles. The **server** is there to provide services and respond to requests coming in from client programs. A typical example is to provide access to files located on the remote machine. A user runs the **client** program on a local machine and, through it, makes various requests. Following our example, a user may request access to one or more files located on a different (remote) machine. Thus, a typical exchange might look something like this:

1. User requests a file.
2. Client sends a request to the server on behalf of the user.
3. Server receives a request from a client and analyzes it.
4. Server copies a file from its auxiliary storage.
5. Server transmits contents of the file back to the client.
6. Client gets file's contents from the server and makes it accessible to the user.

In general, one server may provide service to many clients. Thus, another design issue, particularly for the server, is how the server can handle multiple client requests efficiently. We'll discuss that a bit later; for now we need to worry about how a server handles requests from one client.

SOCKET DATA STRUCTURES

When we eventually discuss some of the socket calls, we will have to describe the parameters passed to them. Some of these parameters have types that are designed specifically for network communications. Therefore, we begin by discussing different data structures required by socket calls. Each of these structures is located in a Linux header file. We will specify which header files are required later.

The first structure we need is

```
struct sockaddr_in {                          where      struct in_addr {
        u_short sin_family;                               u_int s_addr
        u_short sin_port;                                 }
        struct in_addr sin_addr;
        char sin_zero[8]
}
```

Essentially, this is a 16-byte structure that contains a socket address (a combined IP address and port number; we are assuming a TCP/IP network). Table 12.1 specifies what the fields represent.

The next structure is

```
struct hostent {
        char *h_name;
        char **h_alias;
        int h_addrtype;
        int h_length;
        char **h_addr_list
}
```

Table 12.1   Fields of the `sockaddr_in` Structure

FIELD	MEANING
sin_family	This 16-bit integer specifies which protocols will be used to implement the socket connection. In general, sockets can be used with more than just TCP/IP networks, but that's not something we'll discuss here.
sin_port	This 16-bit field specifies a port number identifying an application (recall the definition of port number when we discussed the TCP header).
s_addr	32-bit Internet address (assumes that `sin_family` specifies the TCP/IP protocol).
sin_zero	Unused. Contains all zeros.

Table 12.2   Fields of the `hostent` Structure

FIELD	MEANING
h_name	Null-terminated character string for the text address of a host computer
h_alias	List of alternative names for the host (not important here)
h_addrtype	Type of address (specifies an Internet address in our example)
h_length	Address length
h_addr_list	List of additional addresses for the host (not important here)

Table 12.2 defines the fields of the hostent structure.

SOCKET COMMANDS

There are many different socket-related commands. Table 12.3 lists those we need for our example and provides a short description of each.*

CLIENT/SERVER EXAMPLE

We are now ready to write a client/server protocol used to transfer a file.† The first step is to outline the socket-related calls in each of the client and server programs. This helps us understand their purpose without being burdened with a lot of details. Figure 12.3 shows both a client and server. Keep in mind that both run concurrently

---

* Again, we've made no attempt to be complete because our primary goal is to provide what is necessary for our application.

† Both client and server were tested and run on Red Hat Linux version 7.3.

Table 12.3 Summary of Required Socket Commands

COMMAND	MEANING
socket(int domain, int mode, int protocol)	Creates a socket. The first parameter specifies which domain is used. For example, the symbolic constant AF_INET specifies the Internet domain. AF_UNIX specifies a UNIX domain. The second parameter specifies a mode of communication. For example, the symbolic constant SOCK_STREAM indicates we will use connection-oriented byte streams. SOCK_DGRAM means a connectionless datagram mode of communication. The third parameter specifies a protocol or, if 0, allows the system to rely on a default (in this case, TCP/IP). If this command is successful, it returns an integer (descriptor) of the socket to be used in subsequent commands. At this point the socket is little more than an index to a kernel descriptor table. More is needed to establish an actual connection.
gethostbyname(char *hostname)	Returns a pointer to a hostent structure containing relevant information about the host specified by the text address in hostname.
gethostname(char *hostname, int length)	Puts the character string for the text address of the current host computer into the hostname variable. The second parameter represents the number of available bytes in hostname.
connect(int s, struct sockaddr_in *sa, int size)	Requests a connection with a remote socket. The call must specify the local socket identifier(s) and a structure containing the remote socket address (*sa). This call is needed when a connection-oriented service is required. The third parameter just specifies the size of the *sa structure. As a function, it returns the status of the request.
bind[1] (int s, struct sockaddr *sa, socklen_t length)	Assigns an address and port number (inside *sa) to the socket s. The server will issue this command to make itself accessible to remote clients that connect to this socket.
listen(int s, int n)	Used by a connection-oriented server that responds to requests from remote clients. It indicates that the server is ready for connection requests and listens for them over the socket s. It then puts them into a queue for subsequent processing. The second parameter (n) specifies the number of requests that can be queued. If a request comes in while the queue is full, the server rejects it.
accept(int s, struct sockaddr *sa, socklen_t length)	Allows the server to accept a connection request over the socket s. When accepted, the IP address of the client making the request will be stored in the structure *sa. In addition, this function actually creates and returns a new socket with all of the same properties as s. The reason for this is that after a server accepts a call, it usually forks a child subprocess, which uses the new socket to communicate with the client. Meanwhile, the parent continues to listen over the old socket for any new requests.
send(int s, char *buffer, int length, int flags)	Sends data through a socket s. The location and length of the data correspond to parameters buffer and length, respectively. It does not specify the destination because a previous connect or accept command established who is on the other end of the socket. The flags parameter is not important here.
recv(int s, char *buffer, int length, int flags)	Receives data from a socket and stores it in the specified buffer. The length parameter specifies the buffer's length. As with send, the flags parameter is not important here.
close(int s);	Closes the specified socket.

[1] Note the second parameter. The previously described struct sockaddr_in is a form of a more generalized structure (struct sockaddr) and is used with Internet applications. However, some versions of Linux require that an address to the more general structure be used with certain socket commands. In the sample code that we describe later, we will cast a struct sockaddr_in address as a struct sockaddr address.

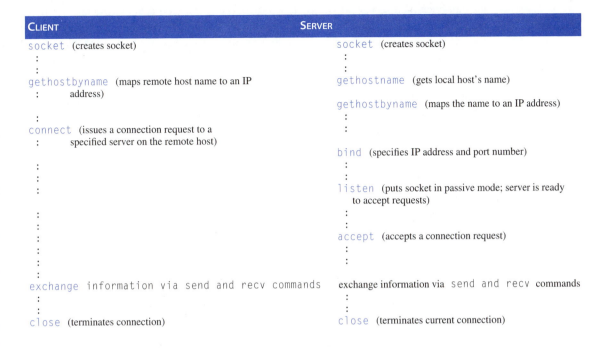

CLIENT	SERVER

```
socket  (creates socket)                         socket  (creates socket)
   :                                                :
   :                                                :
gethostbyname  (maps remote host name to an IP    gethostname  (gets local host's name)
   :          address)
                                                  gethostbyname  (maps the name to an IP address)
   :                                                :
connect  (issues a connection request to a          :
   :       specified server on the remote host)
                                                  bind  (specifies IP address and port number)
   :                                                :
   :                                                :
   :                                              listen  (puts socket in passive mode; server is ready
                                                          to accept requests)
   :                                                :
   :                                                :
   :                                              accept  (accepts a connection request)
   :                                                :
   :                                                :
exchange information via send and recv commands   exchange information via send and recv commands
   :                                                :
   :                                                :
close  (terminates connection)                    close  (terminates current connection)
```

Figure 12.3   Outline of Client and Server Using Socket-Related Commands

on different machines. The only assumption we are making is that both have Internet connections.

The figure shows that the first thing both the client and server do is create a socket with the socket command. After that, the client calls gethostbyname to determine the IP address associated with the text address of the remote host running the server. Once the IP address is known, the client connects to the server. At this point the client is able to exchange messages with the server using send and recv commands. We will have to define the rules governing the exchange and determining when the exchange is done. The last thing the client does is close the socket and quit.

The server, upon creating a socket, must get the name of the host on which it is running (call to gethostname). It then uses the host name and calls gethostbyname to get relevant information about it (i.e., its IP address) and stores it in a hostent structure. It then calls bind to associate an IP address and port number with the socket and begins listening for any incoming calls. When a call arrives, the server accepts the call, and the socket connection with a client is made. At that point it follows the same protocol the client uses to exchange a series of messages. When it is done it closes the socket and quits.

Certainly there are details to fill in, but it helps to understand the framework in which we describe them. Therefore, before you continue, you should make sure you at least understand the reasons for these socket-related calls and the basic organization of client and server programs. The next step is to provide details for working client and server programs. Figures 12.4 and 12.5 contain source code for these programs. You can copy and run them according to the following rules (assuming they are run under Linux):

- Compile the server and run it first. The server must be running so that the client has someone to call.

- We used a port number of 6250 so as not to conflict with any other port numbers in use. You are free to use other available port numbers, but you may have to check with local administration to see if a firewall blocks any communications based on port number.

- Compile the client and assume the executable file is named `myftp`. Run the client by entering the command `myftp text-address-of-host.` For example, if the text address of the host computer is hercules.uwgb.edu, then you run the client by typing `myftp hercules.uwgb.edu.`

- The server will transfer a predetermined file to the client. That is, the server chooses the file name.

- The client will ask you what name you would like to give to the file that it gets from the server.

- The server reads the text file, divides it into packets, and sends them to the client in groups of five. After every fifth packet the server waits for an acknowledgment from the client.

- The client responds accordingly, receiving the packets and extracting file data from them. It stores the data from each packet in a text file. After the last packet arrives, the file transfer is complete. The client also sends an acknowledgment after the receipt of every fifth packet.

- There is no error detection, and flow control is restricted to what we have just described.

We now begin a description of the client and server. For the most part, we will limit the discussion to logic related to the sockets and leave it to the reader to study the details related to the C language. Comments in the source code should help, and we will provide some general descriptions related to tasks that are primarily C oriented.

Client Source Code   The beginning of the client (Figure 12.4) contains header files* that you must include. They contain definitions for the socket-related calls and for the data structures we have described. We have defined a fairly simple protocol packet. The first thing it contains is a `servicetype` field indicating different

---

* This program was tested under Red Hat Linux. Some header files may be different depending on the UNIX variant used.

```
/*****************************/
/*        CLIENT         */
/*        CLIENT         */
/*        CLIENT         */
/*****************************/
/* This program is designed as a client that will call on a server running on another machine. The as-
   sumed protocol is TCP/IP and connections are via the Internet */

#define PACKETSIZE 20
#include <sys/types.h>
#include <stdio.h>
#include <sys/socket.h>
#include <netinet/in.h>
#include <netdb.h>

/define PORTNUM 6250

typedef enum {data, ack} servicetype;

/* transmission unit for this program's protocol */
typedef struct
{
  servicetype service;          /* type of packet */
  int     sequence;             /* packet's sequence number */
  int     datasize;             /* amount of data (in bytes) in packet */
  int     last;                 /* last packet indicator */
  char    data[PACKETSIZE];     /* holds data */
  int     checksum;             /* for error detection */
} PACKET;

/******************************************/
/* open a file and return its identifier */
/******************************************/
FILE * openfile( )

  char * filename;
  FILE * fid;

  printf("This program will copy a file from a remote server\n");
  printf("Enter the name under which the file should be saved>");
  filename = (char *) malloc(30);
  scanf("%s", filename);
  if ((fid = fopen(filename, "w")) == NULL)
  {
    printf("error opening file\n");
    exit (1);
  }
  free(filename);
  return fid;
}

/*******************/
/* create a socket */
/*******************/
int opensocket( )
{
  int s;
  if ((s = socket (AF_INET, SOCK_STREAM, 0)) < 0)
  {
```

Figure 12.4   Client Program

```
    perror ("socket error");
    exit (1);
  }
  return s;
}

/*************************************************************/
/* get remote host information and connect to remote server */
/*************************************************************/
void makeconnection(int argc, char *argv[ ], int s)
{
  struct hostent * ph;                        /* holds remote host name and address information */
  struct sockaddr_in sa;                      /* holds IP address and protocol port */

  memset(&sa,0,sizeof(sa));                   /* zero out the sa structure */
  if (argc !=2)                               /* Be sure the command to run the client contains
                                                 the remote host's text address */
  {
    printf ("Error in command line\n");
    exit (1);
  }
  if ((ph = gethostbyname (argv[1])) == NULL) /* get relevant information about the remote host */
  {
    printf("error in gethostbyname\n");
    exit(1);
  }                                           /* Store remote host's IP address, server's port
                                                 number, protocol type into sa structure */
  memcpy((char*) &sa.sin_addr, ph->h_addr, ph->h_length);
  sa.sin_port = htons ((u_short) PORTNUM);    /* specify port number of remote server */
  sa.sin_family = ph->h_addrtype;
  if (connect (s, &sa, sizeof (sa)) < 0)      /* connect to remote server */
  {
    perror ("connect error");
    exit (1);
  }
}

/*************************************************************/
/* get a file from the remote server in fixed-size packets */
/*************************************************************/
void getfile(FILE * fid, int s)
{
  PACKET * packet;                            /* protocol packet */
  int i;

  packet = (PACKET *) malloc (sizeof(*packet));
  do
  {
    if (recv(s, packet, sizeof(*packet), 0) <= 0)  /* get packet from remote server */
    {
      printf("error reading\n");
      exit(1);
    }
    printf("Received packet %4d: %s\n", packet->sequence, packet->data);
    for (i=0;i < packet->datasize; i++)        /* Store packet's contents into text file */
      putc (packet->data[i], fid);
    if (packet->sequence % 5 == 4)             /* If this was the 5th packet, send an
                                                  acknowledgment */
    {
```

Figure 12.4 Continued

626

```
      printf("acknowledging 5th packet-Press enter to continuen");
      getchar();
      packet->service = ack;
      if (send(s, packet, sizeof(*packet), 0) <= 0)          /* Send the acknowledgment */
        {
        printf("ERROR in send\n");
        exit(1);
        }
      }
    } while (!packet->last);                    /* Continue repeating the above until the last
                                                   packet received */

   fclose(fid);
  }
void main (int argc,char *argv[])
{
  int s;
  FILE * fid;

  fid = openfile();
  s = opensocket();
  makeconnection(argc, argv, s);
  getfile(fid, s);
  close(s);
}
```

Figure 12.4   Continued

Figure 12.5   Server Program

```
/*****************************/
/*          SERVER           */
/*          SERVER           */
/*          SERVER           */
/*****************************/
/* This program is designed to act as a server that will accept calls from a client written on another
   machine. The assumed protocol is TCP/IP and connections are via the Internet */

#define PACKETSIZE 20
#include <sys/types.h>
#include <sys/socket.h>
#include <netinet/in.h>
#include <netdb.h>
#include <stdio.h>
#include <sys/param.h>

#define PORTNUM 6250

typedef enum {data, ack} servicetype;
/* transmission unit for this program's protocol */
typedef struct
{
  servicetype service;          /* type of packet */
  int    sequence;              /* packet's sequence number */
  int    datasize;              /* amount of data (in bytes) in packet */
  int    last;                  /* last packet indicator */
  char   data[PACKETSIZE];      /* holds data */
  int    checksum;              /* for error detection */
} PACKET;
```

```
/**************************************************/
/* get host info for eventual socket connection */
/**************************************************/
struct sockaddr_in gethoststuff()
{
  struct sockaddr_in sa;                          /* holds IP address and protocol port */
  struct hostent * ph;                            /* holds host name and address info */
  char myname[MAXHOSTNAMELEN+1];                  /* host name */

  gethostname(myname, MAXHOSTNAMELEN);            /* Get name of host on which this server is running */

  printf("host name is %s\n", myname);
  if ((ph = gethostbyname(myname)) == NULL)       /* Get relevant information about the host */
  {
    printf("gethostbyname failed\n");
    exit(1);
  }
  memset(&sa, 0, sizeof(struct sockaddr_in));
                                                  /* Put protocol family type and port number into sa
                                                     structure */
  sa.sin_family = ph->h_addrtype;
  sa.sin_port = htons(PORTNUM);
  return sa;
}


/****************************************/
/* Open a file and return its identifier */
/****************************************/
FILE * openfile()
{
  FILE * fid;
  char * filename = "test.dat";

  if (( fid=fopen(filename, "r")) == NULL)
  {
    printf("error opening file\n");
    exit(1);
  }
  return fid;
}


/*******************/
/* Create a socket */
/*******************/
int opensocket()
{
  int s;

  if (( s = socket (AF_INET, SOCK_STREAM, 0)) < 0) /* Create a socket */
  {
    perror ("socket error");
    exit (1);
  }
  return s;
}


/******************************************/
/* Bind and listen for a socket connection*/
/******************************************/
```

Figure 12.5   Continued

```
void bindnlisten (int s, struct sockaddr_in sa)
{
  if (bind (s, (struct sockaddr*) &sa, sizeof (sa)) < 0)   /* Assign IP address and port number with
                                                              socket s */
  {
    perror ("bind error");
    exit (1);
  }
  listen (s,5);                                            /* Listen for incoming client calls */
}
/*****************************/
/* Accept a socket connection */
/*****************************/
int acceptconn(int s)
{
  int sd;
  struct sockaddr_in sa;
  unsigned int sasize;

  sasize = sizeof(sa);
  if ((sd = accept (s, (struct sockaddr*) &sa, &sasize)) < 0)   /* Accept a connection */
  {
    perror ("accept error");
    exit (1);
  }
  printf("connection accepted from: %u\n", sa.sin_addr.s_addr);
  return sd;
}
/*********************************************************/
/* Send the contents of a file using fixed-size packets */
/* Wait for an acknowledgment after every 5th one       */
/*********************************************************/
void sendfile(FILE * fid, int sd)
{
  PACKET * packet;                                        /* protocol packet */
  int i,
  count = 0;                                              /* packet count */
  char c;
  packet = (PACKET *) malloc (sizeof *packet);
  packet->last=0;
  c=getc(fid);
  do
  {
    for (i=0; i<PACKETSIZE && c != EOF; i++,c=getc(fid))  /* Put file data into packet */
      packet->data[i] = c;
    packet->datasize = i;
    if (c==EOF)
      packet->last=1;
    packet->sequence = count++;
    packet->service = data;
    printf("Sending packet %4d: %s\n", packet->sequence, packet->data);
    if (send(sd, packet, sizeof (*packet), 0) <= 0)        /* Send packet to client */
    {
      printf("error in writing to socket\n");
      exit(1);
    }
    if (count % 5 = 0)                                     /* After the 5th packet wait for an
                                                             acknowledgment */
    {
```

Figure 12.5 Continued

629

```
   if (recv(sd, packet, sizeof *packet, 0) < 0)
    {
      printf("socket read failed\n");
      exit(1);
    }
    printf("Receiving acknowledgment \n");
  }
  } while (c != EOF);                          /* Stop when end of file is reached */
  printf("file transfer done\n");
  free(packet);
}

int main (int argc, char *argv[])
{
  int s;                              /* identifies a socket */
  int sd;                             /* identifies connection to socket */
  struct sockaddr_in sa;              /* holds IP address and protocol port */
  int i;                              /* temp variable */
  FILE * fid;                         /* file identifier */

  sa = gethoststuff();
  s = opensocket();
  bindnlisten(s, sa);
  while (1)                           /* This test server will repeatedly accept calls from
                                         clients*/
  {
    sd=acceptconn(s);                 /* call function to accept call. The new socket is
                                         sd*/

    if (fork()==0)/* Create child process to do file transfer */
    {
      close(s);                       /* Close socket s. Child does not need it since it
                                         uses socket sd */

      printf("beginning file transfer\n");
      fid=openfile();
      sendfile(fid,sd);
      fclose(fid);
      close(sd);
      exit (1);
    }
    else
      close(sd);                      /* Close socket sd. Parent does not need it. */
  }
  printf("press enter to quit\n");
  getchar();
  close(s);
}
```

Figure 12.5 Continued

types of packets. In this example, there are only two packet types: Data and Ack (for acknowledgment). It also contains a sequence number, a field indicating how many data bytes it contains, a field indicating which packet is the last in a stream, and a Checksum field (which we don't use here). For simplicity, these fields are type `int`. Finally, the remaining field is an array with a storage capacity of 20 bytes, representing the data in the packet.

A cursory examination of the client shows it has four C functions: `openfile`, `opensocket`, `makeconnection`, and `getfile`. The function `openfile` prompts the user to enter a name under which the client will store the transferred file. Once the user enters the name, the function opens it in write mode. If all goes well, the function returns the file identifier. The second function, `opensocket`, creates a socket. It contains a provision to exit the program if the socket call fails. If successful, the function returns the socket identifier.

The function `makeconnection` gets remote host information and connects to the server running on it associated with the specified port number. Remember, we are assuming that the user enters the text address of the remote host when typing the name of an executable client (e.g., `myftp hercules.uwgb.edu`). As such, the text string `hercules.uwgb.edu` is stored in the main function parameter `argv[1]`, and the other main function parameter, `argc`, has a value of 2. The function calls `gethostbyname` to put relevant remote host information into the `hostent` structure located via the pointer variable `ph`. Then it moves other relevant information, such as the server's port number, into the socket address structure specified by the variable `sa`.* Once variable sa contains necessary information, the function calls the function `connect`, thereby sending a connection request to the server.

The last function is the most complex because it contains the rules governing the file transfer. Yet, mercifully, it is simpler than many other protocols we have described. We are truly beginning to see the advantages of layering now. As mentioned previously, the protocol requires the client to receive five packets, extract their contents, and write them to a file. After receiving every fifth packet, the client creates a packet of type Ack and sends it back to the server. It continues doing this until it receives a packet for which `packet→last` is 1. The function has a few `printf` and `getchar` commands that serve no purpose other than to let the person running it see what is happening. After the last packet arrives, the client closes the file. It then returns to the main program, where it closes the socket and quits. The file has been transferred.

Server Source Code   The server program (Figure 12.5) is a little more complex since it has more to do. Like the client, it must include all necessary headers and define a compatible packet structure. It contains six functions: `gethoststuff`, `openfile`, `opensocket`, `bindnlisten`, `acceptconn`, and `sendfile`. Its main part also is a little more complex, so let's start there. Since this server is strictly for testing, we have designed it to accept precisely three calls and do the same thing each time. This can test its ability to respond to different clients concurrently. Each

---

* The code contains a reference to a function `htons` (host to network short). When dealing with different machines, an incompatibility in the way integers are stored may occur. Some machines store the most significant bits in bytes with a larger address (little endian), whereas some store the most significant bits in bytes with a smaller address (big endian). The `htons` operator makes sure that the network correctly interprets data defined in your program.

time it accepts a connection request, it returns a new socket (sd) with all the same properties as socket s. The server then forks a new child process to handle the details of the file transfer using the socket sd. It is imperative to understand the Linux fork command to see how this works; you should consult a UNIX or Linux book and study it if you are not familiar with this command.

To summarize, the fork command creates a separate child process that executes the code immediately after the line "if (fork() ==0)." This section of code closes the socket s (because this is the socket that the parent uses, the child has no need for it), calls on functions to open a file and return its identifier and to do the file transfer, and quits. Remember, it is the child that quits; the parent process is still running and able to accept more calls. In this case, the parent executes the line after the else that closes the socket returned by the accept call (variable sd). Because this is the socket that the child uses, the parent has no need for it.

The previously mentioned functions perform tasks indicative of their names. The first function, gethoststuff, gets information relevant to the host on which the server is running (for portability, the server code should make no assumptions about the host on which it is running). It also stores necessary information in the socket address structure sa and returns a copy of it. Function openfile opens a specified text file (we are assuming a file named test.dat) for read access and returns the file identifier. This, as you probably guessed, is the file that the server will transfer. The function opensocket creates a socket and returns its identifier. It has a provision to exit if, for some reason, the socket cannot be created. The bindnlisten function assigns the address and port number to the socket and puts the server into a listen mode.

At some point a connection request arrives (as a result of the client's call to connect). When it arrives, the server accepts the connection. The accept call creates a new socket whose identifier is returned and associated with variable sd. As previously mentioned, this socket has all the same properties as socket s. When control returns to the main program, the server forks, thus creating a child that uses sd and closes s. The parent closes sd and returns to the top of the loop to accept another call when it comes in over s.

Finally, the function sendfile reads 20 characters at a time from the text file and deposits them into packets. It sends five packets at a time before it waits for an acknowledgment from the client. As with the client, there are printf statements to let you see what is happening as the program runs. Eventually, the end of the file is reached and the function stops creating packets. At that point, the file transfer is complete.

Sockets are a very powerful and flexible interface to a network. Although they were traditionally developed for UNIX environments and commonly used by C language programs, neither is required any more. For example, the Java language supports sockets and can be implemented in Windows environments. Many of the ideas are, of course, the same but the details differ because of Java's object-oriented nature.

To illustrate the flexibility, extensibility, and platform and language independence of socket connections, reference [Sh02] expands the project from this section to include a Java client and server. The same Java client can download a file from either a Java server or the C server described here. Similarly, the same Java server can respond to download requests from either a Java client or the C client described here. Specifically, this expanded project shows that the client and server

- May be written in the same or different languages (C or Java)
- May be written on the same or different platforms (Windows or Linux)
- May or may not use different language paradigms (object-oriented or non-object-oriented)
- May be written on big endian or little endian environments
- May use byte or Unicode representation of data

A complete copy of the Java and C code for both the client and server can be downloaded from www.uwgb.edu/shayw/courses/files358.htm.

12.3 WORLD WIDE WEB

Almost certainly, the most significant development to occur during the past decade is the **World Wide Web (WWW).** Protocols such as Telnet, FTP, and email have drawn the Internet community together and have made enormous amounts of information available. But the development of the Web has, among other things, made the information much easier to reach. Whether for serious research or simply for fun and games, millions of people have discovered how much the Web has to offer. They have also discovered frustration and delays as the number of websites has grown exponentially. This growth has not only caused vast amounts of traffic throughout the Internet, resulting in delays, but has also often hindered the task of finding useful information because of the sheer volume of information.

There is so much that can be said about the Web that, as with other topics we have discussed, entire books have been written on the subject. These books range from lists of various websites to discussions of Web protocols to helping you develop your own interactive Web pages. Without question the Web is an important topic in this field and should be discussed. The problem is deciding what to discuss. We believe an important goal is to blend some theory with application. This contributes to your overall knowledge base and provides some useful skills as well. Toward this end, the goals of the remaining sections are to provide the following:

- An overview of the Web and its fundamental operational concept.
- An overview of how to create a Web page. We will describe only enough to generate a minimally functional Web page.
- A discussion of the integration of programming and Web page development. This is what we are really aiming for, and the previous items serve as short-term goals needed to do this. We will deal with a client/server model again and will describe how to incorporate programming into both the client and server side of the protocols.

This last item poses some real challenges, primarily because there are several different options and we cannot cover them all. Even within one option there is an enormous amount of material and we have to be selective.

Some of the tools used in Web environments are as follows:

- **HTML (Hypertext Markup Language).** HTML has specifiers or tags that allow the creation and formatting of a Web page.

- **JavaScript.** A scripting language whose code is embedded in an HTML document. The client executes the code to accept and respond to user input.

- **VBScript.** Performs a function similar to JavaScript except it is based on the Visual Basic language.

- **Java applet.** Allows the client to execute routines written in the Java programming language.

- **XML (Extensible Markup Language).** XML is similar to HTML except that HTML deals mainly with the display of information in a Web page, whereas XML defines a standard for describing what the data actually represents.

- **ASP (Active Server Pages).** HTML pages that contain scripts written, for example, in JavaScript or VBScript. The scripts receive information from a client and describe action that a Microsoft Web server takes before returning information back to the client.

- **Perl.** A scripting language often used, for example, in UNIX or Linux environments for CGI programming (described later) to store information into and retrieve information from server text files.

- **C language.** A long-standing language whose compiled code can be called on in a Web environment to perform actions such as searching a database.

We do not have the space to describe all of these tools in detail. However, we will introduce HTML and JavaScript for client-side programming and follow up with examples of Perl and C programs for CGI programming on the server side. We will also provide a couple of working examples representative of many applications on the Web. Although we do not provide all the detail, we can show you enough to get started on your own Web programming.

WEB PAGE ACCESS

We will assume the reader has had some Web experience, at least to the extent of accessing various sites and following (clicking) links to other sites. Indeed, the ease with which anyone can use the Web has been both an enormous advantage and (to some) a disadvantage. We begin by describing the underlying actions that occur when surfing through the Web.

Fundamental to Web operations is **HTTP (Hypertext Transfer Protocol),** a client/server protocol designed to allow the exchange of information over the Web. HTTP defines the types of requests that a browser can make and the types of responses a server returns. Through HTTP, a user can retrieve Web pages from remote servers or store pages on the server if he or she has appropriate access. HTTP also provides the ability to append new information to pages or to delete them altogether. We will focus strictly on the retrieval aspect.

Figure 12.6 shows the basic concepts involved. A user at a personal computer runs a **browser.** Common browsers at the time of this writing are Netscape Navigator and Internet Explorer. The browser runs on the client side and has the ability to display the contents of a Web page.* We'll discuss what a Web page looks like shortly, but for now just assume it is a document (file) that presents information to the user. In addition each Web page has *links* (references) to other Web pages. These pages are stored in auxiliary storage accessible by remote HTTP servers.

A user can follow a link by placing the mouse cursor over some designated text or picture and clicking the mouse button. At that point the local HTTP client sends a request to a remote HTTP server for a specified Web page. The server responds by transferring that page back to the client, where it eventually replaces the old page on the screen (although the old page is usually buffered in case the user wants to return to it). The user can again follow a link from this new page and call up yet another Web page. Another remote HTTP server responds the same way and transfers the requested Web page back to the browser. The user can repeat this process as often as needed. Links can connect documents stored at HTTP servers located all over the world, and with a click of a mouse button a document is transferred to your local computer.

Figure 12.6   Web Overview

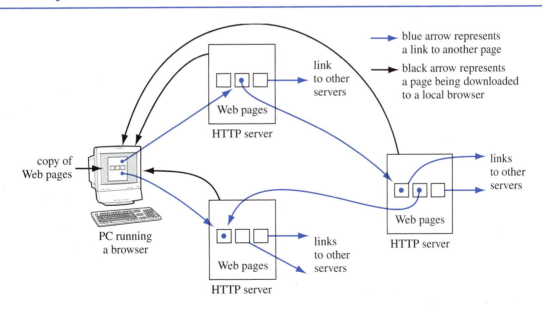

---

* A Web page is perhaps more accurately called an *HTML document,* but we'll discuss that later.

Of course, we have oversimplified things. Perhaps, more correctly stated, we have assumed the existence of TCP, IP, and data link protocols to handle the details of the actual transfer. Thus, from a certain perspective it *is* that simple. Once again, we see the benefits of layered protocols because the tasks at higher layers are much simpler to describe if we assume lower layers exist.

At the heart of all of this is the answer to a question: How does a browser know where to look for a requested page? Every page accessible via the Web must be uniquely named to avoid confusion. To accomplish this, three things are necessary: the page's location, a name unique to that location, and the protocol needed to access that page. Collectively, these three items define the **Uniform Resource Locator (URL)** of the page, which has the form

protocol://site-address/name

For example, you can access the author's Web page (also called the *home page*) via the URL

http://www.uwgb.edu/shayw

The protocol is HTTP,* and the site address is www.uwgb.edu. The last part, shayw, is an indirect reference to a specific file. The string "shayw" represents an account on the host computer www.uwgb.edu. That account contains a file named index.htm. Referencing the above URL causes this file's contents to appear in the browser.† This is a conventional way to access a person's home page without worrying about naming conventions on the host computer. Of course, if you wanted to access a different file, then you would have to indicate it explicitly. For example, the syllabus for our computer networks course is in a file named syll358.htm in the author's Web directory. You can access that page using

http://www.uwgb.edu/shayw/syll358.htm

Of course, making a list of all pages you might want to access and referencing them explicitly is awkward. An alternative to specifying a page directly is to follow a link to it from an entry on another Web page. That's a relatively straightforward thing to do, but first we need to describe how to present the contents of a Web page to someone running a browser.

HYPERTEXT MARKUP LANGUAGE

The next logical step is to describe how to set up a Web page and how to include links in it. The language that allows you to do this is the **Hypertext Markup Language (HTML).** Basically, a user creates a file (usually with a .htm or .html extension) containing HTML elements. This file (also called an **HTML document**), defines

---

* The HTTP protocol is not the only prefix possible in a URL. One can also specify other protocols, such as FTP, Telnet, and email.

† Depending on the site, there are small differences. Some sites require a tilde (~) prior to the user name, others default to a file named index.html (instead of index.htm), and still others require that the files be in a specific subdirectory of the specified account. Check your site to determine the defaults.

how a Web page appears on a browser. (We will ignore the case of text-only browsers here.) However, before we provide a short overview to HTML, the first thing we need to know is just what can be in an HTML document.

When viewing a Web page through a browser, a user can see the following types of content:

- Straight text.

- Graphic or animated images.

- Links to other HTML documents. Typically, links are represented by underlined text that has a different color or by an image. Moving the mouse cursor over the text or image and clicking the mouse button causes a new HTML document to be downloaded and appear on the browser's screen.

In general, HTML can provide some pretty sophisticated-looking pages with fancy formats and color-coordinated backgrounds and images. Because the author has no talent with color coordination (his wife can testify to that), we'll just concentrate on some basic functionality. We'll leave it to the imagination of the reader to generate creative Web pages. We also will make no attempt to be complete in our description of HTML, but we will describe some of the more common elements of it. There are an almost uncountable number of HTML books on the market that can provide all the information you need.

Tags   HTML uses *tags* to indicate what you want to include in an HTML document and how you want to display it. They are typically written as follows:

$$<tag\ options> \ldots \text{some stuff in between} \ldots </tag>$$

Some tags require both a beginning and ending delimiter. Both contain the tag identifier, but the ending delimiter also contains the character /. These delimiters tell the browser what to do with the stuff in between. In some cases, options specified in the beginning delimiter provide additional information.

Figure 12.7 shows a sample HTML document and some typical tags that allow the viewer to see three things: a graphic image, some basic text, and links to other documents. Figure 12.8 shows the actual displayed page. The first and last lines of Figure 12.7 correspond to the HTML tag (<html> and </html>) and indicate that everything in between should be interpreted according to HTML rules. Each HTML document has a *head* and a *body*. The tags <head> and </head> delimit the head, and the tags <body> and </body> delimit the body. The head can contain several things, one of which is a title (delimiters <title> and </title>). The browser takes text that is between the title tags and displays it at the top of the window. Can you see the phrase "The Title Goes Here" in Figure 12.8?

The body is where all of the text information, graphic images, and hypertext links will eventually go. For example, to display an image you must first create an image and store it in a file. The HTML image tag (<img>) specifies that file, and the image is displayed when viewing the document. The option in the image tag of Figure 12.7 specifies the file as "logo.gif." The image in Figure 12.8, which is our university's logo, was created previously and stored in that file. The center tag

```
<html>
<head>
<title>The Title Goes Here</title>
</head>
<body>
<center><img src = "logo.gif"></center>
<hr>
<center> <h1>Links to Courses</h1> </center>
This is a short paragraph containing links to three courses. Each can be
accessed by clicking on the course number. The first one is titled<B> Numerical
Analysis</B> and has a course number of <A HREF = "http://www.uwgb.edu/shayw/
syll350.htm">266-350</A>. The second course is titled <B>Data Structures</B> and
has a course number <A HREF = "http://www.uwgb.edu/shayw/syll351.htm">
266-351</A>. Finally the third course is titled <B> Data Communications and
Computer Networks</B> and has a course number <A HREF = "http://www.uwgb.edu/
shayw/syll358.htm">266-358</A>.
<hr>
If you have any comments or questions you can send them to <A HREF="mailto:
shayw@uwgb.edu"> Bill Shay</A> at the University of Wisconsin-Green Bay
<hr>
</body>
</html>
```

Figure 12.7   Sample HTML Document

Figure 12.8   View of HTML Document in Figure 12.7

delimiters (<center> and </center>) on either side of the image tag cause the image to be centered on the screen. If the center tag delimiters were not present, the image in Figure 12.8 would have appeared on the left side of the screen. The body contains a couple of tags (<hr>) that insert a horizontal rule. Figure 12.8 shows three dim horizontal lines that are used as separators. This is a common visual aid to help separate different parts of a display.

Most of the rest of the body contains text, which appears in Figure 12.8. There are, however, some differences in the way the text is displayed. Some text has a larger typeface, some is in boldface, and some is underlined (which actually corresponds to links). Again, HTML tags make the difference. The header tag delimiters <h1> and </h1> define a level 1 header. They cause any text between them to be displayed in a larger typeface. There are also tags corresponding to <h2>, <h3>, <h4>, <h5>, and <h6>, which have a similar effect except the type sizes vary. Tag <h1> defines the largest, and tag <h6> the smallest. Any text between the bold tags (<B> and </B>) appears in boldface.

The most important tags for our purpose are the *anchor tags* (<A> and </A>), for these define actions the user can choose with a simple click of a mouse button. Anchor tag delimiters have several forms and uses. One possibility is an anchor of the form

<A HREF=url> clickable text </A>

These delimiters serve two functions. The first is to display clickable text.* This means that you can move the mouse cursor over that text and click a mouse button to retrieve a remote document. The second is to define the URL of that document. For example, Figure 12.7 has the following embedded in the body:

<A HREF = "http://www.uwgb.edu/shayw/syll350.htm">266-350</A>

The HREF option defines the URL of a document stored in the author's Web directory. The clickable text in this case is "266-350." Figure 12.8 shows that text as underlined. The user could move the mouse cursor over it, click a button, and retrieve the desired document, in this case a file named syll350.htm in the author's Web directory.

Anchors can also be used to initiate actions besides those used to retrieve an HTML document. Toward the end of Figure 12.7 there is another anchor,

<A HREF="mailto:shayw@uwgb.edu">Bill Shay</A>

In this case, the clickable text corresponds to the author's name. The HREF option identifies a mail server program. When activated, a form appears that allows the user to enter an email message to be sent to the email address specified (in this case, shayw@uwgb.edu). The form also includes a Send button that, when clicked, sends the message.

Table 12.4 contains some other commonly used HTML tags and a brief description of what they do. There are many more tags and many other options to the tags we list. The interested reader can consult any HTML book on the market.

---

* An image tag can be used instead of text, creating a clickable image.

Table 12.4 Some HTML Tags

TAG	MEANING
<A> ... </A>	Anchor. Displays the text located between the delimiters. If there is an image tag between the delimiters, then it is displayed. The anchor also has an option to specify a URL to which a link is made if the user movesf the mouse cursor to the text or image and clicks the mouse button.
<B> ... </B>	Boldface. Text between the delimiters is displayed in boldface.
<body> ... </body>	Delimits the body of an HTML document.

	Line break. Inserts a line break in the Web page. That is, anything after <br> appears beginning on the next line.
<center> ... </center>	Centers the text located between the delimiters.
<font> ... </font>	Options affect the color and size of any text between the delimiters.
<form> ... </form>	Creates and displays a form that allows a user to enter information into specified locations on the form. The form can then be submitted for some action to occur. In some cases the form is also used to display results obtained from the information that was entered.
<h1> ... </h1>	Displays the text located between the delimiters in a large typesize. There are also tags for <h2>, <h3>, <h4>, <h5>, and <h6>, each of which defines a different size for the text.
<head> ... </head>	Delimits the head of an HTML document.
<HR>	Displays a horizontal rule, a line used to visually separate parts of a Web page.
<html> ... </html>	Indicates that everything between the delimiters is to be interpreted according to HTML language rules.
<I> ... </I>	Displays the text located between the delimiters in italics.
<img>	Specifies a file containing a graphic image or animation that is displayed when viewing the Web page.
<input>	Used with a form, it allows a user to enter information.
<li>	Indicates a list element in a list.
<option> ... </option>	Used to provide options in a pop-up menu.
<P>	Indicates the start of a new paragraph in the Web page.
<script> ... </script>	Delimits script language code for client-side programming.
<select> ... </select>	Allows user to select among a list of options in a pop-up menu.
<table> ... </table>	Defines a table to be displayed on the Web page.
<title> ... </title>	Defines the title of an HTML document.
<ul> ... </ul>	Defines an unordered list of elements.

HTML FORMS

As we stated previously, a major goal of this section is to introduce the reader to Web programming, or the capability of a client or server to take certain actions beyond those specified by HTML. We begin by discussing an HTML *form*. You can also think of it as a template for the entering and display of information. Forms are quite common, especially when conducting Internet searches via search engines such as Google or Yahoo. Prior to requesting a search, the user enters keywords or phrases into a form. The user can click a Clear button to erase anything he or she has typed or a Submit or Search button to submit the information to the search engine. Depending on the search engine, the user may also be able to select various options that affect the search results, such as looking specifically for sound or graphic image files.

Submitting forms often requires actions from both the client and server. For example, perhaps your local pizza parlor has a Web page allowing you to order a pizza. You might fill out a form containing your name, address, telephone number, pizza ingredients, and so forth. When the form is submitted, the server should respond with the cost and perhaps an estimated delivery time. The client might also take some action, such as verifying certain information on the form. For example, if someone orders a large pizza with mushroom, pepperoni, and earthworms, the client might recognize one of these as not a viable topping (never did like mushrooms). The idea is to identify certain requests as nonsense before going through all the trouble of submitting the form to the server. In general, this is more efficient because it prevents the Web software from submitting requests that cannot possibly be satisfied.

We begin the discussion of forms by giving an example of a form that can be handled entirely by the client. Figure 12.9 shows a form that allows a user to enter a series of numbers and to calculate any of the largest, smallest, and sum of the numbers. There are some restrictions, as explained in the form's instructions, and eliminating them makes nice assignments. The form contains the following elements:

- Text providing instructions on what to do and how to do it.
- Space (text box) allowing the user to enter a series of numbers.
- Spaces allowing the display of the largest, smallest, or sum of the entered numbers.
- Check boxes allowing the user to determine which of the calculations he or she wants displayed.
- Buttons that cause an action to occur. Possible actions are to make the desired calculations or to clear (erase) all the entered numbers. The latter option exists in case the user made an error and needs to reenter a new set of numbers.

Initially, the form's spaces are blank. Figure 12.9 shows the results after the user has done the following:

1. Entered the numbers 4, 5, 6, 5, 4, and 3.
2. Clicked the check boxes to calculate the total and largest of the entered numbers.
3. Clicked the Calculate button.

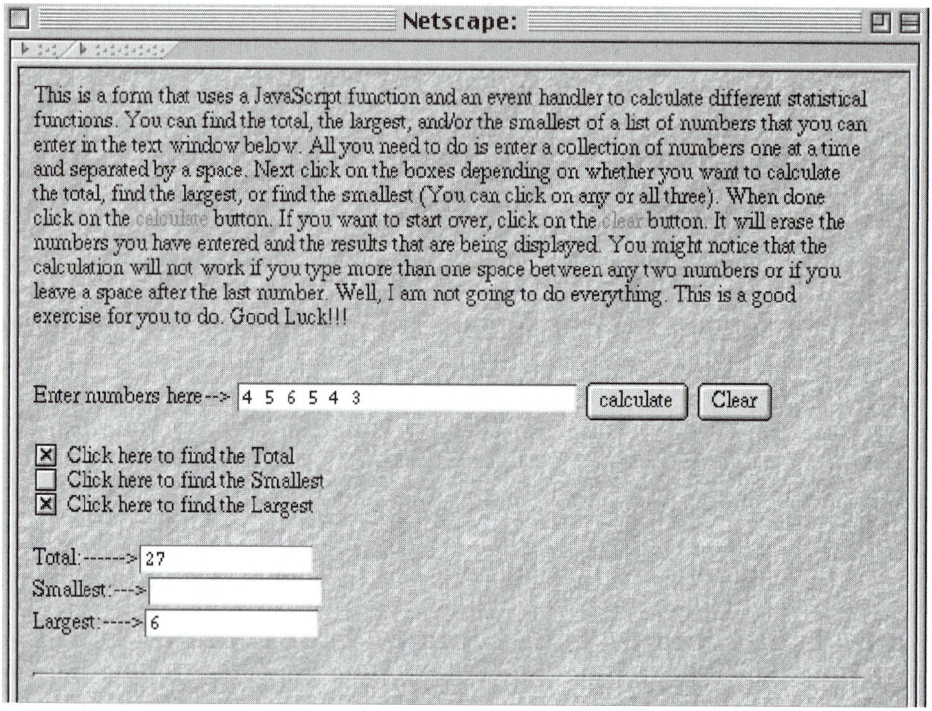

This is a form that uses a JavaScript function and an event handler to calculate different statistical functions. You can find the total, the largest, and/or the smallest of a list of numbers that you can enter in the text window below. All you need to do is enter a collection of numbers one at a time and separated by a space. Next click on the boxes depending on whether you want to calculate the total, find the largest, or find the smallest (You can click on any or all three). When done click on the calculate button. If you want to start over, click on the clear button. It will erase the numbers you have entered and the results that are being displayed. You might notice that the calculation will not work if you type more than one space between any two numbers or if you leave a space after the last number. Well, I am not going to do everything. This is a good exercise for you to do. Good Luck!!!

Enter numbers here --> [4 5 6 5 4 3   ]   [calculate] [Clear]

[X] Click here to find the Total
[ ] Click here to find the Smallest
[X] Click here to find the Largest

Total: ------> [27   ]
Smallest: ---> [   ]
Largest: ----> [6   ]

Figure 12.9   HTML Form for Statistical Calculations

Performing these actions causes the 27 and 6 to be displayed in the Total and Largest boxes, respectively. If the user clicked the Clear button, all of the numbers in Figure 12.9 would disappear. The user could then enter a new collection of numbers and get new results.

If the user does as instructed, the results are returned. But what if the user does *not* do as instructed? Anyone who has programmed for others knows that one of the most difficult aspects of programming is responding to things the user is not supposed to do. For example, what if the user enters numbers but does not select any of the three check boxes before clicking the Calculate button? What if the user clicks the Calculate button but has not yet entered any numbers?

Figure 12.10 indicates possible responses to each of these actions. Figure 12.10a shows a window that appears if the user clicks the Calculate button without having checked any of the boxes. Figure 12.10b shows a window that appears if the user clicks the Calculate button without having entered any numbers. In either case, the user would click the OK button and try again to use the form correctly.

All of the actions described here must be programmed by the person setting up the Web page and can be handled through the use of scripts and a scripting language. A **script** is essentially a program that is automatically executed in response to another action. The **scripting language** is, of course, the language used to write

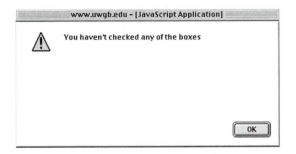

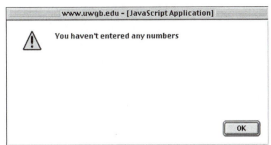

(a) User did not check any boxes

(b) User did not enter any numbers

Figure 12.10 Responses to Unexpected User Actions

the script. What we need to do next is describe how each of the elements in the example can be set up in an HTML document.

The first step is to show how to define a form and how to use it for both input and output. Figure 12.11 shows HTML commands that define the form of Figure 12.9. The first half of the form simply contains the text providing user instructions, as shown in Figure 12.9. Within the text are two font tags with a color option specifying the 24-bit color value (8 bits for each of red, green, and blue) of the delimited

Figure 12.11 HTML Commands to Define the Form of Figure 12.9

```
<form>
This is a form that uses a JavaScript function and an event handler to calculate
different statistical functions. You can find the total, the largest, and/or
the smallest of a list of numbers that you can enter in the text window below.
All you need to do is enter a collection of numbers one at a time and separated
by a space. Next click on the boxes depending on whether you want to calculate
the total, find the largest, or find the smallest. (You can click on any or all
three).
When done click on the <FONT COLOR="ff0000">calculate </FONT>button. If you want
to start over, click on the <FONT COLOR="ff0000">clear </FONT>button. It will
erase the numbers you have entered and the results that are being displayed. You
might notice that the calculation will not work if you type more than one space
between any two numbers or if you leave a space after the last number. Well, I
am not going to do everything. This is a good exercise for you to do. Good
Luck!!!<BR><BR><BR>
<left> Enter numbers here-> <Input type="text" Name="expr" size=30>
<Input Type="button" Value="calculate" Onclick="compute(this.form)">
<Input Type="reset" Value="Clear"><BR><BR></left>
<Input Type="checkbox" Name="gettotal">Click here to find the Total<BR>
<Input Type="checkbox" Name="getmin" >Click here to find the Smallest<BR>
<Input Type="checkbox" Name="getmax">Click here to find the Largest<BR><BR>
Total:——><Input Type="text" name="total" size=15><BR>
Smallest:--><Input Type="text" name="min" size=15><BR>
Largest:—><Input Type="text" name="max" size=15><BR>
</Form>
```

text. In this case the color value of ff0000 means there is only a red component, so the delimited text (in this case, the words *calculate* and *clear*) appears on a Web browser in red.

The lines following the instructions contain *input tags* that define how information is entered into the form. Each box, button, or check box of Figure 12.9 is defined by one input tag. Note that each input tag has several options, or types. The options are as follows:

- **Type = "text".** This is for free-form input and output. It causes a text field to be displayed in which a user can type anything he or she wants. As we will see, a client script can also use this type to display information. In Figure 12.9, the numbers the user enters and the eventual results all correspond to this type.

- **Type = "checkbox".** This allows the user to move the mouse cursor over a box and select it by clicking the mouse button. When selected, an X is displayed (see Figure 12.9). The user may select as many check boxes as he or she wants.

- **Type = "reset".** This option results in the display of a button that, when clicked, erases all information the user may have entered into the form. The input boxes are either cleared or restored to any default values that may have been set up when the form was defined.

- **Type = "button".** This creates a button that, when clicked, will cause some action to occur. We'll soon see how to specify what the action is.

- **Name = "*some_name*".** This assigns a name to the input area (box, button, or check box). The name is not visible to the user but, as we will see later, a scripting language can use these names when examining user input.

- **Value = "*some_value*".** In general, the value option depends on the input type. Here we have used it only with input types "button" and "reset." As Figure 12.9 shows, the string that is assigned to the value is the string that appears on the form's button.

- **Size = *number*.** When used with a text box, this option specifies the size of the box (measured in numbers of characters).

- **OnClick = "*some_action*".** This is an example of an *event handler,* or the specification of some action whenever some event occurs. When applied to a button, this option specifies a script that is automatically executed whenever the button is clicked (the event). Presumably, the script will intercept the form and all it contains and perform some action.

CLIENT-SIDE PROGRAMMING AND JAVASCRIPT

The final step is to explain how to write a script that responds to the form of Figure 12.9. Specifically, we need a script to do the following when the user clicks the Calculate button:

- Determine a value for each check box that was selected and place the result in the appropriate text box

- Generate an alert box (an error message) if the user did not select any check boxes
- Generate an alert box if the user did not type any numbers

Figure 12.12 contains JavaScript code that does this. We will not assume any familiarity with JavaScript, but we will assume that the reader has knowledge of the C language and understands at least the basic concepts of object-oriented programming

Figure 12.12   JavaScript Code for Client-Side Programming

```
<script language = javascript>

function MakeArray(form)
{
  var ind1=0;
  var ind2=0;
  var blank=" ";
  var i = 0;

  while ( (ind2=form.expr.value.indexOf(blank, ind1)) != -1)
    {
      this[++i]= parseInt(form.expr.value.substring(ind1, ind2));
      ind1=ind2+1
    }
  this[++i]=parseInt(form.expr.value.substring(ind1,form.expr.value.length));
  this.length=i;
}

function dototal(myarray, form)
{
  var sum=0;
  for (var i=1; i<=myarray.length; i++)
    sum = sum + myarray[i];
  form.total.value=sum;
}

function domin(myarray, form)
{
  var temp=myarray[1];

  for (var i=2; i<=myarray.length; i++)
    if (myarray[i] < temp)
      temp = myarray[i];
  form.min.value=temp;
}
function domax(myarray, form)
{
  var temp=myarray[1];

  for (var i=2; i<=myarray.length; i++)
  if (myarray[i] > temp)
      temp = myarray[i];
  form.max.value=temp;
}

function compute(form)
{
  var myarray;
```

```
if (form.expr.value.length==0)
  alert("You haven't entered any numbers")
else
if ( !form.gettotal.checked && !form.getmin.checked && !form.getmax.checked )
  alert("You haven't checked any of the boxes")
else
{
  myarray = new MakeArray(form);
  if (form.gettotal.checked)
    dototal(myarray, form);
  if (form.getmin.checked)
    domin(myarray, form);
  if (form.getmax.checked)
    domax(myarray, form);
}
}

</script>
```

Figure 12.12 Continued

and object hierarchies. Furthermore, we will not attempt to provide any details of JavaScript beyond those needed here. References [Fl01] and Go01] provide information on JavaScript.

Before we begin, there are several things to note relevant to the code in Figure 12.12:

- JavaScript code is delimited with <script> and </script> tags.
- The code resides in the head of the HTML document.
- The code contains five functions: compute, MakeArray, dototal, domin, and domax. As specified by the OnClick event handler in Figure 12.11, control will go first to the function compute, which will coordinate the actions the script must take.
- The numbers the user enters exist as a string expression. The JavaScript code must parse this string, locate the numbers, and store them in an array.

JavaScript is an object-oriented language with a complex object hierarchy. We will not describe the entire hierarchy, but it is important to understand at least that part of the hierarchy relevant to the code in Figure 12.12. Figure 12.13 shows the hierarchy that we need. JavaScript sees the form with which we are working as an object. The form is also a property of a *document object* (think of it as our HTML document). In general, a document can have many forms. The form, in turn, also has properties, listed on the third level of the hierarchy in Figure 12.13. Each one corresponds to an input tag defined in the form of Figure 12.11. In fact, if you compare the name options of those tags and the names in Figure 12.13, you'll find they are the same. As we will soon discover, this will allow the script to access objects associated with those tags. There is more to Figure 12.13, but we'll describe it as the need arises.

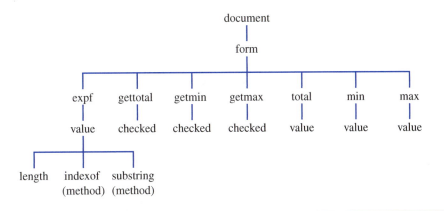

Figure 12.13   JavaScript Object Hierarchy Relevant to Figure 12.12

Recall from Figure 12.11 that the input tag of type "button" has another option of the form Onclick="compute(this.form)". When the user clicks that button, control goes to the JavaScript function named compute. Furthermore, the current form object, along with all of its properties and methods, is passed to the function. The keyword this is commonly used in JavaScript to refer to a current object. Of course, *current* depends on the context in which it is used. In this case, this.form refers to the current form (the one in Figure 12.11) in the current HTML document.

Once control passes to the function compute, the function's parameter allows JavaScript code to access all information about the form through the object named form. The first thing that compute checks is whether the user has entered any numbers in the form. Recall from Figure 12.11 that the form contains an input tag of type "text" that has a name of expr. This is where user input goes, and expr is also a property of the object form (see Figure 12.13). Furthermore, the object hierarchy shows that expr has a value property. It represents the actual string entered through the expr text box. Last, since each string has a length representing the number of characters in it, value has a property named length. If the user enters no characters, the string's length is 0. Consequently, JavaScript checks this condition by comparing form.expr.value.length with 0 (note that the dotted expression corresponds to a sequence of properties defined by the object hierarchy in Figure 12.13). If it is a match, JavaScript calls an alert function, passing the string "you haven't entered any numbers". The alert function causes a window like that in Figure 12.10b to appear. Of course, if the length is not 0, that step is skipped and no alert box appears. Note that a nonzero length does not mean the user has actually entered numbers. It means only that the user has typed something. This script does not check the string for non-numeric characters. We leave it as an exercise to expand the script's error checking capabilities.

Next, JavaScript must determine whether any of the check boxes were selected. Again it uses the object hierarchy to do this. There are three check boxes named gettotal, getmin, and getmax, and each is a property of the object form.

Because each is defined as type "checkbox", each has a property called `checked`. If the user moves the mouse cursor over a check box and clicks a mouse button, the corresponding `checked` property is set to TRUE. Consequently, each `checked` property is either TRUE or FALSE according to whether the corresponding check box was selected by the user. The second `if` statement in `compute` compares the `checked` property of each check box and, if all are FALSE, displays another alert box.

If at least one check box is selected, control passes to the last `else` clause. The first line,

```
myarray = new MakeArray(form)
```

calls a function that parses the user-entered string and stores all the numbers in the array named `myarray`. (We'll see how that works shortly.) The remaining three `if` statements again determine which check boxes were selected. For each one that was selected, JavaScript calls a function to do the designated task. For example, the function `dototal` sums up the values in the array `myarray` using a variable `sum`. The last line in `dototal` stores the sum in `form.total.value`. This latter expression follows the object hierarchy and assigns the sum as the `value` of a text box named `total`. Because of this, the actual sum appears in that box on the form, as shown in Figure 12.9.

The functions `domin` and `domax` determine the smallest and largest values in `myarray`, respectively. They assign the results in a manner similar to `dototal`.

The last piece of the puzzle is to describe how JavaScript extracts the numbers from the user-entered text string. A full understanding of how this happens is probably not possible without a more complete description of JavaScript and its objects and types. We will outline the main ideas and leave it to the reader to consult a textbook on JavaScript for further details on their implementation.

Essentially, the line

```
myarray=new MakeArray(form)
```

(from the function `compute`) calls on a function `MakeArray`, which creates and returns an array object containing the needed numbers. Within that function, JavaScript code assumes the numbers are stored in a text string with a single blank space separating each number. As before, JavaScript refers to the string using the object notation `form.expr.value`. It then calls on a method `form.expr.value.indexOf(blank, ind1)`, which returns the first index (or subscript) of the first blank character located past position `ind1`. Initially, `ind1` is 0, so the first call to this method finds the index of the first blank in the string. As the loop is executed, Figure 12.14 shows how `ind1` and `ind2` relate to the text string. In general, they delimit the characters representing one of the numbers entered by the user. The two index values are used in a `substring` method that extracts a substring consisting of characters between them. Finally, JavaScript uses the function `parseInt` to convert that substring to a numeric format.

As JavaScript goes through the loop, it stores converted substrings into an array object named `this`. As mentioned before, `this` is a keyword used to refer to a calling object. In this case the function `MakeArray` acts much like a constructor for the array object `myarray`. Consequently, used in `this` context this actually corresponds to the object array `myarray`.

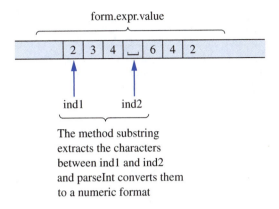

form.expr.value

Figure 12.14   Extracting Numbers from a Text String

12.4 CGI AND SERVER-SIDE PROGRAMMING: SETTING UP A SEARCH ENGINE

The next topic in this chapter addresses server-side programming. For example, during your hours of Web surfing you may have wondered how a search engine works. You know it accepts one or more keywords you give it and that something at another site looks up possible references and sends them back to you. Our task here is to describe how this works and to write a search engine stub. As with previous topics, there are several ways to do server-side programming. Again, however, we will focus on one particular, but fairly standard, technique. Those interested in alternatives should consult a book on HTML programming or on Web development.

We already know that an HTTP server can do some simple tasks, such as sending a requested document back to an HTTP client. However, some activities, such as those found in search engines, require more complexity than HTTP servers are equipped to handle. In such cases the HTTP server relies on a *gateway program* to handle additional logic. Gateway programs may be written in languages such as C or Perl (see references [Fe97], [Gu00], [Me01], or [Sc01]) or even shell scripts such as a Bourne shell script in UNIX. Our task here is to introduce the **Common Gateway Interface (CGI),** which allows a server to communicate with a gateway program. Once done, it is a small step to writing your own gateway programs. We will conclude with a working example.

There are three questions we need to answer:

1. How does a gateway program get information from a client?
2. How does the gateway program do its task?
3. How does the gateway program send information back to the client?

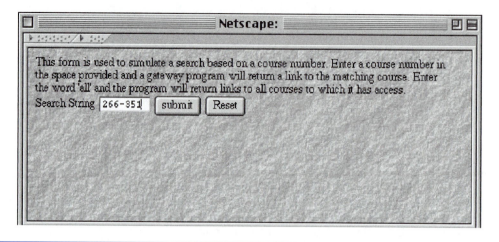

Figure 12.15 Interface Form to a Search Engine

FORMS

The answer to the first item lies in the HTML form. Figure 12.15 shows a simple interface to a search engine, which we will simulate. It contains just the functional parts necessary to request a search: some simple instructions, a text box in which to enter your search words, a button to clear what you have typed, and a button to initiate the search.

Figure 12.16 shows the HTML code to generate this form. It is similar to the HTML code of Figure 12.11 except for two things we have not presented before. First, the input type of "submit" causes a button to appear on the form. Clicking that button causes the form, and information entered in it, to be submitted. Second, the options in the <form> tag indicate how the information is passed (method = "get")* and the URL of the executable file that is the gateway program (action="http://icsc.

Figure 12.16 HTML Code for the Form of Figure 12.15

```
<form method="get" action="http://icsc.uwgb.edu/~shayw/search.cgi">
This form is used to simulate a search based on a course number. Enter a course
number in the space provided and a gateway program will return a link to the
matching course syllabus. Enter the word all and the program will return links
to all courses to which it has access.
<BR><BR>
Search String <Input Type="Text" Name="srch" size=8>
<Input Type="submit" Value = "submit">
<Input Type="reset">
</form>
```

---

* The get method is one way to send information to a gateway program. For alternatives, consult a text on HTML or CGI programming.

uwgb.edu/~shayw/search.cgi").* The latter option indicates that the gateway program is in a file named search.cgi in the shayw subdirectory stored on a Red Hat Linux server.

QUERY STRINGS

When a form is submitted using a `get` method, the HTTP client passes information as a string. The string consists of the referenced URL and a list of name/value pairs, each having the form "*name=value*." There is typically one name/value pair for each input item used to enter information. The name is that defined in the HTML code, and the value is whatever the user has indicated. A question mark character (?) separates the name/value pairs from each other and from the URL. For example, suppose the user entered "266-351" in the example form, as shown in Figure 12.15. The HTTP client sends a character string of the form

```
http://icsc.uwgb.edu/~shayw/search.cgi?srch=266-351
```

Because there is only one input box in which to enter information, the string consists only of the URL and one name/value pair, `srch=266-351`.

Because the `action` option specified a gateway program named search.cgi, the HTTP server passes the string to it. The gateway program must access that string and extract the necessary information. To do this, CGI uses environment variables accessible by the gateway program. There are several different environment variables, but the one of concern here is `QUERY_STRING`.

Figure 12.17 shows a gateway program written in C that does a "search" for whatever the user enters in our form. Examination of the gateway program reveals that this is really just a stub designed to answer two basic questions:

1. Can we get the correct information from the environment variable?
2. Can we return the appropriate information to the user?

EXAMPLE SEARCH ENGINE

The program contains an array of structures hard-coded into it containing the information being sought (lines 16–20). Each structure consists of a course number (e.g., "266-351"), a URL, and a course title. This program will extract a course number from the `QUERY_STRING` environment variable (line 26), search the array for a matching number (lines 56–63), and return both the course name and URL to the client. Through the returned URL, the user sees a reference to the selected course.

For example, if the user entered "266-351" as Figure 12.15 shows, then the response returned would be as shown in Figure 12.18. The search results form echoes the string the user entered and below it displays a link represented by a course name. Using this form, the user can click that name to follow the link. In effect we have mimicked exactly what a search engine does. There is a provision in our gateway program to return all URLs if the user enters the search string "all" instead of a

---

* This URL references a gateway program at the author's site and is subject to change. Attempts at setting up your own gateway programs must be cleared with network personnel at the intended site.

```
 1    #include <string.h>
 2    #include <stdio.h>
 3    #include <stdlib.h>
 4
 5    typedef struct {
 6        char cnum[32];
 7        char url[50];
 8        char cname[32];
 9    } entry;
10
11    void printheading(char *);
12    void listmatches(entry [], char *);
13
14    int main(int argc, char *argv[]) {
15
16      entry mystuff[25]=
17       { "266-350", "http://www.uwgb.edu/shayw/syll350.htm", "Numerical Analysis",
18         "266-351", "http://www.uwgb.edu/shayw/syll351.htm", "Data Structures",
19         "266-358", "http://www.uwgb.edu/shayw/syll358.htm", "Computer Networks",
20         "home",    "http://www.uwgb.edu/shayw/", "My Home Page"};
21
22      int i;
23      int status;
24      char * srchstring;       // search string passed over from html form
25
26      srchstring = getenv("QUERY_STRING");      // gets search string from environment
27      printheading(srchstring);
28
29      if (srchstring = strchr(srchstring, '='))
30        srchstring++;
31
32      listmatches(mystuff, srchstring);
33      return 0;
34    }
35
36    void printheading(char * srchstring)
37    {
38      printf("Content-type: text/html\n\n");
39      printf("<html>\n");
40      printf("<body>\n");
41      printf("<center> <img src=http://icsc.uwgb.edu/~shayw/logo200.gif>\n");
42      printf("<h1>Search results</h1>\n");
43    }
44    void listmatches(entry mystuff[25], char * srchstring)
45    {
46      int i;
47
48      if (strlen(srchstring) == 0)
49      {
50        printf ("No search string is specified\n");
51        exit(0);
52      }
53      printf("<H3>This is a list of links based on your search of</H3>");
54      printf (" <h2>%s</h2></Center>\n\n\n", srchstring);
55
56      for (i=0;i<=3;i++)
57      {
58        if (strstr(mystuff[i].cnum, srchstring)||strstr(srchstring, "all") )
59        {
60           printf("<img src=http://icsc.uwgb.edu/~shayw/cool_fli.gif>");
61           printf("<A href=%s> %s </A>\n<BR>", mystuff[i].url, mystuff[i].cname);
62        }
63      }
64      printf("</body>\n");
65      printf("</html>\n");
66    }
```

Figure 12.17   C Code for Server-Side CGI Programming

Figure 12.18   Results of Search

course number. This was done to test whether the gateway program could return multiple links.

The only step left is to describe how the gateway program of Figure 12.17 generated the results in Figure 12.18. Most of the program is understandable to someone with a knowledge of C, so we will focus on parts that relate strictly to the exchange of information with the client. As previously stated, the first thing the gateway program must do is get the query string. It does this through the following statement on line 26:

```
srchstring = getenv("QUERY_STRING");
```

which puts the string into the C variable srchstring. In this example we are assuming that the form allows only one input box and that the user has entered only a single search phrase (either a course number or the word *all*). This simplifies the program logic; we leave it as an exercise to expand on this program. Since the search string has the form

```
url?srch=phrase
```

the program need only locate the "=" to find the phrase for which it must search. It uses the C string function `strchr` to locate the "=" and redefines the variable `srchstring` to locate the phrase (lines 29–30). Finally, it calls on the function `listmatches` (line 32), passing over the phrase.

This function (lines 44–66) employs a standard linear search of an array to look for the phrase and display the results. However, there is one fundamental difference. Normally, the `printf` statement sends output to a standard output device. When run from the command line, the output usually defaults to the display screen. When run as a CGI program, it sends output to a document that will be interpreted as an HTML document. Examination of these statements reveals that they are producing HTML code.

Inside the loop, the program looks for a match between the phrase and the course numbers of each array item (line 58). When one is found, the statement

```
printf("<A href=%s> %s </A>\n<BR>", mystuff[i].url,
                mystuff[i].cname);
```

sends both the URL and name associated with the matching record to an HTML document. Note that they are contained in an anchor tag. When the program finishes, the HTTP server sends this document back to the client, where the document is displayed according to the rules of HTML. The result is that the user sees the appropriate name, which is actually a clickable reference corresponding to the URL returned. The search is complete, and the user clicks the name to follow the reference.

If the user had entered "all" instead of a course number, he or she would have seen references to all of the URLs listed in the array structure.

12.5 PERL PROGRAMMING: PIZZA ORDERING SYSTEM

We end this chapter with one more example that represents a typical use for CGI scripts. This time we use the Perl language and show how to set up a Web-based pizza ordering program. **Perl (Practical Extension and Report Language)** typically runs on UNIX or Linux systems. Its syntax resembles that of the C language, but Perl is usually interpreted. Perl programs can be run from a UNIX shell or can be accessed from a form on a Web page. The process is the same as that used for accessing a C program in the previous section. The only difference is that the URL specified in the form tag specifies a Perl script file instead of a compiled C program.

The premise is that O'Malley's Pizzeria and Irish Pub has set up a website that allows customers to order a pizza. This website contains some Perl scripts that do some server-side computing. These scripts also create HTML documents that are returned to the client. We assume the reader is familiar with HTML, JavaScript, the C language, interacting with forms, and the general principles of client/server computing. We will not engage in a complete discussion of Perl, but will provide just enough to explain how our scripts work. Additional material on Perl can be found in references [Sc01], [Me01], and [Gu00].

CUSTOMER INTERACTION

When a customer connects to the website of O'Malley's Pizzeria and Irish Pub, the following is a possible sequence of interactions:*

1. The customer enters her phone number into a form (Figure 12.19).

2. The customer clicks the Order button. A Perl script on the server looks for the phone number in a file. If the script does not find the number, the customer is prompted to reenter her phone number. If the number is found, the Perl script produces a customer verification form that displays the customer information (Figure 12.20).†

3. When the verification form appears, the customer has two options. She can update her information by clicking the Change button. This produces the form in Figure 12.21, in which she can change her name or address. She can then click

Figure 12.19   Phone Number Entry Form

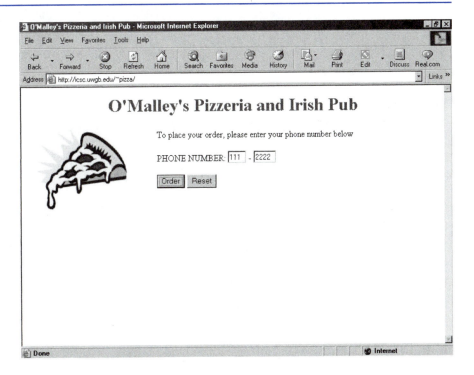

---

* The reader may run this example and access the code through the book's website at www.uwgb.edu/shayw/udcn3. The Perl scripts run on a Linux server (Red Hat Linux version 7.3).

† If you are experimenting with this example, the following phone numbers are stored in the file: 111-2222, 333-4444, 555-6666, and 777-8888.

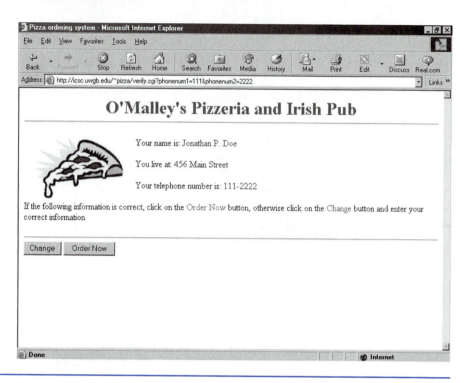

Figure 12.20 Customer Verification Form

Figure 12.21 Customer Update Form

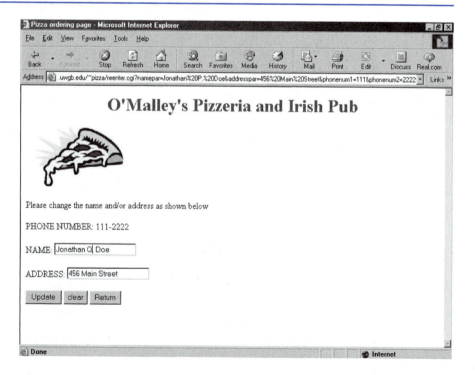

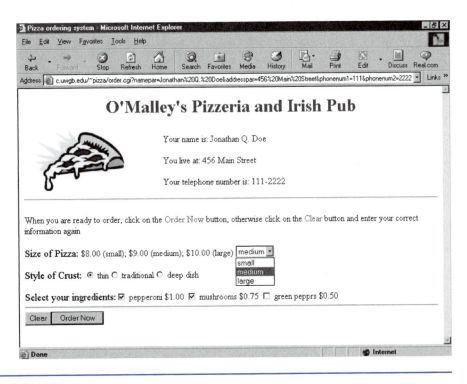

Figure 12.22   Order Form

the Update button to store the change in the server file.* She can also click the Order Now button from Figure 12.20, which produces the order form in Figure 12.22.

4. Once the customer has retrieved the order form, she can select the pizza size, crust style, and toppings. She then clicks the Order Now button to process the order.

5. After the order is processed, the customer sees the Checkout form of Figure 12.23, which echoes the customer information and the pizza ordered. It also displays the total price and an order number. The order number increases by 1 for each order.

These forms and the underlying scripts implement basic functionality; certainly, more can be done to produce a fully functional and robust website. We use the exercises at the end of the chapter to suggest some enhancements, but let's first understand how the scripts perform the required tasks.

---

* For those who access this website, we have disabled the capability to make changes to the file.

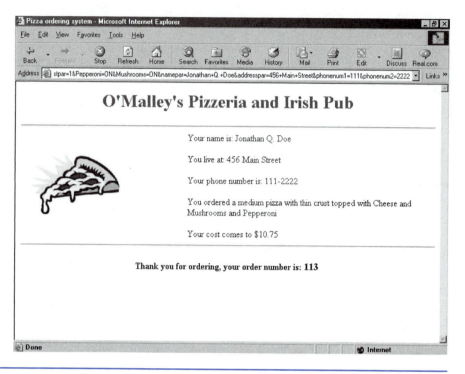

Figure 12.23   Checkout Form

VERIFYING PHONE NUMBERS

It's important that the reader fully understand the user interactions described earlier before we go through the Perl scripts that implement them. If you haven't already done so, we recommend that you access the website listed previously and experiment with it. Suppose a customer enters the phone number 111-2222 into the form of Figure 12.19. The HTML document (index.html in the O'Malley's pizza directory) that produces this form contains items similar to those from previous sections, and we have not reproduced them here. However, when the customer clicks the Order button, the form calls on a CGI script named verify.cgi via a URL similar to the following:

http://icsc.uwgb.edu/~pizza/verify.cgi?phonenum1=111&phonenum2=2222

The important things are the name/value pairs that represent data from the entry form. Figure 12.24 contains the Perl script verify.cgi that accesses the name/value pairs and responds to them. Please note that there are some important but subtle activities occurring here and the explanation requires careful reading. The Perl script runs on the server and searches a server file for the phone number that the customer entered. It also produces an HTML form dependent on the search results. That form

```
1   #!/usr/bin/perl -w
2   use CGI qw(:standard);
3   use CGI::Carp "fatalsToBrowser";
4   # This cgi script will validate data sent to the server and create forms,
5   # depending on the transmitted data., for the client's user
6
7   $phone1 = param("phonenum1");
8   $phone2 = param("phonenum2");
9   $phone = $phone1.$phone2;
10  $address = "";
11  $name = "";
12
13  print header, start_html("Pizza ordering system"),
14   "<h1 align=center> <Font color=RED> O'Malley's Pizzeria and Irish Pub", hr,
15   "</font></h1><img SRC=\"pizza.jpg\" align=left width=200 depth=200></img>";
16
17  print <<END_of_text;
18
19  <script language="JavaScript">
20
21  //*****************************************************************
22  // Will call a cgi script to verify the validity of phone
23  // numbers entered into the form.
24  //*****************************************************************/
25   function reverify(form)
26   {
27    var url; // location of cgi script to verify data
28
29    url = "verify.cgi?phonenum1="+form.phone1.value+
30      "&phonenum2="+form.phone2.value;
31    window.location.href=url;
32   }
33
34  //*****************************************************************
35  // method extracts customer information from the form
36  // and references a url that allows the user to enter new
37  // information.
38  //*****************************************************************/
39   function editForm(form)
40   {
41    var url;       // url for cgi program to enter new data
42
43    url = "reenter.cgi?namepar=" + form.name.value;
44    url = url + "&addresspar=" + form.address.value;
45    window.location.href=url + "&phonenum1=$phone1&phonenum2=$phone2"
46   } //editForm
47
48  //*****************************************************************
49  // method extracts customer information from the form and
50  // references a url that allows the user to order a pizza
51  //*****************************************************************/
52   function placeOrder(form)
53   {
54    var url;       // url for cgi program to take order
55
56    url = "order.cgi?namepar=" + form.name.value;
57    url = url + "&addresspar=" + form.address.value;
58    window.location.href=url + "&phonenum1=$phone1&phonenum2=$phone2"
```

Figure 12.24 CGI Script (verify.cgi) to Verify Form Data

```
59      } //placeOrder
60
61    </script>
62    END_of_text
63
64    # Start execution here
65    # If both phone number fields contain data, search for the phone number
66    if($phone1 && $phone2)
67    {
68      search();
69    }
70    else # one or both phone number fields are empty
71    {
72      createInputForm('Please enter all required fields.');
73    }
74
75    # *********************************************************************
76    # Called when the user did not enter numbers in BOTH
77    # phone number fields or if the phone number entered does
78    # not match one in the database. This method creates a form
79    # with a message indicating which case occurred, displaying
80    # an asterisk next to any field that was left blank. The
81    # form also allows the client's user to re-enter a telephone number.
82    # *********************************************************************/
83    sub createInputForm
84    {
85      print '<form method="get" ACTION="index.html">',
86       p("$_[0] Enter your phone number below"),
87       'PHONE NUMBER:';
88      if($phone1 == "")
89      {
90       print font( {color=>RED}, "*");
91      }
92      print "<input NAME='phone1' VALUE='$phone1' size=3 maxlength=3>-";
93      if($phone2 == "")
94      {
95       print font( {color=>RED}, "*");
96      }
97      print <<END_of_text;
98
99      <input NAME='phone2' VALUE='$phone2' size=4 maxlength=4><p>
100     <input type="button" value="Order" onclick="reverify(this.form)">
101     <input type="submit" value="Reset"
102     end_form()
103     </body>
104     </html>
105
106   END_of_text
107   } # createInputForm
108
109   # *********************************************************
110   # Searches a file, looking for a match to a telephone
111   # number.
112   # *********************************************************/
113   sub search
114   {
115     $found = 0;
116
```

Figure 12.24 Continued

```
117   open (CUSTFILE, "<customers.txt");
118   @data = <CUSTFILE>;
119   $i = 0;
120   while (($i<$#data) && ($found==0))
121   {
122    if($phone == $data[$i])
123    {
124     $name = $data[$i+1];
125     $address = $data[$i+2];
126     $found = 1;
127    }#if
128    $i=$i+3;
129   } # for loop
130   close (CUSTFILE);
131
132   if($found==0)
133   {
134    createInputForm('The number you entered was not found in the database.');
135   }
136   else
137   {
138    createSummaryForm();
139   }
140  } # search
141
142  # *********************************************************************
143  # This method creates a form using customer information that
144  # was found on the server data file. The form allows the client's
145  # user to select a button to change customer information or
146  # another button to proceed with the order.
147  # *********************************************************************/
148  sub createSummaryForm
149  {
150   print <<END_of_text;
151
152    <p> Your name is: <font color=BLUE> $name </font>
153    <p> You live at: <font color=BLUE> $address </font>
154    <p> Your telephone number is: <font color=BLUE> $phone1-$phone2 </font>
155    <FORM method = "get">
156    <p><p><p> If the following information is correct, click on the
157    <font color=RED> Order Now </font> button, otherwise click
158    on the <font color=RED> Change </font> button and enter
159    your correct information <p><hr>
160    <input type=hidden NAME=name value="$name">
161    <input type=hidden NAME=address value="$address">
162    <input type=hidden name=phone1 value=$phone1>
163    <input type=hidden name=phone2 value=$phone2>
164    <input type=button value = "Change" onclick=editForm(this.form)>
165    <input type=button value = "Order Now" onclick =placeOrder(this.form)>
166    </form>
167    </body>
168    </html>
169  END_of_text
170  } # createSummaryForm
```

Figure 12.24   Continued

contains a JavaScript (JS) script that will run on the client when the user clicks a button later. Thus, the Perl script performs not only server file searches but also produces forms that appear on the customer's browser. It also creates a JS script that the browser executes in response to customer actions. The tricky part is that we are using a script (Perl) to generate another script (JavaScript) that will be executed remotely. It's important to keep track of what script executes where.

Lines 1 to 3 are typical of Perl CGI scripts. Line 1 specifies the location of the Perl interpreter, and lines 2 and 3 are similar to C's `#include` statements. They allow the Perl script access to certain variables and functions that facilitate CGI programming and help deal with problems if the Perl script aborts for some reason. For our purposes, just include them, but see the references for more detail. Lines 7 to 11 declare our Perl variables. Lines 7 to 8 provide initial values taken from the query string shown earlier, line 9 concatenates the initial values into one string, and lines 10 to 11 initialize each of the address and name strings to an empty string.

Lines 13 to 62 produce HTML and a JS script that will be sent back to the customer's browser. They define what the customer will see and how the client's browser responds to a subsequent button click. Perl produces HTML documents much like the C programs from the previous section did: It uses a `print` statement. If this script were run from the Linux command line, the `print` statements would display data on the screen. By running it from an HTML form, the output from the `print` statements goes back to the browser. The browser then interprets the output in the same manner it interprets any HTML document.

Line 13 references macros that expand into HTML statements. For example, the command `print header` produces

Content-Type: text/html

and `print start_html("Pizza order system")` produces

<HTML><HEAD><TITLE>Pizza ordering
system</TITLE></HEAD><BODY>

Line 13 prints both of these with one `print` statement. The idea is to group some common HTML tags and define a macro for their use. This reduces the amount of typing that is needed. Lines 14 and 15 produce more HTML tags.

Line 17 is used when the Perl script must print a lot of lines to an HTML document. Rather than having a `print` command on each line, line 17 tells the Perl interpreter that it should treat all subsequent lines as output until it reaches a line containing the `END_of_text` indicator (line 62). Note that Perl requires the line after the print to be blank, and the `END_of_text` indicator must begin in the first column.

Everything from line 19 through 61 is JavaScript and is output to the HTML document that the Perl script is creating. There are three JS functions, each of which corresponds to an OnClick event handler. In each case, the JS function builds a URL that contains the name of a CGI script followed by a query string consisting of name/value pairs generated from the form data. This causes the browser to call that CGI script and pass the query string when the customer clicks a button associated with the event handler. We'll see an example shortly.

The Perl script begins analyzing information extracted from the query string

$$phonenum1 = 111 \& phonenum2 = 2222$$

at line 66. Let's suppose first that the customer did not enter information in one or both fields of Figure 12.19 In that case, one or both of the variables $phone1 or $phone2 are empty strings and the if statement at line 66 returns a FALSE condition. In that case, the script calls a Perl function to create a new input form (lines 83–107). Much of that function contains print statements to produce an HTML document that contains a form almost identical to that in Figure 12.19. However, there is one difference.

A typical response from many scripts when a customer does not fill out all text fields in a form is to provide some type of mark next to a field the user ignored. In this case, if variable $phone1 were an empty string (line 88), the script would print a red asterisk in the form next to the first phone number field (lines 90–92). It proceeds in a similar manner for the $phone2 variable (lines 93–96). Once this function is finished, the Perl script is done and the new form appears in the customer's browser. She can try again to enter the proper phone number. If she clicks the Order button (defined at line 100), the JS function reverify (remember, we're back on the client side now) is called (lines 25–32). This function builds a URL that calls a script named verify.cgi and passes the $phone1 and $phone2 values. Since the script of Figure 12.24 is, in fact, the verify.cgi script, the server starts the above process all over again.

Now let's suppose the customer did enter a phone number in the form of Figure 12.19. The if statement on line 66 returns a TRUE condition and the script calls a Perl function search to determine whether the phone number exists in a server file (lines 113–140). Line 117 opens a file named customers.txt. The character "<" prior to the file name indicates the file is opened for read access. Line 118 reads the entire file into an array of strings,* with each line corresponding to one string in the array. Yes, if the file was large this could cause some problems, but we have used a short file in our example and can get away with this approach. It also reduces the amount of detail we have to cover, a useful fact since we're more interested in how Perl responds to client requests. In this case, each element of the array @data contains one line of the file. In this example, the first three lines contain a phone number, customer name, and customer address for the first customer in the file. The second three lines contain the same information for the second customer. Every set of three lines contains a phone number, name, and address for another customer.

Consequently, the loop defined by lines 119 to 129 compares each of $data[0], $data[3], $data[6], and so on with the current phone number, looking for a match. If a match is found, lines 124 and 125 define the name and address of the customer and line 126 sets $found to 1. This causes the condition on line 120 to be FALSE, and the loop stops. If the script finds no match, then the subscript i will

---

* The @ sign in line 118 is the Perl designation of an array variable. (It's actually a little more general than that, but we'll leave that to the references.) Individual array elements are represented using a $ symbol.

increment to a value larger than the size of the array that is indicated by variable $\$\#data$ in line 120. Again, in this case the condition on line 120 becomes FALSE.

Once the loop finishes, the file is closed. The next step depends on whether the phone number was found. If it was not found, the script calls a Perl function from line 134 that creates a new input form. This is the same action that was taken if the user left one of the text fields of Figure 12.19 blank. If the number was found, the script calls a Perl function to create a summary form (lines 148–170) similar to that in Figure 12.20.

UPDATING CUSTOMER INFORMATION

Upon viewing the form in Figure 12.20, the customer has two choices: Update her information or place the order. If the user clicks the Change button (defined at line 164 of Figure 12.24), the browser calls the JS function editForm (lines 39–46 of Figure 12.24). That function, in turn, builds a URL string containing a CGI script name reenter.cgi. The URL is similar to the following:

http://icsc.uwgb.edu/~pizza/reenter.cgi?namepar=Jonathan%20P.%20Doe& addresspar=456%20Main%20Street&phonenum1=111&phonenum2=2222

The Perl script (reenter.cgi) builds the form of Figure 12.21 and sends it back to the customer's browser. Figure 12.25 shows the contents of reenter.cgi. This is a fairly simple script that extracts customer data from the query string above (lines 3–6) and displays them. It also defines a JS function for each button. The Clear button (line 51) corresponds to a clearForm function (lines 14–18) that just clears the text fields. The Return button (line 52) corresponds to a goback function (lines 20–26) that builds a URL referencing the verify.cgi script we just discussed.

However, suppose the customer changes the text fields and clicks the Update button (line 50). This activates the JS function update (lines 28–34) and builds a URL similar to the following

http://icsc.uwgb.edu/~pizza/update.cgi?namepar=Jonathan%20Q.%20Doe& addresspar=456%20Main%20Street&phonenum1=111&phonenum2=2222

Figure 12.26 shows the CGI script update.cgi. It calls two Perl functions from lines 11 and 12. The makeform function (lines 14–36) produces a simple form (not shown) that just states that the change has been made and includes an OK button that effectively redisplays the form in Figure 12.20 in the customer's browser. The update function (lines 38–60) updates the customer information in the server text file. It works by reading the contents of the file into an array of strings, locating the appropriate customer, making the changes, and writing the results back to the file. Again, a more sophisticated approach is to work with a database, but that requires more explanation.

The first few lines (lines 40–43) initialize variables, open the file, and read the file into an array of strings. The die option in line 41 allows the specified message to appear in a browser if the file could not be opened. The search through the array of strings is similar to a search described previously. The difference is that if the phone number is found at $\$data[\$i]$, then $\$data[\$i+1]$ and $\$data[\$i+2]$ are changed to the new name and address obtained from the query string.

```
1   #!/usr/bin/perl -w
2   use CGI qw(:standard);
3   my $name = param("namepar");
4   my $address = param("addresspar");
5   my $phone1 = param("phonenum1");
6   my $phone2 = param("phonenum2");
7
8   print header, start_html("Pizza ordering page");
9   print "<h1 align=center> <Font color=RED> O'Malley's Pizzeria and Irish Pub";
10  print "<font></h1><img SRC=\"pizza.jpg\" align=CENTER width=200 depth=200>";
11  print <<END_of_text;
12
13  <scriptlanguage="JavaScript">
14  function clearForm(form)
15  {
16    form.name.value="";
17    form.address.value="";
18  }
19
20  function goback(form)
21  {
22    var url;
23    url = "verify.cgi?namepar=" + form.name.value;
24    url = url + "&addresspar=" + form.address.value;
25    window.location.href=url + "&phonenum1=$phone1&phonenum2=$phone2"
26  }
27
28  function update(form)
29  {
30    var url;
31    url = "update.cgi?namepar=" + form.name.value;
32    url = url + "&addresspar=" + form.address.value;
33    window.location.href=url + "&phonenum1=$phone1&phonenum2=$phone2"
34  }
35
36  </script>
37  END_of_text
38
39  CreateEditForm();
40
41  sub createEditForm
42  {
43    print <<END_of_text;
44
45    <form method="get" ACTION="update.cgi">
46    <p>Please change the name and/or address as shown below </p>
47    <p>PHONE NUMBER: $phone1-$phone2
48    <p>NAME:<input NAME="name" VALUE="$name" </p>
49    <p>ADDRESS: <input NAME="address" VALUE="$address" size="20"> </p>
50    <p><input TYPE="button" Value="Update" onclick="update(this.form)">
51    <input TYPE="button" Value="clear" onclick="clearForm((this.form)">
52    <input TYPE="button" Value="Return" onclick="goback(this.form)">
53  END_of_text
54  print end_form();
55  }
```

Figure 12.25   CGI Script (reenter.cgi) That Creates the Form in Figure 12.21

```perl
#!/usr/bin/perl -w
use CGI qw(:standard);
use CGI::Carp "fatalsToBrowser";

my $name = param("namepar");
my $address = param("addresspar");
my $phone1 = param("phonenum1");
my $phone2 = param("phonenum2");
my $phone = $phone1.$phone2;

update();
makeform();

sub makeform
{
  print header, start_html("Pizza Ordering system"),
    "<h1 align=CENTER> <font color=RED> O'Malley's Pizzeria and Irish Pub",
    "</font> </h1> <hr>",
    "<form method='get' ACTION='verify.cgi'>",
    "<input type='hidden' NAME='namepar' value=$name>",
    "<input type='hidden' NAME='addresspar' value=$address>",
    "<input type='hidden' name='phonenum1' value=$phone1>",
    "<input type='hidden' name='phonenum2' value=$phone2>",
    "<table border=0> <tr>",
    "<td>",
    "</font></h1><img SRC='pizza.jpg' align=CENTER width=200 depth=200>",
    "</td>",
    "<td>",
    "Information has been updated. Click on OK to return",
    "<input type='submit' value='OK'>",
    "</td>",
    end_form(),
    "</body>",
    "</html>",
    end_html;
}

sub update
{
  $found = 0;
  open (CUSTFILE, "<customers.txt") || die "Cannot read from file\n";
  @data = <CUSTFILE>;
  $i = 0;
  while (($i<$#data) && ($found==0))
  {
   if($phone == $data[$i])
   {
    $data[$i+1]=$name."\n";
    $data[$i+2]=$address."\n";
    $found = 1;
   } # if
   $i=$i+3;
  } # for loop
  close (CUSTFILE);
# make sure file has write access to world, use chmod command if needed
  open (CUSTFILE, ">customers.txt") || die "cannot open file for write\n;
  flock(CUSTFILE, 2);
  print CUSTFILE @data;
  close (CUSTFILE);
}
```

Figure 12.26 CGI Script (update.cgi) to Update Customer File

The next step is to store the new data into the file. To do this, the script closes the file (line 54) and reopens it (line 56). However, this time the presence of the character ">" indicates the file is opened for write access. Line 57 requests an exclusive lock on the file. This means that while the current script has the lock, no other script will be able to get an exclusive lock. Use of exclusive locks prevents two customers from updating the file concurrently. The remaining two lines write the array of strings back to the file and close the file.

PLACING AN ORDER

Assuming the customer is content with the information in Figure 12.20, she can finally place the order by clicking that form's Order Now button. That results in a call to a CGI script named order.cgi via a URL similar to the following:

http://icsc.uwgb.edu/~pizza/order.cgi?namepar=Jonathan%20Q.%20Doe& addresspar=456%20Main%20Street&phonenum1=111&phonenum2=2222

This script (Figure 12.27) accesses the customer information from the query string (lines 5–8) and calls on a Perl function (lines 20–40) to display it in the form shown in Figure 12.22. It then displays ordering options in the form of a pop-up menu (lines 56–57), radio buttons (lines 58–61), and check boxes (lines 62–68). The form also specifies the CGI script checkout.cgi (line 49) to be the action taken when the customer clicks the Order Now button.

Figure 12.27   CGI Script (order.cgi) to Order Pizza

```perl
1   #!/usr/bin/perl -w
2   use CGI qw(:standard);
3   use CGI::Carp "fatalsToBrowser";
4
5   $name = param("namepar");
6   $address = param("addresspar");
7   $phone1 = param("phonenum1");
8   $phone2 = param("phonenum2");
9
10  displayCustomerData();
11  displayOrderForm();
12
13  print end_html;
14
15  # ****************************************************
16  # Display the order form allowing the customer to
17  # choose pizze size, crust, and toppings and submit
18  # the order
19  # ****************************************************
20  sub displayCustomerData
21  {
```

```
22    print header, start_html("Pizza ordering system");
23    print <<END_of_text;
24
25    <h1 align=CENTER><font color=RED> O'Malley's Pizzeria and Irish Pub
26    </font></h1>
27 <table border=0 width=100%> <tr>
28    <td width=33%>
29    </font></h1><img SRC=\"pizza.jpg\" align=CENTER width=200 depth=200>
30    </td>
31    <td width=67%>
32    <p> Your name is: <font color=BLUE> $name </font>
33    <p> You live at: <font color=BLUE> $address </font>
34    <p> Your telephone number is: <font color=BLUE> $phone1-$phone2 </font>
35
36    </td> <ttr> </table>
37
38    <hr>
39 END_of_text
40    }
41
42 # ********************************************************
43 # Display the order form allowing the customer to
44 # choose pizze size, crust, and toppings and submit
45 # the order
46 # ********************************************************
47 sub displayOrderForm
48 {
49   print ('<FORM method = "get" ACTION='checkout.cgi">');
50   print p, "When you are ready to order, click on the",
51      font( {color=>RED}, "Order Now"), "button, otherwise click",
52      "on the", font ( {color=>RED}, "Clear"),"button and enter",
53      "your correct information again", p;
54   print start_form();
55   print p, font( {size=>4}, "Size of Pizza: ");
56   print "\$8.00 (small); \$9.00 (medium); \$10.00 (large)",
57    popup_menu (sizepar,['small', 'medium', 'large']);
58   print p, font( {size=>4}, "Style of Crust:");
59   print "<input Type='radio' Name='crustpar' value='1' checked> thin";
60   print "<input Type='radio' Name='crustpar' value='2'> traditional";
61   print "<input Type='radio' Name='crustpar' value='3'> deep dish<P>";
62   print font( {size=>4}, "Select your ingredients:");
63   print "<input Type='checkbox' Name='Pepperoni' value 'ON'> pepperoni";
64   print "\$1.00";
65   print "<input Type='checkbox' Name='Mushrooms' value='ON'> mushrooms";
66   print" \$0.75 ";
67   print "<input Type='checkbox' Name='Green peppers' value='ON'> green pepprs";
68   print" \$0.50";
69   print hr;
70   print "<input type=\"hidden\" NAME=namepar value=\"$name\">";
71   print "<input type=\"hidden\" NAME=addresspar value=\"$address\">";
72   print "<input type=\"hidden\" name=phonenum1 value=\"$phone1\">";
73   print "<input type=\"hidden\" name=phonenum2 value=$phone2>";
74   print ('<input type="reset" value = "Clear">');
75   print ('<input type="submit" value = "Order Now">');
76   print end_form();
77 }
```

Figure 12.27 Continued

VERIFYING THE ORDER

Suppose the customer selects the pizza size, crust style, and ingredients shown in Figure 12.22 and clicks the Order Now button. The browser calls the checkout.cgi script via a URL similar to the following:

> http://icsc.uwgb.edu/~pizza/checkout.cgi?sizepar=medium&crustpar=1&
> Pepperoni=ON&Mushrooms=ON&namepar=Jonathan+Q.+Doe&
> addresspar=456+Main+Street&phonenum1=111&phonenum2=2222

Note that in addition to the usual customer information, the query string also contains

> sizepar=medium&crustpar=1&Pepperoni=ON&Mushrooms=ON

which specifies what the user has selected in Figure 12.22. It is up to the checkout.cgi script of Figure 12.28 to access this information, calculate the cost of the pizza, and produce a form similar to that in Figure 12.23 to confirm the customer's order and display the cost.

Lines 4 to 13 extract query string information. The Perl script generates the order number of Figure 12.23 by using a counter stored in a server text file. It's the same concept that many websites use when you see a message such as

> You are visitor number ######

that keeps track of the number of visitors in a text file. The function `update-Counter` defined in lines 25 to 35 shows how to do this. Lines 27 to 30 open the file for read and write access, put an exclusive lock on it (to prevent two customers from accessing the same order number), read the order number into the variable `$ordernumber`, and increment it by 1. The remaining lines reposition the file pointer to the beginning of the file (so new data are not appended to existing data), write the new counter to the file, and close it.

Lines 42 to 107 of the Perl function do the work of determining what the customer ordered, calculating the cost, and displaying the information for the customer in the checkout form of Figure 12.23. The first thing the function does after generating some form output is to determine the style of crust (lines 59–70). Because this does not affect the cost, all the script need do is define a string variable `$Style` that is used for form output. This variable is dependent on `$crust`, a value taken from the query string at line 8. Because the customer chooses crust style by selecting one radio button, the value of `crustpar` in the query string is 1, 2, or 3, depending on which radio button the customer selected. In this case the customer chose a thin crust (the first radio button), and the query string listed previously contains "crustpar=1". Choosing a traditional or deep dish crust would have resulted in `crustpar` being 2 or 3.

Next the script must determine what size pizza the customer ordered. The `$size` variable is determined from the query string at line 9. Its value will equal the string in the pop-up menu that the customer picked. In our case, the customer wanted a medium pizza, so the value associated with `sizepar` and, consequently, `$size`, is "medium". Lines 71 to 82 then calculate the base cost dependent on the size.

Finally, the script must determine the toppings. In this case, the toppings are check boxes and the associated parameters are either ON or OFF. A value of ON

```
1    #!/usr/bin/perl -w
2    use CGI qw(:standard);
3
4    $name = param("namepar");
5    $address = param("addresspar");
6    $phone1 = param("phonenum1");
7    $phone2 = param("phonenum2");
8    $crust = param("crustpar");
9    $size = param("sizepar");
10
11   $topping1 = param("Mushrooms");
12   $topping2 = param("Green peppers");
13   $topping3 = param("Pepperoni");
14
15   $cost = 0;
16   $ordernumber = 0;
17
18   updateCounter();
19   displayCustomerOrder();
20
21   # ********************************************************
22   # Method updates and displays a counter defining
23   # the number of visitors ordering pizza
24   # ********************************************************
25   sub updateCounter
26   {
27     open (FILE, "+<counter.txt")||die "Cannot read from the counter file.\n";
28     flock (FILE, 2);
29     $ordernumber=<FILE>;
30     $ordernumber=$ordernumber+1;
31     seek(FILE, 0, 0);
32     print FILE $ordernumber;
33     flock (FILE, 8);
34     close (FILE);
35   } #updateCounter
36
37   # ********************************************************
38   # Display the order form allowing the customer to
39   # choose pizza size, crust, and toppings and submit
40   # the order
41   # ********************************************************
42   sub displayCustomerCounter
43   {
44     print header, start_html("Pizza ordering system");
45     print <<END_of_text;
46
47     <h1 align=CENTER><font color=RED> O'Malley's Pizzeria and Irish Pub
48     </font></h1><hr>
49     <table border=0> <tr>
50     <td width=40%>
51     </font></h1><img SRC="pizza.jpg" align=CENTER width=200 depth=200>
52     </td>
53     <td>
54     <p> Your name is: <font color=BLUE> $name </font>
55     <p> You live at: <font color=BLUE> $address </font>
56     <p> Your phone number is: <font color=BLUE> $phone1-$phone2 </font>
57
```

Figure 12.28   CGI Script (checkout.cgi) to Process Order

```
58    END_of_text
59    if($crust == 1)
60    {
61      $Style = "thin";
62    }
63    if($crust == 2)
64    {
65      $Style = "traditional";
66    }
67    if($crust == 3)
68    {
69      $Style = "deep dish";
70    }
71    if($size eq "small")
72    {
73      $cost = $cost + 8.00;
74    }
75    if($size eq "medium")
76    {
77      $cost = $cost + 9.00;
78    }
79    if($size eq "large")
80    {
81      $cost = $cost + 10.00;
82    }
83    print "<p> You ordered a <font color=BLUE> $size </font>
84          pizza with <font color=BLUE> $Style </font> crust
85          topped with Cheese";
86    if($topping1 eq "ON")
87    {
88      print" and <font color=BLUE> Mushrooms <font>";
89      $cost = $cost + 0.75;
90    }
91    if($topping2 eq "ON")
92    {
93      print "and <font color=BLUE> Green Peppers </font>";
94      $cost = $cost + 0.50;
95    }
96    if($topping3 eq "ON")
97    {
98      print "and <font color=BLUE> Pepperoni </font>";
99      $cost = $cost + 1.00;
100   }
101
102   print p, "Your cost comes to \$$cost </td> <tr> </table>";
103   print end_html;
104   print hr, "<h4 align=CENTER>
105         Thank you for ordering, your order number is:
106         <font color = BLUE size = 4> $ordernumber </font> </h4>";
107   }
108
109
110
111
```

Figure 12.28 Continued

means the customer checked the box. In this case the customer checked two toppings: pepperoni and mushrooms. Consequently, the query string contains the component

Pepperoni=ON&Mushrooms=ON

The script extracts the ON/OFF values from the query string at lines 11 to 13 and tests those values at lines 86 to 100. Whenever it finds a value of ON, it increments the costs and prints (to the form) a string representing the chosen topping.

Lines 102 to 106 finish up by displaying the final cost, an order number, and a nice polite thank you message in the hopes that the customer will order again.

12.6 SUMMARY

This chapter focused on the development of applications that rely on Internet protocols. All were client/server based but differed in context, the type of interaction between the client and server, and the tools used. Section 12.2 focused on socket programming and the development of a client and server program capable of transferring a file. Some important concepts from that section are as follows:

- A socket is a construct that allows a program to connect to a network for the purpose of sending or receiving data.

- A client can connect to a server program by specifying its IP address and port number from within appropriate socket commands.

- The client and server usually agree on a packet format for the exchange of data. Once this happens and the sockets are established, the client and server need only read and write to the socket to exchange data. Care, however, must be taken to make sure that when one reads the other has written (or will write) something.

The rest of the chapter focused on programming for a Web environment. Section 12.3 introduced the Web, HTTP, and how to create simple HTML documents. However, the important issue from a networking perspective was the ability to use JavaScript for client-side computing. Some important features of JavaScript are as follows:

- A form can be used as a template for the entering and display of information. It can include text fields, check boxes, and other types.

- The form can also include buttons that cause an action when clicked.

- A form button can be associated with a JavaScript function so that when a user clicks the button, the function executes statements that can analyze form data and respond. This is done on the client side and can be used to screen user data before sending it to a server.

Programming can also occur on the server side, and there are several options. One is Common Gateway Interface (or CGI) programming. It involves creating a URL that specifies an executable file on the server. The URL also contains a query string that is used to pass information from the form that called it to the CGI program. The

CGI program extracts information from the query string and can perform needed tasks. Some important features of CGI programs are as follows:

- They can be written in C or Perl. C programs are compiled, and Perl programs are usually interpreted.
- They can create forms that the user's browser displays.
- They can be used to implement search engines. Section 12.4 contained a primitive search engine that showed how a C program can accept a word or phrase from a form and return one or more links to the client's browser.
- They can be used to allow customers to place orders. Section 12.5 explained a pizza ordering system that contained several Perl scripts that verified a telephone number, updated customer information, allowed a customer to order a pizza, and produced a summary of that order.

Review Questions

1. Why use a client/server model as opposed to doing all programming on a single computer?
2. What is a socket?
3. What is the purpose of the socket `bind` command? What would happen if it were not executed?
4. Does the client or the server or both usually execute each of the following socket commands?
   a. `socket()`
   b. `connect()`
   c. `bind()`
   d. `accept()`
   e. `listen()`
   f. `send()`
   g. `recv()`
   h. `close()`
5. The server program of Section 12.2 contains a `fork()` command to create a process to handle a client request. Why not just have the process that gets the request also respond to it?
6. What is the Hypertext Markup Language?
7. What is the Hypertext Transfer Protocol?
8. What is a Uniform Resource Locator?
9. What is an HTML tag?
10. What is the purpose of an HTML form?

11. What is a script?

12. What is an event handler in the context of an HTML form and button?

13. What is a CGI script?

14. What is a query string used for in CGI programming?

15. What is an environment variable?

16. What is the reason for having programming capabilities on both the client and server ends for Web page development?

Exercises

1. Modify the file transfer protocol of Section 12.2 by implementing an error detection mechanism such as a checksum. You can simulate errors by having the server periodically damage a packet immediately prior to sending it over the socket. For example, it might call a random number generator and, based on the number returned, might zero out a packet's bytes. If you would like more random-looking errors, you might have the server add a random number to a random byte in the packet.

2. Use sockets to implement a talk protocol between a client and server program. The protocol would allow a half-duplex mode of communication in which client and server exchange messages defined by what the user types at the keyboard. You will have to figure out who starts "talking" and how to end the conversation.

3. Build a server text file in which each line has a keyword followed by a URL. Write a client program that accepts a keyword as user input and sends the keyword to the server. Write a server that gets a keyword from the client, searches the file to find all instances of the keyword, and returns all the URLs associated with that keyword. The client should display the URLs.

4. Modify the protocol of Section 12.2 by adding any or all of the following capabilities.

   a. The client should ask its user the name of the file on the remote host. The client then sends that name to the server over the socket connection.

   b. Create a Disconnect packet and have the client and server disconnect only after the client sends the server a Disconnect packet and the server acknowledges it.

   c. Build a menu option into the client allowing the user to choose whether the client should request a file transfer or a talk protocol as in Exercise 2.

   d. Have the client and server both send a file to each other concurrently.

   e. Alter the server so that it receives a single packet after accepting a connection. The packet will specify whether the server executes a file transfer or a talk protocol with the client. Of course, the client must send such a packet.

   f. Design the server so that it is capable of transferring a file to one client while, at the same time, it is engaged in a talk protocol with another. It will have to fork child processes to respond to the requests.

5. If you haven't already done so, create a Web page containing at least some text and links to remote URLs. You decide what to put in the page.

6. Modify the JavaScript code of Figure 12.12 so that the user may insert an arbitrary number of spaces between the numbers he or she enters.

7. Create an HTML form that allows a user to enter the dimensions of a rectangle and then uses a script to return the rectangle's area. The script should determine whether the dimensions are positive and, if they are not, generate an alert box.

8. Repeat Exercise 7 but include check boxes to indicate whether the user wants to know the area or perimeter (or both) of the rectangle. The script must make sure the user selects at least one option.

9. Modify the gateway program of Figure 12.17 to allow multiple entries to be made on the form of Figure 12.15. The gateway program should return references matching any one of the numbers entered in the text box.

10. The Perl script of Figure 12.24 is stored in a file verify.cgi and contains a JavaScript function called `reverify`. This function builds a URL that references the CGI script in the file verify.cgi. Is this an example of a recursive call? Why or why not?

11. For the pizza ordering system, comment on the appropriateness of radio buttons, check boxes, or a pop-up menu to allow the user to select the size, crust style, and toppings.

12. This question assumes you have access to a UNIX or Linux server on which you can download and run the Perl scripts of Section 12.5. Make the following changes to the pizza ordering program. Do each independent of the others.

   a. Add an extra large size for $11.00.

   b. Add Chicago Style to the list of crust styles.

   c. Add Onions to the list of toppings at an additional charge of $0.50.

   d. Remove the radio buttons for crust style and use a pop-up menu instead.

   e. Remove the pop-up menu for pizza size and use radio buttons instead.

   f. Assume the prices for toppings are for small pizzas only. For each increment in size beyond small, add $0.25 for each topping chosen. Make sure the customer sees this on the form.

   g. Add a server file that accumulates the cost of all orders placed.

   h. Create a form and script that allows a user to enter his or her phone number, name, and address for the first time into the server file.

   i. The current arrangement requires that a customer order multiple pizzas individually, that is, using a separate form for each. How would you design a form so that a customer could order multiple pizzas?

13. The pizza ordering system contains a Perl script that calculates the cost of the pizza at the server. The script could generate a JavaScript function that would calculate the cost of the pizza on the client side. Is there an advantage in this approach? A disadvantage?

REFERENCES

[Co99] Comer, D. E., and D. Stevens. *Internetworking with TCP/IP. Vol. II. ANSI C Version: Design, Implementation, and Internals,* 3rd ed. Englewood Cliffs, NJ: Prentice-Hall, 1999.

[Co00] Comer, D. E. *Internetworking with TCP/IP. Vol. 1. Principles, Protocols, and Architecture,* 4th ed. Englewood Cliffs, NJ: Prentice-Hall, 2000.

[Fe97] Felton, M. *CGI: Internet Programming in C++ and C.* Englewood Cliffs, NJ: Prentice-Hall, 1997.

[Fl01] Flanagan, D. *JavaScript: The Definitive Guide,* 4th ed. Sebastopol, CA: O'Reilly & Associates, 2001.

[Go01] Goodman, D. *JavaScript Bible,* 4th ed. New York: Wiley, 2001.

[Gu00] Guelich, S., S. Gundavaram, and G. Birznieks. *CGI Programming with Perl,* 2nd ed. Sebastopol, CA: O'Reilly & Associates, 2000.

[Ku03] Kurose, J., and K. Ross. *Computer Networking: A Top-Down Approach Featuring the Internet.* Reading, MA: Addison-Wesley, 2003.

[Me01] Meltzer, K., and B. Michalski. *Writing CGI Applications with Perl.* Reading, MA: Addison-Wesley, 2001.

[Sc01] Schwartz, R., and T. Christiansen. *Learning Perl,* 3rd ed. Sebastopol, CA: O'Reilly & Associates, 2001.

[Sh02] Shay, W. "A Multiplatform/Multilanguage Client/Server Project." In *Proceedings of the 33rd ACM SIGCSE Technical Symposium on Computer Science Education.* New York: ACM Press, 2002, pp. 401–405.

CHAPTER 13

CIRCUIT TECHNOLOGIES

Computers are good at swift, accurate computation and at storing great masses of information. The brain, on the other hand, is not as efficient a number cruncher and its memory is often highly fallible; a basic inexactness is built into its design. The brain's strong point is its flexibility. It is unsurpassed at making shrewd guesses and at grasping the total meaning of information presented to it.
—**Jeremy Campbell,** British journalist

13.1 INTRODUCTION

This final chapter deals with some additional communications protocols that play or have played an important role in the development of communications systems over greater distances. Typically they were developed to implement digital telephone systems, define interfaces to packet-switched networks, or provide several quality of service (QoS) options for a wide variety of applications.

Section 13.2 discusses the Integrated Services Digital Network (ISDN). It was designed at a time when personal computers and workstations were not common and the Internet did not exist. It was intended to be a replacement for the existing telephone system. Many people saw the potential of blending communications and computing and saw the advantages of converting to an all-digital telephone system. The idea behind ISDN was to replace all telephones and their analog circuits with digital devices and communication lines. It faced competition from existing telephone companies who were already implementing digital switches in their networks and was a hard sell to many who saw no advantage in using digital phones rather than analog ones. Indeed, for those who just wanted to make simple phone calls, the advantage was minor to nonexistent.

Sections 13.3 and 13.4 deal with three different virtual circuit technologies. The first, X.25, was also developed before the Internet became popular and was designed for communication systems that crossed international boundaries in Europe. It also assumed that much of the underlying communication system was analog and subject to relatively high error rates. It defined an interface between a DTE (recall the definition of a DTE in Chapter 4) and a public data network and allowed virtual circuits to be established with remote DTEs. Frame relay is another virtual circuit protocol designed for bursty traffic and many see it as the successor to X.25. It operates at only two layers, as opposed to X.25's three layers, and does not include any error or flow control. This simplifies the logic and allows the switches to move frames much more quickly.

The last virtual circuit protocol is Asynchronous Transfer Mode (ATM). It defines fixed-size cells that switches can process quickly. ATM also provides different QoS needs, which makes it suitable not only for standard data transfers but also for real-time applications such as those found in audio or video applications.

13.2 INTEGRATED SERVICES DIGITAL NETWORK

Over 100 years ago, people began stringing wires between houses and towns so they could communicate by telephone. Since then the telephone network has evolved into a global communications system using every communications medium we have described in this book. There is one more feature that distinguishes the telephone system from other networks we have discussed: It has a large analog component. We haven't forgotten that optical fibers and digital switching devices have introduced significant amounts of digital technology into the network. Telephones, however, are still analog devices transmitting analog signals to the local exchange office. This part of the telephone network is often called the **local loop** or the **last mile.** (The latter phrase refers to the largest impediment to an all-digital system.)

Initially, the analog system was a logical choice because the telephone was designed to transmit a person's voice. Since then the two fields of communications and computer science have been merging. Computers are critical to communications systems, and communications systems are commonly used to connect computers. Consequently, the ITU-T developed a standard for a global digital communications system called the **Integrated Services Digital Network (ISDN).** If fully implemented, it would allow the complete integration of both voice and nonvoice (e.g., data, fax, video) transmissions within a single system. We will discuss the numerous advantages of such a system shortly.

Figure 13.1 shows the functionality of ISDN's *basic rate.* It provides three separate channels: two **B channels** transmitting at 64 Kbps and one **D channel** transmitting at 16 Kbps. It is often referred to as 2B+D. The B channels transmit pure data such as pulse code modulated (PCM) voice data or data generated by other devices such as a personal computer. The D channel is used for control and for some low-speed applications such as **telemetry** (remote reading of meters) or alarm systems. The three channels are time-division multiplexed onto a **bit pipe** providing the actual bit transmission.

ITU-T also developed a North American standard for a **primary rate** of 23B+D (23 B channels and one D channel), which fits nicely on the T1 carrier

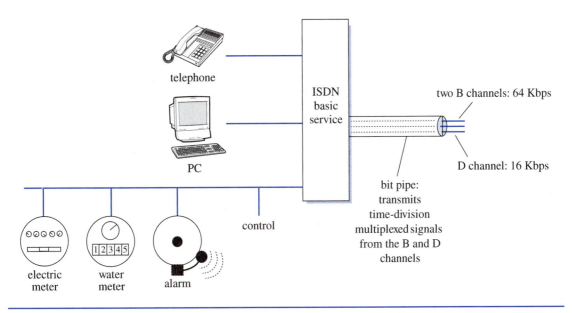

Figure 13.1   ISDN Basic Service

system. Its European standard of 30B+D fits on their 2.048 Mbps channel. The additional data channels provide the capacity for more data from different sources.

Oddly enough, the biggest impediments to eventually implementing a global digital communications system are not the technical problems (but do not underestimate them). The main problems are logistical and economical. One significant problem is convincing telephone users that they will benefit from ISDN and that the conversion costs will be justified. Despite the increase in ISPs and the number of people with personal computers, most people still use their telephone systems for one thing: talking with friends and neighbors. They don't care whether their voice is carried via analog or digital signals. On the other hand, the advantages of providing two data channels in the ISDN basic service are easily articulated. For example, parents would no longer be stuck when their son or daughter monopolized the line, because they automatically would have a second line. (Of course, if they have two children they might still be out of luck.)

SERVICES

This section lists some of the services that an all-digital system provides. Many of them are already available, which is not surprising because much of the telephone network is already completely digital. These services exist because of the digital nature of a communications system, not ISDN per se. ISDN just provides another way to implement them. Furthermore, if the digital components extended onto consumer premises, the services could be implemented without the need for complex modulation methods and potential loss from digital-to-analog conversions.

- One of the B channels can be used to send messages electronically. They can be routed depending on the recipient's telephone number and stored in a local repository near the recipient for eventual access. This is similar to a fax transmission but without the analog-to-digital conversion currently required in fax transmissions.

- Telephone numbers of incoming calls can be displayed even before the telephone is answered (caller ID). Remember, digital systems mean that both outgoing data and incoming signals are digitized. The source number is encoded in the received signals. This feature allows you to decide whether you want to answer the telephone and deters obscene, crank, and telemarketing phone calls. It also facilitates the identification of incoming calls to a 911 emergency system, a particular advantage if the caller is incoherent or a very small child. Because the incoming signals are digital, telephone numbers of incoming calls can also be used as keys to database records. This has applications for professionals who deal with clients or patients (doctors, lawyers, brokers, insurance agents, and so on). Software can use the incoming source number to access the client's record and to display pertinent information on a screen. This feature allows the professional to answer questions quickly and efficiently.

- Voice mail service similar to the service already provided by answering machines allows callers to leave messages. The difference is that messages are recorded and stored in a local repository.

- Every month utility companies send employees to neighborhood homes to read electric, gas, and water meters. ISDN telemetry service allows the meters to be connected to the company and monthly readings accessed via a simple call. In addition, sensors can be placed in a home to detect fires or illegal entries. When they are activated, telephone calls can be made automatically to the nearest fire or police station. At the station, the number of the incoming call can be displayed or used to access a database providing the address from which the call was made.

- Videotex—interactive access to remote databases—allows access to, for example, directory databases providing telephone listings such as those currently found in telephone books. Users can access library databases and query what they have in their collections and access encyclopedias or public records to get information on a particular topic.

- Users can transfer money between bank accounts, shop by entering product codes and credit card numbers, and pay off credit balances by transferring money from their bank accounts—all by telephone.

- Multiple B channels allow some of these activities to be done simultaneously. If a family member is currently using the telephone to talk to a friend, another person can use the other channel to perform another activity.

The potential applications are staggering. Unfortunately, so are the potential abuses. Having so much information available by a simple phone call requires enormous security efforts. It also raises important social and ethical issues. How much information should be available? How do you prevent it from falling into the wrong hands? Could telemetry be extended to monitor (and perhaps control) other events in the home? Capabilities already exist that allow electric companies to remotely turn off power to air conditioners (with the customer's permission) during peak usage times. Could (should) this power be extended to control energy use during an energy crisis? (Who defines when a crisis exists?) These are topics of which any serious student of communications should be aware.

ARCHITECTURE

An ISDN should work with a large variety of users and equipment, especially if it is to be integrated into an office environment. This includes both equipment designed with ISDN in mind and current equipment whose design predates ISDN and has little in common with it. To help in the design of connection strategies and the standardization of interfaces, ITU-T has divided the equipment into *functional groups*. Devices within a group provide specific capabilities. ITU-T has also defined **reference points** to separate these groups, a useful aid to standardizing interfaces. Together the functional groups and reference points help categorize basic connection strategies and provide a basis on which to design more complex architectures. The following list describes the primary functional group designations.

- **NT1 (network termination 1).** Nonintelligent devices concerned with physical and electrical characteristics of the signals. They primarily perform OSI layer 1 functions such as synchronizing and timing. NT1 devices typically form the boundary between a user's site and the ISDN central office. The central office, in turn, functions much as the telephone system's central office, providing access to other sites.

- **NT2 (network termination 2).** Intelligent devices capable of performing functions specified in OSI layers 2 and 3. Among this group's functions are switching, concentration, and multiplexing. A common NT2 device is a digital PBX. It can be used to connect a user's equipment together or to an NT1 to provide access to the ISDN central office.

- **NT12.** Combination of NT1 and NT2 into a single device.

- **TE1 (terminal equipment 1).** ISDN devices such as an ISDN terminal, digital telephone, or computer with an ISDN-compatible interface. Such devices typically connect directly to a network termination device.

- **TE2 (terminal equipment 2).** Non-ISDN devices, including printers, personal computers, analog telephones, or anything that has a non-ISDN interface such as EIA.232 or X.21.

- **TA (terminal adapter).** Device designed to be used with TE2 equipment to convert their signals to an ISDN-compatible format. The purpose is to integrate non-ISDN devices into an ISDN network.

Figure 13.2 shows typical functional groups and how they can be connected. To standardize the interfaces, ITU-T has defined reference points between the groups.

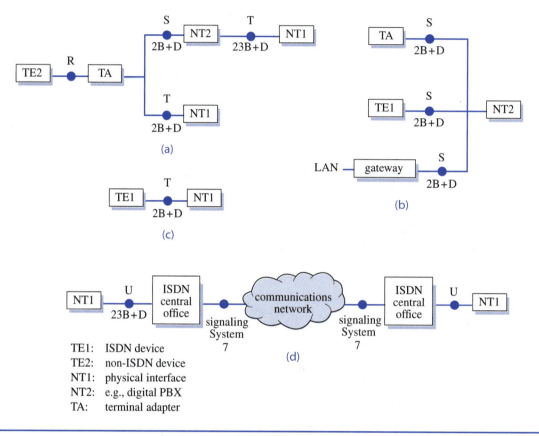

Figure 13.2 ISDN Functional Groups and Reference Points

Although the connections shown are rather simple, they can be combined into much larger and more complex ones. However, the reference points will always divide the functional groups as shown. There are four reference points:

- **Reference point R.** Separates TE2 equipment from the TA (Figure 13.2a). Point R can correspond to several different interfaces according to the TE2's standard.

- **Reference point S.** Separates NT2 equipment from ISDN devices (Figure 13.2a,b). It supports a 2B+D channel and has a bit rate of 192 Kbps.* Effectively, it separates devices dedicated to user functions from devices devoted to communications functions.

- **Reference point T.** The access point to the customer's site (Figure 13.2a,c). Generally, it separates the customer's equipment from the network provider's

---

* The bit rates from the two B channels and the D channel add up to 144 Kbps. Additional overhead bits push the bit rate up to 192 Kbps, as we will show soon.

equipment. Typically, if T is an interface between an NT1 and either terminal equipment or adapter, it corresponds to a 2B+D channel. If it lies between two NT devices, it corresponds to a 23B+D channel.

- **Reference point U.** Defines the connection between an NT1 and the ISDN central office (Figure 13.2d). Communication between different sites can go through one or more *signal transfer points* (a type of routing device) and are handled by a protocol known as Signaling System 7 (described shortly).

PROTOCOLS

On the surface ISDN is similar to the current telephone system. To establish a connection to another site, the user performs some control functions. In the conventional telephone system this means dialing a number; in ISDN it means sending control packets. The telephone uses **in-band signaling;** that is, the tones generated by pressing buttons are sent over the same channel that will later carry your voice. ISDN control information is sent over the D channel. Because this is a different channel from the ones used to carry your voice or data, it is called **out-of-band signaling.** A significant aspect of out-of-band signaling is that after a connection is made for a B channel, the D channel can be used for another purpose. Activities such as telemetry or another call request can be made in parallel with the B channel's transmissions. Another significant aspect is that B channels transmit data (or digital voice) only. That is, ISDN does not specify the content of a B channel and treats all bits as pure data. If two users communicate over the B channel using a particular protocol such as packet switching, they must specify the packet formats and transmit them over the B channel. However, the actual packet format, including headers and control information, is transparent to ISDN.

Several types of connections can be made over a B channel. First is a **circuit-switched connection** similar to that within the telephone system. All signaling and control information exchange occurs over the D channel. A second connection is a **virtual circuit** over a packet-switched network. Again, all control information to establish the call and define the virtual circuit is done over the D channel. The third connection type is similar to a leased line service. The connection is ever present and does not require call establishment prior to sending data.

The D channel is another story. It carries control information such as call establishment or termination, the type of call, and the B channel assigned to that call. Consequently, protocols must be defined to control transmission over the D channel.

A complete description of protocols that form the foundation of ISDN would easily fill at least one book (see references [St99], [Bl97b], [Me03], and [Gr98]). Our approach, then, is to provide an introduction to some of the pertinent protocols and leave it to the reader to see these references if interested in more detail. Relevant to ISDN, ITU-T has developed two separate series of recommendations called the I series and Q series documents. The **I series,** I.100 to I.605, first issued in 1984 and updated in 1988 and 1992, consists of over 60 separate documents and describes topics such as ISDN network architecture, reference configurations, routing principles, and the user–network interface. We will describe a couple of these protocols shortly.

The **Q series,** Q.700 to Q.795, describes a layered protocol known as **Signaling System 7 (SS7).** First issued in 1980, SS7 defines a standard that provides functionality in an *integrated digital network* (IDN). Note the use of the term *IDN* as opposed to *ISDN.* An IDN represents an outgrowth of the old analog telephone system, in which signal transmission and switching were handled separately. With the ability to put all the transmissions in a digital form, the two functions have been integrated. An ISDN uses an IDN but includes the ability to integrate digitized voice with many other types of digital data on the digital links.

Signaling System 7   SS7 is a four-layer protocol (Figure 13.3). The bottom three layers make up the **message transfer part (MTP)** and perform functions similar to the X.25 protocol (discussed in the next section). Unlike X.25, however, SS7 is concerned with internal network functions such as routing and reliability. For example, it provides for the reliable transport of messages using a connectionless mode of transfer. The fourth layer, the *user part,* contains specifications for call control, message formats, various applications, and maintenance.

The lowest layer, the **signaling data link** (ITU-T document Q.702) provides all the physical and electrical specifications and provides a 64 Kbps full-duplex transmission. The second layer, the **signaling link layer** (Q.703), provides reliable communications between two consecutive points in the network. As with other layer 2 protocols, it defines the frame format and provides error checking and flow control. It is similar to HDLC, and another discussion is not useful here.

The third layer, the **signaling network layer** (Q.704), provides reliable message transfer between two signaling points (endpoints). It performs two major functions: routing and management. For example, it determines whether to transfer a message to another network node or to deliver it to the fourth layer (the user part). In the former case, it must determine the next node. In the latter case, it must determine which user part gets the message. Management functions include the exchange of information among nodes regarding routes, error and congestion recovery, and rerouting.

The user part actually consists of a *telephone user part* (TUP) and an *ISDN user part* (ISUP). The TUP (documents Q.721 to Q.725) describes the establishment of circuit-switched connections for telephone calls, including types of control messages and their format. Example messages include those that specify charges for a call, an indication that a call has been answered, and a message that a circuit has been released due to an error.

Figure 13.3   Signaling System 7

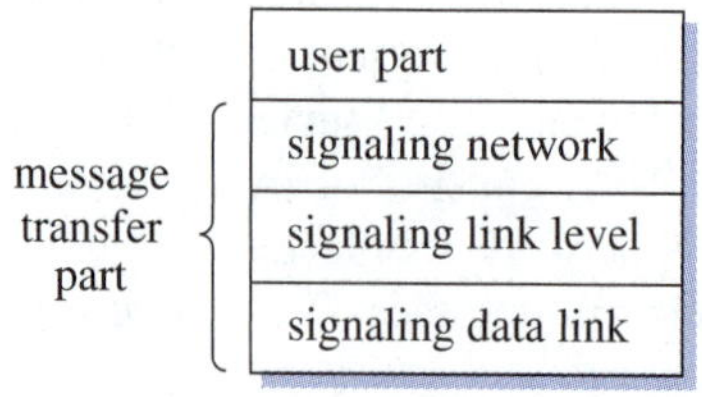

The ISUP (documents Q.761 to Q.766) performs similar functions but is designed to be a service for ISDN users as opposed to telephone users. Some examples of ISUP messages are described in the following list.*

- **Initial Address Message (IAM).** A message sent in the forward direction to initiate seizure of an outgoing circuit and to transmit number and other information relating to the routing and handling of a call.

- **Subsequent Address Message (SAM).** A message that may be sent in the forward direction after an Initial Address Message, to convey additional called party number information.

- **Information Request message (INR).** A message sent by an exchange to request information in association with a call.

- **Information message (INF).** A message sent to convey information in association with a call requested in an INR message.

- **Address Complete Message (ACM).** A message sent in the backward direction indicating that all the address signals required for routing the call to the called party have been received.

- **Call Progress message (CPG).** A message sent in the backward direction indicating that an event has occurred during call setup that should be relayed to the calling party.

- **Answer Message (ANM).** A message sent in the backward direction indicating that the call has been answered. This message is used in conjunction with charging information in order to (1) start metering the charge to the calling customer, and (2) start measuring call duration for international accounting purposes.

- **Facility Request message (FAR).** A message sent from an exchange to another exchange to request activation of a facility.

- **Facility Accepted message (FAA).** A message sent in response to a Facility Request message indicating that the requested facility has been invoked.

- **Facility Reject message (FRJ).** A message sent in response to a Facility Request message to indicate that the facility request has been rejected.

- **User-to-user information message (USR).** A message used for the transport of user-to-user information independent of call-control messages.

- **Call Modification Request message (CMR).** A message sent in either direction indicating a calling or called party request to modify the characteristics of an established call (for example, a change from data to voice).

- **Call Modification Completed message (CMC).** A message sent in response to a Call Modification Request message indicating that the requested call modification (for example, from voice to data) has been completed.

---

* From J. Griffith, *ISDN Explained*, ©1990, pp. 34–35. Reprinted by permission of John Wiley & Sons, New York.

- **Call Modification Reject message (CMRJ).** A message sent in response to a Call Modification Request message indicating that the request has been rejected.

- **Release message (REL).** A message sent in either direction to indicate that the circuit is being released because of the reason (cause) supplied and is ready to be put into the IDLE state on receipt of the Release Complete message. In case the call was forwarded or is to be rerouted, the appropriate indicator is carried in the message together with the redirection address and the redirecting address.

- **Release Complete message (RLC).** A message sent in either direction in response to the receipt of a Release message, or if appropriate, to a Reset Circuit message, when the circuit concerned has been brought into the IDLE condition.

This list merely scratches the surface of SS7. If you would like to read more about SS7, consult any of references [Gr98], [Bl97a], [Bl97b], [Sc86], and [Ap86].

Basic Service Protocols   There are over 60 documents in the ITU-T I series describing ISDN standards. Our approach is to introduce you to the user–network interface recommendations describing a three-layer protocol. The first layer (I.430) describes the physical bit stream for the ISDN basic service. A similar description (I.431) exists for the primary service (ref. [Gr98]).

The physical layer bit stream for the basic service corresponds to that at reference points S or T (see Figure 13.2). Figure 13.4 shows how the basic service

Figure 13.4   ISDN Physical Frame Format

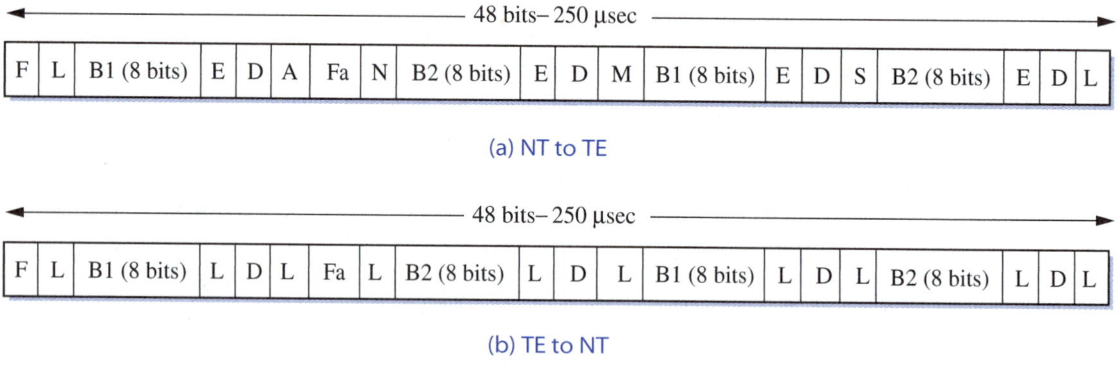

(a) NT to TE

(b) TE to NT

F:	framing	A:	activation bit
L:	DC balancing	Fa:	framing (secondary)
B1:	first B channel	N:	complement of Fa
B2:	second B channel	S:	Future use
D:	D channel	M:	multiframing bit
E:	echo bit		

2B+D channel is multiplexed over the bit pipe. Before we describe it we note several important facts:

- The frame format for frames going from a TE to an NT differs from those going in the reverse direction. We will explain these differences shortly.

- Communications between a TE and an NT are full duplex so that frames going in opposite directions do not collide.

- The word *frame* carries a slightly different meaning from that used many times before. Its format is not defined by a layer 2 (or higher) protocol. Instead, a frame simply defines how bits from the two logical B and D channels are multiplexed into a single physical transmission stream.*

Each frame contains 48 bits and is sent every 250 μsec, resulting in a bit rate of 192 Kbps. Each frame also contains two 8-bit fields from each of the B channels (labeled B1 and B2). A service using the B channel deposits 16 bits into the appropriate fields in each frame. The 16 bits sent every 250 μsec result in a data rate of 64 Kbps for each B channel. Four D bits are stored separately in each frame (labeled D), resulting in a data rate of 16 Kbps for the D channel. This means that when a TE has a packet of information to send over the D channel, it does so 4 bits at a time.

The remaining bits are for some low-level control functions. As we describe them, it is worth noting that ISDN uses a **pseudoternary coding** or **alternate mark inversion** technique in which a 1 bit is represented by zero volts and a 0 bit is represented by either a positive or a negative signal. Furthermore, each 0 bit has polarity opposite that of the most recent 0. This forces the signal representing a string of 0s to alternate between positive and negative.

The *F bit* is a framing bit, a positive signal indicating the beginning of the frame. The *L bit* is a DC balancing bit. After the F bit it is a negative signal. Together they provide timing and synchronization of the incoming frame. The remaining L bits are set to 0 if the number of preceding 0s is odd, and set to 1 otherwise. This is a means of providing electrically balanced signals.

The *E bit* is an echo bit; there is one for each D bit. In general, the NT uses it to echo back each D bit it receives. In cases where several TEs are connected to an NT via a single physical bus (Figure 13.5), the E bit also is used as a primitive form of

Figure 13.5   Multiple TEs Connected to an NT via a Single Bus

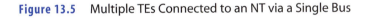

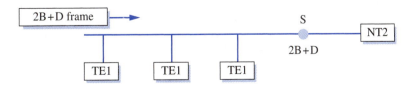

---

* An analogous format exists for a 2B+D channel.

contention for the D channel. When a TE has nothing to send on the D channel, it transmits a steady stream of 1s. Consequently, if none of the TEs is using the D channel, the NT receives all 1s in the D bit positions and echoes them back. Thus, by checking the returning E bits a TE can detect an idle D channel.

When a TE wants to send something on the D channel, it monitors the returning E bits. If they contain 0s, the TE knows that some other TE is using the D channel and waits. If the returning E bits are all 1s, either the D channel is idle or another TE is transmitting a data stream consisting of all 1s along it. However, a higher-layer protocol performs bit stuffing to limit the number of consecutive 1s that can be sent, so if a TE detects a number of 1s exceeding this value, it concludes the D channel is idle and starts sending.

The problem is that another TE might start sending along the D channel as well. However, the mechanism used and the fact that they compete for space in the same physical frame guarantees that one will be successful. To see how this works, suppose the leftmost TE of Figure 13.5 sent a D bit equal to 1 (no signal). Suppose the physical frame reaches the next TE, which then deposits a 0 (high or low signal) into the D bit position. The effect is that the 1 from the first TE is replaced with the 0 from the second TE. Both TEs (and any others that may also be sending) listen to the returning E bits. If a TE detects an E bit different from the D bit it sent, it concludes that some other TE has grabbed the D channel and temporarily abandons its attempt at getting the D channel. If the TE sees its own D bits echoed back as E bits, it continues sending along the D channel. Another contributing factor is that there is a 10-bit delay time between sending a D bit and receiving the corresponding E bit. Thus, because the D bits are more than 10 bits apart in the physical frame, the determination is made before the second D bit is sent. If the first and subsequent D bits from two TEs are the same, both TEs continue sending until there is eventually a difference. At that point the unsuccessful TE stops transmitting.

Of the remaining physical frame bits, the *A bit* is an activation bit and can be used to activate a TE. The *Fa* and *M bits* are used for multiframing, which allows the addition of another channel (Q channel). The *S* and *N bits* are reserved for future use.

The ISDN layer 2 protocol, defined by I.440 and I.441, is known as **Link Access Protocol for channel D (LAP-D).** If you have an absolutely fantastic memory, you might recall its mention in Section 9.2. It is very similar to HDLC, and there is very little to say that has not already been said.

The layer 3 protocol, defined by I.450 and I.451, includes the types and formats of ISDN messages sent over the D channel, protocols for establishing and clearing calls, management functions, and facility support. We will discuss ISDN messages and call control here.

Figure 13.6 shows the ISDN message format. The *protocol discriminator* allows the D channel to send messages from multiple protocols by identifying a protocol corresponding to a message. Currently, the protocol discriminator can specify X.25 messages or the user–network call-control messages that we will describe shortly. However, the capability exists to include other layer 3 protocols in the future.

The *Call Reference field* specifies the call to which the message refers. This is necessary because the D channel is used to set up and clear calls from many other channels. Without it there is no way to specify to which call a control refers. The

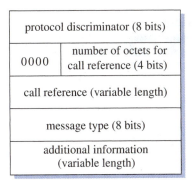

Figure 13.6   ISDN Layer 3 Message Format

4-bit field preceding the Call Reference specifies the number of bytes in the Call Reference field. This is needed because the basic and primary services have different Call Reference lengths. The Message Type field is self-explanatory. The I.451 recommendation specifies about 30 different types of messages, some of which are listed in Table 13.1.

The remaining field's content and format depend on the message type and provide additional information. It contains information similar to that in other message types we have seen before, such as source and destination address. It can also specify a B channel, redirection addresses, reasons for specific messages, and call status.

CALL SETUP

Setting up a call is not terribly different (at this level of discussion) from other initialization procedures we have discussed in this book. Figure 13.7 shows the exchange of messages during a typical setup. While going through this example, keep in mind that each TE is operating on behalf of a user. If it helps to think of the user as someone making a telephone call over a circuit-switched network, go ahead.

When a user wants to place a call, he makes a request to the TE. The telephone analogy would be pushing buttons to specify a number. The TE responds by sending a Setup message to the NT. The Setup message contains information such as the source and destination addresses, channel, whether the source address should be forwarded, and who will be charged for the call. When the network gets the Setup message, it routes it according to the SS7 protocols, thus determining a route to the other end. It also sends a Setup Acknowledge message back to the TE. The latter informs the TE that the call request has been forwarded and requests more information from the TE if the Setup message contained insufficient information.

Once the network has the information it needs, it sends a Call Proceeding message back to the TE. Meanwhile, if all goes well the Setup message travels through the network and reaches the destination TE. The destination TE then does two things. It sends an Alert message back to the caller indicating it has received the

Table 13.1 Some ISDN Layer 3 Messages

CALL	MEANING
Call Establishment	
Alert	Sent to calling TE indicating that the called TE has alerted its user to an incoming call.
Call Proceeding	Sent by the network indicating the call request is in progress.
Connect	Sent to calling TE indicating a call has been accepted.
Connect Acknowledgment	Sent by calling TE indicating receipt of the Connect message.
Setup	Sent by the calling TE requesting call establishment.
Setup Acknowledgment	Sent by the network to the calling TE indicating a previous Setup message has been sent. It also requests that the calling TE send more information to process the call request.
Call Information	
Resume	Resume a suspended call.
Resume Acknowledgment	Previously suspended call has been resumed.
Resume Reject	Previously suspended call could not be resumed.
Suspend	Request suspension of call.
Suspend Acknowledgment	Call has been suspended.
Suspend Reject	Call has not been suspended.
User Information	Used to transfer information between two TEs.
Call Clearing	
Disconnect	Request to disconnect the call. It should be followed by a request to release the B channel.
Release	Request to release a B channel. It is issued after a user "hangs up."
Release Complete	Indicates the B channel is released.

Setup message, and it notifies its user of the incoming call. In the case of a telephone call, it does this by generating the familiar ringing sound. When the Alert message returns to the calling TE, the caller also hears the ringing sound.

When the user being called answers, the called TE sends a Connect message back to the caller. Once the calling TE receives it, the ringing on its end stops and the TE responds with a Connect Acknowledgment. The exchange of the Connect and Connect Acknowledgment messages identifies and confirms the B channel to be used and begins the time during which a charge will accrue. Each TE then routes the PCM-coded voice into the proper B channel, as described in the discussion regarding Figure 13.4, and the conversation begins.

A call ends when one TE sends a Disconnect message to the network, typically after the user hangs up. The network routes the message over the network and sends

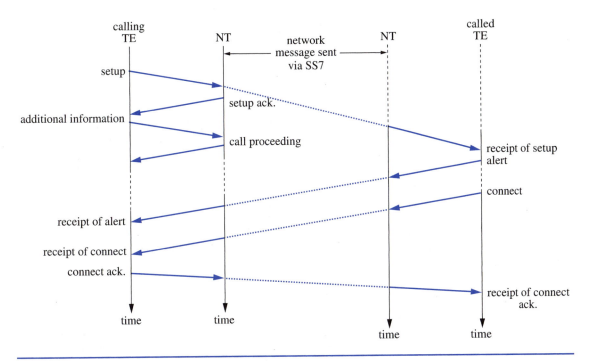

Figure 13.7 ISDN Call Establishment

a Release message back to the TE. The TE then sends a Release Complete message back to the network, clearing the B channel at that end. When the Disconnect message arrives at the other end, the network and TE there also exchange Release and Release Complete messages. This procedure clears the B channel at that end also.

BROADBAND ISDN

The digital nature of ISDN is attractive, but some have criticized the establishment of a 64 Kbps data rate for B channels. Indeed, in an era of gigabit rates for LANs and optical fiber, ISDN's 64 Kbps pales by comparison. In response, ITU-T has developed a set of documents describing **broadband ISDN (B-ISDN).** The intent is to use current high-bandwidth technologies to provide services requiring a high transfer rate.

Several services could be provided by B-ISDN. Videoconferencing and video telephones are two examples. Current ISDN standards could provide videophone service, but only for small screens. For larger screens with a high-quality video image, higher data rates are needed. Another example is pay television, similar to what already exists in many areas. From your television, you choose what you want to watch from a library of movies. At the end of the billing period, you are charged depending on your choices.

One of the issues regarding B-ISDN is the method of transfer. ISDN services use preallocated positions in the layer 1 frames for the channels (recall Figure 13.4). This approach, also called *synchronous transfer mode* (STM), is essentially time-division multiplexing. The disadvantage of it is that unassigned channels result in wasted bandwidth. Could other channels use the unassigned bandwidth to increase their own rates?

Another approach uses Asynchronous Transfer Mode (ATM), a well-established and widely deployed technology. ATM is a very fast packet-switched protocol using small fixed-size packets (called *cells*) optimized for multimedia use. It establishes logical connections similar to X.25 and frame relay (discussed next), but the small fixed size of the packets allows them to be created and routed using underlying hardware. In addition, rather than preassigning slots for a channel's cells, slots are allocated to applications needing them. The advantage is that otherwise empty slots can be used. The disadvantage is the extra complexity and the fact that each slot requires a header. For example, the header would define a virtual circuit so that ATM packets could be routed quickly. We will discuss ATM later in this chapter.

13.3   VIRTUAL CIRCUIT PROTOCOLS: X.25 AND FRAME RELAY

In the 1970s many European countries began to develop **public data networks** (networks available to anyone with a need for network services). The problems they faced were different from those in the United States. In the United States, public networks could be developed in large part by leasing existing telephone lines. In Europe this could not be done easily because of problems inherent in traversing communications systems across international boundaries. Thus, instead of developing separate and incompatible standards, European countries worked under the auspices of the ITU to develop a single standard. The result was the network service interface referred to as the *X series* of protocols, one of which, X.25, is discussed in this section.

The X.25 protocol was designed in the early days of computer networks, and several factors helped motivate its design. For example, personal computers were not common and many people used dumb terminals (terminals with no central processor) as interfaces to the network. Also, many of the communication lines were analog and the error rate was high.

Of course, these conditions no longer hold and X.25 is no longer commonly used. This begs the obvious question: Why study an old protocol? There are many reasons, but one is that it is the basis for another, more commonly used protocol, **frame relay.** In fact, many consider frame relay to be a replacement for X.25. Thus, we provide an overview of X.25 and follow with a discussion of frame relay.

Networks are commonly **packet-switched networks,** represented by the ubiquitous network cloud shown in Figure 13.8. They operate by transporting packets submitted at one part of the "cloud" and routing them to their destinations. Typically, switching logic (circuits) at nodes in the network make routing decisions. However, our concern here is the perspective of someone interacting with the network. Packets enter from point A and exit at points B, C, or D. We do not necessarily know (or care) how they get there. Our main focus is to define the logical connection between the source and the destination.

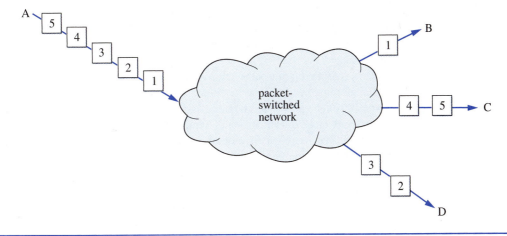

Figure 13.8   Packet-Switched Network

PACKET-SWITCHED NETWORK MODES

Virtual Circuits   Packet-switched networks typically operate in one of two modes. The first is by a **virtual circuit** between two points. It is somewhat analogous to creating a telephone connection between two people. A device connected to the network requests a connection to a device somewhere else. This request is routed through network nodes, establishing a path between the caller and destination. All subsequent packets sent by the caller follow that same path.

The connection is not a physical one, however. The connections between nodes are not dedicated solely to one virtual circuit. In fact, a node and its connection to a neighbor may participate in several virtual circuits. Figure 13.9 shows two overlapping virtual circuits. A and B have both requested and established connections to C

Figure 13.9   Overlapping Virtual Circuits

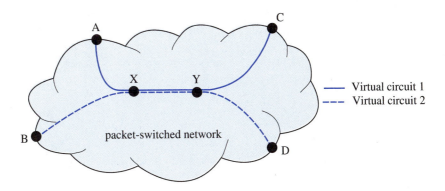

and D, respectively. The paths begin at different locations but overlap at nodes X and Y. X handles packets corresponding to either virtual circuit and routes them to Y. Y, in turn, routes packets differently depending on the virtual circuit on which they arrive.

Because virtual circuit paths can overlap, each node must be able to determine the virtual circuit corresponding to an incoming packet. As the initial connection request goes through each node, the node assigns a virtual circuit number to it, determines the next node to which it will send the request, and makes an entry in its routing table. The routing table contains each virtual circuit number and the next node along the corresponding path.

Note that each node assigns virtual circuit numbers independently, so one virtual circuit may be identified by different numbers at different nodes. Consequently, each node informs the circuit's preceding node of the virtual circuit number it uses for incoming packets. This allows a preceding node to know the virtual circuit number assigned by the next node and to store it in the packet. Thus, incoming packets contain the number of the virtual circuit coming in to the node. The node's routing logic accesses the routing table entry corresponding to it and sends it to the next node. If the next part of the virtual circuit has a different number, the node stores it in the packet as well. For example, Figure 13.10 shows a packet traversing each of the virtual circuits of Figure 13.9. The virtual circuit between A and C is assigned the numbers 1 (by X), 5 (by Y), and 3 (by C). The circuit between B and D is assigned the numbers 2 (by X), 3 (by Y), and 1 (by D).

Table 13.2 shows what the relevant entries of X's and Y's routing tables look like. A packet coming in to X from A contains the virtual circuit number 1. X's routing table indicates that the next node is Y and that it uses 5 as the virtual circuit number. Consequently, X stores 5 into the packet and sends it to Y. A packet entering Y from X will contain a virtual circuit number of 5 or 3. If it is 5, Y's routing table indicates C as the next node and an outgoing virtual circuit number of 3. If it is 3, then D is the next node and the outgoing virtual circuit number is 1.

Figure 13.10   Sending Packets along a Virtual Circuit

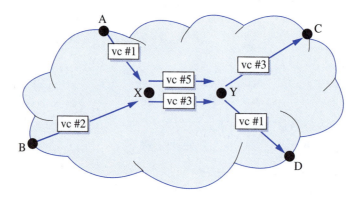

Table 13.2   Routing Tables for Nodes X and Y from Figure 13.9

ROUTING TABLE FOR X			ROUTING TABLE FOR Y		
INCOMING VC NUMBER	OUTGOING VC NUMBER	NEXT NODE	INCOMING VC NUMBER	OUTGOING VC NUMBER	NEXT NODE
1	5	Y	5	3	C
2	3	Y	3	1	D

VC = virtual circuit.

Datagram Service   One advantage of virtual circuits is that routing decisions are made just once for each circuit, eliminating the need to make such decisions for each packet. Your first thought might be that this is particularly beneficial when many packets are sent. The opposite may be true, however, because more packets usually means more time has elapsed since the circuit was established. Consequently, the conditions that may have made the current path a good one may no longer be true. That is, conditions may have changed so that the current path takes longer. The result, in that case, is reduced efficiency.

Another option is a **datagram** service in which each packet contains the source and destination addresses. As packets enter the network, nodes apply routing logic to each packet separately making use of the most current routing information. We have discussed this approach previously and will not elaborate further. Table 13.3 lists some advantages and disadvantages of virtual circuits and datagram services.

Table 13.3   Comparison of Virtual Circuits and Datagrams

VIRTUAL CIRCUIT	DATAGRAM
Helps prevent congestion. Since a node knows it is part of a virtual circuit, it can reserve space for the anticipated arrival of packets.	Unexpected packets make congestion control more difficult.
If a virtual circuit is open too long, the current path may not be the best given current network conditions.	Nodes route each packet using the most current information about the network.
A routing decision is made just once for each set of packets sent along the virtual circuit.	Separate routing decisions are made for each packet.
Packets arrive in the order they were sent.	Packets can arrive out of order, requiring the destination to order them.
A node failure breaks the virtual circuit connection, causing a loss of packets.	If a node fails, packets can be routed around it.

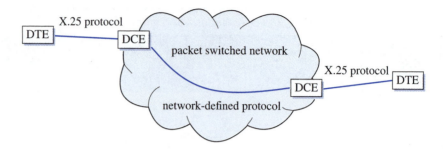

Figure 13.11   X.25 Public Data Network Interface

X.25 INTERFACE STANDARD

An important part of working with networks is their interface. One such interface is the ITU **X.25 standard.** Many people used the term *X.25 network,* causing some to believe mistakenly that X.25 defines the network protocols. It does not. X.25 defines the protocol between a DTE and a DCE connected to a network (Figure 13.11). We note that early versions focused mainly on the asymmetric DTE–DCE relationship. Later versions recognized the need for peer-to-peer communications between two DTEs. Consequently, X.25 can be used strictly as a user-to-network interface or as a user-to-user connection across a network.

X.25 defines a synchronous transmission analogous to the three lowest layers of the OSI (Figure 13.12). The network layer receives user data and puts it into an X.25 packet. The X.25 packet is passed to the data link layer, where it is embedded in an LAPB frame (Section 9.2 defined LAPB). The physical layer then transmits the LAPB frame using the X.21 protocol discussed in Section 4.4. Alternatively,

Figure 13.12   X.25 Protocol Layers

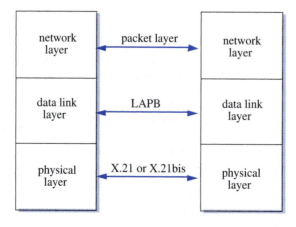

X.25 may use the X.21bis standard, which was designed as an interim standard to connect V series modems with packet-switched networks. The X.21 standard was supposed to replace it, but, as with many plans, it did not happen. A more extensive treatment of X.21bis is found in reference [Bl95]. In some cases, X.25 may even use the EIA-232 protocol.

Since we have already discussed the two lower layers, we will focus here on the network layer's packet protocol.

Packet Format   The first step is defining the packet format. As with previous protocols, formats vary depending on the type of packet. Figure 13.13 shows two primary formats. The relevant packet fields are as follows:

- **Flags.** The first four bits define the *General Format Indicator* (GFI) and, to some extent, define the packet format. For example, two of the bits specify whether 3-bit or 7-bit numbers are used for sequencing and acknowledging. Another bit, called the *D bit,* specifies how to interpret acknowledgments. If the D bit is 0, acknowledgments come from the DCE. If the D bit is 1, they come from the remote DTE. In effect, the D bit determines whether flow control is being managed for a local DTE–DCE connection or for a logical connection with the remote DTE.

- **Logical Group Number** and **Logical Channel Number.** Together these fields define a 12-bit number for a virtual circuit the DTE has established. This allows the DTE to establish up to 4096 virtual circuits.

- **Control** (data packet). Contains either 3-bit or 7-bit sequence and acknowledgment numbers used for flow control. X.25 flow control uses windows and is not significantly different from flow control protocols discussed previously.

Figure 13.13   X.25 Packet Formats

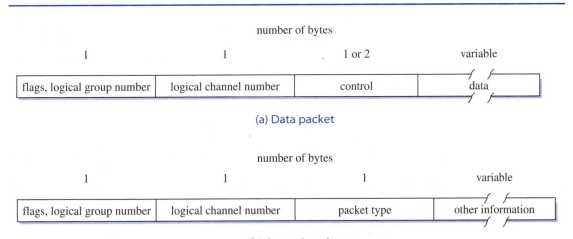

(a) Data packet

(b) Control packet

Table 13.4   X.25 Packet Types

TYPE	FUNCTION
Call Request	When a DTE wants to establish a connection (call another DTE), it sends a Call Request packet.
Call Accepted	If the called DTE accepts the call, it acknowledges it by returning a Call Accepted (or Call Confirmation) packet.
Data	Used to transfer high-level protocol data between the DTEs. There are typically up to 128 bytes of data, but handshake protocols may agree to transfer up to 4096 bytes in a packet.
Clear Request	Sent by a node wanting to terminate a virtual circuit. It can also be used by a DTE not wanting to accept a call. A receiving DTE sees it as a Clear Indication packet.
Clear Confirmation	Sent in response to a Clear Request packet.

This field also contains a bit set in the last of a series of packets to indicate the end of a packet stream.

- **Data** (data packet). Self-explanatory.
- **Packet Type** (control packet). There are several packet types, some of which are defined in Table 13.4.

Virtual Calls   X.25 provides two types of virtual circuits between DTEs. A **permanent virtual circuit** is similar to leasing a telephone line: Either DTE can send data without the overhead of making and establishing a call. It is particularly useful when a high volume of data is transferred. A **virtual call,** the second type, requires a call connection protocol to be performed prior to any data transfer.

Figure 13.14 shows the call connection and termination process between two DTEs. (For brevity, we have not shown the DCEs or the network, but don't forget they are there.) The DTE wanting to make a call constructs a *Call Request packet* containing the virtual call (or logical channel) number and sends it via its DCE and the network. When the receiving DCE gets the packet, it assigns a virtual call number to the request and delivers the packet to the receiving DTE. Note that there is no requirement that the channel numbers be the same at each end. As described previously, they are defined dynamically. If that DTE is willing and able to accept the call, it sends a *Call Accepted packet.* Once the first DTE receives the Call Accepted packet, the virtual call is established.

Next, the DTEs exchange data and acknowledgment packets in a full-duplex mode, using a flow control similar to that used in HDLC (see Section 9.2). When either DTE decides to end the connection (DTE A in Figure 13.14), it creates and sends a *Clear Request packet.* The local DCE responds by doing two things. First, it sends the Clear Request packet to the remote DTE. Second, it responds to its local DTE by sending it a *Clear Confirmation packet.* As far as the local DTE is concerned, the virtual call is terminated and the logical channel number is available for

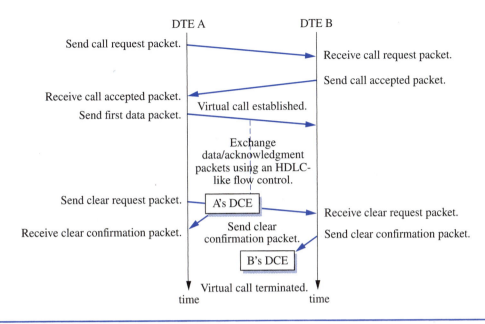

Figure 13.14 Virtual Call

future calls. Eventually, the remote DTE receives the Clear Request packet. It sees it as a Clear Indication packet and responds by sending a Clear Confirmation packet to its DCE. That DCE also clears the channel number, making it available for other calls.

Although once common, X.25 had its critics. For example, one of the strongest criticisms was that X.25-based protocols provided only a connection-oriented service. Another was that its network layer (layer 3) was incomplete and actually contained features found in higher-layer protocols. For example, the OSI layer 3 provides routing capability, but the X.25 layer 3 had no such capability. Furthermore, X.25 provided for some connection-oriented features with the remote DTE. Since end-to-end connections are more typical in layer 4 protocols, some saw this as a blending of two layers into one, thus blurring the distinction between layers as defined by OSI.

FRAME RELAY

Frame relay shares some features with X.25 but also has its own unique ones, such as the following:

- It was designed to be efficient and to maximize frame throughput (number of frames forwarded per unit of time).
- It defines a WAN infrastructure and is commonly provided by phone companies. A typical use is to connect LANs.

- Like X.25, it supports both a *permanent virtual circuit* (PVC) and a **switched virtual circuit (SVC).** (Using X.25 terminology, the latter is a virtual call.)

- Unlike X.25, it provides no error control. The main reason for this is that frame relay runs over digital equipment such as optical fiber. Errors in such equipment are extremely rare.

- It provides no flow control. It assumes that any flow control is handled by higher layers at end-user sites. Because personal computers and servers have replaced dumb terminals for network connections, this assumption is reasonable.

- It was originally designed for T1 speeds but can achieve up to T3 speeds.

- It is designed for bursty data flows. The user may transfer a lot of data over a short period and then nothing for another period of time. This is typical when a client submits database queries or downloads screen images.

- Perhaps the most significant difference is that frame relay operates only at layers 1 and 2, a significant factor in reducing the protocol's overhead. In fact, because it does not implement flow or error control, it does not even implement many of the layer 2 functions we have described previously.

Figure 13.15 shows a common use for frame relay networks. To connect multiple LANs from different organizations, a T1 line might be used as in Figure 13.15a.

Figure 13.15   Using a Frame Relay Network to Connect LANs

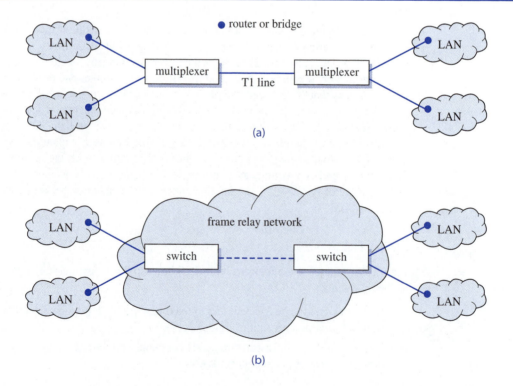

However, there is a potential problem. Recall from our discussion of T1 in Chapter 4 that a channel (part of the T1 bandwidth) is reserved for each connection. This is useful if data are flowing continuously over the connection. However, when data transmission occurs in bursts, there will be times when that portion of the bandwidth is unused and the connection is underutilized. Figure 13.15b shows a frame relay network connecting the LANs. A router from each LAN connects to a frame relay switch and sends it data. Frame relay protocols at each switch in the network transfer the data to their destination. An additional feature is that a customer can purchase a particular data rate over a frame relay network. This means that network protocols are committed to providing the bit rate the customer pays for. The customer that pays more can use the same network to send data at a rate quicker than that of a customer that pays less. We'll describe how this works shortly.

Frame Format   Let's begin by describing the frame relay frame format (Figure 13.16). It resembles the format of an HDLC frame, but this is not surprising because the layer 2 portion of frame relay is based on LAPD, an HDLC variant.

Both Flag fields contain start and end of frame delimiters, just like HDLC. In the event these flags appear in other parts of the frame, bit stuffing is used to make the pattern transparent to the frame relay protocol. The CRC field uses the 16-bit ITU-T V.41 generator polynomial $x^{16} + x^{12} + x^5 + 1$ for error checking. This might seem to contradict what we stated previously about not providing error control. Frame relay does check for errors using the CRC method of Chapter 6; however, if it detects an error it simply discards the frame. This is not as severe as it sounds. The philosophy is that since today's networks are extremely reliable, implementing error control adds overhead with very little gain. If the rare error does occur, just drop the frame. Presumably, a protocol at a higher layer will detect and deal with it. The trade-off is a simpler layer 2 protocol and faster forwarding of frames. The Data field, as usual, is self-explanatory. Maximum sizes vary with the vendor and can go as high as 4096 bytes.

This brings us to the Control field. Some references refer to it as the Address field since it contains routing information. However, it does not contain an address per se and includes some control bits used for special handling or to indicate congestion. The Control field contains the following.

- **Data Link Connection Identifier (DLCI).** Actually, there is a 6-bit DLCI field in the first byte and a 4-bit DLCI field in the second byte. The 4-bit DLCI is an extension of the 6-bit DLCI; together, they specify a 10-bit virtual circuit

Figure 13.16   Frame Relay Frame Format

number of bytes: 1   2   variable   2   1

| flags | control | data | CRC | flags |

number over which the frame is traveling. If the circuit is a PVC, the provider assigns the number. In the case of an SVC, the number is assigned during the call setup. Logic at each frame relay switch examines the 10-bit virtual circuit number and routes accordingly. The approach is very similar to that used by X.25 and we won't repeat it. Why is the DLCI field split up? The explanation of the next field helps answer that.

- **Extended Address (EA).** There is an EA bit at the end of each byte. This allows the Control field to expand and accommodate DLCI values larger than 10 bits (i.e., more virtual circuits). In our current configuration (Figure 13.16), the first EA bit is 0 and the second is 1. If an expanded DLCI were needed, the second EA bit would be 0, indicating a third byte in the Control field (which would have more DLCI bits and another EA bit). If a fourth byte were required, then the third byte's EA bit would be 0 and the fourth byte would have 6 more DLCI bits.

- **Forward Explicit Congestion Notification (FECN)** and **Backward Explicit Congestion Notification (BECN).** One or both bits are set when a frame relay switch detects congestion. We'll discuss congestion control shortly.

- **Discard Eligibility (DE).** A value of 0 indicates a high priority: Frame relay must make every attempt to deliver the frame. A value of 1 indicates a lower priority. A switch may, under the right conditions, drop a low-priority frame. We'll soon see how the protocol uses this to provide specified rates to the customer and to deal with congestion control.

- **Command/Response Indicator (C/R).** A 1-bit field that depends on the higher layer. It might, for example, use the bit to indicate that the frame is a command or a response to a previous command.

Committed Information Rate   An important part of frame relay is the **committed information rate (CIR).** Measured in bits per second, it represents the bandwidth that frame relay is dedicated to providing over a virtual circuit. If a customer leases a PVC, the cost may depend on the CIR. The customer pays more for a higher bit rate. If the customer generates data at or below the CIR, then the bandwidth is available to accommodate them. If the customer generates data at a larger rate, there are no guarantees. The data may or may not be delivered, depending on network conditions.

There are several other parameters we must define to explain how this works:

- Time interval, T, used to measure bit rates and data bursts.

- Committed burst size, B_c, measured in bits. If a customer generates B_c bits during T, there is sufficient bandwidth to deliver them. B_c, T, and CIR are related via the formula CIR $= B_c/T$.

- Excess burst size, B_e. This is a number of bits in excess of B_c that a customer may generate during time T. Frame relay may deliver them if there is sufficient bandwidth.

To see how this works, suppose a customer sends frames to a frame relay switch. The virtual circuit has already been set up and has a CIR associated with it. As long as the total number of bits in the frames do not exceed B_c during time T, they are treated as high-priority frames. That is, the switch sets the DE bit in each frame to 0. This tells other switches in the network that these frames are high priority and that they should make every effort to deliver them. If the number of bits exceeds B_c (but is still smaller than $B_c + B_e$) during time T, the switch sets the DE bit to 1. The frame still travels the virtual circuit; however, a switch may drop a frame that has its DE bit set to 1 if it determines that congestion is building up. If the customer sends more than $B_c + B_e$ bits during time T, the excess frames are dropped immediately.

Figure 13.17 shows an example. Suppose in this case that $T = 1$ second, CIR = 10,000 bps, $B_c = 10,000$ bits, $B_e = 2000$ bits, and that the frame size is 2000 bits. Starting at time $t = 0$, the customer sends five frames. The total number of bits equals B_c, and the switch sets the DE bit in each frame to 0. If the customer sends no more frames, then he is generating data that is within the CIR during a period of length T. However, if the customer sends more frames before time $t = 1$, he is requesting a bit rate in excess of the CIR. Frame relay is willing to allow that up to a point, but makes no guarantees. As a result, the switch sets the DE bit in the sixth frame to 1. However, the B_e value of 2000 bits indicates that this is the last frame during the period T that frame relay will try to deliver. The switch will drop all other frames that the customer delivers before time $t = 1$. Once $t = 1$, the customer will then be allowed to send five more high-priority frames (DE bit = 0) and one low-priority frame (DE bit = 1) until $t = 2$. The fundamental idea is that frame relay has reserved 10,000 bits per second of bandwidth and will try (conditions allowing) to deal with up to 12,000 bits per second. Anything beyond that during a period of length T is dropped.

Congestion Control   Because frame relay implements no flow control between switches, congestion can be a problem. Fortunately, frame relay has some ways of dealing with it. The first logical question might be: How does a switch determine when congestion exists? Each output port has a buffer or queue associated with it. Frames wait in the queue until it is their turn to be forwarded. If the number of

Figure 13.17   Determining Which Frames to Send and Their Priority

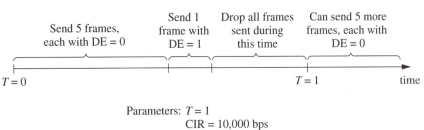

Parameters: $T = 1$
CIR = 10,000 bps
B_c = 10,000 bits
B_e = 2,000 bits
Frame size = 2,000 bits

frames in the queue passes some threshold value, then the queue is in danger of overflowing. In other words, there are too many frames and the outgoing port is becoming congested.

One response to congestion is to just drop any frame with its DE bit set to 1. However, the problem may be caused by end-user protocols feeding too much information into the network. If the corresponding sending and receiving protocols could reduce the amount of frames they exchange (i.e., flow control at a higher layer), this would reduce congestion. Consequently, frame relay contains a way to inform the end-user protocol of congestion problems using the FECN and BECN bits in a frame.

Figure 13.18 shows how this works. Suppose a virtual circuit from a source to a destination goes through the switch in the figure. Suppose also that the outgoing port in the direction of the destination is becoming congested. If a frame is forwarded over that port, the switch sets its FECN bit to 1. When that frame arrives at the destination, the receiving protocols there can determine that the virtual circuit is experiencing congestion in its direction. Now keep in mind that frames travel both ways along a virtual circuit. Consequently, if the switch receives a frame from a congested port, it sets the BECN bit to 1. When that frame arrives at the source, the sending protocols there can determine that the virtual circuit is experiencing congestion in the opposite direction. The important thing is that both ends of a virtual circuit can detect when congestion is occurring and in which direction. Note that congestion may occur in only one direction.

How does this help? It depends on the higher layers. If the sending flow control protocol (at the higher layer) senses congestion, it can reduce its window and reduce the number of frames it sends. It might even stop sending frames altogether for a period of time. If the receiving flow control protocol senses congestion, it may delay sending an acknowledgment. If the corresponding sender waits longer for an acknowledgment, it sends fewer frames per unit of time. If the sender's frames time out, the sender may increase the timer value or decrease the window size or both. Another option (for example, with TCP) is for the receiving protocol to reduce its credit. When the sending side gets the reduced credit, it responds by reducing its window.

Figure 13.18 Setting FECN/BECN Bits due to Congestion

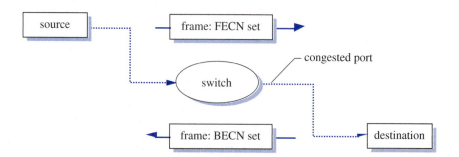

Of course, this is just an introduction to an evolving technology, and there are other issues we did not cover, such as voice over frame relay, more extensive comparisons with X.25 and ATM, configuration issues, and more detail on congestion control. The reader can find more information in references [Bl00], [Hu03], [St99], and [Mc01].

13.4   ASYNCHRONOUS TRANSFER MODE

The impact that the Internet has had on our society is almost beyond measure. It has, without doubt, revolutionized how we communicate with others, seek and organize information, spend our free time, and, in general, how we do our jobs. The previous decade has seen tremendous growth in the Internet, with some estimates having it double in size every 18 months. The Internet is very good at what it was designed to do: provide the means necessary to share vast amounts of information among many diverse systems. However, some have raised questions about its ability to meet the needs of the future. We have already discussed the aging aspects of the Internet Protocol and the development of IPv6 to meet those needs. Developers of IPv6 worked very hard to overcome the aging IP and prepare for the global communications network of the 21st century. Key design issues of IPv6 were developed specifically to increase the speed with which IP packets can be routed through the Internet.

However, the past decade has seen tremendous growth in video and voice communications. For such applications, some claim that IPv6 will still not be adequate, even with such protocols as RTP and RSVP (see Chapter 11). The reader should be aware that we do not refer to situations that allow a user to access a video file (remember MPEG?) and run it locally. The video applications we speak of here refer to the ability to view video in a real-time mode.

One example is video on demand, in which a customer can request a movie from a provider at an arbitrary time. The provider maintains a digitized copy of the movie and transmits it to the customer, who watches as it is being transferred. Another example is videoconferencing. Imagine sitting at a personal computer whose screen is divided into several windows, each containing the image of another individual. Each of them has the same capability. You can speak into a microphone, and each person can see you and hear your words as you speak them. Likewise, you can see them and hear their words. Except for the small images on the screen, it is as if you were all in the same room participating in the conversation. (An additional advantage may be to call on a local program to draw mustaches and Groucho Marx eyebrows on whomever tends to monopolize the conversation.)

Such applications require more than the rapid delivery of digitized voices and images. They require delivery with real-time constraints, that is, a consistent and predictable flow of information. There must be little, if any, noticeable delay, for such delays cause pauses in the sentences or a video effect similar to that in movies from the turn of the century (20th century, that is), where the video images really looked like a sequence of still pictures. Some have argued that IP will not be able to meet these constraints and that a different technology, **Asynchronous Transfer Mode (ATM),** is where the future of audio and video applications lies.

To the user, ATM is designed to resemble the circuit-switching technology of telephone systems in that everything appears to work in real time. However, ATM represents a complete departure from such circuit-switching technology. For example, it maintains the capability of routing individual packets of data. The following items describe the primary attributes of an ATM network and, at a glance, help you see some of its main features.

- Connection oriented.
- Packet switching.
- Fixed-size packets called cells.
- High-speed, low-delay transmission of cells.
- Cells will not arrive out of order.
- Speeds of 155.5 Mbps (this is the data rate necessary for full-motion video) or 622 Mbps (four 155.5 Mbps channels) over SONET. As the technology evolves, the future no doubt will see gigabit per second rates.
- Designed in large part for real-time video and voice applications.
- Heavily promoted by telephone companies.
- Technology used by B-ISDN.

In general, ATM works by initially setting up a connection between two sites during which a virtual circuit between them is established. In ATM terminology this is called *signaling*. It is based on the ITU-T protocol Q.2931, which itself is a subset of Q.931. The virtual circuit corresponds to a specific path determined during signaling, and all cells sent through the virtual circuit follow the same path. When the transmissions are complete, ATM protocols include a disconnect phase.

Much of this may sound similar to topics we have discussed previously, especially X.25. The differences, of course, are in the details and operations. This section provides an overview of ATM and discusses how some of the benefits are realized, some techniques for switching (routing) of cells, cell definition, virtual circuits, connection management, and the layered reference model. Once again, this is a topic that can fill a book and has. Our main goal is to provide the reader with a fundamental understanding of just what ATM is and how it differs from other protocols. Of course, the interested reader is encouraged to seek out additional details in references [Bl99] and [Ha98].

BENEFITS OF SMALL FIXED-SIZE CELLS

One of the key aspects of ATM is that it transmits all information in 53-byte cells (48 bytes of data plus 5 header bytes, whose format we'll describe later). This raises a couple of logical questions. What is so special about transmitting information in fixed-size cells, and why is the size set at 48 bytes of data? The answer to the second question is, Because those involved in developing the protocol wanted something else. As silly as that sounds, the size actually is the result of compromise, a solution in which no one gets what they actually want.

When ATM was in the early stages of development, its committee sought a cell size that would meet several constraints. For example, it had to work well with existing equipment. Cells also had to be small enough so they could pass through intermediate switches quickly and keep internal queues small. The size also had to be small enough to implement error correction techniques efficiently. The committee had a European faction that promoted the use of 32-byte payloads. European countries are relatively small, and a 32-byte payload could be implemented without their telephone companies having to install echo cancelers (circuits that remove signals that echo back from their destination). U.S. telephone companies had been installing echo cancelers anyway and preferred a larger 64-byte payload to decrease the header-to-cell-size ratio. Japan also favored the 64-byte payload. The solution was to take the numerical average of the proposed sizes of 32 and 64 bytes; the 48-byte payload was the result.

Transmitting information in small fixed-size packets has several advantages. First, it is simpler. Programmers learn this fundamental fact early. Writing programs that manipulate fixed-size record structures is easier than writing ones that deal with variable-size structures. There are just fewer checks to make. This, of course, simplifies both the hardware and software required to do the job and also keeps the costs lower.

A second advantage of having small cells is that one cell won't occupy an outgoing link for lengthy periods. For example, suppose a switch just began forwarding a cell when another high-priority cell arrives. High priority typically means it can move to the front of an outgoing queue but it won't interrupt transmission of a cell already in progress. Consequently, it must wait for the transmission to be complete. If that cell is large, then the time the high-priority cell must wait is longer. A smaller cell means the high-priority cell gets out quicker.

Another reason a switch can get small cells through more quickly is the capability to overlap input and output operations. To see how this works, suppose that a cell arrives in its entirety and is buffered before being forwarded. If a cell contains a 1000-byte payload, then all 1000 bytes must be received and buffered before the first byte can be sent through an outgoing link. Figure 13.19 illustrates. Figure 13.19a shows a timeline during which the incoming bytes from a large cell are received. The first bytes are not forwarded until time t_1, after all bytes have arrived. Figure 13.19b shows what happens if a large cell is divided among smaller 48-byte cells. In this case the first cell can be forwarded as soon as it arrives at time t_0 (much earlier than time t_1) because it does not have to wait for all the other cells to arrive. During the timeline of Figure 13.19b, information is being received and forwarded simultaneously, thus increasing the rate at which cells are forwarded toward their final destination.

There are other benefits as well. For example, because information gets forwarded more quickly, less of it is maintained in the switch, which, in turn, contributes to smaller outgoing queues. The result is that the payload spends less time sitting in buffers. Another benefit is that bytes arrive at a more consistent rate at the final destination as opposed to a bursty arrival pattern in which many bytes arrive quickly in one large cell followed by longer wait times between cells. This is especially important in video and voice applications, for which data must arrive quickly and consistently.

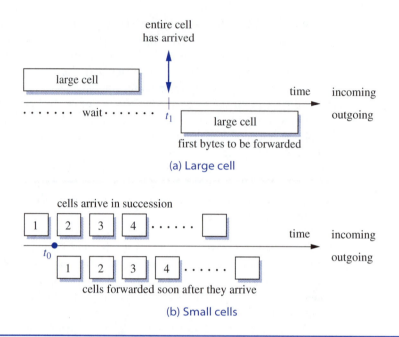

Figure 13.19   Overlapping Cell Input and Output

One last benefit is that small fixed-size cells facilitate designing switches capable of forwarding multiple packets concurrently. This is especially useful because it reduces times when one cell must wait for another cell to be forwarded. How this works is difficult to understand until we have described some switching technologies, so we defer this discussion until a bit later.

OVERVIEW OF ATM NETWORK

We begin by outlining what an ATM network looks like and discussing some of its components. Figure 13.20 shows that an ATM network consists of ATM switches. Generally, the *ATM switch** is analogous to the IP router in that it's responsible for

---

* The difference between a switch and router in this context is not well defined. Some use the term *router* when referring to the Internet and its ability to connect a variety of different technologies. Others use the term *switch* when referring to a collection of homogeneous links connecting similar technologies. This suggests that the difference is whether the device can connect different technologies. However, vendors are advertising switches that are more versatile in their ability to connect different technologies, which blurs this distinction. We also saw previously that *switch* refers to a multiport bridge operating at layer 2. The bottom line is that at this level whatever distinction there may be is not important.

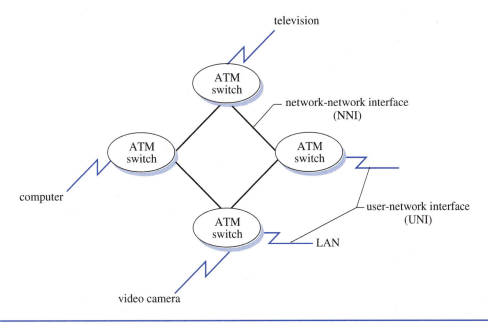

Figure 13.20   ATM Network

receiving incoming cells and forwarding them outward along the correct link. ATM switches have links to one another, forming a network with a variety of paths. Each switch, in turn, can connect to a variety of user-oriented devices such as a computer, television, video camera, or local area network. The figure doesn't show it, but each user device needs an interface card that speaks ATM.

There are two types of links in an ATM network. The *network–network interface* (NNI) connects two ATM switches, and the *user–network interface* (UNI) connects the switch to a user device. There are some differences between the links—for example, how they interpret cells. We'll deal with that shortly. For now we just present them for reference.

SWITCHING

As stated previously, ATM communication is connection oriented. When a site has information to send to another site, it requests a connection by sending a message. The message passes through various switches, setting up a virtual path as it does so. In contrast to IP, subsequent data cells contain a *virtual path ID,* which the switch uses to route the cell through outgoing links. The switch maintains a table in which each entry contains two pairs: an input port/virtual path ID and an output port/ virtual path ID. When a cell arrives over a particular input port, the switch uses that port identifier and the virtual path ID in the cell to locate a table entry. It changes the cell's virtual path ID to the one paired with the associated output port and sends the cell through that port. For example, suppose a table entry contained the following:

Input Port	Virtual Path ID	Output Port	Virtual Path ID
:	:	:	:
C	5	F	8
:	:	:	:

Then a cell containing a virtual path ID of 5 arriving on port C is forwarded over port F with its virtual path ID changed to 8.

The process is really very similar to that described at the beginning of the previous section, and there is little point in elaborating again. The only difference of note is in terminology. X.25 uses a virtual circuit ID in its packets, whereas ATM cells contain virtual path IDs. At this level they play the same role. However, we will see later that ATM also defines a virtual circuit in addition to the virtual path and we will see how they differ.

Banyan Switches   Using routing tables this way allows switches to forward cells very quickly, especially if the table entries are hashed on the incoming port identifier and virtual path ID. Paths are established and released simply by inserting and deleting new entries into the table.

Other techniques exist for providing switching functions in high-speed networks, some of which can make use of switching several cells concurrently. One example is a **Banyan switch.** A Banyan switch has an equal number of input and output lines (typically equal to a power of 2). Inside the switch there are multiple stages. The number of stages is related to the number of output lines. For example, if there are 2^k output lines, then there are k stages in the switch.

Each cell is associated with a *bit string* (also called a *switching string*) of length k, and each bit in the string takes the cell from one stage to the next. This bit string might be in the cell or it might be stored in a table along with a virtual path ID. Its location is not important to the discussion here.

Figure 13.21 shows a Banyan switch with eight inputs and outputs and three stages between them. A cell can enter any one of the eight inputs and pass to one of four switching elements (first stage). Based on the first bit of the switching string, the cell follows one of two possible outputs into one of four elements at the second stage. There, switching logic examines the second bit of the switching string and passes the cell along one of two possible outputs into the third stage. The process is repeated once more using the remaining bit, and the cell is finally forwarded through one of the switch's outputs.

Each output in Figure 13.21 is labeled with a unique 3-bit string that defines the output line over which the cell is forwarded. There are a couple of interesting things about this switch. First, the output depends only on the switching string and is independent of the input line over which a cell arrives. For example, Figure 13.21 highlights three possible paths corresponding to a cell with switching string 100. Cells entering elements A1 and B1 get passed to A2 in the second stage. From there, both

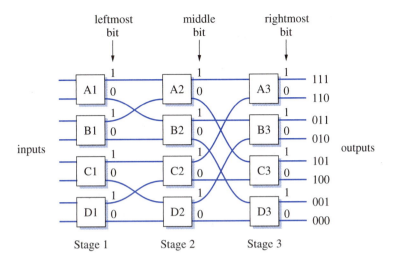

leftmost   middle   rightmost
  bit   bit   bit

inputs   outputs

Stage 1   Stage 2   Stage 3

Figure 13.21   Banyan Switch

would go to C3. The cell entering D1 passes to C2 and then to C3. As you can see, each starts at a different element at the first stage but ends up at the output corresponding to 100.

Another interesting feature is that switching logic can handle multiple cells concurrently. For example, one cell with switching string 100 passes through A1, A2, and C3. Suppose another cell with switching string 110 arrives at D1. It would pass through D1, C2, and A3. Since the two cells involve different elements, the routing can be done concurrently. In other words, one cell does not have to wait for another. This is a particularly important feature because it allows a switch to forward more cells and hence reduce waiting time, a desirable trait for real-time video or voice.

On the other hand, suppose a cell with switching string 100 arrives at A1 and another with string 101 arrives at B1. Each has different inputs and outputs but both must pass through A2. If they arrive at the same time there will be a collision. The important thing here is that the switch may be able to handle two cells concurrently, but there is no guarantee. In the event there is a collision, each switching element must have the ability to decide which cell to pass first and to put the other one in a queue for subsequent passing.

Another switching technology is a **crossbar switch** with n inputs and outputs. The inputs are typically displayed as a series of horizontal lines, and the outputs as a series of vertical lines. Each input line crosses all n output lines, and each output line crosses all n input lines. Each crossing corresponds to a switching element that can switch a cell from an input to an output line. A disadvantage is that there are n^2 switching elements, a lot for a switch.

There is also a *knockout switch,* which is a form of crossbar switch. The problem with the crossbar switch is that two cells destined for the same output at the same time will collide. In addition, the cells may arrive on different input lines and go through different switches to get to the desired output, making it more difficult to handle the collision. With the knockout switch, each output has an *arbiter* that is connected to every input line. If two cells from different inputs are destined for the same output, the crossbar switch part routes them to the arbiter, which then handles the collision by queuing one and sending the other.

REFERENCE MODEL

ATM is actually part of the B-ISDN specification as defined by ITU-T. In addition, the ATM Forum (www.atmforum.com), an international nonprofit organization, has a technical committee that works with standards agencies in selecting appropriate standards and recommending new ones. The committee also works toward interoperability between vendors that market ATM products.

Figure 13.22 shows the layered reference model. Our approach here is to give a brief overview of the model first and follow up with a more detailed discussion of relevant topics. The first thing you might notice about this model when compared with others is the three-dimensional look to it. That's because the combined ATM/B-ISDN model specifies both user-oriented and management functions. For example, the *control plane* specifies how connections are made and released. The *user plane* specifies the transport of data and related issues such as flow control and error detection and correction. Behind the scenes, the *layer management* provides management functions. One of its responsibilities is to provide operations, administration,

Figure 13.22 ATM/B-ISDN Reference Model

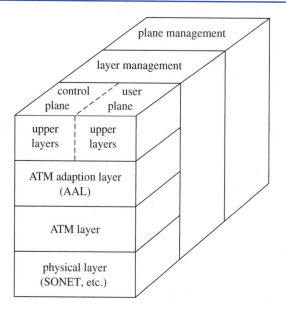

and maintenance (OAM) services through information packets that switches exchange to keep the system running effectively. Management services may also be provided by SNMP or CMIP. Finally, *plane management* makes sure the various planes coordinate their activities properly.

At the bottom of the model, the physical layer specifies the physical characteristics of transmission. Although ATM does not specify rules for physical transmission, it was originally designed with the intention of running over SONET (Synchronous Optical Network). Originally proposed by Bellcore (Bell Communications Research), SONET is an optical network using time-division multiplexing to accommodate simultaneous channels. Controlled by a clock, it transmits bits at rates ranging from about 155.5 Mbps to in excess of 2 Gbps. It defines the way in which telephone companies transmit their data over optical networks. Besides SONET, ATM can also run on top of FDDI, T1 and T3 systems, both shielded and unshielded twisted pair, and even wireless media (ref. [Va97]).

Above the physical layer is the *ATM layer*. It performs activities similar to those found in OSI layers 2 and 3. For example, it defines the cell format and how to respond to information found in the header. It also is responsible for setting up and releasing connections and establishing both virtual circuits and virtual paths (a distinction we will make shortly). Finally, it also performs congestion control.

The **ATM adaptation layer (AAL)** provides the interface between applications and the ATM layer and is divided into two sublayers: the segmentation and reassembly sublayer (lower sublayer) and the convergence sublayer. The *convergence sublayer* provides the interface for a variety of applications to use ATM. What it does depends on the application and the type of traffic it generates. In fact, later we will see that there are several versions of AAL depending on whether the traffic is uncompressed video, compressed video, or a variety of other types. The *segmentation and reassembly sublayer* stores information from higher layers into ATM cells and may add its own header to the payload. On the receiving end, it extracts the payload from each cell and reassembles them into an information stream for the application to process.

CELL DEFINITION

This is a good time to provide some details about how ATM works, and a logical place to start is by defining the ATM cell and describing how ATM handles its contents. As previously mentioned, an ATM cell has 53 bytes, 48 of which are the cell's payload. This leaves just 5 bytes for the cell header. Figure 13.23 outlines

Figure 13.23 ATM Cell Header (NNI)

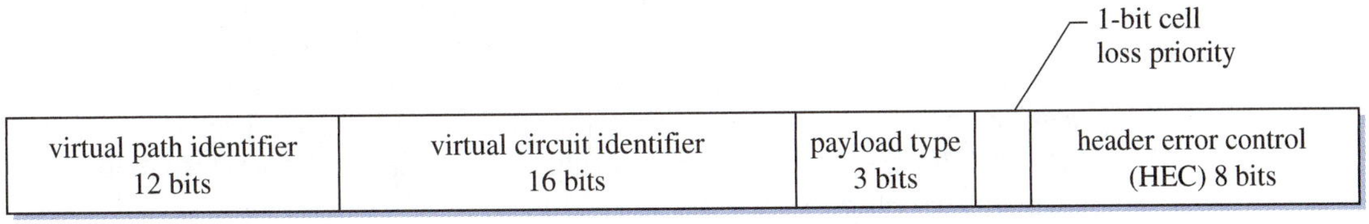

| virtual path identifier 12 bits | virtual circuit identifier 16 bits | payload type 3 bits | | header error control (HEC) 8 bits |

1-bit cell loss priority

what they are as they pass through an NNI. For cells that travel through the UNI, there is a slightly different interpretation of the header's contents. In the latter case, the first 4 bits define a Generic Flow Control (GFC) field, leaving just 8 bits for the virtual path identifier. However, once the cell enters the network, switches may write over the GFC field using a 12-bit virtual path ID.

The GFC is designed to control the flow of traffic from a device into the ATM network (but not in the reverse direction). There are essentially two classes of connections, controlled and uncontrolled, which are either part of the configuration or negotiated during the establishment of a connection. When a connection is *controlled,* the network provides information to the user device regarding how many cells it can send. It's a bit like the credit mechanism used for flow control in TCP. On *uncontrolled* connections, the network simply enables or disables the sending of cells. When enabled, the user device is free to send cells until the network disables it. It's a bit like an X-ON/X-OFF form of flow control.

The small number of header bytes is one factor contributing to ATM's speed: There are fewer things to check in each cell when it arrives at a switch. Let's now examine each field separately.

Header Error Control   The Header Error Control (HEC) field is somewhat self-explanatory: It provides for error checking. However, there are a few noteworthy items. For one thing, it only provides error checking for the other 4 header bytes, leaving the payload unprotected. This, of course, makes error checking, and consequently cell delivery, much faster. (Remember, speed is essential in an ATM network.) Of course, leaving the payload unprotected might at first seem a problem, but, for a couple of reasons, it is not. One reason is that ATM was designed to run on top of optical fiber systems, which are very reliable. Consequently, the odds of errors occurring are very small. Even if they did occur, they could be detected at a higher layer if necessary. Another reason is that many applications involve video or audio. Consequently, an error in a frame that will be displayed for a small fraction of a second will not be noticeable or, at worst, might correspond to a barely perceptible flicker. Would it make sense to wait for a retransmission of such a frame? The answer is no. However, protecting the header is crucial because it contains the virtual path and circuit identifiers that determine where the cell goes.

Another noteworthy item is that the error checking is an adaptive technique based on the CRC method. It can detect over 90% of multiple-bit errors and can even correct single-bit errors. The latter is particularly significant because a study by AT&T and Bellcore published in 1989 (ref. [AT89]) showed that over 99.5% of errors in optical fiber systems are actually single-bit errors.

The HEC field also performs another unrelated function. Recall discussions in Section 9.2 of data link protocols in which frames contained special bit patterns that designated the frame's beginning. ATM defines no such pattern, so a logical question to ask is, How can low-level protocols detect the beginning of a cell? This depends in part on the physical layer. For example, SONET encapsulates ATM cells in an envelope (similar to previous protocols in which a packet was encapsulated in a frame, except that several cells can be in an envelope). Information in the envelope locates the start of the first ATM cell.

However, not all physical layers will provide such an envelope. In fact, with a synchronous medium, cells must be transmitted in a regular pattern defined by a clock. There is no envelope or special bit patterns to locate the start of a cell. They simply arrive at regular intervals, and the receiving device must be able to determine where cell boundaries are. Recognizing where cell boundaries are as a synchronous bit pattern arrives is called *framing*. For example, consider a sequence of ATM cells, each containing information from a video camera. The receiving device must synchronize by locating cell boundaries in order to provide proper viewing.

Although there is no particular bit pattern to identify the start of an ATM cell, one technique uses the fact that every undamaged header has something in common: Applying the error checking method using the 40-bit string that defines the header generates a value consistent with the last 8 bits in that string. Consequently, one technique to locate the cell boundary is as follows:

1. Apply the error checking method using 40 consecutive bits. If it does not generate a result consistent with the last 8 bits, shift one bit and try again (Figure 13.24).

2. Repeat step 1 until a consistent result is found. This indicates that these 40 bits could be a legitimate header. However, random chance could cause a consistent result to be found among 40 other bits (a false header).

3. Once a potential header is found, skip the next 48 bytes (payload) and apply the same technique using the subsequent 40 bits. We are assuming that legitimate headers are each separated by 48 bytes. If the technique does not produce a consistent result, then the previous result was an accident and we must start over.

4. Suppose we find several 40-bit strings, each separated by 48 bytes from an adjacent one, that all generate a consistent HEC value. Then there is a high probability that they are all legitimate headers. In that case, framing has been achieved and the receiving device is now synchronized with incoming cells.

The technique just described sounds complex, but use of circular shift registers similar to those described in Section 4.3 can implement it efficiently. Also, there is the issue of how many consecutive potential headers we should find before we conclude the device is synchronized. Since the HEC field is just 8 bits, the probability of locating a false header is $1/2^8 = 1/256$ for a given 40-bit string. The probability

Figure 13.24   Looking for a Cell Boundary

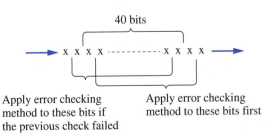

40 bits

x x x x - - - - - - - - - - - - x x x x

Apply error checking method to these bits if the previous check failed

Apply error checking method to these bits first

of locating two consecutive false headers is $1/(256)^2$. In general, the probability of locating n false headers is $1/(256)^n$. Larger values of n take more time but will be less likely to synchronize incorrectly. In fact, if n is just 4, the probability of synchronizing incorrectly is 1 in about 4.3 billion.

Cell Loss Priority   The Cell Loss Priority (CLP) bit indicates a cell's priority level. Whenever congestion occurs, ATM has the option of deleting cells in order to relieve it. It chooses cells with a CLP value of 1 first. It is up to the application to determine which cells are not critical. For example, MPEG-compressed video uses differences between frames and actual compressed frames (recall the difference between I frames and P frames discussed in Section 5.7) in its transmitted images. If those frames that represent small differences were deleted, the overall effect on viewing is likely to be negligible. Consequently, the applications might set the CLP bit for the cells containing those frames to 1.

Payload Type   The Payload Type field provides some specific information about the cell. The leftmost bit specifies whether the payload is user data or OAM information. Switches can exchange OAM messages to provide status checks and keep the system running smoothly. The second bit indicates whether the cell has passed through any congested switches. This lets the receiver know of any congestion problems developing along a particular path. In some cases, the third bit can be used to indicate the last in a sequence of ATM cells.

VIRTUAL CIRCUITS AND PATHS

Prior to this point we have not made any distinction between a virtual circuit and virtual path. This changes with ATM, as Figure 13.25 shows. Conceptually, a *virtual circuit* represents a logical connection between two endpoints. For example, in Figure 13.25 there is a logical connection between A and X, B and Y, and C and Z. However, each connection corresponds to the same **virtual path.**

Each cell contains a 12-bit virtual circuit ID (8 bits across the UNI) and a 16-bit virtual path ID. Thus, from a user's perspective, each connection can be defined by a 24-bit connection identifier that consists of two parts: the circuit ID (8 bits) and path ID (16 bits). It's analogous to Internet addressing, where we indicated that a 32-bit address consisted of a network ID and a host ID. The advantage in that case was that internal routing mechanisms could route based solely on the network ID. The host ID wasn't used until the packet reached the destination network and could be sent directly to the host.

Likewise, ATM switches forward cells based solely on the 16-bit virtual path ID. Making decisions based on a 16-bit number instead of a full 28-bit identifier (remember that when a cell enters the network, the circuit ID expands to 12 bits) allows switching to occur more quickly. Again, this is a major goal of ATM. Using 16-bit numbers instead of 28-bit numbers also keeps internal switching tables smaller (a maximum of 2^{16} entries as opposed to 2^{28} entries). The circuit ID is needed only when the cell arrives at the last ATM switch, which must forward the cell directly to the user.

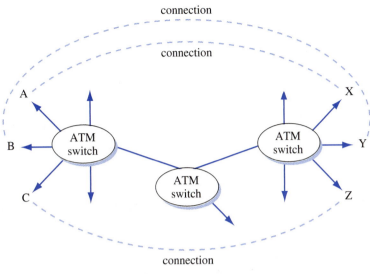

Distinct virtual circuits exist between
A and X, B and Y, C and Z.
All use the same virtual path.

Figure 13.25   Virtual Circuits and Virtual Paths

Another advantage of using both circuit and path IDs is realized if there is a problem in a link. For example, suppose a hundred connections have been established that all use the same path. If a problem develops along the path, a new one must be found. If switching were based on a 28-bit number, then the internal tables for each new switch in the alternate route would require a new entry for each connection. In this case a hundred changes to each table would be made. However, since switching is based on just the path ID and all connections use the same path, each table requires just one change to accommodate all the connections. Clearly, this is a lot quicker.

CONNECTION MANAGEMENT

There are two types of connections: a *permanent virtual circuit* and a *switched virtual circuit*. The permanent circuit is analogous to a leased telephone line, and the switched circuit must be established using a connection protocol. The connection protocol is based on algorithms in ITU-T Q.2931 (itself a subset of Q.931). On the surface, establishing an ATM connection follows procedures similar to those of establishing connections in other protocols we have discussed. One side initiates a call request specifying some of the attributes desired of the connection and waits for an acknowledgment. The control plane is responsible for setting up the connection.

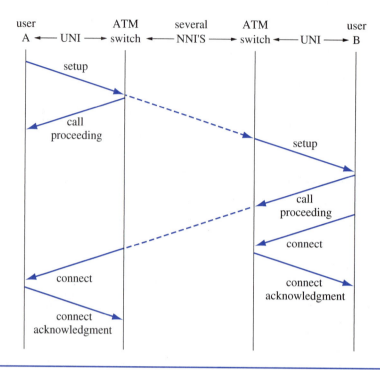

Figure 13.26   Establishing a Connection

Figure 13.26 outlines the connection setup logic when A requests a connection to B. Four different message types are used in setting up a connection; the following steps show how they are used.

1. On behalf of A, the control plane sends a *Setup message* to B across the UNI. This message contains information relevant to the requested connection. For example, it contains B's address and some other items that we'll describe shortly.

2. The switch receiving the Setup message does two things. First, it sends a *Call Proceeding message* back to A informing it that the request has been received and is in progress. This message also contains the virtual circuit and path IDs to be used once the connection is established. Second, the switch forwards the Setup message toward B.

3. The Setup message travels through the network across various NNIs toward B using whatever routing algorithm is implemented (ATM does not specify what it is). The route eventually chosen defines the virtual path and circuit. As a Setup message progresses through switches, each switch responds by returning a Call Proceeding message to the switch that sent the Setup. Consequently, each switch that will eventually be part of the virtual path is aware that a connection is in progress.

4. Eventually B gets the Setup message. B can respond immediately with a *Connect message* or, if it expects a delay, can return a Call Proceeding message. Eventually, if all goes well, B sends the Connect message over the UNI to a switch. The switch returns a *Connect Acknowledgment message.* B is now free to start sending information to A. The Connect message travels back to A through the same switches (in reverse order) that the Setup message traveled. Each switch responds by forwarding it and returning a Connect Acknowledgment. As each switch gets the Connect, it knows it is part of a virtual path and makes an entry associated with the path ID into its tables. It is now prepared to route subsequent cells along the proper path.

5. Eventually the Connect message gets to A and it responds with a Connect Acknowledgment. A is now free to send information to B.

Releasing a connection proceeds similarly. Either side can initiate a release by sending a *Release message.* It travels through the virtual path, with each switch returning a *Release Complete message.* The switches use this to remove path information from their tables and forward the Release to the next switch along the path.

Connection Parameters   Earlier we stated that the Setup message contains information relevant to the requested connection. In general, it specifies the quality of service and type of traffic it expects. For example, a request for video on demand has different expectations than a connection to be used for a file transfer. This is important information to have in the Setup message because one of ATM's goals is to maintain a desired quality of service.

When a Setup message enters the network, each switch must decide whether it can be part of the requested path without adversely affecting the quality of service for existing paths. You can only have so many video-on-demand paths going through a switch. The switch may proceed as described earlier or reject the Setup request. This is where much of the complexity lies. Potentially many possible paths must be investigated before one is found that will provide the needed quality of service. Of course, it is also possible that no such path will be found. The objective is to avoid establishing paths that will have a negative impact on existing users, including the one trying to establish the connection. Effectively, this method guarantees users a certain quality of service and is also a form of congestion control.

We have used the phrase *quality of service* rather generally. Listed here are some specific items that a Setup message might contain.

- **B-ISDN service class.** B-ISDN defines four classes. *Class A traffic* requires a constant bit rate and strict synchronization between the sender and receiver. This is needed for uncompressed video or audio transfer, where the images are to be recorded, transmitted, and then viewed (or heard) as they are received. *Class B* allows a variable bit rate but still requires that the sender and receiver be synchronized. This is typical of compressed video, in which bit rates differ depending on how much compression is being done. However, synchronization is still necessary because it is still being viewed in real time. *Class C* is for connection-oriented traffic with no timing constraints. *Class D* is a connectionless service with no timing constraints. The latter two classes are for the more mundane applications such as file or data transfers that have no real-time constraints.

- **Peak cell rate.** The maximum rate at which cells will be sent.
- **Sustainable cell rate.** An upper bound on the average rate of cell transfer defined over a period of time. The peak cell rate may be higher for short periods, but for an extended period the rate should not exceed what is specified here.
- **Time.** Parameter used to determine the maximum sustainable cell rate.
- **Minimum cell rate.** Specifies the lowest rate at which cells must be received. Anything below that rate is considered unacceptable.
- **AAL version.** We will discuss this topic next.

ADAPTATION LAYERS

We close the section on ATM by describing the **ATM adaptation layer (AAL).** Figure 13.27 shows that it is the interface between higher layers and the ATM layer and consists of two sublayers: the *segmentation and reassembly sublayer* (SAR) and the *convergence sublayer* (CS). The convergence sublayer's responsibilities depend on the type of information the applications at higher levels generate.

Figure 13.28 shows general actions taken by the convergence and SAR sublayers. We intend this to be an overview; there are different types of AAL that may or may not do some of these tasks. We will worry about those differences shortly. Generally, some application at a higher layer generates data, which we view as a byte stream. The convergence sublayer extracts some of those bytes and adds a header and trailer to create its own CS packet. The SAR sublayer gets the CS packet and adds its own header and trailer to create a 48-byte payload that then gets stored into an ATM cell. The figure seems to indicate that the convergence and SAR sublayers do the same things in that they add headers and trailers to data received from a higher layer. Well, that is true, but the difference lies in what those headers and

Figure 13.27   AAL Sublayers

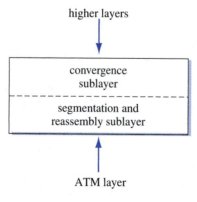

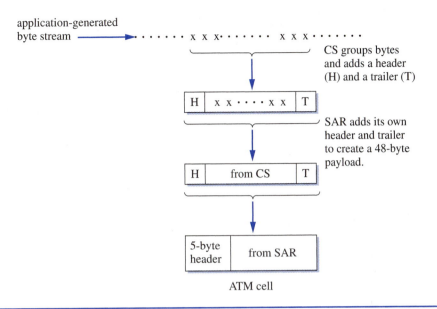

Figure 13.28   General AAL Activities

trailers contain. However, to make that distinction requires that we introduce the different AAL types.

AAL types differ primarily in the classes of traffic they will handle. AAL 1 deals with Class A traffic, and AAL 2 with Class B traffic. The pattern seems to suggest that AAL 3 and AAL 4 deal with Class C and D traffic. To some extent that was true, because ITU-T did develop an AAL 3 and AAL 4. However, as development progressed it became apparent that there were no significant differences in these layers, so ITU-T elected to combine them. One might think the result would be labeled AAL 3.5, but in fact it is called AAL 3/4. After AAL 3/4 was developed, some were concerned about what they perceived as inefficiencies. Consequently, AAL 5 was developed as a successor to AAL 3/4. We won't worry about AAL 3, AAL 4, or AAL 3/4. Reference [Bl95] discusses all the AAL versions. We will, however, briefly discuss AAL 1, AAL 2, and AAL 5.

AAL 1   Figure 13.29 outlines how Class A traffic is handled. A video application generates a real-time uncompressed byte stream. AAL 1 captures 46 or 47 bytes at a time and puts them in an AAL 1 packet. A difference from Figure 13.28 is that only the SAR sublayer creates a header, which is either 1 or 2 bytes long. From there, each packet becomes the payload of an ATM cell, which is then transmitted toward its destination.

Figure 13.30a shows the format of an AAL 1 packet. The first bit indicates whether an optional second header byte is present. This header byte, if present, is

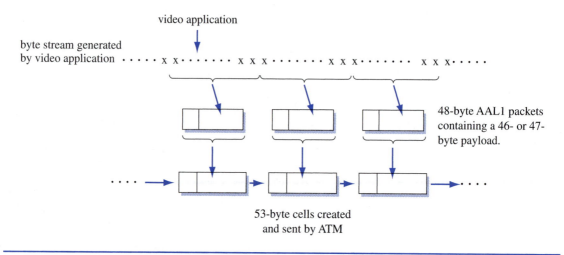

Figure 13.29 Sending Class A Traffic

Figure 13.30 AAL Packet Types

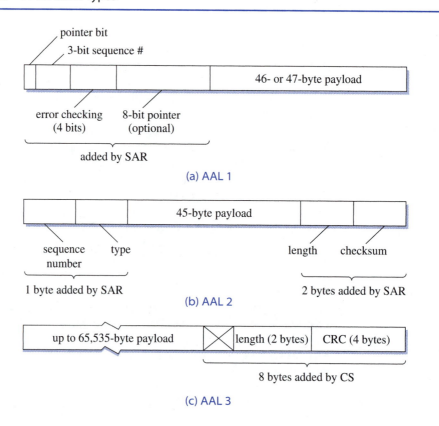

(a) AAL 1

(b) AAL 2

(c) AAL 3

used when the Payload field is not full and locates the data within the Payload field. This method can be used in cases where filling the Payload field to capacity takes more time than the application can tolerate. By only partially filling the Payload field, the information can be passed to the ATM cell and eventually sent more quickly. This may be necessary to maintain the constant bit rate required by Class A traffic. An implication of this is that the convergence sublayer must be synchronized with a clock to deliver the correct amount of data to the SAR sublayer on a timely basis.

Of the remaining 7 bits of the first header byte, 3 are used for a sequence number. The convergence sublayer provides the sequence number, and the SAR sublayer creates the header in which to store it. This allows the receiving CS to detect a loss of information or a misinserted cell. Either of these can occur if an undetected error occurs in the path ID of the cell en route to a destination. The cell could be misdirected to an incorrect location, which would see this error as a misinserted cell. The correct destination would see a gap in arriving sequence numbers that constitutes a loss of information. Any misinserted cells are ignored (imagine seeing bogus images during a touchdown in the last seconds of the Superbowl). If the receiver detects a loss, it notifies the sender but does not request a retransmission. Remember, we are assuming this is a real-time video or audio application, and therefore resending images or sounds serves no useful purpose. The viewer will have to be content with seeing a flicker in the image or hearing a blip in the sound (assuming the loss is even noticeable).

The remaining 4 bits are used for error checking the 3-bit Sequence field. Provided by the SAR sublayer, 3 of the 4 bits correspond to a CRC for the 3 sequence number bits, and the fourth bit establishes parity for the combined sequence number and CRC bits. The parity bit provides an extra measure of protection. In fact, it can correct single-bit errors and detect double-bit errors. Interestingly, the packet's payload is not protected. However, as stated before, ATM generally runs on reliable media. Even if loss does occur, it may not be noticeable. Also, checking only the Sequence field requires less time and helps contribute to timely deliveries of real-time packets.

AAL 2   Figure 13.30b shows the format of an AAL 2 packet. Like AAL 1, only the SAR sublayer adds anything to the payload. In this case, it adds both a header (1 byte) and a trailer (2 bytes). The header's sequence number has the same purpose as the sequence number in an AAL 1 packet. The *Type field* reflects the variable bit rate nature of Class B traffic. With Class A traffic, data are strictly bit streams with no need for message boundaries. Images are displayed as the data that represent them are received. Because Class B traffic includes compressed images, message boundaries are needed to help identify new frames (recall discussions on MPEG sending frames or differences between frames). The Type field helps identify message boundaries by indicating when a cell corresponds to the first, last, or intermediate cell of a message.

The *Length field* specifies the number of data bytes in the payload. Finally, the *Checksum field* provides error checking of the entire packet. AAL 2 is still in the process of development, so there are aspects that are not fully defined yet. For example, the size of the Overhead fields has not yet been specified. In addition, there have been suggestions that the Type field should also contain timing information relevant to audio or video data.

AAL 5   We conclude our discussion of ATM with an outline of AAL 5, whose packet format is described by Figure 13.30c. Perhaps the first thing you will notice is that AAL 5 packets can be considerably larger than other AAL packets. This is partly because AAL 5 was not designed with real-time video or voice in mind; thus, the need for small packets is not so critical. Another difference is that the convergence sublayer adds overhead to the payload instead of the SAR sublayer. Figure 13.31 shows basic steps in sending a potentially large data block. An application generates a block of data and gives it to the CS, which adds an 8-byte trailer and passes the packet to the SAR sublayer. The SAR sublayer divides the packet into 48-byte payloads, each of which is placed into an ATM cell. On the receiving end, the steps are reversed.

Note that Figure 13.31 suggests that the size of the entire packet (data block plus trailer) is a multiple of 48 bytes. Since the amount of data can vary, the data block may actually be padded with anywhere between 1 and 47 extra bytes. The number is chosen to make the packet's size a multiple of 48.

The trailer contains just two items of note. First is a 32-bit CRC field providing error checking on the entire packet. Here is another indication that this format was not designed for real-time audio or video: Using a 32-bit CRC on potentially many thousands of bytes would take too long. The second field specifies the number of bytes in the Payload field.

Because the application runs on top of ATM, the data are still divided into small cells. However, an important aspect is that this division is done at a different layer. In AAL 1 and AAL 2, data were divided into small packets early so that they

Figure 13.31   AAL 5 Dividing a Data Block into ATM Cells

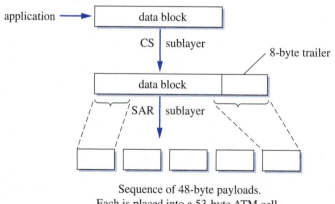

Sequence of 48-byte payloads.
Each is placed into a 53-byte ATM cell.

could be processed and sent as quickly as possible. Here the convergence sublayer deals with a potentially large block and creates the trailer for it. Because of the block's size, this will take longer, which would be unacceptable for Class A or Class B traffic. However, for Class C or Class D traffic such delays are not a problem.

SERVICE-SPECIFIC CONNECTION-ORIENTED PROTOCOL

The AAL protocols we have described deal primarily with data transfer. We have not yet discussed a protocol used primarily for providing a reliable connection. Early developers of ATM recognized that error detection and recovery would be needed for signaling and for certain data applications. Toward this end, AAL was divided into two parts: a common part and a service-specific part. AAL 5 is an example of a common part. Two additional protocols, the *Service-Specific Coordination Function* (SSCF) and the *Service-Specific Connection-Oriented Protocol* (SSCOP), constitute the service-specific part. SSCOP and SSCF lie between AAL 5 and a higher-layer signaling protocol such as Q.2931, with SSCF providing the interface between SSCOP and Q.2931. Together, SSCF and SSCOP are also called the *signaling ATM adaptation layer* (SAAL).

SSCOP is a synchronous bit-oriented protocol whose main functions include flow control and actions to be taken when errors are detected. It uses a form of selective repeat sliding window protocol in which the window sizes can be adjusted dynamically and missing frames can be requested and transmitted explicitly.

The signaling layer (i.e., Q.2931) communicates with SSCOP through the SSCF. The SSCOP creates specific packets, which it sends to the peer SSCOP entity at the other end. The receiving SSCOP extracts information from these packets and, through its SSCF, passes them on to the signaling layer there. SSCOP packets are variable length, with a maximum size of 64 Kbytes.

The following lists most of the SSCOP packet types:

- **Begin** and **Begin Acknowledgment** packets are used to establish and acknowledge the establishment of an SSCOP connection.

- **End** and **End Acknowledgment** packets are used to release and acknowledge the release of an SSCOP connection.

- **Reject** packets are used to reject connection requests by a peer SSCOP entity.

- **Resynchronize** and **Resynchronize Acknowledgment** packets are used to reestablish connections and connection parameters in the event that a connection fails.

- **Sequenced data packets** contain user information. The packet uses 24-bit packet sequence numbers, which, if you recall the discussion on sliding window protocols, allows for potentially large windows. That is significant because small windows can limit the protocol's throughput.

- **Poll packets** are used to request the status of the receiver. SSCOP does not rely on a timer to resend packets that never arrived. This reduces its dependence on timer implementation. Instead, it uses the Poll packet, which contains the successor of the sequence number of the last transmitted packet. This packet also requests that the receiver reply with its status. On receiving the Poll packet, the receiver can tell if any previously sent packets have not arrived.

- **Status packets** are sent by a receiver in response to a Poll packet. The Status packet contains the limiting sequence number of the receiver window, the sequence number of the next expected packet, and sequence numbers of any missing packets. On receipt of the Status packet, the sender knows how many more packets it can send without overflowing the receiver window and which packets have not arrived. It can respond accordingly.

- An **Unsolicited Status packet** is essentially the same as a Status packet except that it is not sent in response to a Poll packet.

To be sure, there is more to SSCOP. The reader is encouraged to consult references [Ha98] and [He95] for additional details on SSCOP and related issues.

GIGABIT ETHERNET VERSUS ATM

The development of Gigabit Ethernet (recall Chapter 9) has elicited comparisons with ATM because ATM is sometimes found as the technology of choice for implementing backbones connecting multiple LANs. We stated earlier that ATM is a protocol that was developed largely in response to emerging audio and video applications. Such applications require a quality of service that differs from that of conventional file transfers, email, or Web applications. The QoS for real-time applications in video and audio demands fast delivery and little or no delay in the delivery of data. Older versions of Ethernet could not guarantee that QoS because of lower speeds and the possibility of collisions. Consequently, it was not unusual to use ATM to implement high-bandwidth links among LANs.

With its new faster speeds and full-duplex modes, Ethernet can now provide the QoS needed for real-time applications. Consequently, it has become a viable choice and has, in fact, begun to replace ATM as a backbone for multiple LANs in many locations. This does not mean the demise of ATM, since it is still the choice of many for connecting metropolitan area networks and even wide area networks. The two technologies are still very different. For example, ATM is connection oriented and Ethernet is not. ATM transmits fixed-size frames, whereas Ethernet frames vary in size.

ATM QoS is implemented using a signaling protocol prior to establishing a connection. Thus, connections are established only if the needed QoS can be maintained. Ethernet was designed to treat all traffic equally. That is, it makes no distinction among frames that carry file data or video data streams. As such, ATM proponents argue that Ethernet really cannot promise the same QoS as ATM. Ethernet proponents counter that the increased bandwidth and additional protocols such as the Resource Reservation Protocol (RSVP) and the Real-Time Transport Protocol (RTP) make Ethernet a viable alternative. Recall from Chapter 11 that RSVP, developed by the IETF, is used by hosts and routers to make QoS requests and reserve resources needed to meet those requests. RTP, also an IETF project, is an end-to-end protocol designed to support real-time applications.

13.5 SUMMARY

This chapter covered several specific protocols that many consider important WAN technologies: ISDN, X.25 packet-switched protocol, frame relay, and ATM. Summaries of each follow.

- ISDN is a long-standing protocol that defines an all-digital communications system. Originally designed in the hopes of replacing the telephone system, it never became entrenched as a common system in part because so many digital components were introduced into the existing telephone system and also in part because the benefits of replacing hundreds of millions of analog telephones and their circuits could not justify the cost.

- X.25 was originally developed for WAN connections across European boundaries and defines a standard for setting up and communicating using virtual circuits. It is a three-layer protocol that defines packet format, call establishment, call termination, flow control, and error control.

- Frame relay is seen by many as the successor to X.25. It performs similar functions but has no flow control or error control. It provides the customer the option of purchasing a bit rate and commits network resources to meeting the bit rates promised to the user. Frame relay takes much of the functionality, such as flow and error control, out of network switches and assumes that end-user devices will deal with them.

- ATM is another virtual circuit technology but offers more quality of service options than were built into frame relay. This makes it suitable not only for standard data traffic but also for audio or video traffic that requires constant bit rates. In contrast to large and variable-size frames, ATM uses a 53-byte cell for all of its transfers. The small size contributes to a switch's ability to process the information in its header and forward it as quickly as possible.

Review Questions

1. What is ISDN?
2. Distinguish between ISDN's basic and primary services.
3. List and summarize the four primary functional groups in ISDN.
4. List and summarize the four reference points in ISDN.
5. What is the difference between out-of-band and in-band signaling?
6. What is Signaling System 7?
7. What is pseudoternary coding?
8. What is broadband ISDN?
9. Are the following statements TRUE or FALSE? Why?
   a. The all-digital capability of ISDN would provide immediate advantages to everyone who uses it.
   b. The X.25 protocol defines packet-switched network operations.

    c. Distinct virtual circuits may overlap.

    d. A datagram service will not deliver packets in the correct order.

    e. Frame relay was designed to work with high-speed digital equipment to provide the quality of service required of real-time applications such as voice and video streaming.

    f. Frame relay's committed information rate provides a guarantee that customer data will reach their destination at the specified rate.

    g. A disadvantage of the small fixed-size cells of ATM is that less information can be put into the headers and therefore switches take longer to forward them.

10. What is a virtual circuit?

11. What is a packet-switched network?

12. Why can't each node in a virtual circuit use the same number to identify the circuit?

13. What is a datagram service?

14. What does the X.25 standard define?

15. List the X.25 packet types related to call establishment.

16. How does a permanent virtual circuit differ from a virtual circuit?

17. What are the similarities between X.25 and frame relay? What are the differences?

18. What is frame relay's committed information rate?

19. How does the DE bit in a frame relay's frame affect its delivery?

20. Frame relay will set either or both of the BECN and FECN bits when congestion occurs. What is the difference between them?

21. How does frame relay deal with congestion?

22. Why do some predict that ATM is the protocol of the future?

23. What is the purpose of having several AAL layers?

24. Distinguish among Class A, B, C, and D traffic on an ATM network.

25. Why are ATM cells 53 bytes long?

26. List some advantages of using small fixed-length cells in ATM.

27. What is the difference between a virtual path and a virtual circuit in ATM, and why is there a distinction?

28. What is the advantage of using a Banyan switch rather than a common routing table?

29. Why does the Header Error Control field in an ATM cell header check only the header and leave the payload unprotected?

30. Describe how the Header Error Control field can also be used to locate an ATM cell's boundary.

31. List some items an ATM Setup message might contain.

32. Why is it acceptable for AAL 5 packets to contain variable-length and potentially large payloads, whereas it is unacceptable for AAL 1 and AAL 2?

Exercises

1. Consider Figure 13.10. Suppose A establishes a virtual circuit to D, and B establishes a virtual circuit to C. If both virtual circuits go through X and Y, what would X's and Y's routing tables look like?

2. Suppose each of the TE1s in the following figure tries sending something to the NT2 at the same time.

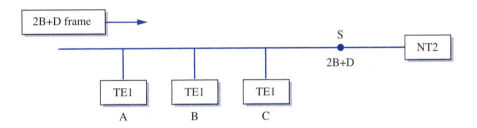

   Suppose also that each is trying to send the following over the D channel:

   • A sends 10011101.

   • B sends 10001100.

   • C sends 10011001.

   Which TE1 wins the contention?

3. ISDN's B channel capacities were designed with the intention of transmitting voice. Section 3.6 showed that to capture most of a voice's characteristics, 8-bit samples taken at a frequency of 8000 samples per second are sufficient and require a bit rate of 64,000 bps. However, some encoding techniques actually allow voice data to be transmitted using 32,000 bps, and others will likely allow 16,000 bps to be sufficient. What effect would this have on the ISDN standard?

4. Draw a diagram similar to that of Figure 13.7 showing the ISDN disconnect procedure.

5. For frame relay flow control, two options of dealing with congestion involve setting the BECN or FECN bit. Which is likely to have a more direct and quicker effect on reducing congestion?

6. Frame relay does much less than X.25 with regard to packet (frame) handling at intermediate switches. What are the advantages of this? Disadvantages?

7. Suppose, for the frame relay protocol, that the CIR = 20,000 bps, frame sizes are 1,000 bits, B_e = 3,000 bits, and rates are calculated over a time duration of 0.5 second. How many frames in a 0.5-second interval will the first switch send with DE set to 0? How many will it send with DE set to 1? How many will it drop?

8. Describe a scenario in which four cells can be routed through the Banyan switch of Figure 13.21 simultaneously with no collisions.

REFERENCES

[Ap86] Appenzeller, H. R. "Signaling System No. 7, ISDN User Part." *IEEE Journal on Selected Areas in Communication,* vol. SAC-4, no. 3 (May 1986), 366–371.

[AT89] AT&T and Bellcore. "Observations of Error Characteristics of Fiber Optic Transmission Systems." *CCITT SG XVIII,* San Diego, CA, January, 1989.

[Bl95] Black, U. *The X Series Recommendations: Standards for Data Communications,* 2nd ed. New York: McGraw-Hill, 1995.

[Bl99] Black, U. *ATM Volume I: Foundation for Broadband Networks,* 2nd ed. Upper Saddle River, NJ: Prentice-Hall, 1999.

[Bl97a] Black, U. *Emerging Communications Technologies,* 2nd ed. Upper Saddle River, NJ: Prentice-Hall, 1997.

[Bl97b] Black, U. *ISDN and SS7: Architectures for Digital Signaling Networks.* Upper Saddle River, NJ: Prentice-Hall, 1997.

[Bl00] Black, U. *QOS in Wide Area Networks.* Upper Saddle River, NJ: Prentice-Hall, 2000.

[Gr98] Griffiths, J. M. *ISDN Explained: Worldwide Network and Applications Technology,* 3rd ed. New York: Wiley, 1998.

[Ha98] Händel, R., M. Huber, and S. Schröder. *ATM Networks: Concepts, Protocols, Applications,* 3rd ed. Reading, MA: Addison-Wesley, 1998.

[He95] Henderson, T. "Design Principles and Performance Analysis of SSCOP: A New ATM Adaptation Layer Protocol." *Computer Communications Review,* vol. 25, no. 2 (April 1995), 47–59.

[Hu03] Hunt, R. "Frame Relay." *Encyclopedia of Information Systems,* vol. II. New York: Academic Press, 2003, 371–390.

[Mc01] McQuerry, S., and K. McGrew. *Cisco Voice over Frame Relay, ATM, and IP.* Upper Saddle River, NJ: Prentice-Hall, 2001.

[Me03] Mesher, G. "Integrated Services Digital Network (Broadband and Narrowband ISDN)." *Encyclopedia of Information Systems,* vol. II. New York: Academic Press, 2003, 627–638.

[Sc86] Schlanger, G. G. "An Overview of Signaling System No. 7." *IEEE Journal on Selected Areas in Communication,* vol. SAC-4, no. 3 (May 1986), 360–365.

[St99] Stallings, W. *ISDN and Broadband ISDN with Frame Relay and ATM,* 4th ed. Upper Saddle River, NJ: Prentice-Hall, 1999.

[Va97] Varshney, U. "Supporting Mobility with Wireless ATM." *Computer,* vol. 30, no. 1 (January 1997), 131–133.

GLOSSARY

10Base2 10 Mbps Ethernet standard for thin coaxial cable.

10Base5 10 Mbps Ethernet standard for thick coaxial cable.

10BaseFx 10 Mbps Ethernet standard for optical fiber.

10BaseT 10 Mbps Ethernet standard for Category 3, 4, or 5 UTP.

100BaseFX 100 Mbps Ethernet standard for optical fiber.

100BaseT4 100 Mbps Ethernet standard for Category 3 UTP.

100BaseTX 100 Mbps Ethernet standard for Category 5 UTP.

1000BaseT Gigabit Ethernet standard for Category 5 UTP.

1000BaseX Gigabit Ethernet standard for optical fiber.

802.3 standard Umbrella term for the many flavors of Ethernet standards over various media.

802.5 standard IEEE standard for a token ring network.

802.11 standard IEEE standard for a wireless LAN.

4B/5B encoding Encoding scheme in which 4-bit values are replaced with 5-bit values.

8B/6T encoding Encoding scheme in which eight bit values are replaced with six trit values.

8B/10B encoding Encoding scheme in which 8-bit values are replaced with 10-bit values.

abort A sudden end to an activity, usually due to some type of error.

Abstract Syntax Notation 1 (ASN.1) Formal language designed expressly for the definition of protocol data unit formats and the representation of and operations on distributed information.

access point A device connected to a wired network that is also capable of communicating with wireless devices.

acknowledgment Indication that a device has received something from another device.

ACK timer Timer used in flow control protocols to determine when to send a separate acknowledgment in the absence of outgoing frames.

adaptive routing Routing strategy that can respond to changes in a network.

add/drop multiplexer Device used to extract traffic from outside a SONET ring and merge it with existing traffic already on the ring.

address learning Capability of a LAN bridge or switch to update its routing tables dynamically.

Address Resolution Protocol See *dynamic binding*.

address spoofing Sending an Internet packet with a source address that is not legitimate.

Advanced Encryption Standard (AES) NIST standard based on the Rijndael algorithm.

Advanced Research Projects Agency Agency of the U.S. Department of Defense.

Advanced Research Projects Agency Network (ARPANET) Network developed by the Advanced Research Projects Agency that evolved into protocols used in the Internet.

Aloha protocol Packet radio protocol in which a device sends a packet and, if it collides with another, will send another after a random amount of time.

alternate mark inversion Digital encoding in which a 1 bit is represented by zero volts and a 0 bit is represented alternately by a positive and a negative signal.

American National Standards Institute (ANSI) Private, nongovernmental standards agency whose members are manufacturers, users, and other interested companies.

American Standard Code for Information Interchange (ASCII) Seven-bit code that assigns a unique combination to every keyboard character and to some special functions.

amplitude Largest magnitude of an analog signal.

amplitude modulation (amplitude shift keying) Method of representing bits using analog signals with different magnitudes.

analog signal Continuously varying signal.

analog-to-digital conversion Process of converting an analog signal to a digital one.

anonymous FTP Application allowing remote users access to a set of files at a given site.

application layer Seventh and highest layer of the OSI protocol, which works directly with a user or with application programs.

application-level gateway Firewall that operates at the application layer.

arbitration The process of making a decision as to which device gains access to a resource.

arithmetic compression Compression method that generates a frequency-dependent code based on interpreting a character string as a single real number.

asymmetric DSL (ADSL) DSL technology in which download and upload bit rates differ.

asynchronous balanced mode Mode for HDLC in which either station can send data, control information, or commands.

asynchronous response mode Mode for HDLC in which a primary station can send data, control information, or commands, and a secondary station can send control information or data only.

Asynchronous Transfer Mode (ATM) Very fast packet-switched protocol using small fixed-size packets optimized for multimedia use.

asynchronous transmission Transmission mode in which bits are divided into small groups (bytes or octets) and sent independently.

ATM adaptation layer (AAL) Component of the ATM protocol that provides the interface between applications and the ATM layer.

attenuation Degradation of a signal as it travels along a medium.

auditory masking Phenomenon that prevents certain sounds from being heard when in the presence of a stronger sound with a similar frequency.

authentication Verifying the sender of a message or the authenticity of a document.

automatic repeat request Error control whereby a device requests the sending device to resend a message if an error occurs.

autonomous system Domain that operates independent of other domains.

B channel ISDN channel capable of transmitting at 64 Kbps.

backbone That part of a network comprising the primary transmission paths.

backward search algorithm Routing algorithm in which a node learns from its neighbors the cheapest route to another node. Also known as a backward learning algorithm.

balanced circuit Circuit using two lines carrying equal but opposite signals.

bandpass filter Device used to extract individual modulated signals.

bandwidth Difference between the highest and lowest frequencies that a medium can transmit.

Banyan switch Switch that connects its input and output ports through a series of internal stages.

baseband mode Mode in which a cable's bandwidth is devoted to a single stream of data.

basic service set (BSS) The set of wireless devices with which a single access point communicates.

Baudot code A five-bit code originally designed for the French telegraph.

baud rate Rate at which signal components can change.

Beacon frame Token ring control frame used to inform devices a problem has occurred and the token-passing protocol has stopped.

beam shaping Process of allowing a satellite signal to be concentrated in a small area.

bel A unit of measurement of signal power relative to noise power.

Bellman-Ford algorithm A type of backward learning algorithm.

binary-coded decimal (BCD) A code used in early IBM mainframes.

binary exponential backoff algorithm Algorithm used to determine when a device should resend a frame after a collision.

binary synchronous communications (BSC) protocol Byte-oriented data link protocol made popular by IBM.

birthday attack Technique used to try to find two documents that produce the same digest value.

bisync See *binary synchronous communications (BSC) protocol.*

bit   Most fundamental unit of information; usually represented by a 0 or 1.

bit-level ciphering   Encryption by bit manipulation.

bit-oriented protocol   A protocol that treats frames as bit streams.

bit pipe   The actual bit transmission in the ISDN protocol.

bit stuffing   The insertion of an extra bit to avoid a long run of the same bit.

block chaining mode   Encryption mode in which the encryption of a block depends in part on the encrypted version of the previous one.

Block Check Character   Character used by the BSC protocol for error checking.

block cipher   Encryption method that divides plaintext into blocks and encrypts each one.

Bluetooth   A technolgy using a microchip containing a radio transmitter/receiver for wireless communication.

Border Gateway Prototol   A protocol that allows routers to implement specific policies or constraints that a route must meet.

bridge   A layer 2 connection between two networks.

bridge port   Bridge to a LAN connection.

bridge protocol data unit (BPDU)   Unit of information exchanged by bridges.

broadband ISDN (B-ISDN)   Protocols that implement ISDN services over a high-speed broadband network.

broadband mode   Mode in which a cable's bandwidth is divided into ranges, each carrying separately coded information.

broadcast address   Address indicating a frame should be sent to all devices on a network.

broadcast domain   Set of devices reachable using a broadcast address.

browser   Program that allows a user to access and display files stored on remote Web servers.

buffering   Temporary storage of information.

burst error   Error affecting a large number of bits.

bus topology   Way of connecting devices so they all communicate via a common cable.

byte multiplexer   Device that combines bytes from different sources into a common data stream.

byte-oriented protocol   Protocol that treats frames as byte streams.

byte stuffing   Insertion of an extra byte to avoid misinterpreting a data byte as a control byte.

cable modem   A device designed to connect a computer with a cable service provider's signals.

Caesar cipher   Simple encryption technique in which a character is replaced by another dependent only on the value of the original character.

Carriage Return   ASCII control character causing a print mechanism or cursor to return to the leftmost print position.

Carrier Sense Multiple Access (CSMA)   Protocol used to sense whether a medium is busy before attempting to transmit.

Carrier Sense Multiple Access with Collision Avoidance (CSMA/CA)   Contention strategy used by the wireless LAN standard defined by 802.11.

Carrier Sense Multiple Access with Collision Detection (CSMA/CD)   Similar to Carrier Sense Multiple Access but also has the ability to detect whether a transmission has collided with another.

carrier signal   Signal that is modulated by an input signal to create another signal.

CAT 5 cable   Grade of UTP used in many networks today that can support 100 megabit per second rates over distances of 100 meters or less.

cell   (1) Geographic region having a reception and transmission station to communicate with cellular telephones. (2) Transmission unit defined by the ATM protocol.

cellular telephone   Portable telephone capable of connecting to the telephone system using radio communications.

centralized routing   Routing using information that is generated and maintained at a single central location.

certificate authority   Agency that creates X.509 certificates.

channel   Bandwidth range.

Cheapernet   IEEE 802.3 network using 10Base2 cable.

checksum   Value used for error detection formed by adding bit strings interpreted as integers.

chipping sequence   Bit string used in the bit expansion of direct-sequence spread spectrum.

Choke packet   Control packet sent to a device causing it to reduce the number of packets it is transmitting.

ciphertext   Message that has been encrypted.

circuit switching   A connection that is dedicated to the communication between two stations.

cladding   Part of an optical fiber that is optically less dense than the core, thus causing light to reflect back into the core.

Class A, B, C addresses Internet addresses in which certain bits represent a network ID and the others are assigned locally with the network.

Class D address Internet address used for multicasting.

classless address Internet address not associated with the traditional class A, B, C, or D address types.

classless interdomain routing (CIDR) Internet routing based on the classless address structure.

client Device or program in a client/server model that sends requests to a server.

client/server model Model of communication between two devices in which each has computing power.

Clipper Chip Controversial encryption device capable of being placed in telephones for the purpose of scrambling conversations.

coaxial cable Conductive wire surrounded by an insulating layer, wire mesh, and a protective outer cover.

code Association of bit patterns with specific information such as characters or actions.

codec Device used to translate an analog signal to a digital equivalent.

collision The result when two or more stations simultaneously send a signal over a medium designed to transmit one signal at a time.

collision avoidance Protocol used by Wireless LAN standard that reduces significantly the number of colliding frames.

collision detection Capability of a device to determine when a collision has occurred.

collision domain Set of devices in a LAN environment whose transmissions have the potential of colliding.

combined station A station that can act as both a primary and a secondary station in the HDLC protocol.

Comité Consultatif International de Télégraphique et Téléphonique (CCITT) Former name of a standards organization whose members include various scientific and industrial organizations, telecommunication agencies, telephone authorities, and the ISO; it has been renamed the ITU-T.

committed information rate Bit rate a carrier is dedicated to providing over a virtual circuit.

common bus topology Way of connecting devices so they all communicate via a common cable.

Common Gateway Interface (CGI) program A server program that can be activated from within an HTML document.

Common Management Information Protocol ISO management protocol.

communications subnet Collection of transmission media and switching elements required for routing and data transmission.

compact disc Storage medium in which information is stored optically by making very small pits in a reflective material.

compression Reduction in the number of bits in a file while retaining most or all of its meaning.

congestion Excessive amount of traffic over a network that causes a degradation of service and response times.

congestion control Protocols used to alleviate congestion in a network.

connection Mechanism through which each of two devices recognize the other for the purpose of exchanging information.

connection management Protocol used to establish, maintain, and release connections.

connection request Request to establish a connection.

connection strategy Strategy used to implement a connection.

content addressable memory Fast method of memory lookup based on the contents of memory.

contention Term used when two or more devices want to transmit over a common medium at the same time.

contention protocol Technique used to control access to a common medium from multiple entry points.

control bits The part of the frame used for control functions such as routing and handling.

control characters Binary codes that identify an action or status.

control-Q Control character used to tell a device to resume sending.

control-S Control character used to tell a device to stop sending.

credit Used in flow control, it specifies the number of bytes a TCP entity can receive from another.

crossbar switch A switching device that contains switching logic for each pair of input and output lines.

crosstalk Interference on a line caused by signals being transmitted along another one.

cyclic redundancy check (CRC) Error detection method based on interpreting bit strings as polynomials with binary coefficients.

daisy chain A connection strategy that connects devices in sequence.

data circuit-terminating equipment (DCE) Device used as an interface between a DTE and a network.

data compression See *compression.*

Data Encryption Standard (DES) Encryption technique developed by IBM and adopted as a standard by the U.S. government. It is no longer secure.

data frame See *frame,* definition (1).

datagram Independent transmission unit in a packet-switching network.

Data Link Escape character Control character used as a toggle switch causing a device to interpret subsequently received characters differently.

data link layer Layer 2 protocol.

data link protocols Protocols operating at layer 2.

data rate Measurement specifying the number of data bits a protocol can transmit per unit of time.

data strobe encoding Communication method used by FireWire that maintains synchronization between two devices using a strobe signal.

data terminal equipment (DTE) Device connected to a communications medium via a DCE.

D channel ISDN channel typically used for control and low-speed applications.

deadlock Situation in which devices are waiting for events to occur that cannot happen because of their own current states.

deadly embrace See *deadlock.*

decibel Measurement related to signal-to-noise ratio.

decryption Process of restoring an encrypted message to its original form.

Deep Space Network NASA facility to allow the monitoring of unmanned deep-space probes at all times.

de facto standards Standards that exist by virtue of their widespread use.

demodulation Restoring a signal that has been modulated to its original form.

denial of service attack An attack on a site that causes an extraordinary amount of traffic to be sent to that site, causing its servers to shut down.

DES Cracker A specially designed computer built to crack the DES cipher.

designated bridge During execution of the spanning tree algorithm for LAN interconnection, a bridge elected to forward frames from a LAN.

destination address Address to which a frame or packet is to be delivered.

differential cryptanalysis Method of analyzing encryption techniques by looking at plaintext block pairs that differ in certain ways.

differential encoding Compression technique in which a frame is represented by the difference between it and a preceding frame.

differential Manchester encoding Manchester encoding technique in which 0 and 1 are distinguished by whether the signal changes at the beginning of a bit interval.

differential phase shift keying Distinguishing an analog signal by measuring its phase shift relative to that of a previous signal.

Differentiated Services Architecture to differentiate among the different types of traffic that travel the Internet.

Diffie-Hellman key exchange A method of key distribution that works by having a sender and receiver exchange calculated values from which an encryption key can be computed.

digital signal Square-wave signal taking on only a high or low value.

digital signature Method of authentication involving encrypting a message in a way only the sender would know.

Digital Subscriber Line (DSL) Technology allowing computer communications over existing telephone lines using frequencies outside the range used by normal telephone use.

Dijkstra's algorithm Algorithm used to find the cheapest (shortest) path between two nodes in a graph.

direct-sequence spread spectrum Spread spectrum method that expands a single bit into many bits and uses a broader frequency range to transmit the resulting signal.

disconnect Termination of a connection.

discrete cosine transforms A calculation used in the first of three phases in the JPEG compression scheme that generates a set of spatial frequencies.

discrete multitone Communication method used by DSL that divides a signal into different ranges (tones) and modulates each one.

distance-vector algorithm See *Bellman-Ford algorithm.*

Distance Vector Multicast Routing Protocol (DVMRP) Protocol used in multicasting during the creation of a multicast tree.

distortion Change in a signal due to electronic noise or interference.

distributed routing Routing strategy in which each node determines and maintains its own routing information.

distribution system Infrastructure used to connect multiple devices and networks.

domain (1) Group of nodes in a network. (2) Logical collection of sites of a particular type in the Internet, grouped for administrative purposes.

Domain Name System Distributed protocol that translates a symbolic Internet address to a 32-bit numeric address.

downlink Connection from a satellite down to a ground station.

downstream neighbor Neighboring node within a ring in the direction the token travels.

DSL access multiplexer (DSLAM) A device that receives DSL signals and routes them to the Internet.

DTE–DCE interface Protocol used to define communication between a DTE and a DCE.

dynamic binding Method used to determine a device's physical address given its IP address.

Dynamic Host Configuration Protocol (DHCP) Protocol that allocates an IP address to a device.

Echo Reply ICMP packet sent in reply to an Echo Request packet.

Echo Request ICMP control packet used to determine whether a particular destination is reachable.

echo suppressor Device that removes electronic echoes from a signal.

e-commerce Term applied to the use the Internet and Web applications for the purposes of conducting business.

effective data rate Measurement specifying the number of actual data bits that can be transmitted per unit of time.

EIA-232 standard Rules defining communication between a DCE and DTE.

electrical ground Voltage level with which all signal voltages are compared.

electromagnetic waves Continuously varying electromagnetic field.

electronic codebook mode Encryption mode in which each block is encrypted independent of others.

Electronic Industries Association (EIA) Standards agency consisting of members from electronics firms and manufacturers of telecommunications equipment; a member of ANSI.

electronic mail (email) Service allowing the sending of files or messages to a person electronically.

Electronic Numerical Integrator and Calculator (ENIAC) First completely electronic computer.

electronic telephone directories Online database providing services similar to that of the conventional telephone directories.

encryption Rendering of information into a different and unintelligible form.

encryption key Data used to encrypt a message.

error Unplanned event affecting accuracy of data or a protocol.

error control Specification of how a device checks frames for errors and what it does if it finds them.

error correction Process of correcting bits in a frame that were changed during transmission.

error detection Process of determining whether bits in a frame have changed during transmission.

error recovery Ability of a protocol to recover in the event of a failure in a network or lower-level protocol.

escape character Control character causing one or more subsequent characters to be associated with some action.

Eskimo pies Warm-weather treat.

ether Imaginary substance that many once believed occupied all of outer space.

Ethernet Any of several local area network protocols based on the IEEE 802.3 standard.

even parity Method of error detection in which an extra bit is added whose value is 0 or 1 in order to make the total number of 1 bits in the transmission unit even.

Extended Binary Coded Decimal Interchange Code (EBCDIC) Eight-bit code for characters and control functions used primarily on IBM mainframes.

Exterior Gateway Protocol Protocol that exchanges routing information between two autonomous networks in an internetwork.

exterior routing protocol A protocol for routing across autonomous system boundaries.

extremely low frequency (ELF) Communication signals with a frequency less than 300 Hz.

facsimile compression Method combining run-length and Huffman encoding techniques.

facsimile (fax) machine Device that scans and digitizes images for transmission over telephone lines.

Fast Ethernet   Ethernet standard capable of 100 Mbps rates.

Federal Communications Commission (FCC)   Federal agency that regulates and licenses communications.

Federal Information Processing Standards (FIPS)   Set of publications on computer security produced by NIST.

file server   Device responsible for the maintenance and security of a network's files.

file transfer protocol   Rules for the access and exchange of files between two sites.

filter   Device that allows signals of a certain frequency to pass.

filter bank   Collection of filters, each of which creates a stream representing signal components within a specified frequency range.

fingerd   UNIX utility that allows users to obtain information about others.

finite state machine   Formal model describing the set of all possible states and state transitions of a system.

firewall   Device that separates a site from the Internet and controls the flow of information in and out of the site.

FireWire   A peer-to-peer technology that allows multiple devices to be connected, frequently with a personal computer.

fixed routing   Routing techniques based on information that does not change except by reprogramming.

flooding algorithm   Routing algorithm that transmits a message to all possible locations.

flow control   Protocol that regulates the exchange of information between two devices.

foil-electret condenser microphone   A method used by some telephones to convert sound into electricity through the use of a vibrating diaphragm that causes varying electric fields between it and a backplate in the mouthpiece.

forwarding database   Information used by a device to route frames from one network to another.

forward search algorithm   See *Dijkstra's algorithm.*

Fourier series   Mathematical formula used to describe an arbitrary periodic signal.

fragmentation   Process of dividing a packet into pieces to maintain compatibility with a network's protocol.

frame   (1) Unit of information exchanged by low-level protocols. (2) In USB, a 1-millisecond slice of time.

frame bursting   Method of combining frames in the Gigabit Ethernet standard.

frame check sequence   Field in a frame used for error checking.

frame relay   A protocol that implements virtual circuits.

frame timer   Timer used in flow control protocols to determine when to resend a frame if it has not been acknowledged.

free space optics (FSO)   Method of communicating using lasers that are unconstrained by optical fiber.

frequency   Rate at which a signal repeats.

frequency-dependent code   Compression code that takes advantage of the fact that certain characters appear with a higher frequency than others.

frequency-division multiplexing   Process of accepting analog signals within distinct bandwidths and combining them into a more complex signal with a larger bandwidth.

frequency-hopping spread spectrum   Spread spectrum method that transmits using different frequencies at different times.

frequency modulation (frequency shift keying)   Method of representing bits using analog signals with different frequencies.

full duplex   Transmission mode in which a device can send and receive simultaneously.

fully connected topology   Connection strategy in which every device in a network is connected directly to every other one.

gateway   OSI layer 7 connection between two networks.

generator polynomial   Polynomial used as a divisor in the CRC method of error detection.

geosynchronous orbit   Orbit at which a satellite moves at the same speed that the earth rotates, thus appearing stationary to a ground observer.

Gigabit Ethernet   Ethernet standard capable of 1 Gbps rates.

go-back-*n* protocol   Sliding window flow control protocol in which the receiver must receive frames in order.

graded-index multimode fiber   Optical fiber whose cladding has a variable refractive index.

graph   Mathematical model consisting of nodes and edges connecting the nodes.

Graphics Interchange Form at (GIF)   Format used for graphic images containing relatively few colors and sharply defined boundaries.

gremlin   Mythical creature responsible for all lost frames in a network.

group address Address specifying several stations in a predefined group.

guard band Unused frequencies between two adjacent channels.

guest station Secondary station in the HDLC protocol.

hacker Person who likes to program just for the sheer enjoyment of doing so.

half duplex Transmission mode in which a device must alternate between sending and receiving.

Hamming code Error correction method performed by doing several parity checks in prescribed positions.

handshake Process of defining and setting up a connection.

hash function Function used to calculate a message digest value.

hash value See *message digest value.*

hertz (Hz) Signal measurement specifying the number of cycles per second.

hierarchical routing Routing technique in which nodes are divided into groups called domains.

high-definition television Television technology providing a much sharper image than conventional television.

High-level Data Link Control (HDLC) Data link protocol defined by ISO.

hop count A measurement in a routing technique that counts the number of devices along a route.

horn antenna Device used for microwave transmission.

host A computer attached to a network and capable of running network applications.

hot pluggable A feature that allows new devices to be plugged (and unplugged) without powering off the system or loading new software to make them work.

HTML document File that defines what the user sees in a browser window.

hub A layer 1 device that receives a signal over one port, regenerates it, and sends it out all other ports.

Huffman code Frequency-dependent compression technique.

Hypertext Markup Language (HTML) Language used to create Web documents.

Hypertext Transfer Protocol (HTTP) Application layer protocol used in the World Wide Web to access and transfer Web documents.

IEEE 802 standards Set of network standards for local and metropolitan area networks.

in-band signaling Signaling technique in which the signals are sent in the same channel or bit stream as data.

index of refraction Measurement specifying how much light will bend as it travels from one medium to another.

infrared waves That part of the electromagnetic wave spectrum whose frequencies are just below those of visible light.

initialization vector Data that affects the encryption of the first data block in block chaining mode.

Institute of Electrical and Electronic Engineers (IEEE) Professional organization that publishes journals, runs conferences, and develops standards.

Integrated Services Digital Network (ISDN) Standard for a global digital communications system.

interior routing protocol Protocol for routing within an autonomous system.

intermedia synchronization Real-time application characteristic in which video and audio data are synchronized.

International Organization for Standardization (ISO) Worldwide organization consisting of standards bodies from many countries.

International Telecommunications Union (ITU) Standards organization whose members include various scientific and industrial organizations, telecommunications agencies, telephone authorities, and the ISO; formerly known as CCITT.

Internet Collection of networks that run the TCP/IP protocol.

Internet address A 32-bit or 128-bit number identifying a device on the Internet.

Internet Assigned Numbers Authority (IANA) Federally funded organization once responsible for managing and allocating IP addresses.

Internet Control Message Protocol (ICMP) Internet protocol for error reporting and providing routers updates on conditions that can develop in the Internet.

Internet Corporation for Assigned Names and Numbers (ICANN) Nonprofit organization responsible for managing and allocating IP addresses.

Internet Engineering Task Force (IETF) An international community whose members include network designers, vendors, and researchers, all of whom have an interest in the stable operation of the Internet and in its evolution.

Internet Group Management Protocol (IGMP) Protocol that operates between a host and a local router that allows the host to join and leave various multicast groups.

Internet Protocol (IP) Network layer protocol originally developed by the Advanced Research Projects Agency.

Internet Protocol version 6 (Ipv6) An updated version of the current Internet Protocol (IPv4).

Internet Radio An application allowing personal computer users to tune in and listen to a radio station through the computer and the Internet.

Internet Security Association and Key Management Protocol Protocol that defines packet formats and the rules for exchanging packets containing encryption key information.

Internet service provider (ISP) Organization that provides access to the Internet for its customers.

Internet worm Famous intrusion into the Internet that clogged systems and forced many to shut down.

IPSec Protocol designed to provide secure transmission at the packet level.

I series Set of documents describing ISDN architecture, configurations, routing principles, and interfaces.

isochronous transmission Real-time transmission mode in which data arrive at a specified rate.

JavaScript A language used to write client-side scripts for Web applications.

JPEG compression A compression standard for both grayscale and photographic-quality color images, developed by the Joint Photographic Experts Group (JPEG).

key distribution (key exchange) Problem of sending encryption keys to those receiving encrypted messages.

key escrow agency An agency responsible for storing private encryption keys.

laser Very pure and narrow beam of light.

last mile Term applying to the copper wires that connect residences' telephones to the telephone network.

Lempel-Ziv compression Compression technique that replaces repeated strings with certain codes.

light-emitting diode (LED) Device that produces less concentrated light than a laser and is often used as an alternative to a laser in fiber optic communication.

Link Access Protocol (LAP) Data link layer protocol that handles logical links between devices.

link state routing A routing strategy in which routers send and forward packets specifying the status of a link between two specified routers; each router uses the accumulated information to build routing tables.

local area network (LAN) Network spanning a relatively small geographic area connecting a variety of devices.

local exchange Local office containing switching logic to route telephone calls.

local loop Wires connecting telephones to the local exchange office.

lock-up See *deadlock*.

logical link control (LLC) IEEE standard data link protocol used in local area networks that handles logical links between devices.

lossless compression Compression method for which no information is lost during compression.

lossy compression Compression method for which some loss of information occurs during compression.

low earth orbit (LEO) satellites Satellites orbiting at low altitudes used to define a worldwide communications network.

machine state Collection of values associated with a system at an instant in time.

Management Information Base (MIB) Database used by SNMP that describes routers and hosts.

Manchester code Digital encoding scheme in which the digital signal always changes state in the middle of an interval.

man-in-the-middle attack An attack in which a perpetrator places himself between two communicating entities, posing as a legitimate entity to each.

maximum transfer unit (MTU) Maximum frame size that can be transferred over a network.

MBone Network within the Internet that supports class D address routing.

medium access control (MAC) Lower sublayer of the data link protocol that controls access to the transmission medium.

medium independent interface (MII) Ethernet term referring to the connection between a network interface card and a transceiver.

memory-resident viruses Computer virus that waits in memory for an executable file to be placed there.

Menehune Central facility used in the Hawaiian Islands' Aloha (packet radio) system.

message age timer Timer maintained by a bridge specifying a maximum time during which it expects to hear from the root bridge elected by the spanning tree algorithm.

message digest value A number calculated from the contents of a document.

message switching Alternative to packet switching or circuit switching in which a transmitted message is stored at each node, but different messages may travel different routes.

microwave transmissions Method of transmission using electromagnetic waves with a frequency below that of infrared light.

modal dispersion Phenomenon resulting from light reflecting at different angles in an optical fiber, causing some of the light to take a bit longer to get to the other end of the fiber.

modem Device that converts analog signals to digital ones and vice versa.

modulation Process of using one signal to change another one.

monitor station Token ring station that has some maintenance and control responsibilities.

monoalphabetic cipher Primitive encryption technique in which a text character is replaced by another that is chosen dependent only on the character being replaced.

Morse code Transmission code developed for telegraph systems in which each character is represented by a series of dots and dashes.

Moving Pictures Expert Group (MPEG) Often used to refer to a compression method for video files; more accurately, the group that defines standards for video compression.

MP3 Compression method commonly applied to audio files.

multicast Sending information to a particular group of host computers.

multicast address Address that identifies a group of host computers.

multicast tree Collection of routers participating in a multicast.

Multilevel Line Transmission–Three Levels (MLT-3) Signaling scheme in Fast Ethernet that uses a three-state signal.

multiplexer Device combining signals from several inputs and sending them out over a single channel.

multiport repeater Synonym for *hub*.

mux See *multiplexer*.

National Institute of Standards and Technology (NIST) A standards-making agency of the United States Department of Commerce.

near-end crosstalk (NEXT) Interference on a line caused by signals being transmitted along another one.

negative acknowledgment (NAK) Flow control indication that a frame was not received correctly or was not received at all.

network Collection of devices running software allowing them to communicate via some transmission medium.

network interface card (NIC) Logic circuit placed into a personal computer for the purpose of interfacing with a network.

network layer Layer 3 protocol responsible for routing packets through a network.

network termination 1 (NT1) ISDN designation for nonintelligent devices concerned with physical and electrical characteristics of a transmission signal.

network termination 2 (NT2) ISDN designation for intelligent devices capable of performing functions specified in OSI layers 2 and 3.

network topology Manner in which network devices are connected physically.

noise Unwanted signals that interfere with a transmitted signal.

noiseless channel Channel impervious to noise.

noisy lines Lines having more than a typical amount of noise.

nonbroadcast frame Frame destined for a specific destination.

non-data-J and non-data-K Digital signal that do not conform to any Manchester code for defining bits.

nonpersistent CSMA Protocol in which, after a collision has occurred, the device does not monitor the transmission medium, instead waiting for one time slot before checking for activity.

nonreturn to zero (NRZ) Digital encoding scheme in which 0s and 1s are represented by specific voltage levels.

no-prefix property Property stating that the bit code for a character never appears as the prefix of another code.

normal response mode HDLC mode in which the primary station controls the communication.

null modem Device used to connect two DTEs directly.

Nyquist theorem Theoretical result that relates the data rate to a signal's baud rate and the number of signal components.

octet Group of eight bits.

odd parity Method of error detection in which an extra bit is added whose value is 0 or 1 in order to make the total number of 1 bits in the transmission unit odd.

one-time pad   An unbreakable encryption technique that uses a key whose length is equal to the plaintext and is used only once.

one-way hash function   Hash function that always produces a unique digest value from each document.

Open Shortest Path First (OSPF)   Variation of link state routing that provides additional features including authentication and load balancing.

open system   Set of protocols that would allows any two different systems to communicate regardless of their underlying architecture.

Open Systems Interconnect (OSI)   Protocol standard developed by the International Standards Organization to implement an open system.

operation, administration, and maintenance (OAM)   Protocols used to maintain, monitor, and troubleshoot communications.

optical fiber   Communications medium consisting of a thin strand of glass through which light travels.

orphan frame   Token ring frame circulating endlessly because no device will remove it from the ring.

out-of-band signaling   Signaling technique in which the signals are sent in a separate channel or outside the data bit stream.

outstanding frames   Frames that have been sent but not yet acknowledged by a flow control protocol.

packet   (1) Transmission unit for a specified protocol. (2) In USB, a packaged group of bits.

packet elimination   Congestion control scheme that eliminates some packets if there is an excessive buildup of them at a node.

packet filtering   Method used by a firewall to restrict packets based on their content.

packet header   Control information in a packet.

packet jitter   Side effect of real-time applications in which delays in a network cause packets to arrive at irregular intervals.

packet sniffer   A program that looks through data packets as they travel the network.

packet-switched network   Network over which messages are divided into pieces called packets and transmitted separately.

parabolic dish reflector   Microwave antenna whose dish is parabolic in shape.

parallel transmission   Transmission mode in which several bits are transmitted simultaneously.

parity bit   Extra bit in an error detection mechanism whose value is 0 or 1 in order to make the total number of 1 bits in the checked stream either even or odd.

path   Sequence of nodes in a network through which data must pass as they travel from sender to receiver.

peer-to-peer networking   Capability to allow a group of computers to all communicate without the use of a centralized server.

peer-to-peer protocol   Protocol allowing multiple devices to communicate with anyone initiating the connection to another without the need for a central coordinating device.

period   Time required for a periodic signal to repeat a pattern once.

periodic signal   Signal that varies with time but repeats a certain pattern continually.

Perl   Scripting language common in Unix and Linux environments.

permanent virtual circuit (PVC)   Type of virtual circuit for which no call establishment protocol is needed prior to transferring data.

personal area network   Collection of small consumer devices equipped with radio transceivers capable of communicating with one another.

Petri net   Way to model a protocol using a graph to represent states and transitions.

phase modulation   Method of altering a signal by changing its phase shift.

phase shift   Horizontal shift in a periodic signal.

phase shift keying   See *phase modulation*.

physical layer   Layer 1 protocol responsible for defining the electrical and physical properties of the transmission medium.

physical medium dependent sublayer   Ethernet term referring to where signals are generated.

picture element   See *pixel*.

piggyback acknowledgment   Technique of sending an acknowledgment within a data frame.

pixel   Smallest visible component of an image on a television or video screen.

plaintext   Unencrypted message.

point-to-point link   HDLC link in which a primary station communicates with one secondary station.

Poll bit   HDLC flag allowing a primary station to request a response from a secondary station.

polyalphabetic cipher Encryption technique in which each occurrence of a text character is replaced by a different character depending on the original character and its position in the message.

polymorphic virus A virus capable of mutating or changing in order to avoid detection when it infects a file.

polynomial Mathematical expression formed by adding terms, each of which is a constant multiplied by an unknown term raised to a positive integral power.

port number TCP value that identifies a server application.

p-persistent CSMA Protocol in which, after a collision has occurred, the station monitors the transmission medium and, when it is quiet, transmits with probability p $(0 \le p \le 1)$.

preamble Special bit pattern appearing at the beginning of some frame formats.

presentation layer OSI layer 6 protocol.

Pretty Good Privacy Package that can be used with email for encrypting and digitally signing messages.

primary rate ITU standard for ISDN consisting of 23 B channels and 1 D channel.

primary station Type of station designated by HDLC that manages data flow by issuing commands to other stations and acting on their responses.

private branch exchange (PBX) Private telephone system.

protocol Set of rules by which two or more devices communicate.

protocol converters Logic to convert one protocol to another.

pseudoternary coding See *alternate mark inversion.*

psychoacoustic model Model based on auditory senses that specifies what sounds are masked by other sounds and can be removed with little or no perceptive loss.

public data networks Packet-switched networks managed by a government or public utility.

public key cryptosystem Encryption technique for which there is no attempt to protect the identity of the encryption key.

pulse amplitude modulation Technique of sampling an analog signal at regular intervals and generating pulses with amplitude equal to that of the sampled signal.

pulse code modulation Similar to pulse amplitude modulation, except the amplitude of the pulse must be one of a set of predefined values.

pure Aloha Protocol developed at the University of Hawaii for a packet radio system.

Purge frame Token ring control frame that clears the ring of any extraneous signals.

Q series Series of ITU-T documents describing a layered protocol called Signaling System 7, a standard providing functionality in integrated digital networks.

quadrature amplitude modulation Modulation technique in which bits are assigned to an analog signal dependent on a combination of its amplitude and phase shift.

quality of service (QoS) Specification of the type of service required by an application.

Real-Time Transport Protocol (RTP) Transport layer protocol designed to support real-time applications.

reassembly deadlock Deadlock caused by running out of buffer space while accepting packets from multiple sources.

reassembly timer Timer used by the Internet Protocol specifying the time in which it expects to receive all fragments from a packet.

receiving window Flow control parameter specifying which frames can be received.

Record Route option Internet protocol parameter specifying that the route a packet takes be placed in the packet.

reference points (R, S, T, U) ITU-T-defined reference points used to divide ISDN functional groups.

refraction Phenomenon relating to the changing direction of light as it passes from one medium to another.

Relative encoding See *differential encoding.*

remote login Process of logging in to a computer at a remote site.

Remote Monitoring (RMON) Network management protocol.

repeater Layer 1 connection that receives signals and regenerates them before sending them on.

replay attack Unauthorized copying of legitimate packets in order to send them later to mimic a legitimate activity.

reply Message sent in response to another.

Request for Comments (RFC) Series of documents containing research notes.

reservation system Token ring protocol mechanism allowing a device to try to reserve a token on its next pass.

Resource Reservation Protocol (RSVP) Protocol for transport messages that contain information about a particular data flow and request that sufficient resources be reserved to meet a specified quality of service.

reverse-path broadcasting   Protocol used in multicasting in which a router determines the source of a received packet and broadcasts it only if the packet arrived from the direction of that source.

Rijndael Algorithm   Complex encryption standard based on a variety of bit-level operations combined with higher-level mathematics.

ring topology   Circular arrangement of devices each capable of communicating directly with its neighbor.

roaming   Feature that allows a network to track the location of a moving device.

root bridge   Specially designated bridge determined by the spanning tree algorithm corresponding to the root of the spanning tree.

root port   Bridge port corresponding to the cheapest path to the root bridge in a spanning tree.

route   Sequence of devices through which a packet or frame must travel from its source to its destination.

routed   Routing program developed at the University of California at Berkeley to do routing on their local area network.

route designators   Sequence of LAN and bridge IDs specifying a path.

route discovery   Process used by source-routing bridges to determine the path to a particular device.

route learning   Process by which a bridge or switch learns what to put in its routing table.

router   Layer 3 connection between two networks.

routing algorithm   Method used to determine a route.

routing directory   See *routing table*.

Routing Information Protocol (RIP)   Routing strategy that uses a hop count to determine the path in a network.

routing matrix   Matrix specifying the next node in a route between pairs of nodes.

routing table   Database used by a bridge or router to decide where to send frames it receives.

RS-232 standard   See *EIA-232 standard*.

run-length encoding   Compression technique that replaces a run of bits (or bytes) by the number of bits (or bytes) in the run.

sampling frequency   Rate at which analog signals are sampled.

satellite   Object orbiting the earth.

satellite radio   A service by which radio signals are broadcast to earth providing listening opportunities for subscribers.

satellite transmission   Microwave transmission to or from an orbiting satellite.

S-box   Structure that defines how one byte is substituted for another during encryption.

script   File containing a collection of commands to be executed.

scripting language   A language whose source code is interpreted as it is executed.

secondary station   Type of station designated by HDLC that responds to a primary station.

Secure Copy (scp)   Secure file transfer protocol.

Secure Hash Algorithm (SHA)   One-way hash function used in authenticating documents.

Secure Shell (ssh)   Secure remote login protocol.

Secure Sockets Layer (SSL)   Protocol that authenticates sites and negotiates encryption strategies between them.

security   Pertaining to the protection or hiding of information from unauthorized people.

segment   A formatted collection of information items for a protocol (usually TCP).

selective repeat protocol   Sliding window flow control protocol in which the sender and receiver defines a window specifying frames each can send or receive.

self-synchronizing code   Digital encoding scheme in which the signal always changes state in the middle of a bit interval.

sending window   Flow control parameter specifying which frames can be sent.

sequence number   Number used for ordering frames or packets.

serial transmission   Mode of transmission in which all bits are sent in sequence.

server   Network device whose function is to respond to requests from the network users.

session   Logical connection between two end users.

session layer   OSI layer 5 protocol.

Shamir's method   Method of key distribution in which a specified number of people must be present to determine the key.

shielded twisted pair   Two conducting wires wrapped around each other, both of which have a metal sheathing protecting the wire from outside electrical interference.

shift register   Part of a circuit used to implement cyclic redundancy checks.

shortest-path algorithm Logic used to determine the shortest path between two points.

signal constellation Diagram using plotted points to define all legitimate signal changes recognized by a modem.

signal ground Voltage level against which all other signals are measured.

signaling data link Lowest layer of Signaling System 7, providing physical and electrical specifications.

signaling link layer Second layer of Signaling System 7, providing reliable communications between two adjacent points in the network.

signaling network layer Third layer of Signaling System 7, providing reliable message transfer between two signaling points.

signal speed Speed at which a signal travels through a medium.

Signaling System 7 Four-layer protocol that defines a standard for functionality in an integrated digital network.

signal-to-noise ratio Measurement used to quantify how much noise there is in the presence of a signal.

Simple Mail Transfer Protocol (SMTP) Standard mail protocol in the TCP/IP suite.

Simple Network Management Protocol (SNMP) Management protocol designed to make sure network protocols and devices work well.

simplex communication Mode in which communication goes only one way.

single-bit error Error affecting just one bit.

single-mode fiber Optical fiber with a very small diameter designed to reduce the number of angles at which light reflects off the cladding to one angle.

sliding window protocol Flow control protocol in which the sending and receiving devices restrict the frames they can send or receive.

slotted Aloha protocol Aloha protocol requiring a device to transmit at the beginning of a slot.

slow start Part of the startup process in the TCP flow control algorithm, in which the sending entity tries to determine how much it can send before congestion causes delays.

smurf attack A type of denial of service attack.

socket UNIX construct and a mechanism used to read and write to a network.

source address Address of a device sending a packet or frame.

Source Quench ICMP control message requesting a reduction in the rate at which packets are sent.

source-routing bridge Bridge that routes a frame based on the contents of the frame's route designator.

spanning tree algorithm Distributed algorithm executed by bridges or switches to determine a connection among all participating LANs that contains no redundant paths.

spatial frequencies Values in the JPEG compression scheme that relate directly to how much the pixel values change as a function of their position in a block.

split horizon Modification of a routing algorithm in which a node does not send information it received from a neighboring node back to that node.

splitter Device that splits a signal into different components.

spoofing see *address spoofing*.

spot beam Type of antenna allowing satellite signals to be broadcast to only a very small area.

spread spectrum Mode of wireless transmission that spreads the signal's spectral energy over a wider range of frequencies.

spyware A program that inserts itself into your system without your knowledge and logs what you do.

stacking station Token ring station that has raised the token's priority.

standard Agreed-on way of doing something.

start bit Single-bit signal used in asynchronous transmission alerting the receiver that data is arriving.

start of frame delimiter Special bit pattern indicating the start of a frame.

star topology Arrangement of devices in which all communication goes through a central device.

stateful inspection Method used by a firewall to restrict packets based on their content and the context of what has occurred previously.

state transition Changing of a system from one state to another due to the occurrence of some event.

state transition diagram Model of a system depicting all possible states and the events that cause the system to change states.

static routing Routing strategy that uses information that does not change with time.

statistical multiplexer Time-division multiplexer that creates a variable-sized frame.

step-index multimode fiber Optical fiber with a larger diameter allowing several angles at which light reflects off the cladding.

stop-and-wait protocol Flow control protocol in which a sender sends a frame and waits for the acknowledgment to return before sending the next frame.

stop bit Single-bit signal used in asynchronous transmission indicating the end of the transmission.

store and forward Network protocol in which a message is stored in its entirety at each intermediate node along the path to the destination.

store-and-forward deadlock Deadlock caused by a situation in which none in a circular list of nodes can send because the next one's buffers are full.

strobe signal A signal that stays constant when a data signal changes and changes when the data signal does not.

study The process by which one reads material, lists what one does not understand, rereads the material to gain further insight, makes another list of what one still does not understand, and repeats this process as often as necessary until the list is empty.

subnet An independent physical network that is also a component of a larger network.

subnet mask Bit string of 1s that determine which bits in an address determine the subnet ID.

supernetting Grouping several smaller networks and visualizing them as a single larger network.

supervisory frame Frame used by HDLC to indicate a station's status or to send negative acknowledgments.

switch A layer 2 device capable of forwarding frames from one network to another. The term is usually applied to cases in which the connected networks have similar technologies.

switched Ethernet Ethernet connection strategy in which switches are used to connect all the devices.

switched virtual circuit (SVC) Type of virtual circuit that requires a call establishment protocol.

SYN character Character used in byte-oriented protocols to indicate the start of a frame.

Synchronous Data Link Control (SDLC) Bit-oriented data link protocol developed by IBM and similar to HDLC.

Synchronous Digital Hierarchy (SDH) An optical carrier system similar to SONET.

Synchronous Optical Network (SONET) An optical network using time-division multiplexing to accommodate simultaneous channels. Controlled by a clock, it transmits bits at rates ranging from about 155.5 Mbps to in excess of 2 Gbps.

synchronous payload envelope (SPE) Data stored in a SONET frame.

synchronous transmission Mode of transmission in which bits are placed into frames and sent in sequence.

T1 A digital carrier service with 24 channels and a bit rate of 1.544 Mbps.

teleconferencing Communication system allowing people at different sites to not only hear but see each other as well.

telegraph Primitive communication device consisting of a power source, switch, and sensor.

telemetry Sensing of status or reading of data at remote sites.

telepresence Concept of projecting one's senses into a remote location.

Telnet Application layer virtual terminal protocol allowing remote logins.

temporal redundancy Redundancy defined by the presence of similar data in successive frames.

terminal adapter Device designed to be used with ISDN TE2 equipment to convert their signals to an ISDN-compatible format.

terminal equipment 1 (TE1) ISDN primary functional group designation for ISDN devices.

terminal equipment 2 (TE2) ISDN primary functional group designation for non-ISDN devices.

terminators Electronic devices placed at the end of a medium preventing any electronic echoing of signals.

ThickNet A thick, less flexible coaxial cable used in older local area networks.

ThinNet A thinner, more flexible coaxial cable used in local area networks; once commonly used to connect network devices together.

three-way handshake Mechanism to establish a connection consisting of a connection request, acknowledgment of the request, and an acknowledgment of the acknowledgment.

time-division multiplexing Process of accepting digital signals from several sources, storing them in a single frame, and sending the frame over a single channel.

Time Exceeded ICMP control message sent to a source device when a packet or unassembled fragments are dropped from the network due to a timer expiration.

Timestamp Reply ICMP control message sent in response to a Timestamp Request.

Timestamp Request ICMP control message sent to a remote host when a local host wants to estimate the round-trip time between it and the remote host.

Time to Live Internet Protocol packet field specifying the maximum amount of time the packet can remain in the network.

token Special frame circulating among all devices in a network used to determine when a device can send information over the network.

token ring network Ring topology network that controls access to the ring by using a token-passing protocol.

traceroute Utility to trace the route an Internet packet will take.

transceiver Logic circuit in a network card that implements some of the protocols needed to access the network.

Transmission Control Protocol (TCP) Transport protocol used in the Internet.

transparent bridge Bridge that creates and updates its own routing tables.

transparent data Mode of transmission in which a receiving device does not react to the contents of incoming bytes.

transponder Satellite device that accepts a signal within one frequency and retransmits it over another.

transport layer Layer 4 protocol responsible for end-to-end communications.

Transport Layer Security (TLS) Protocol that authenticates sites and negotiates encryption strategies between them.

transposition cipher Encryption technique that rearranges the plaintext characters.

triple DES Encryption method defined by applying DES three times in succession.

trit Unit of information having three possible values.

tunneling Embedding of a IPv6 packet inside an IPv4 packet for the purpose of transmitting an IPv6 packet through a collection of routers that are not IPv6 compatible.

twisted pair Communication circuit consisting of two insulated wires twisted around each other.

two-way handshake Mechanism to establish a connection consisting of a connection request and an acknowledgment to the request.

unbalanced circuit Circuit using one line for signal transmission and a common ground.

unicast address Address that identifies one host.

Unicode Sixteen-bit code allowing a wide variety of different characters and symbols from different languages.

Uniform Resource Locator (URL) A text string specifying an Internet location and a protocol used to access a document at that location.

universal serial bus (USB) A master/slave protocol that allows multiple devices to be connected to a personal computer.

unrestricted flow control Essentially a lack of flow control; the sending device sends frames and makes no effort to limit the number it sends.

unshielded twisted pair Two conducting wires wrapped around each other, neither of which has a metal sheathing protecting the wire from outside electrical interference.

uplink Connection from a ground station to a satellite.

upstream neighbor Token-passing term applying to the device from which a token is received.

urgent data Data in a TCP segment that must be delivered to higher layers as quickly as possible.

Urgent Pointer TCP segment field pointing to urgent data.

User Datagram Protocol (UDP) Connectionless transport layer protocol.

very high frequency (VHF) Television transmission using electromagnetic waves between 30 MHz and 300 MHz.

very small aperture terminal (VSAT) system Satellite communication system using small antenna dishes.

videoconferencing System allowing people in different locations to see and hear each other in a real-time setting.

virtual call Type of virtual circuit that requires a call establishment protocol prior to data transfer.

virtual circuit (route) Logical connection that is established prior to any packet-switched data transfer and for which all packets travel through the same network nodes.

virtual file structure File structure supported by a network for the purpose of file transfer.

virtual LAN (VLAN) A group of devices that are logically grouped independent of their physical locations.

virtual path In ATM, a sequence of ATM switches along a virtual circuit.

virtual terminal protocol Protocol defining communication between an application and terminal, independent of terminal characteristics.

virus Unauthorized set of instructions that spreads from one computer to another, either through a network or through peripheral transfers.

voice over IP Delivery of voice data via IP packets.

waveguide Cylindrical tube that is part of a horn antenna.

wave-division multiplexing Combining signals represented by different frequencies of visible light.

well-known ports TCP port numbers assigned to common Internet applications.

wide area network (WAN) Network spanning a large geographic distance, often connecting many smaller networks running a variety of different protocols.

window Abstract concept defining a subset of frames for the purpose of flow control between two devices.

Wired Equivalency Privacy A security protocol used in the 802.11 wireless LAN standard.

wireless communications Communication independent of a physical connection.

wireless fidelity (Wi-Fi) Variation of 802.11 standard that uses radio waves in the 2.4 GHz range.

wireless LAN LAN protocol that allows devices to communicate independent of physical connections such as wire, cable, or fiber.

World Wide Web Term applied to a collection of documents, links to other documents, and protocols to access them via the Internet.

worm Program that intrudes into a system and has the potential to damage the system's security.

X.21 interface standard Standard used to allow a DTE and DCE to communicate.

X.25 standard Standard for connecting devices to a packet-switched network.

X.509 certificate Certificate signed by an authority, used to verify the identity of a host.

X-OFF Flow control character causing incoming data to stop.

X-ON Flow control character causing incoming data to resume.

ACRONYMS

2B1Q Two binary, one quarternary

3DES Triple DES

AAL ATM adaptation layer

ABM Asynchronous balanced mode

ACK Acknowledgment

ADSL Asymmetric DSL

AES Advanced Encryption Standard

AM Amplitude modulation

ANSI American National Standards Institute

AP Access point

ARM Asynchronous response mode

ARP Address Resolution Protocol

ARPA Advanced Research Projects Agency

ARQ Automatic repeat request

AS Autonomous system

ASCII American Standard Code For Information Interchange

ASK Amplitude shift keying

ASN.1 Abstract Syntax Notation 1

AT&T American Telephone and Telegraph

ATM Asynchronous Transfer Mode

AUI Attachment unit interface

BCC Block Check Character

BCD Binary-coded decimal

BCDIC Binary-coded decimal interchange code

BGP Border Gateway Protocol

B-ISDN Broadband ISDN

BPDU Bridge protocol data unit

BSC Binary synchronous communication

BSS Basic service set

CA Certificate authority

CATV Cable TV

CBX Computer branch exchange

CCITT Comité Consultatif International de Télégraphique et Téléphonique

CGI Common Gateway Interface

CIDR Classless interdomain routing

CIR Committed information rate

CMIP Common Management Information Protocol

CMOT CMIP over TCP

CPU Central processing unit

CRC Cyclic redundancy check

CS Convergence sublayer

CSMA Carrier Sense Multiple Access

CSMA/CA Carrier Sense Multiple Access with Collision Avoidance

CSMA/CD Carrier Sense Multiple Access with Collision Detection

DCE Data circuit-terminating equipment

DCF Distributed Coordination Function

DCT Discrete cosine transform

DES Data Encryption Standard

DHCP Dynamic Host Configuration Protocol

DIFS DCF interframe space

DLE Data Link Escape

DNS Domain Name System

DoD Department of Defense

DoS Denial of service

DPSK Differential phase shift keying

DS Distributed system

DSL   Digital Subscriber Line

DSLAM   DSL access multiplexer

DSN   Deep Space Network

DSS   Digital Signature Standard

DSSS   Direct-sequence spread spectrum

DTE   Data terminal equipment

DVMRP   Distance Vector Multicast Routing Protocol

EBCDIC   Extended Binary-Coded Decimal Interchange Code

EGP   Exterior Gateway Protocol

EIA   Electronic Industries Association

ELF   Extremely low frequency

ENIAC   Electronic Numerical Integrator and Calculator

ESP   Encapsulating Security Payload

FCC   Federal Communications Commission

FDM   Frequency-division multiplexing

FHSS   Frequency-hopping spread spectrum

FM   Frequency modulation

FSK   Frequency shift keying

FSO   Free space optics

FTP   File Transfer Protocol

GIF   Graphics Interchange Format

GMII   Gigabit medium independent interface

HDLC   High-level Data Link Control

HDSL   High-bit-rate DSL

HDTV   High-definition television

HTML   Hypertext Markup Language

HTTP   Hypertext Transfer Protocol

IANA   Internet Assigned Numbers Authority

IBM   International Business Machines

ICANN   Internet Corporation for Assigned Names and Numbers

ICMP   Internet Control Message Protocol

IEC   International Electrotechnical Commission

IEEE   Institute of Electrical and Electronic Engineers

IETF   Internet Engineering Task Force

IGMP   Internet Group Management Protocol

IKE   Internet Key Exchange

IP   Internet Protocol

IPv6   Internet Protocol version 6

ISAKMP   Internet Security Association and Key Management Protocol

ISDN   Integrated Services Digital Network

ISO   International Organization for Standardization

ITU   International Telecommunications Union

JPEG   Joint Photographic Experts Group

LAN   Local area network

LAP   Link Access Protocol

LED   Light-emitting diode

LEO   Low earth orbit

LLC   Logical link control

MAC   Medium access control

MaGIC   Media-accelerated Global Information Carrier

MII   Medium independent interface

MLT-3   Multilevel Line Transmission–Three Levels

MP3   MPEG audio layer 3

MPEG   Moving Pictures Expert Group

MTSO   Mobile telephone switching office

MTU   Maximum transfer unit

NAK   Negative acknowledgment

NASA   National Aeronautics and Space Administration

NBS   National Bureau of Standards

NEXT   Near-end crosstalk

NIC   Network interface card

NIST   National Institute of Standards and Technology

NNI   Network–network interface

NRM   Normal response mode

NRZ   Nonreturn to zero

NRZI   Nonreturn to zero inverted

NSA   National Security Agency *or* No Such Agency

NTSC   National Television Standards Committee

OAM   Operations, administration, and maintenance

OC-*n*   Optical carrier *n*

ONU   Optical network unit

OSI   Open Systems Interconnect

OSPF   Open Shortest Path First

PABX   Private automatic branch exchange

PAM   Pulse amplitude modulation

PAM5   Pulse amplitude modulation with five levels

PAN   Personal area network

PBX   Private branch exchange

PC   Personal computer

PCM   Pulse code modulation

PCS   Physical coding sublayer

PDU   Protocol data unit

Perl   Practical Extension and Report Language

PGP   Pretty Good Privacy

PIN   Personal identification number

PM   Phase modulation

PMD   Physical medium dependent

POTS   Plain old telephone service

PSK   Phase shift keying

PVC   Permanent virtual circuit

QAM   Quadrature amplitude modulation

QoS   Quality of service

QPSK   Quaternary phase shift keying

RADSL   Rate-adaptive asymmetric DSL

RFC   Request for Comments

RIP   Routing Information Protocol

RMON   Remote Monitoring

RPB   Reverse-path broadcasting

RSA   Rivest, Shamir, Adelman

RSVP   Resource Reservation Protocol

RTCP   RTP Control Protocol

RTP   Real-Time Transport Protocol

SAR   Segmentation and reassembly sublayer

SDH   Synchronous Digital Hierarchy

SDLC   Synchronous Data Link Control

SDSL   Symmetric DSL or single-wire DSL

SHA-1   Secure Hash Algorithm 1

SHDSL   Single-pair high-speed DSL

SIFS   Short interframe space

SIPP   Simple Internet Protocol Plus

SMTP   Simple Mail Transfer Protocol

SNMP   Simple Network Management Protocol

SONET   Synchronous Optical Network

SPE   Synchronous payload envelope

SSCF   Service-Specific Coordination Function

SSCOP   Service-Specific Connection-Oriented Protocol

ssh   Secure Shell

SSL   Secure Sockets Layer

SS7   Signaling System 7

STD   State transition diagram

STP   Shielded twisted pair

STS-*n*   Synchronous transport signal *n*

SVC   Switched virtual circuit

TCP   Transmission Control Protocol

TCP/IP   Transmission Control Protocol/Internet Protocol

TIA   Telecommunications Industry Association

TDM   Time-division multiplexing

TLS   Transport Layer Security

TPDU   Transport protocol data unit

UDP   User Datagram Protocol

UHF   Ultra-high frequency

UNI   User–network interface

URL   Uniform Resource Locator

USB   Universal serial bus

UTP   Unshielded twisted pair

VDSL   Very high data rate DSL

VHF   Very high frequency

VLAN   Virtual LAN

VLSI   Very large-scale integration

VSAT   Very small aperture terminal

WAN   Wide area network

WEP   Wired Equivalent Privacy

WDDM   Wave-division demultiplexer

WDM   Wave-division multiplexing

Wi-Fi   Wireless fidelity

WIS   WAN interface sublayer

WLAN   Wireless LAN

WWW   World Wide Web

XAUI   XGMJI attachment unit interface

XGMIII   10-Gigabit medium independent interface

INDEX